Stephen P. Robbins • Timothy A. Judge

Essentials of Organizational Behavior

Custom Edition for Ashworth College

Taken from:
Essentials of Organizational Behavior, Twelfth Edition
by Stephen P. Robbins and Timothy A. Judge

Cover Art: Courtesy of Digital Vision, Photodisc, Rubberball Productions, Stockbyte/Getty Images.

Taken from:

Essentials of Organizational Behavior, Twelfth Edition
by Stephen P. Robbins and Timothy A. Judge
Copyright © 2014, 2012, 2010 by Pearson Education
Published by Pearson Education, Inc.
Boston, Massachusetts 02116

This special edition published in cooperation with Pearson Learning Solutions.

All trademarks, service marks, registered trademarks, and registered service marks are the property of their respective owners and are used herein for identification purposes only.

Pearson Learning Solutions, 501 Boylston Street, Suite 900, Boston, MA 02116
A Pearson Education Company
www.pearsoned.com

Printed in the United States of America

7 8 9 10 11 V0UD 20 19 18 17 16

000200010271777679

SR

ISBN 10: 1-269-33138-8
ISBN 13: 978-1-269-33138-8

*This book is dedicated to our friends and colleagues in
The Organizational Behavior Teaching Society
who, through their teaching, research, and commitment
to the leading process, have significantly
improved the ability of students
to understand and apply OB concepts.*

BRIEF CONTENTS

CONTENTS

PREFACE

This book was created as an alternative to the 600- or 700-page comprehensive textbook in organizational behavior (OB). It attempts to provide balanced coverage of all the key elements comprising the discipline of OB in a style that readers will find both informative and interesting. We're pleased to say that this text has achieved a wide following in short courses and executive programs as well as in traditional courses as a companion volume with experiential, skill development, case, and readings books. It is currently used at more than 500 colleges and universities in the United States, Canada, Latin America, Europe, Australia, and Asia. It has also been translated into Spanish, Portuguese, Japanese, Chinese, Dutch, Polish, Turkish, Danish, and Bahasa Indonesian.

KEY CHANGES TO THE TWELFTH EDITION

- New chapter on diversity in organizations including information on current U.S. workforce demographics, discrimination, biographical characteristics, abilities, and implementing diversity management strategies.
- Improved integration of contemporary global implications: with the explosion of international research, global OB research is now woven into each chapter, rather than contained in a stand-alone section at the end of the chapter.
- Summary and Implications for Managers section revised to bring the topics together with the application for managers.
- New end of chapter assisted-graded writing question located in MyManagmentLab provides support for developing students' critical thinking skills.
- Six new videos added demonstrating the real-world applications of OB concepts. Companies and topics include: East Haven Fire Department on Emotions and Moods and Managing Stress, Gordon Law Group on Conflict and Negotiation, Orpheus Group Casting on Social Perception and Attribution, Power and Political Behavior, and Verizon on Diversity.
- Thoroughly updated examples and figures illustrating the latest data pertaining to Organizational Behavior.

RETAINED FROM THE PREVIOUS EDITION

What do readers like about this book? Surveys of users have found general agreement about the following features. Needless to say, they've all been retained in this edition.

- **Length.** Since its inception in 1984, we've tried diligently to keep this book in the range of 300 to 400 pages. Users tell us this length allows them considerable flexibility in assigning supporting materials and projects.
- **Balanced topic coverage.** Although short in length, this book continues to provide balanced coverage of all the key concepts in OB. This includes not only traditional topics, such as personality, motivation, and leadership, but also cutting-edge issues such as emotions, diversity, negotiation, and teamwork.
- **Writing style.** This book is frequently singled out for its fluid writing style and extensive use of examples. Users regularly tell us that they find this book "conversational," "interesting," "student friendly," and "very clear and understandable."

- *Practicality.* This book has never been solely about theory. It's about *using* theory to better explain and predict the behavior of people in organizations. In each edition of this book, we have focused on making sure that readers see the link between OB theories, research, and implications for practice.
- *Absence of pedagogy.* Part of the reason we've been able to keep this book short in length is that it doesn't include review questions, cases, exercises, or similar teaching/learning aids. It continues to provide only the basic core of OB knowledge, allowing instructors the maximum flexibility in designing and shaping their courses. Exercises and other teaching/learning aids can be found online on MyManagementLab.
- *Integration of globalization, diversity, and ethics.* The topics of globalization and cross-cultural differences, diversity, and ethics are discussed throughout this book. Rather than being presented in stand-alone chapters, these topics have been woven into the context of relevant issues. Users tell us they find that this integrative approach makes these topics more fully part of OB and reinforces their importance.
- *Comprehensive supplements.* Although this book may be short in length, it's not short on supplements. It comes with a complete, high-tech support package for both faculty and students. This includes a comprehensive Instructor's Manual, Test Item File and computerized Test Generator, DVD, PowerPoints, Blackboard and Web CT Courses and MyManagementLab. The Self-Assessment Library provides students with insights into their skills, abilities, and interests. These supplements are described in detail later in this preface.

CHAPTER-BY-CHAPTER CHANGES

Chapter 1 (What Is Organizational Behavior?)

- Defines *organizational behavior* with current data, business examples, and research
- New OB model, with better integration with pedagogy (structure) of book

Chapter 2 (Diversity in Organizations)

- Describes the two major forms of workplace diversity, covering surface-level diversity and deep-level diversity
- Explores the biographical characteristics of age, gender, race, disability, and length of service as some of the most obvious ways employees differ, and how those identities impact the workplace
- Discusses other biographical characteristics such as tenure, religion, sexual orientation, and gender identity as additional sources of workplace diversity
- Explores the role of intellectual ability and physical ability on employee performance
- Provides diversity management strategies for attracting, selecting, developing, and retaining diverse employees

Chapter 3 (Attitudes and Job Satisfaction)

- Describes how the social relationships one has at work contribute to job satisfaction
- Updated research on organizational commitment and employee engagement

- Review of recent studies on within-person variation in job attitudes
- Updated material on organizational citizenship behaviors
- New perspectives on attitudes and organizational performance
- Exploration of job satisfaction across cultures, including a look at Eastern and Western cultural differences

Chapter 4 (Emotions and Moods)

- Revised introduction to the topic
- Enhanced discussion of emotional intelligence
- Review of research on moods and employee attachment
- New section on "moral emotions"
- Discussion of emotion regulation strategies and their consequences
- New research on gender and emotions
- Updated content on emotional displays at work
- Integration of international cultural considerations
- Research discussion on positive and negative affect in Western and Eastern cultures

Chapter 5 (Personality and Values)

- Introduces concepts related to dispositional self- and other-orientation
- New material regarding vocational choices
- New discussion of values and reaction to violations of employee values
- Major revision regarding Hofstede's model of culture and its consequences
- Updated information on personality and expatriate success

Chapter 6 (Perception and Individual Decision Making)

- Review of recent work on self-serving biases
- New information on stereotyping processes
- Discussion of latest trends in decision errors research
- Updated discussion of culture and perceptions

Chapter 7 (Motivation Concepts)

- New material on psychological need theories
- Increased discussion of employee engagement
- Updates to the discussion on goal-setting theory
- New perspectives on equity and organizational justice
- Discussion of the impact of various cultures on the hierarchy of needs theory and McClelland's theory of needs. Exploration of the implications of equity theory in different cultures

Chapter 8 (Motivation: From Concepts to Applications)

- Updated discussion of job characteristics
- New coverage of flextime, telecommuting, and related work practices
- Revised discussion of employee empowerment and its effects
- Discussions of innovations in gainsharing practices
- Integration of international cultural considerations

- Consideration of job rotation in international manufacturing settings, a discussion of the success of employee involvement programs in non-U.S. countries, and the adoption of flexible benefits programs in Canada and the United Kingdom

Chapter 9 (Foundations of Group Behavior)

- New information on defining and classifying groups
- New material on dysfunctional behavior in teams
- Discussion of minority influence on group decision making
- New section on temporary groups with deadlines
- Updated information on group decision errors and groupthink
- Introduction of Group Property 6: Diversity
- New information on international variations in group behavior integration of international cultural considerations
- Discussion of social loafing in various cultures and the impact of group member diversity on group performance

Chapter 10 (Understanding Work Teams)

- Updated discussion of strategies to improve team performance
- Review of research on team decision-making strategies
- New perspectives on creativity in teams
- New material on team proactivity
- Discussion on diversity created by national differences
- Discussion on diversity in teams of members from various cultures, and research on teams in the United Kingdom and China

Chapter 11 (Communication)

- New section on social networking
- New section on blogs
- New section on lying
- Discussion of how to frame messages for maximum impact
- Discussion of the effects of authority, expertise, and liking on communication effectiveness
- Updated discussion of body language in communication
- Introduces new ideas about the effect of electronic communication
- Integration of international communication cultural considerations

Chapter 12 (Leadership)

- Expanded discussion of leader effects on employee attitudes
- New perspectives on culture and leadership
- New material regarding emotional intelligence and leadership
- Consideration of "servant leadership"
- Discussion of how leaders can increase employee productivity
- The GLOBE Framework for Assessing Cultures is discussed as it relates to behavioral theories of leadership
- Discussion of leadership internationally including transformational leadership and servant leadership

Chapter 13 (Power and Politics)

- Coverage of latest research on influence tactics
- Revised discussion of sexual harassment
- Updated discussion of political behavior in organizations
- Revision to discussion of international issues in power and politics
- Added discussions and research on the use of organizational power tactics and organizational political behavior across cultures

Chapter 14 (Conflict and Negotiation)

- Updated material on gender and negotiation styles
- New material on individual differences in negotiation styles
- Discussion of emotions in negotiation
- New information on suspicion and deception in negotiation
- Updates to discussion on conflict and conflict management processes
- Discussion of the effect of conflict on group productivity on team performance and the effectiveness of conflict resolution strategies in different cultures.
- Discussion on negotiation strategies within and across cultures

Chapter 15 (Foundations of Organization Structure)

- Latest research on boundaryless organizations and their functioning
- Discussion of technology's influence on organizational structure
- Updated review of the relationship between organizational structure and attitudes
- Updated examples from businesses and OB research
- Research on the role of various power-distance cultures on how structure affects employee performance and satisfaction

Chapter 16 (Organizational Culture)

- New review of basic issues in organizational culture and subcultures
- Enhanced discussion of ethical culture
- Review of culture and organizational performance
- Revised discussion of organizational socialization practices and outcomes
- Updated examples from businesses and OB research

Chapter 17 (Organizational Change and Stress Management)

- Updated review of research on individual readiness for organizational change
- Discussion of maladaptive behavioral response to stress at work
- Updated discussion of coping strategies
- Implications of the stress–health relationship
- Exploration of how idea champions are successful in various cultures. Research ideas on the impact of work stress on physical well-being across cultures.

SUPPLEMENTS PACKAGE

Essentials of Organizational Behavior continues to be supported with an extensive supplements package for both students and faculty.

Faculty Resources

All of the following supplements can be downloaded from our Instructor Resource Center. Request your user name and password from your Pearson Sales Representative. www.pearsonhighered.com/irc

If you ever need assistance, our dedicated technical support team is ready to help with the media supplements that accompany this text. Visit **http://247pearsoned .custhelp.com** for answers to frequently asked questions and user support.

INSTRUCTOR'S MANUAL

This instructor's manual includes chapter overview, chapter objectives lecture outlines, discussion questions and possible answers, and additional activities and assignments for your students.

TEST ITEM FILE

This Test Item File contains more than 1,000 questions, including multiple-choice, true/false, and essay. Each question is followed by the correct answer, the learning objective it ties to, AACSB category, course learning objective, question type (concept, application, critical-thinking, or synthesis), and difficulty rating. It has been thoroughly reviewed by an assessment expert.

TESTGEN

The software is PC/Mac compatible and preloaded with all of the Test Item File questions. You can manually or randomly view test questions and drag and drop to create a test. You can add or modify test-bank questions as needed.

INSTRUCTOR POWERPOINTS

This presentation includes basic outlines and key points from each chapter. It includes figures from the text but no forms of rich media, which makes the file size manageable and easier to share online or via e-mail. This set was also designed for the professor who prefers to customize PowerPoints and who wants to be spared from having to strip out animation, embedded files, and other media-rich features.

LEARNING MANAGEMENT SYSTEMS

Our TestGens are converted for use in BlackBoard and WebCT. These standard course cartridges contain the Instructor's Manual, TestGen, Instructor PowerPoints, and when available, Student PowerPoints and Student Data Files.

VIDEO LIBRARY

Videos illustrating the most important subject topics are available in two formats:

DVD—available for classroom use by instructors; includes videos mapped to Pearson textbooks.
MyLab—available for instructors and students, provides round-the-clock instant access to videos and corresponding assessment and simulations for Pearson textbooks.

Contact your local Pearson representative to request access to either format.

Student Resources

PEARSON'S SELF-ASSESSMENT LIBRARY (SAL)

The Self-Assessment Library is available with this text in print, CD-ROM, and online. It contains more than 60 self-scoring exercises that provide insights into your skills, abilities, and interests. To order *Essentials of Organizational Behavior* with the Self-Assessment Library, use ISBN 0-13-336521-2.

COURSESMART ETEXTBOOKS

CourseSmart eTextbooks were developed for students looking to save on required or recommended textbooks. Students simply select their eText by title or author and purchase immediate access to the content for the duration of the course using any major credit card. With a CourseSmart eText, students can search for specific keywords or page numbers, take notes online, print out reading assignments that incorporate lecture notes, and bookmark important passages for later review. For more information or to purchase a CourseSmart eTextbook, visit www.coursesmart.com.

ACKNOWLEDGMENTS

We owe a debt of gratitude to all those at Pearson who have supported this text over the past 25 years and who have worked so hard on the development of this latest edition. On the editorial side, we want to thank Editor-in-Chief Stephanie Wall, Senior Editor Kris Ellis-Levy, Director of Editorial Services Ashley Santora, Editorial Project Manager Sarah Holle, and Editorial Assistant Bernard Ollila. On the production side, Project Manager Becca Groves did an outstanding job. The authors are grateful for Lori Ehrman Tinkey for her invaluable assistance in manuscript editing and preparation. Last but not least, we would like to thank Senior Marketing Manager Erin Gardner and Director of Marketing Maggie Moylan and their sales staff who have been selling this book over its many editions. Thank you for the attention you've given this book.

ABOUT THE AUTHORS

Stephen P. Robbins
Ph.D. University of Arizona

Stephen P. Robbins is professor emeritus of management at San Diego State University and the world's best-selling textbook author in the areas of both management and organizational behavior. His books are used at more than a thousand U.S. colleges and universities, have been translated into 19 languages, and have adapted editions for Canada, Australia, South Africa, and India. Dr. Robbins is also the author of the best-selling books *The Truth About Managing People*, 2nd ed. (Financial Times/Prentice Hall, 2008) and *Decide & Conquer* (Financial Times/Prentice Hall, 2004).

In his "other life," Dr. Robbins actively participates in masters' track competitions. Since turning 50 in 1993, he's won 18 national championships; 12 world titles; and set numerous U.S. and world age-group records at 60, 100, 200, and 400 meters. In 2005, Dr. Robbins was elected into the USA Masters' Track & Field Hall of Fame.

Timothy A. Judge
Ph.D. University of Illinois at Urbana-Champaign

Timothy A. Judge is currently the Franklin D. Schurz Professor of Management at the Mendoza College of Business, University of Notre Dame. He has held academic positions at the University of Florida, University of Iowa, Cornell University, Charles University in the Czech Republic, Comenius University in Slovakia, and University of Illinois at Urbana-Champaign. Dr. Judge's primary research interests are in (1) personality, moods, and emotions; (2) job attitudes; (3) leadership and influence behaviors; and (4) careers (person–organization fit, career success).

Dr. Judge has published more than 150 articles in these and other major topics in journals such as the *Academy of Management Journal* and the *Journal of Applied Psychology*. He is a fellow of several organizations, including the American Psychological Association and the Academy of Management. In 1995, Dr. Judge received the Distinguished Early Career Contributions Award from the Society for Industrial and Organizational Psychology, and in 2001, he received the Larry L. Cummings Award for midcareer contributions from the Organizational Behavior Division of the Academy of Management. He is a coauthor of *Organizational Behavior*, 13th ed., with Stephen P. Robbins and *Staffing Organizations*, 6th ed., with Herbert G. Heneman III. He is married and has three children, a daughter who was recently graduated with her a masters degree, a daughter currently in college, and a son in elementary school.

PART 1: Prologue

1
■ ■ ■
Introduction to Organizational Behavior

After studying this chapter, you should be able to:

- Define *organizational behavior* (*OB*).
- Show the value to OB of systematic study.
- Identify the major behavioral science disciplines that contribute to OB.
- Demonstrate why few absolutes apply to OB.
- Identify the challenges and opportunities managers have in applying OB concepts.
- Identify the three levels of analysis in OB.

MyManagementLab™
⭐ **Improve Your Grade!**

Over 10 million students improved their results using the Pearson MyLabs. Visit **mymanagementlab.com** for simulations, tutorials, and end-of-chapter problems.

If you ask managers to describe their most frequent or troublesome problems, the answers you get tend to exhibit a common theme. The managers most often describe people problems. They talk about their bosses' poor communication skills, employees' resistance to a company reorganization, and similar concerns. It may surprise you to learn that only recently have courses in people skills become an important part of business school programs.

Until the late 1980s, business school curricula emphasized the technical aspects of management, focusing on economics, accounting, finance, and quantitative techniques. Course work in human behavior and people skills received relatively less attention. Over the past three decades, business school faculty have come to realize the significant role understanding human behavior plays in determining a manager's effectiveness; required courses on people skills have therefore been added to many curricula.

Developing managers' interpersonal skills also helps organizations attract and keep high-performing employees. Regardless of labor market conditions, outstanding employees are always in short supply.[1] Companies known as good places to work—such as Starbucks, Adobe Systems, Cisco, Whole Foods, Google, American Express, Amgen, Pfizer, and Marriott—have a big advantage. A recent survey of hundreds of workplaces, and more than 200,000 respondents, showed the social relationships among co-workers and supervisors were strongly related to overall job satisfaction. Positive social relationships also were associated with lower stress at work and lower intentions to quit.[2] Having managers with good interpersonal skills is likely to make the workplace more pleasant, which in turn makes it easier to hire and keep qualified people. Creating a pleasant workplace also appears to make good economic sense. Companies with reputations as good places to work (such as *Forbes'* "100 Best Companies to Work for in America") have been found to generate superior financial performance.[3]

We have come to understand that in today's competitive and demanding workplace, managers can't succeed on their technical skills alone. They also have to have good people skills. This book has been written to help both managers and potential managers develop those people skills.

ENTER ORGANIZATIONAL BEHAVIOR

OB's goal is to understand and predict human behavior in organizations; the complexities of human behavior are not easy to predict, but neither are they random—certain fundamental consistencies underlie the behavior of all individuals.

We've made the case for the importance of people skills. But neither this book nor the discipline on which it is based is called "people skills." The term that is widely used to describe the discipline is *organizational behavior.*

Organizational behavior (often abbreviated OB) is a field of study that investigates the impact individuals, groups, and structure have on behavior within organizations, for the purpose of applying such knowledge toward improving an organization's effectiveness. That's a mouthful, so let's break it down.

Organizational behavior is a field of study, meaning that it is a distinct area of expertise with a common body of knowledge. What does it study? It studies three determinants of behavior in organizations: individuals, groups, and structure. In addition, OB applies the knowledge gained about individuals, groups, and the effect of structure on behavior in order to make organizations work more effectively.

To sum up our definition, OB is the study of what people do in an organization and how their behavior affects the organization's performance. And because OB is concerned specifically with employment-related situations, it emphasizes behavior as related to concerns such as jobs, work, absenteeism, employment turnover, productivity, human performance, and management. Although debate exists about the relative importance of each, OB includes the core topics:

- Motivation
- Leader behavior and power
- Interpersonal communication
- Group structure and processes
- Attitude development and perception
- Change processes
- Conflict and negotiation
- Work design[4]

COMPLEMENTING INTUITION WITH SYSTEMATIC STUDY

Each of us is a student of behavior. Whether you've explicitly thought about it before, you've been "reading" people almost all your life, watching their actions and trying to interpret what you see or predict what people might do under different conditions. Unfortunately, the casual or common-sense approach to reading others can often lead to erroneous predictions. However, you can improve your predictive ability by supplementing intuition with a more systematic approach.

The systematic approach in this book will uncover important facts and relationships and provide a base from which to make more accurate predictions of behavior. Underlying this systematic approach is the belief that behavior is not random. Rather, we can identify fundamental consistencies underlying the behavior of all individuals and modify them to reflect individual differences.

These fundamental consistencies are very important. Why? Because they allow predictability. Behavior is generally predictable, and the *systematic study* of behavior is a means to making reasonably accurate predictions. When we use the term **systematic study**, we mean looking at relationships, attempting to attribute causes and effects, and basing our conclusions on scientific evidence—that is, on data gathered under controlled conditions and measured and interpreted in a reasonably rigorous manner.

Evidence-based management (EBM) complements systematic study by basing managerial decisions on the best available scientific evidence. For example, we want doctors to make decisions about patient care based on the latest available evidence, and EBM argues that managers should do the same, becoming more scientific in how they think about management problems. A manager might pose a managerial question, search for the best available evidence, and apply the relevant information to the question or case at hand. You might think it difficult to argue against this (what manager would say decisions shouldn't be based on evidence?), but the vast majority of management decisions are still made "on the fly," with little or systematic study of available evidence.[5]

Systematic study and EBM add to **intuition**, or those "gut feelings" about what makes others (and ourselves) "tick." Of course, the things you have come to believe in an unsystematic way are not necessarily incorrect. Jack Welch (former CEO of GE) noted, "The trick, of course, is to know when to go with your gut." But if we make *all* decisions with intuition or gut instinct, we're likely working with incomplete information—like making an investment decision with only half the data.

DISCIPLINES THAT CONTRIBUTE TO THE OB FIELD

Organizational behavior is an applied behavioral science built on contributions from a number of behavioral disciplines, mainly psychology and social psychology, sociology, and anthropology. Psychology's contributions have been mainly at the individual or micro level of analysis, whereas the other disciplines have contributed to our understanding of macro concepts such as group processes and organization. Exhibit 1-1 is an overview of the major contributions to the study of organizational behavior.

Several social science disciplines contribute to OB, but none are more important than psychology.

Psychology

Psychology seeks to measure, explain, and sometimes change the behavior of humans and other animals. Those who have contributed and continue to add to the knowledge

EXHIBIT 1-1
Toward an OB Discipline

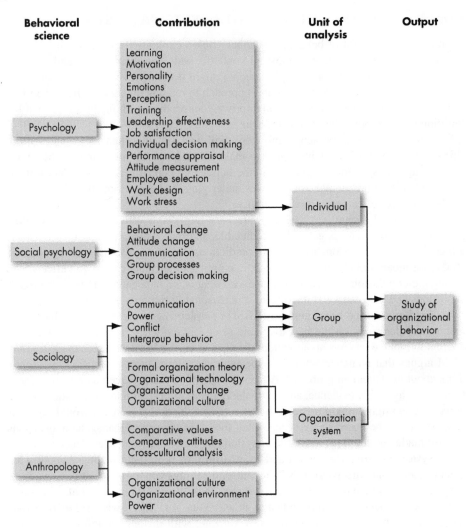

Behavioral science	Contribution	Unit of analysis	Output

Psychology →
Learning
Motivation
Personality
Emotions
Perception
Training
Leadership effectiveness
Job satisfaction
Individual decision making
Performance appraisal
Attitude measurement
Employee selection
Work design
Work stress
→ Individual

Social psychology →
Behavioral change
Attitude change
Communication
Group processes
Group decision making

Sociology →
Communication
Power
Conflict
Intergroup behavior
→ Group

Formal organization theory
Organizational technology
Organizational change
Organizational culture

Anthropology →
Comparative values
Comparative attitudes
Cross-cultural analysis
→ Organization system

Organizational culture
Organizational environment
Power

→ Study of organizational behavior

of OB are learning theorists, personality theorists, counseling psychologists, and, most important, industrial and organizational psychologists.

Early industrial/organizational psychologists studied the problems of fatigue, boredom, and other working conditions that could impede efficient work performance. More recently, their contributions have expanded to include learning, perception, personality, emotions, training, leadership effectiveness, needs and motivational forces, job satisfaction, decision-making processes, performance appraisals, attitude measurement, employee-selection techniques, work design, and job stress.

Social Psychology

Social psychology, generally considered a branch of psychology, blends concepts from both psychology and sociology to focus on people's influence on one another. One major study area is *change*—how to implement it and how to reduce barriers to its acceptance. Social psychologists also contribute to measuring, understanding, and changing attitudes;

identifying communication patterns; and building trust. Finally, they have made important contributions to our study of group behavior, power, and conflict.

Sociology

Whereas psychology focuses on the individual, **sociology** studies people in relation to their social environment or culture. Sociologists have contributed to OB through their study of group behavior in organizations, particularly formal and complex organizations. Perhaps most important, sociologists have studied organizational culture, formal organization theory and structure, organizational technology, communications, power, and conflict.

Anthropology

Anthropology is the study of societies to learn about human beings and their activities. Anthropologists' work on cultures and environments has helped us understand differences in fundamental values, attitudes, and behavior between people in different countries and within different organizations. Much of our current understanding of organizational culture, organizational environments, and differences among national cultures is a result of the work of anthropologists or those using their methods.

THERE ARE FEW ABSOLUTES IN OB

Laws in the physical sciences—chemistry, astronomy, physics—are consistent and apply in a wide range of situations. They allow scientists to generalize about the pull of gravity or to be confident about sending astronauts into space to repair satellites. But as a noted behavioral researcher observed, "God gave all the easy problems to the physicists." Human beings are complex, and few, if any, simple and universal principles explain organizational behavior. Because we are not alike, our ability to make simple, accurate, and sweeping generalizations is limited. Two people often act very differently in the same situation, and the same person's behavior changes in different situations. Not everyone is motivated by money, and people may behave differently at a religious service than they do at a party.

That doesn't mean, of course, that we can't offer reasonably accurate explanations of human behavior or make valid predictions. It does mean that OB concepts must reflect situational, or contingency, conditions. We can say *x* leads to *y,* but only under conditions specified in *z*—the **contingency variables**. The science of OB was developed by applying general concepts to a particular situation, person, or group. For example, OB scholars would avoid stating that everyone likes complex and challenging work (the general concept). Why? Because not everyone wants a challenging job. Some people prefer routine over varied, or simple over complex. A job attractive to one person may not be to another; its appeal is contingent on the person who holds it.

As you proceed through this book, you'll encounter a wealth of research-based theories about how people behave in organizations. But don't expect to find a lot of straightforward cause-and-effect relationships. There aren't many! Organizational behavior theories mirror the subject matter with which they deal, and people are complex and complicated.

CHALLENGES AND OPPORTUNITIES FOR OB

Understanding organizational behavior has never been more important for managers. Take a quick look at the dramatic changes in organizations. The typical employee is getting older; more women and people of color are in the workplace; corporate downsizing and the heavy use of temporary workers are severing the bonds of loyalty that tied many employees to their employers; and global competition requires employees to become more flexible and cope with rapid change. The global recession has brought to the forefront the challenges of working with and managing people during uncertain times.

In short, today's challenges bring opportunities for managers to use OB concepts. In this section, we review some of the most critical issues confronting managers for which OB offers solutions—or at least meaningful insights toward solutions.

Responding to Economic Pressures

When the U.S. economy plunged into a deep and prolonged recession in 2008, virtually all other large economies around the world followed suit. Layoffs and job losses were widespread, and those who survived the ax were often asked to accept pay cuts.

During difficult economic times, effective management is often at a premium. Anybody can run a company when business is booming because the difference between good and bad management reflects the difference between making a lot of money and making a lot more money. When times are bad, though, managers are on the front lines with employees who must be fired, who are asked to make do with less, and who worry about their futures. The difference between good and bad management can be the difference between profit and loss or, ultimately, between survival and failure.

There are many reasons why it is more important than ever to learn OB concepts.

Managing employees well when times are tough is just as hard as when times are good—if not more so. But the OB approaches sometimes differ. In good times, understanding how to reward, satisfy, and retain employees is at a premium. In bad times, issues like stress, decision making, and coping come to the fore.

Responding to Globalization

Organizations are no longer constrained by national borders. Burger King is owned by a British firm, and McDonald's sells hamburgers in more than 100 countries in six continents. ExxonMobil, a so-called U.S. company, reported that less than 6 percent of their 2011 earnings were from gas and products sales in the United States.[6] New employees at Finland-based phone maker Nokia are increasingly being recruited from India, China, and other developing countries—non-Finns now outnumber Finns at their renowned research center in Helsinki. And all major automobile makers now manufacture cars outside their borders: Honda builds cars in Ohio, Ford in Brazil, Volkswagen in Mexico, and both Mercedes and BMW in South Africa.

The world has become a global village. In the process, the manager's job has changed.

INCREASED FOREIGN ASSIGNMENTS   If you're a manager, you are increasingly likely to find yourself in a foreign assignment—transferred to your employer's operating division or subsidiary in another country. Once there, you'll have to manage a workforce very different in needs, aspirations, and attitudes from those you are used to back home.

WORKING WITH PEOPLE FROM DIFFERENT CULTURES   Even in your own country, you'll find yourself working with bosses, peers, and other employees born and raised in different cultures. What motivates you may not motivate them. Or your communication style may be straightforward and open, which others may find uncomfortable and threatening. To work effectively with people from different cultures, you need to understand how their culture, geography, and religion have shaped them and how to adapt your management style to their differences.

OVERSEEING MOVEMENT OF JOBS TO COUNTRIES WITH LOW-COST LABOR   It's increasingly difficult for managers in advanced nations, where minimum wages are typically $6 or more an hour, to compete against firms that rely on workers from China and other developing nations where labor is available for 30 cents an hour. It's not by chance that many people in the United States wear clothes made in China, work on computers whose microchips came from Taiwan, and watch movies filmed in Canada. In a global economy, jobs tend to flow where lower costs give businesses a comparative advantage, though labor groups, politicians, and local community leaders see exporting jobs as undermining the job market at home. Managers face the difficult task of balancing the interests of their organizations with their responsibilities to the communities in which they operate.

Managing Workforce Diversity

One of the most important challenges for organizations is *workforce diversity,* the concept that organizations are becoming more heterogeneous in terms of gender, age, race, ethnicity, sexual orientation, and inclusion of other diverse groups. Whereas globalization focuses on differences among people *from* different countries, workforce diversity addresses differences among people *within* given countries.

Workforce diversity acknowledges a workforce of women and men; many racial and ethnic groups; individuals with a variety of physical or psychological abilities; and people who differ in age and sexual orientation. Managing this diversity is a global concern. For example, most European countries have experienced dramatic growth in immigration from the Middle East. Argentina and Venezuela host a significant number of migrants from other South American countries, and nations from India to Iraq to Indonesia find great cultural diversity within their borders.

The most significant change in the U.S. labor force during the last half of the twentieth century was the rapid increase in the number of female workers. In 1950, for instance, only 29.6 percent of the workforce was female. By 2008, it was 46.5 percent. The first half of the twenty-first century will be notable for changes in racial and ethnic composition and an aging baby-boom generation. By 2050, Hispanics will grow from today's 11 percent of the workforce to 24 percent, blacks will increase from 12 to 14 percent, and Asians from 5 to 11 percent. Meanwhile, in the near term the labor force will be aging. The 55-and-older age group, currently 13 percent of the labor force, will increase to 20 percent by 2014.[7]

Though we have more to say about workforce diversity in the next chapter, suffice it to say here that it presents great opportunities and poses challenging questions for managers and employees in all countries. How can we leverage differences within groups for competitive advantage? Should we treat all employees alike? Should we recognize individual and cultural differences? How can we foster cultural awareness in employees without lapsing into political correctness? What are the legal requirements in each country? Does diversity even matter? Exhibit 1-2 outlines the major workforce diversity issues employers need to ensure they are addressed in their organizations.

EXHIBIT 1-2
Major Workforce Diversity Categories

GENDER

Nearly half of the U.S. workforce is now made up of women, and women are a growing percentage of the workforce in most countries throughout the world. Organizations need to ensure that hiring and employment policies create equal access and opportunities to individuals, regardless of gender.

RACE

The percentage of Hispanics, blacks, and Asians in the U.S. workforce continues to increase. Organizations need to ensure that policies provide equal access and opportunities, regardless of race.

NATIONAL ORIGIN

A growing percentage of U.S. workers are immigrants or come from homes where English is not the primary language spoken. Because employers in the United States have the right to demand that English be spoken at the workplace during job-related activities, communication problems can occur when employees' English-language skills are weak.

AGE

The U.S. workforce is aging, and recent polls indicate that an increasing percentage of employees expect to work past the traditional retirement age of 65. Organizations cannot discriminate on the basis of age and need to make accommodations for the needs of older workers.

DISABILITY

Organizations need to ensure that jobs and workplaces are accessible to the mentally, physically, and health challenged.

DOMESTIC PARTNERS

An increasing number of gay and lesbian employees, as well as employees with live-in partners of the opposite sex, are demanding the same rights and benefits for their partners that organizations have provided for traditional married couples.

RELIGION

Organizations need to be sensitive to the customs, rituals, and holidays, as well as the appearance and attire, of individuals of non-Christian faiths such as Judaism, Islam, Hinduism, Buddhism, and Sikhism, and ensure that these individuals suffer no adverse impact as a result of their appearance or practices.

Improving Customer Service

Today, the majority of employees in developed countries work in service jobs, including 80 percent in the United States. In Australia, 73 percent work in service industries. In the United Kingdom, Germany, and Japan, the percentages are 69, 68, and 65, respectively. Service jobs include technical support representatives, fast-food counter workers, sales clerks, waiters and waitresses, nurses, automobile repair technicians, consultants, credit representatives, financial planners, and flight attendants. The common characteristic of these jobs is substantial interaction with an organization's customers. Many an organization has failed because its employees failed to please customers. Management needs to create a customer-responsive culture. OB can provide considerable guidance in helping managers create such cultures—in which employees are friendly and courteous, accessible, knowledgeable, prompt in responding to customer needs, and willing to do what's necessary to please the customer.[8]

Improving People Skills

As you proceed through the chapters of this book, we'll present relevant concepts and theories that can help you explain and predict the behavior of people at work. You'll also gain insights into specific people skills that you can use on the job. For instance, you'll learn ways to design motivating jobs, techniques for improving your listening skills, and how to create more effective teams.

Stimulating Innovation and Change

Whatever happened to Montgomery Ward, Woolworth, Smith Corona, TWA, Bethlehem Steel, and WorldCom? All these giants went bust. Why have other giants, such as General Motors, Sears, Boeing, and Lucent Technologies, implemented huge cost-cutting programs and eliminated thousands of jobs? The answer is to avoid going broke.

Today's successful organizations must foster innovation and master the art of change, or they'll become candidates for extinction. Victory will go to the organizations that maintain their flexibility, continually improve their quality, and beat their competition to the marketplace with a constant stream of innovative products and services. Domino's single-handedly brought on the demise of small pizza parlors whose managers thought they could continue doing what they had been doing for years. Amazon. com is putting a lot of independent bookstores out of business as it proves you can successfully sell books (and most anything else) from a website. After years of lackluster performance, Boeing realized it needed to change its business model. The result was its 787 Dreamliner and a return to being the world's largest airplane manufacturer.

An organization's employees can be the impetus for innovation and change, or they can be a major stumbling block. The challenge for managers is to stimulate their employees' creativity and tolerance for change. The field of OB provides a wealth of ideas and techniques to aid in realizing these goals.

Coping with "Temporariness"

Globalization, expanded capacity, and advances in technology have required organizations to be fast and flexible if they are to survive. The result is that most managers and employees today work in a climate best characterized as "temporary."

Workers must continually update their knowledge and skills to perform new job requirements. Production employees at companies such as Caterpillar, Ford, and Alcoa need to keep up with changes in CAD/CAM equipment. That was not part of their job descriptions 20 years ago. In the past, employees were assigned to a specific work group, gaining a considerable amount of security working with the same people day in, day out. That predictability has been replaced by temporary work groups, with members from different departments, and the increased use of employee rotation to fill constantly changing work assignments. Finally, organizations are in a state of flux. They continually reorganize their various divisions, sell off poorly performing businesses, downsize operations, subcontract noncritical services and operations to other organizations, and replace permanent employees with temporary workers.

Today's managers and employees must learn to cope with temporariness, flexibility, spontaneity, and unpredictability. The study of OB can help you better understand a work world of continual change, overcome resistance to change, and create an organizational culture that thrives on change. What we are advising is to use evidence as much as possible to inform your intuition and experience. That is the promise of OB.

Working in Networked Organizations

Networked organizations allow people to communicate and work together even though they may be thousands of miles apart. Independent contractors can telecommute via computer to workplaces around the globe and change employers as the demand for their services changes. Software programmers, graphic designers, systems analysts, technical writers, photo researchers, book and media editors, and medical transcribers are just a few examples of people who can work from home or other nonoffice locations.

The manager's job is different in a networked organization. Motivating and leading people and making collaborative decisions online requires different techniques than when individuals are physically present in a single location. As more employees do their jobs by linking to others through networks, managers must develop new skills. OB can provide valuable insights to help with honing those skills.

Helping Employees Balance Work–Life Conflicts

The typical employee in the 1960s or 1970s showed up at a specified workplace Monday through Friday and worked for clearly defined 8- or 9-hour chunks of time. That's no longer true for a large segment of today's workforce. Employees are increasingly complaining that the line between work and nonwork time has become blurred, creating personal conflicts and stress.[9] At the same time, today's workplace presents opportunities for workers to create and structure their own roles.

How do work–life conflicts come about? First, the creation of global organizations means the world never sleeps. Many employees of global firms are "on call" 24 hours a day because they need to consult with colleagues or customers 8 or 10 time zones away. Second, communication technology allows many technical and professional employees to do their work at home, in their cars, or on the beach in Tahiti—but it also means many feel like they never really get away from the office. Third, organizations are asking employees to put in longer hours. Over a recent 10-year period, the average U.S. workweek increased from 43 to 47 hours; and the number of people working 50 or more hours a week jumped from 24 to 37 percent. Finally, the rise of the dual-career couple makes it difficult for married employees to find time to fulfill commitments to home, spouse, children, parents, and friends. Millions of single-parent households and employees with dependent parents have even more significant challenges in balancing work and family responsibilities.

Employees increasingly recognize that work infringes on their personal lives, and they're not happy about it. Recent studies suggest employees want jobs that give them flexibility in their work schedules so they can better manage work–life conflicts.[10] In fact, balancing work and life demands now surpasses job security as an employee priority.[11]

The next generation of employees is likely to show similar concerns.[12] Most college and university students say attaining a balance between personal life and work is a primary career goal; they want "a life" as well as a job. Organizations that don't help their people achieve work–life balance will find it increasingly difficult to attract and retain the most capable and motivated employees.

As you'll see in later chapters, the field of OB offers a number of suggestions to guide managers in designing workplaces and jobs that can help employees deal with work–life conflicts.

Improving Ethical Behavior

In an organizational world characterized by cutbacks, expectations of increasing productivity, and tough competition, it's not surprising many employees feel pressured to cut corners, break rules, and engage in other questionable practices.

Increasingly they face **ethical dilemmas** and **ethical choices**, in which they are required to identify right and wrong conduct. What constitutes good ethical behavior has never been clearly defined, and, in recent years, the line differentiating right from wrong has blurred. Employees see people all around them engaging in unethical practices— elected officials pad expense accounts or take bribes; corporate executives inflate profits so they can cash in lucrative stock options; and university administrators look the other way when winning coaches encourage scholarship athletes to take easy courses. When caught, these people give excuses such as "Everyone does it" or "You have to seize every advantage nowadays." Determining the ethically correct way to behave is especially difficult in a global economy because different cultures have different perspectives on certain ethical issues.[13] Fair treatment of employees in an economic downturn varies considerably across cultures, for instance. Is it any wonder employees are expressing decreased confidence in management and increasing uncertainty about what is appropriate ethical behavior in their organizations?[14]

Managers and their organizations are responding to the problem of unethical behavior in a number of ways.[15] They're writing and distributing codes of ethics to guide employees through dilemmas. They're offering seminars, workshops, and other training programs to try to improve ethical behaviors. They're providing in-house advisors who can be contacted, in many cases anonymously, for assistance in dealing with issues, and they're creating protection mechanisms for employees who reveal internal unethical practices.

Today's manager must create an ethically healthy climate for her employees, where they can do their work productively with minimal ambiguity about right versus wrong behaviors. Companies that promote a strong ethical mission, encourage employees to behave with integrity, and provide strong leadership can influence employee decisions to behave ethically.[16] In upcoming chapters, we'll discuss the actions managers can take to create an ethically healthy climate and help employees sort through ambiguous situations.

THE PLAN OF THIS BOOK

How is this book going to help you better explain, predict, and control behavior? Our approach uses a building-block process. As illustrated in Exhibit 1-3, OB is characterized by three levels of analysis. As we move from the individual level to the organization system level, we increase in an additive fashion our understanding of behavior in organizations.

EXHIBIT 1-3
Levels of OB
Analysis

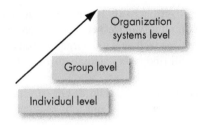

Chapters 2 through 8 deal with the individual in the organization. We begin by looking at such foundations of individual behavior as personality and values. Then we consider perceptions, decision making, and attitudes. Next, we focus on the fundamental role of motivational states to individual behavior. We conclude this section with a discussion of moods and emotions.

The behavior of people in groups is something more than the sum total of each individual acting in his own way. People's behavior in groups is different from their behavior when alone. Chapters 9 through 14 address group behavior. We introduce basic group concepts, discuss ways to make teams more effective, consider communication issues and group decision making, and then investigate the important topics of leadership, power, politics, conflict, and negotiation.

OB reaches its highest level of sophistication when we add the formal organization system to our knowledge of individual and group behavior. Just as groups are more than the sum of their individual members, organizations are not necessarily merely the summation of the behavior of a number of groups. In Chapters 15 through 17, we discuss how an organization's structure affects behavior, how each organization has its own culture that acts to shape the behavior of its members, and the various organizational change and development techniques managers can use to affect behavior for the organization's benefit.

SUMMARY AND IMPLICATIONS FOR MANAGERS

Managers need to develop their interpersonal, or people, skills to be effective in their jobs. Organizational behavior (OB) investigates the impact that individuals, groups, and structure have on behavior within an organization, and it applies that knowledge to make organizations work more effectively. Specifically, OB focuses on how to improve productivity; reduce absenteeism, turnover, and deviant workplace behavior; and increase organizational citizenship behavior and job satisfaction. Here are a few specific implications for managers:

- Some generalizations provide valid insights into human behavior, but many are erroneous. Organizational behavior uses systematic study to improve predictions of behavior over intuition alone.
- Because people are different, we need to look at OB in a contingency framework, using situational variables to explain cause-and-effect relationships.
- Organizational behavior offers specific insights to improve a manager's people skills.
- It helps managers to see the value of workforce diversity and practices that may need to be changed in different countries.

- It can improve quality and employee productivity by showing managers how to empower their people, design and implement change programs, improve customer service, and help employees balance work–life conflicts.
- It can help managers cope in a world of temporariness and learn how to stimulate innovation.
- Finally, OB can guide managers in creating an ethically healthy work climate.

MyManagementLab

Go to **MyManagementLab.com** to access study plans, interactive lectures, and videos as well as Auto-graded writing questions and the following Assisted-graded writing question.

1-1. MyManagementLab Only—comprehensive writing assignment for this chapter.

PART 2: The Individual in the Organization

2
■ ■ ■
Diversity in Organizations

After studying this chapter, you should be able to:

- Describe the two major forms of workforce diversity.
- Recognize stereotypes and understand how they function in organizational settings.
- Identify the key biographical characteristics and describe how they are relevant to OB.
- Define *intellectual ability* and demonstrate its relevance to OB.
- Contrast intellectual and physical ability.
- Describe how organizations manage diversity effectively.

MyManagementLab™
⭐ **Improve Your Grade!**
Over 10 million students improved their results using the Pearson MyLabs. Visit
mymanagementlab.com for simulations, tutorials, and end-of-chapter problems.

DIVERSITY

We aren't all the same. This is obvious enough, but managers sometimes forget they need to recognize and capitalize on differences to get the most from their employees. Effective diversity management increases an organization's access to the widest possible pool of skills, abilities, and ideas. Managers also need to recognize that differences among people can lead to miscommunication, misunderstanding, and conflict. In this chapter, we'll learn about how individual characteristics like age, gender, race, ethnicity, and abilities can influence employee performance. We'll also see how managers can develop awareness about these characteristics and manage a diverse workforce effectively.

Demographic Characteristics of the U.S. Workforce

In the past, OB textbooks noted that rapid change was about to occur as the predominantly White, male managerial workforce gave way to a gender-balanced, multiethnic workforce. Today, that change is no longer happening: it has happened, and it is increasingly reflected in the makeup of managerial and professional jobs. Compared to 1976, women today are much more likely to be employed full-time, have more education, and earn wages comparable to those of men.[1] In addition, over the past 50 years, the earnings gap between Whites and other racial and ethnic groups has decreased significantly; past differences between Whites and Asians have disappeared or been reversed.[2] Workers over the age of 55 are an increasingly large portion of the workforce as well. This permanent shift toward a diverse workforce means organizations need to make diversity management a central component of their policies and practices. At the same time, however, differences in wages across genders and racial and ethnic groups persist, and executive positions in *Fortune* 500 corporations continue to be held by White males in numbers far beyond their representation in the workforce in general.

A survey by the Society for Human Resources Management shows some major employer concerns and opportunities resulting from the demographic makeup of the U.S. workforce.[3] The aging of the workforce was consistently the most significant concern of HR managers. The loss of skills resulting from the retirement of many baby boomers, increased medical costs due to an aging workforce, and many employees' needs to care for elderly relatives topped the list of issues. Other issues include developing multilingual training materials and providing work–life benefits for dual-career couples.

Levels of Diversity

Although much has been said about diversity in age, race, gender, ethnicity, religion, and disability status, experts now recognize these demographic characteristics are just the tip of the iceberg.[4] Demographics mostly reflect **surface-level diversity**, not thoughts and feelings, and can lead employees to perceive one another through stereotypes and assumptions. However, evidence has shown that as people get to know one another, they become less concerned about demographic differences if they see themselves as sharing more important characteristics, such as personality and values, that represent **deep-level diversity**.[5]

To understand this difference between surface- and deep-level diversity, consider a few examples. Luis and Carol are co-workers who seem to have little in common at first glance. Luis is a young, recently hired male college graduate with a business degree, raised in a Spanish-speaking neighborhood in Miami. Carol is an older, long-tenured woman raised in rural Kansas, who achieved her current level in the organization by starting as a high school graduate and working her way up the hierarchy. At first, these co-workers may experience some differences in communication based on their surface-level differences in education, ethnicity, regional background, and gender. However, as they get to know each other, they may find they are both deeply committed to their families, share a common way of thinking about important work problems, like to work collaboratively, and are interested in international assignments in the future. These deep-level similarities will overshadow the more superficial differences between them, and research suggests they will work well together.

On the other hand, Steve and Dave are two unmarried White male college graduates from Oregon who recently started working together. Superficially, they seem well matched. But Steve is highly introverted, prefers to avoid risks, solicits the opinions of others before making decisions, and likes the office quiet, whereas Dave is extraverted, risk-seeking, and assertive, and likes a busy, active, and energetic work environment. Their surface-level similarity will not necessarily lead to positive interactions because they have such fundamental, deep-level differences. It will be a challenge for them to collaborate regularly at work, and they'll have to make some compromises to get things done together.

Throughout this book, we will encounter differences between deep- and surface-level diversity in various contexts. Individual differences in personality and culture shape preferences for rewards, communication styles, reactions to leaders, negotiation styles, and many other aspects of behavior in organizations.

Discrimination

Although diversity does present many opportunities for organizations, effective diversity management also means working to eliminate unfair **discrimination**. To discriminate is to note a difference between things, which in itself isn't necessarily bad. Noticing one employee is more qualified is necessary for making hiring decisions; noticing another is taking on leadership responsibilities exceptionally well is necessary for making promotion decisions. Usually when we talk about discrimination, though, we mean allowing our behavior to be influenced by stereotypes about *groups* of people. Rather than looking at individual characteristics, unfair discrimination assumes everyone in a group is the same. This discrimination is often very harmful to organizations and employees.

Exhibit 2-1 provides definitions and examples of some forms of discrimination in organizations. Although many of these actions are prohibited by law, and therefore aren't part of almost any organization's official policies, thousands of cases of employment discrimination are documented every year, and many more go unreported. As discrimination has increasingly come under both legal scrutiny and social disapproval, most overt forms have faded, which may have resulted in an increase in more covert forms like incivility or exclusion.[6]

As you can see, discrimination can occur in many ways, and its effects can be just as varied depending on the organizational context and the personal biases of its members. Some forms, like exclusion or incivility, are especially hard to root out because they are impossible to observe and may occur simply because the actor isn't aware of the effects of his or her actions. Whether intentional or not, discrimination can lead to serious negative consequences for employers, including reduced productivity and citizenship behavior, negative conflicts, and increased turnover. Unfair discrimination also leaves qualified job candidates out of initial hiring and promotions. Even if an employment discrimination lawsuit is never filed, a strong business case can be made for aggressively working to eliminate unfair discrimination.

Diversity is a broad term, and the phrase *workplace diversity* can refer to any characteristic that makes people different from one another. The following section covers some important surface-level characteristics that differentiate members of the workforce.

BIOGRAPHICAL CHARACTERISTICS

Biographical characteristics such as age, gender, race, disability, and length of service are some of the most obvious ways employees differ. As discussed in Chapter 1, this textbook is essentially concerned with finding and analyzing the variables that affect employee productivity, absence, turnover, deviance, citizenship, and satisfaction. Many organizational concepts—motivation, say, or power and politics, or organizational

Type of Discrimination	Definition	Examples from Organizations
Discriminatory Policies or Practices	Actions taken by representatives of the organization that deny equal opportunity to perform or unequal rewards for performance	Older workers may be targeted for layoffs because they are highly paid and have lucrative benefits.
Sexual Harassment	Unwanted sexual advances and other verbal or physical conduct of a sexual nature that create a hostile or offensive work environment	Salespeople at one company went on company-paid visits to strip clubs, brought strippers into the office to celebrate promotions, and fostered pervasive sexual rumors.
Intimidation	Overt threats or bullying directed at members of specific groups of employees	African-American employees at some companies have found nooses hanging over their work stations.
Mockery and Insults	Jokes or negative stereotypes; sometimes the result of jokes taken too far	Arab-Americans have been asked at work whether they were carrying bombs or were members of terrorist organizations.
Exclusion	Exclusion of certain people from job opportunities, social events, discussions, or informal mentoring; can occur unintentionally	Many women in finance claim they are assigned to marginal job roles or are given light workloads that don't lead to promotion.
Incivility	Disrespectful treatment, including behaving in an aggressive manner, interrupting the person, or ignoring his or her opinions	Female lawyers note that male attorneys frequently cut them off or do not adequately address their comments.

EXHIBIT 2-1

Forms of Discrimination

Source: J. Levitz and P. Shishkin, "More Workers Cite Age Bias after Layoffs," *Wall Street Journal* (March 11, 2009), pp. D1–D2; W. M. Bulkeley, "A Data-Storage Titan Confronts Bias Claims," *Wall Street Journal* (September 12, 2007), pp. A1, A16; D. Walker, "Incident with Noose Stirs Old Memories," *McClatchy-Tribune Business News* (June 29, 2008); D. Solis, "Racial Horror Stories Keep EEOC Busy," *Knight-Ridder Tribune Business News,* July 30, 2005, p. 1; H. Ibish and A. Stewart, *Report on Hate Crimes and Discrimination Against Arab Americans: The Post-September 11 Backlash, September 11, 2001–October 11, 2001* (Washington, DC: American-Arab Anti-Discrimination Committee, 2003); A. Raghavan, "Wall Street's Disappearing Women," *Forbes* (March 16, 2009), pp. 72–78; and L. M. Cortina, "Unseen Injustice: Incivility as Modern Discrimination in Organizations," *Academy of Management Review* 33, no. 1 (2008), pp. 55–75.

culture—are hard to assess. Let's begin, then, by looking at factors that are easily definable and readily available—data that can be obtained, for the most part, from an employee's human resources (HR) file. Variations in these surface-level characteristics may be the basis for discrimination against classes of employees, so it is worth knowing how closely related they actually are to important work outcomes. Many are not as important as people believe, and far more variation occurs *within* groups sharing biographical characteristics than between them.

Age

The relationship between age and job performance is likely to be an issue of increasing importance during the next decade for at least three reasons. First, belief is widespread that job performance declines with increasing age. Regardless of whether this is true, a lot of people believe it and act on it. Second, the workforce is aging. Many employers recognize older workers represent a huge potential pool of high-quality applicants. Companies such as the Vanguard Group have sought to increase their attractiveness to older workers by providing targeted training that meets their needs, and by offering flexible work schedules and part-time work to draw in those who are semiretired.[7] The third reason is U.S. legislation that, for all intents and purposes, outlaws mandatory retirement. Most U.S. workers today no longer have to retire at age 70.

What is the perception of older workers? Employers hold mixed feelings.[8] They see a number of positive qualities older workers bring to their jobs, such as experience, judgment, a strong work ethic, and commitment to quality. But older workers are also perceived as lacking flexibility and resisting new technology. And when organizations are actively seeking individuals who are adaptable and open to change, the negatives associated with age clearly hinder the initial hiring of older workers and increase the likelihood they will be let go during cutbacks.

Now let's take a look at the evidence. What effect does age actually have on turnover, absenteeism, productivity, and satisfaction? The older you get, the less likely you are to quit your job. That conclusion is based on studies of the age–turnover relationship.[9] Of course, this shouldn't be too surprising. As workers get older, they have fewer alternative job opportunities as their skills have become more specialized to certain types of work. Their long tenure also tends to provide them with higher wage rates, longer paid vacations, and more attractive pension benefits.

It's tempting to assume that age is also inversely related to absenteeism. After all, if older workers are less likely to quit, won't they also demonstrate higher stability by coming to work more regularly? Not necessarily. Most studies do show an inverse relationship, but close examination finds it is partially a function of whether the absence is avoidable or unavoidable.[10] In general, older employees have lower rates of avoidable absence than do younger employees. However, they have equal rates of unavoidable absence, such as sickness absences.

How does age affect productivity? Many believe productivity declines with age. It is often assumed that skills like speed, agility, strength, and coordination decay over time and that prolonged job boredom and lack of intellectual stimulation contribute to reduced productivity. The evidence, however, contradicts those assumptions. During a 3-year period, a large hardware chain staffed one of its stores solely with employees over age 50 and compared its results with those of five stores with younger employees. The store staffed by the over-50 employees was significantly more productive (in terms of sales generated against labor costs) than two of the stores and held its own against the other three.[11] Other reviews of the research find that age and job task performance are unrelated and that older workers are more likely to engage in citizenship behavior.[12]

Our final concern is the relationship between age and job satisfaction, where the evidence is mixed. A review of more than 800 studies found that older workers tend to be more satisfied with their work, report better relationships with co-workers, and are more committed to their employing organizations.[13] Other studies, however, have found a U-shaped relationship, meaning that job satisfaction increases up to middle age, at which point it begins to drop off.[14] Several explanations could clear up these results, the most plausible being that these studies are intermixing professional and nonprofessional employees. When we separate the two types, satisfaction tends to continually increase among professionals as they age, whereas it falls among nonprofessionals during middle age and then rises again in the later years.

What are the effects of discrimination against individuals on the basis of age? One large-scale study of more than 8,000 employees in 128 companies found that an organizational climate favoring age discrimination was associated with lower levels of commitment to the company. This lower commitment was, in turn, related to lower levels of organizational performance.[15] Such results suggest that combating age discrimination may be associated with higher levels of organizational performance.

Gender

Few issues initiate more debates, misconceptions, and unsupported opinions than whether women perform as well on jobs as men do.

The best place to begin to consider this is with the recognition that few, if any, important differences between men and women affect job performance. There are no consistent male–female differences in problem-solving ability, analytical skills, competitive drive, motivation, sociability, or learning ability.[16] Psychological studies have found women are more agreeable and willing to conform to authority, whereas men are more aggressive and more likely to have expectations of success; but those differences are minor. Given the significantly increased female participation in the workforce over the past 40 years and the rethinking of what constitutes male and female roles, we can assume no significant difference in job productivity between men and women.[17]

Unfortunately, gender roles still affect our perceptions. For example, women who succeed in traditionally male domains are perceived as less likable, more hostile, and less desirable as supervisors.[18] Interestingly, research also suggests that women believe gender-based discrimination is more prevalent than do male employees, and these beliefs are especially pronounced among women who work with a large proportion of men.[19]

One issue that does seem to differ between men and women, especially when the employee has preschool-age children, is preference for work schedules.[20] Working mothers are more likely to prefer part-time work, flexible work schedules, and telecommuting in order to accommodate their family responsibilities. Women also prefer jobs that encourage work–life balance, which has the effect of limiting their options for career advancement. An interview study showed many of the work–life issues found in U.S. business contexts are also common in France, despite government subsidies for child care.[21]

What about absence and turnover rates? Are women less stable employees than men? First, evidence from a study of nearly 500,000 professional employees indicates significant differences, with women more likely to turn over than men.[22] Women also have higher rates of absenteeism than men do.[23] The most logical explanation is that the research was conducted in North America, and North American culture has historically placed home and family responsibilities on women. When a child is ill or someone needs to stay home to wait for a plumber, the woman has traditionally taken time from work. However, this research is also undoubtedly time-bound.[24] The role of women has definitely changed over the past generation. Men are increasingly sharing responsibility for child care, and an increasing number report feeling a conflict between their home responsibilities and their work lives.[25] One interesting finding is that regardless of gender, parents were rated lower in job commitment, achievement striving, and dependability than individuals without children, but mothers were rated especially low in competence.[26]

Again, it is worth asking what the implications of gender discrimination are for individuals. Research has shown that workers who experience sexual harassment have higher levels of psychological stress, and these feelings in turn are related to lower levels of organizational commitment and job satisfaction, and higher intentions to turn over.[27] As with age discrimination, the evidence suggests that combating gender discrimination may be associated with better performance for the organization as a whole.

Race and Ethnicity

Race is a controversial issue. In many cases, even bringing up the topic of race and ethnicity is enough to create an uncomfortable silence. Indeed, evidence suggests that some people find interacting with other racial groups uncomfortable unless there are clear behavioral scripts to guide their behavior.[28]

Most people in the United States identify themselves according to racial groups. The U.S. Bureau of the Census classifies individuals according to seven broad racial categories: American Indian and Alaska Native, Asian, Black or African American, Native Hawaiian or Other Pacific Islander, Some Other Race, White, and Two or More Races. An ethnicity distinction is also made between native English speakers and Hispanics: Hispanics can be of any race. We define *race* in this book as the biological heritage people use to identify themselves; *ethnicity* is the additional set of cultural characteristics that often overlaps with race. This definition allows each individual to define his or her race and ethnicity.

Race and ethnicity have been studied as they relate to employment outcomes such as hiring decisions, performance evaluations, pay, and workplace discrimination. Most research has concentrated on the differences in outcomes and attitudes between Whites and African Americans, with little study of issues relevant to Asian, Native American, and Hispanic populations. Doing justice to all this research isn't possible here, so let's summarize a few points.

First, in employment settings, individuals tend to slightly favor colleagues of their own race in performance evaluations, promotion decisions, and pay raises, although such differences are not found consistently, especially when highly structured methods of decision making are employed.[29] Second, substantial racial differences exist in attitudes toward affirmative action, with African Americans approving of such programs to a greater degree than Whites.[30] This difference may reflect the fact that African Americans and Hispanics perceive discrimination to be more prevalent in the workplace.[31] Third, African Americans generally fare worse than Whites in employment decisions. They receive lower ratings in employment interviews, receive lower job performance ratings, are paid less, and are promoted less frequently.[32] Yet there are no statistically significant differences between African Americans and Whites in observed absence rates, applied social skills at work, or accident rates. African Americans and Hispanics also have higher turnover rates than Whites.

Employers' major concern about using mental-ability tests for selection, promotion, training, and similar employment decisions is that these tests may have an unnecessary negative impact on racial and ethnic groups, discriminating against employees whom they consider qualified.[33] Evidence suggests that "despite group differences in mean test performance, there is little convincing evidence that well-constructed tests are more predictive of educational, training, or occupational performance for members of the majority group than for members of minority groups."[34] Observed differences in IQ test scores by racial or ethnic group are smaller in more recent samples.[35] The issue of racial differences in general mental-ability tests continues to be hotly debated.[36]

Does racial and ethnic discrimination lead to negative workplace outcomes? The evidence isn't entirely clear. As we will see in our discussion of groups and teams, considerable evidence suggests that diversity tends to interfere with group cohesion and decision making, at least in the early stages of group formation. On the other hand, some research suggests that having a positive climate for diversity overall can lead to increased sales.[37] Moreover, for many employers, diversity is a value imperative—they believe they must increase the diversity of their workforce for legal or ethical reasons.

Disability

With the passage of the Americans with Disabilities Act (ADA) in 1990, representation of individuals with disabilities in the U.S. workforce rapidly increased.[38] According to the ADA, employers are required to make reasonable accommodations so their workplaces will be accessible to individuals with physical or mental disabilities.

Making inferences about the relationship between disability and employment outcomes is difficult because the term *disability* is so broad. The U.S. Equal Employment Opportunity Commission classifies a person as disabled who has any physical or mental impairment that substantially limits one or more major life activities. Examples include missing limbs, seizure disorder, Down syndrome, deafness, schizophrenia, alcoholism, diabetes, and chronic back pain. These conditions share almost no common features, so there's no generalization about how each condition is related to employment. Some jobs obviously cannot be accommodated to some disabilities—the law and common sense recognize that a blind person could not be a bus driver, a person with severe cerebral palsy could not be a surgeon, and a person with profound mobility constraints probably could not be a police patrol officer. However, the increasing presence of computer technology and other adaptive devices is shattering many traditional barriers to employment.

One of the most controversial aspects of the ADA is the provision that requires employers to make reasonable accommodations for people with psychiatric disabilities.[39] Most people have very strong biases against those with mental illnesses, who may be therefore reluctant to disclose this information to employers. Many who notify their employers report negative consequences.

The impact of disabilities on employment outcomes has been explored from a variety of perspectives. On the one hand, a review of the evidence suggests workers with disabilities receive higher performance evaluations, whether or not the evaluations would be considered as objective. This same review found that despite these higher performance ratings, individuals with disabilities tend to encounter lower performance expectations and are less likely to be hired.[40] These negative effects are much stronger for individuals with mental disabilities, and there is some evidence to suggest mental disabilities may impair performance more than physical disabilities: Individuals with such common mental health issues as depression and anxiety are significantly more likely to be absent from work.[41]

Several studies have examined participants who received résumés that were identical, except that some mentioned a disability. The résumés that mentioned mental illness or a physical disability were associated with much lower ratings for perceived employability, especially in jobs requiring a great deal of personal contact with the public.[42] Employability ratings for individuals with mental illnesses were especially low. Similarly, when given randomly manipulated academic portfolios, students preferred not to avoid working with individuals who had a learning disability even though there were no effects of disability on performance ratings or expectations.[43]

Contrast these selection-oriented results with studies showing that the accomplishments of those with disabilities are often rated as more impressive than the same accomplishments of people without disabilities. Participants watched three individuals completing a carpentry task, one of whom was described as recently hospitalized for a debilitating mental illness.[44] The raters consistently gave that person higher performance ratings. In this case, it may be that the disabled individual was being treated as a person in need of special consideration. Similarly, when disability status is randomly manipulated among hypothetical candidates, disabled individuals are rated as having superior personal qualities like dependability and potency.[45]

Other Biographical Characteristics: Tenure, Religion, Sexual Orientation, and Gender Identity

The last set of biographical characteristics we'll look at includes tenure, religion, sexual orientation, and gender identity.

TENURE   Except for gender and racial differences, few issues are more subject to misconceptions and speculations than the impact of seniority on job performance.

Extensive reviews have been conducted of the seniority–productivity relationship.[46] If we define *seniority* as time on a particular job, the most recent evidence demonstrates a positive relationship between seniority and job productivity. So *tenure*, expressed as work experience, appears to be a good predictor of employee productivity.

The research relating tenure to absence is quite straightforward. Studies consistently show seniority is negatively related to absenteeism.[47] In fact, in terms of both frequency of absence and total days lost at work, tenure is the single most important explanatory variable.[48]

Tenure is also a potent variable in explaining turnover. The longer a person is in a job, the less likely she is to quit.[49] Moreover, consistent with research suggesting past behavior is the best predictor of future behavior, evidence indicates tenure at an employee's previous job is a powerful predictor of that employee's future turnover.[50]

Evidence indicates tenure and job satisfaction are positively related.[51] In fact, when age and tenure are treated separately, tenure appears a more consistent and stable predictor of job satisfaction than age.

RELIGION   Not only do religious and nonreligious people question each other's belief systems; often people of different religious faiths conflict. As the war in Iraq and the past conflict in Northern Ireland demonstrate, violent differences can erupt among sects of the same religion. U.S. federal law prohibits employers from discriminating against employees based on their religion, with very few exceptions. However, that doesn't mean religion is a nonissue in OB.

Perhaps the greatest religious diversity issue in the United States today revolves around Islam. Nearly two million Muslims live in the United States, and across the world Islam is one of the most prevalent religions. There is a wide variety of perspectives on Islam. As one Islamic scholar has noted, "There is no such thing as a single American Muslim community, much as there is no single Christian community. Muslims vary hugely by ethnicity, faith, tradition, education, income, and degree of religious observance."[52] For the most part, U.S. Muslims have attitudes similar to those of other U.S. citizens (though the differences tend to be greater for younger U.S. Muslims). Still, there are both perceived and real differences. Nearly 4 in 10 U.S. adults admit they harbor negative feelings or prejudices toward U.S. Muslims, and 52 percent believe U.S. Muslims are not respectful of women. Some take these general biases a step further. Motaz Elshafi, a 28-year-old software engineer for Cisco Systems, born and raised in New Jersey, received an e-mail from a co-worker addressed "Dear Terrorist." Research has shown that job applicants in Muslim-identified religious attire who applied for hypothetical retail jobs in the United States had shorter, more interpersonally negative interviews than applicants who did not wear Muslim-identified attire.[53]

Faith can be an employment issue when religious beliefs prohibit or encourage certain behaviors. Many Christians do not believe they should work on Sundays, and many conservative Jews believe they should not work on Saturdays. Religious individuals may also believe they have an obligation to express their beliefs in the workplace, and those who do not share those beliefs may object. Perhaps as a result of different perceptions of religion's role in the workplace, religious discrimination claims have been a growing source of discrimination claims in the United States.

SEXUAL ORIENTATION AND GENDER IDENTITY Employers differ widely in their treatment of sexual orientation. Federal law does not prohibit discrimination against employees based on sexual orientation, though many states and municipalities do. In general, observers note that even in the absence of federal legislation requiring nondiscrimination, many organizations have implemented policies and procedures protecting employees on the basis of sexual orientation.[54]

Raytheon, builder of Tomahawk cruise missiles and other defense systems, offers domestic-partner benefits, supports a wide array of gay rights groups, and wants to be an employer of choice for gays. The firm believes these policies give it an advantage in the ever-competitive market for engineers and scientists. Raytheon is not alone. More than half the *Fortune* 500 companies offer domestic-partner benefits for gay couples, including American Express, IBM, Intel, Morgan Stanley, Motorola, and Walmart. Some companies oppose domestic-partner benefits or nondiscrimination clauses for gay employees. Among these are Alltel, ADM, ExxonMobil, H. J. Heinz, Nissan, Nestlé, and Rubbermaid.[55] Despite some gains, many lesbian, gay, and bisexual employees keep their gender identity from their co-workers for fear of being discriminated against.[56]

As for gender identity, companies are increasingly putting in place policies to govern how their organization treats employees who change genders (often called *transgender employees*). In 2001, only eight companies in the *Fortune* 500 had policies on gender identity. By 2006, that number had swelled to 124. IBM is one of them. Brad Salavich, a diversity manager for IBM, says, "We believe that having strong transgender and gender identification policies is a natural extension of IBM's corporate culture." Dealing with transgender employees requires some special considerations, such as for bathrooms, employee names, and so on.[57]

ABILITY

We've so far covered surface characteristics unlikely, on their own, to directly relate to job performance. Now we turn to deep-level abilities that *are* closely related to job performance. Contrary to what we were taught in grade school, we weren't all created equal in our abilities. Most people are to the left or the right of the median on some normally distributed ability curve. For example, regardless of how motivated you are, it's unlikely you can act as well as Scarlett Johansson, play basketball as well as LeBron James, write as well as J. K. Rowling, or play the guitar as well as Pat Metheny. Of course, just because we aren't all equal in abilities does not imply that some individuals are inherently inferior. Everyone has strengths and weaknesses that make him relatively superior or inferior to others in performing certain tasks or activities. From management's standpoint, the issue is not whether people differ in terms of their abilities. They clearly do. The issue is using the knowledge that people differ to increase the likelihood an employee will perform his or her job well.

What does *ability* mean? As we use the term, **ability** is an individual's current capacity to perform the various tasks in a job. Overall abilities are essentially made up of two sets of factors: intellectual and physical.

Intellectual Abilities

Intellectual abilities are abilities needed to perform mental activities—thinking, reasoning, and problem solving. Most societies place a high value on intelligence, and for good reason. Smart people generally earn more money and attain higher levels of education. They are also more likely to emerge as leaders of groups. Intelligence quotient (IQ) tests, for example, are designed to ascertain a person's general intellectual abilities. So, too, are popular college admission tests, such as the SAT and ACT and graduate admission tests in business (GMAT), law (LSAT), and medicine (MCAT). Testing firms don't claim their tests assess intelligence, but experts know they do.[58] The seven most frequently cited dimensions making up intellectual abilities are number aptitude, verbal comprehension, perceptual speed, inductive reasoning, deductive reasoning, spatial visualization, and memory.[59] Exhibit 2-2 describes these dimensions.

Intelligence dimensions are positively related, so if you score high on verbal comprehension, for example, you're more likely to also score high on spatial visualization. The correlations aren't perfect, meaning people do have specific abilities that predict important work-related outcomes when considered individually.[60] However, they are high enough that researchers also recognize a general factor of intelligence, **general mental ability (GMA)**. Evidence strongly supports the idea that the structures and measures of intellectual abilities generalize across cultures. Thus, someone in Venezuela or Sudan does not have a different set of mental abilities than a U.S. or Czech worker. There is some evidence that IQ scores vary to some degree across cultures, but those differences are much smaller when we take into account educational and economic differences.[61]

Jobs differ in the demands they place on intellectual abilities. The more complex a job in terms of information-processing demands, the more general intelligence and verbal abilities will be necessary to perform successfully.[62] Where employee behavior is highly routine and there are few or no opportunities to exercise discretion, a high IQ is

Dimension	Description	Job Example
Number aptitude	Ability to do speedy and accurate arithmetic	Accountant: Computing the sales tax on a set of items
Verbal comprehension	Ability to understand what is read or heard and the relationship of words to each other	Plant manager: Following corporate policies on hiring
Perceptual speed	Ability to identify visual similarities and differences quickly and accurately	Fire investigator: Identifying clues to support a charge of arson
Inductive reasoning	Ability to identify a logical sequence in a problem and then solve the problem	Market researcher: Forecasting demand for a product in the next time period
Deductive reasoning	Ability to use logic and assess the implications of an argument	Supervisor: Choosing between two different suggestions offered by employees
Spatial visualization	Ability to imagine how an object would look if its position in space were changed	Interior decorator: Redecorating an office
Memory	Ability to retain and recall past experiences	Salesperson: Remembering the names of customers

EXHIBIT 2-2
Dimensions of Intellectual Ability

not as important to performing well. However, that does not mean people with high IQs cannot have an impact on traditionally less complex jobs.

It might surprise you that the most widely used intelligence test in hiring decisions takes only 12 minutes to complete. It's the Wonderlic Cognitive Ability Test. There are different forms, and each has 50 questions. Here are a few examples:

- When rope is selling at $0.10 a foot, how many feet can you buy for $0.60?
- Assume the first two statements are true. Is the final one:
  1. True.
  2. False.
  3. Not certain.
     a. The boy plays baseball.
     b. All baseball players wear hats.
     c. The boy wears a hat.

The Wonderlic measures both speed (almost nobody has time to answer every question) and power (questions get harder as you go along), so the average score is pretty low—about 21/50. And because it is able to provide valid information cheaply (for $5 to $10/applicant), more companies are using the Wonderlic in hiring decisions. The Factory Card & Party Outlet, with 182 stores nationwide, uses it. So do Subway, Peoples Flowers, Security Alarm, Workforce Employment Solutions, and many others. Most of these companies don't give up other hiring tools, such as application forms or interviews. Rather, they add the Wonderlic for its ability to provide valid data on applicants' intelligence levels.

Interestingly, although intelligence is a big help in performing a job well, it doesn't make people happier or more satisfied with their jobs. The correlation between intelligence and job satisfaction is about zero. Why? Research suggests that although intelligent people perform better and tend to have more interesting jobs, they are also more critical when evaluating their job conditions. Thus, smart people have it better, but they also expect more.[63]

Physical Abilities

Though the changing nature of work suggests intellectual abilities are increasingly important for many jobs, **physical abilities** have been and will remain valuable. Research on hundreds of jobs has identified nine basic abilities needed in the performance of physical tasks.[64] These are described in Exhibit 2-3. Individuals differ in the extent to which they have each of these abilities. Not surprisingly, there is also little relationship among them: a high score on one is no assurance of a high score on others. High employee performance is likely to be achieved when management has ascertained the extent to which a job requires each of the nine abilities and then ensures that employees in that job have those abilities.

Strength Factors	
1. Dynamic strength	Ability to exert muscular force repeatedly or continuously over time
2. Trunk strength	Ability to exert muscular strength using the trunk (particularly abdominal) muscles
3. Static strength	Ability to exert force against external objects
4. Explosive strength	Ability to expend a maximum of energy in one or a series of explosive acts
Flexibility Factors	
5. Extent flexibility	Ability to move the trunk and back muscles as far as possible
6. Dynamic flexibility	Ability to make rapid, repeated flexing movements
Other Factors	
7. Body coordination	Ability to coordinate the simultaneous actions of different parts of the body
8. Balance	Ability to maintain equilibrium despite forces pulling off balance
9. Stamina	Ability to continue maximum effort requiring prolonged effort over time

EXHIBIT 2-3
Nine Basic Physical Abilities

The Role of Disabilities

The importance of ability at work obviously creates problems when we attempt to formulate workplace policies that recognize diversity in terms of disability status. As we have noted, recognizing that individuals have different abilities that can be taken into account when making hiring decisions is not problematic. However, it is discriminatory to make blanket assumptions about people on the basis of a disability. It is also possible to make accommodations for disabilities.

IMPLEMENTING DIVERSITY MANAGEMENT STRATEGIES

Having discussed a variety of ways in which people differ, we now look at how a manager can and should manage these differences. **Diversity management** makes everyone more aware of and sensitive to the needs and differences of others. This definition highlights the fact that diversity programs include and are meant for everyone. Diversity is much more likely to be successful when we see it as everyone's business than if we believe it helps only certain groups of employees.

Attracting, Selecting, Developing, and Retaining Diverse Employees

One method of enhancing workforce diversity is to target recruiting messages to specific demographic groups underrepresented in the workforce. This means placing advertisements in publications geared toward specific demographic groups; recruiting at colleges, universities, and other institutions with significant numbers of underrepresented minorities; and forming partnerships with associations like the Society for Women Engineers or the Graduate Minority Business Association. These efforts can be successful, and research has shown that women and minorities do have greater interest in employers that make special efforts to highlight a commitment to diversity in their recruiting materials. Advertisements depicting groups of diverse employees are seen as more attractive to women and racioethnic minorities, which is probably why most organizations depict workforce diversity prominently in their recruiting materials. Diversity advertisements that fail to show women and minorities in positions of organizational leadership send a negative message about the diversity climate at an organization.[65]

The selection process is one of the most important places to apply diversity efforts. Managers who hire need to value fairness and objectivity in selecting employees and focus on the productive potential of new recruits. Fortunately, ensuring that hiring is bias-free does appear to work. Where managers use a well-defined protocol for assessing applicant talent and the organization clearly prioritizes nondiscrimination policies, qualifications become far more important in determining who gets hired than demographic characteristics.[66] Organizations that do not discourage discriminatory behavior are more likely to see problems.

Similarity in personality appears to affect career advancement. Those whose personality traits are similar to those of their co-workers are more likely to be promoted than those whose personalities are different.[67] There's an important qualifier to these results: in collectivistic cultures, similarity to supervisors is more important for predicting advancement, whereas in individualistic cultures, similarity to peers is more important. Once again, deep-level diversity factors appear to be more important in shaping people's reactions to one another than surface-level characteristics.

Evidence from a study of more than 6,000 workers in a major retail organization indicated that in stores with a less supportive diversity climate, African Americans or Hispanics made significantly fewer sales than White employees, but when the diversity climate was positive, Hispanics and Whites sold about the same amount and African Americans made more sales than Whites.[68] Whites sold about the same amount whether there was a positive diversity climate or not, but African Americans and Hispanics sold far more when there was. There are obvious bottom-line implications of this research: stores that fostered a positive diversity climate were able to capitalize on their diverse workforce and make more money.

Some data suggest individuals who are demographically different from their co-workers are more likely to feel low commitment and to turn over: women are more likely to turn over from predominantly male work groups and men from predominantly female work groups; non-Whites are more likely to turn over from predominantly White work groups and Whites from predominantly non-White work groups.[69] However, this behavior is more prominent among new hires. After people become better acquainted with one another, demographic differences are less consistently related to turnover. One very large-scale study showed a positive diversity climate was related to higher organizational commitment and lower turnover intentions among African-American, Hispanic, *and* White managers.[70] In other words, all workers appeared to prefer an organization that values diversity.

Diversity in Groups

Most contemporary workplaces require extensive work in group settings. When people work in groups, they need to establish a common way of looking at and accomplishing the major tasks, and they need to communicate with one another often. If they feel little sense of membership and cohesion in their groups, all these group attributes are likely to suffer.

Does diversity help or hurt group performance? The answer is "yes." In some cases, diversity in traits can hurt team performance, whereas in others it can facilitate it.[71] Whether diverse or homogeneous teams are more effective depends on the characteristic of interest. Demographic diversity (in gender, race, and ethnicity) does not appear to either help or hurt team performance in general. On the other hand, teams of individuals who are highly intelligent, conscientious, and interested in working in team settings are more effective. Thus diversity on these variables is likely to be a bad thing—it makes little sense to try to form teams that mix in members who are lower in intelligence, conscientiousness, and uninterested in teamwork. In other cases, differences can be a strength. Groups of individuals with different types of expertise and education are more effective than homogeneous groups. Similarly, a group made entirely of assertive people who want to be in charge, or a group whose members all prefer to follow the lead of others, will be less effective than a group that mixes leaders and followers.

Regardless of the composition of the group, differences can be leveraged to achieve superior performance. The most important way is to emphasize the higher-level similarities among members.[72] In other words, groups of diverse individuals will be much more effective if leaders can show how members have a common interest in the group's success. Evidence also shows transformational leaders (who emphasize higher-order goals and values in their leadership style) are more effective in managing diverse teams.[73]

Effective Diversity Programs

Organizations use a variety of efforts to capitalize on diversity, including the recruiting and selection policies we have already discussed, as well as training and development practices. Effective, comprehensive workforce programs encouraging diversity have three distinct components. First, they teach managers about the legal framework for equal employment opportunity and encourage fair treatment of all people regardless of their demographic characteristics. Second, they teach managers how a diverse workforce will be better able to serve a diverse market of customers and clients. Third, they foster personal development practices that bring out the skills and abilities of all workers, acknowledging how differences in perspective can be a valuable way to improve performance for everyone.[74]

Much concern about diversity has to do with fair treatment.[75] Most negative reactions to employment discrimination are based on the idea that discriminatory treatment is unfair. Regardless of race or gender, people are generally in favor of diversity-oriented programs, including affirmative action, if they believe the policies ensure everyone a fair opportunity to show their skills and abilities.

A major study of the consequences of diversity programs came to what might seem a surprising conclusion.[76] Organizations that provided diversity training were not consistently more likely to have women and minorities in upper management positions than organizations that did not. On closer examination though, these results are not surprising. Experts have long known that one-shot training sessions without strategies to encourage effective diversity management back on the job are not likely to be very effective. Some diversity programs are truly effective in improving representation in management. They include strategies to measure the representation of women and minorities in managerial positions, and they hold managers accountable for achieving more demographically diverse management teams. Researchers also suggest that diversity experiences are more likely to lead to positive adaptation for all parties if (1) the diversity experience undermines stereotypical attitudes, (2) if the perceiver is motivated and able to consider a new perspective on others, (3) if the perceiver engages in stereotype suppression and generative thought in response to the diversity experience, and (4) if the positive experience of stereotype undermining is repeated frequently.[77] Diversity programs based on these principles are likely to be more effective than traditional classroom learning.

Organizational leaders should examine their workforce to determine whether target groups have been underutilized. If groups of employees are not proportionally represented in top management, managers should look for any hidden barriers to advancement. They can often improve recruiting practices, make selection systems more transparent, and provide training for those employees who have not had adequate exposure to certain material in the past. The organization should also clearly communicate its policies to employees so they can understand how and why certain practices are followed. Communications should focus as much as possible on qualifications and job performance; emphasizing certain groups as needing more assistance could well backfire. A case study of the multinational Finnish company TRANSCO found it was possible to develop a consistent global philosophy for diversity management. However, differences in legal and cultural factors across nations forced TRANSCO to develop unique policies to match the cultural and legal frameworks of each country in which it operated.[78]

To ensure the top-level management team represents the diversity of its workforce and client base, Safeway implemented the Retail Leadership Development (RLD) program, a formal career development program. This program is open to all employees, so it is inclusive, but women and underrepresented racial or ethnic groups are particularly encouraged to participate. Interested individuals take a series of examinations to determine whether they have management potential. Those who perform well on the tests are provided with work in roles that expose them to managerial opportunities. The program's comprehensive nature is underscored by its additional support activities: All managers attend workshops that help them bring diversity concerns front and center in their staff meetings. They are also charged with providing promising RLD participants with additional training and development opportunities to ensure they have the skills needed for advancement. The program incorporates the type of accountability we have said is crucial to the success of diversity efforts; performance bonuses are provided to managers who meet concrete diversity goals. This program has shown real success: the number of White women store managers has increased by 31 percent since its inception, and the number of women-of-color store managers has increased by 92 percent.[79]

SUMMARY AND IMPLICATIONS FOR MANAGERS

This chapter looked at diversity from many perspectives. We paid particular attention to three variables—biographical characteristics, ability, and diversity programs. Let's summarize what we found and consider its importance for a manager trying to understand organizational behavior.

- We can readily observe biographical characteristics, but that doesn't mean we should explicitly use them in management decisions. Most research shows fairly minimal effects of biographical characteristics on job performance. We also need to be aware of implicit biases we or other managers may have.
- An effective selection process will improve the fit between employees and job requirements. A job analysis will provide information about jobs currently being done and the abilities individuals need to perform the jobs adequately. Applicants can then be tested, interviewed, and evaluated on the degree to which they possess the necessary abilities.
- Promotion and transfer decisions affecting individuals already in the organization's employ should reflect candidates' abilities. As with new employees, care should be taken to assess critical abilities incumbents will need in the job and match those with the organization's human resources.
- To accommodate employees with disabilities, managers can improve the fit by fine-tuning the job to better match an incumbent's abilities. Often, modifications with no significant impact on the job's basic activities, such as changing equipment or reorganizing tasks within a group, can better adapt work to the specific talents of a given employee.
- Diversity management must be an ongoing commitment that crosses all levels of the organization. Group management, recruiting, hiring, retention, and development practices can all be designed to leverage diversity for the organization's competitive advantage.
- Policies to improve the climate for diversity can be effective, so long as they are designed to acknowledge all employees' perspectives. One-shot diversity training sessions are less likely to be effective than comprehensive programs that address the climate for diversity at multiple levels.

MyManagementLab

Go to **MyManagementLab.com** to access study plans, interactive lectures, and videos as well as Auto-graded writing questions and the following Assisted-graded writing question.

2-1. MyManagementLab Only—comprehensive writing assignment for this chapter.

3

Attitudes and Job Satisfaction

After studying this chapter, you should be able to:

- Contrast the three components of an attitude.
- Summarize the relationship between attitudes and behavior.
- Compare and contrast the major job attitudes.
- Define *job satisfaction* and show how we can measure it.
- Summarize the main causes of job satisfaction.
- Identify four employee responses to dissatisfaction.

We seem to have attitudes toward everything, whether it's about our leaders, our college or university, our families, or ourselves. In this chapter, we look at attitudes, their link to behavior, and how employee's satisfaction or dissatisfaction with their jobs affects the workplace.

ATTITUDES

Attitudes are evaluative statements—either favorable or unfavorable—about objects, people, or events. They reflect how we feel about something. For example, when you say "I like my job," you are expressing your attitude about work.

Attitudes are complex. If you ask people about their attitude toward religion, Lady Gaga, or the organization they work for, you may get a simple response, but the reasons underlying are probably complicated. In order to fully understand attitudes, we must consider their fundamental properties or components.

What Are the Main Components of Attitudes?

Typically, researchers have assumed that attitudes have three components: cognition, affect, and behavior.[1] Let's look at each.

The statement "My pay is low" is the **cognitive component** of an attitude—a description of or belief in the way things are. It sets the stage for the more critical part of an attitude—its **affective component**. Affect is the emotional or feeling segment of an attitude and is reflected in the statement "I am angry over how little I'm paid." Affect can lead to behavioral outcomes. The **behavioral component** of an attitude describes an intention to behave in a certain way toward someone or something—to continue the example, "I'm going to look for another job that pays better."

Viewing attitudes as having three components—cognition, affect, and behavior—is helpful in understanding their complexity and the potential relationship between attitudes and behavior. It is important to keep in mind that these components are closely related, and cognition and affect in particular are inseparable in many ways. For example, imagine you realized that someone has just treated you unfairly. Aren't you likely to have feelings about that, occurring virtually instantaneously with the realization? Thus, cognition and affect are intertwined.

Exhibit 3-1 illustrates how the three components of an attitude are related. In this example, an employee didn't get a promotion he thought he deserved; a co-worker got it instead. The employee's attitude toward his supervisor is illustrated as follows: the employee thought he deserved the promotion (cognition), he strongly dislikes his supervisor (affect), and he has complained and taken action (behavior). As we've noted, although we often think cognition causes affect, which then causes behavior, in reality these components are often difficult to separate.

In organizations, attitudes are important for their behavioral component. If workers believe, for example, that supervisors, auditors, bosses, and time-and-motion engineers are all in conspiracy to make employees work harder for the same or less money, it

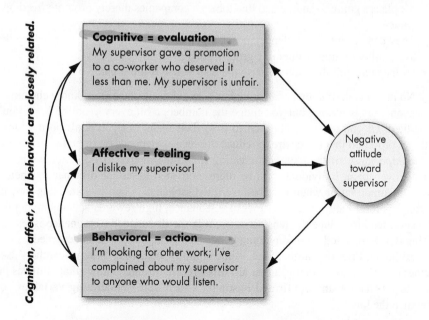

EXHIBIT 3-1

**The Components
of an Attitude**

makes sense to try to understand how these attitudes formed, how they relate to actual job behavior, and how they might be changed.

Does Behavior Always Follow from Attitudes?

Early research on attitudes assumed they were causally related to behavior—that is, the attitudes people hold determine what they do. Common sense, too, suggests a relationship. Isn't it logical that people watch television programs they like, or that employees try to avoid assignments they find distasteful?

However, in the late 1960s, a review of the research challenged this assumed effect of attitudes on behavior.[2] One researcher—Leon Festinger—argued that attitudes *follow* behavior. Did you ever notice how people change what they say so it doesn't contradict what they do? Perhaps a friend of yours has consistently argued that the quality of U.S. cars isn't up to that of imports and that he'd never own anything but a Japanese or German car. Then his dad gives him a late-model Ford Mustang, and suddenly he says U.S. cars aren't so bad. Festinger proposed that cases of attitude following behavior illustrate the effects of **cognitive dissonance**,[3] any incompatibility an individual might perceive between two or more attitudes or between behavior and attitudes. Festinger argued that any form of inconsistency is uncomfortable and that individuals will therefore attempt to reduce it. They will seek a stable state, which is a minimum of dissonance.

Research has generally concluded that people do seek consistency among their attitudes and between their attitudes and their behavior.[4] They either alter the attitudes or the behavior, or they develop a rationalization for the discrepancy. Tobacco executives provide an example.[5] How, you might wonder, do these people cope with the continuing revelations about the health dangers of smoking?

- They can deny any clear causation between smoking and cancer.
- They can brainwash themselves by continually articulating the benefits of tobacco.
- They can acknowledge the negative consequences of smoking but rationalize that people are going to smoke and that tobacco companies merely promote freedom of choice.
- They can accept the evidence and make cigarettes less dangerous or reduce their availability to more vulnerable groups, such as teenagers.
- Or they can quit their job because the dissonance is too great.

No individual, of course, can completely avoid dissonance. You know cheating on your income tax is wrong, but you fudge the numbers a bit every year and hope you're not audited. Or you tell your children to floss their teeth, but you don't do it yourself. Festinger proposed that the desire to reduce dissonance depends on three factors, including the *importance* of the elements creating it and the degree of *influence* we believe we have over them. Individuals will be more motivated to reduce dissonance when the attitude is important or when they believe the dissonance is due to something they can control. The third factor is the *rewards* of dissonance; high rewards accompanying high dissonance tend to reduce the tension inherent in the dissonance (dissonance is less distressing if accompanied with something good, such as higher pay than deserved).

Although Festinger argued that attitudes follow behavior, other researchers asked whether there was any relationship at all. More recent research shows that attitudes predict future behavior and confirmed Festinger's idea that "moderating variables" can strengthen the link.[6]

MODERATING VARIABLES   The most powerful moderators of the attitudes relationship are the *importance* of the attitude, its *correspondence to behavior,* its *accessibility,* the presence of *social pressures,* and whether a person has *direct experience* with the attitude.[7]

Important attitudes reflect our fundamental values, self-interest, or identification with individuals or groups we value. These attitudes tend to show a strong relationship to our behavior.

Specific attitudes tend to predict specific behaviors, whereas general attitudes tend to best predict general behaviors. For instance, asking someone about her intention to stay with an organization for the next 6 months is likely to better predict turnover for that person than asking her how satisfied she is with her job overall. On the other hand, overall job satisfaction would better predict a general behavior, such as whether the individual was engaged in her work or motivated to contribute to her organization.[8]

Attitudes that our memories can easily access are more likely to predict our behavior. Interestingly, you're more likely to remember attitudes you frequently express. So the more you talk about your attitude on a subject, the more likely you are to remember it, and the more likely it is to shape your behavior.

Discrepancies between attitudes and behavior tend to occur when social pressures to behave in certain ways hold exceptional power, as in most organizations. This may explain why an employee who holds strong antiunion attitudes attends prounion organizing meetings, or why tobacco executives, who are not smokers and who tend to believe the research linking smoking and cancer, don't actively discourage others from smoking.

Finally, the attitude–behavior relationship is likely to be much stronger if an attitude refers to something with which we have direct personal experience. Asking college students with no significant work experience how they would respond to working for an authoritarian supervisor is far less likely to predict actual behavior than asking that same question of employees who have actually worked for such an individual.

What Are the Major Job Attitudes?

We each have thousands of attitudes, but OB focuses our attention on a very limited number of work-related attitudes. These tap positive or negative evaluations that employees hold about aspects of their work environments. Most of the research in OB has looked at three attitudes: job satisfaction, job involvement, and organizational commitment.[9] A few other important attitudes are perceived organizational support and employee engagement.

Individuals have many kinds of attitudes about their job. Of the main job attitudes, organizational commitment and job satisfaction are the most widely studied.

JOB SATISFACTION   When people speak of employee attitudes, they usually mean **job satisfaction**, which describes a positive feeling about a job, resulting from an evaluation of its characteristics. A person with a high level of job satisfaction holds positive feelings about his or her job, whereas a person with a low level holds negative feelings. Because OB researchers give job satisfaction high importance, we'll review this attitude in detail later in the chapter.

JOB INVOLVEMENT   Related to job satisfaction is **job involvement**,[10] which measures the degree to which people identify psychologically with their jobs and consider their perceived performance levels important to self-worth.[11] Employees with a high level of job involvement strongly identify with and really care about the kind of work they do. Another closely related concept is **psychological empowerment**, employees' beliefs in the degree to which they influence their work environments, their competencies, the meaningfulness of their jobs, and their perceived autonomy.[12] One study of nursing managers in Singapore found that good leaders empower their employees by involving them in decisions, making them feel their work is important, and giving them discretion to "do their own thing."[13]

High levels of both job involvement and psychological empowerment are positively related to organizational citizenship behavior (known as OCB, this is discretionary behavior that is not part of an employee's formal job requirements but contributes to the psychological and social environment of the workplace) and job performance.[14] High job involvement is also related to reduced absences and lower resignation rates.[15]

ORGANIZATIONAL COMMITMENT   In **organizational commitment**, an employee identifies with a particular organization and its goals and wishes to remain a member. Most research has focused on emotional attachment to an organization and belief in its values as the "gold standard" for employee commitment.[16]

A positive relationship appears to exist between organizational commitment and job productivity, but it is a modest one.[17] A review of 27 studies suggested the relationship between commitment and performance is strongest for new employees, and considerably weaker for more experienced employees.[18] Interestingly, research indicates that employees who feel their employers fail to keep promises to them feel less committed, and these reductions in commitment, in turn, lead to lower levels of creative performance.[19] And, as with job involvement, the research evidence demonstrates negative relationships between organizational commitment and both absenteeism and turnover.[20]

Theoretical models propose that employees who are committed will be less likely to engage in work withdrawal even if they are dissatisfied, because they have a sense of organizational loyalty or attachment. On the other hand, employees who are not committed, who feel less loyal to the organization, will tend to show lower levels of attendance at work across the board. Research confirms this theoretical proposition.[21] It does appear that even if employees are not currently happy with their work, they are willing to make sacrifices for the organization if they are committed enough.

PERCEIVED ORGANIZATIONAL SUPPORT   **Perceived organizational support (POS)** is the degree to which employees believe the organization values their contributions and cares about their well-being (for example, an employee believes his organization would accommodate him if he had a child care problem or would forgive an honest mistake on his part). Research shows that people perceive their organizations as supportive when rewards are deemed fair, when employees have a voice in decisions, and when they see their supervisors as supportive.[22] Employees with strong POS perceptions have been found more likely to have higher levels of organizational citizenship behaviors, lower levels of tardiness, and better customer service.[23] This seems to hold true mainly in countries where the power distance, the degree to which people in a country accept that power in institutions and organizations is distributed unequally, is lower. In these countries, like the United States, people are more likely to view work as an exchange than a moral obligation. This isn't to say POS can't be a predictor anywhere on a situation-specific basis. Though little cross-cultural research has been done, one study found POS predicted the job performance and citizenship behaviors of untraditional or low power-distance Chinese employees—in short, those more likely to think of work as an exchange rather than a moral obligation.[24]

EMPLOYEE ENGAGEMENT   A new concept is **employee engagement**, an individual's involvement with, satisfaction with, and enthusiasm for, the work she does. To evaluate this, we might ask employees about the availability of resources and the opportunities to learn new skills, whether they feel their work is important and meaningful, and whether their interactions with co-workers and supervisors are rewarding.[25] Highly engaged employees have a passion for their work and feel a deep connection to their companies; disengaged employees have essentially checked out—putting time but not energy or attention into their work. Engagement becomes a real concern for most organizations because surveys indicate that few employees—between 17 percent and 29 percent—are highly engaged by their work. A study of nearly 8,000 business units in 36 companies found that those whose employees reported high-average levels of engagement had higher levels of customer satisfaction, were more productive, brought in higher profits, and experienced lower levels of turnover and accidents than at other companies.[26] Molson Coors, for example, found engaged employees were five times less likely to have safety incidents, and when one did occur, it was much less serious and less costly for the engaged employee than for a disengaged one ($63 per incident versus $392).[27] Caterpillar set out to increase employee engagement and recorded a resulting 80 percent drop in grievances and a 34 percent increase in highly satisfied customers.[28]

Such promising findings have earned employee engagement a following in many business organizations and management consulting firms. However, the concept is relatively new and still generates active debate about its usefulness. One set of researchers concluded, "The meaning of employee engagement is ambiguous among both academic researchers and among practitioners who use it in conversations with clients." Another reviewer called engagement "an umbrella term for whatever one wants it to be."[29] More recent research has set out to clarify the dimensions of employee engagement. This work has demonstrated that engagement is distinct from job satisfaction and job involvement and incrementally predicts job behaviors after we take these traditional job attitudes into account.

ARE THESE JOB ATTITUDES REALLY ALL THAT DISTINCT?   You might wonder whether the above job attitudes are really distinct. If people feel deeply engaged by their job (high job involvement), isn't it probable they like it too (high job satisfaction)? Won't people who think their organization is supportive (high perceived organizational support) also feel committed to it (strong organizational commitment)?

Evidence suggests these attitudes *are* highly related, perhaps to a troubling degree. For example, the correlation between perceived organizational support and affective commitment is very strong.[30] That means the variables may be redundant—if you know someone's affective commitment, you know her perceived organizational support. Why is redundancy troubling? Because it is inefficient and confusing. Why have two steering wheels on a car when you need only one? Why have two concepts—going by different labels—when you need only one?

Although we OB researchers like proposing new attitudes, often we haven't been good at showing how they compare and contrast with each other. There is some distinctiveness among them, but they overlap greatly, for various reasons including the employee's personality. Some people are predisposed to be positive or negative about almost everything. If someone tells you she loves her company, it may not mean a lot if she is positive about everything else in her life. Or the overlap may mean some organizations are just all-around better places to work than others. If you as a manager know someone's level of job satisfaction, taking this into account, you know most of what you need to know about how that person sees the organization—and can predict the employee's effectiveness.

JOB SATISFACTION

We have already discussed job satisfaction briefly. Now let's dissect the concept more carefully. How do we measure job satisfaction? What causes an employee to have a high level of job satisfaction? Moreover, how do dissatisfied and satisfied employees affect an organization?

Measuring Job Satisfaction

Our definition of job satisfaction—a positive feeling about a job resulting from an evaluation of its characteristics—is clearly broad.[31] Yet that breadth is appropriate. A job is more than just shuffling papers, writing programming code, waiting on customers, or driving a truck. Jobs require interacting with co-workers and bosses, following organizational rules and policies, meeting performance standards, living with working conditions, and the like.[32] An employee's assessment of his satisfaction with the job is thus a complex summation of many discrete elements. How, then, do we measure it?

   Two approaches are popular. The single global rating is a response to one question, such as, "All things considered, how satisfied are you with your job?" Respondents circle a number between 1 and 5 on a scale from "highly satisfied" to "highly dissatisfied." The second method, the summation of job facets, is more sophisticated. It identifies key elements in a job such as the nature of the work, supervision, present pay, promotion opportunities, and relationships with co-workers.[33] Respondents rate these on a standardized scale, and researchers add the ratings to create an overall job satisfaction score.

   Is one of these approaches superior? Intuitively, summing up responses to a number of job factors seems likely to achieve a more accurate evaluation of job satisfaction. Research, however, doesn't support the intuition.[34] This is one of those rare instances in which simplicity seems to work as well as complexity, making one method essentially as valid as the other. The best explanation is that the concept of job satisfaction is so broad a single question captures its essence. Both methods are helpful. The single global rating method isn't very time consuming, and the summation of job facets helps managers zero in on problems and deal with them faster and more accurately.

How Satisfied Are People in Their Jobs?

Are most people satisfied with their jobs? The answer seems to be a qualified "yes" in the United States and most other developed countries. Independent studies conducted among U.S. workers over the past 30 years generally indicate more workers are satisfied with their jobs than not. But a caution is in order. Recent data show a dramatic drop-off in average job satisfaction levels during the economic contraction that started in late 2007, so much so that only about half of workers report being satisfied with their jobs now.[35]

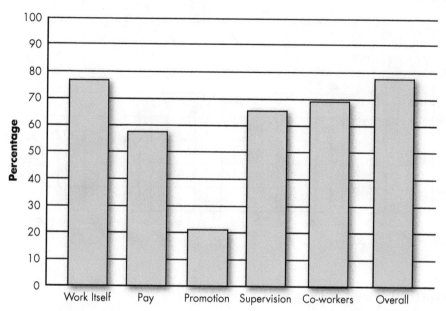

EXHIBIT 3-2
Average Job Satisfaction Levels by Facet

Research also shows satisfaction levels vary a lot, depending on which facet of job satisfaction you're talking about. As shown in Exhibit 3-2, people have typically been more satisfied with their jobs overall, with the work itself, and with their supervisors and co-workers than they have been with their pay and with promotion opportunities. It's not really clear why people dislike their pay and promotion possibilities more than other aspects of their jobs.[36]

Although job satisfaction appears relevant across cultures, that doesn't mean there are no cultural differences in job satisfaction. Evidence suggests employees in Western cultures have higher levels of job satisfaction than those in Eastern cultures.[37] Exhibit 3-3 provides the results of a global study of job satisfaction levels of workers in 15 countries. (This study included 23 countries, but for presentation purposes we report the results for only the largest.) As the exhibit shows, the highest levels appear in the United States and Western Europe. Do employees in Western cultures have better jobs? Or are they simply more positive (and less self-critical)? Although both factors are probably at play, evidence suggests that individuals in Eastern cultures find negative emotions less aversive more than do individuals in Western cultures, who tend to emphasize positive emotions and individual happiness.[38] That may be why employees in Western cultures such as the United States and Scandinavia are more likely to have higher levels of satisfaction.

What Causes Job Satisfaction?

Think about the best job you've ever had. What made it so? Chances are you liked the work you did and the people with whom you worked. Interesting jobs that provide training, variety, independence, and control satisfy most employees.[39] There is also a strong correspondence between how well people enjoy the social context of their workplace and how satisfied they are overall. Interdependence, feedback, social support, and interaction

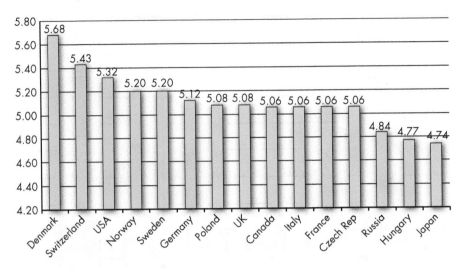

EXHIBIT 3-3

Average Level of Job Satisfaction by Country

Note: Scores represent average job satisfaction levels in each country as rated on a 1 = very dissatisfied to 10 = very satisfied scale.

Source: M. Benz and B. S. Frey, "The Value of Autonomy: Evidence from the Self-Employed in 23 Countries," *Journal of Economic Behavior and Organization* 68, (2008), pp. 445–455.

with co-workers outside the workplace are strongly related to job satisfaction even after accounting for characteristics of the work itself.[40]

You've probably noticed that pay comes up often when people discuss job satisfaction. For people who are poor or who live in less wealthy countries, pay does correlate with job satisfaction and overall happiness. But once an individual reaches a level of comfortable living (in the United States, that occurs at about $40,000 a year, depending on the region and family size), the relationship between pay and job satisfaction virtually disappears. People who earn $80,000 are, on average, no happier with their jobs than those who earn closer to $40,000. Take a look at Exhibit 3-4. It shows the relationship between the average pay for a job and the average level of job satisfaction. As you can see, there isn't much of a relationship there. Handsomely compensated jobs have average satisfaction levels no higher than those that pay much less. One researcher even found no significant difference when he compared the overall well-being of the richest people on the *Forbes'* 400 list with that of Maasai herders in East Africa.[41]

Money does motivate people, as we will discover in a later chapter. But what motivates us is not necessarily the same as what makes us happy. A recent poll by University of California at Los Angeles and the American Council on Education found that entering college freshmen rated becoming "very well off financially" first on a list of 19 goals, ahead of choices such as helping others, raising a family, or becoming proficient in an academic pursuit. Maybe your goal isn't to be happy. But if it is, money's probably not going to do much to get you there.[42]

Job satisfaction is not just about job conditions. Personality also plays a role. Research has shown that people who have positive **core self-evaluations (CSE)**—who

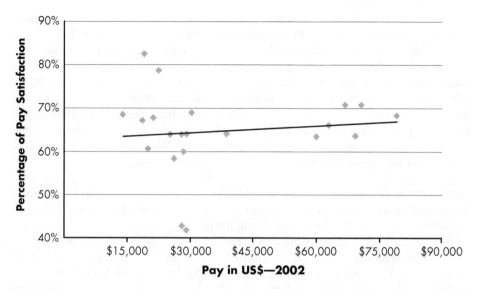

EXHIBIT 3-4

Relationship Between Average Pay in a Job Satisfaction of Employees in That Job

Source: Judge, T. A., Piccolo, R. F., Podsakoff, N. P., Shaw, J. C., and Rich, B. L., "The Relationship Between Pay and Job Satisfaction: A Meta-Analysis of the Literature," *Journal of Vocational Behavior* 77 (2010), pp. 157–167.

believe in their inner worth and basic competence—are more satisfied with their jobs than those with negative CSE. Not only do they see their work as more fulfilling and challenging, they are more likely to gravitate toward challenging jobs in the first place. Those with negative CSE set less ambitious goals and are more likely to give up when confronting difficulties. Thus, they're more likely to be stuck in boring, repetitive jobs than those with positive CSE.[43]

The Impact of Satisfied and Dissatisfied Employees on the Workplace

What happens when employees like their jobs, and when they dislike their jobs? One theoretical model—the *exit–voice–loyalty–neglect framework*—is helpful in understanding the consequences of dissatisfaction. The framework's four responses differ along two dimensions: constructive/destructive and active/passive. The responses are as follows:[44]

Most employees are satisfied with their jobs; when they're not, however, a host of actions in response to the dissatisfaction might be expected.

- *Exit.* The **exit** response directs behavior toward leaving the organization, including looking for a new position as well as resigning.
- *Voice.* The **voice** response includes actively and constructively attempting to improve conditions, including suggesting improvements, discussing problems with superiors, and undertaking some forms of union activity.
- *Loyalty.* The **loyalty** response means passively but optimistically waiting for conditions to improve, including speaking up for the organization in the face of external criticism and trusting the organization and its management to "do the right thing."
- *Neglect.* The **neglect** response passively allows conditions to worsen and includes chronic absenteeism or lateness, reduced effort, and increased error rate.

Exit and neglect behaviors encompass our performance variables—productivity, absenteeism, and turnover. But this model expands employee response to include voice and loyalty—constructive behaviors that allow individuals to tolerate unpleasant situations or revive satisfactory working conditions. It helps us understand situations, such as we sometimes find among unionized workers, for whom low job satisfaction is coupled with low turnover.[45] Union members often express dissatisfaction through the grievance procedure or formal contract negotiations. These voice mechanisms allow them to continue in their jobs while convincing themselves they are acting to improve the situation.

As helpful as this framework is, it's quite general. We now discuss more specific outcomes of job satisfaction and dissatisfaction in the workplace.

JOB SATISFACTION AND JOB PERFORMANCE   As several studies have concluded, happy workers are more likely to be productive workers. Some researchers used to believe the relationship between job satisfaction and job performance was a myth. But a review of 300 studies suggested the correlation is pretty strong.[46] As we move from the individual to the organizational level, we also find support for the satisfaction–performance relationship.[47] When we gather satisfaction and productivity data for the organization as a whole, we find organizations with more satisfied employees tend to be more effective than organizations with fewer.

JOB SATISFACTION AND OCB   It seems logical to assume job satisfaction should be a major determinant of an employee's **organizational citizenship behavior (OCB)**, the discretionary behavior that is not part of an employee's formal job requirements, and that contributes to the psychological and social environment of the workplace.[48] Satisfied employees would seem more likely to talk positively about the organization, help others, and go beyond the normal expectations of their job, perhaps because they want to reciprocate their positive experiences. Consistent with this thinking, evidence suggests job satisfaction *is* moderately correlated with OCB; people who are more satisfied with their jobs are more likely to engage in OCB.[49] Why? Fairness perceptions help explain the relationship.[50] Also, those who feel their co-workers support them are more likely to engage in helpful behaviors, whereas those who have antagonistic relationships with co-workers are less likely to do so.[51] Individuals with certain personality traits are also more satisfied with their work, which in turn leads them to engage in more OCB.[52] Finally, research shows that when people are in a good mood, they are more likely to engage in OCB.[53]

JOB SATISFACTION AND CUSTOMER SATISFACTION   As we noted in Chapter 1, employees in service jobs often interact with customers. Because service organization managers should be concerned with pleasing those customers, it is reasonable to ask, Is employee satisfaction related to positive customer outcomes? For frontline employees who have regular customer contact, the answer is "yes." Satisfied employees increase customer satisfaction and loyalty.[54]

A number of companies are acting on this evidence. The first core value of on-line retailer Zappos, "Deliver WOW through service," seems fairly obvious, but the way in which Zappos does it is not. Employees are encouraged to "create fun and a little weirdness" and are given unusual discretion in making customers satisfied; they are encouraged to use their imaginations, including sending flowers to disgruntled customers; and Zappos even offers a $2,000 bribe to quit the company after training (to weed out the half-hearted).[55] Other organizations seem to work the other end of the spectrum by ignoring the effect job satisfaction has on the customer's experience. In the airline industry, for example, two independent reports—one on the Transportation Security Administration (TSA) and the other on airline passenger complaints—argue that low employee morale was a major factor undermining passenger satisfaction. At US Airways, employees have posted comments on blogs such as "Our plans [sic] smell filthy" and, from another, "How can I take pride in this product?"[56]

JOB SATISFACTION AND ABSENTEEISM   We find a consistent negative relationship between satisfaction and absenteeism, but it is moderate to weak.[57] Although it certainly makes sense that dissatisfied employees are more likely to miss work, other factors affect the relationship. Organizations that provide liberal sick leave benefits are encouraging all their employees—including those who are highly satisfied—to take days off. You can find work satisfying yet still want to enjoy a three-day weekend if those days come free with no penalties. When numerous alternative jobs are available, dissatisfied employees have high absence rates, but when there are few, they have the same (low) rate of absence as satisfied employees.[58]

JOB SATISFACTION AND TURNOVER   The relationship between job satisfaction and turnover is stronger than between satisfaction and absenteeism.[59] The satisfaction–turnover relationship also is affected by alternative job prospects. If an employee is presented with an unsolicited job offer, job dissatisfaction is less predictive of turnover because the employee is more likely leaving in response to "pull" (the lure of the other job) than "push" (the unattractiveness of the current job). Similarly, job dissatisfaction is more likely to translate into turnover when employment opportunities are plentiful because employees perceive it is easy to move. Finally, when employees have high "human capital" (high education, high ability), job dissatisfaction is more likely to translate into turnover because they have, or perceive, many available alternatives.[60]

JOB SATISFACTION AND WORKPLACE DEVIANCE   Job dissatisfaction and antagonistic relationships with co-workers predict a variety of behaviors organizations find undesirable, including unionization attempts, substance abuse, stealing at work, undue socializing, and tardiness. Researchers argue these behaviors are indicators of a broader syndrome called *deviant behavior in the workplace* (or *counterproductive behavior* or *employee withdrawal*).[61] If employees don't like their work environments, they'll respond somehow, though it is not always easy to forecast exactly *how*. One worker might quit. Another might use work time to surf the internet or take work supplies home for personal use. In short, workers who don't like their jobs "get even" in various ways—and because those ways can be quite creative, controlling only one behavior, such as with an absence control policy, leaves the root cause untouched. To effectively control the undesirable consequences of job dissatisfaction, employers should attack the source of the problem—the dissatisfaction—rather than try to control the different responses.

MANAGERS OFTEN "DON'T GET IT"   Given the evidence we've just reviewed, it should come as no surprise that job satisfaction can affect the bottom line. One study by a management consulting firm separated large organizations into high morale (more than 70 percent of employees expressed overall job satisfaction) and medium or low morale (fewer than 70 percent). The stock prices of companies in the high-morale group grew 19.4 percent, compared with 10 percent for the medium-or low-morale group. Despite these results, many managers are unconcerned about employee job satisfaction. Still others overestimate how satisfied employees are with their jobs, so they don't think there's a problem when there is. In one study of 262 large employers, 86 percent of senior managers believed their organizations treated employees well, but only 55 percent of employees agreed. Another study found 55 percent of managers thought morale was good in their organizations, compared to only 38 percent of employees.[62]

Regular surveys can reduce gaps between what managers *think* employees feel and what they *really* feel. This can impact the bottom line in small franchise sites as well as in large companies. For instance, Jonathan McDaniel, manager of a KFC restaurant in Houston, surveys his employees every 3 months. Some results led him to make changes, such as giving employees greater say about which workdays they have off. Moreover, McDaniel believes the process itself is valuable. "They really love giving their opinions," he says. "That's the most important part of it—that they have a voice and that they're heard." Surveys are no panacea, but if job attitudes are as important as we believe, organizations need to find out where they can be improved.[63]

SUMMARY AND IMPLICATIONS FOR MANAGERS

Job satisfaction is related to organizational effectiveness—a large study found that business units whose employees had high-average levels of engagement had higher levels of customer satisfaction and lower levels of turnover and accidents. All else equal, it clearly behooves organizations to have a satisfied workforce.

Managers should be interested in their employees' attitudes because attitudes give warnings of potential problems and influence behavior. Creating a satisfied workforce is hardly a guarantee of successful organizational performance, but evidence strongly suggests that whatever managers can do to improve employee attitudes will likely result in heightened organizational effectiveness all the way to high customer satisfaction—and profits. Some takeaway lessons from the study of attitudes include the following:

- *Positivity.* Satisfied and committed employees have lower rates of turnover, absenteeism, and withdrawal behaviors. They also perform better on the job. Given that managers want to keep resignations and absences down—especially among their most productive employees—they'll want to do things that generate positive job attitudes.
- *Valid measurement.* Managers will also want to measure job attitudes effectively so they can tell how employees are reacting to their work. As one review put it, "A sound measurement of overall job attitude is one of the most useful pieces of information an organization can have about its employees."[64]
- *Job appeal.* The most important thing managers can do to raise employee satisfaction is focus on the intrinsic parts of the job, such as making the work challenging and interesting.
- *More than money.* Although paying employees poorly will likely not attract high-quality employees to the organization or keep high performers, managers should realize that high pay alone is unlikely to create a satisfying work environment.

MyManagementLab

Go to **MyManagementLab.com** to access study plans, interactive lectures, and videos as well as Auto-graded writing questions and the following Assisted-graded writing question.

3-1. MyManagementLab Only—comprehensive writing assignment for this chapter.

4

∎ ∎ ∎

Emotions and Moods

After studying this chapter, you should be able to:

- Differentiate emotions from moods and list the basic emotions and moods.
- Identify the sources of emotions and moods.
- Show the impact emotional labor has on employees.
- Contrast the evidence for and against the existence of emotional intelligence.
- Apply concepts about emotions and moods to specific OB issues.
- Contrast the experience, interpretation, and expression of emotions across cultures.

MyManagementLab™
⭐ Improve Your Grade!
Over 10 million students improved their results using the Pearson MyLabs. Visit **mymanagementlab.com** for simulations, tutorials, and end-of-chapter problems.

Given the obvious role emotions play in our lives, it might surprise you that, until recently, the field of OB has given the topic of emotions little attention.[1] Why? We offer two possible explanations.

First is the myth of rationality.[2] Until recently, the protocol of the work world kept a damper on emotions. A well-run organization didn't allow employees to express emotions as they were thought to be the antithesis of rationality. Though researchers and managers knew emotions were an inseparable part of everyday life, they tried to create organizations that were emotion-free.

The second explanation is the belief that emotions were disruptive.[3] Researchers looked at strong negative emotions—especially anger—that interfered with an employee's ability to work effectively. They rarely viewed emotions as constructive or positive.

Certainly emotions exhibited at the wrong time can hinder performance. But employees do bring their emotions to work every day, and no study of OB would be comprehensive without considering their role in workplace behavior.

WHAT ARE EMOTIONS AND MOODS?

In our analysis, we'll need three terms that are closely intertwined: *affect, emotions*, and *moods*.

Affect is a generic term that covers a broad range of feelings people experience, including both emotions and moods.[4] **Emotions** are intense feelings directed at someone or something.[5] **Moods** are less intense feelings than emotions and often (though not always) arise without a specific event acting as a stimulus.[6] Exhibit 4-1 shows the characteristics of each and the relationship between them.

Most experts believe emotions are more fleeting than moods.[7] For example, if someone is rude to you, you'll feel angry. That intense feeling probably comes and goes fairly quickly, maybe in a matter of seconds. Bad moods, though, can linger for several hours.

Emotions are reactions to a person or an event. You show your emotions when you're "happy about something, angry at someone, afraid of something."[8] Moods, in contrast, aren't usually directed at a person or an event. But emotions can turn into moods when you lose focus on the event or object that started the feeling. And, by the same token, good or bad moods can make you more emotional in response to an event. So when a colleague criticizes how you spoke to a client, you might show emotion toward a specific object, but as the specific emotion dissipates, you might just feel generally dispirited. You can't attribute this feeling to any single event; you're just not your normal self. You might then overreact to other events. This affect state describes a mood.

First, as the exhibit shows, *affect* is a broad term that encompasses emotions and moods. Second, there are differences between emotions and moods. Some of these differences are more subtle than the ones discussed previously. For example, unlike moods, emotions tend to be more clearly revealed by facial expressions. Also, some emotions may be more action-oriented—they may lead us to some immediate action—while moods may be more cognitive, meaning they may cause us to think or brood.[9]

Finally, emotions and moods are closely connected and can influence each other. Getting your dream job may generate the emotion of joy, which can put you in a good

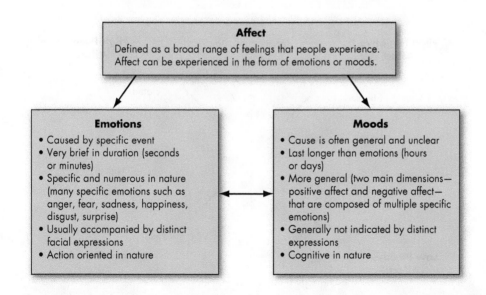

Affect
Defined as a broad range of feelings that people experience. Affect can be experienced in the form of emotions or moods.

Emotions
- Caused by specific event
- Very brief in duration (seconds or minutes)
- Specific and numerous in nature (many specific emotions such as anger, fear, sadness, happiness, disgust, surprise)
- Usually accompanied by distinct facial expressions
- Action oriented in nature

Moods
- Cause is often general and unclear
- Last longer than emotions (hours or days)
- More general (two main dimensions—positive affect and negative affect—that are composed of multiple specific emotions)
- Generally not indicated by distinct expressions
- Cognitive in nature

EXHIBIT 4-1
Affect, Emotions, and Moods

mood for several days. Similarly, if you're in a good or bad mood, you might experience a more intense positive or negative emotion than is typical.

Affect, emotions, and moods are separable in theory; in practice the distinction isn't always crystal-clear. In some areas, researchers have studied mostly moods, in other areas mainly emotions. So, when we review the OB topics on emotions and moods, you may see more information about emotions in one area and about moods in another. This is simply the state of the research.

The Basic Emotions

Because there is such a wide range of emotions, researchers have tried to limit them to a fundamental set.[10] But some argue that it makes no sense to think in terms of "basic" emotions because even emotions we rarely experience, such as shock, can have a powerful effect on us.[11]

It's unlikely psychologists or philosophers will ever completely agree on one set of basic emotions. Still, many researchers agree on six essentially universal emotions—anger, fear, sadness, happiness, disgust, and surprise.[12] Some even plot them along a continuum: happiness—surprise—fear—sadness—anger—disgust.[13] The closer two emotions are to each other on this continuum, the more likely people will confuse them. We sometimes mistake happiness for surprise, but rarely do we confuse happiness and disgust. In addition, as we'll see later on, cultural factors can also influence interpretations.

The Basic Moods: Positive and Negative Affect

One way to classify emotions is by whether they are positive or negative.[14] Positive emotions—such as joy and gratitude—express a favorable evaluation or feeling. Negative emotions—such as anger or guilt—express the opposite. Keep in mind that emotions can't be neutral. Being neutral is being nonemotional.[15]

When we group emotions into positive and negative categories, they become mood states because we are now looking at them more generally instead of isolating one particular emotion. In Exhibit 4-2, excited is a pure marker of high positive affect, whereas

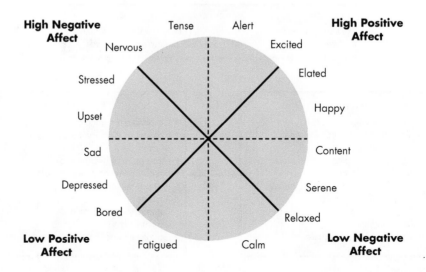

EXHIBIT 4-2
The Structure of Mood

boredom is a pure marker of low positive affect. Nervous is a pure marker of high negative affect; relaxed is a pure marker of low negative affect. Finally, some emotions—such as contentment (a mixture of high positive affect and low negative affect) and sadness (a mixture of low positive affect and high negative affect)—are in between. Some emotions, such as surprise, don't fit well into this model because they're not as clearly positive or negative.

So, we can think of **positive affect** as a mood dimension consisting of positive emotions such as excitement and cheerfulness at the high end, and boredom and tiredness at the low end. **Negative affect** is a mood dimension consisting of nervousness, stress, and anxiety at the high end, and relaxation and poise at the low end. (*Note:* Positive and negative affect *are* moods. We're using these labels, rather than *positive mood* and *negative mood*, because that's how researchers label them.)

Negative emotions are likely to become negative moods. People think about events that created strong negative emotions five times as long as they do about events that created strong positive ones.[16] So, we should expect people to recall negative experiences more readily than positive ones. Perhaps one reason is that negative experiences are generally more unusual. Indeed, research finds a **positivity offset**, meaning that at zero input (when nothing in particular is going on), most individuals experience a mildly positive mood.[17] So, for most people, positive moods are more common than negative moods.

Does the degree to which people experience these positive and negative emotions vary across cultures? Yes. In China, people report experiencing fewer positive and negative emotions than people in other cultures, and the emotions they experience are less intense. People in most cultures appear to experience certain positive and negative emotions, but the frequency and intensity varies to some degree.[18] Despite these differences, people from all over the world interpret negative and positive emotions in much the same way. We all view negative emotions as dangerous and destructive, and we desire positive emotions such as love and happiness. However, some cultures value certain emotions more than others. Pride, for example, is generally a positive emotion in Western individualistic cultures such as the United States, but Eastern cultures like China view pride as undesirable.[19]

The Function of Emotions

DO EMOTIONS MAKE US IRRATIONAL? Famous astronomer Carl Sagan once indicated that when people have powerful emotions they tend to be less honest with themselves. This observation suggests rationality and emotion are in conflict, and that if you exhibit emotion you are likely to act irrationally. Some posit that displaying emotions such as sadness to the point of crying is so toxic to a career that we should leave the room rather than allow others to witness it.[20] These perspectives suggest the demonstration or even experience of emotions can make us seem irrational. However, research is increasingly showing that emotions are actually critical to rational thinking.[21]

Consider Phineas Gage, a railroad worker in Vermont. One September day in 1848, while Gage was setting an explosive charge at work, a 3-foot, 7-inch iron bar flew into his lower-left jaw and out through the top of his skull. Remarkably, Gage survived his injury. He was still able to read and speak, and he performed well above average on cognitive ability tests. However, it became clear he had lost his ability to experience emotion. Gage's inability to express emotion eventually took away his ability to reason. Despite being an intelligent man whose intellectual abilities were unharmed by the accident, he started making irrational choices about his life, often behaving erratically and against his self-interests. In commenting on Gage's condition, one expert noted, "Reason may not be as pure as most of us think it is or wish it were . . . emotions and feelings may not be intruders in the bastion of reason at all: they may be enmeshed in its networks, for worse *and* for better."[22]

The example of Phineas Gage shows emotions are critical to rational thinking. We must have the ability to experience emotions to be rational. Why? Because our emotions provide important information about how we understand the world around us. The key to good decision making is to employ both thinking *and* feeling in our decisions.

DO EMOTIONS MAKE US ETHICAL?   A growing body of research has begun to examine the relationship between emotions and moral attitudes.[23] It was previously believed that, like decision making in general, most ethical decision making was based on higher-order cognitive processes, but research on moral emotions increasingly questions this perspective. Examples of moral emotions include sympathy for the suffering of others, guilt about our own immoral behavior, anger about injustice done to others, contempt for those who behave unethically, and disgust at violations of moral norms. Numerous studies suggest that these reactions are largely based on feelings rather than cold cognition. People who are behaving ethically are at least partially making decisions based on their emotions and feelings, and this emotional reaction will often be a good thing.

Sources of Emotions and Moods

Have you ever said "I got up on the wrong side of the bed today"? Have you ever snapped at a co-worker or family member for no particular reason? If you have, it probably makes you wonder where emotions and moods come from. Here we discuss some of the primary influences.

PERSONALITY   Moods and emotions have a trait component: most people have built-in tendencies to experience certain moods and emotions more frequently than others do. People also experience the same emotions with different intensities. Contrast former coach Bobby Knight to Microsoft former CEO Bill Gates. The first is easily moved to anger, whereas the other is relatively distant and unemotional. Knight and Gates probably differ in **affect intensity**, or how strongly they experience their emotions.[24] Affectively intense people experience both positive and negative emotions more deeply: When they're sad, they're really sad, and when they're happy, they're really happy.

DAY OF THE WEEK AND TIME OF THE DAY   As Exhibit 4-3 shows, people tend to be in their worst moods (highest negative affect and lowest positive affect) early in the week, and in their best moods (highest positive affect and lowest negative affect) late in the week.[25]

What about time of the day? (See Exhibit 4-4.) We often think we are either "morning" or "evening" people. However, most of us actually follow the same pattern. Regardless of what time we go to bed at night or get up in the morning, levels of positive affect tend to peak at around the halfway point between waking and sleeping. Negative affect, however, shows little fluctuation throughout the day.

What does this mean for organizational behavior? Monday morning is probably not the best time to ask someone for a favor or to convey bad news. Our workplace

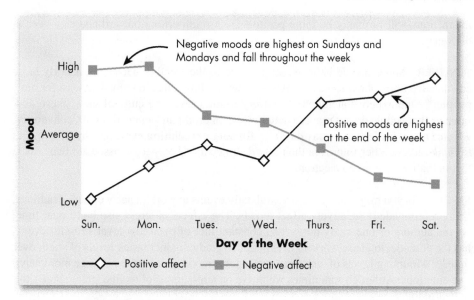

Negative moods are highest on Sundays and Mondays and fall throughout the week

Positive moods are highest at the end of the week

Mood

High

Average

Low

Sun. Mon. Tues. Wed. Thurs. Fri. Sat.

Day of the Week

◇── Positive affect   ■── Negative affect

EXHIBIT 4-3
Our Moods Are Affected by the Days of the Week

Source: D. Watson, *Mood and Temperament* (New York: Guilford Press, 2000). Reprinted by permission.

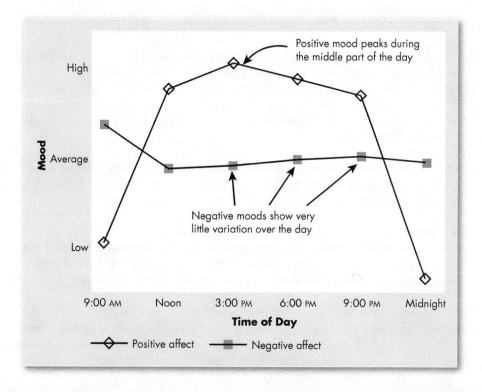

Positive mood peaks during the middle part of the day

Negative moods show very little variation over the day

Mood

High

Average

Low

9:00 AM Noon 3:00 PM 6:00 PM 9:00 PM Midnight

Time of Day

◇── Positive affect   ■── Negative affect

EXHIBIT 4-4
Our Moods Are Affected by the Time of the Day

Source: D. Watson, *Mood and Temperament* (New York: Guilford Press, 2000). Reprinted by permission.

interactions will probably be more positive from midmorning onward and also later in the week.

WEATHER   Many people believe mood is tied to the weather. However, a fairly large and detailed body of evidence suggests weather has little effect on mood, at least for most people.[26] One expert concluded, "Contrary to the prevailing cultural view, these data indicate that people do not report a better mood on bright and sunny days (or, conversely, a worse mood on dark and rainy days)."[27] **Illusory correlation** explains why people tend to *think* nice weather improves their mood. It occurs when people associate two events that in reality have no connection.

STRESS   As you might imagine, stressful daily events at work (a nasty e-mail, deadlines, being reprimanded) negatively affect moods. The effects of stress also build over time. As the authors of one study note, "[A] constant diet of even low-level stressful events has the potential to cause workers to experience gradually increasing levels of strain over time."[28] Mounting levels of stress can worsen our moods, and we experience more negative emotions. Although sometimes we thrive on stress, most of us find stress takes a toll on our mood.

SOCIAL ACTIVITIES   For most people, social activities increase positive mood and have little effect on negative mood. But do people in positive moods seek out social interactions, or do social interactions cause people to be in good moods? It seems both are true.[29] Does the *type* of social activity matter? Indeed it does. Research suggests activities that are physical (skiing or hiking with friends), informal (going to a party), or epicurean (eating with others) are more strongly associated with increases in positive mood than events that are formal (attending a meeting) or sedentary (watching TV with friends).[30]

SLEEP   U.S. adults report sleeping less than adults a generation ago.[31] This is important to note as sleep quality does affect mood. Undergraduates and adult workers who are sleep-deprived report greater feelings of fatigue, anger, and hostility.[32] One reason is that poor or reduced sleep impairs decision making and makes it difficult to control emotions.[33] Poor sleep also impairs job satisfaction because people feel fatigued, irritable, and less alert.[34]

EXERCISE   Research consistently shows exercise enhances people's positive mood.[35] While not terribly strong overall, the effects are strongest for those who are depressed. So exercise may help put you in a better mood, but its influence is limited.

AGE   One study of people ages 18 to 94 revealed that negative emotions seem to occur less as people get older. Periods of highly positive moods lasted longer for older individuals, and bad moods faded more quickly.[36] The study implies emotional experience improves with age; as we get older, we experience fewer negative emotions.

SEX   Evidence confirms women are more *emotionally expressive* than men;[37] they experience emotions more intensely, tend to "hold onto" emotions longer than men, and display more frequent expressions of both positive and negative emotions, except anger.[38] Evidence from a study of participants from 37 different countries found that men consistently report higher levels of powerful emotions like anger, whereas women report more powerless emotions like sadness and fear. Thus, there are some sex differences in the experience and expression of emotions.[39]

People also tend to attribute men's and women's emotions in ways that might be based on stereotypes of what typical emotional reactions are. One study showed that participants who read about emotional expressions interpreted women's reactions as being dispositional (related to personality), whereas men's reactions were interpreted as being due to the situation around them.[40] Another study showed that participants were faster at detecting angry expressions on male faces and happy expressions on female faces; neutral faces in men were attributed as more angry and neutral faces in women were interpreted as happy.[41]

EMOTIONAL LABOR

Every employee expends physical and mental labor by putting body and mind, respectively, into the job. But jobs also require **emotional labor**, an employee's expression of organizationally desired emotions during interpersonal transactions at work.

The concept of emotional labor emerged from studies of service jobs. Airlines expect their flight attendants to be cheerful; we expect funeral directors to be sad, and doctors emotionally neutral. But emotional labor is relevant to almost every job. At the least, your managers expect you to be courteous, not hostile, in your interactions with co-workers. The true challenge arises when employees have to project one emotion while feeling another.[42] This disparity is **emotional dissonance**, and it can take a heavy toll. Emotional dissonance is like cognitive dissonance as discussed in a previous chapter, except that emotional dissonance concerns feelings rather than thinking. With emotional dissonance, bottled-up feelings of frustration and resentment can lead to emotional exhaustion and burnout.[43] It's from the increasing importance of emotional labor as a key component of effective job performance that we have come to understand the relevance of emotion within the field of OB.

It can help you, on the job especially, if you separate emotions into felt or *displayed emotions*.[44] **Felt emotions** are an individual's actual emotions. In contrast, **displayed emotions** are those that the organization requires workers to show and considers appropriate in a given job. They're not innate; they're learned. "The ritual look of delight on the face of the first runner-up as the new Miss America is announced is a product of the display rule that losers should mask their sadness with an expression of joy for the winner."[45] Similarly, most of us know how we're expected to act at funerals and weddings, regardless of our actual feelings.

Research suggests that at U.S. workplaces, it is expected that we should typically display positive emotions like happiness and excitement and suppress negative emotions like fear and anger.[46] Effective managers have learned to be serious when giving an employee a negative performance evaluation and to hide their anger when they've been passed over for promotion. A salesperson who hasn't learned to smile and appear friendly, despite his true feelings at the moment, typically won't last long in the job. How we *experience* an emotion isn't always the same as how we show it.[47]

Displaying fake emotions requires us to suppress real ones. **Surface acting** is hiding inner feelings and forgoing emotional expressions in response to display rules. A worker who smiles at a customer even when he doesn't feel like it is surface acting.

Deep acting is trying to modify our true inner feelings based on display rules. A health care provider trying to genuinely feel more empathy for her patients is deep acting.[48] Surface acting deals with *displayed* emotions, and deep acting deals with *felt* emotions. Research shows that surface acting is more stressful to employees because it entails denying their true emotions.[49] Displaying emotions we don't really feel is exhausting, so it is important to give employees who engage in surface displays a chance to relax and recharge. A study found that in hospital work groups where there were heavy emotional display demands, for instance, burnout was higher than in other hospital work groups.[50] As well, the quality of breaks matters to the ability to recover. A study that looked at how cheerleading instructors spent their breaks from teaching found those who used their breaks to rest and relax were more effective instructors after their breaks.[51] Instructors who did chores during their breaks were only about as effective after their break as they were before.

EMOTIONAL INTELLIGENCE

People who know their own emotions and are good at reading others' emotions may be more effective in their jobs.

Diane Marshall is an office manager. Her awareness of her own and others' emotions is almost nil. She's moody and unable to generate much enthusiasm or interest in her employees. She doesn't understand why employees get upset with her. She often overreacts to problems and chooses the most ineffectual responses to emotional situations. Diane has low emotional intelligence.

Emotional intelligence (EI) is a person's ability to (1) perceive emotions in the self and others, (2) understand the meaning of these emotions, and (3) regulate one's emotions accordingly in a cascading model, as shown in Exhibit 4-5. People who know their own emotions and are good at reading emotional cues—for instance, knowing why they're angry and how to express themselves without violating norms—are most likely to be effective.[52]

EI has been a controversial concept in OB, with supporters and detractors. In the following sections, we review the arguments for and against its viability.

The Case for EI

The arguments in favor of EI include its intuitive appeal, the fact that it predicts criteria that matter, and the idea that it is biologically based.

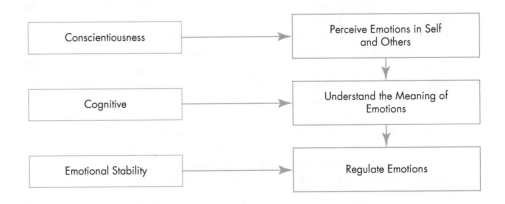

EXHIBIT 4-5

A Cascading Model of Emotional Intelligence

INTUITIVE APPEAL   Almost everyone agrees it is good to possess social intelligence. Intuition suggests people who can detect emotions in others and control their own emotions will have an advantage in the business world. For example, partners in a multinational consulting firm who scored above the median on an EI measure delivered $1.2 million more in business than did the other partners.[53]

EI PREDICTS CRITERIA THAT MATTER   Evidence suggests a high level of EI means a person will perform well on the job. For example, one study found EI predicted the performance of employees in a cigarette factory in China.[54] Another study found the ability to recognize emotions in others' facial expressions, and to pick up subtle signals about people's emotions, predicted peer ratings of how valuable people were to their organization.[55] Finally, a review of studies indicated that, overall, EI weakly but consistently positively correlated with job performance, even after researchers took cognitive ability, conscientiousness, and neuroticism into account.[56]

EI IS BIOLOGICALLY BASED   In one study, people with damage to the brain area that governs emotional processing (part of the prefrontal cortex) scored no lower on standard measures of intelligence than people without similar damage. But they scored significantly lower on EI tests and were impaired in normal decision making. This suggests EI is neurologically based in a way that's unrelated to standard measures of intelligence, as we will discuss in more depth in the next chapter.[57] There is also evidence EI is genetically influenced, further supporting the idea that it measures a real underlying biological factor.[58]

The Case Against EI

For all its supporters, EI has just as many critics who say it's vague and impossible to measure, and they question its validity.

EI RESEARCHERS DO NOT AGREE ON DEFINITIONS   To many researchers, it's not clear what EI is because researchers use different definitions of the construct.[59] Some researchers have focused on emotional intelligence via tests with right and wrong answers, scoring the ability to recognize and control emotions. This is the ability-based perspective on EI. Others focus on EI as a broad variety of constructs that can be measured by self-reports and are connected primarily by the fact that they are not redundant with cognitive intelligence. Not only are these two definitions different, but the measures used by each perspective are barely correlated with one another.[60]

EI CAN'T BE MEASURED   Many have raised questions about measuring EI, arguing because it's a form of intelligence, there must be right and wrong answers on tests. Some tests do have right and wrong answers, although the validity of some questions is doubtful. One measure asks you to associate feelings with colors, as if purple always makes us feel cool and not warm. Other measures are self-reported, such as "I'm good at 'reading' other people," and have no right or wrong answers. However, these self-report measures could reflect a variety of nonability-related constructs like general self-esteem or self-efficacy. The measures of EI are diverse, and researchers have not subjected them to as much rigorous study as they have measures of personality and general intelligence.[61]

EI IS NOTHING BUT PERSONALITY WITH A DIFFERENT LABEL   Some critics argue that because EI is so closely related to intelligence and personality, once you control for these factors, it has nothing unique to offer. There is some foundation to this argument. EI appears to be correlated with measures of personality, especially emotional stability.[62] If this is true, then the evidence for a biological component to EI is spurious, and biological markers like brain activity and heritability are attributable to other well-known and much better researched psychological constructs. To some extent, researchers have resolved this issue by noting that EI is a construct partially determined by traits like cognitive intelligence, conscientiousness, and emotional stability, as shown in Exhibit 4-5, so it makes sense that EI is correlated with these characteristics.[63]

Although the field is progressing in its understanding of EI, many questions have not been answered. Still, EI is wildly popular among consulting firms and in the popular press. One consulting firm's promotional materials for an EI measure claimed, "EI accounts for more than 85 percent of star performance in top leaders."[64] To say the least, it's difficult to validate this statement with the research literature.

Emotion Regulation

Have you ever tried to cheer yourself up when you're feeling down, or calm yourself when you're feeling angry? If so, you have engaged in *emotion regulation*—identifying and modifying the emotions you feel. Strategies to change your emotions include thinking about more pleasant things, suppressing negative thoughts, distracting yourself, or engaging in relaxation techniques.

While it might seem desirable to regulate your emotions, research suggests there is a downside to trying to change the way you feel. Changing your emotions takes effort, and this effort can be exhausting. Sometimes attempts to change an emotion actually make the emotion stronger; for example, trying to talk yourself out of being afraid can make you focus more on what scares you, making you more afraid.[65] Also, emotion suppression appears to be especially difficult to do effectively and can lead to more negative emotions.[66] From another perspective, research suggests that avoiding negative emotional experiences is less likely to lead to positive moods than seeking out positive emotional experiences.[67] For example, you're more likely to experience a positive mood if you have a pleasant conversation with a friend than you would be if you avoided an unpleasant conversation with a hostile co-worker.

OB APPLICATIONS OF EMOTIONS AND MOODS

Positive emotions can increase problem-solving skills and help us understand and analyze new information.

In this section, we assess how an understanding of emotions and moods can improve our ability to explain and predict the selection process in organizations, decision making, creativity, motivation, leadership, interpersonal conflict, negotiation, customer service, job attitudes, and deviant workplace behaviors. We also look at how managers can influence our moods.

Selection

One implication from the evidence on EI is that employers should consider it a factor in hiring employees, especially in jobs that demand a high degree of social interaction. In fact, more employers are starting to use EI measures to hire people. In fact, a study of U.S. Air Force recruiters showed that top-performing recruiters exhibited high levels of EI.

Decision Making

As you will see in Chapter 6, traditional approaches to the study of decision making in organizations have emphasized rationality. But OB researchers are increasingly finding that moods and emotions have important effects on decision making.

Positive moods and emotions seem to help people make sound decisions. People in good moods or experiencing positive emotions are more likely than others to use heuristics, or rules of thumb,[68] to help make good decisions quickly. Positive emotions also enhance problem-solving skills, so positive people find better solutions to problems.[69]

OB researchers continue to debate the role of negative emotions and moods in decision making. Although one often-cited study suggested depressed people reach more accurate judgments,[70] more recent evidence hints they make poorer decisions. Why? Because depressed people are slower at processing information and tend to weigh all possible options rather than the most likely ones.[71] They search for the perfect solution, when there rarely is one.

Creativity

People in good moods tend to be more creative than people in bad moods.[72] They produce more ideas and more options.[73] It seems people experiencing positive moods or emotions are more flexible and open in their thinking, which may explain why they're more creative.[74] Supervisors should actively try to keep employees happy because doing so creates more good moods, which in turn leads people to be more creative.[75]

Some researchers, however, do not believe a positive mood makes people more creative. They argue that when people are in positive moods, they may relax and not engage in the critical thinking necessary for some forms of creativity.[76] The answer may lie in thinking of moods somewhat differently. Rather than looking at positive or negative affect, it's possible to conceptualize moods as active feelings like anger or elation and contrast these with deactivating moods like sorrow or serenity. All the activating moods, whether positive *or* negative, seem to lead to more creativity, whereas deactivating moods, as shown in Exhibit 4-2, as those with low affect, lead to less.[77]

Motivation

Several studies have highlighted the importance of moods and emotions on motivation. One study set two groups of people to solving word puzzles. The first group saw a funny video clip, intended to put the subjects in a good mood first. The other group was not shown the clip and started working on the puzzles right away. The results? The positive-mood group reported higher expectations of being able to solve the puzzles, worked harder at them, and solved more puzzles as a result.[78]

The second study found that giving people performance feedback—whether real or fake—influenced their mood, which then influenced their motivation.[79] So a cycle can exist in which a positive mood causes people to be more creative, which leads to positive feedback from those observing their work. This positive feedback further reinforces the positive mood, which may make people perform even better, and so on.

Another study looked at the moods of insurance sales agents in Taiwan.[80] Agents in a good mood were more helpful toward their co-workers, and also felt better about themselves. These two factors in turn led to superior performance in the form of higher sales and better supervisor reports of performance.

Leadership

Effective leaders rely on emotional appeals to help convey their messages.[81] In fact, the expression of emotions in speeches is often the critical element that makes us accept or reject a leader's message. Politicians, as a case in point, have learned to show enthusiasm when talking about their chances of winning an election, even when polls suggest otherwise.

Corporate executives know emotional content is critical if employees are to buy into their vision of the company's future and accept change. When higher-ups offer new visions with vague or distant goals, it is often difficult for employees to accept the changes they'll bring. By arousing emotions and linking them to an appealing vision, leaders increase the likelihood that managers and employees alike will accept change.[82] Leaders who focus on inspirational goals also generate greater optimism and enthusiasm in employees, leading to more positive social interactions with co-workers and customers.[83]

Negotiation

Negotiation is an emotional process; however, we often say a skilled negotiator has a "poker face." Several studies have shown that a negotiator who feigns anger has an advantage over their opponent. Why? Because when a negotiator shows anger, the opponent concludes the negotiator has conceded all she can and so gives in.[84] However, anger should be used selectively in negotiation: angry negotiators who have less information or less power than their opponents experience significantly worse outcomes.[85] It appears that a powerful, better-informed individual will be less willing to share information or meet an angry opponent halfway.

Displaying a negative emotion (such as anger) can be effective, but feeling bad about your performance appears to impair future negotiations. Individuals who do poorly in a negotiation experience negative emotions, develop negative perceptions of their counterpart, and are less willing to share information or be cooperative in future negotiations.[86] Interestingly, then, while moods and emotions have benefits at work, in negotiation—unless we're putting up a false front like feigning anger—emotions may impair negotiator performance. A 2005 study found people who suffered damage to the emotional centers of their brains (the same part that was injured in Phineas Gage) may be the *best* negotiators, because they're not likely to overcorrect when faced with negative outcomes.[87]

Customer Service

A worker's emotional state influences customer service, which influences levels of repeat business and of customer satisfaction.[88] Providing high-quality customer service makes demands on employees because it often puts them in a state of emotional dissonance. Long-term emotional dissonance is a predictor for job burnout, declines in job performance, and lower job satisfaction.[89]

Employees' emotions can transfer to the customer. Studies indicate a matching effect between employee and customer emotions called **emotional contagion**—the "catching" of emotions from others.[90] When someone experiences positive emotions and laughs and smiles at you, you tend to respond positively. Emotional contagion is important because customers who catch the positive moods or emotions of employees shop longer. Negative emotions and moods are contagious too. When an employee feels unfairly treated by a customer, for example, it's harder for him to display the positive emotions his organization expects of him.[91]

Job Attitudes

Ever hear the advice "Never take your work home with you," meaning you should forget about work once you go home? That's easier said than done. Several studies have shown people who had a good day at work tend to be in a better mood at home that evening, and vice versa.[92] People who have a stressful day at work also have trouble relaxing after they get off work.[93] One study had married couples describing their moods throughout the course of the day. As one might suspect, if one member of the couple was in a negative mood during the workday, that mood spilled over to the spouse at night.[94] Even though people do emotionally take their work home with them, by the next day the effect is usually gone.[95]

Deviant Workplace Behaviors

Anyone who has spent much time in an organization realizes people often behave in ways that violate established norms and threaten the organization, its members, or both. These actions are called *workplace deviant behaviors*.[96] Many can be traced to negative emotions.

For instance, envy is an emotion that occurs when you resent someone for having something you don't have but strongly desire and it can lead to malicious behaviors. An envious employee could backstab another employee, negatively distort others' successes, and positively distort his own accomplishments.[97] Angry people look for other people to blame for their bad mood, interpret other people's behavior as hostile, and have trouble considering others' point of view.[98] It's not hard to see how these thought processes can lead to verbal or physical aggression.

Evidence suggests people who feel negative emotions, particularly anger or hostility, are more likely than others to engage in short-term deviant behavior at work such as gossiping or searching the internet.[99] Once aggression starts, it's likely that other people will become angry and aggressive, so the stage is set for a serious escalation of negative behavior.

Safety and Injury at Work

Research relating negative affectivity to increased injuries at work suggests employers might improve health and safety by ensuring workers aren't engaged in potentially dangerous activities when they're in a bad mood as these moods can contribute to injury in several ways.[100] Individuals in negative moods tend to be more anxious, which can make them less able to cope effectively with hazards. A person who is always fearful will be more pessimistic about the effectiveness of safety precautions because she feels she'll just get hurt anyway, or she might panic or freeze up when confronted with a threatening situation. Negative moods also make people more easily distracted, and distractions can obviously lead to careless behaviors.

How Managers Can Influence Moods

You can usually improve a friend's mood by sharing a funny video clip, giving the person a small bag of candy, or even offering a pleasant beverage.[101] But what can companies do to improve employees' moods? Managers can use humor and give their employees small tokens of appreciation for work well done. Also, when leaders themselves are in good moods, group members are more positive, and as a result they cooperate better.[102]

Finally, selecting positive team members can have a contagion effect because positive moods transmit from team member to team member. One study of professional cricket teams found players' happy moods affected the moods of their team members and positively influenced their performance.[103] It makes sense, then, for managers to select team members predisposed to experience positive moods.

SUMMARY AND IMPLICATIONS FOR MANAGERS

Emotions and moods are similar in that both are affective in nature. But they're also different—moods are more general and less contextual than emotions. And events do matter. The time of day and day of the week, stressful events, social activities, and sleep patterns are some of the factors that influence emotions and moods.

Emotions and moods have proven relevant for virtually every OB topic we study, and they have implications for managerial practice.

- Increasingly, organizations are relying on research to select employees they believe have high levels of emotional intelligence.
- Emotions and positive moods appear to facilitate effective decision making and creativity.
- Research suggests mood is linked to motivation, especially through feedback.
- Leaders rely on emotions to increase their effectiveness.
- The display of emotions is important to social behavior like negotiation and customer service.
- The experience of emotions is closely linked to job attitudes and behaviors that follow from attitudes, such as deviant workplace behavior.
- Our final managerial implication is a question: Can managers control colleagues' and employees' emotions and moods? Certainly there are limits, practical and ethical. Emotions and moods are a natural part of an individual's makeup. Where managers err is in ignoring co-workers' and employees' emotions and assessing others' behavior as if it were completely rational. As one consultant aptly put it, "You can't divorce emotions from the workplace because you can't divorce emotions from people."[104] Managers who understand the role of emotions and moods will significantly improve their ability to explain and predict their co-workers' and employees' behavior.

MyManagementLab

Go to **MyManagementLab.com** to access study plans, interactive lectures, and videos as well as Auto-graded writing questions and the following Assisted-graded writing question.

4-1. MyManagementLab Only—comprehensive writing assignment for this chapter.

5

■ ■ ■

Personality and Values

After studying this chapter, you should be able to:

- Define *personality,* describe how it is measured, and explain the factors that determine an individual's personality.
- Describe the Myers-Briggs Type Indicator personality framework and assess its strengths and weaknesses.
- Identify the key traits in the Big Five personality model and demonstrate how the Big Five traits predict behavior at work.
- Identify other personality traits relevant to OB.
- Define *values,* demonstrate the importance of values, and contrast terminal and instrumental values.
- Identify Hofstede's five value dimensions of national culture.

MyManagementLab™
⭐ **Improve Your Grade!**

Over 10 million students improved their results using the Pearson MyLabs. Visit **mymanagementlab.com** for simulations, tutorials, and end-of-chapter problems.

PERSONALITY

Why are some people quiet and passive, while others are loud and aggressive? Are certain personality types better adapted than others for certain job types? Before we can answer these questions, we need to address a more basic one: What is personality?

What Is Personality?

When we talk of personality, we don't mean a person has charm, a positive attitude toward life, or a constantly smiling face. When psychologists talk of personality, they mean a dynamic concept describing the growth and development of a person's whole psychological system.

DEFINING PERSONALITY The definition of *personality* we most frequently use was produced by Gordon Allport nearly 70 years ago. Allport said personality is "the dynamic organization within the individual of those psychophysical systems that determine his unique adjustments to his environment."[1] For our purposes, you should think of **personality** as the sum total of ways in which an individual reacts to and interacts with others. We most often describe it in terms of the measurable traits a person exhibits.

MEASURING PERSONALITY The most important reason managers need to know how to measure personality is that research has shown personality tests are useful in hiring decisions and help managers forecast who is best for a job.[2] The most common means of measuring personality is through self-report surveys, with which individuals evaluate themselves on a series of factors, such as "I worry a lot about the future." Though self-report measures work well when well constructed, one weakness is that the respondent might lie or practice impression management to create a good impression. When people know their personality scores are going to be used for hiring decisions, they rate themselves as about half a standard deviation more conscientious and emotionally stable than if they are taking the test just to learn more about themselves.[3] Another problem is accuracy. A perfectly good candidate could have been in a bad mood when taking the survey, and that will make the scores less accurate.

PERSONALITY DETERMINANTS An early debate in personality research centered on whether an individual's personality was the result of heredity or of environment. It appears to be a result of both. However, it might surprise you that research tends to support the importance of heredity over the environment.

    Heredity refers to factors determined at conception. Physical stature, facial attractiveness, gender, temperament, muscle composition and reflexes, energy level, and biological rhythms are generally considered to be either completely or substantially influenced by who your parents are—that is, by their biological, physiological, and inherent psychological makeup. The heredity approach argues that the ultimate explanation of an individual's personality is the molecular structure of the genes, located in the chromosomes.

    Researchers in many different countries have studied thousands of sets of identical twins who were separated at birth and raised separately.[4] If heredity played little or no part in determining personality, you would expect to find few similarities between the separated twins. But twins raised apart have much in common, and a significant part of the behavioral similarity between them turns out to be associated with genetic factors. One set of twins separated for 39 years and raised 45 miles apart were found to drive the same model and color car. They chain-smoked the same brand of cigarette, owned dogs with the same name, and regularly vacationed within three blocks of each other in

Personality—the sum total of ways in which an individual reacts to and interacts with others—is partly genetic in origins; yet, personality can be easily measured by various methods, including self-report surveys.

a beach community 1,500 miles away. Researchers have found that genetics accounts for about 50 percent of the personality similarities between twins and more than 30 percent of the similarities in occupational and leisure interests.

Interestingly, twin studies have suggested parents don't add much to our personality development. The personalities of identical twins raised in different households are more similar to each other than to the personalities of siblings with whom the twins were raised. Ironically, the most important contribution our parents may make to our personalities is giving us their genes!

This is not to suggest that personality never changes. People's scores on measures of dependability tend to increase over time, as when young adults take on roles like starting a family and establishing a career that require great responsibility. However, strong individual differences in dependability remain; everyone tends to change by about the same amount, so their rank order stays roughly the same.[5] An analogy to intelligence may make this clearer. Children become smarter as they age, so nearly everyone is smarter at age 20 than at age 10. Still, if Madison is smarter than Blake at age 10, she is likely to be so at age 20, too. Consistent with the notion that the teenage years are periods of great exploration and change, research has shown that personality is more changeable in adolescence and more stable among adults.[6]

Early work on the structure of personality tried to identify and label enduring characteristics that describe an individual's behavior, including shy, aggressive, submissive, lazy, ambitious, loyal, and timid. When someone exhibits these characteristics in a large number of situations, we call them **personality traits** of that person.[7] The more consistent the characteristic over time, and the more frequently it occurs in diverse situations, the more important that trait is in describing the individual.

Early efforts to identify the primary traits that govern behavior[8] often resulted in long lists that were difficult to generalize from and provided little practical guidance to organizational decision makers. Two exceptions are the Myers-Briggs Type Indicator and the Big Five Model, now the dominant frameworks for identifying and classifying traits.

The Myers-Briggs Type Indicator

The **Myers-Briggs Type Indicator (MBTI)** is the most widely used personality-assessment instrument in the world.[9] It is a 100-question personality test that asks people how they usually feel or act in particular situations. Respondents are classified as extraverted or introverted (E or I), sensing or intuitive (S or N), thinking or feeling (T or F), and judging or perceiving (J or P). These terms are defined as follows:

- *Extraverted (E) Versus Introverted (I).* Extraverted individuals are outgoing, sociable, and assertive. Introverts are quiet and shy.
- *Sensing (S) Versus Intuitive (N).* Sensing types are practical and prefer routine and order. They focus on details. Intuitives rely on unconscious processes and look at the "big picture."
- *Thinking (T) Versus Feeling (F).* Thinking types use reason and logic to handle problems. Feeling types rely on their personal values and emotions.
- *Judging (J) Versus Perceiving (P).* Judging types want control and prefer their world to be ordered and structured. Perceiving types are flexible and spontaneous.

These classifications together describe 16 personality types, identifying every person by one trait from each of the four pairs. For example, Introverted/Intuitive/Thinking/Judging (INTJ) people are visionaries with original minds and great drive. They are skeptical, critical, independent, determined, and often stubborn. ESTJs are organizers. They are realistic, logical, analytical, and decisive and have a natural head for business or mechanics. The ENTP type is a conceptualizer, innovative, individualistic, versatile, and attracted to entrepreneurial ideas. This person tends to be resourceful in solving challenging problems but may neglect routine assignments.

The MBTI has been widely used by organizations including Apple Computer, AT&T, Citigroup, GE, 3M Co., many hospitals and educational institutions, and even the U.S. Armed Forces. Evidence is mixed about its validity as a measure of personality, however; most of the evidence is against it.[10] One problem is that it forces a person into one type or another; that is, you're either introverted or extraverted. There is no in between, though in reality people can be both extraverted and introverted to some degree. The best we can say is that the MBTI can be a valuable tool for increasing self-awareness and providing career guidance. But because results tend to be unrelated to job performance, managers probably shouldn't use it as a selection test for job candidates.

The Big Five Personality Model

The MBTI may lack strong supporting evidence, but an impressive body of research supports the thesis of the **Big Five Model**—that five basic dimensions underlie all others and encompass most of the significant variation in human personality.[11] Moreover, test scores of these traits do a very good job of predicting how people behave in a variety of real-life situations.[12] The following are the Big Five factors:

- *Extraversion.* The **extraversion** dimension captures our comfort level with relationships. Extraverts tend to be gregarious, assertive, and sociable. Introverts tend to be reserved, timid, and quiet.
- *Agreeableness.* The **agreeableness** dimension refers to an individual's propensity to defer to others. Highly agreeable people are cooperative, warm, and trusting. People who score low on agreeableness are cold, disagreeable, and antagonistic.
- *Conscientiousness.* The **conscientiousness** dimension is a measure of reliability. A highly conscientious person is responsible, organized, dependable, and persistent. Those who score low on this dimension are easily distracted, disorganized, and unreliable.
- *Emotional Stability.* The **emotional stability** dimension—often labeled by its converse, neuroticism—taps a person's ability to withstand stress. People with positive emotional tability tend to be calm, self-confident, and secure. Those with high negative scores tend to be nervous, anxious, depressed, and insecure.
- *Openness to Experience.* The **openness to experience** dimension addresses range of interests and fascination with novelty. Extremely open people are creative, curious, and artistically sensitive. Those at the other end of the category are conventional and find comfort in the familiar.

The Big Five personality traits are related to many OB criteria; each of the five traits has proven its usefulness to understanding individual behavior in organizations.

HOW DO THE BIG FIVE TRAITS PREDICT BEHAVIOR AT WORK? Research has found relationships between these personality dimensions and job performance.[13] As the authors of the most-cited review put it, "The preponderance of evidence shows that individuals who are dependable, reliable, careful, thorough, able to plan, organized, hardworking, persistent, and achievement-oriented tend to have higher job performance in most if not all occupations."[14] In addition, employees who score higher in conscientiousness develop higher levels of job knowledge, probably because highly conscientious people learn more (a review of 138 studies revealed conscientiousness was rather strongly related to GPA).[15] Higher levels of job knowledge then contribute to higher levels of job performance. Conscientious individuals who are more interested in learning than in just performing on the job are also exceptionally good at maintaining performance in the face of negative feedback.[16] There can be "too much of a good thing," however, as extremely conscientious individuals typically do not perform better than those who are simply above average in conscientiousness.[17]

Conscientiousness is as important for managers as for front-line employees. A study of the personality scores of 313 CEO candidates in private equity companies (of whom 225 were hired, and their company's performance later correlated with their personality scores) found conscientiousness—in the form of persistence, attention to detail, and setting of high standards—was more important than other traits. These results attest to the importance of conscientiousness to organizational success.

Interestingly, conscientious people live longer because they take better care of themselves (they eat better and exercise more) and engage in fewer risky behaviors like smoking, drinking and drugs, and risky sexual or driving behavior.[18] Still, probably because they're so organized and structured, conscientious people don't adapt as well to changing contexts. They are generally performance oriented and have more trouble learning complex skills early in the training process because their focus is on performing well rather than on learning. Finally, they are often less creative than less conscientious people, especially artistically.[19]

Although conscientiousness is most consistently related to job performance, the other Big Five traits are also related to aspects of performance and have other implications for work and for life. Let's look at them one at a time. Exhibit 5-1 summarizes.

Of the Big Five traits, emotional stability is most strongly related to life satisfaction, job satisfaction, and low stress levels. This is probably true because high scorers are more likely to be positive and optimistic and experience fewer negative emotions. They are happier than those who score low. People low on emotional stability are hypervigilant (looking for problems or impending signs of danger) and are especially vulnerable to the physical and psychological effects of stress.

Extraverts tend to be happier in their jobs and in their lives as a whole. They experience more positive emotions than do introverts, and they more freely express these feelings. They also tend to perform better in jobs that require significant interpersonal interaction, perhaps because they have more social skills—they usually have more friends and spend more time in social situations than introverts. Finally, extraversion is a relatively strong predictor of leadership emergence in groups; extraverts are more socially dominant, "take charge" sorts of people, and they are generally more assertive than introverts.[20] One downside is that extraverts are more impulsive than introverts; they are more likely to be absent from work and engage in risky behavior such as unprotected sex, drinking, and other impulsive or sensation-seeking acts.[21] One study also found extraverts were more likely than introverts to lie during job interviews.[22]

You might expect agreeable people to be happier than disagreeable people. They are, but only slightly. When people choose romantic partners, friends, or organizational

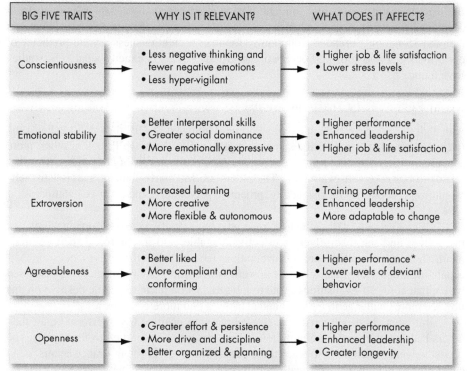

EXHIBIT 5-1
Model of How
Big Five Traits
Influence OB
Criteria

BIG FIVE TRAITS	WHY IS IT RELEVANT?	WHAT DOES IT AFFECT?
Conscientiousness	• Less negative thinking and fewer negative emotions • Less hyper-vigilant	• Higher job & life satisfaction • Lower stress levels
Emotional stability	• Better interpersonal skills • Greater social dominance • More emotionally expressive	• Higher performance* • Enhanced leadership • Higher job & life satisfaction
Extroversion	• Increased learning • More creative • More flexible & autonomous	• Training performance • Enhanced leadership • More adaptable to change
Agreeableness	• Better liked • More compliant and conforming	• Higher performance* • Lower levels of deviant behavior
Openness	• Greater effort & persistence • More drive and discipline • Better organized & planning	• Higher performance • Enhanced leadership • Greater longevity

*In jobs requiring significant teamwork or frequent interpersonal interactions.

team members, agreeable individuals are usually their first choice. Agreeable individuals are better liked than disagreeable people, which explains why they tend to do better in interpersonally oriented jobs such as customer service. They also are more compliant and rule abiding and less likely to get into accidents as a result. People who are agreeable are more satisfied in their jobs and contribute to organizational performance by engaging in citizenship behavior.[23] They are also less likely to engage in organizational deviance. One downside is that agreeableness is associated with lower levels of career success (especially earnings).

Individuals who score high on openness to experience are more creative in science and art than those who score low. Because creativity is important to leadership, open people are more likely to be effective leaders, and more comfortable with ambiguity and change. They cope better with organizational change and are more adaptable in changing contexts. Recent evidence also suggests, however, that they are especially susceptible to workplace accidents.

The five personality factors identified in the Big Five model appear in almost all cross-cultural studies.[24] These studies have included a wide variety of diverse cultures—such as China, Israel, Germany, Japan, Spain, Nigeria, Norway, Pakistan, and the United States. Differences are complex but tend to be primarily about whether countries are predominantly individualistic or collectivistic. Chinese managers use the category of conscientiousness more often and agreeableness less often than do U.S. managers. And the Big Five appear to predict a bit better in individualistic than in collectivist cultures.[25]

But there is a surprisingly high amount of agreement, especially across individuals from developed countries. A comprehensive review of studies covering people from what was then the 15-nation European Community found conscientiousness a valid predictor of performance across jobs and occupational groups.[26] This is exactly what U.S. studies have found.

Other Personality Traits Relevant to OB

Although the Big Five traits have proven highly relevant to OB, they don't exhaust the range of traits that can describe someone's personality. Now we'll look at other, more specific, attributes that are powerful predictors of behavior in organizations. The first relates to our core self-evaluation. The others are Machiavellianism, narcissism, self-monitoring, propensity for risk taking, proactive personality, and other-orientation.

CORE SELF-EVALUATIONS (CSE)   People who have positive **core self-evaluations** like themselves and see themselves as effective, capable, and in control of their environment. Those with negative core self-evaluations tend to dislike themselves, question their capabilities, and view themselves as powerless over their environment.[27] We discussed before that core self-evaluations relate to job satisfaction because people positive on this trait see more challenge in their job and actually attain more complex jobs.

But what about job performance? People with positive CSE perform better than others because they set more ambitious goals, are more committed to their goals, and persist longer in attempting to reach these goals. One study of life insurance agents found core self-evaluations were critical predictors of performance. Ninety percent of life insurance sales calls end in rejection, so an agent has to believe in herself to persist. In fact, this study showed the majority of successful salespersons did have positive CSE.[28] Such people also provide better customer service, are more popular co-workers, and have careers that both begin on better footing and ascend more rapidly over time. [29] Some evidence suggests that individuals high in CSE perform especially well if they also feel their work provides meaning and is helpful to others.[30]

Can we be *too* positive? What happens when someone thinks he is capable but is actually incompetent? One study of *Fortune* 500 CEOs showed that many are overconfident, and their perceived infallibility often causes them to make bad decisions.[31] Teddy Forstmann, chairman of the sports marketing giant IMG, said of himself, "I know God gave me an unusual brain. I can't deny that. I have a God-given talent for seeing potential."[32] We might say people like Forstmann are overconfident, but very often we humans sell ourselves short and are less happy and effective than we could be because of it. If we decide we can't do something, for example, we won't try, and not doing it only reinforces our self-doubts.

MACHIAVELLIANISM   Kuzi is a young bank manager in Taiwan. He's had three promotions in the past 4 years and makes no apologies for the aggressive tactics he's used to propel his career upward. "I'm prepared to do whatever I have to do to get ahead," he says. Kuzi would properly be called Machiavellian.

The personality characteristic of **Machiavellianism** (often abbreviated *Mach*) is named after Niccolo Machiavelli, who wrote in the sixteenth century on how to gain and use power. An individual high in Machiavellianism is pragmatic, maintains emotional distance, and believes ends can justify means. "If it works, use it" is consistent with a high-Mach perspective. A considerable amount of research has found high Machs manipulate more, win more, are persuaded less, and persuade others more than do low Machs.[33] They like their jobs less, are more stressed by their work, and engage in more deviant work behaviors.[34] Yet high-Mach outcomes are moderated by situational factors. High Machs flourish (1) when they interact face to face with others rather than indirectly; (2) when the situation has minimal rules and regulations, allowing latitude for improvisation; and (3) when emotional involvement with details irrelevant to winning distracts low Machs.[35] Thus, in jobs that require bargaining skills (such as labor negotiation) or that offer substantial rewards for winning (such as commissioned sales), high Machs will be productive. But if ends can't justify the means, there are absolute standards of behavior, or the three situational factors we noted are not in evidence, our ability to predict a high Mach's performance will be severely curtailed.

NARCISSISM   Hans likes to be the center of attention. He looks at himself in the mirror a lot, has extravagant dreams, and considers himself a person of many talents. Hans is a narcissist. The term is from the Greek myth of Narcissus, a man so vain and proud he fell in love with his own image. In psychology, **narcissism** describes a person who has a grandiose sense of self-importance, requires excessive admiration, has a sense of entitlement, and is arrogant. Evidence suggests that narcissists are more charismatic and thus more likely to emerge as leaders, and they may even display better psychological health (at least as they self-report).[36]

Despite having some advantages, most evidence suggests that narcissism is undesirable. A study found that while narcissists thought they were *better* leaders than their colleagues, their supervisors actually rated them as *worse*. An Oracle executive described that company's CEO Larry Ellison as follows: "The difference between God and Larry is that God does not believe he is Larry."[37] Because narcissists often want to gain the admiration of others and receive affirmation of their superiority, they tend to "talk down" to those who threaten them, treating others as if they were inferior. Narcissists also tend to be selfish and exploitive and believe others exist for their benefit.[38] Their bosses rate them as less effective at their jobs than others, particularly when it comes to helping people.[39] Research using data compiled over 100 years has shown that narcissistic CEOs of baseball organizations tend to generate higher levels of manager turnover, although curiously, members of external organizations see them as more influential.[40]

SELF-MONITORING   Joyce McIntyre is always in trouble at work. Though she's competent, hardworking, and productive, in performance reviews she is rated no better than average, and she seems to have made a career of irritating bosses. Joyce's problem is that she's politically inept. She's unable to adjust her behavior to fit changing situations. As she puts it, "I'm true to myself. I don't remake myself to please others." We would describe Joyce as a low self-monitor.

Self-monitoring refers to an individual's ability to adjust behavior to external, situational factors.[41] Individuals high in self-monitoring show considerable adaptability in adjusting their behavior to external situational factors. They are highly sensitive to external cues and can behave differently in different situations, sometimes presenting striking contradictions between their public persona and their private self. Low self-monitors, like Joyce, can't disguise themselves in that way. They tend to display their true dispositions and attitudes in every situation; hence, there is high behavioral consistency between who they are and what they do.

Evidence indicates high self-monitors pay closer attention to the behavior of others and are more capable of conforming than are low self-monitors.[42] They also receive better performance ratings, are more likely to emerge as leaders, and show less commitment to their organizations.[43] In addition, high self-monitoring managers tend to be more mobile in their careers, receive more promotions (both internal and cross-organizational), and are more likely to occupy central positions in an organization.[44]

RISK TAKING   Donald Trump stands out for his willingness to take risks. He started with almost nothing in the 1960s. By the mid-1980s, he had made a fortune by betting on a resurgent New York City real estate market. Then, trying to capitalize on his successes, Trump overextended himself. By 1994, he had a *negative* net worth of $850 million. Never fearful of taking chances, "The Donald" leveraged the few assets he had left on several New York, New Jersey, and Caribbean real estate ventures and hit it big again. In 2011, when Trump was contemplating a presidential run, *The Atlantic* estimated his net worth at more than $7 billion.[45]

People differ in their willingness to take chances, a quality that affects how much time and information they need to make a decision. For instance, 79 managers worked on simulated exercises that required them to make hiring decisions.[46] High risk-taking managers made more rapid decisions and used less information than did the low risk takers. Interestingly, decision accuracy was the same for both groups.

Although previous studies have shown managers in large organizations to be more risk averse than growth-oriented entrepreneurs who actively manage small businesses, recent findings suggest managers in large organizations may actually be more willing to take risks than entrepreneurs.[47] The work population as a whole also differs in risk propensity.[48] It makes sense to recognize these differences and even consider aligning them with specific job demands. A high risk-taking propensity may lead to more effective performance for a stock trader in a brokerage firm because that type of job demands rapid decision making. On the other hand, a willingness to take risks might prove a major obstacle to an accountant who performs auditing activities.

PROACTIVE PERSONALITY   Did you ever notice that some people actively take the initiative to improve their current circumstances or create new ones? These are proactive personalities.[49] Those with a **proactive personality** identify opportunities, show initiative, take action, and persevere until meaningful change occurs, compared to others who passively react to situations. Proactives create positive change in their environment, regardless of, or even in spite of, constraints or obstacles.[50] Not surprisingly, they have many desirable behaviors that organizations covet. They are more likely than others to be seen as leaders and to act as change agents.[51] Proactive individuals are more likely to be satisfied with work and help others more with their tasks, largely because they build more relationships with others.[52]

Proactives are also more likely to challenge the status quo or voice their displeasure when situations aren't to their liking.[53] If an organization requires people with entrepreneurial initiative, proactives make good candidates; however, they're also more likely to leave an organization to start their own business.[54] As individuals, proactives are more likely than others to achieve career success.[55] They select, create, and influence work situations in their favor. They seek out job and organizational information, develop contacts in high places, engage in career planning, and demonstrate persistence in the face of career obstacles.

OTHER-ORIENTATION   Some people just naturally seem to think about other people a lot, being concerned about their well-being and feelings. Others behave like "economic actors," primarily rational and self-interested. These differences reflect varying levels of other-orientation, a personality trait that reflects the extent to which decisions are affected by social influences and concerns as opposed to our own well-being and outcomes.[56]

What are the consequences of having a high level of other-orientation? Those who are other-oriented feel more obligated to help others who have helped them (pay me back), whereas those who are more self-oriented will help others when they expect to be helped in the future (pay me forward).[57] Employees high in other-orientation also exert especially high levels of effort when engaged in helping work or prosocial behavior.[58] In sum, it appears that having a strong orientation toward helping others does affect some behaviors that actually matter for organizations. However, research is still needed to clarify this emerging construct and its relationship with agreeableness.

Having discussed personality traits—the enduring characteristics that describe a person's behavior—we now turn to values. Values are often very specific and describe belief systems rather than behavioral tendencies. Some beliefs or values don't say much about a person's personality, and we don't always act consistently with our values.

VALUES

Is capital punishment right or wrong? If a person likes power, is that good or bad? The answers to these questions are value laden. Some might argue capital punishment is right because it is an appropriate retribution for crimes such as murder and treason. Others might argue, just as strongly, that no government has the right to take anyone's life.

Values represent basic convictions that "a specific mode of conduct or end-state of existence is personally or socially preferable to an opposite or converse mode of conduct or end-state of existence."[59] They contain a judgmental element in that they carry an individual's ideas as to what is right, good, or desirable. Values have both content and intensity attributes. The content attribute says a mode of conduct or end-state of existence is *important*. The intensity attribute specifies *how important* it is. When we rank an individual's values in terms of their intensity, we obtain that person's **value system**. All of us have a hierarchy of values that forms our value system. We find it in the relative importance we assign to values such as freedom, pleasure, self-respect, honesty, obedience, and equality.

Are values fluid and flexible? Generally speaking, no. They tend to be relatively stable and enduring.[60] A significant portion of the values we hold is established in our early years—by parents, teachers, friends, and others. As children, we are told certain behaviors or outcomes are *always* desirable or *always* undesirable, with few gray areas. You were never taught to be just a little bit honest or a little bit responsible, for example. It is this absolute, or "black-or-white," learning of values that ensures their stability and endurance. If we question our values, of course, they may change, but more often they are reinforced. There is also evidence linking personality to values, implying our values may be partly determined by our genetically transmitted traits.[61]

The Importance of Values

Values lay the foundation for our understanding of people's attitudes and motivation and influence our perceptions. We enter an organization with preconceived notions of what "ought" and "ought not" to be. These notions are not value-free; on the contrary, they contain our interpretations of right and wrong and our preference for certain behaviors or outcomes over others. As a result, values cloud objectivity and rationality; they influence attitudes and behavior.[62]

Suppose you enter an organization with the view that allocating pay on the basis of performance is right, while allocating pay on the basis of seniority is wrong. How will you react if you find the organization you've just joined rewards seniority and not performance? You're likely to be disappointed—and this can lead to job dissatisfaction and a decision not to exert a high level of effort because "It's probably not going to lead to more money anyway." Would your attitudes and behavior be different if your values aligned with the organization's pay policies? Most likely.

Terminal Versus Instrumental Values

Can we classify values? Yes. In this section, we review two approaches to developing value typologies.

ROKEACH VALUE SURVEY   Milton Rokeach created the Rokeach Value Survey (RVS).[63] It consists of two sets of values, each containing 18 individual value items. One set, called **terminal values**, refers to desirable end-states. These are the goals a person would like to achieve during a lifetime. The other set, called **instrumental values**, refers to preferable modes of behavior, or means of achieving the terminal values. Some examples of terminal values in the RVS include: prosperity and economic success, freedom, health and well-being, world peace, social recognition, and meaning in life. The types of instrumental values illustrated in RVS are self-improvement, autonomy and self-reliance, personal discipline, kindness, ambition, and goal-orientation.

Several studies confirm that RVS values vary among groups.[64] People in the same occupations or categories (corporate managers, union members, parents, students) tend to hold similar values. One study compared corporate executives, members of the steelworkers' union, and members of a community activist group. Although there was a good deal of overlap among them,[65] there were also significant differences (see Exhibit 5-2).

The activists ranked "equality" as their most important terminal value; executives and union members ranked this value 12 and 13, respectively. Activists ranked "helpful" as their second-highest instrumental value. The other two groups both ranked it 14. Because executives, union members, and activists all have a vested interest in what corporations do, these differences can create serious conflicts when groups contend with each other over an organization's economic and social policies.[66]

EXHIBIT 5-2
Terminal and Instrumental Values in the Rokeach Value Survey

Terminal Values	Instrumental Values
Prosperity and economic success	Self-improvement
Freedom	Autonomy and self-reliance
Health and well-being	Personal discipline
World peace	Kindness
Social recognition	Ambition
Meaning in life	Goal-orientation

LINKING AN INDIVIDUAL'S PERSONALITY AND VALUES TO THE WORKPLACE

Thirty years ago, organizations were concerned only with personality because their primary focus was to match individuals to specific jobs. That concern has expanded to include how well the individual's personality *and* values match the organization. Why? Because managers today are less interested in an applicant's ability to perform a *specific* job than with their *flexibility* to meet changing situations and commitment to the organization.

We'll now discuss person–job fit and person–organization fit in more detail.

Person–Job Fit

The effort to match job requirements with personality characteristics is best articulated in John Holland's **personality–job fit theory**.[67] Holland presents six personality types and proposes that satisfaction and the propensity to leave a position depend on how well individuals match their personalities to a job. Exhibit 5-3 describes the six types, their personality characteristics, and examples of the congruent occupations for each.

Holland developed the Vocational Preference Inventory questionnaire, which contains 160 occupational titles. Respondents indicate which they like or dislike, and their answers form personality profiles. Research strongly supports the resulting hexagonal diagram shown in Exhibit 5-4.[68] The closer two fields or orientations are in the hexagon,

Type	Personality Characteristics	Congruent Occupations
Realistic: Prefers physical activities that require skill, strength, and coordination	Shy, genuine, persistent, stable, conforming, practical	conforming, practical, assembly-line worker, farmer
Investigative: Prefers activities that involve thinking, organizing, and understanding	Analytical, original, curious, independent	Biologist, economist, mathematician, news reporter
Social: Prefers activities that involve helping and developing others	Sociable, friendly, cooperative, understanding	Social worker, teacher, counselor, clinical psychologist
Conventional: Prefers rule-regulated, orderly, and unambiguous activities	Conforming, efficient, practical, unimaginative, inflexible	Accountant, corporate manager, bank teller, file clerk
Enterprising: Prefers verbal activities in which there are opportunities to influence others and attain power	Self-confident, ambitious, energetic, domineering	Lawyer, real estate agent, public relations specialist, small business manager
Artistic: Prefers ambiguous and unsystematic activities that allow creative expression	Imaginative, disorderly, idealistic, emotional, impractical	Painter, musician, writer, interior decorator

EXHIBIT 5-3

Holland's Typology of Personality and Congruent Occupations

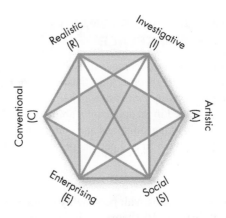

EXHIBIT 5-4
Relationships Among Occupational Personality Types

Source: Reprinted by special permission of the publisher, Psychological Assessment Resources, from *Making Vocational Choices*, © 1973, 1985, 1992 by Psychological Assessment Resources. All rights reserved.

the more compatible they are. Adjacent categories are quite similar, whereas diagonally opposite ones are highly dissimilar.

What does all this mean? The theory argues that satisfaction is highest and turnover lowest when personality and occupation are in agreement. A realistic person in a realistic job is in a more congruent situation than a realistic person in an investigative job. A realistic person in a social job is in the most incongruent situation possible. The key points of this model are that (1) there do appear to be intrinsic differences in personality among individuals, (2) there are different types of jobs, and (3) people in jobs congruent with their personality should be more satisfied and less likely to voluntarily resign than people in incongruent jobs. Evidence supports the value of assessing vocational interests in the selection process, with a match between interests and job requirements predicting job knowledge, performance, and low likelihood of turnover.[69]

As you might expect, Holland types relate to personality scales. One study found individuals higher in openness to experience as children were more likely to take jobs high on the investigative and artistic dimensions as adults, and those higher in conscientiousness as children were more likely to work in conventional jobs as adults.[70]

Person–Organization Fit

We've noted that researchers have looked at matching people to organizations as well as to jobs. If an organization faces a dynamic and changing environment and requires employees able to readily change tasks and move easily between teams, it's more important that employees' personalities fit with the overall organization's culture than with the characteristics of any specific job.

The person–organization fit essentially argues that people are attracted to and selected by organizations that match their values, and they leave organizations that are not compatible with their personalities.[71] Using the Big Five terminology, for instance, we could expect that people high on extraversion fit well with aggressive and team-oriented cultures, that people high on agreeableness match up better with a supportive organizational climate than one focused on aggressiveness, and that people high on openness to experience fit better in organizations that emphasize innovation rather than standardization.[72] Following these guidelines at the time of hiring should identify new employees who fit better with the organization's culture, which should, in turn, result in higher employee satisfaction and reduced turnover. Research on person–organization fit has also looked at whether people's values match the organization's culture. This match predicts job satisfaction, commitment to the organization, and low turnover.[73] Interestingly, some research found that person-organization fit was more important in predicting turnover in a collectivistic nation (India) than in a more individualistic nation (the United States).[74]

International Values

One of the most widely referenced approaches for analyzing variations among cultures was done in the late 1970s by Geert Hofstede.[75] He surveyed more than 116,000 IBM employees in 40 countries about their work-related values and found that managers and employees vary on five value dimensions of national culture:

Values do appear to vary across cultures, meaning that, on average, people's values in one nation tend to differ from those in another; however, there is substantial variability in values within a culture.

- *Power Distance.* **Power distance** describes the degree to which people in a country accept that power in institutions and organizations is distributed unequally. A high rating on power distance means that large inequalities of power and wealth exist and are tolerated in the culture, as in a class or caste system that discourages upward mobility. A low power-distance rating characterizes societies that stress equality and opportunity.
- *Individualism Versus Collectivism.* **Individualism** is the degree to which people prefer to act as individuals rather than as members of groups and believe in individual rights above all else. **Collectivism** emphasizes a tight social framework in which people expect others in groups of which they are a part to look after them and protect them.
- *Masculinity Versus Femininity.* Hofstede's construct of **masculinity** is the degree to which the culture favors traditional masculine roles such as achievement, power, and control, as opposed to viewing men and women as equals. A high masculinity rating indicates the culture has separate roles for men and women, with men dominating the society. A high **femininity** rating means the culture sees little differentiation between male and female roles and treats women as the equals of men in all respects.
- *Uncertainty Avoidance.* The degree to which people in a country prefer structured over unstructured situations defines their **uncertainty avoidance**. In cultures that score high on uncertainty avoidance, people have an increased level of anxiety about uncertainty and ambiguity and use laws and controls to reduce uncertainty. People in cultures low on uncertainty avoidance are more accepting of ambiguity, are less rule oriented, take more risks, and more readily accept change.
- *Long-Term Versus Short-Term Orientation.* This newest addition to Hofstede's typology measures a society's devotion to traditional values. People in a culture with **long-term orientation** look to the future and value thrift, persistence, and tradition. In a **short-term orientation**, people value the here and now; they accept change more readily and don't see commitments as impediments to change.

How do different countries score on Hofstede's dimensions? Exhibit 5-5 shows the ratings for the countries for which data are available. For example, power distance is higher in Malaysia than in any other country. The United States is very individualistic; in fact, it's the most individualistic nation of all (closely followed by Australia and Great Britain). The United States also tends to be short term in orientation and low in power

Country	Power Distance		Individualism Versus Collectivism		Masculinity Versus Femininity		Uncertainty Avoidance		Long- versus Short-Term Orientation	
	Index	Rank	Index	Rank	Index	Rank	Index	Rank	Index	Rank
Argentina	49	35–36	46	22–23	56	20–21	86	10–15		
Australia	36	41	90	2	61	16	51	37	31	22–24
Austria	11	53	55	18	79	2	70	24–25	31	22–24
Belgium	65	20	75	8	54	22	94	5–6	38	18
Brazil	69	14	38	26–27	49	27	76	21–22	65	6
Canada	39	39	80	4–5	52	24	48	41–42	23	30
Chile	63	24–25	23	38	28	46	86	10–15		
Colombia	67	17	13	49	64	11–12	80	20		
Costa Rica	35	42–44	15	46	21	48–49	86	10–15		
Denmark	18	51	74	9	16	50	23	51	46	10
Ecuador	78	8–9	8	52	63	13–14	67	28		
El Salvador	66	18–19	19	42	40	40	94	5–6		
Finland	33	46	63	17	26	47	59	31–32	41	14
France	68	15–16	71	10–11	43	35–36	86	10–15	39	17
Germany	35	42–44	67	15	66	9–10	65	29	31	22–24
Great Britain	35	42–44	89	3	66	9–10	35	47–48	25	28–29
Greece	60	27–28	35	30	57	18–19	112	1		
Guatemala	95	2–3	6	53	37	43	101	3		
Hong Kong	68	15–16	25	37	57	18–19	29	49–50	96	2
India	77	10–11	48	21	56	20–21	40	45	61	7
Indonesia	78	8–9	14	47–48	46	30–31	48	41–42		
Iran	58	29–30	41	24	43	35–36	59	31–32		
Ireland	28	49	70	12	68	7–8	35	47–48	43	13
Israel	13	52	54	19	47	29	81	19		
Italy	50	34	76	7	70	4–5	75	23	34	19
Jamaica	45	37	39	25	68	7–8	13	52		
Japan	54	33	46	22–23	95	1	92	7	80	4
Korea (South)	60	27–28	18	43	39	41	85	16–17	75	5
Malaysia	104	1	26	36	50	25–26	36	46		
Mexico	81	5–6	30	32	69	6	82	18		
The Netherlands	38	40	80	4–5	14	51	53	35	44	11–12
New Zealand	22	50	79	6	58	17	49	39–40	30	25–26
Norway	31	47–48	69	13	8	52	50	38	44	11–12
Pakistan	55	32	14	47–48	50	25–26	70	24–25	0	34
Panama	95	2–3	11	51	44	34	86	10–15		
Peru	64	21–23	16	45	42	37–38	87	9		
Philippines	94	4	32	31	64	11–12	44	44	19	31–32
Portugal	63	24–25	30	33–35	31	45	104	2	30	25–26
Singapore	74	13	20	39–41	48	28	8	53	48	9
South Africa	49	35–36	65	16	63	13–14	49	39–40		

EXHIBIT 5-5

Hofstede's Cultural Values by Nation

Source: Copyright © Geert Hofstede BV, hofstede@bovt.nl. Reprinted with permission.

Country	Power Distance		Individualism Versus Collectivism		Masculinity Versus Femininity		Uncertainty Avoidance		Long- Versus Short-Term Orientation	
	Index	Rank	Index	Rank	Index	Rank	Index	Rank	Index	Rank
Spain	57	31	51	20	42	37–38	86	10–15	19	31–32
Sweden	31	47–48	71	10–11	5	53	29	49–50	33	20
Switzerland	34	45	68	14	70	4–5	58	33	40	15–16
Taiwan	58	29–30	17	44	45	32–33	69	26	87	3
Thailand	64	21–23	20	39–41	34	44	64	30	56	8
Turkey	66	18–19	37	28	45	32–33	85	16–17		
United States	40	38	91	1	62	15	46	43	29	27
Uruguay	61	26	36	29	38	42	100	4		
Venezuela	81	5–6	12	50	73	3	76	21–22		
Yugoslavia	76	12	27	33–35	21	48–49	88	8		
Regions:										
Arab countries	80	7	38	26–27	53	23	68	27		
East Africa	64	21–23	27	33–35	41	39	52	36	25	28–29
West Africa	77	10–11	20	39–41	46	30–31	54	34	16	33

EXHIBIT 5-5   Continued

distance (people in the United States tend not to accept built-in class differences between people). It is also relatively low on uncertainty avoidance, meaning most adults are relatively tolerant of uncertainty and ambiguity. The United States scores relatively high on masculinity; most people emphasize traditional gender roles (at least relative to countries such as Denmark, Finland, Norway, and Sweden).

You'll notice regional differences. Western and northern nations such as Canada and the Netherlands tend to be more individualistic. Less wealthy countries such as Mexico and the Philippines tend to be higher on power distance. South American nations tend to be higher than other countries on uncertainty avoidance, and Asian countries tend to have a long-term orientation.

Hofstede's culture dimensions have been enormously influential on OB researchers and managers. Nevertheless, his research has been criticized. First, although the data have since been updated, the original work is more than 30 years old and was based on a single company (IBM). A lot has happened on the world scene since then. Some of the most obvious changes include the fall of the Soviet Union, the transformation of central and eastern Europe, the end of apartheid in South Africa, and the rise of China as a global power. Second, few researchers have read the details of Hofstede's methodology closely and are therefore unaware of the many decisions and judgment calls he had to make (for example, reducing the number of cultural values to just five). Some results are unexpected. Japan, which is often considered a highly collectivist nation, is considered only average on collectivism under Hofstede's dimensions.[76] Despite these concerns, Hofstede has been one of the most widely cited social scientists ever, and his framework has left a lasting mark on OB.

Recent research across 598 studies with more than 200,000 respondents has investigated the relationship of cultural values and a variety of organizational criteria at both the individual and national level of analysis.[77] Overall, the five original culture dimensions were equally strong predictors of relevant outcomes, meaning researchers and practicing managers need to think about culture holistically and not just focus on one or two dimensions. Cultural values were more strongly related to organizational commitment, citizenship behavior, and team-related attitudes than were personality scores. On the other hand, personality was more strongly related to behavioral criteria like performance, absenteeism, and turnover. The researchers also found that individual scores were much better predictors of most outcomes than assigning all people in a country the same cultural values. In sum, this research suggests that Hofstede's value framework may be a valuable way of thinking about differences among people, but we should be cautious about assuming all people from a country have the same values.

THE GLOBE FRAMEWORK FOR ASSESSING CULTURES   Begun in 1993, the Global Leadership and Organizational Behavior Effectiveness (GLOBE) research program is an ongoing cross-cultural investigation of leadership and national culture. Using data from 825 organizations in 62 countries, the GLOBE team identified nine dimensions on which national cultures differ.[78] Some—such as power distance, individualism/collectivism, uncertainty avoidance, gender differentiation (similar to masculinity versus femininity), and future orientation (similar to long-term versus short-term orientation)—resemble the Hofstede dimensions. The main difference is that the GLOBE framework added dimensions, such as humane orientation (the degree to which a society rewards individuals for being altruistic, generous, and kind to others) and performance orientation (the degree to which a society encourages and rewards group members for performance improvement and excellence).

Which framework is better? That's hard to say, and each has its adherents. We give more emphasis to Hofstede's dimensions here because they have stood the test of time and the GLOBE study confirmed them. However, researchers continue to debate the differences between them, and future studies may favor the more nuanced perspective of the GLOBE study. [79]

SUMMARY AND IMPLICATIONS FOR MANAGERS

PERSONALITY   What value, if any, does the Big Five model provide to managers? From the early 1900s through the mid-1980s, researchers sought a link between personality and job performance. However, the past 20 years have been more promising, largely due to the findings about the Big Five.

- Screening job candidates for high conscientiousness—as well as the other Big Five traits, depending on the criteria an organization finds most important—should pay dividends. Of course, managers still need to take situational factors into consideration.[80]
- Factors such as job demands, the degree of required interaction with others, and the organization's culture are examples of situational variables that moderate the personality–job performance relationship.
- You need to evaluate the job, the work group, and the organization to determine the optimal personality fit.
- Other traits, such as core self-evaluation or narcissism, may be relevant in certain situations, too.
- Although the MBTI has been widely criticized, it may have a place in organizations. In training and development, it can help employees better understand themselves,

help team members better understand each other, and open up communication in work groups and possibly reduce conflicts.

VALUES   Why is it important to know an individual's values? Values often underlie and explain attitudes, behaviors, and perceptions. So knowledge of an individual's value system can provide insight into what makes the person "tick."

- Employees' performance and satisfaction are likely to be higher if their values fit well with the organization. The person who places great importance on imagination, independence, and freedom is likely to be poorly matched with an organization that seeks conformity from its employees.
- Managers are more likely to appreciate, evaluate positively, and allocate rewards to employees who fit in, and employees are more likely to be satisfied if they perceive they do fit in. This argues for management to seek job candidates who have not only the ability, experience, and motivation to perform but also a value system compatible with the organization's.

MyManagementLab

Go to **MyManagementLab.com** to access study plans, interactive lectures, and videos as well as Auto-graded writing questions and the following Assisted-graded writing question.

5-1. MyManagementLab Only—comprehensive writing assignment for this chapter.

6
■ ■ ■
Perception and Individual Decision Making

After studying this chapter, you should be able to:

- Define *perception* and explain the factors that influence it.
- Identify the shortcuts individuals use in making judgments about others.
- Explain the link between perception and decision making.
- List and explain the common decision biases or errors.
- Contrast the three ethical decision criteria.
- Define *creativity* and discuss the three-component model of creativity.

MyManagementLab™
✪ Improve Your Grade!
Over 10 million students improved their results using the Pearson MyLabs. Visit **mymanagementlab.com** for simulations, tutorials, and end-of-chapter problems.

WHAT IS PERCEPTION?

Perception is a process by which individuals organize and interpret their sensory impressions in order to give meaning to their environment. However, what we perceive can be substantially different from objective reality. For example, all employees in a firm may view it as a great place to work—favorable working conditions, interesting job assignments, good pay, excellent benefits, understanding and responsible management—but, as most of us know, it's very unusual to find such agreement.

Why is perception important in the study of OB? Simply because people's behavior is based on their perception of what reality is, not on reality itself. *The world as it is perceived is the world that is behaviorally important.*

Factors That Influence Perception

How do we explain the fact that individuals may look at the same thing yet perceive it differently? A number of factors operate to shape and sometimes distort perception.

These factors can reside in the *perceiver*; in the object, or *target*, being perceived; or in the context of the *situation* in which the perception is made.

- *Perceiver.* When you look at a target and attempt to interpret what you see, your interpretation is heavily influenced by your personal characteristics—your attitudes, personality, motives, interests, past experiences, and expectations. For instance, if you expect police officers to be authoritative or young people to be lazy, you may perceive them as such, regardless of their actual traits.
- *Target.* Characteristics of the target also affect what we perceive. Loud people are more likely to be noticed in a group than quiet ones. So, too, are extremely attractive or unattractive individuals. Because we don't look at targets in isolation, the relationship of a target to its background also influences perception, as does our tendency to group close things and similar things together. We often perceive women, men, Whites, African Americans, Asians, or members of any other group that has clearly distinguishable characteristics as alike in other, unrelated ways as well.
- *Situation.* Context matters too. The time at which we see an object or event can influence our attention, as can location, light, heat, or any number of situational factors. At a nightclub on Saturday night, you may not notice a guest "dressed to the nines." Yet that same person so attired for your Monday morning management class would certainly catch your attention (and that of the rest of the class). Neither the perceiver nor the target has changed between Saturday night and Monday morning, but the situation is different.

People have inherent biases in how they see others (perception) and in how they make decisions (decision making). We can better understand people by understanding these biases.

PERSON PERCEPTION: MAKING JUDGMENTS ABOUT OTHERS

Now we turn to the application of perception concepts most relevant to OB—*person perception*, or the perceptions people form about each other.

Attribution Theory

Nonliving objects such as desks, machines, and buildings are subject to the laws of nature, but they have no beliefs, motives, or intentions. People do. That's why when we observe people, we attempt to explain why they behave in certain ways. Our perception and judgment of a person's actions, therefore, will be significantly influenced by the assumptions we make about that person's internal state of mind.

Attribution theory tries to explain the ways in which we judge people differently, depending on the meaning we attribute to a given behavior.[1] It suggests that when we observe an individual's behavior, we attempt to determine whether it was internally or externally caused. That determination, however, depends largely on three factors: (1) distinctiveness, (2) consensus, and (3) consistency. First, let's clarify the differences between internal and external causation, and then explore each of the three determining factors.

Internally caused behaviors are those an observer believes to be under the personal behavioral control of another individual. *Externally* caused behavior is what we imagine the situation forced the individual to do. If one of your employees is late for work, you might attribute that to his partying into the wee hours and then oversleeping. This is an internal attribution. But if you attribute lateness to an automobile accident that tied up traffic, you are making an external attribution.

Now let's discuss the three determining factors.

1. *Distinctiveness. Distinctiveness* refers to whether or not an individual displays different behaviors in different situations. Is the employee who arrives late today also one who regularly "blows off" commitments? What we want to know is whether this behavior is unusual, relative to others. If it is, we are likely to give it an external attribution. If it's not, we will probably judge the behavior to be internal.

2. *Consensus.* If everyone who faces a similar situation responds in the same way, we can say the behavior shows *consensus.* The behavior of our tardy employee meets this criterion if all employees who took the same route were also late. From an attribution perspective, if consensus is high, you would probably give an external attribution to the employee's tardiness, whereas if other employees who took the same route made it to work on time, you would attribute his lateness to an internal cause.

3. *Consistency.* Finally, an observer looks for *consistency* in a person's actions. Does the person respond the same way over time? Coming in 10 minutes late for work is not perceived in the same way for an employee who hasn't been late for several months as it is for an employee who is late two or three times a week. The more consistent the behavior over time, the more we are inclined to attribute it to internal causes.

Exhibit 6-1 summarizes the key elements in attribution theory. It tells us, for instance, that if an employee, Kim, generally performs at about the same level on related tasks as she does on her current task (low distinctiveness), other employees frequently perform differently—better or worse—than Kim on that task (low consensus), and Kim's performance on this current task is consistent over time (high consistency), then anyone judging Kim's work will likely hold her primarily responsible for her task performance (internal attribution).

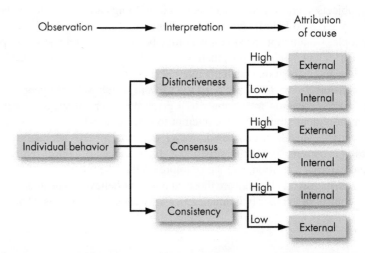

EXHIBIT 6-1
Attribution
Theory

One of the most interesting findings from attribution theory research is that errors or biases distort attributions. When we make judgments about the behavior of other people, we tend to underestimate the influence of external factors and overestimate the influence of internal or personal factors.[2] This **fundamental attribution error** can explain why a sales manager is prone to attribute the poor performance of her sales agents to laziness rather than to the innovative product line introduced by a competitor. Individuals and organizations also tend to attribute their own successes to internal factors such as ability or effort, while blaming failure on external factors such as bad luck or noisy co-workers. People also tend to attribute ambiguous information as relatively flattering and accept positive feedback while rejecting negative feedback. This is the **self-serving bias**.[3]

The evidence on cultural differences in perception is mixed, but most suggest there *are* differences across cultures in the attributions people make.[4] One study found Korean managers less likely to use the self-serving bias—they tended to accept responsibility for group failure "because I was not a capable leader" instead of attributing failure to group members.[5] On the other hand, Asian managers are more likely to blame institutions or whole organizations, whereas Western observers believe individual managers should get blame or praise.[6] That probably explains why U.S. newspapers prominently report the names of individual executives when firms do poorly, whereas Asian media cover how the firm as a whole has failed. This tendency to make group-based attributions also explains why individuals from Asian cultures are more likely to make group-based stereotypes.[7] Attribution theory was developed largely based on experiments with U.S. and Western European workers. But these studies suggest caution in making attribution theory predictions in non-Western societies, especially in countries with strong collectivist traditions.

Differences in attribution tendencies don't mean the basic concepts of attribution and blame completely differ across cultures, though. Self-serving biases may be less common in East Asian cultures, but evidence suggests they still operate across cultures.[8] Recent studies indicate Chinese managers assess blame for mistakes using the same distinctiveness, consensus, and consistency cues Western managers use.[9] They also become angry and punish those deemed responsible for failure, a reaction shown in many studies of Western managers. This means the basic process of attribution applies across cultures, but that it takes more evidence for Asian managers to conclude someone else should be blamed.

Common Shortcuts in Judging Others

The shortcuts we use in judging others are frequently valuable: They allow us to make accurate perceptions rapidly and provide valid data for making predictions. However, they are not foolproof. They can and do get us into trouble when they result in significant distortions.

SELECTIVE PERCEPTION   Any characteristic that makes a person, an object, or an event stand out will increase the probability we will perceive it. Why? Because it is impossible for us to assimilate everything we see; we can take in only certain stimuli. This explains why you're more likely to notice cars like your own, or why a boss may reprimand some people and not others doing the same thing. Because we can't observe everything going on about us, we engage in *selective perception*. **Selective perception** allows us to "speed-read" others, but not without the risk of drawing an inaccurate picture. Because we see what we want to see, we can draw unwarranted conclusions from an ambiguous situation.

HALO EFFECT   When we draw a general impression about an individual on the basis of a single characteristic, such as intelligence, sociability, or appearance, a **halo effect** is operating.[10] The reality of the halo effect was confirmed in a classic study in which subjects were given a list of traits such as intelligent, skillful, practical, industrious, determined, and warm and asked to evaluate the person to whom those traits applied.[11] Subjects judged the person to be wise, humorous, popular, and imaginative. When the same list was modified to include "cold" instead of "warm," a completely different picture emerged. Clearly, the subjects were allowing a single trait to influence their overall impression of the person they were judging.

CONTRAST EFFECTS   An old adage among entertainers is "Never follow an act that has kids or animals in it." Why? Audiences love children and animals so much that you'll look bad in comparison. This example demonstrates how a **contrast effect** can distort perceptions. We don't evaluate a person in isolation. Our reaction is influenced by other persons we have recently encountered.

STEREOTYPING   When we judge someone on the basis of our perception of the group to which he belongs, we are using the shortcut called **stereotyping**.[12]

We rely on generalizations every day because they help us make decisions quickly; they are a means of simplifying a complex world. It's less difficult to deal with an unmanageable number of stimuli if we use *heuristics* or stereotypes. For example, it does make sense to assume that Tre, the new employee from accounting, is going to know something about budgeting, or that Allie from finance will be able to help you figure out a forecasting problem. The problem occurs, of course, when we generalize inaccurately or too much. In organizations, we frequently hear comments that represent stereotypes based on gender, age, race, religion, ethnicity, and even weight:[13] "Men aren't interested in child care," "Older workers can't learn new skills," "Asian immigrants are hardworking and conscientious." An accumulating amount of research suggests stereotypes operate emotionally and often below the level of conscious awareness, making them particularly hard to challenge and change.[14]

Stereotypes can be deeply ingrained and powerful enough to influence life-and-death decisions. One study, controlling for a wide array of factors (such as aggravating or mitigating circumstances), showed that the degree to which black defendants in murder trials looked "stereotypically black" essentially doubled their odds of receiving a death sentence if convicted.[15] Another experimental study found that students who read scenarios describing leaders tended to assign higher scores for leadership potential and effective leadership to Whites than to minorities even though the content of the scenarios was equivalent, supporting the idea of a stereotype of Whites as better leaders.[16]

One problem of stereotypes is that they are widespread and often useful generalizations, though they may not contain a shred of truth when applied to a particular person or situation. So we constantly have to check ourselves to make sure we're not unfairly or inaccurately applying a stereotype in our evaluations and decisions. Stereotypes are an example of the warning "The more useful, the more danger from misuse."

THE LINK BETWEEN PERCEPTION AND INDIVIDUAL DECISION MAKING

Individuals in organizations make **decisions**, choices from among two or more alternatives. Top managers determine their organization's goals, what products or services to offer, how best to finance operations, or where to locate a new manufacturing plant. Middle- and lower-level managers set production schedules, select new employees, and decide how to allocate pay raises. Organizations have begun empowering their nonmanagerial employees with decision-making authority historically reserved for managers alone. Individual decision making is thus an important part of organizational behavior. But the way individuals make decisions and the quality of their choices are largely influenced by their perceptions.

Decision making occurs as a reaction to a **problem**.[17] That is, a discrepancy exists between the current state of affairs and some desired state, requiring us to consider alternative courses of action. If your car breaks down and you rely on it to get to work, you have a problem that requires a decision on your part. Unfortunately, most problems don't come neatly labeled "problem." One person's *problem* is another person's *satisfactory state of affairs*. One manager may view her division's 2 percent decline in quarterly sales to be a serious problem requiring immediate action on her part. In contrast, her counterpart in another division, who also had a 2 percent sales decrease, might consider that quite acceptable. So awareness that a problem exists and that a decision might or might not be needed is a perceptual issue.

Every decision requires us to interpret and evaluate information. We typically receive data from multiple sources and need to screen, process, and interpret them. Which data are relevant to the decision and which are not? Our perceptions will answer that question. We also need to develop alternatives and evaluate their strengths and weaknesses. Again, our perceptual process will affect the final outcome. Finally, throughout the entire decision-making process, perceptual errors often surface that can bias analysis and conclusions.

DECISION MAKING IN ORGANIZATIONS

Business schools generally train students to follow rational decision-making models. Although models have considerable merit, they don't always describe how people actually make decisions. This is where OB enters the picture: to improve the way we make decisions in organizations, we must understand the decision-making errors people commit (in addition to the perception errors we've discussed). Next we describe these errors, beginning with a brief overview of the rational decision-making model.

The Rational Model, Bounded Rationality, and Intuition

In OB, there are three generally accepted constructs of decision making each of us employs to make determinations: rational decision making, bounded rationality, and intuition. Though their processes outwardly make sense, they may not lead to the most accurate (or best) decisions. More importantly, there are times when one strategy may lead to a better outcome than another in a given situation.

RATIONAL DECISION MAKING
We often think the best decision maker is **rational** and makes consistent, value-maximizing choices within specified constraints.[18] These decisions follow a six-step **rational decision-making model**.[19] The six steps are listed in Exhibit 6-2 on the next page.

1. Define the problem.

2. Identify the decision criteria.

3. Allocate weights to the criteria.

4. Develop the alternatives.

5. Evaluate the alternatives.

6. Select the best alternative.

EXHIBIT 6-2

Steps in the Rational Decision-Making Model

Source: For a review of the rational decision-making model, see E. F. Harrison, *The Managerial Decision-Making Process*, 5th ed. (Boston: Houghton Mifflin, 1999), pp. 75–102.

The rational decision-making model relies on a number of assumptions, including that the decision maker has complete information, is able to identify all the relevant options in an unbiased manner, and chooses the option with the highest utility.[20] As you might imagine, most decisions in the real world don't follow the rational model. People are usually content to find an acceptable or reasonable solution to a problem rather than an optimal one. Choices tend to be limited to the neighborhood of the problem symptom and the current alternative. As one expert in decision making put it, "Most significant decisions are made by judgment, rather than by a defined prescriptive model."[21] What's more, people are remarkably unaware of making suboptimal decisions.[22]

BOUNDED RATIONALITY   Our limited information-processing capability makes it impossible to assimilate and understand all the information necessary to optimize.[23] So most people respond to a complex problem by reducing it to a level at which they can readily understand it. Also many problems don't have an optimal solution because they are too complicated to fit the rational decision-making model. So people satisfice; they seek solutions that are satisfactory and sufficient.

Because the human mind cannot formulate and solve complex problems with full rationality, we operate within the confines of **bounded rationality**. We construct simplified models that extract the essential features from problems without capturing all their complexity.[24] We can then behave rationally within the limits of the simple model.

Perceptual and decision-making biases and heuretics are not necessarily bad. They allow us to process information more quickly and efficiently. The key is to be self-aware enough to see when a bias or shortcut may be counterproductive.

How does bounded rationality work for the typical individual? Once we've identified a problem, we begin to search for criteria and alternatives. But the criteria are unlikely to be exhaustive. We identify choices that are easy to find and highly visible and that usually represent familiar criteria and tried-and-true solutions. Next, we begin reviewing them, focusing on alternatives that differ little from the choice currently in effect until we identify one that is "good enough"—that meets an acceptable level of performance. That ends our search. So the solution represents a satisficing choice—the first *acceptable* one we encounter—rather than an optimal one.

Satisficing is not always a bad idea—a simple process may frequently be more sensible than the traditional rational decision-making model.[25] To use the rational model in the real world, you need to gather a great deal of information about all the options, compute applicable weights, and then calculate values across a huge number of criteria. All of these processes can cost time, energy, and money. And if there are many unknown weights and preferences, the fully rational model may not be any more accurate than a best guess. Sometimes a fast-and-frugal process of solving problems might be your best option.

INTUITION   Perhaps the least rational way of making decisions is **intuitive decision making**, an unconscious process created from distilled experience.[26] It occurs outside conscious thought; it relies on holistic associations, or links between disparate pieces of information; it's fast; and it's *affectively charged*, meaning it usually engages the emotions.[27]

While intuition isn't rational, it isn't necessarily wrong. Nor does it always contradict rational analysis; rather, the two can complement each other. But nor is intuition superstition, or the product of some magical or paranormal sixth sense. As one recent review noted, "Intuition is a highly complex and highly developed form of reasoning that is based on years of experience and learning."[28]

Common Biases and Errors in Decision Making

Decision makers engage in bounded rationality, but they also allow systematic biases and errors to creep into their judgments.[29] To minimize effort and avoid difficult trade-offs, people tend to rely too heavily on experience, impulses, gut feelings, and convenient rules of thumb. These shortcuts can be helpful. However, they can also distort rationality. Following are the most common biases in decision making. Exhibit 6-3 provides some suggestions for how to avoid falling into these biases and errors.

Focus on Goals. Without goals, you can't be rational, you don't know what information you need, you don't know which information is relevant and which is irrelevant, you'll find it difficult to choose between alternatives, and you're far more likely to experience regret over the choices you make. Clear goals make decision making easier and help you eliminate options that are inconsistent with your interests.

Look for Information That Disconfirms Your Beliefs. One of the most effective means for counteracting overconfidence and the confirmation and hindsight biases is to actively look for information that contradicts your beliefs and assumptions. When we overtly consider various ways we could be wrong, we challenge our tendencies to think we're smarter than we actually are.

Don't Try to Create Meaning out of Random Events. The educated mind has been trained to look for cause-and-effect relationships. When something happens, we ask why. And when we can't find reasons, we often invent them. You have to accept that there are events in life that are outside your control. Ask yourself if patterns can be meaningfully explained or whether they are merely coincidence. Don't attempt to create meaning out of coincidence.

Increase Your Options. No matter how many options you've identified, your final choice can be no better than the best of the option set you've selected. This argues for increasing your decision alternatives and for using creativity in developing a wide range of diverse choices. The more alternatives you can generate, and the more diverse those alternatives, the greater your chance of finding an outstanding one.

EXHIBIT 6-3

Reducing Biases and Errors

OVERCONFIDENCE BIAS It's been said that "no problem in judgment and decision making is more prevalent and more potentially catastrophic than overconfidence."[30] When we're given factual questions and asked to judge the probability that our answers are correct, we tend to be far too optimistic. When people say they're 90 percent confident about the range a certain number might take, their estimated ranges contain the correct answer only about 50 percent of the time—and experts are no more accurate in setting up confidence intervals than are novices.[31] When people say they're 100 percent sure of an outcome, they tend to be 70 to 85 percent correct.[32]

Individuals whose intellectual and interpersonal abilities are *weakest* are most likely to overestimate their performance and ability.[33] There's also a negative relationship between entrepreneurs' optimism and the performance of their new ventures: the more optimistic, the less successful.[34] The tendency to be too confident about their ideas might keep some from planning how to avoid problems that arise.

ANCHORING BIAS The **anchoring bias** is a tendency to fixate on initial information and fail to adequately adjust for subsequent information.[35] Anchors are widely used by people in professions in which persuasion skills are important—advertising, management, politics, real estate, and law. Any time a negotiation takes place, so does anchoring. When a prospective employer asks how much you made in your prior job, your answer typically anchors the employer's offer. (Remember this when you negotiate your salary, but set the anchor only as high as you realistically can.) Finally, the more precise your anchor, the smaller the adjustment. Some research suggests people think of making an adjustment after an anchor is set as rounding off a number. If you suggest a target salary of $55,000, your boss will consider $50,000 to $60,000 a reasonable range for negotiation, but if you mention $55,650, your boss is more likely to consider $55,000 to $56,000 the range of likely values.[36]

CONFIRMATION BIAS The rational decision-making process assumes we objectively gather information. But we don't. We *selectively* gather it. The **confirmation bias** represents a specific case of selective perception: We seek out information that reaffirms our past choices, and we discount information that contradicts them.[37] We also tend to accept at face value information that confirms our preconceived views, while we are critical and skeptical of information that challenges them. Therefore, the information we gather is typically biased toward supporting views we already hold. Interestingly, we are most prone to the confirmation bias when we believe we have good information and strongly believe in our opinions. Fortunately, those who feel there is a strong need to be accurate in making a decision are less prone to the confirmation bias.

AVAILABILITY BIAS More people fear flying than fear driving in a car. But if flying on a commercial airline really were as dangerous as driving, the equivalent of two 747s filled to capacity would crash every week, killing all aboard. Because the media give much more attention to air accidents, we tend to overstate the risk of flying and understate the risk of driving.

The **availability bias** is our tendency to base judgments on information readily available.[38] Events that evoke emotions, are particularly vivid, or are more recent tend to be more available in our memory, leading us to overestimate the chances of unlikely events such as an airplane crash. The availability bias can also explain why managers doing performance appraisals give more weight to recent employee behaviors than to behaviors of 6 or 9 months earlier, or why credit-rating agencies such as Moody's or Standard & Poor's may issue overly positive ratings by relying on information presented by debt issuers, who have an incentive to offer data favorable to their case.[39]

ESCALATION OF COMMITMENT   Another distortion that creeps into decisions is a tendency to escalate commitment.[40] **Escalation of commitment** refers to staying with a decision even when there is clear evidence it's wrong. Consider a friend who has been dating someone for several years. Although he admits things aren't going too well, he says he is still going to marry her. His justification: "I have a lot invested in the relationship!"

Individuals escalate commitment to a failing course of action when they view themselves as responsible for the failure.[41] They "throw good money after bad" to demonstrate their initial decision wasn't wrong and to avoid admitting they made a mistake.[42] In fact, people who carefully gather and consider information consistent with the rational decision-making model are *more* likely to engage in escalation of commitment than those who spend less time thinking about their choices.[43] Perhaps they have invested so much time and energy in making their decisions that they have convinced themselves they're taking the right course of action and don't update their knowledge in the face of new information. Many an organization has suffered because a manager determined to prove her original decision right continued to commit resources to a lost cause.

RANDOMNESS ERROR   Most of us like to think we have some control over our world and our destiny. Our tendency to believe we can predict the outcome of random events is the **randomness error**.

Decision making suffers when we try to create meaning in random events, particularly when we turn imaginary patterns into superstitions.[44] These can be completely contrived ("I never make important decisions on Friday the 13th") or can evolve from a reinforced past pattern of behavior (Tiger Woods often wears a red shirt during a golf tournament's final round because he won many junior tournaments wearing red shirts). Superstitious behavior can be debilitating when it affects daily judgments or biases major decisions.

RISK AVERSION   Mathematically, we should find a 50–50 flip of the coin for $100 to be worth as much as a sure promise of $50. After all, the expected value of the gamble over a number of trials is $50. However, nearly everyone but committed gamblers would rather have the sure thing than a risky prospect.[45] For many people, a 50–50 flip of a coin even for $200 might not be worth as much as a sure promise of $50, even though the gamble is mathematically worth twice as much! This tendency to prefer a sure thing over a risky outcome is **risk aversion**.

Risk aversion has important implications. To offset the risks inherent in a commission-based wage, companies pay commissioned employees considerably more than they do those on straight salaries. Risk-averse employees will stick with the established way of doing their jobs, rather than taking a chance on innovative or creative methods. Sticking with a strategy that has worked in the past does minimize risk, but in the long run it will lead to stagnation. Ambitious people with power that can be taken away (most managers) appear to be especially risk averse, perhaps because they don't want to lose on a gamble everything they've worked so hard to achieve.[46] CEOs at risk of being terminated are also exceptionally risk averse, even when a riskier investment strategy is in their firms' best interests.[47]

HINDSIGHT BIAS The **hindsight bias** is the tendency to believe falsely, after the outcome is known, that we'd have accurately predicted it.[48] When we have accurate feedback on the outcome, we seem pretty good at concluding it was obvious.

Over the past 10 years, the home video rental industry has been collapsing fast as online distribution outlets have eaten away at the market.[49] Hollywood Video declared bankruptcy in May 2010 and began liquidating its assets; Blockbuster filed for bankruptcy in September 2010. Some have suggested that if only these organizations had leveraged their brand and distribution resources effectively and sooner to develop web-based delivery, as Netflix does, and low-cost distribution in grocery and convenience stores, which Redbox offers, they could have avoided failure. Although that might seem obvious now, many experts with good information failed to see these two major trends that would upend the industry.

Of course, after the fact, it is easy to see that a combination of automated and mail-order distribution would outperform the traditional brick-and-mortar movie rental business. Similarly, former Merrill Lynch CEO John Thain—and many other Wall Street executives—took blame for failing to see what now seems obvious (that housing prices were inflated, too many risky loans were made, and the values of many "securities" were based on fragile assumptions). Though the criticisms may have merit, things are often all too clear in hindsight.

APPLICATION: FINANCIAL DECISION MAKING This discussion of decision-making errors may have you thinking about how organizations and individuals make financial decisions. Did decision errors influence capital markets and even lead to crises like the financial meltdown of 2008? How are financial decisions affected by errors and biases? Experts have identified several ways this can occur.[50]

One of the core problems that created the financial crisis was that large loans were made to individuals who could not repay them, and finance companies purchased these bad debts without realizing how poor the prospects of repayment were. Thus, overconfidence bias by both lenders and borrowers about the ability to pay back loans was clearly a major factor. Most studies suggest that people are more willing to buy on credit and spend more money when they feel confident. Although experts were no more accurate at predicting financial outcomes than were people without knowledge or skills in finance, they *were* more confident in their predictions. Unfortunately, as confidence decreases in the face of poor economic data, businesses and consumers become more conservative in their spending. This further decreases demand for products and services, which deepens the economic crisis in a vicious cycle.

Overconfidence isn't the only decision error implicated in the financial crisis. Investors deliberately avoid negative information about investments, an example of the confirmation bias. Lenders may have overlooked potential problems with borrowers' accounts when making loans, and stock traders may have ignored information about potential problems with complex derivatives when making purchasing decisions. Once a loan has been paid off, lenders also selectively ignore the negative effects of debt, making them more likely to make unwise loans in the future.

What might prevent these situations from occurring in the future? Both investors and consumers may need to more carefully consider whether their confidence level is aligned with their actual future ability to pay. It is also always a good idea to seek information that goes against your initial inclinations, to ensure you're getting the whole picture. Be careful not to commit the hindsight bias and conclude after financial crises have dissipated that it should have been obvious problems were about to occur.

ORGANIZATIONAL CONSTRAINTS ON DECISION MAKING

Having examined the rational decision-making model, bounded rationality, and some of the most salient biases and errors in decision making, we turn here to a discussion of organizational constraints. Organizations can constrain decision makers, creating deviations from the rational model. For instance, managers shape their decisions to reflect the organization's performance evaluation and reward system, to comply with its formal regulations, and to meet organizationally imposed time constraints. Precedent can also limit decisions.

PERFORMANCE EVALUATION   Managers are strongly influenced by the criteria on which they are evaluated. If a division manager believes the manufacturing plants under his responsibility are operating best when he hears nothing negative, we shouldn't be surprised to find his plant managers spending a good part of their time ensuring that negative information doesn't reach him.

REWARD SYSTEMS   The organization's reward system influences decision makers by suggesting which choices have better personal payoffs. If the organization rewards risk aversion, managers are more likely to make conservative decisions. From the 1930s through the mid-1980s, General Motors consistently gave promotions and bonuses to managers who kept a low profile and avoided controversy. These executives became adept at dodging tough issues and passing controversial decisions on to committees.

FORMAL REGULATIONS   David Gonzalez, a shift manager at a Taco Bell restaurant in San Antonio, Texas, describes constraints he faces on his job: "I've got rules and regulations covering almost every decision I make—from how to make a burrito to how often I need to clean the restrooms. My job doesn't come with much freedom of choice." David's situation is not unique. All but the smallest organizations create rules and policies to program decisions and get individuals to act in the intended manner. And of course, in so doing, they limit decision choices.

SYSTEM-IMPOSED TIME CONSTRAINTS   Almost all important decisions come with explicit deadlines. A report on new-product development may have to be ready for executive committee review by the first of the month. Such conditions often make it difficult, if not impossible, for managers to gather all the information they might like before making a final choice.

HISTORICAL PRECEDENTS   Decisions aren't made in a vacuum; they have a context. In fact, individual decisions are points in a stream of choice. Those made in the past are like ghosts that haunt and constrain current choices. It's common knowledge that the largest determinant of the size of any given year's budget is last year's budget.[51] Choices made today are largely a result of choices made over the years.

WHAT ABOUT ETHICS AND CREATIVITY IN DECISION MAKING?

Ethical considerations should be an important criterion in all organizational decision making. In this section, we present three ways to frame decisions ethically.[52] As well, all managers need to understand the important role creativity should play in the decision process; the best managers employ strategies to increase the creative potential of their employees and harvest the ideas for organizational application.

Three Ethical Decision Criteria

The first ethical yardstick is **utilitarianism**, which proposes making decisions solely on the basis of their *outcomes*, ideally to provide the greatest good for the greatest number. This view dominates business decision making. It is consistent with goals such as efficiency, productivity, and high profits.

Another ethical criterion is to make decisions consistent with fundamental liberties and privileges, as set forth in documents such as the Bill of Rights. An emphasis on *rights* in decision making means respecting and protecting the basic rights of individuals, such as the right to privacy, free speech, and due process. This criterion protects **whistleblowers** when they reveal an organization's unethical practices to the press or government agencies, using their right to free speech.

A third criterion is to impose and enforce rules fairly and impartially to ensure *justice* or an equitable distribution of benefits and costs. Union members typically favor this view. It justifies paying people the same wage for a given job regardless of performance differences and using seniority as the primary determination in layoff decisions.

Each criterion has advantages and liabilities. A focus on utilitarianism promotes efficiency and productivity, but it can sideline the rights of some individuals, particularly those with minority representation. The use of rights protects individuals from injury and is consistent with freedom and privacy, but it can create a legalistic environment that hinders productivity and efficiency. A focus on justice protects the interests of the underrepresented and less powerful, but it can encourage a sense of entitlement that reduces risk taking, innovation, and productivity.

Decision makers, particularly in for-profit organizations, feel comfortable with utilitarianism. The "best interests" of the organization and its stockholders can justify a lot of questionable actions, such as large layoffs. But many critics feel this perspective needs to change.[53] Public concern about individual rights and social justice suggests managers should develop ethical standards based on nonutilitarian criteria. This presents a challenge because satisfying individual rights and social justice creates far more ambiguities than utilitarian effects on efficiency and profits. However, while raising prices, selling products with questionable effects on consumer health, closing down inefficient plants, laying off large numbers of employees, and moving production overseas to cut costs can be justified in utilitarian terms, that may no longer be the single measure by which good decisions are judged.

Improving Creativity in Decision Making

Creativity allows the decision maker to more fully appraise and understand the problem, including seeing problems others can't see.

Although the rational decision-making model will often improve decisions, a rational decision maker also needs **creativity**, the ability to produce novel and useful ideas.[54] These are different from what's been done before but appropriate to the problem presented.

L'Oreal puts its managers through creative exercises such as cooking or making music, and the University of Chicago requires MBA students to make short movies about their experiences.

CREATIVE POTENTIAL Most people have useful creative potential. But to unleash it, they have to escape the psychological ruts many of us fall into and learn how to think about a problem in divergent ways.

Exceptional creativity is scarce. We all know of creative geniuses in science (Albert Einstein), art (Pablo Picasso), and business (Steve Jobs). But what about the typical individual? Intelligent people and those who score high on openness to experience are more likely to be creative.[55] Other traits of creative people are independence, self-confidence, risk taking, an internal locus of control, tolerance for ambiguity, a low need for structure, and perseverance.[56] Exposure to a variety of cultures can also improve creativity.[57] So taking an international assignment, or even an international vacation, could jump-start your creative process.

THREE-COMPONENT MODEL OF CREATIVITY What can individuals and organizations do to stimulate employee creativity? The best answer lies in the **three-component model of creativity**,[58] which proposes that individual creativity essentially requires expertise, creative-thinking skills, and intrinsic task motivation. Studies confirm that the higher the level of each, the higher the creativity.

Expertise is the foundation for all creative work. Film writer, producer, and director Quentin Tarantino spent his youth working in a video rental store, where he built up an encyclopedic knowledge of movies. The potential for creativity is enhanced when individuals have abilities, knowledge, proficiencies, and similar expertise in their field of endeavor. You wouldn't expect someone with minimal knowledge of programming to be very creative as a software engineer.

The second component is *creative-thinking skills*. This encompasses personality characteristics associated with creativity, the ability to use analogies, and the talent to see the familiar in a different light.

A meta-analysis of 102 studies found positive moods increase creativity, but it depends on what sort of positive mood was considered.[59] Moods such as happiness that encourage interaction with the world are more conducive to creativity than passive moods such as calm. This means the common advice to relax and clear your mind to develop creative ideas may be misplaced. It would be better to get in an upbeat mood and then frame your work as an opportunity to have fun and experiment. Negative moods also don't always have the same effects on creativity. Passive negative moods such as sadness don't seem to have much effect, but avoidance-oriented negative moods such as fear and anxiety decrease creativity. Feeling threatened reduces your desire to try new activities; risk aversion increases when you're scared. Active negative moods, such as anger, however, do appear to enhance creativity, especially if you are taking your task seriously.

Being around creative others can make us more inspired, especially if we're creatively "stuck."[60] One study found that having "weak ties" to creative people—knowing them but not well—facilitates creativity because the people are there as a resource if we need them but not so close as to stunt our own independent thinking.[61]

Analogies allow decision makers to apply an idea from one context to another. One of the most famous examples was Alexander Graham Bell's observation that it might be possible to apply the way the ear operates to his "talking box." Bell noticed the bones in the ear are operated by a delicate, thin membrane. He wondered why a thicker and stronger membrane shouldn't be able to move a piece of steel. From that analogy, the telephone was conceived. Thinking in terms of analogies is a complex intellectual skill, which helps explain why cognitive ability is related to creativity. Demonstrating this effect, one study found children who got high scores on cognitive ability tests at age 13 were significantly more likely to have made creative achievements in their professional lives 25 years later.[62]

The final component in the three-component model of creativity is *intrinsic task motivation*. This is the desire to work on something because it's interesting, involving, exciting, satisfying, or personally challenging. It's what turns creativity *potential* into *actual* creative ideas. Environmental stimulants that foster creativity include a culture that encourages the flow of ideas; fair and constructive judgment of ideas; rewards and recognition for creative work; sufficient financial, material, and information resources; freedom to decide what work is to be done and how to do it; a supervisor who communicates effectively, shows confidence in others, and supports the work group; and work group members who support and trust each other.[63]

International Differences

There are no global ethical standards,[64] as contrasts between Asia and the West illustrate.[65] Because bribery is commonplace in countries such as China, a Canadian working in China might face a dilemma: Should I pay a bribe to secure business if it is an accepted part of that country's culture? A manager of a large U.S. company operating in China once caught an employee stealing. Following company policy, she fired him and turned him over to the local authorities. Later, she was horrified to learn the employee had been summarily executed.[66]

Although ethical standards may seem ambiguous in the West, criteria defining right and wrong are actually much clearer there than in Asia, where few issues are black and white and most are gray. Global organizations must establish ethical principles for decision makers in countries such as India and China and modify them to reflect cultural norms if they want to uphold high standards and consistent practices.

SUMMARY AND IMPLICATIONS FOR MANAGERS

PERCEPTION   Individuals base their behavior not on the way their external environment actually is but rather on what they see or believe it to be.

- Whether a manager successfully plans and organizes the work of employees and actually helps them to structure their work more efficiently and effectively is far less important than how employees perceive the manager's efforts.
- Employees judge issues such as fair pay, performance appraisals, and working conditions in very individual ways. To influence productivity, we need to assess how workers perceive their jobs.
- Absenteeism, turnover, and job satisfaction are also reactions to an individual's perception. Dissatisfaction with working conditions and the belief that an organization lacks promotion opportunities are judgments based on attempts to create meaning in the job.
- The employee's conclusion that a job is good or bad is an interpretation. Managers must spend time understanding how each individual interprets reality and, when there is a significant difference between what someone sees and what exists, try to eliminate the distortions.

INDIVIDUAL DECISION MAKING   Individuals think and reason before they act. This is why an understanding of how people make decisions can be helpful for explaining and predicting their behavior.

In some decision situations, people follow the rational decision-making model. But few important decisions are simple or unambiguous enough for the rational model's assumptions to apply. So we find individuals looking for solutions that satisfice rather than optimize, injecting biases and prejudices into the decision process, and relying on intuition.

What can managers do to improve their decision making? We offer four suggestions.

- Analyze the situation. Adjust your decision-making approach to the national culture you're operating in and to the criteria your organization evaluates and rewards. If you're in a country that doesn't value rationality, don't feel compelled to follow the rational decision-making model or to try to make your decisions appear rational. Similarly, organizations differ in the importance they place on risk, the use of groups, and the like. Adjust your decision approach to ensure it's compatible with the organization's culture.
- Second, be aware of biases. Then try to minimize their impact.
- Third, combine rational analysis with intuition. These are not conflicting approaches to decision making. By using both, you can actually improve your decision-making effectiveness. As you gain managerial experience, you should feel increasingly confident in imposing your intuitive processes on top of your rational analysis.
- Finally, try to enhance your creativity. Actively look for novel solutions to problems, attempt to see problems in new ways, and use analogies. Try to remove work and organizational barriers that might impede your creativity.

MyManagementLab

Go to **MyManagementLab.com** to access study plans, interactive lectures, and videos as well as Auto-graded writing questions and the following Assisted-graded writing question.

6-1. MyManagementLab Only—comprehensive writing assignment for this chapter.

7

■ ■ ■

Motivation Concepts

After studying this chapter, you should be able to:

- Describe the three key elements of motivation.
- Identify early theories of motivation and evaluate their applicability today.
- Contrast goal-setting theory and management by objectives.
- Demonstrate how organizational justice is a refinement of equity theory.
- Apply the key tenets of expectancy theory to motivating employees.

MyManagementLab™

⭐ **Improve Your Grade!**

Over 10 million students improved their results using the Pearson MyLabs. Visit **mymanagementlab.com** for simulations, tutorials, and end-of-chapter problems.

Debates about motivation can occupy a central role in important public policy debates, and as we will see, they also rank among the most important questions managers need to answer.

Motivation is one of the most frequently researched topics in OB.[1] A recent Gallup poll revealed one reason—a majority of U.S. employees (54 percent) are not actively engaged in their work, and another portion (17 percent) are actively disengaged.[2] In another study, workers reported wasting roughly 2 hours per day, not counting lunch and scheduled breaks (usually Internet surfing and talking with co-workers).[3] Clearly, motivation is an issue. The good news is that all this research provides useful insights into how to improve it.

In this chapter, we'll review the basics of motivation, assess motivation theories, and provide an integrative model that fits the best of these theories together.

DEFINING MOTIVATION

Some individuals seem driven to succeed. But the same student who struggles to read a textbook for more than 20 minutes may devour a Harry Potter book in a day. The difference is the situation. So as we analyze the concept of motivation, keep in mind that the level of motivation varies both between individuals and within individuals at different times.

We define **motivation** as the processes that account for an individual's intensity, direction, and persistence of effort toward attaining a goal.[4] Although general motivation is concerned with effort toward *any* goal, we'll narrow the focus to *organizational* goals in order to reflect our singular interest in work-related behavior.

The three key elements in our definition are intensity, direction, and persistence. *Intensity* describes how hard a person tries. This is the element most of us focus on when we talk about motivation. However, high intensity is unlikely to lead to favorable job-performance outcomes unless the effort is channeled in a *direction* that benefits the organization. Therefore, we consider the quality of effort as well as its intensity. Effort directed toward, and consistent with, the organization's goals is the kind of effort we should be seeking. Finally, motivation has a *persistence* dimension. This measures how long a person can maintain effort. When motivated, individuals stay with a task long enough to achieve their goal.

EARLY THEORIES OF MOTIVATION

Four theories of employee motivation formulated during the 1950s, although now of questionable validity, are probably still the best known. We will discuss more valid explanations later, but these four represent a foundation on which contemporary theories have grown, and practicing managers still use them and their terminology.

Hierarchy of Needs Theory

The best-known theory of motivation is Abraham Maslow's **hierarchy of needs**.[5] Maslow hypothesized that within every human being, there exists a hierarchy of five needs:

1. *Physiological.* Includes hunger, thirst, shelter, sex, and other bodily needs.
2. *Safety.* Security and protection from physical and emotional harm.
3. *Social.* Affection, belongingness, acceptance, and friendship.
4. *Esteem.* Internal factors such as self-respect, autonomy, and achievement, and external factors such as status, recognition, and attention.
5. *Self-actualization.* Drive to become what we are capable of becoming; includes growth, achieving our potential, and self-fulfillment.

Although no need is ever fully gratified, a substantially satisfied need no longer motivates. Thus as each becomes substantially satisfied, the next one becomes dominant. So if you want to motivate someone, according to Maslow, you need to understand what level of the hierarchy that person is currently on and focus on satisfying needs at or above that level, moving up the steps in Exhibit 7-1.

Maslow separated the five needs into higher and lower orders. Physiological and safety needs, where the theory says people start, were **lower-order needs**, and social, esteem, and **self-actualization** were **higher-order needs**. Higher-order needs are satisfied internally (within the person), whereas lower-order needs are predominantly satisfied externally (by things such as pay, union contracts, and tenure).

The hierarchy, if it applies at all, aligns with U.S. culture. In Japan, Greece, and Mexico, where uncertainty-avoidance characteristics are strong, security needs would be on top of the hierarchy, or first priority. Countries that score high on nurturing characteristics—Denmark, Sweden, Norway, the Netherlands, and Finland—would have social needs and

EXHIBIT 7-1
Maslow's Hierarchy of Needs

Source: A. H. Maslow, *Motivation and Personality*, 3rd ed., R. D. Frager and J. Fadiman (eds.). © 1997. Adapted by permission of Pearson Education, Inc., Upper Saddle River, New Jersey.

self-actualization on top.[6] Group work will motivate employees more when the country's culture scores high on the nurturing criterion.

Maslow's theory has received wide recognition, particularly among practicing managers. It is intuitively logical and easy to understand. When introduced, it provided a compelling alternative to behaviorist theories that posited only physiological and safety needs as important. Unfortunately, however, research does not validate it. Maslow provided no empirical substantiation, and several studies that sought to validate it found no support for it.[7] There is little evidence that need structures are organized as Maslow proposed, that unsatisfied needs motivate, or that a satisfied need activates movement to a new need level.[8] But old theories, especially intuitively logical ones, apparently die hard.

Some researchers have attempted to revive components of the need hierarchy concept, using principles from evolutionary psychology.[9] They propose that lower-level needs are the chief concern of immature animals or those with primitive nervous systems, whereas higher needs are more frequently observed in mature animals with more developed nervous systems. They also note distinct underlying biological systems for different types of needs. Time will tell whether these revisions to Maslow's hierarchy will be useful to practicing managers.

Theory X and Theory Y

Douglas McGregor proposed two distinct views of human beings: one basically negative, labeled Theory X, and the other basically positive, labeled Theory Y.[10] After studying managers' dealings with employees, McGregor concluded that the managers' views of the nature of human beings are based on certain assumptions that mold the managers' behavior toward the employees.

Under **Theory X**, managers believe employees inherently dislike work and must therefore be directed or even coerced into performing it. Under **Theory Y**, in contrast, managers assume employees can view work as being as natural as rest or play, and therefore the average person can learn to accept, and even seek, responsibility.

To understand more fully, think in terms of Maslow's hierarchy. Theory Y assumes higher-order needs dominate individuals. McGregor himself believed Theory Y assumptions were more valid than Theory X. Therefore, he proposed such ideas as participative decision making, responsible and challenging jobs, and good group relations to maximize an employee's job motivation.

Unfortunately, no evidence confirms that *either* set of assumptions is valid or that acting on Theory Y assumptions will lead to more motivated workers. OB theories need empirical support before we can accept them. Theory X and Theory Y lack such support as much as the hierarchy of needs.

Two-Factor Theory

Believing an individual's relationship to work is basic, and that attitude toward work can determine success or failure, psychologist Frederick Herzberg wondered, "What do people want from their jobs?" He asked people to describe, in detail, situations in which they felt exceptionally *good* or *bad* about their jobs. The responses differed significantly and led Hertzberg to his **two-factor theory**—also called *motivation-hygiene theory*.[11]

As shown in Exhibit 7-2 intrinsic factors such as advancement, recognition, responsibility, and achievement seem related to job satisfaction. Respondents who felt good about their work tended to attribute these factors to themselves, while dissatisfied respondents tended to cite extrinsic factors, such as supervision, pay, company policies, and working conditions.

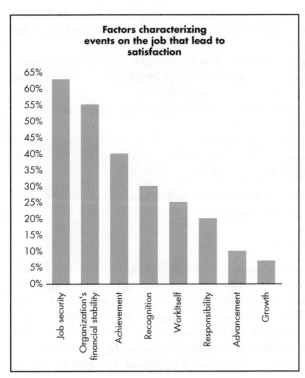 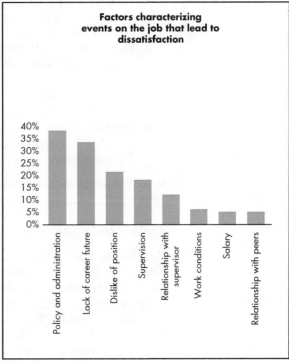

EXHIBIT 7-2

Comparison of Satisfiers and Dissatisfiers

Source: Data compiled from Harvard Business Review. "Comparison of Satisfiers and Dissatisfiers"; an exhibit from One More Time: How Do You Motivate Employees? by Frederick Herzberg, January 2003; http://www.careervision.org/about/pdfs/mr_jobsatisfaction.pdf; http://www.shrm.org/research/surveyfindings/articles/documents/11-0618%20job_satisfaction_fnl.pdf.

To Hertzberg, the data suggest that the opposite of satisfaction is not dissatisfaction, as was traditionally believed. Removing dissatisfying characteristics from a job does not necessarily make the job satisfying. Herzberg proposed a dual continuum: The opposite of "satisfaction" is "no satisfaction," and the opposite of "dissatisfaction" is "no dissatisfaction."

According to Herzberg, the factors that lead to job satisfaction are separate and distinct from those that lead to job dissatisfaction. Therefore, managers who seek to eliminate factors that can create job dissatisfaction may bring about peace, but not necessarily motivation. They will be placating rather than motivating their workers. As a result, Herzberg characterized conditions such as quality of supervision, pay, company policies, physical working conditions, relationships with others, and job security as **hygiene factors**. When they're adequate, people will not be dissatisfied; neither will they be satisfied. If we want to *motivate* people on their jobs, Herzberg suggested emphasizing factors associated with the work itself or with outcomes directly derived from it, such as promotional opportunities, personal growth opportunities, recognition, responsibility, and achievement. These are the characteristics people find intrinsically rewarding.

The two-factor theory has not been well supported in OB research, and it has many detractors.[12] Criticisms include the following:

1. Herzberg's methodology is limited because it relies on self-reports. When things are going well, people tend to take credit. Contrarily, they blame failure on the extrinsic environment.
2. The reliability of Herzberg's methodology is questionable. Raters have to make interpretations, so they may contaminate the findings by interpreting one response in one manner while treating a similar response differently.
3. No overall measure of satisfaction was utilized. A person may dislike part of a job yet still think the job is acceptable overall.
4. Herzberg assumed a relationship between satisfaction and productivity, but he looked only at satisfaction. To make his research relevant, we must assume a strong relationship between satisfaction and productivity.

Regardless of the criticisms, Herzberg's theory has been quite influential, and few managers are unfamiliar with its recommendations.

McClelland's Theory of Needs

You have one beanbag and five targets set up in front of you, each farther away than the last. Target A sits almost within arm's reach. If you hit it, you get $2. Target B is a bit farther out, but about 80 percent of the people who try can hit it. It pays $4. Target C pays $8, and about half the people who try can hit it. Very few people can hit Target D, but the payoff is $16 for those who do. Finally, Target E pays $32, but it's almost impossible to achieve. Which would you try for? If you selected C, you're likely to be a high achiever. Why? Read on.

McClelland's theory of needs was developed by David McClelland and his associates.[13] It looks at three needs:

- **Need for achievement (nAch)** is the drive to excel, to achieve in relationship to a set of standards.
- **Need for power (nPow)** is the need to make others behave in a way they would not have otherwise.
- **Need for affiliation (nAff)** is the desire for friendly and close interpersonal relationships.

McClelland and subsequent researchers focused most of their attention on nAch. High achievers perform best when they perceive their probability of success as 0.5—that is, a 50–50 chance. They dislike gambling with high odds because they get no achievement satisfaction from success that comes by pure chance. Similarly, they dislike low odds (high probability of success) because then there is no challenge to their skills. They like to set goals that require stretching themselves a little.

Relying on an extensive amount of research, we can predict some relationships between achievement need and job performance. First, when jobs have a high degree of personal responsibility and feedback and an intermediate degree of risk, high achievers are strongly motivated. They are successful in entrepreneurial activities such as running their own businesses, for example, and managing self-contained units within large organizations.[14] Second, a high need to achieve does not necessarily make someone a good manager, especially in large organizations. People with a high achievement need are interested in how well they do personally, and not in influencing others to do well. High-nAch salespeople do not necessarily make good sales managers, and the good general manager in a large organization does not typically have a high need to achieve.[15] Third, needs for affiliation and power tend to be closely related to managerial success. The best managers are high in their need for power and low in their need for affiliation.[16] In fact, a high power motive may be a requirement for managerial effectiveness.[17]

The view that a high achievement need acts as an internal motivator presupposes two U.S. cultural characteristics—willingness to accept a moderate degree of risk (which excludes countries with strong uncertainty-avoidance characteristics) and concern with performance (which applies to countries with strong achievement characteristics). This combination is found in Anglo-American countries such as the United States, Canada, and Great Britain,[18] and much less in Chile and Portugal.

Among the early theories of motivation, McClelland's has garnered the best research support. Unfortunately, it has less practical effect than the others. Because McClelland argued that the three needs are subconscious—we may rank high on them but not know it—measuring them is not easy. In the most common approach, a trained expert presents pictures to individuals, asks them to tell a story about each, and then scores their responses in terms of the three needs. However, the process is time consuming and expensive, and few organizations have been willing to invest in measuring McClelland's concept.

CONTEMPORARY THEORIES OF MOTIVATION

Early theories of motivation either have not held up under close examination or have fallen out of favor. In contrast, contemporary theories have one thing in common: each has a reasonable degree of valid supporting documentation. This doesn't mean they are unquestionably right. We call them "contemporary theories" because they represent the current state of thinking in explaining employee motivation.

Self-Determination Theory

"It's strange," said Marcia. "I started work at the Humane Society as a volunteer. I put in 15 hours a week helping people adopt pets. And I loved coming to work. Then, 3 months ago, they hired me full-time at $11 an hour. I'm doing the same work I did before. But I'm not finding it nearly as much fun."

Does Marcia's reaction seem counterintuitive? There's an explanation for it. It's called **self-determination theory**, which proposes that people prefer to feel they have control over their actions, so anything that makes a previously enjoyed task feel more like an obligation than a freely chosen activity will undermine motivation.[19] Much research on self-determination theory in OB has focused on **cognitive evaluation theory**, which hypothesizes that extrinsic rewards will reduce intrinsic interest in a task. When people are paid for work, it feels less like something they *want* to do and more like something they have to do. Self-determination theory also proposes that in addition to being driven by a need for autonomy, people seek ways to achieve competence and positive connections to others. A large number of studies support self-determination theory.[20] As we'll show, its major implications relate to work rewards.

When organizations use extrinsic rewards as payoffs for superior performance, employees feel they are doing a good job less because of their own intrinsic desire to excel than because that's what the organization wants. Eliminating extrinsic rewards can also shift an individual's perception of why she works on a task from an external to an internal explanation. If you're reading a novel a week because your English literature instructor requires you to, you can attribute your reading behavior to an external source. However, if you find yourself continuing to read a novel a week after the course is over, your natural inclination is to say, "I must enjoy reading novels because I'm still reading one a week." Applying extrinsic rewards is therefore all in the approach.

Studies examining how extrinsic rewards increases motivation for some creative tasks suggest we might need to place cognitive evaluation theory's predictions into a broader context.[21] Goal setting is more effective in improving motivation, for instance, when we provide rewards for achieving the goals. The original authors of self-determination theory acknowledge that extrinsic rewards such as verbal praise and feedback about competence can improve even intrinsic motivation under specific circumstances. Deadlines and specific work standards do, too, if people believe they are in control of their behavior.[22] This is consistent with the central theme of self-determination theory: rewards and deadlines diminish motivation if people see them as coercive.

What does self-determination theory suggest for providing rewards? If a senior sales representative really enjoys selling and making the deal, a commission indicates she's been doing a good job and increases her sense of competence by providing feedback that could improve intrinsic motivation. On the other hand, if a computer programmer values writing code because she likes to solve problems, then a reward for working to an externally imposed standard she does not accept, such as writing a certain number of lines of code every day, could feel coercive, and her intrinsic motivation would suffer. She would be less interested in the task and might reduce her effort.

A recent outgrowth of self-determination theory is **self-concordance**, which considers how strongly people's reasons for pursuing goals are consistent with their interests and core values. If individuals pursue goals because of an intrinsic interest, they are more likely to attain their goals and are happy even if they do not. Why? Because the process of striving toward them is fun. In contrast, people who pursue goals for extrinsic reasons (money, status, or other benefits) are less likely to attain their goals and less happy even when they do. Why? Because the goals are less meaningful to them.[23] OB research suggests that people who pursue work goals for intrinsic reasons are more satisfied with their jobs, feel they fit into their organizations better, and may perform better.[24]

What does all this mean? For individuals, it means choose your job for reasons other than extrinsic rewards. For organizations, it means managers should provide intrinsic as well as extrinsic incentives. They need to make the work interesting, provide recognition, and support employee growth and development. Employees who feel what they do is within their control and a result of free choice are likely to be more motivated by their work and committed to their employers.[25]

Job Engagement

When nurse Melissa Jones comes to work, it seems that everything else in her life goes away, and she becomes completely absorbed in what she is doing. Her emotions, her thoughts, and her behavior are all directed toward patient care. In fact, she can get so caught up in her work that she isn't even aware of how long she's been there. As a result of this total commitment, she is more effective in providing patient care and feels uplifted by her time at work.

Melissa has a high level of **job engagement**, the investment of an employee's physical, cognitive, and emotional energies into job performance.[26] Practicing managers and scholars alike have lately become interested in facilitating job engagement, believing something deeper than liking a job or finding it interesting drives performance. Many studies attempt to measure this deeper level of commitment.

The Gallup organization has been using 12 questions to assess the extent to which employee engagement is linked to positive work outcomes for millions of employees over the past 30 years.[27] There are far more engaged employees in highly successful than in average organizations, and groups with more engaged employees have higher levels of productivity, fewer safety incidents, and lower turnover. Academic studies have also found positive outcomes. One particularly large study examined multiple business units for their level of engagement and found a positive relationship with a variety of practical outcomes.[28] Another reviewed 91 distinct investigations and found higher levels of engagement associated with task performance and citizenship behavior.[29]

What makes people more likely to be engaged in their jobs? As we discussed in Chapter 3 in relation to the major job attitudes, one key is the degree to which an employee believes it is meaningful to engage in work. This is partially determined by job characteristics and access to sufficient resources to work effectively.[30] Another factor is a match between the individual's values and those of the organization.[31] Leadership behaviors that inspire workers to a greater sense of mission also increase employee engagement.[32]

One of the critiques of engagement is that the construct is partially redundant with job attitudes like satisfaction or stress.[33] However, engagement questionnaires usually assess motivation and absorption in a task, quite unlike job satisfaction questionnaires. Engagement may also predict important work outcomes better than traditional job attitudes.[34] Other critics note there may be a "dark side" to engagement, as evidenced by positive relationships between engagement and workfamily conflict.[35] Individuals might grow so engaged in their work roles that family responsibilities become an unwelcome intrusion. Further research exploring how engagement relates to these negative outcomes may help clarify whether some highly engaged employees might be getting "too much of a good thing."

Goal-Setting Theory

Gene Broadwater, coach of the Hamilton High School cross-country team, gave his squad these last words before they approached the starting line for the league championship race: "Each one of you is physically ready. Now, get out there and do your best. No one can ever ask more of you than that."

You've heard the sentiment a number of times yourself: "Just do your best. That's all anyone can ask." But what does "do your best" mean? Do we ever know whether we've

In general, managers should make goals specific and difficult—managers should set the highest goals to which employees will commit.

achieved that vague goal? Would the cross-country runners have recorded faster times if Coach Broadwater had given each a specific goal? Research on **goal-setting theory** in fact reveals impressive effects of goal specificity, challenge, and feedback on performance.

In the late 1960s, Edwin Locke proposed that intentions to work toward a goal are a major source of work motivation.[36] That is, goals tell an employee what needs to be done and how much effort is needed.[37] Evidence strongly suggests that specific goals increase performance; that difficult goals, when accepted, result in higher performance than do easy goals; and that feedback leads to higher performance than does nonfeedback.[38]

Specific goals produce a higher level of output than the generalized goal "do your best." Why? Specificity itself seems to act as an internal stimulus. When a trucker commits to making 12 round-trip hauls between Toronto and Buffalo, New York, each week, this intention gives him a specific objective to attain. All things being equal, he will outperform a counterpart with no goals or the generalized goal "do your best."

If factors such as acceptance of the goals are held constant, the more difficult the goal, the higher the level of performance. Of course, it's logical to assume easier goals are more likely to be accepted. But once a hard task is accepted, we can expect the employee to exert a high level of effort to try to achieve it.

But why are people motivated by difficult goals?[39] First, challenging goals get our attention and thus tend to help us focus. Second, difficult goals energize us because we have to work harder to attain them. Do you study as hard for an easy exam as you do for a difficult one? Probably not. Third, when goals are difficult, people persist in trying to attain them. Finally, difficult goals lead us to discover strategies that help us perform the job or task more effectively. If we have to struggle to solve a difficult problem, we often think of a better way to go about it.

People do better when they get feedback on how well they are progressing toward their goals, because it helps identify discrepancies between what they have done and what they want to do next—that is, feedback guides behavior. But all feedback is not equally potent. Self-generated feedback—with which employees are able to monitor their own progress—is more powerful than externally generated feedback.[40]

If employees can participate in the setting of their own goals, will they try harder? The evidence is mixed.[41] In some cases, participatively set goals yielded superior performance; in others, individuals performed best when assigned goals by their boss. But a major advantage of participation may be that it increases acceptance of the goal as a desirable one toward which to work.[42] Commitment is important. Without participation, the individual assigning the goal needs to clearly explain its purpose and importance.[43]

In addition to feedback, three other factors influence the goals—performance relationship: *goal commitment, task characteristics,* and *national culture.*

Goal-setting theory assumes an individual is committed to the goal and determined not to lower or abandon it. The individual (1) believes she can achieve the goal and (2) wants to achieve it.[44] Goal commitment is most likely to occur when goals are made public, when the individual has an internal locus of control, and when the goals are self-set rather than assigned.[45] Goals themselves seem to affect performance more strongly when tasks are simple rather than complex, well learned rather than novel, and independent rather than interdependent.[46] On interdependent tasks, group goals are preferable.

Finally, setting specific, difficult, individual goals may have different effects in different cultures. Most goal-setting research has been done in the United States and Canada, where individual achievement and performance are most highly valued. To date, research has not shown that group-based goals are more effective in collectivists than in individualist cultures. In collectivistic and high-power-distance cultures, achievable moderate goals can be more highly motivating than difficult ones.[47] Finally, assigned goals appear to generate greater goal commitment in high than in low power-distance cultures.[48] More research is needed to assess how goal constructs might differ across cultures.

Although goal-setting has positive outcomes, some goals may be *too* effective.[49] When learning something is important, goals related to performance undermine adaptation and creativity because people become too focused on outcomes and ignore changing conditions. In this case, a goal to learn and generate alternative solutions will be more effective than a goal to perform. Some authors argue that goals can lead employees to focus on a single standard and exclude all others. Consider the narrow focus on boosting short-term stock prices in many businesses—it may have led organizations to ignore long-term success and even to engage in such unethical behavior as accounting fraud or excessively risky investments. (Of course, organizations can establish goals for ethical performance.) Other studies show that employees low in conscientiousness and emotional stability experience greater emotional exhaustion when their leaders set goals.[50] Despite differences of opinion, most researchers do agree that goals are powerful in shaping behavior. Managers should make sure they are actually aligned with the company's objectives.

Research has begun to examine subconscious goals—that is, goals we are not even aware of setting.[51] One study primed people to think about goals by having them assemble scrambled words into sentences with achievement themes, whereas other people assembled sentences without achievement themes. The people who made the achievement sentences were subconsciously primed. That might not sound like a very strong manipulation, but this group performed more effectively in a brainstorming task than those given easier goals. Another study found similar results when a picture of a woman winning a race was the subconscious prime rather than assembling sentences. Interestingly, these studies do not find that conscious and subconscious goal-setting are related, meaning that we sometimes are driven by goals we don't even know we have.

IMPLEMENTING GOAL-SETTING?   As a manager, how do you make goal-setting theory operational? That's often left up to the individual. Some managers set aggressive performance targets—what General Electric called "stretch goals." Some CEOs, such as Procter Gamble's A. G. Lafley and SAP AG's Hasso Plattner, are known for the demanding performance goals they set. But many managers don't set goals. When asked whether their job had clearly defined goals, only a minority of employees in a recent survey said yes.[52]

A more systematic way to utilize goal-setting is with **management by objectives (MBO)**, an initiative most popular in the 1970s, but still used today. MBO emphasizes participatively set goals that are tangible, verifiable, and measurable. As in Exhibit 7-3, the organization's overall objectives are translated into specific objectives for each level (divisional, departmental, individual). But because lower-unit managers jointly participate in setting their own goals, MBO works from the bottom up as well as from the top down. The result is a hierarchy that links objectives at one level to those at the next. And for the individual employee, MBO provides specific personal performance objectives.

Four ingredients are common to MBO programs: goal specificity, participation in decision making (including the setting of goals or objectives), an explicit time period, and performance feedback.[53] Many elements in MBO programs match propositions of goal-setting theory. For example, having an explicit time period to accomplish objectives matches goal-setting theory's emphasis on goal specificity. Similarly, we noted

EXHIBIT 7-3
Cascading of Objectives

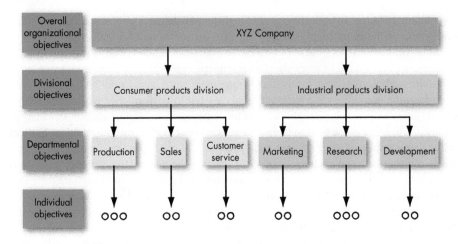

previously that feedback about goal progress is a critical element of goal-setting theory. The only area of possible disagreement between MBO and general goal-setting theory is participation: MBO strongly advocates it, whereas goal-setting theory demonstrates that managers' assigned goals are usually just as effective.

Self-Efficacy Theory

Managers will increase employees' motivation by increasing their confidence in successfully completing the task (self-efficacy).

Self-efficacy (also known as *social cognitive theory or social learning theory*) refers to an individual's belief that he is capable of performing a task.[54] The higher your self-efficacy, the more confidence you have in your ability to succeed. So, in difficult situations, people with low self-efficacy are more likely to lessen their effort or give up altogether, while those with high self-efficacy will try harder to master the challenge.[55] Self-efficacy can create a positive spiral in which those with high efficacy become more engaged in their tasks and then, in turn, increase performance, which increases efficacy further.[56] Changes in self-efficacy over time are related to changes in creative performance as well.[57] In addition, individuals high in self-efficacy also seem to respond to negative feedback with increased effort and motivation, while those low in self-efficacy are likely to lessen their effort after negative feedback.[58] How can managers help their employees achieve high levels of self-efficacy? By bringing goal-setting theory and self-efficacy theory together.

Goal-setting theory and self-efficacy theory don't compete; they complement each other. As Exhibit 7-4 shows, employees whose managers set difficult goals for them will have a higher level of self-efficacy and set higher goals for their own performance. Why? Setting difficult goals for people communicates your confidence in them. Imagine you learn your boss sets a higher goal for you than for your co-workers. How would you interpret this? As long as you didn't feel you were being picked on, you would probably think, "Well, I guess my boss thinks I'm capable of performing better than others." This sets in motion a psychological process in which you're more confident in yourself (higher self-efficacy) and you set higher personal goals, performing better both inside and outside the workplace.

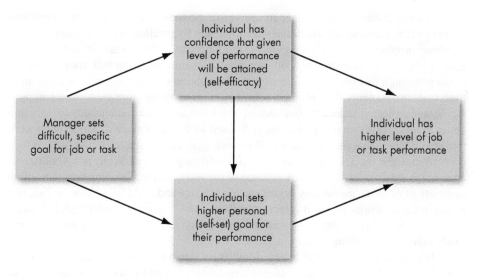

EXHIBIT 7-4
Joint Effects of Goals and Self-Efficacy on Performance

Source: Based on E. A. Locke and G. P. Latham, "Building a Practically Useful Theory of Goal Setting and Task Motivation: A 35-Year Odyssey," *American Psychologist*, September 2002, pp. 705–717.

The researcher who developed self-efficacy theory, Albert Bandura, proposes four ways self-efficacy can be increased:[59]

1. Enactive mastery
2. Vicarious modeling
3. Verbal persuasion
4. Arousal

According to Bandura, the most important source of increasing self-efficacy is *enactive mastery*—that is, gaining relevant experience with the task or job. If you've been able to do the job successfully in the past, you're more confident you'll be able to do it in the future.

The second source is *vicarious modeling*—becoming more confident because you see someone else doing the task. If your friend slims down, it increases your confidence that you can lose weight, too. Vicarious modeling is most effective when you see yourself as similar to the person you are observing. Watching Tiger Woods play a difficult golf shot might not increase your confidence in being able to play the shot yourself, but if you watch a golfer with a handicap similar to yours, it's persuasive.

The third source is *verbal persuasion*: becoming more confident because someone convinces you that you have the skills necessary to be successful. Motivational speakers use this tactic.

Finally, Bandura argues that *arousal* increases self-efficacy. Arousal leads to an energized state, so the person gets "psyched up" and performs better. But if the task requires a steady, lower-key perspective (say, carefully editing a manuscript), arousal may in fact hurt performance.

The best way for a manager to use verbal persuasion is through the *Pygmalion effect* or the *Galatea effect*. As discussed earlier, the **Pygmalion effect** is a form of self-fulfilling prophecy in which believing something can make it true. In some studies, teachers were told their students had very high IQ scores when, in fact, they spanned a range from high to low. Consistent with the Pygmalion effect, the teachers spent more time with the students they *thought* were smart, gave them more challenging assignments, and expected more of them—all of which led to higher student self-efficacy and better grades.[60] This strategy also has been used in the workplace.[61] Sailors who were told convincingly that they would not get seasick were in fact much less likely to do so.[62]

What are the OB implications of self-efficacy theory? Well, it's a matter of applying Bandura's sources of self-efficacy to the work setting. Training programs often make use of enactive mastery by having people practice and build their skills. In fact, one reason training works is that it increases self-efficacy.[63] Individuals with higher levels of self-efficacy also appear to reap more benefits from training programs and are more likely to use their training on the job.[64]

Intelligence and personality are absent from Bandura's list, but they can increase self-efficacy.[65] People who are intelligent, conscientious, and emotionally stable are so much more likely to have high self-efficacy that some researchers argue self-efficacy is less important than prior research would suggest.[66] They believe it is partially a by-product in a smart person with a confident personality. Although Bandura strongly disagrees with this conclusion, more research is needed.

Equity Theory/Organizational Justice

Jane Pearson graduated from State University last year with a degree in accounting. After interviews with a number of organizations on campus, she accepted a position with a top public accounting firm and was assigned to its Boston office. Jane was very pleased with the offer she received: challenging work with a prestigious firm, an excellent opportunity to gain valuable experience, and the highest salary any accounting major at State was offered last year—$4,550 per month—but Jane was the top student in her class. She was articulate and mature, and she fully expected to receive a commensurate salary.

Twelve months have passed. The work has proved to be as challenging and satisfying as Jane had hoped. Her employer is extremely pleased with her performance; in fact, Jane recently received a $200-per-month raise. However, her motivational level has dropped dramatically in the past few weeks. Why? Jane's employer has just hired a fresh graduate out of State University who lacks the year of experience Jane has gained, for $4,800 per month—$50 more than Jane now makes! Jane is irate. She is even talking about looking for another job.

Jane's situation illustrates the role that equity plays in motivation. Employees perceive what they get from a job situation (salary levels, raises, recognition) in relationship to what they put into it (effort, experience, education, competence), and then they compare their outcome—input ratio with that of relevant others. This is shown in Exhibit 7-5. If we perceive our ratio to be equal to that of the relevant others with whom we compare ourselves, a state of equity exists; we perceive that our situation is fair and justice prevails. When we see the ratio as unequal and we feel underrewarded, we experience equity tension that creates anger. When we see ourselves as overrewarded, tension creates guilt. J. Stacy Adams proposed that this negative state of tension provides the motivation to do something to correct it.[67]

Ratio Comparisons*	Perception
$\dfrac{O}{I} < \dfrac{O}{I_B}$	Inequity due to being underrewarded
$\dfrac{O}{I} = \dfrac{O}{I_B}$	Equity
$\dfrac{O}{I} > \dfrac{O}{I_B}$	Inequity due to being overrewarded

*Where $\dfrac{O}{I}$ represents the employee; and $\dfrac{O}{I_B}$ represents relevant others

EXHIBIT 7-5
Equity Theory

The referent an employee selects adds to the complexity of **equity theory**.[68] There are four referent comparisons:

1. *Self-inside.* An employee's experiences in a different position inside the employee's current organization.
2. *Self-outside.* An employee's experiences in a situation or position outside the employee's current organization.
3. *Other-inside.* Another individual or group of individuals inside the employee's organization.
4. *Other-outside.* Another individual or group of individuals outside the employee's organization.

Employees might compare themselves to friends, neighbors, co-workers, or colleagues in other organizations or compare their present job with past jobs. Which referent an employee chooses will be influenced by the information the employee holds about referents as well as by the attractiveness of the referent. Four moderating variables are gender, length of tenure, level in the organization, and amount of education or professionalism.[69]

Based on equity theory, employees who perceive inequity will make one of six choices:[70]

1. Change inputs (exert less effort if underpaid or more if overpaid).
2. Change outcomes (individuals paid on a piece-rate basis can increase their pay by producing a higher quantity of units of lower quality).
3. Distort perceptions of self ("I used to think I worked at a moderate pace, but now I realize I work a lot harder than everyone else.").
4. Distort perceptions of others ("Mike's job isn't as desirable as I thought.").
5. Choose a different referent ("I may not make as much as my brother-in-law, but I'm doing a lot better than my Dad did when he was my age.").
6. Leave the field (quit the job).

Some of these propositions have been supported, but others haven't.[71] First, inequities created by overpayment do not seem to significantly affect behavior in most work situations. Apparently, people have more tolerance of overpayment inequities than of underpayment inequities or are better able—to rationalize them. It's pretty damaging to a theory when half the equation falls apart. Second, not all people are equity sensitive.[72] A few actually prefer outcome—input ratios lower than the referent comparisons. Predictions from equity theory are not likely to be very accurate about these "benevolent types."

Finally, recent research has expanded the meaning of *equity*, or *fairness*.[73] Historically, equity theory focused on **distributive justice**, the employee's perceived fairness of the amount of rewards among individuals and who received them. But **organizational justice** draws a bigger picture. Employees perceive their organizations as just when they believe rewards and the way they are distributed are fair. In other words, fairness or equity can be subjective; what one person sees as unfair, another may see as perfectly appropriate. In general, people see allocations or procedures favoring themselves as fair.[74]

Most of the equity theory research we've described proposes a fairly rational, calculative way of estimating what is fair and unfair. But few people really make mathematical calculations of their inputs relative to the outcomes of others. Instead, they base distributive judgments on a feeling or an emotional reaction to how they think they are treated relative to others, and their reactions are often emotional as well.[75] Our discussion has also focused on reactions to personal mistreatment. However, people also react emotionally to injustices committed against others, prompting them to take retributive actions.[76]

Beyond perceptions of fairness, the other key element of organizational justice is the view that justice is multidimensional. How much we get paid relative to what we think we should be paid (distributive justice) is obviously important. But, according to researchers, how we get paid is just as important. Thus, the model of organizational justice in Exhibit 7-6 includes **procedural justice**—the perceived fairness of the *process*

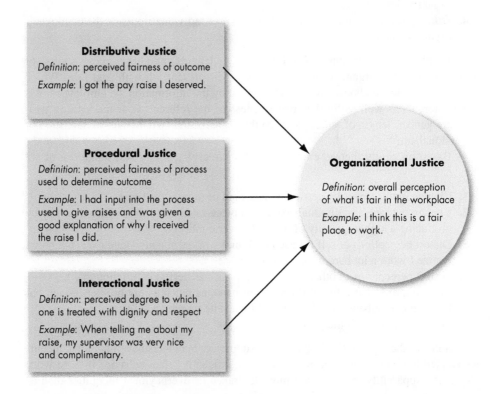

Distributive Justice

Definition: perceived fairness of outcome

Example: I got the pay raise I deserved.

Procedural Justice

Definition: perceived fairness of process used to determine outcome

Example: I had input into the process used to give raises and was given a good explanation of why I received the raise I did.

Interactional Justice

Definition: perceived degree to which one is treated with dignity and respect

Example: When telling me about my raise, my supervisor was very nice and complimentary.

Organizational Justice

Definition: overall perception of what is fair in the workplace

Example: I think this is a fair place to work.

EXHIBIT 7-6
Model of Organizational Justice

used to determine the distribution of rewards. Two key elements of procedural justice are process control and explanations. *Process control* is the opportunity to present your point of view about desired outcomes to decision makers. *Explanations* are clear reasons management gives for the outcome. Therefore, for employees to see a process as fair, they need to feel they have some control over the outcome and that they were given an adequate explanation about why the outcome occurred. It's also important that a manager is consistent (across people and over time), is *unbiased*, makes decisions based on *accurate information*, and is *open to appeals*.[77]

The effects of procedural justice become more important when distributive justice is lacking. This makes sense. If we don't get what we want, we tend to focus on *why*. If your supervisor gives a cushy office to a co-worker instead of to you, you're much more focused on your supervisor's treatment of you than if you had gotten the office. Explanations are beneficial when they take the form of post hoc excuses ("I know this is bad, and I wanted to give you the office, but it wasn't my decision") rather than justifications ("I decided to give the office to Sam, but having it isn't a big deal").[78]

Interactional justice describes an individual's perception of the degree to which she is treated with dignity, concern, and respect. When people are treated in an unjust manner (at least in their own eyes), they retaliate (for example, badmouthing a supervisor).[79] Because people intimately connect interactional justice or injustice to the conveyer of the information, we would expect perceptions of injustice to be more closely related to the supervisor. Generally, that's what the evidence suggests.[80]

Of these three forms of justice, distributive justice is most strongly related to organizational commitment and satisfaction with outcomes such as pay. Procedural justice relates most strongly to job satisfaction, employee trust, withdrawal from the organization, job performance, and citizenship behaviors. There is less evidence about interactional justice.[81]

Equity theory has gained a strong following in the United States because U.S.-style reward systems assume workers are highly sensitive to equity in reward allocations. And in the United States, equity is meant to closely tie pay to performance. However, in collectivist cultures, employees expect rewards to reflect their individual needs as well as their performance.[82] Other research suggests that inputs and outcomes are valued differently in various cultures.[83] Some cultures emphasize status over individual achievement as a basis for allocating resources. Materialistic cultures are more likely to see cash compensation and rewards as the most relevant outcomes of work, whereas relational cultures will see social rewards and status as important outcomes. International managers must consider the cultural preferences of each group of employees when determining what is "fair" in different contexts.

Studies suggest that managers are motivated to foster employees' perceptions of justice because they wish to ensure compliance, maintain a positive identity, and establish fairness at work.[84] To enhance perceptions of justice, they should realize that employees are especially sensitive to unfairness in procedures when bad news has to be communicated (that is, when distributive justice is low). If employees feel they have been treated unjustly, having opportunities to express their frustration has been shown to reduce their desire for retribution.[85] Meta-analytic evidence shows individuals in both individualistic and collectivistic cultures prefer an equitable distribution of rewards (the most effective workers get paid the most) over an equal division (everyone gets paid the

To promote fairness in the workplace, managers should consider openly sharing information on how allocation decisions are made. Fair and open procedures are especially important when the outcome is likely to be viewed negatively by some or all employees.

same regardless of performance).[86] Across nations, the same basic principles of procedural justice are respected, and workers around the world prefer rewards based on performance and skills over rewards based on seniority.[87] Thus, it's especially important to openly share information about how allocation decisions are made, follow consistent and unbiased procedures, and engage in similar practices to increase the perception of procedural justice. Second, when addressing perceived injustices, managers need to focus their actions on the source of the problems.

Expectancy Theory

One of the most widely accepted explanations of motivation is Victor Vroom's **expectancy theory**.[88] Although it has its critics, most of the evidence supports the theory.[89]

Expectancy theory argues that the strength of our tendency to act a certain way depends on the strength of our expectation of a given outcome and its attractiveness. In more practical terms, employees will be motivated to exert a high level of effort when they believe it will lead to a good performance appraisal; that a good appraisal will lead to organizational rewards such as salary increases, and/or intrinsic rewards; and that the rewards will satisfy the employees' personal goals. The theory, therefore, focuses on three relationships (see Exhibit 7-7):

1. *Effort–Performance Relationship.* The probability perceived by the individual that exerting a given amount of effort will lead to performance.
2. *Performance–Reward Relationship.* The degree to which the individual believes performing at a particular level will lead to the attainment of a desired outcome.
3. *Rewards–Personal Goals Relationship.* The degree to which organizational rewards satisfy an individual's personal goals or needs and the attractiveness of those potential rewards for the individual.[90]

Expectancy theory helps explain why a lot of workers aren't motivated on their jobs and do only the minimum necessary to get by. Let's frame the theory's three relationships as questions employees need to answer in the affirmative if their motivation is to be maximized.

First, *if I give a maximum effort, will it be recognized in my performance appraisal?* For many employees, the answer is no. Why? Their skill level may be deficient, which means no matter how hard they try, they're not likely to be high performers. The organization's performance appraisal system may be designed to assess nonperformance factors such as loyalty, initiative, or courage, which means more effort won't necessarily result in a higher evaluation. Another possibility is that employees, rightly or wrongly, perceive the boss doesn't like them. As a result, they expect a poor appraisal, regardless of effort. These examples suggest one possible source of motivation is employees' belief that, no matter how hard they work, the likelihood of getting a good performance appraisal is low.

EXHIBIT 7-7
Expectancy Theory

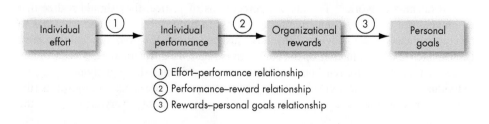

Individual effort → (1) → Individual performance → (2) → Organizational rewards → (3) → Personal goals

(1) Effort–performance relationship
(2) Performance–reward relationship
(3) Rewards–personal goals relationship

Second, *if I get a good performance appraisal, will it lead to organizational rewards?* Many organizations reward things besides performance. When pay is based on factors such as having seniority, being cooperative, or "kissing up" to the boss, employees are likely to see the performance–reward relationship as weak and demotivating.

Finally, *if I'm rewarded, are the rewards attractive to me?* The employee works hard in the hope of getting a promotion but gets a pay raise instead. Or the employee wants a more interesting and challenging job but receives only a few words of praise. Unfortunately, many managers are limited in the rewards they can distribute, which makes it difficult to tailor rewards to individual employee needs. Some incorrectly assume all employees want the same thing, thus overlooking the motivational effects of differentiating rewards. In either case, employee motivation is submaximized.

As a vivid example of how expectancy theory can work, consider stock analysts. They make their living trying to forecast a stock's future price; the accuracy of their buy, sell, or hold recommendations is what keeps them in work or gets them fired. But it's not quite that simple. Analysts place few sell ratings on stocks, although in a steady market, by definition, as many stocks are falling as are rising. Expectancy theory provides an explanation: analysts who place a sell rating on a company's stock have to balance the benefits they receive by being accurate against the risks they run by drawing that company's ire. What are these risks? They include public rebuke, professional blackballing, and exclusion from information. When analysts place a buy rating on a stock, they face no such trade-off because, obviously, companies love it when analysts recommend that investors buy their stock. So the incentive structure suggests the expected outcome of buy ratings is higher than the expected outcome of sell ratings, and that's why buy ratings vastly outnumber sell ratings.[91]

Does expectancy theory work? Some critics suggest it has only limited use and is more valid where individuals clearly perceive effort—performance and performance—reward linkages.[92] Because few individuals do, the theory tends to be idealistic. If organizations actually rewarded individuals for performance rather than for seniority, effort, skill level, and job difficulty, expectancy theory might be much more valid. However, rather than invalidating it, this criticism can explain why a significant segment of the workforce exerts low effort on the job.

SUMMARY AND IMPLICATIONS FOR MANAGERS

The motivation theories in this chapter differ in their predictive strength. Here, we (1) review the most established to determine their relevance in explaining turnover, productivity, and other outcomes and (2) assess the predictive power of each.[93]

- *Need theories.* Maslow's hierarchy, McClelland's needs, and the two-factor theory focus on needs. None has found widespread support, although McClelland's is the strongest, particularly regarding the relationship between achievement and productivity. In general, need theories are not very valid explanations of motivation.
- *Self-Determination Theory and Cognitive Evaluation Theory.* As research on the motivational effects of rewards has accumulated, it increasingly appears extrinsic rewards can undermine motivation if they are seen as coercive. They can increase motivation if they provide information about competence and relatedness.
- *Goal-Setting Theory.* Clear and difficult goals lead to higher levels of employee productivity, supporting goal-setting theory's explanation of this dependent variable. The theory does not address absenteeism, turnover, or satisfaction, however.

- *Equity Theory/Organizational Justice.* Equity theory deals with productivity, satisfaction, absence, and turnover variables. However, its strongest legacy is that it provided the spark for research on organizational justice, which has more support in the literature.
- *Expectancy Theory.* Expectancy theory offers a powerful explanation of performance variables such as employee productivity, absenteeism, and turnover. But it assumes employees have few constraints on decision making, such as bias or incomplete information, and this limits its applicability. Expectancy theory has some validity because, for many behaviors, people consider expected outcomes.

MyManagementLab

Go to **MyManagementLab.com** to access study plans, interactive lectures, and videos as well as Auto-graded writing questions and the following Assisted-graded writing question.

7-1. MyManagementLab Only—comprehensive writing assignment for this chapter.

8

■ ■ ■

Motivation: From Concepts to Applications

After studying this chapter, you should be able to:

- Describe the job characteristics model and evaluate the way it motivates by changing the work environment.
- Compare and contrast the main ways jobs can be redesigned.
- Give examples of employee involvement measures and show how they can motivate employees.
- Demonstrate how the different types of variable-pay programs can increase employee motivation.
- Show how flexible benefits turn benefits into motivators.
- Identify the motivational benefits of intrinsic rewards.

MyManagementLab™

⭐ **Improve Your Grade!**

Over 10 million students improved their results using the Pearson MyLabs. Visit **mymanagementlab.com** for simulations, tutorials, and end-of-chapter problems.

In the last chapter, we focused on motivation theories. In this chapter, we start applying motivation concepts to practices such as employee involvement and skill-based pay. Why? Because it's one thing to know specific theories; it's quite another to see how, as a manager, you can use them.

MOTIVATING BY CHANGING THE NATURE OF THE WORK ENVIRONMENT

Increasingly, research on motivation focuses on approaches that link motivational concepts to changes in the way work is structured. Research in **job design** suggests the way the elements in a job are organized can increase or decrease effort and also suggests what those elements are. We'll first review the job characteristics model and then discuss some ways jobs can be redesigned. Finally, we'll explore alternative work arrangements.

The Job Characteristics Model

Developed by J. Richard Hackman and Greg Oldham, the **job characteristics model (JCM)** says we can describe any job in terms of five core job dimensions:[1]

Though there are individual differences, most people respond well to intrinsic job characteristics; the job characteristics model does a good job of summarizing what intrinsic job characteristics might be altered to make the work more interesting and intrinsically motivating for employees.

1. *Skill Variety.* **Skill variety** is the degree to which a job requires a variety of different activities so the worker can use a number of different skills and talents. The work of a garage owner-operator who does electrical repairs, rebuilds engines, does bodywork, and interacts with customers scores high on skill variety. The job of a bodyshop worker who sprays paint 8 hours a day scores low on this dimension.
2. *Task Identity.* **Task identity** is the degree to which a job requires completion of a whole and identifiable piece of work. A cabinetmaker who designs a piece of furniture, selects the wood, builds the object, and finishes it to perfection has a job that scores high on task identity. A job scoring low on this dimension is operating a factory lathe solely to make table legs.
3. *Task Significance.* **Task significance** is the degree to which a job affects the lives or work of other people. The job of a nurse handling the diverse needs of patients in a hospital intensive care unit scores high on task significance; sweeping floors in a hospital scores low.
4. *Autonomy.* **Autonomy** is the degree to which a job provides the worker freedom, independence, and discretion in scheduling work and determining the procedures in carrying it out. A salesperson who schedules his own work each day and decides on the most effective sales approach for each customer without supervision has a highly autonomous job. A salesperson who is given a set of leads each day and is required to follow a standardized sales script with each potential customer has a job low on autonomy.
5. *Feedback.* **Feedback** is the degree to which carrying out work activities generates direct and clear information about your own performance. A job with high feedback is assembling iPads and testing them to see whether they operate properly. A factory worker who assembles iPads but then routes them to a quality-control inspector for testing and adjustments receives low feedback from her activities.

Exhibit 8-1 presents the job characteristics model (JCM). Note how the first three dimensions—skill variety, task identity, and task significance—combine to create meaningful work the incumbent will view as important, valuable, and worthwhile. Note, too, that jobs with high autonomy give incumbents a feeling of personal responsibility for the results and that, if a job provides feedback, employees will know how effectively they are performing. From a motivational standpoint, the JCM proposes that individuals obtain internal rewards when they learn (knowledge of results) that they personally (experienced responsibility) have performed well on a task they care about (experienced meaningfulness).[2] The more these three psychological states are present, the greater will be employees' motivation, performance, and satisfaction, and the lower their absenteeism and likelihood of leaving. As Exhibit 8-1 also shows, individuals with a high growth need are more likely to experience the critical psychological states when their jobs are enriched—and respond to them more positively—than are their counterparts with low growth need.

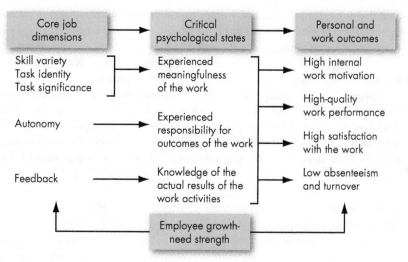

EXHIBIT 8-1

The Job Characteristics Model

Source: J. R. Hackman and G. R. Oldham, *Work Redesign* (Upper Saddle River, NJ: Pearson Education) pp. 78–80, © 1980. Adapted by permission of Pearson Education, Inc., Upper Saddle River, New Jersey.

Much evidence supports the JCM concept that the presence of a set of job characteristics—variety, identity, significance, autonomy, and feedback—does generate higher and more satisfying job performance.[3] But apparently we can better calculate motivating potential by simply adding the characteristics rather than using the multiplicative formula.[4] Think about your job. Do you have the opportunity to work on different tasks, or is your day pretty routine? Are you able to work independently, or do you constantly have a supervisor or co-worker looking over your shoulder? What do you think your answers to these questions say about your job's motivating potential?

A few studies have tested the job characteristics model in different cultures, but the results aren't very consistent. One study suggested that when employees are "other oriented" (concerned with the welfare of others at work), the relationship between intrinsic job characteristics and job satisfaction was weaker. The fact that the job characteristics model is relatively individualistic (considering the relationship between the employee and his work) suggests job enrichment strategies may not have the same effects in collectivistic cultures as in individualistic cultures (such as the United States).[5] However, another study suggested the degree to which jobs had intrinsic job characteristics predicted job satisfaction and job involvement equally well for U.S., Japanese, and Hungarian employees.[6]

How Can Jobs Be Redesigned?

"Every day was the same thing," Frank Greer said. "Stand on that assembly line. Wait for an instrument panel to be moved into place. Unlock the mechanism and drop the panel into the Jeep Liberty as it moved by on the line. Then I plugged in the harnessing wires.

I repeated that for eight hours a day. I don't care that they were paying me twenty-four dollars an hour. I was going crazy. I did it for almost a year and a half. Finally, I just said to my wife that this isn't going to be the way I'm going to spend the rest of my life. My brain was turning to JELL-O on that Jeep assembly line. So I quit. Now I work in a print shop and I make less than fifteen dollars an hour. But let me tell you, the work I do is really interesting. The job changes all the time, I'm continually learning new things, and the work really challenges me! I look forward every morning to going to work again."

The repetitive tasks in Frank Greer's job at the Jeep plant provided little variety, autonomy, or motivation. In contrast, his job in the print shop is challenging and stimulating. Let's look at some of the ways to put JCM into practice to make jobs more motivating.

JOB ROTATION   If employees suffer from overroutinization of their work, one alternative is **job rotation**, or the periodic shifting of an employee from one task to another with similar skill requirements at the same organizational level (also called *cross-training*). Many manufacturing firms have adopted job rotation as a means of increasing flexibility and avoiding layoffs.[7] Managers at Apex Precision Technologies, a custom-machine shop in Indiana, train workers on all the company's equipment so they can move around as needed in response to incoming orders. Although job rotation has often been conceptualized as an activity for assembly-line and manufacturing employees, many organizations use job rotation for new managers to help them get a picture of the whole business as well.[8] At Singapore Airlines, for instance, a ticket agent may take on the duties of a baggage handler. Extensive job rotation is among the reasons Singapore Airlines is rated one of the best airlines in the world and a highly desirable place to work.

The strengths of job rotation are that it reduces boredom, increases motivation, and helps employees better understand how their work contributes to the organization. An indirect benefit is that employees with a wider range of skills give management more flexibility in scheduling work, adapting to changes, and filling vacancies.[9] International evidence from Italy, Britain, and Turkey does show that job rotation is associated with higher levels of organizational performance in manufacturing settings.[10] However, job rotation has drawbacks. Training costs increase, and moving a worker into a new position reduces productivity just when efficiency at the prior job is creating organizational economies. Job rotation also creates disruptions when members of the work group have to adjust to the new employee. And supervisors may also have to spend more time answering questions and monitoring the work of recently rotated employees.

JOB ENRICHMENT   **Job enrichment** expands jobs by increasing the degree to which the worker controls the planning, execution, and evaluation of the work. An enriched job organizes tasks to allow the worker to do a complete activity, increases the employee's freedom and independence, increases responsibility, and provides feedback so individuals can assess and correct their own performance.[11]

How does management enrich an employee's job? Exhibit 8-2 offers suggested guidelines based on the job characteristics model. *Combining tasks* puts fractionalized tasks back together to form a new and larger module of work. *Forming natural work units* makes an employee's tasks create an identifiable and meaningful whole. *Establishing client relationships* increases the direct relationships between workers and their clients (clients can be internal as well as outside the organization). *Expanding jobs vertically*

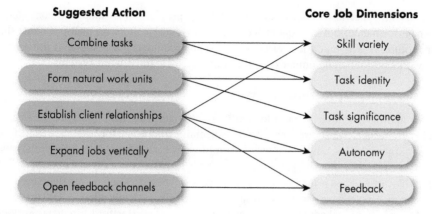

EXHIBIT 8-2
Guidelines for Enriching a Job

Source: J. R. Hackman and J. L. Suttle (eds.), *Improving Life at Work* (Glenview, IL: Scott Foresman, 1977), p. 138. Reprinted by permission of Richard Hackman and J. Lloyd Suttle.

gives employees responsibilities and control formerly reserved for management. *Opening feedback channels* lets employees know how well they are doing and whether their performance is improving, deteriorating, or remaining constant.

Some newer versions of job enrichment concentrate specifically on improving the meaningfulness of work. One method is to relate employee experiences to customer outcomes, by providing employees with stories from customers who benefited from the company's products or services. The medical device manufacturer Medtronic invites people to describe how Medtronic products have improved, or even saved, their lives and shares these stories with employees during annual meetings, providing a powerful reminder of the impact of their work. Researchers recently found that when university fund-raisers briefly interacted with the undergraduates who would receive the scholarship money they raised, they persisted 42 percent longer, and raised nearly twice as much money, as those who didn't interact with potential recipients.[12]

Another method for improving the meaningfulness of work is providing employees with mutual assistance programs.[13] Employees who can help each other directly through their work come to see themselves, and the organizations for which they work, in more positive, pro-social terms. This, in turn, can increase employee affective commitment.

Many organizations provide job enrichment through cross-training to learn new skills, and through job rotation to perform new tasks in another position. Employees typically work with managers to set job enrichment goals, identify desired competencies, and find appropriate placement. For example, an employee who usually works in handling client records might receive cross-training to learn about the organization's purchasing and accounting systems. Then an accounting employee might learn about client data processes. These two employees could then rotate through one another's jobs, allowing them to cover for one another and prepare for possible future promotions.

The evidence on job enrichment shows it reduces absenteeism and turnover costs and increases satisfaction, but not all programs are equally effective.[14] A review of 83 organizational interventions designed to improve performance management showed that frequent, specific feedback related to solving problems was linked to consistently higher performance, but infrequent feedback that focused more on past problems than future solutions was much less effective.[15] Some recent evidence suggests job enrichment works best when it compensates for poor feedback and reward systems.[16]

Alternative Work Arrangements

Another approach to motivation is to alter work arrangements with flextime, job sharing, or telecommuting. These are likely to be especially important for a diverse workforce of dual-earner couples, single parents, and employees caring for sick or aging relatives.

FLEXTIME   Susan Ross is the classic "morning person." She rises at 5:00 AM sharp each day, full of energy. However, as she puts it, "I'm usually ready for bed right after the 7:00 PM news."

Susan's work schedule as a claims processor at The Hartford Financial Services Group is flexible. Her office opens at 6:00 AM and closes at 7:00 PM. It's up to her how she schedules her 8-hour day within this 13-hour period. Because Susan is a morning person and also has a 7-year-old son who gets out of school at 3:00 PM every day, she opts to work from 6:00 AM to 3:00 PM. "My work hours are perfect. I'm at the job when I'm mentally most alert, and I can be home to take care of my son after he gets out of school."

Susan's schedule is an example of **flextime**, short for "flexible work time." Employees must work a specific number of hours per week but are free to vary their hours of work within certain limits. As in Exhibit 8-3, each day consists of a common core, usually 6 hours, with a flexibility band surrounding it. The core may be 9:00 AM to 3:00 PM, with the office actually opening at 6:00 AM and closing at 6:00 PM. All employees are required to be at their jobs during the common core period, but they may accumulate their other 2 hours before, after, or before *and* after that. Some flextime programs allow employees to accumulate extra hours and turn them into a free day off each month.

Flextime has become extremely popular; according to the Bureau of Labor Statistics, nearly 26 percent of working women with children have flexible work schedules, compared to just 14 percent in 1991.[17] And this is not just a U.S. phenomenon. In Germany, for instance, 29 percent of businesses offer flextime, and such practices are becoming more widespread in Japan as well.[18]

Claimed benefits include reduced absenteeism, increased productivity, reduced overtime expenses, reduced hostility toward management, reduced traffic congestion around work sites, elimination of tardiness, and increased autonomy and responsibility for employees—any of which may increase employee job satisfaction.[19] But what's flextime's actual record?

Most of the evidence stacks up favorably. Flextime tends to reduce absenteeism and frequently improves worker productivity,[20] probably for several reasons. Employees can schedule their work hours to align with personal demands, reducing tardiness and absences, and they can work when they are most productive. Flextime can also help employees balance work and family lives; it is a popular criterion for judging how "family friendly" a workplace is.

Flextime's major drawback is that it's not applicable to every job or every worker. It works well with clerical tasks for which an employee's interaction with people outside his department is limited. It is not a viable option for receptionists, sales personnel in retail stores, or people whose service jobs require them to be at their workstations at predetermined times. It also appears that people who have a stronger desire to separate their

EXHIBIT 8-3
Example of
a Flextime
Schedule

Schedule 1	
Percent Time:	100% = 40 hours per week
Core Hours:	9:00 AM–5:00 PM, Monday through Friday (1-hour lunch)
Work Start Time:	Between 8:00 AM and 9:00 AM
Work End Time:	Between 5:00 PM and 6:00 PM

Schedule 2	
Percent Time:	100% = 40 hours per week
Work Hours:	8:00 AM–6:30 PM, Monday through Thursday (1/2-hour lunch)
	Friday off
Work Start Time:	8:00 AM
Work End Time:	6:30 PM

Schedule 3	
Percent Time:	90% = 36 hours per week
Work Hours:	8:30 AM–5:00 PM, Monday through Thursday (1/2-hour lunch)
	8:00 AM–Noon Friday (no lunch)
Work Start Time:	8:30 AM (Monday–Thursday); 8:00 AM (Friday)
Work End Time:	5:00 PM (Monday–Thursday); Noon (Friday)

Schedule 4	
Percent Time:	80% = 32 hours per week
	8:00 AM–6:00 PM, Monday through Wednesday (1/2-hour lunch)
Work Hours:	8:00 AM–11:30 AM Thursday (no lunch)
	Friday off
Work Start Time:	Between 8:00 AM and 9:00 AM
Work End Time:	Between 5:00 PM and 6:00 PM

work and family lives are less prone to take advantage of opportunities for flextime.[21] Overall, employers need to consider the appropriateness of both the work and the workers before implementing flextime schedules.

JOB SHARING **Job sharing** allows two or more individuals to split a traditional 40-hour-a-week job. One might perform the job from 8:00 AM to noon and the other from 1:00 PM to 5:00 PM, or the two could work full but alternate days. For example, top Ford engineers Julie Levine and Julie Rocco engage in a job-sharing program that allows both of them to spend time with their families while working on the time-intensive job of redesigning the Explorer crossover. Typically, one of the pair will work late afternoons and evenings while the other works mornings. They both agree that the program has worked well, although making such a relationship work requires a great deal of time and preparation.[22]

Approximately 19 percent of large organizations now offer job sharing.[23] Reasons it is not more widely adopted are likely the difficulty of finding compatible partners to share a job and the historically negative perceptions of individuals not completely committed to their jobs and employers.

Job sharing allows an organization to draw on the talents of more than one individual in a given job. A bank manager who oversees two job sharers describes it as an opportunity to get two heads but "pay for one."[24] It also opens the opportunity to acquire skilled workers—for instance, women with young children and retirees—who might not be available on a full-time basis.[25] Many Japanese firms are increasingly considering job sharing—but for a very different reason.[26] Because Japanese executives are extremely reluctant to fire people, job sharing is seen as a potentially humanitarian means of avoiding layoffs due to overstaffing.

From the employee's perspective, job sharing increases flexibility and can increase motivation and satisfaction when a 40-hour-a-week job is just not practical. But the major drawback is finding compatible pairs of employees who can successfully coordinate the intricacies of one job.[27]

TELECOMMUTING   It might be close to the ideal job for many people. No commuting, flexible hours, freedom to dress as you please, and few or no interruptions from colleagues. It's called **telecommuting**, and it refers to working at home at least 2 days a week on a computer linked to the employer's office.[28] (A closely related term—the *virtual office*—describes working from home on a relatively permanent basis.)

The U.S. Department of the Census estimated there was a 25 percent increase in self-employed home-based workers from 1999 to 2005, and a 20 percent increase in employed workers who work exclusively from home.[29] One recent survey of more than 5,000 HR professionals found that 35 percent of organizations allowed employees to telecommute at least part of the time, and 21 percent allowed employees to telecommute full-time.[30] Well-known organizations that actively encourage telecommuting include AT&T, IBM, American Express, Sun Microsystems, and a number of U.S. government agencies.[31]

What kinds of jobs lend themselves to telecommuting? There are three categories: routine information-handling tasks, mobile activities, and professional and other knowledge-related tasks.[32] Writers, attorneys, analysts, and employees who spend the majority of their time on computers or the telephone—such as telemarketers, customer-service representatives, reservation agents, and product-support specialists—are natural candidates. As telecommuters, they can access information on their computers at home as easily as in the company's office.

The potential pluses of telecommuting include a larger labor pool from which to select, higher productivity, less turnover, improved morale, and reduced office-space costs. A positive relationship exists between telecommuting and supervisor performance ratings, but any relationship between telecommuting and potentially lower turnover intentions has not been substantiated in research to date.[33] The major downside for management is less direct supervision of employees. In today's team-focused workplace, telecommuting may make it more difficult to coordinate teamwork and can reduce knowledge transfer in organizations.[34] From the employee's standpoint, telecommuting can offer a considerable increase in flexibility and job satisfaction—but not without costs.[35] For employees with a high social need, telecommuting can increase feelings of isolation and reduce job satisfaction. And all telecommuters are vulnerable to the "out of sight, out of mind" effect.[36] Employees who aren't at their desks, who miss meetings, and who don't share in day-to-day informal workplace interactions may be at a disadvantage when it comes to raises and promotions.

The Social and Physical Context of Work

Robin and Chris both graduated from college a couple years ago with degrees in elementary education and became first-grade teachers in different school districts. Robin immediately confronted a number of obstacles: several long-term employees were hostile to her hiring, there was tension between administrators and teachers, and students had little interest in learning. Chris, conversely, had a colleague who was excited to work with a new graduate, students who were excited about academics, and a highly supportive principal. Not surprisingly, at the end of the first year, Chris had become a considerably more effective teacher than Robin.

The job characteristics model shows most employees are more motivated and satisfied when their intrinsic work tasks are engaging. However, having the most interesting workplace characteristics in the world may not always lead to satisfaction if you feel isolated from your co-workers, and having good social relationships can make even the most boring and onerous tasks more fulfilling. Research demonstrates that social aspects and work context are as important as other job design features.[37] Policies such as job rotation, worker empowerment, and employee participation have positive effects on productivity, at least partially because they encourage more communication and a positive social environment.

Some social characteristics that improve job performance include interdependence, social support, and interactions with other people outside work. Social interactions are strongly related to positive moods and give employees more opportunities to clarify their work roles and how well they are performing. Social support gives employees greater opportunities to obtain assistance with their work. Constructive social relationships can bring about a positive feedback loop as employees assist one another in a "virtuous circle."

The work context is also likely to affect employee satisfaction. Hot, loud, and dangerous work is less satisfying than work conducted in climate-controlled, relatively quiet, and safe environments. This is probably why most people would rather work in a coffee shop than a metalworking foundry. Physical demands make people physically uncomfortable, which is likely to show up in lower levels of job satisfaction.

To assess why an employee is not performing to her best level, see whether the work environment is supportive. Does the employee have adequate tools, equipment, materials, and supplies? Does the employee have favorable working conditions, helpful co-workers, supportive work rules and procedures, sufficient information to make job-related decisions, and adequate time to do a good job? If not, performance will suffer.

EMPLOYEE INVOLVEMENT

Employee involvement is a participative process that uses employees' input to increase their commitment to the organization's success. The logic is that if we engage workers in decisions that affect them and increase their autonomy and control over their work lives, they will become more motivated, more committed to the organization, more productive, and more satisfied with their jobs.[38]

Employee involvement programs differ among countries.[39] A study of four nations, including the United States and India, confirmed the importance of modifying practices to reflect culture.[40] Although U.S. employees readily accepted employee involvement programs, managers in India who tried to empower their employees were rated low by those employees. These reactions are consistent with India's high power–distance culture, which accepts and expects differences in authority. Similarly, Chinese workers who were very accepting of traditional Chinese values showed few benefits from participative decision making, but workers who were less traditional were more satisfied and had higher performance ratings under participative management.[41]

Examples of Employee Involvement Programs

Let's look at two major forms of employee involvement—participative management and representative participation—in more detail.

PARTICIPATIVE MANAGEMENT   Common to all **participative management** programs is joint decision making, in which subordinates share a significant degree of decision-making power with their immediate superiors. Participative management has, at times, been promoted as a panacea for poor morale and low productivity. But for it to work, employees must be engaged in issues relevant to their interests so they'll be motivated, they must have the competence and knowledge to make a useful contribution, and trust and confidence must exist among all parties.[42]

Studies of the participation–performance relationship have yielded mixed findings.[43] Organizations that institute participative management do have higher stock returns, lower turnover rates, and higher estimated labor productivity, although these effects are typically not large.[44] A careful review of research at the individual level shows participation typically has only a modest influence on employee productivity, motivation, and job satisfaction. Of course, this doesn't mean participative management can't be beneficial under the right conditions. However, it is not a sure means for improving performance.

REPRESENTATIVE PARTICIPATION   Almost every country in western Europe requires companies to practice **representative participation**, called "the most widely legislated form of employee involvement around the world."[45] Its goal is to redistribute power within an organization, putting labor on a more equal footing with the interests of management and stockholders by letting workers be represented by a small group of employees who actually participate.

The two most common forms are works councils and board representatives.[46] Works councils are groups of nominated or elected employees who must be consulted when management makes decisions about employees. Board representatives are employees who sit on a company's board of directors and represent employees' interests.

The influence of representative participation on working employees seems to be minimal.[47] Works councils are dominated by management and have little impact on employees or the organization. Although participation might increase the motivation and satisfaction of employee representatives, there is little evidence this trickles down to the employees they represent. Overall, "the greatest value of representative participation is symbolic. If one is interested in changing employee attitudes or in improving organizational performance, representative participation would be a poor choice."[48]

Linking Employee Involvement Programs and Motivation Theories

As opposed to research on the job characteristics model and work redesign, which is mostly favorable, the research evidence on employee involvement programs is decidedly mixed. It is not clear that employee involvement programs have fulfilled their promise.

Employee involvement draws on a number of the motivation theories we discussed in Chapters 7. Theory Y is consistent with participative management and Theory X with the more traditional autocratic style of managing people. In terms of two-factor theory, employee involvement programs could provide intrinsic motivation by increasing opportunities for growth, responsibility, and involvement in the work itself. The opportunity to make and implement decisions—and then see them work out—can help satisfy an employee's needs for responsibility, achievement, recognition, growth, and enhanced self-esteem. And extensive employee involvement programs clearly have the potential to increase employee intrinsic motivation in work tasks.

USING REWARDS TO MOTIVATE EMPLOYEES

As we saw in Chapters 3, pay is not a primary factor driving job satisfaction. However, it does motivate people, and companies often underestimate its importance in keeping top talent. A 2006 study found that while 45 percent of employers thought pay was a key factor in losing top talent, 71 percent of top performers called it a top reason.[49]

Given that pay is so important, will the organization lead, match, or lag the market in pay? How will individual contributions be recognized? In this section, we consider (1) what to pay employees (decided by establishing a pay structure), (2) how to pay individual employees (decided through variable pay plans and skill-based pay plans), (3) what benefits and choices to offer (such as flexible benefits), and (4) how to construct employee recognition programs.

What to Pay: Establishing a Pay Structure

There are many ways to pay employees. The process of initially setting pay levels entails balancing *internal equity*—the worth of the job to the organization (usually established through a technical process called job evaluation)—and *external equity*—the external competitiveness of an organization's pay relative to pay elsewhere in its industry (usually established through pay surveys). Obviously, the best pay system pays what the job is worth (internal equity) while also paying competitively relative to the labor market.

Some organizations prefer to pay above the market, while some may lag the market because they can't afford to pay market rates, or they are willing to bear the costs of paying below market (namely, higher turnover as people are lured to better-paying jobs). Walmart, for example, pays less than its competitors and often outsources jobs overseas. Chinese workers in Shenzhen earn $120 a month (that's $1,440 per year) to make stereos for Walmart. Of the 6,000 factories that are worldwide suppliers to Walmart, 80 percent are located in China. In fact, one-eighth of all Chinese exports to the United States go to Walmart.[50]

Variable-pay plans, when properly designed and administered, do appear to enhance employee motivation.

Pay more, and you may get better-qualified, more highly motivated employees who will stay with the organization longer. A study covering 126 large organizations found employees who believed they were receiving a competitive pay level had higher morale and were more productive, and customers were more satisfied as well.[51] But pay is often the highest single operating cost for an organization, which means paying too much can make the organization's products or services too expensive. It's a strategic decision an organization must make, with clear trade-offs.

How to Pay: Rewarding Individual Employees Through Variable-Pay Programs

"Why should I put any extra effort into this job?" asked Anne Garcia, a fourth-grade elementary schoolteacher in Denver, Colorado. "I can excel or I can do the bare minimum. It makes no difference. I get paid the same. Why do anything above the minimum to get by?" Comments like Anne's have been voiced by schoolteachers for decades because pay increases were tied to seniority. Recently, however, a number of states have revamped their compensation systems to motivate people like Anne by tying teacher pay levels to results in the classroom in various ways, and other states are considering such programs.[52]

A number of organizations are moving away from paying solely on credentials or length of service. Piece-rate plans, merit-based pay, bonuses, skill-based pay, profit sharing, gainsharing, and employee stock ownership plans are all forms of a **variable-pay program**, which bases a portion of an employee's pay on some individual and/or organizational measure of performance. Earnings therefore fluctuate up and down.[53]

The fluctuation in variable pay is what makes these programs attractive to management. It turns part of an organization's fixed labor costs into a variable cost, thus reducing expenses when performance declines. When the U.S. economy encountered a recession in 2001 and 2008, companies with variable pay were able to reduce their labor costs much faster than others.[54] When pay is tied to performance, the employee's earnings also recognize contribution rather than being a form of entitlement. Over time, low performers' pay stagnates, while high performers enjoy pay increases commensurate with their contributions.

Let's examine the different types of variable-pay programs in more detail.

1. *Piece-Rate Pay.* The **piece-rate pay plan** has long been popular as a means of compensating production workers with a fixed sum for each unit of production completed. A pure piece-rate plan provides no base salary and pays the employee only for what she produces. Ballpark workers selling peanuts and soda are frequently paid this way. If they sell 40 bags of peanuts at $1 each, their take is $40. The harder they work and the more peanuts they sell, the more they earn. The limitation of these plans is that they're not feasible for many jobs. Surgeons earn significant salaries regardless of their patients' outcomes. Would it be better to pay them only if their patients fully recover? It seems unlikely that most would accept such a deal, and it might cause unanticipated consequences as well (such as surgeons avoiding patients with complicated or terminal conditions). So, although incentives are motivating and relevant for some jobs, it is unrealistic to think they can constitute the only piece of some employees' pay.

2. *Merit-Based Pay.* A **merit-based pay plan** pays for individual performance based on performance appraisal ratings. A main advantage is that people thought to be high performers can get bigger raises. If designed correctly, merit-based plans let individuals perceive a strong relationship between their performance and their rewards.[55] Despite their intuitive appeal, merit pay plans have several limitations. One is that they are typically based on an annual performance appraisal and thus are only as valid as the performance ratings. Another limitation is that the pay-raise pool fluctuates on economic or other conditions that have little to do with individual performance. One year, a colleague at a top university who performed very well in teaching and research was given a pay raise of $300. Why? Because the pay-raise pool was very small. Yet that is hardly pay-for-performance. Finally, unions typically resist merit pay plans. Relatively few teachers are covered by merit pay for this reason. Instead, seniority-based pay, where all employees get the same raises, predominates.

3. *Bonuses.* An annual **bonus** is a significant component of total compensation for many jobs. The incentive effects of performance bonuses should be higher than those of merit pay because, rather than paying for performance years ago (that was rolled into base pay), bonuses reward recent performance. When times are bad, firms can cut bonuses to reduce compensation costs. Steel company Nucor, for example, guarantees employees only about $10 per hour, but bonuses can be substantial. In 2006, the average Nucor worker made roughly $91,000. When the recession hit, bonuses were cut dramatically: in 2009, total pay had dropped 40 percent.[56] This example also highlights the downside of bonuses: employees' pay is more vulnerable to cuts. This is problematic when bonuses are a large percentage of total pay or when employees take bonuses for granted.

4. *Skill-Based Pay.* **Skill-based pay** (also called *competency-based* or *knowledge-based pay*) is an alternative to job-based pay that centers pay levels on how many skills employees have or how many jobs they can do.[57] For employers, the lure of skill-based pay plans is increased flexibility of the workforce: staffing is easier when employee skills are interchangeable. Skill-based pay also facilitates communication across the organization because people gain a better understanding of each other's jobs. One study found that across 214 different organizations, skill-based pay was related to higher levels of workforce flexibility, positive attitudes, membership behaviors, and productivity.[58] Another study found that over 5 years, a skill-based pay plan was associated with higher levels of individual skill change and skill maintenance.[59] These results suggest that skill-based pay plans are effective in achieving their stated goals. What about the downsides? People can "top out"—that is, they can learn all the skills the program calls for them to learn. This can frustrate employees after they've been challenged by an environment of learning, growth, and continual pay raises. Finally, skill-based plans don't address level of performance but only whether someone can perform the skill. Perhaps reflecting these weaknesses, one study of 97 U.S. companies using skill-based pay plans found that 39 percent had switched to a more traditional market-based pay plan 7 years later.[60]

5. *Profit-Sharing Plans.* A **profit-sharing plan** distributes compensation based on some established formula designed around a company's profitability. Compensation can be direct cash outlays or, particularly for top managers, allocations of stock options. When you read about executives like Oracle's Larry Ellison earning $75.33 million in pay, it almost all (88.8 percent in Ellison's case) comes from cashing in stock options previously granted based on company profit performance. Not all profit-sharing plans are so grand in scale. Jacob Luke, age 13, started his own lawn-mowing business after getting a mower from his uncle. Jacob employs his brother, Isaiah, and friend, Marcel Monroe, and pays them each 25 percent of the profits he makes on each yard. Profit-sharing plans at the organizational level appear to have positive impacts on employee attitudes; employees report a greater feeling of psychological ownership.[61]

6. *Gainsharing.* **Gainsharing**[62] is a formula-based group incentive plan that uses improvements in group productivity from one period to another to determine the total amount of money allocated. Its popularity seems narrowly focused among large manufacturing companies, although some health care organizations have experimented with it as a cost-saving mechanism. Gainsharing differs from profit sharing

in tying rewards to productivity gains rather than profits, so employees can receive incentive awards even when the organization isn't profitable. Because the benefits accrue to groups of workers, high performers pressure weaker ones to work harder, improving performance for the group as a whole.[63]

7. ***Employee Stock Ownership Plans.*** An **employee stock ownership plan (ESOP)** is a company-established benefit plan in which employees acquire stock, often at below-market prices, as part of their benefits. Research on ESOPs indicates they increase employee satisfaction and innovation.[64] But their impact on performance is less clear. ESOPs have the potential to increase employee job satisfaction and work motivation, but employees need to psychologically experience ownership.[65] That is, in addition to their financial stake in the company, they need to be kept regularly informed of the status of the business and have the opportunity to influence it in order to significantly improve the organization's performance.[66] ESOP plans for top management can reduce unethical behavior. CEOs are more likely to manipulate firm earnings reports if unfavorable to make themselves look good in the short run when they don't have an ownership share, even though this manipulation may eventually lead to lower stock prices. However, when CEOs own a large amount of stock, they report earnings accurately, partly because they view themselves as company owners; also, they don't want the greater potential negative consequences such as the loss of their positions if exposed.[67]

EVALUATION OF VARIABLE PAY Do variable-pay programs increase motivation and productivity? Studies generally support the idea that organizations with profit-sharing plans have higher levels of profitability than those without them.[68] Profit-sharing plans have also been linked to higher levels of employee affective commitment, especially in small organizations.[69] Similarly, gainsharing has been found to improve productivity in a majority of cases and often has a positive impact on employee attitudes.[70] Economist Ed Lazear seems generally right when he says, "Workers respond to prices just as economic theory predicts. Claims by sociologists and others that monetizing incentives may actually reduce output are unambiguously refuted by the data." But that doesn't mean everyone responds positively to variable-pay plans.[71] A study found that whereas piece-rate pay-for-performance plans stimulated higher levels of productivity, this positive effect was not observed for risk-averse employees.

You'd probably think individual pay systems such as merit pay or pay-for-performance work better in individualistic cultures such as the United States or that group-based rewards such as gainsharing or profit sharing work better in collectivistic cultures. Unfortunately, there isn't much research on the issue. One recent study did suggest that employee beliefs about the fairness of a group incentive plan were more predictive of pay satisfaction in the United States than in Hong Kong. This could mean that U.S. employees are more critical in appraising a group pay plan, and therefore, it's more important that the plan be communicated clearly and administered fairly.[72]

Flexible Benefits: Developing a Benefits Package

Consistent with expectancy theory's thesis that organizational rewards should be linked to employees' individual goals, **flexible benefits** individualize rewards by allowing each employee to choose the compensation package that best satisfies his current needs and situation. These plans replace the "one-benefit-plan-fits-all" programs designed for a male with a wife and two children at home that dominated organizations for more than 50 years.[73] Fewer than 10 percent of employees now fit this image: about 25 percent are single, and one-third are part of two-income families with no children. Flexible benefits can accommodate differences in employee needs based on age, marital status, partner's benefit status, and number and age of dependents.

Today, almost all major corporations in the United States offer flexible benefits. And they're becoming the norm in other countries and in small companies, too. A recent survey of 211 Canadian organizations found that 60 percent offer flexible benefits, up from 41 percent in 2005.[74] A similar survey of firms in the United Kingdom found that nearly all major organizations were offering flexible benefits programs, with options ranging from private supplemental medical insurance to holiday trading (with co-workers), discounted bus travel, and child-care assistance.[75]

Intrinsic Rewards: Employee Recognition Programs

Laura Schendell makes only $8.50 per hour working at her fast-food job in Pensacola, Florida, and the job isn't very challenging or interesting. Yet Laura talks enthusiastically about the job, her boss, and the company that employs her. "What I like is the fact that Guy [her supervisor] appreciates the effort I make. He compliments me regularly in front of the other people on my shift, and I've been chosen Employee of the Month twice in the past six months. Did you see my picture on that plaque on the wall?"

Organizations are increasingly recognizing what Laura knows: important work rewards can be both intrinsic and extrinsic. Rewards are intrinsic in the form of employee recognition programs and extrinsic in the form of compensation systems. In this section, we deal with ways in which managers can reward and motivate employee performance.

Employee recognition programs range from a spontaneous and private thank-you to widely publicized formal programs in which specific types of behavior are encouraged and the procedures for attaining recognition are clearly identified. Some research suggests financial incentives and benefits may be more motivating in the short term, but in the long run it's nonfinancial incentives.[76]

A few years ago, 1,500 employees were surveyed in a variety of work settings to find out what they considered the most powerful workplace motivator. Their response? Recognition, recognition, and more recognition.

An obvious advantage of recognition programs is that they are inexpensive, since praise is free![77] As companies and government organizations face tighter budgets, nonfinancial incentives become more attractive. Everett Clinic in Washington State uses a combination of local and centralized initiatives to encourage managers to recognize employees.[78] Employees and managers give "Hero Grams" and "Caught in the Act" cards to colleagues for exceptional accomplishments at work. Part of the incentive is simply to receive recognition, but there are also drawings for prizes based on the number of cards a person receives. Managers are trained to use the programs frequently and effectively to reward good performance. Multinational corporations like Symantec Corporation have also increased their use of recognition programs. Centralized programs across multiple offices in different countries can help ensure that all employees, regardless of where they work, can be recognized for their contribution to the work environment.[79] Another study found that recognition programs are common in both Canadian and Australian firms as well.[80]

Despite the increased popularity of employee recognition programs, critics argue they are highly susceptible to political manipulation by management. When applied to jobs for which performance factors are relatively objective, such as sales, recognition programs are likely to be perceived by employees as fair. However, in most jobs, the criteria for good performance aren't self-evident, which allows managers to manipulate the system and recognize their favorites. Abuse can undermine the value of recognition programs and demoralize employees.

SUMMARY AND IMPLICATIONS FOR MANAGERS

Although it's always dangerous to synthesize a large number of complex ideas, the following suggestions summarize what we know about motivating employees in organizations.

- *Recognize Individual Differences.* Managers should be sensitive to individual differences. For example, employees from Asian cultures prefer not to be singled out as special because it makes them uncomfortable. Spend the time necessary to understand what's important to each employee. This allows you to individualize goals, level of involvement, and rewards to align with individual needs. Design jobs to align with individual needs and maximize their motivation potential.
- *Use Goals and Feedback.* Employees should have firm, specific goals, and they should get feedback on how well they are faring in pursuit of those goals.
- *Allow Employees to Participate in Decisions That Affect Them.* Employees can contribute to setting work goals, choosing their own benefits packages, and solving productivity and quality problems. Participation can increase employee productivity, commitment to work goals, motivation, and job satisfaction.
- *Link Rewards to Performance.* Rewards should be contingent on performance, and employees must perceive the link between the two. Regardless of how strong the relationship is, if individuals perceive it to be weak, the results will be low performance, a decrease in job satisfaction, and an increase in turnover and absenteeism.
- *Check the System for Equity.* Employees should perceive that experience, skills, abilities, effort, and other obvious inputs explain differences in performance and hence in pay, job assignments, and other obvious rewards.

MyManagementLab

Go to **MyManagementLab.com** to access study plans, interactive lectures, and videos as well as Auto-graded writing questions and the following Assisted-graded writing question.

8-1. MyManagementLab Only—comprehensive writing assignment for this chapter.

PART 3: Groups in the Organization

9
■ ■ ■
Foundations of Group Behavior

After studying this chapter, you should be able to:

- Define *group* and distinguish the different types of groups.
- Identify the five stages of group development.
- Show how role requirements change in different situations.
- Demonstrate how norms and status exert influence on an individual's behavior.
- Contrast the strengths and weaknesses of group decision making.

DEFINING AND CLASSIFYING GROUPS

We define a **group** as two or more individuals, interacting and interdependent, who have come together to achieve particular objectives. Groups can be either formal or informal.

By a **formal group**, we mean one defined by the organization's structure, with designated work assignments establishing tasks. In formal groups, the behaviors team members should engage in are stipulated by and directed toward organizational goals. The six members of an airline flight crew are a formal group, for example. In contrast, an **informal group** is neither formally structured nor organizationally determined. Informal groups are natural formations in the work environment that appear in response to the need for social contact. Three employees from different departments who regularly have lunch or coffee together are an informal group. These types of interactions among individuals, though informal, deeply affect their behavior and performance.

Groups can be formal as well as informal; regardless of the type of group, group norms, roles, and identities have powerful effects on individuals' behavior.

It's possible to further subclassify groups as command, task, interest, or friendship groups.[1] Command and task groups are dictated by formal organization, whereas interest and friendship groups are informal alliances.

A **command group** is determined by the organization chart. It is composed of the individuals who report directly to a given manager. An elementary school principal and her 18 teachers form a command group, as do a director of postal audits and his five inspectors.

A **task group**, also organizationally determined, represents individuals working together to complete a job task. However, a task group's boundaries are not limited to its immediate hierarchical superior; the group can cross command relationships. If a college student is accused of a campus crime, dealing with the problem might require coordination among the dean of academic affairs, the dean of students, the registrar, the director of security, and the student's advisor. Such a formation constitutes a task group. All command groups are also task groups. But because task groups can cut across the organization, they are not always command groups.

Whether they are together or not in command groups or task groups, people may affiliate to attain a specific objective with which each individual is concerned. This creates an **interest group**. Employees who band together to have their vacation schedules altered, to support a peer who has been fired, or to seek improved working conditions have formed a united body to further their common interest.

Groups often develop because individual members have one or more common characteristics. We call these formations **friendship groups**. Social alliances, which frequently extend outside the work situation, can be based on common age or ethnic heritage, support for Notre Dame football, interest in the same alternative rock band, or similar political views, to name just a few such characteristics.

There is no single reason individuals join groups. Because most people belong to a number of groups, it's obvious that different groups provide different benefits to their members. Exhibit 9-1 summarizes the most popular reasons people have for joining groups.

Security.   By joining a group, individuals can reduce the insecurity of "standing alone." People feel stronger, have fewer self-doubts, and are more resistant to threats when they are part of a group.

Status.   Inclusion in a group that is viewed as important by others provides recognition and status for its members.

Self-esteem.   Groups can provide people with feelings of self-worth. That is, in addition to conveying status to those outside the group, membership can also give increased feelings of worth to the group members.

Affiliation.   Groups can fulfill social needs. People enjoy the regular interactiorn that comes with group membership. For many people, these on-the-job interactions are their primary sources for fulfilling their needs for affiliation.

Power.   What cannot be achieved individually often becomes possible through group action. There is power in numbers.

Goal achievement.   There are times when it takes more than one person to accomplish a particular task—there is a need to pool talents, knowledge, or power in order to complete a job. In such instances, management will rely on the use of a formal group.

EXHIBIT 9-1

Why Do People Join Groups?

STAGES OF GROUP DEVELOPMENT

Groups generally pass through a predictable sequence in their evolution. Although not all groups follow this five-stage model,[2] it is a useful framework for understanding group development. In this section, we describe the five-stage model and an alternative for temporary groups with deadlines.

The Five-Stage Model

As shown in Exhibit 9-2, the **five-stage group-development model** characterizes groups as proceeding through the distinct stages of forming, storming, norming, performing, and adjourning.[3]

The first stage, **forming stage**, is characterized by a great deal of uncertainty about the group's purpose, structure, and leadership. Members "test the waters" to determine what types of behaviors are acceptable. This stage is complete when members have begun to think of themselves as part of a group.

The **storming stage** is one of intragroup conflict. Members accept the existence of the group but resist the constraints it imposes on individuality. There is conflict over who will control the group. When this stage is complete, there will be a relatively clear hierarchy of leadership within the group.

In the third stage, close relationships develop and the group demonstrates cohesiveness. There is now a strong sense of group identity and camaraderie. This **norming stage** is complete when the group structure solidifies and the group has assimilated a common set of expectations of what defines correct member behavior.

The fourth stage is **performing**. The structure at this point is fully functional and accepted. Group energy has moved from getting to know and understand each other to performing the task at hand.

For permanent work groups, performing is the last stage in development. However, for temporary committees, teams, task forces, and similar groups that have a limited task to perform, the **adjourning stage** is for wrapping up activities and preparing to disband. Some group members are upbeat, basking in the group's accomplishments. Others may be depressed over the loss of camaraderie and friendships gained during the work group's life.

Many interpreters of the five-stage model have assumed a group becomes more effective as it progresses through the first four stages. Although this may be generally true, what makes a group effective is actually more complex.[4] First, groups proceed through the stages of group development at different rates. Those with a strong sense of purpose and strategy rapidly achieve high performance and improve over time, whereas those with less sense of purpose actually see their performance worsen over time. Similarly, groups that begin with a positive social focus (reward) appear to achieve the "performing"stage more rapidly. Nor do groups always proceed clearly from one stage to the next. Storming and performing can occur simultaneously, and groups can even regress to previous stages.

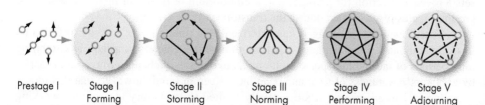

| Prestage I | Stage I Forming | Stage II Storming | Stage III Norming | Stage IV Performing | Stage V Adjourning |

EXHIBIT 9-2
Stages of Group Development

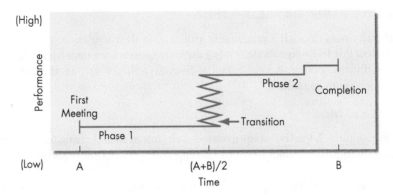

EXHIBIT 9-3

Groups and Deviant Behavior

Source: A. Erez, H. Elms, and E. Fong, "Lying, Cheating, Stealing: Groups and the Ring of Gyges,"paper presented at the Academy of Management Annual Meeting, Honolulu, HI, August 8, 2005. Reprinted by permission of the authors.

An Alternative Model for Temporary Groups with Deadlines

Temporary groups with deadlines don't seem to follow the usual five stage model. Studies indicate they have their own unique sequencing of actions (or inaction): (1) their first meeting sets the group's direction, (2) this first phase of group activity is one of inertia, (3) a transition takes place exactly when the group has used up half its allotted time, (4) this transition initiates major changes, (5) a second phase of inertia follows the transition, and (6) the group's last meeting is characterized by markedly accelerated activity.[5] This pattern, called the **punctuated-equilibrium model**, is shown in Exhibit 9-3.

The first meeting sets a framework of behavioral patterns and assumptions through which the group will approach its project emerges, sometimes in the first few seconds of the group's existence. Once set, the group's direction is solidified and is unlikely to be reexamined throughout the first half of its life. This is a period of inertia—the group tends to stand still or become locked into a fixed course of action even if it gains new insights that challenge initial patterns and assumptions.

One of the most interesting discoveries[6] was that each group experienced its transition precisely halfway between its first meeting and its official deadline—whether members spent an hour on their project or 6 months. The midpoint appears to work like an alarm clock, heightening members' awareness that project time is limited and they need to get moving. This transition ends phase 1 and is characterized by a concentrated burst of changes, dropping of old patterns, and adoption of new perspectives. The transition sets a revised direction for phase 2, a new equilibrium or period of inertia in which the group executes plans created during the transition period.

The group's last meeting is characterized by a final burst of activity to finish its work. In summary, the punctuated-equilibrium model characterizes groups as exhibiting long periods of inertia interspersed with brief revolutionary changes triggered primarily by members' awareness of time and deadlines. Keep in mind, however, that this model doesn't apply to all groups. It's essentially limited to temporary task groups working under a time-constrained completion deadline.[7]

GROUP PROPERTIES: ROLES, NORMS, STATUS, SIZE, COHESIVENESS, AND DIVERSITY

Work groups are not unorganized mobs; they have properties that shape members' behavior and help explain and predict individual behavior within the group as well as the performance of the group itself. Some of these properties are roles, norms, status, size, cohesiveness, and diversity.

Group Property 1: Roles

Shakespeare said, "All the world's a stage, and all the men and women merely players." Using the same metaphor, all group members are actors, each playing a **role**. By this term, we mean a set of expected behavior patterns attributed to someone occupying a given position in a social unit. Our understanding of role behavior would be dramatically simplified if each of us could choose one role and play it regularly and consistently. Instead, we are required to play a number of diverse roles, both on and off our jobs. As we'll see, one of the tasks in understanding behavior is grasping the role a person is currently playing.

Bill Patterson is a plant manager with EMM Industries, a large electrical equipment manufacturer in Phoenix. He fulfills a number of roles—EMM employee, member of middle management, electrical engineer, and primary company spokesperson in the community. Off the job, Bill Patterson finds himself in still more roles: husband, father, Catholic, tennis player, member of the Thunderbird Country Club, and president of his homeowners' association. Many of these roles are compatible; some create conflicts. How does Bill's religious commitment influence his managerial decisions regarding layoffs, expense account padding, and provision of accurate information to government agencies? A recent offer of promotion requires Bill to relocate, yet his family wants to stay in Phoenix. Can the role demands of his job be reconciled with the demands of his husband and father roles?

Like Bill Patterson, we are all required to play a number of roles, and our behavior varies with each. Different groups impose different role requirements on individuals.

ROLE PERCEPTION   Our view of how we're supposed to act in a given situation is a **role perception**. We get role perceptions from stimuli all around us—for example, friends, books, films, television, as when we form an impression of the work of doctors from watching *Grey's Anatomy*. Apprenticeship programs allow beginners to watch an expert so they can learn to act as they should.

ROLE EXPECTATIONS   **Role expectations** are the way others believe you should act in a given context. The role of a U.S. federal judge is viewed as having propriety and dignity, whereas a football coach is seen as aggressive, dynamic, and inspiring to his players.

ROLE CONFLICT   When compliance with one role requirement may make it difficult to comply with another, the result is **role conflict**.[8] For example, if you were asked to provide feedback on your supervisor's performance, your role as evaluator for that task and employee of that person would conflict. At the extreme, two or more role expectations are mutually contradictory.

Group Property 2: Norms

Did you ever notice that golfers don't speak while their partners are putting on the green or that employees don't criticize their bosses in public? Why not? The answer is norms.

All groups have established **norms**—acceptable standards of behavior shared by their members that express what they ought and ought not to do under certain circumstances. When agreed to and accepted by the group, norms influence members' behavior with a minimum of external controls. Different groups, communities, and societies have different norms, but they all have them.[9]

Norms can cover virtually any aspect of group behavior.[10] Probably the most common is a *performance norm,* providing explicit cues about how hard members should work, what the level of output should be, how to get the job done, what level of tardiness is appropriate, and the like. These norms are extremely powerful and are capable of significantly modifying a performance prediction based solely on ability and level of personal motivation. Other norms include *appearance norms* (dress codes, unspoken rules about when to look busy), *social arrangement norms* (with whom to eat lunch, whether to form friendships on and off the job), and *resource allocation norms* (assignment of difficult jobs, distribution of resources like pay or equipment).

THE HAWTHORNE STUDIES   Full-scale appreciation of the influence of norms on worker behavior did not occur until the early 1930s, following studies undertaken between 1924 and 1932 at the Western Electric Company's Hawthorne Works in Chicago.[11]

The Hawthorne researchers began by examining the relationship between the physical environment and productivity. As they increased the light level for the experimental group of workers, output rose for that unit and the control group. But to their surprise, as they dropped the light level in the experimental group, productivity continued to increase in both groups. In fact, productivity in the experimental group decreased only when the light intensity had been reduced to that of moonlight.

As a follow-up, the researchers began a second set of experiments at Western Electric. A small group of women assembling telephone relays was isolated from the main work group so their behavior could be more carefully observed. Observations covering a multiyear period found this small group's output increased steadily. The number of personal and out-sick absences was approximately one-third that recorded by women in the regular production department. It became evident this group's performance was significantly influenced by its status as "special." The members thought being in the experimental group was fun, that they were in an elite group, and that management showed concern about their interests by engaging in such experimentation. In essence, workers in both the illumination and assembly-test-room experiments were really reacting to the increased attention they received.

A third study, in the bank wiring observation room, was introduced to study the effect of a sophisticated wage incentive plan for the group. The most important finding was that employees did not individually maximize their outputs. Rather, their output became controlled by a group norm that determined what was a proper day's work even with the awareness of the share of incentive each would earn. Interviews determined the group was operating well below its capability and was leveling output to protect itself. Members were afraid that if they significantly increased their output, the unit incentive rate would be eliminated, the expected daily output would be increased, layoffs might occur, or slower workers would be reprimanded. So the group established its idea of a fair output—neither too much nor too little. Members helped each other ensure their reports were nearly level.

The norms the group established included a number of "don'ts." *Don't* be a rate-buster, turning out too much work. *Don't* be a chiseler, turning out too little work. *Don't* squeal on any of your peers. How did the group enforce these norms? The methods included sarcasm, name-calling, ridicule, and even punches to the upper arm of any member who violated the group's norms. Members also ostracized individuals whose behavior was against the group's interest.

CONFORMITY   As a member of a group, you desire acceptance by the group. Thus you are susceptible to conforming to the group's norms. Considerable evidence suggests groups can place strong pressures on individual members to change their attitudes and behaviors to conform to the group's standard.[12] There are numerous reasons for conformity, with recent research highlighting the importance of a desire to develop meaningful social relationships with others or to maintain a favorable self-concept.

The impact that group pressures for **conformity** can have on an individual member's judgment was demonstrated in now-classic studies by Solomon Asch.[13] Asch made up groups of seven or eight people who were asked to compare two cards held by the experimenter. One card had one line, and the other had three lines of varying length, one of which was identical to the line on the one-line card, as Exhibit 9-4 shows. The difference in line length was quite obvious; in fact, under ordinary conditions, subjects made fewer than 1 percent errors in announcing aloud which of the three lines matched the single line. But what happens if members of the group begin giving incorrect answers? Will pressure to conform cause an unsuspecting subject (USS) to alter an answer? Asch arranged the group so only the USS was unaware the experiment was rigged. The seating was prearranged so the USS was one of the last to announce a decision.

The experiment began with several sets of matching exercises. All the subjects gave the right answers. On the third set, however, the first subject gave an obviously wrong answer—for example, saying "C" in Exhibit 9-4. The next subject gave the same wrong answer, and so did the others. Now the dilemma confronting the USS was this: publicly state a perception that differs from the announced position of the others in the group, or give an incorrect answer in order to agree with the others.

The results over many experiments and trials showed 75 percent of subjects gave at least one answer that conformed—that they knew was wrong but was consistent with the replies of other group members—and the average conformer gave wrong answers 37 percent of the time. What meaning can we draw from these results? They suggest group norms press us toward conformity. We desire to be one of the group and therefore avoid being visibly different.

Conformity is a problem with groups; managers should encourage group leaders to actively seek input from all members and avoid expressing their own opinions, especially in the early stages of deliberation.

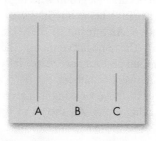

EXHIBIT 9-4

The Punctuated-Equilibrium Model

This research was conducted more than 50 years ago. Has time altered the conclusions' validity? And should we consider them generalizable across cultures? Evidence indicates levels of conformity have steadily declined since Asch's studies in the early 1950s, and his findings *are* culture-bound to the United States.[14] Conformity to social norms is even higher in collectivist cultures, but it is obviously or conclusively still a powerful force in groups in individualistic countries.

Do individuals conform to the pressures of all the groups to which they belong? Obviously not, because people belong to many groups, and their norms vary and sometimes are contradictory. So what do people do? We conform to the important groups (according to our perception) to which we belong or hope to belong. These important groups are **reference groups**, in which a person is aware of other members, defines himself as a member or would like to be a member, and feels group members are significant to him. The implication, then, is that all groups cannot impose equal conformity pressures on their members, since their importance is in the eye of the perceiver.

DEVIANT WORKPLACE BEHAVIOR LeBron Hunt is frustrated by a co-worker who constantly spreads malicious and unsubstantiated rumors about him. Debra Hundley is tired of a member of her work team who, when confronted with a problem, takes out his frustration by yelling and screaming at her and other members. And Mi Cha Kim recently quit her job as a dental hygienist after being constantly sexually harassed by her employer.

What do these three episodes have in common? They represent employees exposed to acts of deviant workplace behavior.[15] As we've briefly discussed in a previous chapter, **deviant workplace behavior** (also called *counterproductive behavior* or *employee withdrawal*) is voluntary behavior that violates significant organizational norms and, in doing so, threatens the well-being of the organization or its members.

Few organizations will admit to creating or condoning conditions that encourage and maintain deviant norms. Yet they exist. Employees report an increase in rudeness and disregard toward others by bosses and co-workers in recent years. And nearly half of employees who have suffered this incivility say it has led them to think about changing jobs; 12 percent actually quit because of it.[16] A study of nearly 1,500 respondents found that in addition to increasing turnover intentions, incivility at work increased reports of psychological stress and physical illness.[17]

Like norms in general, individual employees' antisocial actions are shaped by the group context within which they work. Evidence demonstrates deviant workplace behavior is likely to flourish where it's supported by group norms.[18] For example, workers who socialize either at or outside work with people who are frequently absent from work are more likely to be absent themselves.[19] What this means for managers is that when deviant workplace norms surface, employee cooperation, commitment, and motivation are likely to suffer.

What are the consequences of workplace deviance for teams? Some research suggests a chain reaction occurs in a group with high levels of dysfunctional behavior.[20] The process begins with negative behaviors like shirking, undermining co-workers, or being generally uncooperative. As a result of these behaviors, the team collectively starts to have negative moods. These negative moods then result in poor coordination of effort and lower levels of group performance, especially when there is a lot of nonverbal negative communication between members.

One study suggests those working in a group are more likely to lie, cheat, and steal than individuals working alone. As shown in Exhibit 9-5, in this study, no individual working alone lied, but 22 percent of those working in groups did. They also were more likely to cheat on a task (55 percent versus 23 percent of individuals working alone) and steal (29 percent compared to 10 percent working alone).[21] Groups provide a shield of anonymity, so someone who might ordinarily be afraid of getting caught can rely on the fact that other group members had the same opportunity, creating a false sense of confidence that may result in more aggressive behavior. Thus, deviant behavior depends on the accepted norms of the group—or even whether an individual is part of a group.[22]

Group Property 3: Status

STATUS   **Status**—a socially defined position or rank given to groups or group members by others—permeates every society. Even the smallest group will develop roles, rights, and rituals to differentiate its members. Status is a significant motivator and has major behavioral consequences when individuals perceive a disparity between what they believe their status is and what others perceive it to be.

WHAT DETERMINES STATUS?   According to **status characteristics theory**, status tends to derive from one of three sources:[23]

1. *The Power a Person Wields Over Others.* Because they likely control the group's resources, people who control the outcomes tend to be perceived as high status.
2. *A Person's Ability to Contribute to a Group's Goals.* People whose contributions are critical to the group's success tend to have high status. Some thought NBA star Kobe Bryant had more say over player decisions than his coaches (though not as much as Bryant wanted!).
3. *An Individual's Personal Characteristics.* Someone whose personal characteristics are positively valued by the group (good looks, intelligence, money, or a friendly personality) typically has higher status than someone with fewer valued attributes.

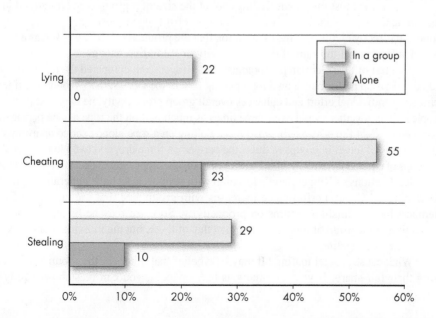

EXHIBIT 9-5

Example of Cards Used in Asch's Study

STATUS AND NORMS Status has some interesting effects on the power of norms and pressures to conform. High-status individuals are often given more freedom to deviate from norms than are other group members.[24] Physicians actively resist administrative decisions made by lower-ranking insurance company employees.[25] High-status people are also better able to resist conformity pressures than their lower-status peers. An individual who is highly valued by a group but doesn't need or care about the group's social rewards is particularly able to disregard conformity norms.[26]

These findings explain why many star athletes, celebrities, top-performing salespeople, and outstanding academics seem oblivious to appearance and social norms that constrain their peers. As high-status individuals, they're given a wider range of discretion as long as their activities aren't severely detrimental to group goal achievement.[27]

STATUS AND GROUP INTERACTION High-status people tend to be more assertive group members.[28] They speak out more often, criticize more, state more commands, and interrupt others more often. But status differences actually inhibit diversity of ideas and creativity in groups, because lower-status members tend to participate less actively in group discussions. When they possess expertise and insights that could aid the group, failure to fully utilize these members reduces the group's overall performance.

Group Property 4: Size

Does the size of a group affect the group's overall behavior? Yes, but the effect depends on what dependent variables we look at. Smaller groups are faster at completing tasks than larger ones, and individuals perform better in smaller groups.[29] However, in problem solving, large groups consistently get better marks than their smaller counterparts.[30] Translating these results into specific numbers is a bit more hazardous, but groups with a dozen or more members are good for gaining diverse input. So if the goal is fact-finding, larger groups should be more effective. Smaller groups of about seven members are better at doing something productive.

One of the most important findings about the size of a group concerns **social loafing**, the tendency for individuals to expend less effort when working collectively than alone.[31] It directly challenges the assumption that the productivity of the group as a whole should at least equal the sum of the productivity of the individuals in it.

As a test of this, German psychologist Max Ringelmann compared the results of individual and group performance on a rope-pulling task in the late 1920s.[32] Wondering if team spirit spurs individual effort and enhances overall group productivity, he expected that three people pulling together would exert three times as much pull on the rope as one person, and eight people eight times as much. One person pulling on a rope alone exerted an average of 63 kilograms of force. In groups of three, the per-person force dropped to 53 kilograms. And in groups of eight, it fell to only 31 kilograms per person, supporting the social loafing theory.

Replications of Ringelmann's research with similar tasks have generally supported his findings.[33] Group performance increases with group size, but the addition of new members has diminishing returns on productivity. So more may be better in that total productivity of a group of four is greater than that of three, but the individual productivity of each member declines.

What causes social loafing? It may be a belief that others in the group are not carrying their fair share. If you see others as lazy or inept, you can reestablish equity by reducing your effort. Another explanation is the dispersion of responsibility. Because group results cannot be attributed to any single person, the relationship between an individual's input and the group's output is clouded. Individuals may then be tempted to become free riders and coast on the group's efforts. The implications for OB are significant. When managers use collective work situations to enhance morale and improve teamwork, they must also be able to identify individual efforts. Otherwise, they must weigh the potential losses in productivity from using groups against the possible gains in worker satisfaction.[34]

Social loafing appears to have a Western bias. It's consistent with individualistic cultures, such as the United States and Canada, that are dominated by self-interest. It is *not* prevalent in collective societies, in which individuals are motivated by in-group goals. In studies comparing U.S. employees with employees from the People's Republic of China and Israel, the Chinese and Israelis showed no propensity to engage in social loafing and actually performed better in a group than alone.

There are several ways to prevent social loafing: (1) Set group goals, so the group has a common purpose to strive toward; (2) increase intergroup competition, which again focuses on the shared outcome; (3) engage in peer evaluation so each person evaluates each other person's contribution; (4) select members who have high motivation and prefer to work in groups, and (5) if possible, base group rewards in part on each member's unique contributions.[35] Although no magic bullet will prevent social loafing in all cases, these steps should help minimize its effect.

Group Property 5: Cohesiveness

Groups differ in their **cohesiveness**—the degree to which members are attracted to each other and motivated to stay in the group. Some work groups are cohesive because the members have spent a great deal of time together, or the group's small size or purpose facilitates high interaction, or external threats have brought members close together.

Cohesiveness affects group productivity.[36] Studies consistently show that the relationship between cohesiveness and productivity depends on the group's performance-related norms.[37] If norms for quality, output, and cooperation with outsiders, for instance, are high, a cohesive group will be more productive than will a less cohesive group. But if performance norms are low and cohesiveness is high, productivity will be low. If performance norms are high and cohesiveness is low, productivity increases, but less than in the high-norms/high-cohesiveness situation. When performance-related norms and cohesiveness are both low, productivity tends to fall into the low-to-moderate range.

What can you do to encourage group cohesiveness? (1) Make the group smaller, (2) encourage agreement with group goals, (3) increase the time members spend together, (4) increase the group's status and the perceived difficulty of attaining membership, (5) stimulate competition with other groups, (6) give rewards to the group rather than to individual members, and (7) physically isolate the group.[38]

Group Property 6: Diversity

The final property of groups we consider is **diversity** in the group's membership, the degree to which members of the group are similar to, or different from, one another. A great deal of research is being done on how diversity influences group performance. Some research looks at cultural diversity and some at racial, gender, and other differences. Overall, studies identify both benefits and costs from group diversity.

Diversity appears to increase group conflict, especially in the early stages of a group's tenure, which often lowers group morale and raises dropout rates. One study compared groups that were culturally diverse (composed of people from different countries) and homogeneous (composed of people from the same country). On a wilderness survival exercise, the groups performed equally well, but the diverse groups were less satisfied with their groups, were less cohesive, and had more conflict.[39] Another study examined the effect of differences in tenure on the performance of 67 engineering research and development groups.[40] When most people had roughly the same level of tenure, performance was high, but as tenure diversity increased, performance dropped off. There was an important qualifier: higher levels of tenure diversity were not related to lower performance for groups when there were effective team-oriented human resources practices. In other words, teams in which members' values or opinions differ tend to experience more conflict, but leaders who can get the group to focus on the task at hand and encourage group learning are able to reduce these conflicts and enhance discussion of group issues.[41] It seems diversity can be bad for performance even in creative teams, but appropriate organizational support and leadership might offset these problems.

However, culturally and demographically diverse groups may perform better over time—if they can get over their initial conflicts. Why might this be so?

Surface-level diversity—in observable characteristics such as national origin, race, and gender—alerts people to possible deep-level diversity—in underlying attitudes, values, and opinions. One researcher argues, "The mere presence of diversity you can see, such as a person's race or gender, actually cues a team that there's likely to be differences of opinion."[42] Although those differences can lead to conflict, they also provide an opportunity to solve problems in unique ways.

One study of jury behavior found diverse juries more likely to deliberate longer, share more information, and make fewer factual errors when discussing evidence. Two studies of MBA student groups found surface-level diversity led to greater openness even without deep-level diversity. Here, surface-level diversity may subconsciously cue team members to be more open-minded in their views.[43]

The impact of diversity on groups is mixed. It is difficult to be in a diverse group in the short term. However, if members can weather their differences, over time, diversity may help them to be more open-minded and creative and to do better. But even positive effects are unlikely to be especially strong. As one review stated, "The business case (in terms of demonstrable financial results) for diversity remains hard to support based on the extant research."[44]

GROUP DECISION MAKING

The belief—characterized by juries—that two heads are better than one has long been accepted as a basic component of the U.S. legal system and those of many other countries. Today, many decisions in organizations are made by groups, teams, or committees.[45] We'll discuss the advantages of group decision making, along with the unique challenges group dynamics bring to the decision-making process. Finally, we'll offer some techniques for maximizing the group decision-making opportunity.

Groups Versus the Individual

Decision-making groups may be widely used in organizations, but are group decisions preferable to those made by an individual alone? The answer depends on a number of factors. Let's begin by looking at the strengths and weaknesses of group decision making.[46]

STRENGTHS OF GROUP DECISION MAKING Groups generate *more complete information and knowledge.* By aggregating the resources of several individuals, groups bring more input as well as heterogeneity into the decision process. They offer *increased diversity of views.* This opens up the opportunity to consider more approaches and alternatives. Finally, groups lead to increased *acceptance of a solution.* Group members who participated in making a decision are more likely to enthusiastically support and encourage others to accept it.

WEAKNESSES OF GROUP DECISION MAKING Group decisions are time consuming because groups typically take more time to reach a solution. There are *conformity pressures.* The desire by group members to be accepted and considered an asset to the group can squash any overt disagreement. Group discussion can be *dominated by one or a few members.* If they're low- and medium-ability members, the group's overall effectiveness will suffer. Finally, group decisions suffer from *ambiguous responsibility.* In an individual decision, it's clear who is accountable for the final outcome. In a group decision, the responsibility of any single member is diluted.

EFFECTIVENESS AND EFFICIENCY Whether groups are more effective than individuals depends on how you define effectiveness. Group decisions are generally more *accurate* than the decisions of the average individual in a group, but less accurate than the judgments of the most accurate person.[47] In terms of *speed,* individuals are superior. If *creativity* is important, groups tend to be more effective. And if effectiveness means the degree of *acceptance* the final solution achieves, the nod again goes to the group.[48]

But we cannot consider effectiveness without also assessing efficiency. With few exceptions, group decision making consumes more work hours than an individual tackling the same problem alone. The exceptions tend to be the instances in which, to achieve comparable quantities of diverse input, the single decision maker must spend a great deal of time reviewing files and talking to other people. In deciding whether to use groups, then, managers must assess whether increases in effectiveness are more than enough to offset the reductions in efficiency.

Groupthink and Groupshift

Two by-products of group decision making have the potential to affect a group's ability to appraise alternatives objectively and arrive at high-quality solutions.

The first, called **groupthink**, relates to norms. It describes situations in which group pressures for conformity deter the group from critically appraising unusual, minority, or unpopular views. Groupthink is a disease that attacks many groups and can dramatically hinder their performance. The second phenomenon is **groupshift**, which describes the way group members tend to exaggerate the initial positions they hold when discussing a given set of alternatives and arriving at a solution. In some situations, caution dominates and there is a conservative shift, whereas in other situations groups tend toward a risky shift. Let's look at each phenomenon in detail.

Group decision making is not always better than individual decision making.

GROUPTHINK   Have you ever felt like speaking up in a meeting, a classroom, or an informal group but decided against it? One reason may have been shyness. Or you may have been a victim of groupthink, which occurs when the norm for consensus overrides the realistic appraisal of alternative courses and the full expression of deviant, minority, or unpopular views. The individual's mental efficiency, reality testing, and moral judgment deteriorate as a result of group pressures.[49]

We have all seen the symptoms of groupthink:

1. Group members rationalize any resistance to the assumptions they've made. No matter how strongly the evidence may contradict their basic assumptions, they behave so as to reinforce them.
2. Members apply direct pressure on those who momentarily express doubts about any of the group's shared views, or who question the validity of arguments supporting the alternative favored by the majority.
3. Members who have doubts or differing points of view seek to avoid deviating from what appears to be group consensus by keeping silent about misgivings and even minimizing to themselves the importance of their doubts.
4. There is an illusion of unanimity. If someone doesn't speak, it's assumed he is in full accord. Abstention becomes a "yes" vote.[50]

Groupthink appears closely aligned with the conclusions Solomon Asch drew in his experiments with a lone dissenter. Individuals who hold a position different from that of the dominant majority are under pressure to suppress, withhold, or modify their true feelings and beliefs. As members of a group, we find it more pleasant to be in agreement—to be a positive part of the group—than to be a disruptive force, even if disruption is necessary to improve the effectiveness of the group's decisions. Groups that are more focused on performance than on learning are especially likely to fall victim to groupthink and to suppress the opinions of those who do not agree with the majority.[51]

Does groupthink attack all groups? No. It seems to occur most often when there is a clear group identity, when members hold a positive image of their group that they want to protect, and when the group perceives a collective threat to this positive image.[52] So groupthink is not a dissenter-suppression mechanism as much as it's a means for a group to protect its positive image. One study also showed that those influenced by groupthink were more confident about their course of action early on.[53] Groups that believe too strongly in the correctness of their course of action are more likely to suppress dissent and encourage conformity than are groups that are more skeptical about their course of action.

What can managers do to minimize groupthink?[54] First, they can monitor group size. People grow more intimidated and hesitant as group size increases and, although there is no magic number that will eliminate groupthink, individuals are likely to feel less personal responsibility when groups get larger than about 10 members. Managers should also encourage group leaders to play an impartial role. Leaders should actively seek input from all members and avoid expressing their own opinions, especially in the early stages of deliberation. In addition, managers should appoint one group member to play the role of devil's advocate, overtly challenging the majority position and offering divergent perspectives. Still another suggestion is to use exercises that stimulate active discussion of diverse alternatives without threatening the group or intensifying identity protection. Have group members delay discussion of possible gains so they can first talk about the dangers or risks inherent in a decision. Requiring members to first focus on the negatives of an alternative makes the group less likely to stifle dissenting views and more likely to gain an objective evaluation.

GROUPSHIFT OR GROUP POLARIZATION   There are differences between group decisions and the individual decisions of group members.[55] As discussed previously, what appears to happen in groups is that discussion leads members toward more extreme views of the positions they already held. Conservatives become more cautious, and more aggressive types take on more risk. The group discussion tends to exaggerate the initial position of the group.

We can view group polarization as a special case of groupthink. The group's decision reflects the dominant decision-making norm that develops during discussion. Whether the shift in the group's decision is toward greater caution or more risk depends on the dominant prediscussion norm.

The shift toward polarization has generated several explanations.[56] It's been argued, for instance, that discussion makes the members more comfortable with each other and, thus, more willing to express extreme versions of their original positions. Another argument is that the group diffuses responsibility. Group decisions free any single member from accountability for the group's final choice, so a more extreme position can be taken. It's also likely that people take on extreme positions because they want to demonstrate how different they are from the out-group.[57] People on the fringes of political or social movements take on ever-more extreme positions just to prove they are really committed to the cause, whereas those who are more cautious tend to take exceptionally moderate positions to demonstrate how reasonable they are.

So how should you use the findings on groupshift? Recognize that group decisions exaggerate the initial position of the individual members, that the shift has been shown more often to be toward greater risk, and that which way a group will shift is a function of the members' prediscussion inclinations.

We now turn to the techniques by which groups make decisions. These reduce some of the dysfunctional aspects of group decision making.

Group Decision-Making Techniques

The most common form of group decision making takes place in **interacting groups**. Members meet face to face and rely on both verbal and non verbal interaction to communicate. But as our discussion of groupthink demonstrated, interacting groups often censor themselves and pressure individual members toward conformity of opinion. Brainstorming and the nominal group technique can reduce problems inherent in the traditional interacting group.

Brainstorming can overcome the pressures for conformity that dampen creativity[58] by encouraging any and all alternatives while withholding criticism. In a typical brainstorming session, a half-dozen to a dozen people sit around a table. The group leader states the problem in a clear manner so all participants understand. Members then freewheel as many alternatives as they can in a given length of time. To encourage members to "think the unusual," no criticism is allowed, even of the most bizarre suggestions, and all ideas are recorded for later discussion and analysis.

Brainstorming may indeed generate ideas—but not in a very efficient manner. Research consistently shows individuals working alone generate a greater number of ideas than a group in a brainstorming session (though the ideas may not be more creative in scope). One reason for this is "production blocking." When people are generating ideas in a group, many are talking at once, which blocks the thought process and eventually impedes the sharing of ideas.[59] The following two techniques go further than brainstorming by helping groups arrive at a preferred solution.[60]

The **nominal group technique** restricts discussion or interpersonal communication during the decision-making process, hence the term *nominal.* Group members are all physically present, as in a traditional committee meeting, but they operate independently. Specifically, a problem is presented and then the group takes the following steps:

1. Before any discussion takes place, each member independently writes down ideas on the problem.
2. After this silent period, each member presents one idea to the group. No discussion takes place until all ideas have been presented and recorded.
3. The group discusses the ideas for clarity and evaluates them.
4. Each group member silently and independently rank-orders the ideas. The idea with the highest aggregate ranking determines the final decision.

The chief advantage of the nominal group technique is that it permits a group to meet formally but does not restrict independent thinking, as does an interacting group. Research generally shows nominal groups outperform brainstorming groups.[61]

Brainstorming and the nominal group technique both have their own set of strengths and weaknesses. The choice depends on what criteria you want to emphasize and the cost–benefit trade-off. An interacting group is good for achieving commitment to a solution, brainstorming develops group cohesiveness, and the nominal group technique is an inexpensive means for generating a large number of ideas.

SUMMARY AND IMPLICATIONS FOR MANAGERS

Several implications can be drawn from our discussion of groups. The next chapter will explore several of these in greater depth.

- Role perception and an employee's performance evaluation are positively related.[62] The degree of congruence between the employee's and the boss's perception of the employee's job influences the degree to which the boss will judge that employee effective. An employee whose role perception fulfills the boss's role expectations will receive a higher performance evaluation.
- Norms control behavior by establishing standards of right and wrong. The norms of a given group can help explain members' behaviors for managers. When norms support high output, managers can expect markedly higher individual performance than when they aim to restrict output. Norms that support antisocial behavior increase the likelihood that individuals will engage in deviant workplace activities.
- Status inequities create frustration and can adversely influence productivity and willingness to remain with an organization. Incongruence is likely to reduce motivation and motivate a search for ways to bring about fairness. Because lower-status people tend to participate less in group discussions, groups with high status differences are likely to inhibit input from lower-status members and reduce their potential.
- The impact of size on a group's performance depends on the type of task. Larger groups are more effective at fact-finding activities, and smaller groups are more effective at action-taking tasks. Our knowledge of social loafing suggests that managers using larger groups should also provide measures of individual performance.
- Cohesiveness can influence a group's level of productivity or not, depending on the group's performance-related norms.

- Diversity appears to have a mixed impact on group performance, with some studies suggesting that diversity can help performance and others suggesting it can hurt it. It appears the situation makes a difference in whether positive or negative results predominate.
- High congruence between a boss's and an employee's perception of the employee's job correlates strongly with high employee satisfaction.[63] Role conflict is associated with job-induced tension and job dissatisfaction.[64]
- Most people prefer to communicate with others at their own status level or a higher one rather than with those below them.[65] As a result, we should expect satisfaction to be greater among employees whose job minimizes interaction with individuals lower in status than themselves.
- The group size–satisfaction relationship is what we would intuitively expect: larger groups are associated with lower satisfaction.[66] As size increases, opportunities for participation and social interaction decrease, as does the ability of members to identify with the group's accomplishments. Also, having more members prompts dissension, conflict, and the formation of subgroups, which all act to make the group a less pleasant entity of which to be a part.

MyManagementLab

Go to **MyManagementLab.com** to access study plans, interactive lectures, and videos as well as Auto-graded writing questions and the following Assisted-graded writing question.

9-1. MyManagementLab Only—comprehensive writing assignment for this chapter.

10
■ ■ ■

Understanding Work Teams

After studying this chapter, you should be able to:

- Contrast groups and teams and analyze the growing popularity of teams in organizations.
- Compare and contrast four types of teams.
- Identify the characteristics of effective teams.
- Show how organizations can create team players.
- Decide when to use individuals instead of teams.
- Show how our understanding of teams differs in a global context.

MyManagementLab™
⭐ Improve Your Grade!
Over 10 million students improved their results using the Pearson MyLabs. Visit **mymanagementlab.com** for simulations, tutorials, and end-of-chapter problems.

WHY HAVE TEAMS BECOME SO POPULAR?

Decades ago, when companies such as W. L. Gore, Volvo, and General Foods introduced teams into their production processes, it made news because no one else was doing it. Today, it's just the opposite. The organization that *doesn't* use teams has become newsworthy. Teams are everywhere.

How do we explain the current popularity of teams? As organizations have restructured themselves to compete more effectively and efficiently, they have turned to teams as a better way to use employee talents. Teams are more flexible and responsive to changing events than traditional departments or other forms of permanent groupings. They can quickly assemble, deploy, refocus, and disband. But don't overlook the motivational properties of teams. Consistent with our discussion of employee involvement as a motivator, teams facilitate employee participation in operating decisions. So another explanation for their popularity is that they are an effective means for management to democratize organizations and increase employee motivation.

The fact that organizations have turned to teams doesn't necessarily mean they're always effective. Decision makers, as humans, can be swayed by fads and herd mentality. Are teams truly effective? What conditions affect their potential? How do members work together? These are some of the questions we'll answer in this chapter.

DIFFERENCES BETWEEN GROUPS AND TEAMS

Groups and teams are not the same thing. In this section, we define and clarify the difference between work groups and work teams.[1]

In Chapter 9, we defined a *group* as two or more individuals, interacting and interdependent, who have come together to achieve particular objectives. A **work group** is a collective of any size that interacts primarily to share information and make decisions to help each member perform within his area of responsibility.

Work groups have no need or opportunity to engage in collaborative work that requires joint effort. So their performance is merely the summation of each group member's individual contribution. There is no positive synergy that would create an overall level of performance greater than the sum of the inputs.

A **work team**, on the other hand, generates positive synergy through coordinated effort. The individual efforts result in a level of performance greater than the sum of those individual inputs. With both work groups and work teams, there are often behavioral expectations of members, collective normalization efforts, active group dynamics, and some level of decision making (even if just informally about the scope of membership). Both work groups and work teams may be called upon to generate ideas, pool resources, or coordinate logistics such as work schedules; for the work group, however, this will be limited to information gathering for decision makers outside the group (not team actionable).

Whereas a work team may be thought of as a subset of a work group, the team is constructed to be purposeful (symbiotic) in its member interaction. The distinction should be kept even when the terms are mentioned interchangeably in differing contexts. Exhibit 10-1 highlights the differences between work groups and work teams.

These definitions help clarify why so many organizations have recently restructured work processes around teams. Management is looking for positive synergy that will allow the organizations to increase performance. The extensive use of teams creates the *potential* for an organization to generate greater outputs with no increase in inputs. Notice, however, we said *potential*. There is nothing inherently magical that ensures the achievement of positive synergy in the creation of teams. Merely calling a *group a team* doesn't automatically improve its performance. As we show later in this chapter, effective teams have certain common characteristics. If management hopes to gain increases in organizational performance through the use of teams, its teams must possess these.

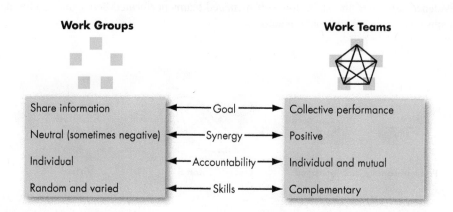

Work Groups		Work Teams
Share information	←— Goal —→	Collective performance
Neutral (sometimes negative)	←—Synergy—→	Positive
Individual	←—Accountability—→	Individual and mutual
Random and varied	←— Skills —→	Complementary

EXHIBIT 10-1
Comparing Work Groups and Work Teams

TYPES OF TEAMS

Teams can make products, provide services, negotiate deals, coordinate projects, offer advice, and make decisions.[2] In this section, we describe the four most common types of teams in an organization: *problem-solving teams, self-managed work teams, cross-functional teams,* and *virtual teams* (see Exhibit 10-2).

Problem-Solving Teams

In the past, teams were typically composed of 5 to 12 hourly employees from the same department who met for a few hours each week to discuss ways of improving quality, efficiency, and the work environment.[3] These **problem-solving teams** rarely have the authority to unilaterally implement any of their suggestions. Merrill Lynch created a problem-solving team to figure out ways to reduce the number of days it took to open a new cash management account.[4] By suggesting cutting the number of steps from 46 to 36, the team reduced the average number of days from 15 to 8.

Self-Managed Work Teams

Problem-solving teams only make recommendations. Some organizations have gone further and created teams that not only solve problems but implement solutions and take responsibility for outcomes.

    Self-managed work teams are groups of employees (typically 10 to 15 in number) who perform highly related or interdependent jobs and take on many of the responsibilities of their former supervisors.[5] Typically, these tasks are planning and scheduling work, assigning tasks to members, making operating decisions, taking action on problems, and working with suppliers and customers. Fully self-managed work teams even select their own members and evaluate each other's performance. Supervisory positions take on decreased importance and are sometimes even eliminated.

    But research on the effectiveness of self-managed work teams has not been uniformly positive.[6] Self-managed teams do not typically manage conflicts well. When disputes arise, members stop cooperating and power struggles ensue, which leads to lower group performance.[7] Moreover, although individuals on these teams report higher levels of job satisfaction than other individuals, they also sometimes have higher absenteeism and turnover rates. One large-scale study of labor productivity in British establishments found that although using teams in general does improve labor productivity, no evidence supported the claim that self-managed teams performed better than traditional teams with less decision-making authority.[8]

  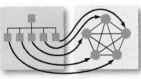 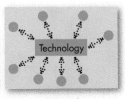

EXHIBIT 10-2
Four Types of Teams

Problem-solving **Self-managed**   **Cross-functional**   **Virtual**

Cross-Functional Teams

Starbucks created a team of individuals from production, global PR, global communications, and U.S. marketing to develop its Via brand of instant coffee. The team's suggestions resulted in a product that would be cost-effective to produce and distribute and that was marketed through a tightly integrated, multifaceted strategy.[9] This example illustrates the use of **cross-functional teams**, made up of employees from about the same hierarchical level but different work areas, who come together to accomplish a task.

Many organizations have used horizontal, boundary-spanning teams for decades. In the 1960s, IBM created a large task force of employees from across departments to develop its highly successful System 360. Today, cross-functional teams are so widely used it is hard to imagine a major organizational undertaking without one. All the major automobile manufacturers—Toyota, Honda, Nissan, BMW, GM, Ford, and Chrysler—currently use this form of team to coordinate complex projects. Cisco relies on specific cross-functional teams to identify and capitalize on new trends in several areas of the software market. Cisco's teams are the equivalent of social-networking groups that collaborate in real time to identify new business opportunities in the field and then implement them from the bottom up.[10]

Cross-functional teams are an effective means of allowing people from diverse areas within or even between organizations to exchange information, develop new ideas, solve problems, and coordinate complex projects. Of course, cross-functional teams are no picnic to manage. Their early stages of development are often long, as members learn to work with diversity and complexity. It takes time to build trust and teamwork, especially among people from varying backgrounds with different experiences and perspectives.

Virtual Teams

The teams described in the preceding section do their work face to face. **Virtual teams** use computer technology to unite physically dispersed members and achieve a common goal.[11] They collaborate online—using communication links such as wide-area networks, videoconferencing, or e-mail—whether they're a room away or continents apart. Virtual teams are so pervasive, and technology has advanced so far, that it's probably a bit of a misnomer to call them "virtual." Nearly all teams today do at least some of their work remotely.

Despite their ubiquity, virtual teams face special challenges. They may suffer because there is less social rapport and direct interaction among members. Evidence from 94 studies entailing more than 5,000 groups found that virtual teams are better at sharing unique information (information held by individual members but not the entire group), but they tend to share less information overall.[12] As a result, low levels of virtuality in teams results in higher levels of information sharing, but high levels of virtuality hinder it. For virtual teams to be effective, management should ensure that (1) trust is established among members (one inflammatory remark in an e-mail can severely undermine team trust), (2) team progress is monitored closely (so the team doesn't lose sight of its goals and no team member "disappears"), and (3) the efforts and products of the team are publicized throughout the organization (so the team does not become invisible).[13]

CREATING EFFECTIVE TEAMS

Many have tried to identify factors related to team effectiveness.[14] However, some studies have organized what was once a "veritable laundry list of characteristics"[15] into a relatively focused model.[16] Exhibit 10-3 summarizes what we currently know about what makes teams effective. As you'll see, it builds on many of the group concepts introduced in Chapter 9.

The following discussion is based on the model in Exhibit 10-3. Keep in mind two points. First, teams differ in form and structure. The model attempts to generalize across all varieties of teams, but avoid rigidly applying its predictions to all teams.[17] Use it as a guide. Second, the model assumes teamwork is preferable to individual work. Creating "effective" teams when individuals can do the job better is like perfectly solving the wrong problem.

We can organize the key components of effective teams into three general categories. First are the resources and other *contextual* influences that make teams effective. The second relates to the team's *composition*. Finally, *process* variables are events within the team that influence effectiveness. What does *team effectiveness* mean in this model? Typically, it has included objective measures of the team's productivity, managers' ratings of the team's performance, and aggregate measures of member satisfaction.

Context: What Factors Determine Whether Teams Are Successful?

The four contextual factors most significantly related to team performance are adequate resources, effective leadership, a climate of trust, and a performance evaluation and reward system that reflects team contributions.

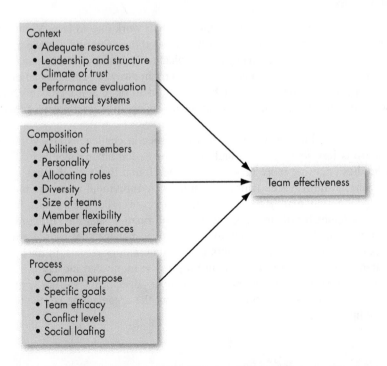

EXHIBIT 10-3

Team Effectiveness Model

ADEQUATE RESOURCES   Teams are part of a larger organization system; every work team relies on resources outside the group to sustain it. A scarcity of resources directly reduces the ability of a team to perform its job effectively and achieve its goals. As one study concluded, after looking at 13 factors related to group performance, "perhaps one of the most important characteristics of an effective work group is the support the group receives from the organization."[18] This support includes timely information, proper equipment, adequate staffing, encouragement, and administrative assistance.

LEADERSHIP AND STRUCTURE   Teams can't function if they can't agree on who is to do what and ensure all members share the workload. Agreeing on the specifics of work and how they fit together to integrate individual skills requires leadership and structure, either from management or from the team members themselves. It's true in self-managed teams that team members absorb many of the duties typically assumed by managers. However, a manager's job then becomes managing *outside* (rather than inside) the team.

Leadership is especially important in **multiteam systems**, in which different teams coordinate their efforts to produce a desired outcome. Here, leaders need to empower teams by delegating responsibility to them, and they play the role of facilitator, making sure the teams work together rather than against one another.[19] Teams that establish shared leadership by effectively delegating it are more effective than teams with a traditional single-leader structure.[20]

CLIMATE OF TRUST   Members of effective teams trust each other. They also exhibit trust in their leaders.[21] Interpersonal trust among team members facilitates cooperation, reduces the need to monitor each others' behavior, and bonds members around the belief that others on the team won't take advantage of them. Team members are more likely to take risks and expose vulnerabilities when they believe they can trust others on their team. And, as we will discuss later in the book, trust is the foundation of leadership. It allows a team to accept and commit to its leader's goals and decisions.

PERFORMANCE EVALUATIONS AND REWARD SYSTEMS   How do you get team members to be both individually and jointly accountable? Individual performance evaluations and incentives may interfere with the development of high-performance teams. So, in addition to evaluating and rewarding employees for their individual contributions, management should modify the traditional, individually oriented evaluation and reward system to reflect team performance and focus on hybrid systems that recognize individual members for their exceptional contributions and reward the entire group for positive outcomes.[22] Group-based appraisals, profit sharing, gainsharing, small-group incentives, and other system modifications can reinforce team effort and commitment.

Team Composition

The team composition category includes variables that relate to how teams should be staffed—the abilities and personalities of team members, allocation of roles and diversity, size of the team, and members' preferences for teamwork.

Team composition matters—the optimal way to construct teams depends on the ability, skill, or trait under consideration.

ABILITIES OF MEMBERS   Part of a team's performance depends on the knowledge, skills, and abilities of its individual members.[23] It's true we occasionally read about an athletic team of mediocre players who, because of excellent coaching, determination, and precision teamwork, beat a far more talented group. But such cases make the news precisely because they are unusual. A team's performance is not merely the summation of its individual members' abilities. However, these abilities set limits on what members can do and how effectively they will perform on a team.

Research reveals some insights into team composition and performance. First, when the task entails considerable thought (solving a complex problem such as reengineering an assembly line), high-ability teams—composed of mostly intelligent members—do better than lower-ability teams, especially when the workload is distributed evenly. That way, team performance does not depend on the weakest link. High-ability teams are also more adaptable to changing situations; they can more effectively apply existing knowledge to new problems.

The ability of the team's leader also matters. Smart team leaders help less intelligent team members when they struggle with a task. This is due in part because the leader is able to contribute to successful completion of team goals on his own. A less intelligent leader can neutralize the effect of a high-ability team.[24]

PERSONALITY OF MEMBERS We demonstrated previously that personality significantly influences individual employee behavior. Many of the dimensions identified in the Big Five personality model are also relevant to team effectiveness; a review of OB literature identified three.[25] Specifically, teams that rate higher on mean levels of conscientiousness and openness to experience tend to perform better, and the minimum level of team member agreeableness also matters: teams did worse when they had one or more highly disagreeable members. Perhaps one bad apple *can* spoil the whole bunch!

Research has also provided us with a good idea about why these personality traits are important to teams. Conscientious people are good at backing up other team members, and they're also good at sensing when their support is truly needed. One study found that specific behavioral tendencies such as personal organization, cognitive structuring, achievement orientation, and endurance were all related to higher levels of team performance.[26] Open team members communicate better with one another and throw out more ideas, which makes teams composed of open people more creative and innovative.[27]

Suppose an organization needs to create 20 teams of 4 people each and has 40 highly conscientious people and 40 who score low on conscientiousness. Would the organization be better off (1) forming 10 teams of highly conscientious people and 10 teams of members low on conscientiousness, or (2) "seeding" each team with 2 people who scored high and 2 who scored low on conscientiousness? Perhaps surprisingly, evidence suggests option 1 is the best choice; performance across the teams will be higher if the organization forms 10 highly conscientious teams and 10 teams low in conscientiousness. This is because the team of highly conscientious members will set and keep high group performance expectations, while the team comprised of members of varying conscientiousness levels will not work to the peak performance of the highly conscientious members. Instead, a resentment or group normalization dynamic will complicate interactions and force the highly conscientious members to lower their expectations, thus adversely affecting the group's performance. In cases like this, it does appear to make sense to "put all of one's eggs [conscientious team members] into one basket [into teams with other conscientious members].[28]

By matching individual preferences with team role demands, managers increase the likelihood that the team members will work well together.

ALLOCATION OF ROLES Teams have different needs, and members should be selected to ensure all the various roles are filled. A study of 778 major league baseball teams over a 21-year period highlights the importance of assigning roles appropriately.[29] As you might expect, teams with more experienced and skilled members performed better. However, the experience and skill of those in core roles who handle more of the workflow of the team, and who are central to all work processes (in this case, pitchers and catchers), were especially vital. In other words, put your most able, experienced, and conscientious workers in the most central roles in a team.

We can identify nine potential team roles. Successful work teams have selected people to play all these roles based on their skills and preferences.[30] (On many teams, individuals will play multiple roles.) To increase the likelihood the team members will work well together, managers need to understand the individual strengths each person can bring to a team, select members with their strengths in mind, and allocate work assignments that fit with members' preferred styles.

DIVERSITY OF MEMBERS   There is a great deal of discussion and research on the effect of diversity on groups. How does *team* diversity affect *team* performance? The degree to which members of a work unit (group, team, or department) share a common demographic attribute, such as age, sex, race, educational level, or length of service in the organization, is the subject of **organizational demography**. Organizational demography suggests that attributes such as age or the date of joining should help us predict turnover. The logic goes like this: Turnover will be greater among those with dissimilar experiences because communication is more difficult and conflict is more likely. Increased conflict makes membership less attractive, so employees are more likely to quit. Similarly, the losers in a power struggle are more apt to leave voluntarily or be forced out.[31]

Many of us hold the optimistic view that diversity should be a good thing—diverse teams should benefit from differing perspectives. Two meta-analytic reviews of the research literature show, however, that demographic diversity is essentially unrelated to team performance overall, while a third actually suggests that race and gender diversity are negatively related to team performance.[32] One qualifier is that gender and ethnic diversity have more negative effects in occupations dominated by white or male employees, but in more demographically balanced occupations, diversity is less of a problem. Diversity in function, education, and expertise are positively related to group performance, but these effects are quite small and depend on the situation.

Proper leadership can also improve the performance of diverse teams.[33] When leaders provide an inspirational common goal for members with varying types of education and knowledge, teams are very creative. When leaders don't provide such goals, diverse teams fail to take advantage of their unique skills and are actually *less* creative than teams with homogeneous skills. Even teams with diverse values can perform effectively, however, if leaders provide a focus on work tasks rather than leading based on personal relationships.

We have discussed research on team diversity in race or gender. But what about diversity created by national differences? Like the earlier research, evidence here indicates elements of diversity interfere with team processes, at least in the short term.[34] Cultural diversity does seem to be an asset for tasks that call for a variety of viewpoints. But culturally heterogeneous teams have more difficulty learning to work with each other and solving problems. The good news is that these difficulties seem to dissipate with time. Although newly formed culturally diverse teams underperform newly formed culturally homogeneous teams, the differences disappear after about 3 months.[35] Fortunately, some team performance-enhancing strategies seem to work well in many cultures. One study found that teams in the European Union made up of members from collectivist and individualist countries benefited equally from having group goals.[36]

SIZE OF TEAMS   Most experts agree, keeping teams small is a key to improving group effectiveness.[37] Generally speaking, the most effective teams have five to nine members. And experts suggest using the smallest number of people who can do the task. Unfortunately, managers often err by making teams too large. It may require only four or five members to develop diversity of views and skills, while coordination problems can increase exponentially as team members are added. When teams have excess members, cohesiveness and mutual accountability decline, social loafing increases, and people communicate less. Members of large teams have trouble coordinating with one another, especially under time pressure. If a natural working unit is larger and you want a team effort, consider breaking the group into subteams when it's difficult to develop effective coordination processes.[38]

MEMBER PREFERENCES   Not every employee is a team player. Given the option, many employees will select themselves *out* of team participation. When people who prefer to work alone are required to team up, there is a direct threat to the team's morale and to individual member satisfaction.[39] This result suggests that, when selecting team members, managers should consider individual preferences along with abilities, personalities, and skills. High-performing teams are likely to be composed of people who prefer working as part of a group.

Team Processes

The final category related to team effectiveness is process variables such as member commitment to a common purpose, establishment of specific team goals, team efficacy, a managed level of conflict, and minimized social loafing. These will be especially important in larger teams and in teams that are highly interdependent.[40]

Why are processes important to team effectiveness? Let's return to the topic of social loafing. We found that 1+1+1 doesn't necessarily add up to 3. When each member's contribution is not clearly visible, individuals tend to decrease their efforts. Social loafing, in other words, illustrates a process loss from using teams. But teams should create outputs greater than the sum of their inputs, as when a diverse group develops creative alternatives. Exhibit 10-4 illustrates how group processes can have an impact on actual effectiveness.[41]

Teams are often used in research laboratories because they can draw on the diverse skills of various individuals to produce more meaningful research than researchers working independently—that is, they produce positive synergy, and their process gains exceed their process losses.

Effective teams maintain a common plan and purpose to their actions that guides their actions and concentrates their energies.

COMMON PLAN AND PURPOSE   Effective teams begin by analyzing the team's mission, developing goals to achieve that mission, and creating strategies for achieving the goals. Teams that consistently perform better have established a clear sense of what needs to be done and how.[42]

EXHIBIT 10-4
Effects of Group Processes

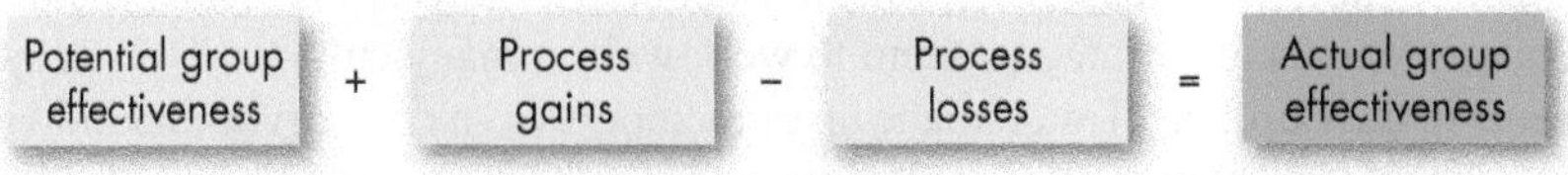

Potential group effectiveness + Process gains − Process losses = Actual group effectiveness

Members of successful teams put a tremendous amount of time and effort into discussing, shaping, and agreeing on a purpose that belongs to them both collectively and individually. This common purpose, when accepted by the team, becomes what GPS is to a ship captain: it provides direction and guidance under any and all conditions. Like a ship following the wrong course, teams that don't have good planning skills are doomed; perfectly executing the wrong plan is a lost cause.[43] Teams should also agree on whether their goal is to learn about and master a task or simply to perform the task; evidence suggests that diverging perspectives on learning versus performance goals lead to lower levels of team performance overall.[44] It appears that these differences in goal orientation have their effects by reducing discussion and sharing of information. In sum, having all employees on a team strive for the same *type* of goal is important.

Effective teams also show **reflexivity**, meaning they reflect on and adjust their master plan when necessary. A team has to have a good plan, but it also has to be willing and able to adapt when conditions call for it.[45] Interestingly, some evidence does suggest that teams high in reflexivity are better able to adapt to conflicting plans and goals among team members.[46]

SPECIFIC GOALS   Successful teams translate their common purpose into specific, measurable, and realistic performance goals. Specific goals facilitate clear communication. They also help teams maintain their focus on getting results.

Consistent with the research on individual goals, team goals should also be challenging. Difficult but achievable goals raise team performance on those criteria for which they're set. So, for instance, goals for quantity tend to raise quantity, goals for accuracy raise accuracy, and so on.[47]

TEAM EFFICACY   Effective teams have confidence in themselves; they believe they can succeed. We call this *team efficacy*.[48] Teams that have been successful raise their beliefs about future success, which, in turn, motivates them to work harder. What can management do to increase team efficacy? Two options are helping the team achieve small successes that build confidence and providing training to improve members' technical and interpersonal skills. The greater the abilities of team members, the more likely the team will develop confidence and the ability to deliver on that confidence.

MENTAL MODELS   Effective teams share accurate **mental models**—organized mental representations of the key elements within a team's environment that team members share.[49] If team members have the wrong mental models, which is particularly likely with teams under acute stress, their performance suffers.[50] In the Iraq War, for instance, many military leaders said they underestimated the power of the insurgency and the infighting among Iraqi religious sects. The similarity of team members' mental models matters, too. If team members have different ideas about how to do things, the team will fight over methods rather than focus on what needs to be done.[51] One review of 65 independent studies of team cognition found that teams with shared mental models engaged in more frequent interactions with one another, were more motivated, had more positive attitudes toward their work, and had higher levels of objectively rated performance.[52]

CONFLICT LEVELS   Conflict on a team isn't necessarily bad. As we discuss later in this book, conflict has a complex relationship with team performance. *Relationship conflicts*— those based on interpersonal incompatibilities, tension, and animosity toward others—are almost always dysfunctional. However, when teams are performing nonroutine activities, disagreements about task content (called *task conflicts*) stimulate discussion, promote critical assessment of problems and options, and can lead to better team decisions. A study conducted in China found that moderate levels of task conflict during the initial phases of team performance were positively related to team creativity, but both very low and very high levels of task conflict were negatively related to team performance.[53] In other words, both too much and too little disagreement about how a team should initially perform a creative task can inhibit performance.

The way conflicts are resolved can also make the difference between effective and ineffective teams. A study of ongoing comments made by 37 autonomous work groups showed that effective teams resolved conflicts by explicitly discussing the issues, whereas ineffective teams had conflicts focused more on personalities and the way things were said.[54]

SOCIAL LOAFING   As we noted previously, individuals can engage in social loafing and coast on the group's effort when their particular contributions can't be identified. Effective teams undermine this tendency by making members individually and jointly accountable for the team's purpose, goals, and approach.[55] Therefore, members should be clear on what they are individually responsible for and what they are jointly responsible for on the team.

TURNING INDIVIDUALS INTO TEAM PLAYERS

We've made a strong case for the value and growing popularity of teams. But many people are not inherently team players, and many organizations have historically nurtured individual accomplishments. Finally, teams fit well in countries that score high on collectivism. But what if an organization wants to introduce teams into a work population of individuals born and raised in an individualistic society? A veteran employee of a large company, who had done well working in an individualistic company in an individualist country, described the experience of joining a team: "I'm learning my lesson. I just had my first negative performance appraisal in 20 years."[56]

So what can organizations do to enhance team effectiveness—to turn individual contributors into team members? Here are options for managers trying to turn individuals into team players.

Selecting: Hiring Team Players

Some people already possess the interpersonal skills to be effective team players. When hiring team members, be sure candidates can fulfill their team roles as well as technical requirements.[57]

When faced with job candidates who lack team skills, managers have three options. First, don't hire them. If you have to hire them, assign them to tasks or positions that don't require teamwork. If that is not feasible, the candidates can undergo training to make them into team players. In established organizations that decide to redesign jobs around teams, some employees will resist being team players and may be untrainable. Unfortunately, they typically become casualties of the team approach.

Creating teams often means resisting the urge to hire the best talent no matter what. Personal traits also appear to make some people better candidates for working in diverse teams. Teams made up of members who like to work through difficult mental puzzles also seem more effective at capitalizing on the multiple points of view that arise from diversity in age and education.[58]

Training: Creating Team Players

Training specialists conduct exercises that allow employees to experience the satisfaction teamwork can provide. Workshops help employees improve their problem solving, communication, negotiation, conflict-management, and coaching skills. L'Oréal, for example, found that successful sales teams required much more than being staffed with high-ability salespeople: management had to focus much of its efforts on team building. "What we didn't account for was that many members of our top team in sales had been promoted because they had excellent technical and executional skills," said L'Oréal's senior VP of sales, David Waldock. As a result of the focus on team training, Waldock says, "We are no longer a team just on paper, working independently. We have a real group dynamic now, and it's a good one."[59] Employees also learn the five-stage group development model described in the previous chapter. Developing an effective team doesn't happen overnight—it takes time.

Rewarding: Providing Incentives to Be a Good Team Player

An organization's reward system must be reworked to encourage cooperative efforts rather than competitive ones.[60] Hallmark Cards Inc. added to its basic individual-incentive system an annual bonus based on achievement of team goals. Whole Foods directs most of its performance-based rewards toward team performance. As a result, teams select new members carefully so they will contribute to team effectiveness (and thus team bonuses).[61] It is usually best to set a cooperative tone as soon as possible in the life of a team. As we already noted, teams that switch from a competitive to a cooperative system do not immediately share information, and they still tend to make rushed, poor-quality decisions.[62] Apparently, the low trust typical of the competitive group will not be readily replaced by high trust with a quick change in reward systems. These problems are not seen in teams that have consistently cooperative systems.

Promotions, pay raises, and other forms of recognition should be given to individuals who work effectively as team members by training new colleagues, sharing information, helping resolve team conflicts, and mastering needed new skills. This doesn't mean individual contributions should be ignored; rather, they should be balanced with selfless contributions to the team.

Finally, don't forget the intrinsic rewards, such as camaraderie, that employees can receive from teamwork. It's exciting to be part of a successful team. The opportunity for personal development of self and teammates can be a very satisfying and rewarding experience.

BEWARE! TEAMS AREN'T ALWAYS THE ANSWER

Teamwork takes more time and often more resources than individual work. Teams have increased communication demands, conflicts to manage, and meetings to run. So, the benefits of using teams have to exceed the costs, and that's not always the case.[63] Before you rush to implement teams, carefully assess whether the work requires or will benefit from a collective effort.

How do you know whether the work of your group would be better done in teams? You can apply three tests.[64] First, can the work be done better by more than one person? A good indicator is the complexity of the work and the need for different perspectives. Simple tasks that don't require diverse input are probably better left to individuals. Second, does the work create a common purpose or set of goals for the people in the group that is more than the aggregate of individual goals? Many service departments of new-vehicle dealers have introduced teams that link customer service people, mechanics, parts specialists, and sales representatives. Such teams can better manage collective responsibility for ensuring customer needs are properly met.

The final test is to determine whether the members of the group are interdependent. Using teams makes sense when there is interdependence among tasks—the success of the whole depends on the success of each one, *and* the success of each one depends on the success of the others. Soccer, for instance, is an obvious *team* sport. Success requires a great deal of coordination between interdependent players. Conversely, except possibly for relays, swim teams are not really teams. They're groups of individuals performing individually, whose total performance is merely the aggregate summation of their individual performances.

SUMMARY AND IMPLICATIONS FOR MANAGERS

Few trends have influenced jobs as much as the massive movement to introduce teams into the workplace. The shift from working alone to working on teams requires employees to cooperate with others, share information, confront differences, and sublimate personal interests for the greater good of the team.

- Effective teams have common characteristics. They have adequate resources, effective leadership, a climate of trust, and a performance evaluation and reward system that reflects team contributions. These teams have individuals with technical expertise as well as problem-solving, decision-making, and interpersonal skills and the right traits, especially conscientiousness and openness.
- Effective teams also tend to be small—with fewer than 10 people, preferably of diverse backgrounds. They have members who fill role demands and who prefer to be part of a group. And the work that members do provides freedom and autonomy, the opportunity to use different skills and talents, the ability to complete a whole and identifiable task or product, and work that has a substantial impact on others.
- Effective teams have members who believe in the team's capabilities and are committed to a common plan and purpose, an accurate shared mental model of what is to be accomplished, specific team goals, a manageable level of conflict, and a minimal degree of social loafing.
- Because individualistic organizations and societies attract and reward individual accomplishments, it can be difficult to create team players in these environments. To make the conversion, management should try to select individuals who have the interpersonal skills to be effective team players, provide training to develop teamwork skills, and reward individuals for cooperative efforts.

MyManagementLab

Go to **MyManagementLab.com** to access study plans, interactive lectures, and videos as well as Auto-graded writing questions and the following Assisted-graded writing question.

10-1. MyManagementLab Only—comprehensive writing assignment for this chapter.

11

■ ■ ■

Communication

After studying this chapter, you should be able to:

- Describe the communication process and distinguish between formal and informal communication.
- Contrast downward, upward, and lateral communication, and provide examples of each.
- Contrast oral, written, and nonverbal communication.
- Identify common barriers to effective communication.
- Show how to overcome the potential problems in cross-cultural communication.

MyManagementLab™
⭐ **Improve Your Grade!**

Over 10 million students improved their results using the Pearson MyLabs. Visit **mymanagementlab.com** for simulations, tutorials, and end-of-chapter problems.

No individual, group, or organization can exist without sharing meaning among its members. It is only then that we can convey information and ideas. Communicating, however, is more than merely imparting meaning; that meaning must also be understood. If one group member speaks only German and the others do not know the language, the German speaker will not be fully understood. Therefore, **communication** must include both the *transfer and the understanding of meaning.*

Before making too many generalizations concerning communication and problems in communicating effectively, we need to describe the communication process.

THE COMMUNICATION PROCESS

Before communication can take place it needs a purpose, a message to be conveyed between a sender and a receiver. The sender encodes the message (converts it to a symbolic form) and passes it through a medium (channel) to the receiver, who decodes it. The result is transfer of meaning from one person to another.[1]

Exhibit 11-1 depicts this **communication process**. The key parts of this model are (1) the sender, (2) encoding, (3) the message, (4) the channel, (5) decoding, (6) the receiver, (7) noise, and (8) feedback.

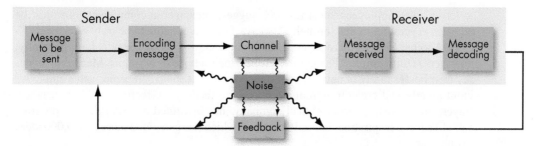

EXHIBIT 11-1
The Communication Process

The *sender* initiates a message by encoding a thought. The *message* is the actual physical product of the sender's *encoding*. When we speak, the speech is the message. When we write, the writing is the message. When we gesture, the movements of our arms and the expressions on our faces are the message. The *channel* is the medium through which the message travels. The sender selects it, determining whether to use a formal or informal channel. **Formal channels** are established by the organization and transmit messages related to the professional activities of members. They traditionally follow the authority chain within the organization. Other forms of messages, such as personal or social, follow **informal channels**, which are spontaneous and emerge as a response to individual choices.[2] The *receiver* is the person(s) to whom the message is directed, who must first translate the symbols into understandable form. This step is the *decoding* of the message. *Noise* represents communication barriers that distort the clarity of the message, such as perceptual problems, information overload, semantic difficulties, or cultural differences. The final link in the communication process is a feedback loop. *Feedback* is the check on how successful we have been in transferring our messages as originally intended. It determines whether or not understanding has been achieved.

DIRECTION OF COMMUNICATION

Communication can flow vertically or laterally. We further subdivide the vertical dimension into downward and upward directions.[3]

Downward Communication

Communication that flows from one level of a group or organization to a lower level is *downward communication*. Group leaders and managers use it to assign goals, provide job instructions, explain policies and procedures, point out problems that need attention, and offer feedback about performance.

    When engaging in downward communication, managers must explain the reasons *why* a decision was made. One study found employees were twice as likely to be committed to changes when the reasons behind them were fully explained. Although this may seem like common sense, many managers feel they are too busy to explain things or that explanations will "open up a big can of worms." Evidence clearly indicates, though, that explanations increase employee commitment and support of decisions.[4] Moreover, although managers might think that sending a message one time is enough to get through

Downward, upward, and lateral directions of communication have their own challenges; understand and manage these unique challenges.

to lower-level employees, most research suggests managerial communications must be repeated several times and through a variety of different media to be truly effective.[5]

Another problem in downward communication is its one-way nature; generally, managers inform employees but rarely solicit their advice or opinions. Many employees say their bosses rarely or never ask for their advice. Yet some companies value employee input greatly and create programs to maximize feedback effectiveness. For instance, Bayer, the German pharmaceutical company, has instituted a corporatewide program called Triple-i: Inspiration, Ideas, Innovation, which has generated more than 9,000 ideas in one year.[6]

The best communicators explain the reasons behind their downward communications but also solicit communication from the employees they supervise. That leads us to the next direction: upward communication.

Upward Communication

Upward communication flows to a higher level in the group or organization. It's used to provide feedback to higher-ups, inform them of progress toward goals, and relay current problems. Upward communication keeps managers aware of how employees feel about their jobs, co-workers, and the organization in general. Managers also rely on upward communication for ideas on how conditions can be improved.

Given that most managers' job responsibilities have expanded, upward communication is increasingly difficult because managers are overwhelmed and easily distracted. To engage in effective upward communication, try to reduce distractions (meet in a conference room if you can, rather than your boss's office or cubicle), communicate in headlines not paragraphs (your goal is to get your boss's attention, not to engage in a meandering discussion), support your headlines with actionable items (what you believe should happen), and prepare an agenda to make sure you use your boss's attention well.[7]

Lateral Communication

When communication takes place among members of the same work group, members of work groups at the same level, managers at the same level, or any other horizontally equivalent workers, we describe it as *lateral communication.*

Why is lateral communication needed if a group or an organization's vertical communications are effective? Lateral communication saves time and facilitates coordination. Some lateral relationships are formally sanctioned. More often, they are informally created to short-circuit the vertical hierarchy and expedite action. So from management's viewpoint, lateral communications can be good or bad. Because strictly adhering to the formal vertical structure for all communications can be inefficient, lateral communication occurring with management's knowledge and support can be beneficial. But it can create dysfunctional conflicts when the formal vertical channels are breached, when members go above or around their superiors to get things done, or when bosses find actions have been taken or decisions made without their knowledge.

INTERPERSONAL COMMUNICATION

How do group members transfer meaning between and among each other? They essentially rely on oral, written, and nonverbal communication.

Oral Communication

The chief means of conveying messages is oral communication. Speeches, formal one-on-one and group discussions, and the informal rumor mill or grapevine are popular forms of oral communication.

Oral, written, and nonverbal communication forms or mediums of communication have their unique purposes, and specific limitations; utilize each medium when optimal, and try to avoid their limitations.

The advantages of oral communication are speed and feedback. We can convey a verbal message and receive a response in minimal time. If the receiver is unsure of the message, rapid feedback allows the sender to quickly detect and correct it. As one professional put it, "Face-to-face communication on a consistent basis is still the best way to get information to and from employees."[8]

The major disadvantage of oral communication surfaces whenever a message has to pass through a number of people: the more people, the greater the potential distortion. If you've ever played the game "Telephone," you know the problem. Each person interprets the message in her own way. The message's content, when it reaches its destination, is often very different from the original. In an organization, where decisions and other communiqués are verbally passed up and down the authority hierarchy, considerable opportunities arise for messages to become distorted.

Written Communication

Written communications include memos, letters, fax transmissions, e-mail, instant messaging, organizational periodicals, notices placed on bulletin boards (including electronic ones), and any other device that transmits via written words or symbols.

Why would a sender choose written communication? It's often tangible and verifiable. Both the sender and receiver have a record of the communication; and the message can be stored for an indefinite period. If there are questions about its content, the message is physically available for later reference. This feature is particularly important for complex and lengthy communications. The marketing plan for a new product, for instance, is likely to contain a number of tasks spread out over several months. By putting it in writing, those who have to initiate the plan can readily refer to it over its lifespan. A final benefit of all written communication comes from the process itself. People are usually forced to think more thoroughly about what they want to convey in a written message than in a spoken one. Thus, written communications are more likely to be well thought out, logical, and clear.

Of course, written messages have drawbacks. They're time consuming. You could convey far more information to a college instructor in a 1-hour oral exam than in a 1-hour written exam. In fact, what you can say in 10 to 15 minutes might take you an hour to write. The other major disadvantage is lack of a built-in feedback mechanism. Oral communication allows the receiver to respond rapidly to what he thinks he hears. But e-mailing a memo or sending an instant message provides no assurance it has been received or that the recipient will interpret it as the sender intended.

Nonverbal Communication

Every time we deliver a verbal message, we also impart a nonverbal message.[9] Sometimes the nonverbal component may stand alone. In a singles bar, a glance, a stare, a smile, a frown, and a provocative body movement all convey meaning. No discussion of communication would thus be complete without consideration of *nonverbal communication*—which includes body movements, the intonations or emphasis we give to words, facial expressions, and the physical distance between the sender and receiver.

We could argue that every *body movement* has meaning, and no movement is accidental (though some are unconscious). Through body language, we say, "Help me, I'm lonely"; "Take me, I'm available"; and "Leave me alone, I'm depressed." We act out our state of being with nonverbal body language. We lift one eyebrow for disbelief. We rub our noses for puzzlement. We clasp our arms to isolate ourselves or to protect ourselves. We shrug our shoulders for indifference, wink for intimacy, tap our fingers for impatience, slap our forehead for forgetfulness.[10]

The two most important messages body language conveys are (1) the extent to which we like another and are interested in the other person's views and (2) the perceived status between a sender and receiver.[11] We're more likely to position ourselves closer to people we like and touch them more often. Similarly, if you feel you're of higher status than another, you're more likely to display body movements—such as crossed legs or a slouched seated position—that reflect a casual and relaxed manner.[12]

Body language adds to, and often complicates, verbal communication. A body position or movement can communicate something of the emotion behind a message, but when it is linked with spoken language, it gives fuller meaning to a sender's message.

If you read the verbatim minutes of a meeting, you wouldn't grasp the impact of what was said the same way as if you had been there or could see the meeting on video. Why? There is no record of nonverbal communication. The emphasis given to words or phrases is missing. Exhibit 11-2 illustrates how *intonations* can change the meaning of a message. *Facial expressions* also convey meaning. A snarling face says something different from a smile. Facial expressions, along with intonations, can show arrogance, aggressiveness, fear, shyness, and other characteristics.

Physical distance also has meaning. What is considered proper spacing between people largely depends on cultural norms. A businesslike distance in some European countries feels intimate in many parts of North America. If someone stands closer to you than is considered appropriate, it may indicate aggressiveness or sexual interest; if farther away, it may signal disinterest or displeasure with what is being said.

It's important to be alert to these nonverbal aspects of communication and look for nonverbal cues as well as the literal meaning of a sender's words. You should particularly be aware of contradictions between the messages. Someone who frequently glances at her wristwatch is giving the message that she would prefer to terminate the conversation

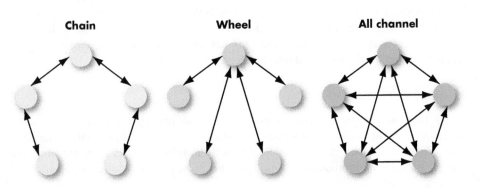

EXHIBIT 11-2
**Three Common
Small-Group
Networks**

Chain   **Wheel**   **All channel**

EXHIBIT 11-3
**Intonations:
It's the Way You
Say It!**

Change your tone and you change your meaning:	
Placement of the emphasis	**What it means**
Why don't I take **you** to dinner tonight?	I was going to take someone else.
Why don't **I** take you to dinner tonight?	Instead of the guy you were going with.
Why **don't** I take you to dinner tonight?	I'm trying to find a reason why I **shouldn't** take you.
Why don't I take you to dinner tonight?	Do you have a problem with me?
Why don't I **take** you to dinner tonight?	Instead of going on your own.
Why don't I take you to **dinner** tonight?	Instead of lunch tomorrow.
Why don't I take you to dinner **tonight**?	Not tomorrow night.

no matter what she actually says. We misinform others when we express one message verbally, such as trust, but nonverbally communicate a contradictory message that reads, "I don't have confidence in you."

ORGANIZATIONAL COMMUNICATION

In this section, we move from interpersonal communication to organizational communication. Our first focus will be to describe and distinguish formal networks and the grapevine. Then we discuss technological innovations in communication.

Formal Small-Group Networks

Formal organizational networks can be very complicated, including hundreds of people and a half-dozen or more hierarchical levels. To simplify our discussion, we've condensed these networks into three common small groups of five people each (see Exhibit 11-3): chain, wheel, and all channel.

The *chain* rigidly follows the formal chain of command; this network approximates the communication channels you might find in a rigid three-level organization. The *wheel* relies on a central figure to act as the conduit for all the group's communication; it simulates the communication network you would find on a team with a strong leader. The *all-channel* network permits all group members to actively communicate with each other; it's most often characterized in practice by self-managed teams, in which all group members are free to contribute and no one person takes on a leadership role.

As Exhibit 11-4 demonstrates, the effectiveness of each network depends on the dependent variable that concerns you. The structure of the wheel facilitates the emergence

Criteria	Chain	Networks Wheel	All Channel
Speed	Moderate	Fast	Fast
Accuracy	High	High	Moderate
Emergence of a leader	Moderate	High	None
Member satisfaction	Moderate	Low	High

EXHIBIT 11-4
**Small-Group
Networks and
Effective Criteria**

of a leader, the all-channel network is best if you desire high member satisfaction, and the chain is best if accuracy is most important. Exhibit 11-4 leads us to the conclusion that no single network will work best for all occasions.

The Grapevine

The informal communication network in a group or organization is called the **grapevine**.[13] Although the rumors and gossip transmitted through the grapevine may be informal, it's still an important source of information. A recent report shows that grapevine or word-of-mouth information from peers about a company has important effects on whether job applicants join an organization.[14]

One of the most famous studies of the grapevine investigated communication patterns among 67 managers in a small manufacturing firm.[15] The study asked each communication recipient how he or she first received a given piece of information and then traced it back to its source. Although the grapevine was important, only 10 percent of the executives acted as liaison individuals (that is, passed the information to more than one other person). When one executive decided to resign to enter the insurance business, 81 percent of the others knew about it, but only 11 percent told someone else. This lack of spreading information through the grapevine is interesting in light of how often individuals claim to receive information that way.

It's frequently assumed rumors start because they make good gossip. This is rarely the case. Rumors emerge as a response to situations that are *important* to us, when there is *ambiguity,* and under conditions that arouse *anxiety.*[16] The fact that work situations frequently contain these three elements explains why rumors flourish in organizations. The secrecy and competition that typically prevail in large organizations—around the appointment of new bosses, the relocation of offices, downsizing decisions, or the realignment of work assignments—encourage and sustain rumors on the grapevine. A rumor will persist until either the wants and expectations creating the uncertainty are fulfilled or the anxiety has been reduced.

What can we conclude about the grapevine? Certainly it's an important part of any group or organization communication network and is well worth understanding. It gives managers a feel for the morale of their organization, identifies issues employees consider important, and helps tap into employee anxieties. The grapevine also serves employees' needs: small talk creates a sense of closeness and friendship among those who share information, although research suggests it often does so at the expense of those in the "out" group.[17] There is also evidence that gossip is driven largely by employee social networks that managers can study to learn more about how positive and negative information is flowing through their organization.[18] Thus, although the grapevine may not be sanctioned or controlled by the organization, it can be understood.

Can managers entirely eliminate rumors? No. What they should do, however, is minimize the negative consequences of rumors by limiting their range and impact. Exhibit 11-5 offers a few practical suggestions.

Electronic Communications

An indispensable—and in about 71 percent of cases, the primary—medium of communication in today's organizations is electronic. Electronic communications include e-mail, text messaging, networking software, blogs, and videoconferencing. Let's discuss each.

EXHIBIT 11-5
**Suggestions
for Reducing
the Negative
Consequences
of Rumors**

1. **Provide** information—in the long run, the best defense against rumors is a good offense (in other words, rumors tend to thrive in the absence of formal communication).
2. **Explain** actions and decisions that may appear inconsistent, unfair, or secretive.
3. **Refrain** from shooting the messenger—rumors are a natural fact of organizational life, so respond to them calmly, rationally, and respectfully.
4. **Maintain** open communication channels—constantly encourage employees to come to you with concerns, suggestions, and ideas.

E-MAIL   E-mail uses the Internet to transmit and receive computer-generated text and documents. Its growth has been spectacular, and its use is now so pervasive it's hard to imagine life without it. E-mail messages can be quickly written, edited, and stored. They can be distributed to one person or thousands with a click of a mouse. And the cost of sending formal e-mail messages to employees is a fraction of the cost of printing, duplicating, and distributing a comparable letter or brochure.[19]

E-mail is not without drawbacks. The following are some of its most significant limitations and what organizations should do to reduce or eliminate them:

- *Risk of misinterpreting the message.* It's true we often misinterpret verbal messages, but the potential to misinterpret e-mail is even greater. One research team at New York University found we can accurately decode an e-mail's intent and tone only 50 percent of the time, yet most of us vastly overestimate our ability to send and interpret clear messages. If you're sending an important message, make sure you reread it for clarity.[20]
- *Drawbacks for communicating negative messages.* E-mail may not be the best way to communicate negative information. When Radio Shack decided to lay off 400 employees, it drew an avalanche of scorn inside and outside the company by doing it via e-mail. Employees need to be careful when communicating negative messages via e-mail, too. Justen Deal, 22, wrote an e-mail critical of some strategic decisions made by his employer, pharmaceutical giant Kaiser Permanente, and questioned the financing of several information technology projects. Within hours, Deal's computer was seized; he was later fired.[21]
- *Time-consuming nature.* An estimated 62 trillion e-mails are sent every year, of which approximately 60 percent, or 36 trillion, are non-spam messages that someone has to answer![22] Some people, such as venture capitalist and Dallas Mavericks owner Mark Cuban, receive more than a thousand messages a day (Cuban says 10 percent are of the "I want" variety). Although you probably don't receive *that* many, most of us have trouble keeping up with all e-mail, especially as we advance in our career. Experts suggest the following strategies:
- *Don't check e-mail in the morning.* Take care of important tasks before getting ensnared in e-mails. Otherwise, you may never get to those tasks.
- *Check e-mail in batches.* Don't check e-mail continually throughout the day. Some experts suggest twice a day. "You wouldn't want to do a new load of laundry every time you have a dirty pair of socks," says one expert.
- *Unsubscribe.* Stop newsletters and other subscriptions you don't really need.

- *Stop sending e-mail.* The best way to receive lots of e-mail is to send lots of e-mail, so send less. Shorter e-mails garner shorter responses. "A well-written message can and should be as concise as possible," says one expert.
- *Declare e-mail bankruptcy.* Some people, like recording artist Moby and venture capitalist Fred Wilson, become so overwhelmed by e-mail they declare "e-mail bankruptcy." They wipe out their entire inbox and start over.

  Although some of these steps may not work for you, keep in mind that e-mail can be less productive than it seems: we often seem busy but get less accomplished through e-mail than we might think.[23]

- *Limited expression of emotions.* We tend to think of e-mail as a sort of sterile, faceless form of communication. Some researchers say the lack of visual and vocal cues means emotionally positive messages, like those including praise, will be seen as more emotionally neutral than the sender intended.[24] But as you no doubt know, e-mails are often highly emotional. E-mail tends to have a disinhibiting effect on people; without the recipient's facial expression to temper their emotional expression, senders write things they'd never be comfortable saying in person. When others send flaming messages, remain calm and try not to respond in kind. And, as hard as it might sometimes be, try to see the flaming message from the other party's point of view. That may calm your nerves.[25]
- *Privacy concerns.* There are two privacy issues with e-mail.[26] First, your e-mails may be, and often are, monitored. You can't always trust the recipient of your e-mail to keep it confidential, either. For these reasons, you shouldn't write anything you wouldn't want made public. Second, you need to exercise caution in forwarding e-mail from your company's e-mail account to a personal or "public" e-mail account (for example, Gmail, Yahoo!, MSN). These accounts often aren't as secure as corporate accounts, so when you forward a company e-mail to them, you may be violating your organization's policy or unintentionally disclosing confidential data. Many employers hire vendors to sift through e-mails, using software to catch not only obvious key words ("insider trading") but also the vague ("that thing we talked about") or the guilt-ridden ("regret"). Another survey revealed nearly 40 percent of companies have employees whose only job is to read other employees' e-mail.[27]

INSTANT MESSAGING AND TEXT MESSAGING Like e-mail, instant messaging (IM) and text messaging (TM) use electronic media. Unlike e-mail, though, IM and TM either occur in real time (IM) or use portable communication devices (TM). In just a few years, IM and TM have become pervasive. As you no doubt know from experience, IM is usually sent via computer, whereas TM is transmitted via cell phones or handheld devices such as BlackBerrys and iPhones.

Despite their advantages, IM and TM aren't going to replace e-mail. E-mail is still probably a better device for conveying long messages that must be saved. IM is preferable for one- or two-line messages that would just clutter up an e-mail inbox. On the downside, some IM and TM users find the technology intrusive and distracting. Its continual presence can make it hard for employees to concentrate and stay focused. A survey of managers revealed that in 86 percent of meetings, at least some participants checked TM, and another survey revealed 20 percent of managers report having been scolded for using wireless devices during meetings.[28] Finally, because instant messages can be intercepted easily, many organizations are concerned about the security of IM and TM.[29]

One other point: it's important to not let the informality of text messaging ("omg! r u serious? brb") spill over into business e-mails. Many prefer to keep business communication relatively formal. A survey of employers revealed that 58 percent rate grammar, spelling, and punctuation as "very important" in e-mail messages.[30] By making sure your professional communications are, well, professional, you'll show yourself to be mature and serious. Avoid jargon and slang, use formal titles, use formal e-mail addresses for yourself (losethatpartygirl@yahoo.com), and take care to make your message concise and well written. None of this means, of course, that you have to give up TM or IM; you just need to maintain the differences between the way you communicate with your friends and the way you communicate professionally.

SOCIAL NETWORKING Nowhere has communication been more transformed than in the rise of social networking. You are doubtlessly familiar with and perhaps a user of social networking platforms such as Facebook and LinkedIn. Rather than being one huge site, Facebook, which has more than 600 million active users, is actually composed of separate networks based on schools, companies, or regions. Individuals older than age 25 are now its fastest-growing group of users. In a desire to maintain control over employee use of social networking for professional purposes, many organizations have developed their own in-house social networking applications. The research and advisory firm Gartner Inc. estimates that social networking will soon replace e-mail as the primary form of business communication for 20 percent or more of business users.[31]

To get the most from social networks and avoid irritating your contacts, reserve them for high-value items only—not as an everyday or even every-week tool. Remember that a prospective employer might check your Facebook entries. Some entrepreneurs have developed software that mines such websites on behalf of companies (or individuals) that want to check up on a job applicant (or potential date). So keep in mind that what you post may be read by people other than your intended contacts.[32]

BLOGS A **blog (web log)** is a website about a single person or company. Experts estimate that more than 156 million blogs now exist. Millions of U.S. workers have blogs. And, of course, many organizations and organizational leaders have blogs that speak for the organization.

Twitter is a hybrid social networking service that allows users to post "micro-blog" entries to their subscribers about any topic, including work. Many organizational leaders send Twitter messages ("tweets"), but they can also come from any employee about any work topic, leaving organizations with less control over the communication of important or sensitive information.

Although some companies have policies governing the content of blogs and Twitter feeds, many don't, and many posters say they have blogged or tweeted comments that could be construed as harmful to their company's reputation. Many think their personal blogs are outside their employer's purview, but if someone else in the company happens to read a critical or negative blog entry or post, there is nothing to keep him or her from sharing that information with others, and the employee could be dismissed as a result.

One legal expert notes, "Employee bloggers mistakenly believe the First Amendment gives them the right to say whatever they want on their personal blogs.

Wrong!" Also, beware of posting personal blog entries from work. More than three-quarters of employers actively monitor employees' website connections. In short, if you are going to have a personal blog, maintain a strict work–personal "firewall."[33]

VIDEOCONFERENCING *Videoconferencing* permits employees in an organization to have real-time meetings with people at different locations. Live audio and video images let participants see, hear, and talk with each other without being physically in the same location.

Peter Quirk, a program manager with EMC Corporation, uses videoconferencing to hold monthly meetings of employees at various locations and many other meetings as well. Doing so saves travel expenses and time. However, Quirk notes, it's especially important to stimulate questions and involve all participants in order to avoid someone who is linked in but disengaged. Sun Microsystem's Karen Rhode agrees special efforts must be made to engage remote participants, suggesting, "You can poll people, people can ask questions, you can do an engaging presentation."[34]

Managing Information

We all have more information at our disposal than ever. It brings us many benefits, but also two important challenges: information overload and threats to information security. We consider each in turn.

DEALING WITH INFORMATION OVERLOAD Do you find yourself bombarded with information—from e-mail, blogs, Internet surfing, IMs, cell phones, and televisions? You're not alone. Basex, a company that looks at worker efficiency, found the largest part of an average worker's day—43 percent—is spent on matters that are neither important nor urgent, such as responding to noncrucial e-mails and surfing the web. (Basex also found 25 percent of an employee's time was spent composing and responding to *important* e-mail.)

Intel designed an 8-month experiment to see how limiting this **information overload** might aid productivity. One group of employees was told to limit both digital and in-person contact for 4 hours on Tuesdays, while another group followed its usual routine. The first group was more productive, and 75 percent of its members suggested the program be expanded. "It's huge. We were expecting less," remarked Nathan Zeldes, an Intel engineer who led the experiments. "When people are uninterrupted they can sit back and design chips and really think."[35]

We have already reviewed some ways of reducing the time sunk into e-mails. More generally, as the Intel study shows, it may make sense to connect to technology less frequently, to, in the words of one article, "avoid letting the drumbeat of digital missives constantly shake up and reorder to-do lists." For instance, Lynaia Lutes, an account supervisor for a small Texas company, was able to think much more strategically by taking a break from digital information each day. In the past, she said, "I basically completed an assignment" but didn't approach it strategically. By creating such breaks for yourself, you may be better able to prioritize, think about the big picture, and thereby be more effective.[36]

BARRIERS TO EFFECTIVE COMMUNICATION

A number of barriers can retard or distort effective communication. In this section, we highlight the most important.

Filtering

Filtering refers to a sender's purposely manipulating information so the receiver will see it more favorably. A manager who tells his boss what he feels the boss wants to hear is filtering information.

The more vertical levels in the organization's hierarchy, the more opportunities there are for filtering. But some filtering will occur wherever there are status differences. Factors such as fear of conveying bad news and the desire to please the boss often lead employees to tell their superiors what they think they want to hear, thus distorting upward communications.

Selective Perception

We have mentioned selective perception before in this book. It appears again here because the receivers in the communication process selectively see and hear based on their needs, motivations, experience, background, and other personal characteristics. Receivers also project their interests and expectations into communications as they decode them. An employment interviewer who expects a female job applicant to put her family ahead of her career is likely to see that in all female applicants, regardless of whether they actually feel that way. As we said in the chapter on perception, we don't see reality; we interpret what we see and call it reality.

Information Overload

Individuals have a finite capacity for processing data. When the information we have to work with exceeds our processing capacity, the result is information overload. We've seen that dealing with it has become a huge challenge for individuals and for organizations. It's a challenge you can manage—to some degree—by following the steps outlined earlier in this chapter.

What happens when individuals have more information than they can sort and use? They tend to select, ignore, pass over, or forget. Or they may put off further processing until the overload situation ends. In any case, lost information and less effective communication results, making it all the more important to deal well with overload.

Emotions

You may interpret the same message differently when you're angry or distraught than when you're happy. For example, individuals in positive moods are more confident about their opinions after reading a persuasive message, so well-crafted arguments have stronger impacts on their opinions.[37] People in negative moods are more likely to scrutinize messages in greater detail, whereas those in positive moods tend to accept communications at face value.[38] Extreme emotions such as jubilation or depression are most likely to hinder effective communication. In such instances, we are most prone to disregard our rational and objective thinking processes and substitute emotional judgments.

Language

Even when we're communicating in the same language, words mean different things to different people. Age and context are two of the biggest factors that influence such differences.

For instance, when Michael Schiller, a business consultant, was talking with his 15-year-old daughter about where she was going with her friends, he told her, "You need to recognize your KPIs and measure against them." Schiller said that in response, his daughter "looked at him like he was from outer space." (For the record, KPI stands for key performance indicators.) Those new to corporate lingo may find acronyms such as *KPI*, words such as *deliverables* (verifiable outcomes of a project), and phrases such as *get the low-hanging fruit* (deal with the easiest parts first) bewildering, in the same way parents may be mystified by teen slang.[39]

In short, our use of language is far from uniform. If we knew how each of us modified the language, we could minimize communication difficulties, but we usually don't know. Senders tend to assume the words and terms they use mean the same to the receiver as to them. This assumption is often incorrect.

Silence

It's easy to ignore silence or lack of communication, precisely because it is defined by the absence of information. However, research suggests silence and withholding communication are both common and problematic.[40] One survey found that more than 85 percent of managers reported remaining silent about at least one issue of significant concern.[41] Employee silence means managers lack information about ongoing operational problems. And silence regarding discrimination, harassment, corruption, and misconduct means top management cannot take action to eliminate this behavior. Finally, employees who are silent about important issues may also experience psychological stress.

Silence is less likely where minority opinions are treated with respect, work group identification is high, and high procedural justice prevails.[42] Practically, this means managers must make sure they behave in a supportive manner when employees voice divergent opinions or concerns, and they must take these under advisement. One act of ignoring or belittling an employee for expressing concerns may well lead the employee to withhold important future communication.

Communication Apprehension

An estimated 5 to 20 percent of the population suffers debilitating **communication apprehension**, or social anxiety.[43] These people experience undue tension and anxiety in oral communication, written communication, or both.[44] They may find it extremely difficult to talk with others face to face or may become extremely anxious when they have to use the phone, relying on memos or e-mails when a phone call would be faster and more appropriate.

Studies show oral-communication apprehensives avoid situations, such as teaching, for which oral communication is a dominant requirement.[45] But almost all jobs require *some* oral communication. Of greater concern is evidence that high oral-communication apprehensives distort the communication demands of their jobs in order to minimize the need for communication. So be aware some people severely limit their oral communication and rationalize their actions by telling themselves communicating isn't necessary for them to do their jobs effectively.

Lying

The final barrier to effective communication is outright misrepresentation of information, or lying. People differ in their definition of what constitutes a lie. For example, is deliberately withholding information about a mistake you made a lie, or do you have to actively deny your role in the mistake to pass the threshold of deceit? Although the definition of a lie will continue to befuddle both ethicists and social scientists, there is no denying the prevalence of lying. In one diary study, the average person reported telling one to two lies per day, with some individuals telling considerably more.[46] Compounded across a large organization, this is an enormous amount of deception happening every single day! Evidence also shows people are more comfortable lying over the phone than face to face, and more comfortable lying in e-mails than when they have to write with pen and paper.[47]

Can you detect liars? Despite a great deal of investigation, research generally suggests most people are not very good at detecting deception in others.[48] The problem is, there are no nonverbal or verbal cues unique to lying—averting your gaze, pausing, and shifting your posture, although possibly thought to be indicators of lying, can also be signals of nervousness, shyness, or doubt. Moreover, most people who lie take a number of steps to guard against being detected, so they might deliberately look a person in the eye when lying because they know that direct eye contact is (incorrectly) assumed to be a sign of truthfulness. Finally, many lies are embedded in truths; liars usually give a somewhat true account with just enough details changed to avoid detection.

In sum, the frequency of lying and the difficulty in detecting liars makes this an especially strong barrier to effective communication in organizations.

GLOBAL IMPLICATIONS

Effective communication is difficult under the best of conditions. Cross-cultural factors clearly create the potential for increased communication problems. A gesture that is well understood and acceptable in one culture can be meaningless or lewd in another. Only 18 percent of companies have documented strategies for communicating with employees across cultures, and only 31 percent require that corporate messages be customized for consumption in other cultures. Procter & Gamble seems to be an exception; more than half the company's employees don't speak English as their first language, so the company focuses on simple messages to make sure everyone knows what's important.[49]

Cultural Barriers

Researchers have identified a number of problems related to language difficulties in cross-cultural communications.[50]

First are *barriers caused by semantics*. Words mean different things to different people, particularly people from different national cultures. Some words don't translate between cultures. The Finnish word *sisu* means something akin to "guts" or "dogged persistence" but is essentially untranslatable into English. The new capitalists in Russia may have difficulty communicating with British or Canadian counterparts because English terms such as *efficiency, free market,* and *regulation* have no direct Russian equivalents.

Second are *barriers caused by word connotations*. Words imply different things in different languages. Negotiations between U.S. and Japanese executives can be difficult because the Japanese word *hai* translates as "yes," but its connotation is "Yes, I'm listening" rather than "Yes, I agree."

A number of barriers—such as culture—often retard or distort effective communication; understand these barriers as a means of overcoming them.

Third are *barriers caused by tone differences.* In some cultures, language is formal; in others, it's informal. In some cultures, the tone changes depending on the context: People speak differently at home, in social situations, and at work. Using a personal, informal style when a more formal style is expected can be embarrassing.

Fourth are *differences in tolerance for conflict and methods for resolving conflicts.* Individuals from individualist cultures tend to be more comfortable with direct conflicts and will make the source of their disagreements overt. Collectivists are more likely to acknowledge conflict only implicitly and avoid emotionally charged disputes. They may attribute conflicts to the situation more than to the individuals and therefore may not require explicit apologies to repair relationships, whereas individualists prefer explicit statements accepting responsibility for conflicts and public apologies to restore relationships.

Cultural Context

Cultures tend to differ in the degree to which context influences the meaning individuals take from communication.[51] In **high-context cultures** such as China, Korea, Japan, and Vietnam, people rely heavily on nonverbal and subtle situational cues in communicating with others, and a person's official status, place in society, and reputation carry considerable weight. What is *not* said may be more significant than what *is* said. In contrast, people from Europe and North America reflect their **low-context cultures**. They rely essentially on spoken and written words to convey meaning; body language and formal titles are secondary.

These contextual differences actually mean quite a lot in terms of communication. Communication in high-context cultures implies considerably more trust by both parties. What may appear to be casual and insignificant conversation in fact reflects the desire to build a relationship and create trust. Oral agreements imply strong commitments in high-context cultures. And who you are—your age, seniority, rank in the organization—is highly valued and heavily influences your credibility. But in low-context cultures, enforceable contracts tend to be in writing, precisely worded, and highly legalistic. Similarly, low-context cultures value directness. Managers are expected to be explicit and precise in conveying intended meaning. It's quite different in high-context cultures, in which managers tend to "make suggestions" rather than give orders.

A Cultural Guide

When communicating with people from a different culture, what can you do to reduce misinterpretations? Begin by trying to assess the cultural context. You're likely to have fewer difficulties if it's similar to yours. The following rules can be helpful:[52]

1. *Assume differences until similarity is proven.* Most of us assume others are more similar to us than they actually are. You are less likely to err if you assume they are different from you until proven otherwise.
2. *Emphasize description rather than interpretation or evaluation.* Interpreting or evaluating what someone has said or done draws more on your own culture and background than on the observed situation. So delay judgment until you've had sufficient time to observe and interpret the situation from the differing perspectives of all concerned.
3. *Practice empathy.* Before sending a message, put yourself in the recipient's shoes. What are his values, experiences, and frames of reference? What do you know

about his education, upbringing, and background that can give you added insight? Try to see the other person as he really is.

4. ***Treat your interpretations as a working hypothesis.*** Once you've developed an explanation for a new situation or think you empathize with someone from a foreign culture, treat your interpretation as a hypothesis that needs further testing rather than as a certainty. Carefully assess the feedback recipients provide you, to see whether it confirms your hypothesis. For important decisions or communiqués, check with other foreign and home-country colleagues to make sure your interpretations are on target.

SUMMARY AND IMPLICATIONS FOR MANAGERS

You've probably discovered the link between communication and employee satisfaction in this chapter: the less uncertainty, the greater the satisfaction. Distortions, ambiguities, and incongruities between verbal and nonverbal messages all increase uncertainty and reduce satisfaction.[53]

- The less distortion, the more employees will receive goals, feedback, and other management messages as intended.[54] This, in turn, should reduce ambiguities and clarify the group's task.
- Extensive use of vertical, lateral, and informal channels also increases communication flow, reduces uncertainty, and improves group performance and satisfaction.
- Perfect communication is unattainable, yet a positive relationship exists between effective communication and worker productivity.[55] Choosing the correct channel, being an effective listener, and using feedback can make for more effective communication.
- Whatever the sender's expectations, the message as decoded in the receiver's mind represents his reality. And this reality will determine performance, along with the individual's level of motivation and degree of satisfaction.
- Because we gather so much meaning from the way a message is communicated, the potential for misunderstanding in electronic communication is great despite its advantages.
- We sometimes process messages relatively automatically, whereas at other times we use a more effortful, controlled process. Make sure you use communication strategies appropriate to your audience and the type of message you're sending.
- Finally, by keeping in mind communication barriers such as gender and culture, we can overcome them and increase our communication effectiveness.

MyManagementLab

Go to **MyManagementLab.com** to access study plans, interactive lectures, and videos as well as Auto-graded writing questions and the following Assisted-graded writing question.

11-1. MyManagementLab Only—comprehensive writing assignment for this chapter.

12
▪▪▪
Leadership

After studying this chapter, you should be able to:

- Define *leadership* and contrast leadership and management.
- Summarize the conclusions of trait theories of leadership.
- Assess contingency theories of leadership by their level of support.
- Compare and contrast *charismatic* and *transformational leadership*.
- Address challenges to the effectiveness of leadership.
- Assess whether or not charismatic and transformational leadership generalize across cultures.

MyManagementLab™
⭐ **Improve Your Grade!**
Over 10 million students improved their results using the Pearson MyLabs. Visit **mymanagementlab.com** for simulations, tutorials, and end-of-chapter problems.

In this chapter, we look at what makes an effective leader and what differentiates leaders from nonleaders. First, we'll present trait theories of leadership. Then, we'll discuss challenges to the meaning and importance of leadership. But before we review these approaches, let's clarify what we mean by the term *leadership*.

WHAT IS LEADERSHIP?

In today's dynamic world, leadership has the ability to influence a group toward the achievement of a vision or set of goals.

We define **leadership** as the ability to influence a group toward the achievement of a vision or set of goals. The source of this influence may be formal, such as that provided by managerial rank in an organization. But not all leaders are managers, nor, for that matter, are all managers leaders. Just because an organization provides its managers with certain formal rights is no assurance they will lead effectively. Nonsanctioned leadership—the ability to influence that arises outside the formal structure of the organization—is often as important or more important than formal influence. In other words, leaders can emerge from within a group as well as by formal appointment.

Organizations need strong leadership *and* strong management for optimal effectiveness. We need leaders today to challenge the status quo, create visions of the future, and inspire organizational members to want to achieve the visions. We also need managers to formulate detailed plans, create efficient organizational structures, and oversee day-to-day operations.

TRAIT THEORIES

Throughout history, strong leaders—Buddha, Napoléon, Mao, Churchill, Roosevelt, Reagan—have been described in terms of their traits. **Trait theories of leadership** thus focus on personal qualities and characteristics. We recognize leaders like South Africa's Nelson Mandela, Virgin Group CEO Richard Branson, Apple co-founder Steve Jobs, and American Express Chairman Ken Chenault as *charismatic, enthusiastic,* and *courageous.* The search for personality, social, physical, or intellectual attributes that differentiate leaders from nonleaders goes back to the earliest stages of leadership research.

Early research efforts to isolate leadership traits resulted in a number of dead ends. A review in the late 1960s of 20 different studies identified nearly 80 leadership traits, but only five were common to four or more of the investigations.[1] By the 1990s, after numerous studies and analyses, about the best we could say was that most leaders "are not like other people," but the particular traits that characterized them varied a great deal from review to review.[2] It was a confusing state of affairs.

A breakthrough, of sorts, came when researchers began organizing traits around the Big Five personality (ambition and energy are part of extraversion, for instance), giving strong support to traits as predictors of leadership.

A comprehensive review of the leadership literature, when organized around the Big Five, has found extraversion to be the most important trait of effective leaders,[3] but it is more strongly related to the way leaders emerge than to their effectiveness. Sociable and dominant people are more likely to assert themselves in group situations, but leaders need to make sure they're not too assertive—one study found leaders who scored very high on assertiveness were less effective than those who scored moderately high.[4]

Unlike agreeableness and emotional stability, conscientiousness and openness to experience also showed strong relationships to leadership, though not quite as strong as extraversion. Overall, the trait approach does have something to offer. Leaders who like being around people and are able to assert themselves (extraverted), who are disciplined and able to keep commitments they make (conscientious), and who are creative and flexible (open) do have an apparent advantage when it comes to leadership, suggesting good leaders do have key traits in common.

One reason is that conscientiousness and extraversion are positively related to leaders' self-efficacy, which explained most of the variance in subordinates' ratings of leader performance.[5] People are more likely to follow someone who is confident she's going in the right direction.

Another trait that may indicate effective leadership is emotional intelligence (EI), discussed in Chapter 4. Advocates of EI argue that without it, a person can have outstanding training, a highly analytical mind, a compelling vision, and an endless supply of terrific ideas but still not make a great leader. This may be especially true as individuals move up in an organization.[6] Why is EI so critical to effective leadership? A core component of EI is empathy. Empathetic leaders can sense others' needs, listen to what followers say (and don't say), and read the reactions of others. A leader who effectively displays and manages emotions will find it easier to influence the feelings of followers, by both expressing genuine sympathy and enthusiasm for good performance and by using irritation for those who fail to perform.[7]

The link between EI and leadership effectiveness may be worth investigating in greater detail.[8] Some recent research has demonstrated that people high in EI are more likely to emerge as leaders, even after taking cognitive ability and personality into account, which helps to answer some of the most significant criticisms of this research.[9]

Based on the latest findings, we offer two conclusions. First, contrary to what we believed 20 years ago and thanks to the Big Five, we can say that traits can predict leadership. Second, traits do a better job predicting the emergence of leaders and the appearance of leadership than actually distinguishing between *effective* and *ineffective* leaders.[10] The fact that an individual exhibits the traits and that others consider her a leader does not necessarily mean the leader is successful at getting the group to achieve its goals.

BEHAVIORAL THEORIES

The failures of early trait studies led researchers in the late 1940s through the 1960s to wonder whether there was something unique in the way effective leaders *behave.* Trait research provides a basis for *selecting* the right people for leadership. In contrast, **behavioral theories of leadership** implied we could *train* people to be leaders.

The most comprehensive theories resulted from the Ohio State Studies in the late 1940s,[11] which sought to identify independent dimensions of leader behavior. Beginning with more than a thousand dimensions, the studies narrowed the list to two that substantially accounted for most of the leadership behavior described by employees: *initiating structure* and *consideration.*

Initiating structure is the extent to which a leader is likely to define and structure her role and those of employees in the search for goal attainment. It includes behavior that attempts to organize work, work relationships, and goals. A leader high in initiating structure is someone who "assigns group members to particular tasks," "expects workers to maintain definite standards of performance," and "emphasizes the meeting of deadlines."

Consideration is the extent to which a person's job relationships are characterized by mutual trust, respect for employees' ideas, and regard for their feelings. A leader high in consideration helps employees with personal problems, is friendly and approachable, treats all employees as equals, and expresses appreciation and support. In a recent survey, when asked to indicate what most motivated them at work, 66 percent of employees mentioned appreciation.[12]

Leadership studies at the University of Michigan's Survey Research Center had similar objectives: to locate behavioral characteristics of leaders that appeared related to performance effectiveness. The Michigan group also came up with two behavioral dimensions: the **employee-oriented leader** emphasized interpersonal relationships by taking a personal interest in the needs of employees and accepting individual differences among them, and the **production-oriented leader** emphasized the technical or task aspects of the job, focusing on accomplishing the group's tasks. These dimensions are closely related to the Ohio State dimensions. Employee-oriented leadership is similar to consideration, and production-oriented leadership is similar to initiating structure. In fact, most leadership researchers use the terms synonymously.[13]

At one time, the results of testing behavioral theories were thought to be disappointing. However, a more recent review of 160 studies found the followers of leaders high in consideration were more satisfied with their jobs, were more motivated, and had more respect for their leader. Initiating structure was more strongly related to higher levels of group and organization productivity and more positive performance evaluations.

Some research from the GLOBE program, a study on cultural values (that also focused on cultural differences in leadership) we mentioned in Chapter 5, suggests there are international differences in preference for initiating structure and consideration.[14] Based on the values of Brazilian employees, a U.S. manager leading a team in Brazil would need to be team oriented, participative, and humane. Leaders high in consideration would succeed best in this culture. As one Brazilian manager said in the GLOBE study, "We do not prefer leaders who take self-governing decisions and act alone without engaging the group. That's part of who we are." Compared to U.S. employees, the French have a more bureaucratic view of leaders and are less likely to expect them to be humane and considerate. A leader high in initiating structure (relatively task oriented) will do best and can make decisions in a relatively autocratic manner. A manager who scores high on consideration (people oriented) may find that style backfiring in France. According to the GLOBE study, Chinese culture emphasizes being polite, considerate, and unselfish, but it also has a high-performance orientation. Thus, consideration and initiating structure may both be important.

Summary of Trait Theories and Behavioral Theories

Leaders who have certain traits and who display consideration and structuring behaviors do appear to be more effective. Perhaps you're wondering whether conscientious leaders (trait) are more likely to be structuring (behavior) and extraverted leaders (trait) to be considerate (behavior). Unfortunately, we can't be sure there is a connection. Future research is needed to integrate these approaches.

Some leaders may have the right traits or display the right behaviors and still fail. As important as traits and behaviors are in identifying effective or ineffective leaders, they do not guarantee success. The context matters, too.

CONTINGENCY THEORIES

Some tough-minded leaders seem to gain a lot of admirers when they take over struggling companies and help lead them out of the doldrums. Home Depot and Chrysler didn't hire former CEO Bob Nardelli for his winning personality. However, such leaders also seem to be quickly dismissed when the situation stabilizes.

The rise and fall of leaders like Bob Nardelli illustrate that predicting leadership success is more complex than isolating a few traits or behaviors. In their cases, what worked in very bad times and in very good times didn't seem to translate into long-term success. When researchers looked at situational influences, it appeared that under condition *a,* leadership style *x* would be appropriate, whereas style *y* was more suitable for condition *b,* and style *z* for condition *c.* But what *were* conditions *a, b,* and *c?* We next consider three approaches to isolating situational variables: the Fiedler model, the situational theory, the path–goal theory, and the leader-participation model.

The Fiedler Model

Fred Fiedler developed the first comprehensive contingency model for leadership.[15] The **Fiedler contingency model** proposes that effective group performance depends on the proper match between the leader's style and the degree to which the situation gives the leader control.

IDENTIFYING LEADERSHIP STYLE   Fiedler believes a key factor in leadership success is the individual's basic leadership style. He created the **least preferred co-worker (LPC) questionnaire** to identify that style by measuring whether a person is task or relationship oriented. The LPC questionnaire asks respondents to think of all the co-workers they have ever had and describe the one they *least enjoyed* working with by rating that person on a scale of 1 to 8 for each of 16 sets of contrasting adjectives (such as pleasant–unpleasant, efficient–inefficient, open–guarded, supportive–hostile). If you describe the person you are least able to work with in favorable terms (a high LPC score), Fiedler would label you *relationship oriented.* If you see your least-preferred co-worker in unfavorable terms (a low LPC score), you are primarily interested in productivity and are *task oriented.* About percent of respondents score in the middle range[16] and thus fall outside the theory's predictions. The rest of our discussion relates to the 84 percent who score in either the high or low range of the LPC questionnaire.

Fiedler assumes an individual's leadership style is fixed. This means if a situation requires a task-oriented leader and the person in the leadership position is relationship oriented, either the situation has to be modified or the leader has to be replaced to achieve optimal effectiveness.

DEFINING THE SITUATION   After assessing an individual's basic leadership style through the LPC questionnaire, we match the leader with the situation. Fiedler has identified three contingency or situational dimensions:

1. **Leader–member relations** is the degree of confidence, trust, and respect members have in their leader.
2. **Task structure** is the degree to which the job assignments are procedurized (that is, structured or unstructured).
3. **Position power** is the degree of influence a leader has over power variables such as hiring, firing, discipline, promotions, and salary increases.

The next step is to evaluate the situation in terms of these three variables. Fiedler states that the better the leader–member relations, the more highly structured the job, and the stronger the position power, the more control the leader has. A very favorable situation (in which the leader has a great deal of control) might include a payroll manager who is well respected and whose employees have confidence in her (good leader–member relations); who manages activities that are clear and specific—such as wage computation, check writing, and report filing (high task structure); and who is provided considerable freedom to reward and punish employees (strong position power). An unfavorable situation might be that of the disliked chairperson of a volunteer United Way fundraising team. In this job, the leader has very little control.

MATCHING LEADERS AND SITUATIONS   Combining the three contingency dimensions yields eight possible situations in which leaders can find themselves (Exhibit 12-1). The

Fiedler model proposes matching an individual's LPC score and these eight situations to achieve maximum leadership effectiveness.[17] Fiedler concluded that task-oriented leaders perform better in situations very favorable to them and very unfavorable. So, when faced with a category I, II, III, VII, or VIII situation, task-oriented leaders perform better. Relationship-oriented leaders, however, perform better in moderately favorable situations—categories IV, V, and VI. In recent years, Fiedler has condensed these eight situations down to three.[18] He now says task-oriented leaders perform best in situations of high and low control, whereas relationship-oriented leaders perform best in moderate control situations.

How would you apply Fiedler's findings? You would match leaders—in terms of their LPC scores—with the type of situation—in terms of leader–member relationships, task structure, and position power—for which they were best suited. But remember that Fiedler views an individual's leadership style as fixed. Therefore, there are only two ways to improve leader effectiveness.

First, you can change the leader to fit the situation—as a baseball manager puts a right- or left-handed pitcher into the game depending on the hitter. If a group situation rates highly unfavorable but is currently led by a relationship-oriented manager, the group's performance could be improved under a manager who is task oriented. The second alternative is to change the situation to fit the leader by restructuring tasks or increasing or decreasing the leader's power to control factors such as salary increases, promotions, and disciplinary actions.

EVALUATION   Studies testing the overall validity of the Fiedler model find considerable evidence to support substantial parts of it.[19] If we use only three categories rather than the original eight, ample evidence supports Fiedler's conclusions.[20] But the logic underlying the LPC questionnaire is not well understood, and respondents' scores are not stable.[21] The contingency variables are also complex and difficult for practitioners to assess.[22]

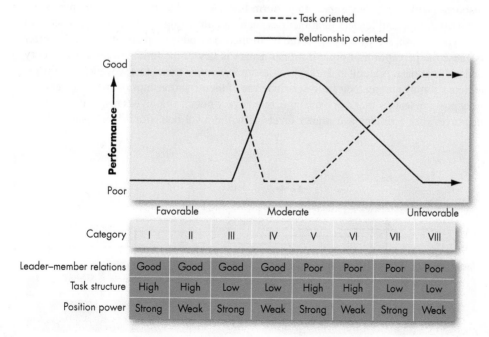

Category	I	II	III	IV	V	VI	VII	VIII
Leader–member relations	Good	Good	Good	Good	Poor	Poor	Poor	Poor
Task structure	High	High	Low	Low	High	High	Low	Low
Position power	Strong	Weak	Strong	Weak	Strong	Weak	Strong	Weak

EXHIBIT 12-1

Findings from the Fiedler Model

LEADER-MEMBER EXCHANGE (LMX) THEORY

Think of a leader you know. Did this leader have favorites who made up his in-group? If you answered yes, you're acknowledging the foundation of leader–member exchange theory.[23] **Leader–member exchange (LMX) theory** argues that, because of time pressures, leaders establish special relationships with small groups of their followers. These individuals make up the in-group—they are trusted, get a disproportionate amount of the leader's attention, and are more likely to receive special privileges. Other followers fall into the out-group.

The theory proposes that early in the history of the interaction between a leader and a given follower, the leader implicitly categorizes the follower as an "in" or an "out" and that relationship is relatively stable over time. Leaders induce LMX by rewarding those employees with whom they want a closer linkage and punishing those with whom they do not.[24] But for the LMX relationship to remain intact, the leader and the follower must invest in the relationship.

Just how the leader chooses who falls into each category is unclear, but there is evidence in-group members have demographic, attitude, and personality characteristics similar to those of their leader or a higher level of competence than out-group members[25] (see Exhibit 12-2). Leaders and followers of the same gender tend to have closer (higher LMX) relationships than those of different genders.[26] Even though the leader does the choosing, the follower's characteristics drive the categorizing decision.

Research to test LMX theory has been generally supportive, with substantive evidence that leaders do differentiate among followers; these disparities are far from random; and followers with in-group status will have higher performance ratings, engage in more helping or "citizenship" behaviors at work, and report greater satisfaction with their superiors.[27] These positive findings for in-group members shouldn't be surprising, given our knowledge of self-fulfilling prophecy (see Chapter 6). Leaders invest their resources with those they expect to perform best. And believing in-group members are the most competent, leaders treat them as such and unwittingly fulfill their prophecy. In this type of case, we would expect the performance of out-group members would suffer because the perception of organizational justice is key to the link between LMX theory and performance. A study in Turkey, for instance, demonstrated that when leaders differentiate strongly among their followers in terms of their relationships (some followers had very positive leader–member exchange, others very poor), employees respond with more negative work attitudes and higher levels of withdrawal behavior when organizational

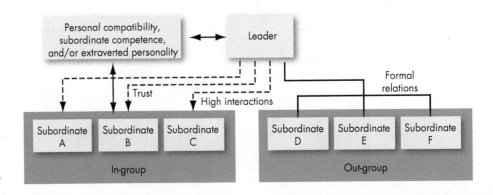

EXHIBIT 12-2
Leader–Member Exchange Theory

justice is perceived to be low.[28] Leader–follower relationships may be stronger when followers have a more active role in shaping their own job performance. Research on 287 software developers and 164 supervisors showed leader–member relationships have a stronger impact on employee performance and attitudes when employees have higher levels of autonomy and a more internal locus of control.[29]

CHARISMATIC LEADERSHIP AND TRANSFORMATIONAL LEADERSHIP

In this section, we present two contemporary leadership theories—charismatic leadership and transformational leadership—with a common theme: they view leaders as individuals who inspire followers through their words, ideas, and behaviors.

Charismatic Leadership

John F. Kennedy, Martin Luther King Jr., Ronald Reagan, Bill Clinton, Mary Kay Ash (founder of Mary Kay Cosmetics), and Steve Jobs (cofounder of Apple Computer) are frequently cited as charismatic leaders. What do they have in common?

WHAT IS CHARISMATIC LEADERSHIP? Max Weber, a sociologist, defined *charisma* (from the Greek for "gift") more than a century ago as "a certain quality of an individual personality, by virtue of which he is set apart from ordinary people and treated as endowed with supernatural, superhuman, or at least specifically exceptional powers or qualities. These are not accessible to the ordinary person and are regarded as of divine origin or as exemplary, and on the basis of them the individual concerned is treated as a leader."[30] Weber argued that charismatic leadership was one of several ideal types of authority.

The first researcher to consider charismatic leadership in terms of OB was Robert House. According to House's **charismatic leadership theory**, followers attribute heroic or extraordinary leadership abilities when they observe certain behaviors.[31] A number of studies have attempted to identify the characteristics of charismatic leaders: they have a vision, they are willing to take personal risks to achieve that vision, they are sensitive to follower needs, and they exhibit extraordinary behaviors[32] (see Exhibit 12-3).

ARE CHARISMATIC LEADERS BORN OR MADE? Are charismatic leaders born with their qualities? Or can people actually learn to be charismatic leaders? Yes, and yes.

---

1. *Vision and articulation.* Has a vision—expressed as an idealized goal—that proposes a future better than the status quo; and is able to clarify the importance of the vision in terms that are understandable to others.
2. *Personal risk.* Willing to take on high personal risk, incur high costs, and engage in self-sacrifice to achieve the vision.
3. *Sensitivity to follower needs.* Perceptive of others' abilities and responsive to their needs and feelings.
4. *Unconventional behavior.* Engages in behaviors that are perceived as novel and counter to norms.

EXHIBIT 12-3
Key Characteristics of Charismatic Leaders

Individuals *are* born with traits that make them charismatic. In fact, studies of identical twins have found they score similarly on charismatic leadership measures, even if they were raised in different households and had never met. Personality is also related to charismatic leadership; charismatic leaders are likely to be extraverted, self-confident, and achievement oriented.[33] Consider Presidents Barack Obama and Ronald Reagan: like them or not, they are often compared because both possess the qualities of charismatic leaders.

Most experts believe individuals can be trained to exhibit charismatic behaviors.[34] After all, just because we inherit certain tendencies doesn't mean we can't learn to change. One set of authors proposes a three-step process.[35] First, develop an aura of charisma by maintaining an optimistic view; using passion as a catalyst for generating enthusiasm; and communicating with the whole body, not just with words. Second, draw others in by creating a bond that inspires them to follow. Third, bring out the potential in followers by tapping into their emotions.

The approach seems to work, according to researchers who have asked undergraduate business students to "play" charismatic.[36] The students were taught to articulate an overarching goal, communicate high-performance expectations, exhibit confidence in the ability of followers to meet these expectations, and empathize with the needs of their followers; they learned to project a powerful, confident, and dynamic presence; and they practiced using a captivating and engaging voice. They were also trained to evoke charismatic nonverbal characteristics: they alternated between pacing and sitting on the edges of their desks, leaned toward the subjects, maintained direct eye contact, and had relaxed postures and animated facial expressions. Their followers had higher task performance, task adjustment, and adjustment to the leader and the group than did followers of noncharismatic leaders.

HOW CHARISMATIC LEADERS INFLUENCE FOLLOWERS How do charismatic leaders actually influence followers? Evidence suggests a four-step process.[37] It begins with articulating an appealing **vision**, a long-term strategy for attaining a goal by linking the present with a better future for the organization. Desirable visions fit the times and circumstances and reflect the uniqueness of the organization. Steve Jobs championed the iPod at Apple, noting, "It's as Apple as anything Apple has ever done." People in the organization must also believe the vision is challenging yet attainable.

Second, a vision is incomplete without an accompanying **vision statement**, a formal articulation of an organization's vision or mission. Charismatic leaders may use vision statements to imprint on followers an overarching goal and purpose. They build followers' self-esteem and confidence with high-performance expectations and belief that followers can attain them. Next, through words and actions, the leader conveys a new set of values and sets an example for followers to imitate. One study of Israeli bank employees showed charismatic leaders were more effective because their employees personally identified with them. Charismatic leaders also set a tone of cooperation and mutual support. A study of 115 government employees found they had a stronger sense of personal belonging at work when they had charismatic leaders, increasing their willingness to engage in helping and compliance-oriented behavior.[38]

Finally, the charismatic leader engages in emotion-inducing and often unconventional behavior to demonstrate courage and conviction about the vision. Followers "catch" the emotions their leader is conveying.[39]

DOES EFFECTIVE CHARISMATIC LEADERSHIP DEPEND ON THE SITUATION? Research shows impressive correlations between charismatic leadership and high performance and satisfaction among followers.[40] People working for charismatic leaders are motivated to exert extra effort and, because they like and respect their leaders, express greater satisfaction. Organizations with charismatic CEOs are more profitable, and charismatic college professors enjoy higher course evaluations.[41] However, charisma appears most successful when the follower's task has an ideological component or the environment includes a high degree of stress and uncertainty.[42] Even in laboratory studies, when people are psychologically aroused, they are more likely to respond to charismatic leaders.[43] This may explain why, when charismatic leaders surface, it's likely to be in politics or religion, or during wartime, or when a business is in its infancy, or facing a life-threatening crisis. Franklin D. Roosevelt offered a vision to get the United States out of the Great Depression in the 1930s. In 1997, when Apple Computer was floundering and lacking direction, the board persuaded charismatic cofounder Steve Jobs to return as interim CEO and return the company to its innovative roots.

Another situational factor apparently limiting charisma is level in the organization. Top executives create vision; it's more difficult to utilize a person's charismatic leadership qualities in lower-level management jobs or to align her vision with the larger goals of the organization.

Finally, people are especially receptive to charismatic leadership when they sense a crisis, when they are under stress, or when they fear for their lives. Charismatic leaders are able to reduce stress for their employees, perhaps because they help make work seem more meaningful and interesting.[44] And some people's personalities are especially susceptible to charismatic leadership.[45] Consider self-esteem. An individual who lacks self-esteem and questions his self-worth is more likely to absorb a leader's direction rather than establish his own way of leading or thinking.

THE DARK SIDE OF CHARISMATIC LEADERSHIP Charismatic business leaders like AIG's Hank Greenberg, GE's Jack Welch, Tyco's Dennis Kozlowski, Southwest Airlines' Herb Kelleher, Disney's Michael Eisner, and HP's Carly Fiorina became celebrities on the order of David Beckham and Madonna. Every company wanted a charismatic CEO, and to attract them, boards of directors gave them unprecedented autonomy and resources—the use of private jets and multimillion-dollar penthouses, interest-free loans to buy beach homes and artwork, security staffs, and similar benefits befitting royalty. One study showed charismatic CEOs were able to leverage higher salaries even when their performance was mediocre.[46]

Unfortunately, charismatic leaders who are larger than life don't necessarily act in the best interests of their organizations.[47] Many have allowed their personal goals to override the goals of the organization. The results at companies such as Enron, Tyco, WorldCom, and HealthSouth were disastrous; leaders recklessly used organizational resources for their personal benefit, and executives violated laws and ethical boundaries to inflate stock prices, allowing them to cash in millions of dollars in stock options. It's little wonder research has shown that individuals who are narcissistic are also higher in some behaviors associated with charismatic leadership.[48]

It's not that charismatic leadership isn't effective; overall, it is. But a charismatic leader isn't always the answer. Success depends, to some extent, on the situation and on the leader's vision. Some charismatic leaders—Hitler, for example—are all too successful at convincing their followers to pursue a vision that can be ruinous.

Transformational Leadership

A stream of research has focused on differentiating transformational from transactional leaders.[49] The Ohio State studies, Fiedler's model, and path–goal theory describe **transactional leaders**, who guide their followers toward established goals by clarifying role and task requirements. **Transformational leaders** inspire followers to transcend their self-interests for the good of the organization and can have an extraordinary effect on their followers. Andrea Jung at Avon, Richard Branson of the Virgin Group, and Jim McNerney of Boeing are all transformational leaders. They pay attention to the concerns and needs of individual followers; they change followers' awareness of issues by helping them look at old problems in new ways; and they excite and inspire followers to put out extra effort to achieve group goals. Exhibit 12-4 briefly identifies and defines the characteristics that differentiate these two types of leaders.

Transactional and transformational leadership complement each other; they aren't opposing approaches to getting things done.[50] Transformational leadership *builds on* transactional leadership and produces levels of follower effort and performance beyond what transactional leadership alone can do. But the reverse isn't true. So if you are a good transactional leader but do not have transformational qualities, you'll likely only be a mediocre leader. The best leaders are transactional *and* transformational.

FULL RANGE OF LEADERSHIP MODEL   Exhibit 12-5 shows the **full range of leadership model**. Laissez-faire is the most passive and therefore least effective of leader behaviors.[51] Management by exception—active or passive—is slightly better, but it's still considered

---

Transactional Leader

Contingent Reward: Contracts exchange of rewards for effort, promises rewards for good performance, recognizes accomplishments.

Management by Exception (active): Watches and searches for deviations from rules and standards, takes correct action.

Management by Exception (passive): Intervenes only if standards are not met.

Laissez-Faire: Abdicates responsibilities, avoids making decisions.

Transformational Leader

Idealized Influence: Provides vision and sense of mission, instills pride, gains respect and trust.

Inspirational Motivation: Communicates high expectations, uses symbols to focus efforts, expresses important purposes in simple ways.

Intellectual Stimulation: Promotes intelligence, rationality, and careful problem solving.

Individualized Consideration: Gives personal attention, treats each employee individually, coaches, advises.

EXHIBIT 12-4

Characteristics of Transactional and Transformational Leaders

Source: Based on B. M. Bass, "From Transactional to Transformational Leadership: Learning to Share the Vision," *Organizational Dynamics* (Winter 1990), p. 22; A. H. Eagly, M. C. Johannesen-Schmidt, and M. L. Van Engen. "Transformational, Transactional, and Laissez-faire Leadership Styles: A Meta-analysis Comparing Women and Men," *Psychological Bulletin* 129 (2003), pp. 569–591; and T. A. Judge and J. E. Bono, "Five Factor Model of Personality and Transformational Leadership," *Journal of Applied Psychology* 85 (2000), pp. 751–765.

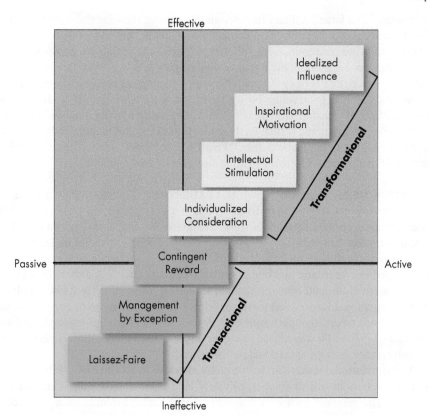

EXHIBIT 12-5
Full Range of Leadership Model

ineffective. Management by exception leaders tend to be available only when there is a problem, which is often too late. Contingent reward leadership can be an effective style of leadership but will not get employees to go above and beyond the call of duty.

Only with the four remaining styles—all aspects of transformational leadership—are leaders able to motivate followers to perform above expectations and transcend their self-interest for the sake of the organization. Individualized consideration, intellectual stimulation, inspirational motivation, and idealized influence (known as the four I's) all result in extra effort from workers, higher productivity, higher morale and satisfaction, higher organizational effectiveness, lower turnover, lower absenteeism, and greater organizational adaptability. Based on this model, leaders are generally most effective when they regularly use each of the four transformational behaviors.

HOW TRANSFORMATIONAL LEADERSHIP WORKS   Transformational leaders are more effective because they are more creative, but also because they encourage those who follow them to be creative, too.[52] Companies with transformational leaders have greater decentralization of responsibility, managers have more propensity to take risks, and compensation plans are geared toward long-term results—all of which facilitate corporate entrepreneurship.[53] One study of information technology workers in China, for instance, found empowering leadership behavior led to feelings of positive personal control among workers, which increased their creativity at work.[54]

Companies with transformational leaders also show greater agreement among top managers about the organization's goals, which yields superior organizational performance.[55] The Israeli military has seen similar results, showing that transformational leaders improve performance by building consensus among group members.[56] Transformational leaders are able to increase follower self-efficacy, giving the group a "can do" spirit.[57] Followers are more likely to pursue ambitious goals, agree on the strategic goals of the organization, and believe the goals they are pursuing are personally important.[58]

Just as vision helps explain how charismatic leadership works, it also explains part of the effect of transformational leadership. One study found vision was even more important than a charismatic (effusive, dynamic, lively) communication style in explaining the success of entrepreneurial firms.[59] Finally, transformational leadership engenders commitment on the part of followers and instills greater trust in the leader.[60]

EVALUATION OF TRANSFORMATIONAL LEADERSHIP Transformational leadership has been impressively supported at diverse job levels and occupations (school principals, teachers, marine commanders, ministers, presidents of MBA associations, military cadets, union shop stewards, sales reps). One study of R&D firms found teams whose project leaders scored high on transformational leadership produced better-quality products as judged one year later and higher profits five years later.[61] Another study looking at employee creativity and transformational leadership more directly found employees with transformational leaders had more confidence in their ability to be creative at work and higher levels of creative performance.[62] A review of 117 studies testing transformational leadership found it was related to higher levels of individual follower performance, team performance, and organizational performance.[63]

Transformational leadership isn't equally effective in all situations. It has a greater impact on the bottom line in smaller, privately held firms than in more complex organizations.[64] The personal nature of transformational leadership may be most effective when leaders can directly interact with the workforce and make decisions than when they report to an external board of directors or deal with a complex bureaucratic structure. Another study showed transformational leaders were more effective in improving group potency in teams higher in power distance and collectivism.[65] Other recent research using a sample of employees both in China and the United States found that transformational leadership had a positive relationship with perceived procedural justice, especially among individuals who were lower in power distance orientation.[66] Transformational leaders also obtain higher levels of trust, which reduces stress for followers.[67] In short, transformational leadership works through a number of different processes.

One study examined how different types of transformational leadership can be effective depending on whether work is evaluated at the team or the individual level.[68] Individual-focused transformational leadership is behavior that empowers individual followers to develop, enhance their abilities, and increase self-efficacy. Team-focused transformational leadership emphasizes group goals, shared values and beliefs, and unified efforts. Evidence from a sample of 203 team members and 60 leaders in a business unit found individual transformational leadership associated with higher individual-level performance, whereas team-focused transformational leadership drew higher group-level performance.

Transformational leadership theory is not perfect. Contingent reward leadership may not characterize transactional leaders only. And contrary to the full range of leadership model, the four I's in transformational leadership are not always superior in effectiveness to transactional leadership (contingent reward leadership sometimes works as well as transformational leadership).

In summary, transformational leadership is more strongly correlated than transactional leadership with lower turnover rates, higher productivity, lower employee stress and burnout, and higher employee satisfaction.[69] Like charisma, it can be learned. One study of Canadian bank managers found branches managed by those who underwent transformational leadership training performed significantly better than branches whose managers did not receive training. Other studies show similar results.[70]

The GLOBE study—of 18,000 leaders from 825 organizations in 62 countries—links a number of elements of transformational leadership with effective leadership, regardless of country.[71] This conclusion is very important because it disputes the contingency view that leadership style needs to adapt to cultural differences.

What elements of transformational leadership appear universal? Vision, foresight, providing encouragement, trustworthiness, dynamism, positiveness, and proactiveness top the list. The GLOBE team concluded that "effective business leaders in any country are expected by their subordinates to provide a powerful and proactive vision to guide the company into the future, strong motivational skills to stimulate all employees to fulfill the vision, and excellent planning skills to assist in implementing the vision."[72]

A vision is important in any culture, then, but the way it is formed and communicated may need to vary by culture. A GE executive who used his U.S. leadership style in Japan recalls, "Nothing happened. I quickly realized that I had to adapt my approach, to act more as a consultant to my colleagues and to adopt a team-based motivational decision-making process rather than the more vocal style which tends to be common in the West. In Japan the silence of a leader means far more than a thousand words uttered by somebody else."[73]

AUTHENTIC LEADERSHIP: ETHICS AND TRUST

Although theories have increased our understanding of effective leadership, they do not explicitly deal with the role of ethics and trust, which some argue is essential to complete the picture. Here, we consider these two concepts under the rubric of authentic leadership.[74]

If we're looking for the best possible leader, it is not enough to be charismatic or visionary—one must also be ethical and authentic.

What Is Authentic Leadership?

Mike Ullman, former JCPenney CEO, argues that leaders have to be selfless, listen well, and be honest. Consistent with this, Campbell Soup's CEO Douglas R. Conant is decidedly understated. When asked to reflect on the strong performance of Campbell Soup, he says, "We're hitting our stride a little bit more (than our peers)." He regularly admits mistakes and often says, "I can do better." Ullman and Conant appear to be good exemplars of authentic leadership.[75]

Authentic leaders know who they are, know what they believe in and value, and act on those values and beliefs openly and candidly. Their followers consider them ethical people. The primary quality produced by authentic leadership, therefore, is trust. Authentic leaders share information, encourage open communication, and stick to their ideals. The result: people come to have faith in them.

Because the concept is relatively new, there has been less research on authentic leadership than on other forms of leadership. However, it's a promising way to think about ethics and trust in leadership because it focuses on the moral aspects of being a leader. Transformational or charismatic leaders can have a vision and communicate it persuasively, but sometimes the vision is wrong (as in the case of Hitler), or the leader is more concerned with his or her own needs or pleasures, as were Dennis Kozlowski (ex-CEO of Tyco), Jeff Skilling (ex-CEO of Enron), and Raj Rajaratnam (founder of the Galleon Group).[76]

Ethics and Leadership

Only recently have researchers begun to consider the ethical implications in leadership.[77] Why now? One reason may be the growing interest in ethics throughout the field of management. Another may be the recognition that many past leaders—such as Martin Luther King Jr., John F. Kennedy, and Thomas Jefferson—suffered ethical shortcomings. Some companies, like Boeing, are tying executive compensation to ethics to reinforce the idea that, in CEO Jim McNerney's words, "there's no compromise between doing things the right way and performance."[78]

Ethics and leadership intersect at a number of junctures. We can think of transformational leaders as fostering moral virtue when they try to change the attitudes and behaviors of followers.[79] Charisma, too, has an ethical component. Unethical leaders use their charisma to enhance power over followers, directed toward self-serving ends. Ethical leaders use it in a socially constructive way to serve others.[80] Leaders who treat their followers with fairness, especially by providing honest, frequent, and accurate information, are seen as more effective.[81] Leaders rated highly ethical tend to have followers who engage in more organizational citizenship behaviors and who are more willing to bring problems to the leaders' attention.[82] Because top executives set the moral tone for an organization, they need to set high ethical standards, demonstrate them through their own behavior, and encourage and reward integrity in others while avoiding abuses of power such as giving themselves large raises and bonuses while seeking to cut costs by laying off longtime employees.

Leadership is not value-free. In assessing its effectiveness, we need to address the *means* a leader uses in trying to achieve goals, as well as the content of those goals. Scholars have tried to integrate ethical and charismatic leadership by advancing the idea of **socialized charismatic leadership**—leadership that conveys other-centered (not self-centered) values by leaders who model ethical conduct.[83] Socialized charismatic leaders are able to bring employee values in line with their own values through their words and actions.[84]

Servant Leadership

Scholars have recently considered ethical leadership from a new angle by examining **servant leadership**.[85] Servant leaders go beyond their own self-interest and focus on opportunities to help followers grow and develop. They don't use power to achieve ends; they emphasize persuasion. Characteristic behaviors include listening, empathizing, persuading, practicing stewardship, and actively developing followers' potential. Because servant leadership focuses on serving the needs of others, research has focused on its outcomes for the well-being of followers.

What are the effects of servant leadership? One study of 123 supervisors found it resulted in higher levels of commitment to the supervisor, self-efficacy, and perceptions of justice, which all were related to organizational citizenship behavior.[86] This relationship between servant leadership and follower organizational citizenship behavior appears to be stronger when followers are focused on being dutiful and responsible.[87] Second, servant leadership increases **team potency** (a belief that one's team has above-average skills and abilities), which in turn leads to higher levels of group performance.[88] Third, a study with a nationally representative sample of 250 workers found higher levels of citizenship associated with a focus on growth and advancement, which in turn was associated with higher levels of creative performance.[89]

Servant leadership may be more prevalent and more effective in certain cultures.[90] When asked to draw images of leaders, U.S. subjects tend to draw them in front of the group, giving orders to followers. Singaporeans tend to draw leaders at the back of the group, acting more to gather a group's opinions together and then unify them from the rear. This suggests the East Asian prototype is more like a servant leader, which might mean servant leadership is more effective in these cultures.

Trust and Leadership

Trust is a psychological state that exists when you agree to make yourself vulnerable to another because you have positive expectations about how things are going to turn out.[91] Even though you aren't completely in control of the situation, you are willing to take a chance that the other person will come through for you.

Trust is a primary attribute associated with leadership; breaking it can have serious adverse effects on a group's performance.[92] As one author noted, "Part of the leader's task has been, and continues to be, working with people to find and solve problems, but whether leaders gain access to the knowledge and creative thinking they need to solve problems depends on how much people trust them. Trust and trust-worthiness modulate the leader's access to knowledge and cooperation."[93]

Followers who trust a leader are confident their rights and interests will not be abused.[94] Transformational leaders create support for their ideas in part by arguing that their direction will be in everyone's best interests. People are unlikely to look up to or follow someone they perceive as dishonest or likely to take advantage of them. Thus, as you might expect, transformational leaders do generate higher levels of trust from their followers, which in turn is related to higher levels of team confidence and, ultimately, higher levels of team performance.[95]

In a simple contractual exchange of goods and services, your employer is legally bound to pay you for fulfilling your job description. But today's rapid reorganizations, diffusion of responsibility, and collaborative team-based work style mean employment relationships are not stable long-term contracts with explicit terms. Rather, they are more fundamentally based on trusting relationships than ever before. You have to trust that if you show your supervisor a creative project you've been working on, she won't steal the credit behind your back. You have to trust that extra work you've been doing will be recognized in your performance appraisal. In contemporary organizations, where the scope of work is broader, voluntary employee contribution based on trust is absolutely necessary. And only a trusted leader will be able to encourage employees to reach beyond themselves to a transformational goal.

What Are the Consequences of Trust?

Trust between supervisors and employees has a number of important advantages. Here are just a few that research has shown:

- *Trust Encourages Taking Risks.* Whenever employees decide to deviate from the usual way of doing things, or to take their supervisors' word on a new direction, they are taking a risk. In both cases, a trusting relationship can facilitate that leap.

- *Trust Facilitates Information Sharing.* One big reason employees fail to express concerns at work is because they don't feel psychologically safe revealing their views. When managers demonstrate they will give employees' ideas a fair hearing and actively make changes, employees are more willing to speak out.[96]
- *Trusting Groups Are More Effective.* When a leader sets a trusting tone in a group, members are more willing to help each other and exert extra effort for one another, which further increases trust. Conversely, members of mistrusting groups tend to be suspicious of each other, constantly guard against exploitation, and restrict communication with others in the group. These actions tend to undermine and eventually destroy the group.
- *Trust Enhances Productivity.* The bottom-line interest of companies also appears positively influenced by trust. Employees who trust their supervisors tend to receive higher performance ratings. This is partially because the trust fosters employee responses conducive to good job performance.[97] People respond to mistrust by concealing information and secretly pursuing their own interests.

CHALLENGES TO THE LEADERSHIP CONSTRUCT

Jim Collins, a leading business consultant, says, "In the 1500s, people ascribed all events they didn't understand to God. Why did the crops fail? God. Why did someone die? God. Now our all-purpose explanation is leadership."[98] But much of an organization's success or failure is due to factors outside the influence of leadership. Sometimes it's just a matter of being in the right or wrong place at a given time. In this section, we present two perspectives and one technological change that challenge accepted beliefs about the value of leadership.

Leadership as an Attribution

As you may remember from Chapter 6, attribution theory examines how people try to make sense of cause-and-effect relationships. The **attribution theory of leadership** says leadership is merely an attribution people make about other individuals.[99] Thus we attribute to leaders intelligence, outgoing personality, strong verbal skills, aggressiveness, understanding, and industriousness.[100] At the organizational level, we tend to see leaders, rightly or wrongly, as responsible for extremely negative or extremely positive performance.[101]

One longitudinal study of 128 major U.S. corporations found that whereas perceptions of CEO charisma did not lead to objective company performance, company performance did lead to perceptions of charisma.[102] Employee perceptions of their leaders' behaviors are significant predictors of whether they blame the leader for failure, regardless of how the leader assesses himself.[103] A study of more than 3,000 employees from Western Europe, the United States, and the Middle East found people who tended to "romanticize" leadership in general were more likely to believe their own leaders were transformational.[104]

When Merrill Lynch began to lose billions in 2008 as a result of its investments in mortgage securities, it wasn't long before CEO Stan O'Neal lost his job. He appeared before the House Oversight and Government Reform Committee of the U.S. Congress for what one committee member termed "a public flogging." Some called him a "criminal," and still others suggested company losses represented "attempted destruction."[105]

Whether O'Neal was responsible for the losses at Merrill Lynch or deserved his nine-figure severance package are difficult questions to answer. However, it is not difficult to argue that he probably changed very little between 2004 when *Fortune* described him as a "turnaround genius" and 2009 when he was fired. What did change was the performance of the organization he led. It's not necessarily wrong to terminate a CEO for failing or flagging financial performance. However, O'Neal's story illustrates the power of the attribution approach to leadership: hero and genius when things are going well, villain when they aren't.

We also make demographic assumptions about leaders. Respondents in a study assumed a leader described with no identifying racial information was white at a rate beyond the base rate of white employees in a company. In scenarios where identical leadership situations are described but the leaders' race is manipulated, white leaders are rated as more effective than leaders of other racial groups.[106] One large-scale summary study (a meta-analysis) found that many individuals hold stereotypes of men as having more leader characteristics than women, although as you might expect, this tendency to equate leadership with masculinity has decreased over time.[107] Other data suggest women's perceived success as transformational leaders may be based on demographic characteristics. Teams prefer male leaders when aggressively competing against other teams, but they prefer female leaders when the competition is within teams and calls for improving positive relationships within the group.[108]

Attribution theory suggests what's important is projecting the *appearance* of being a leader rather than focusing on *actual accomplishments*. Leader-wannabes who can shape the perception that they're smart, personable, verbally adept, aggressive, hardworking, and consistent in their style can increase the probability their bosses, colleagues, and employees will view them as effective leaders.

Substitutes for and Neutralizers of Leadership

One theory of leadership suggests that in many situations leaders' actions are irrelevant.[109] Experience and training are among the **substitutes** that can replace the need for a leader's support or ability to create structure. Organizational characteristics such as explicit formalized goals, rigid rules and procedures, and cohesive work groups can also replace formal leadership, while indifference to organizational rewards can neutralize its effects. **Neutralizers** make it impossible for leader behavior to make any difference to follower outcomes (see Exhibit 12-6).

This observation shouldn't be too surprising. After all, we've introduced a number of variables—such as attitudes, personality, ability, and group norms—that affect employee performance and satisfaction. It's simplistic to think employees are guided to goal accomplishments solely by the actions of their leader. Leadership is simply another independent variable in our overall OB model.

Sometimes the difference between substitutes and neutralizers is fuzzy. If I'm working on a task that's intrinsically enjoyable, theory predicts leadership will be less important because the task itself provides enough motivation. But does that mean intrinsically enjoyable tasks neutralize leadership effects, or substitute for them, or both? Another problem is that while substitutes for leadership (such as employee characteristics, the nature of the task, and so forth) matter to performance, that doesn't necessarily mean leadership doesn't.[110]

Defining Characteristics	Relationship-Oriented Leadership	Task-Oriented Leadership
Individual		
Experience/training	No effect on	Substitutes for
Professionalism	Substitutes for	Substitutes for
Indifference to rewards	Neutralizes	Neutralizes
Job		
Highly structured task	No effect on	Substitutes for
Provides its own feedback	No effect on	Substitutes for
Intrinsically satisfying	Substitutes for	No effect on
Organization		
Explicit formalized goals	No effect on	Substitutes for
Rigid rules and procedures	No effect on	Substitutes for
Cohesive work groups	Substitutes for	Substitutes for

EXHIBIT 12-6

Substitutes for and Neutralizers of Leadership

Source: Based on S. Kerr and J. M. Jermier, "Substitutes for Leadership: Their Meaning and Measurement," *Organizational Behavior and Human Performance* (December 1978), p. 378.

Online Leadership

How do you lead people who are physically separated from you and with whom you communicate electronically? This question needs attention from OB researchers.[111] Today's managers and employees are increasingly linked by networks rather than geographic proximity.

We propose that online leaders have to think carefully about what actions they want their digital messages to initiate. They confront unique challenges, the greatest of which appears to be developing and maintaining trust. **Identification-based trust**, based on a mutual understanding of each other's intentions and appreciation of the other's wants and desires, is particularly difficult to achieve without face-to-face interaction.[112] And online negotiations can also be hindered because parties express lower levels of trust.[113]

We tentatively conclude that good leadership skills will soon include the abilities to communicate support, trust, and inspiration through keyboarded words and accurately read emotions in others' messages. In electronic communication, writing skills are likely to become an extension of interpersonal skills.

SUMMARY AND IMPLICATIONS FOR MANAGERS

Leadership plays a central part in understanding group behavior, because it's the leader who usually directs us toward our goals. Knowing what makes a good leader should thus be valuable in improving group performance.

- The early search for a set of universal leadership traits failed. However, recent efforts using the Big Five personality framework show strong and consistent relationships between leadership and extraversion, conscientiousness, and openness to experience.

- The behavioral approach's major contribution was narrowing leadership into task-oriented (initiating structure) and people-oriented (consideration) styles. By considering the situation in which the leader operates, contingency theories promised to improve on the behavioral approach, but only LPC theory has fared well in leadership research.

- Research on charismatic and transformational leadership has made major contributions to our understanding of leadership effectiveness. Organizations want managers who can exhibit transformational leadership qualities and who have vision and the charisma to carry it out.

- Effective managers must develop trusting relationships with followers because, as organizations have become less stable and predictable, strong bonds of trust are replacing bureaucratic rules in defining expectations and relationships.

MyManagementLab

Go to **MyManagementLab.com** to access study plans, interactive lectures, and videos as well as Auto-graded writing questions and the following Assisted-graded writing question.

12-1. MyManagementLab Only—comprehensive writing assignment for this chapter.

13
■ ■ ■
Power and Politics

After studying this chapter, you should be able to:

- Define *power* and contrast leadership and power.
- Contrast the five bases of power.
- Identify nine power or influence tactics and their contingencies.
- Identify the causes and consequences of political behavior.
- Apply impression management techniques.
- Show the influence of culture on the uses and perceptions of politics.

MyManagementLab™
⭐ **Improve Your Grade!**
Over 10 million students improved their results using the Pearson MyLabs. Visit
mymanagementlab.com for simulations, tutorials, and end-of-chapter problems.

In both research and practice, *power* and *politics* have been described as the last dirty words. It is easier for most of us to talk about sex or money than about power or political behavior. People who have power deny it, people who want it try not to look like they're seeking it, and those who are good at getting it are secretive about how they do so.[1]

In this chapter, we show that power determines what goals a group will pursue and how the group's resources will be distributed among its members. Further, we show how group members with good political skills use their power to influence the distribution of resources in their favor.

A DEFINITION OF POWER

Power refers to a capacity that *A* has to influence the behavior of *B* so *B* acts in accordance with *A*'s wishes.[2]

Someone can thus have power but not use it; it is a capacity or potential. Probably the most important aspect of power is that it is a function of **dependence**. The greater *B*'s dependence on *A*, the greater *A*'s power in the relationship. Dependence, in turn, is based on alternatives that *B* perceives and the importance *B* places on the alternative(s) *A* controls. A person can have power over you only if he controls something you desire. If you want a college degree and have to pass a certain course to get it, and your current instructor is the only faculty member in the college who teaches that course, he has power over you. Your alternatives are highly limited, and you place a high degree of importance on obtaining a passing grade. Similarly, if you're attending college on funds totally provided by your parents, you probably recognize the power they hold over you. You're dependent on them for financial support. But once you're out of school, have a job, and are making a good income, your parents' power is reduced significantly. Who among us has not known or heard of a rich relative who is able to control a large number of family members merely through the implicit or explicit threat of "writing them out of the will"?

As anyone with young children (one of the most dependent groups) has doubtlessly noted, dependency increases the incentive to lie. But is the link as strong in less overt or ongoing situations? One study explored the link between dependency and lying in a controlled experiment with adults who had no outside relationship with one another. Researchers gave one group of research subjects bigger offices and more authority, whereas another group received smaller offices and less authority. Then half the subjects in each condition were told to steal a $100 bill and convince an interviewer they hadn't taken it. If they were able to fool the interviewer, they could keep the money. In the interviews, those in positions of power showed fewer signs of dishonesty and stress like shoulder shrugs and stuttering when lying—perhaps because they felt less dependent on others. Recall that this simulation involved only hypothetical, experimentally manipulated power, so imagine the effects when real power is on the line.[3] This study also suggests that powerful people might be better liars because they are more confident in their status, and less willing to acknowledge dependency on others.

Another study on the dependency variable relating to power investigated how people respond to the poor performance of a subordinate dependent on them in a work context.[4] In this experiment, a laboratory mockup of a performance review was developed, and participants acted the part of either powerful or unpowerful managers. The result? Powerful managers were more likely to respond to poor performers by either directly confronting them or frankly encouraging them to get training to improve. Less powerful managers enacted strategies not to confront the poor performer, like compensating for poor performance or avoiding the individual altogether. In other words, they were less likely to actively engage in a potential conflict with the subordinate, possibly because they would be more vulnerable if the subordinate wanted to "get revenge" for the negative feedback.

Power involves dependency, but as we've explored, the dynamic range is wide. Managers do well to acknowledge the roles of dependency and power in their relationships with employees, as well as to minimize situations that escalate the pressure for employees to engage in workplace deviant behavior.

CONTRASTING LEADERSHIP AND POWER

A careful comparison of our description of power with our description of leadership in Chapter 12 reveals the concepts are closely intertwined. Leaders use power as a means of attaining group goals.

How are the two terms different? *Power* does not require goal compatibility, merely dependence. Leadership, on the other hand, requires some congruence between the goals of the leader and those being led. A second difference relates to the direction of influence. Leadership focuses on the downward influence on followers. It minimizes the importance of lateral and upward influence patterns. Power does not. In still another difference, leadership research, for the most part, emphasizes style. It seeks answers to questions such as these: How supportive should a leader be? How much decision making should be shared with followers? In contrast, the research on power focuses on tactics for gaining compliance. It goes beyond the individual as the exerciser of power, because groups as well as individuals can use power to control other individuals or groups.

BASES OF POWER

Where does power come from? What gives an individual or a group influence over others? We answer by dividing the bases or sources of power into two general groupings—formal and personal—and then breaking each of these down into more specific categories.[5]

Formal Power

Formal power is based on an individual's position in an organization. It can come from the ability to coerce or reward, or from formal authority.

COERCIVE POWER   The **coercive power** base depends on fear of the negative results from failing to comply. It rests on the application, or the threat of application, of physical sanctions such as the infliction of pain, frustration through restriction of movement, or the controlling by force of basic physiological or safety needs.

   At the organizational level, *A* has coercive power over *B* if *A* can dismiss, suspend, or demote *B,* assuming *B* values her job. If *A* can assign *B* work activities *B* finds unpleasant, or treat *B* in a manner *B* finds embarrassing, *A* possesses coercive power over *B.* Coercive power can also come from withholding key information. People in an organization who have data or knowledge others need can make those others dependent on them.

REWARD POWER   The opposite of coercive power is **reward power**, with which people comply because it produces positive benefits; someone who can distribute rewards others view as valuable will have power over them. These rewards can be either financial—such as controlling pay rates, raises, and bonuses—or nonfinancial, including recognition, promotions, interesting work assignments, friendly colleagues, and preferred work shifts or sales territories.[6]

LEGITIMATE POWER   In formal groups and organizations, probably the most common access to one or more of the power bases is through **legitimate power**. It represents the formal authority to control and use organizational resources based on structural position in the organization.

   Legitimate power is broader than the power to coerce and reward. Specifically, it includes members' acceptance of the authority of a position. We associate power so closely with the concept of hierarchy that just drawing longer lines in an organization chart leads people to infer the leaders are especially powerful, and when a powerful executive is described, people tend to put the person at a higher position when drawing an organization chart.[7] When school principals, bank presidents, or army captains speak (assuming their directives are viewed as within the authority of their positions), teachers, tellers, and first lieutenants listen and usually comply.

Personal Power

Many of the most competent and productive chip designers at Intel have power, but they aren't managers and have no formal power. What they have is **personal power**, which comes from an individual's unique characteristics. There are two bases of personal power: expertise and the respect and admiration of others.

Formal power can come from the ability to coerce or reward, or it can come from formal authority. However, evidence suggests that informal power, expert and reference power, are the most important to acquire.

EXPERT POWER   **Expert power** is influence wielded as a result of expertise, special skill, or knowledge. As jobs become more specialized, we become increasingly dependent on experts to achieve goals. It is generally acknowledged that physicians have expertise and hence expert power: most of us follow our doctor's advice. Computer specialists, tax accountants, economists, industrial psychologists, and other specialists wield power as a result of their expertise.

REFERENT POWER   **Referent power** is based on identification with a person who has desirable resources or personal traits. If I like, respect, and admire you, you can exercise power over me because I want to please you.

Referent power develops out of admiration of another and a desire to be like that person. It helps explain, for instance, why celebrities are paid millions of dollars to endorse products in commercials. Marketing research shows people such as LeBron James and Tom Brady have the power to influence your choice of athletic shoes and credit cards. With a little practice, you and I could probably deliver as smooth a sales pitch as these celebrities, but the buying public doesn't identify with you and me. Some people who are not in formal leadership positions nonetheless have referent power and exert influence over others because of their charismatic dynamism, likability, and emotional effects on us.

Which Bases of Power Are Most Effective?

Of the three bases of formal power (coercive, reward, legitimate) and two bases of personal power (expert, referent), which are most important to have? Research suggests clearly that personal sources of power are most effective. Both expert and referent power are positively related to employees' satisfaction with supervision, their organizational commitment, and their performance, whereas reward and legitimate power seem to be unrelated to these outcomes. One source of formal power—coercive power—actually can backfire in that it is negatively related to employee satisfaction and commitment.[8]

Consider Steve Stoute's company, Translation, which matches pop-star spokespersons with corporations that want to promote their brands. Stoute has paired Gwen Stefani with HP, Justin Timberlake with McDonald's, Beyoncé Knowles with Tommy Hilfiger, and Jay-Z with Reebok. Stoute's business seems to be all about referent power. His firm's work aims to use the credibility of these artists and performers to reach youth culture.[9] In other words, people buy products associated with cool figures because they wish to identify with and emulate them.

Power and Perceived Justice

Just as relational dependency potentially distorts the perception of those in power, there are potential distortions in the perception of justice related to individuals in power. Commonly, for instance, people in positions of power are to be blamed for their failures and credited for their successes to a greater degree than those who have less power. Studies also suggest that leaders and managers in positions of power pay greater costs for unfairness and reap greater benefits for fairness.[10] The perception of organizational justice reflects upon powerful leaders in them well. Specifically, authorities are given greatest trust when they have a lot of power and their organizations are seen as operating fairly, and the least trust when they have a lot of power and their organizations are seen as operating unfairly. Thus, it appears that people think powerful leaders should have the discretion to shape organizational policies and change unfair rules, and if they fail to do so, they will be regarded especially negatively.

POWER TACTICS

Political influence behaviors are one important means of gaining power and influence. The most effective influence behaviors—consultation and inspirational appeal—tend to be the least widely used. You should make these influence tactics part of your repertoire.

What **power tactics** do people use to translate power bases into specific actions? What options do they have for influencing their bosses, co-workers, or employees? In this section, we review popular tactical options and the conditions that may make one more effective than another.

Research has identified nine distinct influence tactics:[11]

1. *Legitimacy.* Relying on your authority position or making a request accords with organizational policies or rules.
2. *Rational Persuasion.* Presenting logical arguments and factual evidence to demonstrate a request is reasonable.
3. *Inspirational Appeals.* Developing emotional commitment by appealing to a target's values, needs, hopes, and aspirations.
4. *Consultation.* Increasing the target's support by involving him in deciding how you will accomplish your plan.
5. *Exchange.* Rewarding the target with benefits or favors in exchange for following a request.
6. *Personal Appeals.* Asking for compliance based on friendship or loyalty.
7. *Ingratiation.* Using flattery, praise, or friendly behavior prior to making a request.
8. *Pressure.* Using warnings, repeated demands, and threats.
9. *Coalitions.* Enlisting the aid or support of others to persuade the target to agree.

Some tactics are more effective than others. Rational persuasion, inspirational appeals, and consultation tend to be the most effective, especially when the audience is highly interested in the outcomes of a decision process. Pressure tends to backfire and is typically the least effective of the nine tactics.[12] You can also increase your chance of success by using two or more tactics together or sequentially, as long as your choices are compatible.[13] Using both ingratiation and legitimacy can lessen negative reactions to your appearing to dictate outcomes, but only when the audience does not really care about the outcome of a decision process or the policy is routine.[14]

Let's consider the most effective way of getting a raise. You can start with rational persuasion: figure out how your pay compares to that of peers, or land a competing job offer, or show objective results that testify to your performance. Kitty Dunning, a vice president at Don Jagoda Associates, landed a 16 percent raise when she e-mailed her boss numbers showing she had increased sales.[15] You can also make good use of salary calculators such as Salary.com to compare your pay with others in the same occupation.

But the effectiveness of some influence tactics depends on the direction of influence.[16] As Exhibit 13-1 shows, rational persuasion is the only tactic effective across

Upward Influence	Downward Influence	Lateral Influence
Rational persuasion	Rational persuasion	Rational persuasion
	Inspirational appeals	Consultation
	Pressure	Ingratiation
	Consultation	Exchange
	Ingratiation	Legitimacy
	Exchange	Personal appeals
	Legitimacy	Coalitions

EXHIBIT 13-1
**Preferred
Power Tactics
by Influence
Direction**

organizational levels. Inspirational appeals work best as a downward-influencing tactic with subordinates. When pressure works, it's generally downward only. Personal appeals and coalitions are most effective as lateral influence. Other factors that affect the effectiveness of influence include the sequencing of tactics, a person's skill in using the tactics, and the organizational culture.

You're more likely to be effective if you begin with "softer" tactics that rely on personal power, such as personal and inspirational appeals, rational persuasion, and consultation. If these fail, you can move to "harder" tactics, such as exchange, coalitions, and pressure, which emphasize formal power and incur greater costs and risks.[17] Interestingly, a single soft tactic is more effective than a single hard tactic, and combining two soft tactics or a soft tactic and rational persuasion is more effective than any single tactic or combination of hard tactics.[18] The effectiveness of tactics depends on the audience.[19] People especially likely to comply with soft power tactics tend to be more reflective and intrinsically motivated; they have high self-esteem and greater desire for control. Those likely to comply with hard power tactics are more action-oriented and extrinsically motivated and are more focused on getting along with others than on getting their own way.

People in different countries prefer different power tactics.[20] Those from individualistic countries tend to see power in personalized terms and as a legitimate means of advancing their personal ends, whereas those in collectivistic countries see power in social terms and as a legitimate means of helping others.[21] A study comparing managers in the United States and China found that U.S. managers prefer rational appeal, whereas Chinese managers preferred coalition tactics.[22] These differences tend to be consistent with the values in these two countries. Reason is consistent with the U.S. preference for direct confrontation and rational persuasion to influence others and resolve differences, while coalition tactics align with the Chinese preference for meeting difficult or controversial requests with indirect approaches. Research also has shown that individuals in Western, individualistic cultures tend to engage in more self-enhancement behaviors (such as self-promotion) than individuals in more collectivistic Eastern cultures.[23]

People differ in their **political skill**, or their ability to influence others to enhance their own objectives. The politically skilled are more effective users of all the influence tactics. Political skill also appears more effective when the stakes are high—such as when the individual is accountable for important organizational outcomes. Finally, the politically skilled are able to exert their influence without others detecting it, a key element in being effective (it's damaging to be labeled political).[24] However, these individuals also appear most able to use their political skills in environments marked by low levels of procedural and distributive justice. When an organization is run with open and fairly applied rules, free of favoritism or biases, political skill is actually negatively related to job performance ratings.[25]

Finally, we know cultures within organizations differ markedly—some are warm, relaxed, and supportive; others are formal and conservative. Some encourage participation and consultation, some encourage reason, and still others rely on pressure. People who fit the culture of the organization tend to obtain more influence.[26] Specifically, extraverts tend to be more influential in team-oriented organizations, and highly conscientious people are more influential in organizations that value working alone on technical tasks. People who fit the culture are influential because they can perform especially well in the domains deemed most important for success. In other words, they are influential because they are competent. Thus, the organization will influence which subset of power tactics is viewed as acceptable for use.

POLITICS: POWER IN ACTION

When people get together in groups, power will be exerted. People want to carve out a niche from which to exert influence, earn rewards, and advance their careers. When employees in organizations convert their power into action, we describe them as being engaged in **politics**. Those with good political skills have the ability to use their bases of power effectively.[27]

Definition of Organizational Politics

There is no shortage of definitions of **organizational politics**. Essentially, this type of politics focuses on the use of power to affect decision making in an organization, or on self-serving and organizationally unsanctioned behaviors.[28] For our purposes, **political behavior** in organizations consists of activities that are not required as part of an individual's formal role but that influence, or attempt to influence, the distribution of advantages and disadvantages within the organization.[29]

This definition encompasses what most people mean when they talk about organizational politics. Political behavior is outside specified job requirements. It requires some attempt to use power bases. It includes efforts to influence the goals, criteria, or processes used for decision making. Our definition is broad enough to include varied political behaviors such as withholding key information from decision makers, joining a coalition, whistle-blowing, spreading rumors, leaking confidential information to the media, exchanging favors with others in the organization for mutual benefit, and lobbying on behalf of or against a particular individual or decision alternative.

The Reality of Politics

Interviews with experienced managers show that most believe political behavior is a major part of organizational life.[30] Many managers report some use of political behavior is both ethical and necessary, as long as it doesn't directly harm anyone else. They describe politics as a necessary evil and believe someone who *never* uses political behavior will have a hard time getting things done. Most also indicate they had never been trained to use political behavior effectively. But why, you may wonder, must politics exist? Isn't it possible for an organization to be politics free? It's *possible*—but unlikely.

Organizations are made up of individuals and groups with different values, goals, and interests.[31] This sets up the potential for conflict over the allocation of limited resources, such as departmental budgets, space, project responsibilities, and salary adjustments.[32] If resources were abundant, then all constituencies within the organization could satisfy their goals. But because resources are limited, not everyone's interests can be satisfied. Furthermore, gains by one individual or group are often *perceived* as coming at the expense of others within the organization (whether they are or not). These forces create real competition among members for the organization's limited resources.

Maybe the most important factor leading to politics within organizations is the realization that most of the "facts" used to allocate the limited resources are open to interpretation. What, for instance, is *good* performance? What's an *adequate* improvement? What constitutes an *unsatisfactory* job? One person's "selfless effort to benefit the organization" is seen by another as a "blatant attempt to further one's interest."[33] The manager of any major league baseball team knows a .400 hitter is a high performer and a .125 hitter is a poor performer. You don't need to be a baseball genius to know you should play your .400 hitter and send the .125 hitter back to the minors. But what if you have to choose between players who hit .280 and .290? Then less objective factors come into play: fielding expertise, attitude, potential, ability to perform in a clutch, loyalty to the team, and so on. More managerial decisions resemble the choice between a .280 and a .290 hitter than between a .125 hitter and a .400 hitter. It is in this large and ambiguous middle ground of organizational life—where the facts *don't* speak for themselves—that politics flourish.

Finally, because most decisions have to be made in a climate of ambiguity—where facts are rarely fully objective and thus are open to interpretation—people within organizations will use whatever influence they can to taint the facts to support their goals and interests. That, of course, creates the activities we call **politicking**.

Therefore, to answer the question whether or not it is possible for an organization to be politics-free, we can say yes—if all members of that organization hold the same goals and interests, if organizational resources are not scarce, and if performance outcomes are completely clear and objective. But that doesn't describe the organizational world in which most of us live.

CAUSES AND CONSEQUENCES OF POLITICAL BEHAVIOR

Factors Contributing to Political Behavior

Not all groups or organizations are equally political. In some organizations, for instance, politicking is overt and rampant, whereas in others politics plays a small role in influencing outcomes. Why this variation? Recent research and observation have identified a number of factors that appear to encourage political behavior. Some are individual characteristics, derived from the unique qualities of the people the organization employs; others are a result of the organization's culture or internal environment. Both individual and organizational factors can increase political behavior and provide favorable outcomes (increased rewards and averted punishments) for both individuals and groups in the organization.

INDIVIDUAL FACTORS   At the individual level, researchers have identified certain personality traits, needs, and other factors likely to be related to political behavior. In terms of traits, we find that employees who are high self-monitors, possess an internal locus of control, and have a high need for power are more likely to engage in political behavior.[34] The high self-monitor is more sensitive to social cues, exhibits higher levels of social conformity, and is more likely to be skilled in political behavior than the low self-monitor. Because they believe they can control their environment, individuals with an internal locus of control are more prone to take a proactive stance and attempt to manipulate situations in their favor. Not surprisingly, the Machiavellian personality—characterized by the will to manipulate and the desire for power—is comfortable using politics as a means to further her self-interest.

In addition, an individual's investment in the organization, perceived alternatives, and expectations of success influence the degree to which she will pursue illegitimate means of political action.[35] The more a person expects increased future benefits from the organization, the more that person has to lose if forced out and the less likely she is to use illegitimate means. The more alternative opportunities an individual has—due to a favorable job market or the possession of scarce skills or knowledge, a prominent reputation, or influential contacts outside the organization—the more likely that individual is to risk illegitimate political actions. Finally, an individual with low expectations of success from illegitimate means is unlikely to use them. High expectations of success from such measures are most likely to be the province of both experienced and powerful individuals with polished political skills and inexperienced, and naïve employees who misjudge their chances.

ORGANIZATIONAL FACTORS   Although we acknowledge the role individual differences can play, the evidence more strongly suggests that certain situations and cultures promote politics. Specifically, when an organization's resources are declining, when the existing pattern of resources is changing, and/or when there is opportunity for promotions, politicking is more likely to surface.[36] When organizations downsize to improve efficiency, resources must be reduced, and people may engage in political actions to safeguard what they have. But *any* changes, especially those that imply significant reallocation of resources within the organization, are likely to stimulate conflict and increase politicking. For instance, the opportunity for promotions or advancement has consistently been found to encourage competition for a limited resource as people try to positively influence the decision outcome.

Cultures characterized by low trust, role ambiguity, unclear performance evaluation systems, zero-sum (win-lose) reward allocation practices, democratic decision making, high pressures for performance, and self-serving senior managers will also create breeding grounds for politicking.[37] The less trust within the organization, the higher the level of political behavior and the more likely it will be of the illegitimate kind. So, high trust should suppress political behavior in general and inhibit illegitimate actions in particular.

Role ambiguity, wherein the prescribed employee behaviors are not clear, allows fewer limits to the scope and functions of the employee's political actions. Because political activities are defined as those not required as part of the employee's formal role, the greater the role ambiguity, the more employees can engage in perhaps unnoticed political activity.

Performance evaluation is far from a perfect science. The more organizations use subjective criteria in the appraisal, emphasize a single outcome measure, or allow significant time to pass between the time of an action and its appraisal process, the greater the likelihood that an employee can get away with politicking. Subjective performance criteria create ambiguity. The use of a single outcome measure encourages individuals to do whatever is necessary to "look good" on that measure, but often at the cost of good performance on other important parts of the job not appraised.

The more an organization's culture emphasizes the zero-sum or win–lose approach to reward allocations, the more employees will be motivated to engage in politicking. The **zero-sum approach** treats the reward "pie" as fixed, so any gain one person or group achieves has to come at the expense of another person or group. If $15,000 in annual raises is to be distributed among five employees, any employee who gets more than $3,000 takes money away from one or more of the others. Such a practice encourages making others look bad and increasing the visibility of what you do.

Finally, when employees see the people on top engaging in political behavior, especially doing so successfully and being rewarded for it, a climate is created that supports politicking. This in a sense gives those lower in the organization permission to play politics by implying that such behavior is acceptable and even rewarded.

How Do People Respond to Organizational Politics?

Trish O'Donnell loves her job as a writer on a weekly television comedy series but hates the internal politics. "A couple of the writers here spend more time kissing up to the executive producer than doing any work. And our head writer clearly has his favorites. Although they pay me a lot and I get to really use my creativity, I'm sick of having to be on alert for backstabbers and constantly having to self-promote my contributions. I'm tired of doing most of the work and getting little of the credit." Are Trish O'Donnell's comments typical of people who work in highly politicized workplaces? We all know friends or relatives who regularly complain about the politics at their job. But how do people in general react to organizational politics? Let's look at the evidence.

In our earlier discussion in this chapter of factors that contribute to political behavior, we focused on favorable outcomes. But for most people—who have modest political skills or are unwilling to play the politics game—outcomes tend to be predominantly negative. Exhibit 13-2 summarizes the extensive research (mostly conducted in the United States) on the relationship between organizational politics and individual outcomes.[38] Very strong evidence indicates, for instance, that perceptions of organizational politics are negatively related to job satisfaction.[39] The perception of politics also tends to increase job anxiety and stress, possibly because people believe they may be losing ground to others who are active politickers or, conversely, because they feel additional pressures from entering into and competing in the political arena.[40] Politics may lead to

EXHIBIT 13-2

Employee Responses to Organizational Politics

self-reported declines in employee performance, perhaps because employees perceive political environments to be unfair, which demotivates them.[41] Not surprisingly, when politicking becomes too much to handle, it can lead employees to quit.[42]

When employees of two agencies in a recent study in Nigeria viewed their work environments as political, they reported higher levels of job distress and were less likely to help their co-workers. Thus, although developing countries such as Nigeria are perhaps more ambiguous and more political environments in which to work, the negative consequences of politics appear to be the same as in the United States.[43]

Researchers have also noted several interesting qualifiers. First, the politics–performance relationship appears to be moderated by an individual's understanding of the "hows" and "whys" of organizational politics. "An individual who has a clear understanding of who is responsible for making decisions and why they were selected to be the decision makers would have a better understanding of how and why things happen the way they do than someone who does not understand the decision-making process in the organization."[44] When both politics and understanding are high, performance is likely to increase because the individual will see political actions as an opportunity. This is consistent with what you might expect among individuals with well-honed political skills. But when understanding is low, individuals are more likely to see politics as a threat, which can have a negative effect on job performance.[45]

Second, political behavior at work moderates the effects of ethical leadership.[46] One study found that male employees were more responsive to ethical leadership and showed the most citizenship behavior when levels of both politics and ethical leadership were high. Women, on the other hand, appear most likely to engage in citizenship behavior when the environment is consistently ethical and *apolitical.*

Third, when employees see politics as a threat, they often respond with **defensive behaviors**—reactive and protective behaviors to avoid action, blame, or change.[47] (Exhibit 13-3 provides some examples of these behaviors.) And defensive behaviors are often associated with negative feelings toward the job and work environment.[48] In the short run, employees may find defensiveness protects their self-interest, but in the long run it wears them down. People who consistently rely on defensiveness find that, eventually, it is the only way they know how to behave. At that point, they lose the ability to approach their work proactively, and the trust and support of their peers, bosses, employees, and clients is negatively compromised.

Impression Management

Impression management is a specific type of political behavior, designed to alter other's immediate perceptions of us; evidence suggests that the effectiveness of impression management techniques depends on the setting (i.e., self-promotion works better in the interview than for performance evaluation).

We know people have an ongoing interest in how others perceive and evaluate them. For example, North Americans spend billions of dollars on diets, health club memberships, cosmetics, and plastic surgery—all intended to make them more attractive to others.[49] Being perceived positively by others should have benefits for people in organizations. It might, for instance, help them initially to get the jobs they want in an organization and, once hired, to get favorable evaluations, superior salary increases, and fast promotions. In a political context, it might help sway the distribution of advantages in their favor. The process by which individuals attempt to control the impression others form of them is called **impression management (IM)**.[50]

Who might we predict will engage in IM? No surprise here. It's our old friend, the high self-monitor.[51] High self-monitors are good at reading situations and molding their appearances and behavior to fit each situation. In contrast, low self-monitors tend to present

EXHIBIT 13-3
Defensive
Behaviors

AVOIDING ACTION

Overconforming. Strictly interpreting your responsibility by saying things like "The rules clearly state . . ." or "This is the way we've always done it."

Buck passing. Transferring responsibility for the execution of a task or decision to someone else.

Playing dumb. Avoiding an unwanted task by falsely pleading ignorance or inability.

Stretching. Prolonging a task so that one person appears to be occupied—for example, turning a two-week task into a 4-month job.

Stalling. Appearing to be more or less supportive publicly while doing little or nothing privately.

AVOIDING BLAME

Buffing. This is a nice way to refer to "covering your rear." It describes the practice of rigorously documenting activity to project an image of competence and thoroughness.

Playing safe. Evading situations that may reflect unfavorably. It includes taking on only projects with a high probability of success, having risky decisions approved by superiors, qualifying expressions of judgment, and taking neutral positions in conflicts.

Justifying. Developing explanations that lessen one's responsibility for a negative outcome and/ or apologizing to demonstrate remorse, or both.

Scapegoating. Placing the blame for a negative outcome on external factors that are not entirely blameworthy.

Misrepresenting. Manipulation of information by distortion, embellishment, deception, selective presentation, or obfuscation.

AVOIDING CHANGE

Prevention. Trying to prevent a threatening change from occurring.

Self-protection. Acting in ways to protect one's self-interest during change by guarding information or other resources.

images of themselves that are consistent with their personalities, regardless of the beneficial or detrimental effects for them. If you want to control the impression others form of you, what IM techniques can you use? Exhibit 13-4 summarizes some of the most popular.

Keep in mind that when people engage in IM, they are sending a false message that might be true under other circumstances.[52] Excuses, for instance, may be offered with sincerity. Referring to the example in Exhibit 13-4, you can *actually* believe that ads contribute little to sales in your region. But in saying so, you are attempting to change your manager's impression of the situation by minimizing the impact of your failure to perform.

Misrepresentation can have a high cost. If you "cry wolf" once too often, no one is likely to believe you when the wolf really comes. So the impression manager must be cautious not to be perceived as insincere or manipulative.[53] Consider the effect of implausible name-dropping as an example of this principle. Participants in a study in Switzerland disliked an experimental confederate who claimed to be a personal friend of the well-liked Swiss tennis star Roger Federer, but they generally liked confederates who just said they were fans.[54] Another study found that when managers attributed an

CONFORMITY

Agreeing with someone else's opinion to gain his or her approval is a form of ingratiation.

Example: A manager tells his boss, "You're absolutely right on your reorganization plan for the western regional office. I couldn't agree with you more."

FAVORS

Doing something nice for someone to gain that person's approval is a form of ingratiation.

Example: A salesperson says to a prospective client, "I've got two tickets to the theater tonight that I can't use. Take them. Consider it a thank-you for taking the time to talk with me."

EXCUSES

Explanations of a predicament-creating event aimed at minimizing the apparent severity of the predicament is a defensive IM technique.

Example: A sales manager says to her boss, "We failed to get the ad in the paper on time, but no one responds to those ads anyway."

APOLOGIES

Admitting responsibility for an undesirable event and simultaneously seeking to get a pardon for the action is a defensive IM technique.

Example: An employee says to his boss, "I'm sorry I made a mistake on the report. Please forgive me."

SELF-PROMOTION

Highlighting one's best qualities, downplaying one's deficits, and calling attention to one's achievements is a self-focused IM technique.

Example: A salesperson tells his boss, "Matt worked unsuccessfully for three years to try to get that account. I sewed it up in six weeks. I'm the best closer this company has."

ENHANCEMENT

Claiming that something you did is more valuable than most other members of the organizations would think is a self-focused IM technique.

Example: A journalist tells his editor, "My work on this celebrity divorce story was really a major boost to our sales" (even though the story only made it to page 3 in the entertainment section).

FLATTERY

Complimenting others about their virtues in an effort to make oneself appear perceptive and likeable is an assertive IM technique.

Example: A new sales trainee says to her peer, "You handled that client's complaint so tactfully! I could never have handled that as well as you did."

EXEMPLIFICATION

Doing more than you need to in an effort to show how dedicated and hardworking you are is an assertive IM technique.

Example: An employee sends e-mails from his work computer when he works late so that his supervisor will know how long he's been working.

EXHIBIT 13-4

Impression Management Techniques

Source: Based on B. R. Schlenker, *Impression Management* (Monterey, CA: Brooks/Cole, 1980); W. L. Gardner and M. J. Martinko, "Impression Management in Organizations," *Journal of Management,* June 1988, p. 332; and R. B. Cialdini, "Indirect Tactics of Image Management Beyond Basking" in R. A. Giacalone and P. Rosenfeld (eds.), *Impression Management in the Organization* (Hillsdale, NJ: Lawrence Erlbaum, 1989), pp. 45–71.

employee's citizenship behaviors to impression management, they actually felt angry (probably because they felt manipulated) and gave subordinates lower performance ratings. When managers attributed the same **citizenship** behaviors to prosocial values and concern about the organization, they felt happy and gave higher performance ratings.[55] In sum, people don't like to feel others are manipulating them through impression management, so such tactics should be employed with caution.

Are there *situations* in which individuals are more likely to misrepresent themselves or more likely to get away with it? Yes—situations characterized by high uncertainty or ambiguity provide relatively little information for challenging a fraudulent claim and reduce the risks associated with misrepresentation.[56] The increasing use of telework may be increasing the use of IM. Individuals who work remotely from their supervisors engage in high levels of IM relative to those who work closely with their supervisors.[57]

Most of the studies undertaken to test the effectiveness of IM techniques have related it to two criteria: interview success and performance evaluations. Let's consider each of these.

The evidence indicates most job applicants use IM techniques in interviews[58] and that it works.[59] In one study, for instance, interviewers felt applicants for a position as a customer service representative who used IM techniques performed better in the interview, and they seemed somewhat more inclined to hire these people.[60] Moreover, when the researchers considered applicants' credentials, they concluded it was the IM techniques alone that influenced the interviewers—it didn't seem to matter whether applicants were well or poorly qualified. If they used IM techniques, they did better in the interviews.

Some IM techniques work better in interviews than others. Researchers have compared applicants whose IM techniques focused on promoting their accomplishments (called *self-promotion*) to those who focused on complimenting the interviewer and finding areas of agreement (referred to as *ingratiation*). In general, applicants appear to use self-promotion more than ingratiation.[61] As well, self-promotion tactics may be more important to interviewing success than ingratiation, though both contribute. Applicants who work to create an appearance of competence by enhancing their accomplishments, taking credit for successes, and explaining away failures do better in interviews. These effects reach beyond the interview: applicants who use more self-promotion tactics also seem to get more follow-up job-site visits, even after adjusting for grade-point average, gender, and job type. Ingratiation also works well in interviews; applicants who compliment the interviewer, agree with his opinions, and emphasize areas of fit do better than those who don't.[62]

In terms of performance ratings, the picture is quite different. Ingratiation is positively related to performance ratings, meaning those who ingratiate with their supervisors get higher performance evaluations. However, self-promotion appears to backfire: those who self-promote actually seem to receive *lower* performance evaluations.[63] There is an important qualifier to this general result. It appears that individuals high in political skill are able to translate IM into higher performance appraisals, whereas those lower in political skill are more likely to be hurt by their IM attempts.[64] For example, a study of 760 boards of directors found that individuals who ingratiate themselves to current board members (express agreement with the director, point out shared attitudes and opinions, compliment the director) increase their chances of landing on a board.[65]

What explains these results? If you think about them, they make sense. Ingratiating always works because everyone—both interviewers and supervisors—likes to be treated nicely. However, self-promotion may work only in interviews and backfire on the job because, whereas the interviewer has little idea whether you're blowing smoke about your accomplishments, the supervisor knows because it's her job to observe you. Thus, if you're going to self-promote, remember that what works in an interview won't always work once you're on the job, and stick to the truth.

Are our conclusions about responses to politics globally valid? Should we expect employees in Israel, for instance, to respond the same way to workplace politics that employees in the United States do? Almost all our conclusions on employee reactions to organizational politics are based on studies conducted in North America. The few studies that have included other countries suggest some minor modifications.[66] One study of managers in U.S. culture and three Chinese cultures (People's Republic of China, Hong Kong, and Taiwan) found U.S. managers evaluated "gentle persuasion" tactics such as consultation and inspirational appeal as more effective than did their Chinese counterparts.[67] Other research suggests that effective U.S. leaders achieve influence by focusing on personal goals of group members and the tasks at hand (an analytical approach), whereas influential East Asian leaders focus on relationships among group members and meeting the demands of the people around them (a holistic approach).[68]

As another example, Israelis and the British seem to generally respond as do North Americans—their perception of organizational politics relates to decreased job satisfaction and increased turnover.[69] But in countries that are more politically unstable, such as Israel, employees seem to demonstrate greater tolerance of intense political processes in the workplace, perhaps because they are used to power struggles and have more experience in coping with them.[70] This suggests people from politically turbulent countries in the Middle East or Latin America might be more accepting of organizational politics, and even more willing to use aggressive political tactics in the workplace, than people are from countries such as Great Britain or Switzerland.

THE ETHICS OF BEHAVING POLITICALLY

There are some questions you should consider when engaging in politicking behaviors. For example, what is the utility of engaging in the effort? Sometimes we do it for little good reason. Major league baseball player Al Martin claimed he played football at USC when in fact he never did. As a baseball player, he had little to gain by pretending to have played football. Outright lies like this may be a rather extreme example of impression management, but many of us have at least distorted information to make a favorable impression. One thing to keep in mind is whether it's really worth the risk. Another question to ask is this: how does the utility of engaging in the political behavior balance out any harm (or potential harm) it will do to others? Complimenting a supervisor on his appearance in order to curry favor is probably much less harmful than grabbing credit for a project that others deserve.

Finally, does the political activity conform to standards of equity and justice? Sometimes it is difficult to weigh the costs and benefits of a political action, but its ethical implications are clear. The department head who inflates the performance evaluation of a favored employee and deflates the evaluation of a disfavored employee—and then uses these evaluations to justify giving the former a big raise and nothing to the latter—has treated the disfavored employee unfairly.

Unfortunately, powerful people can become very good at explaining self-serving behaviors in terms of the organization's best interests. They can persuasively argue that unfair actions are really equitable and just. Our point is that immoral people can justify almost any behavior. Those who are powerful, articulate, and persuasive are most vulnerable to ethical lapses because they are likely to be able to get away with unethical practices successfully. When faced with an ethical dilemma regarding organizational politics, try to consider whether playing politics is worth the risk and whether others might be harmed in the process. If you have a strong power base, recognize the ability of power to corrupt. Remember that it's a lot easier for the powerless to act ethically, if for no other reason than they typically have very little political discretion to exploit.

SUMMARY AND IMPLICATIONS FOR MANAGERS

If you want to get things done in a group or an organization, it helps to have power. Here are several suggestions for how to deal with power in your own work life:

- As a manager who wants to maximize your power, you will want to increase others' dependence on you. You can, for instance, increase your power in relation to your boss by developing knowledge or a skill she needs and for which she perceives no ready substitute. But you will not be alone in attempting to build your power bases. Others, particularly employees and peers, will be seeking to increase your dependence on them, while you are trying to minimize it and increase their dependence on you. The result is a continual battle.
- Few employees relish being powerless in their jobs and organizations. Try to avoid putting others in a position where they feel they have no power.
- People respond differently to the various power bases. Expert and referent power are derived from an individual's personal qualities. In contrast, coercion, reward, and legitimate power are essentially organizationally derived. Competence especially appears to offer wide appeal, and its use as a power base results in high performance by group members. The message for managers seems to be "Develop and use your expert power base!"
- An effective manager accepts the political nature of organizations. By assessing behavior in a political framework, you can better predict the actions of others and use that information to formulate political strategies that will gain advantages for you and your work unit.
- Some people are significantly more politically astute than others, meaning they are aware of the underlying politics and can manage impressions. Those who are good at playing politics can be expected to get higher performance evaluations and, hence, larger salary increases and more promotions than the politically naïve or inept. The politically astute are also likely to exhibit higher job satisfaction and be better able to neutralize job stressors.
- Employees who have poor political skills or are unwilling to play the politics game generally relate perceived organizational politics to lower job satisfaction and self-reported performance, increased anxiety, and higher turnover.

MyManagementLab

Go to **MyManagementLab.com** to access study plans, interactive lectures, and videos as well as Auto-graded writing questions and the following Assisted-graded writing question.

13-1. MyManagementLab Only—comprehensive writing assignment for this chapter.

14

∎∎∎

Conflict and Negotiation

After studying this chapter, you should be able to:

- Define *conflict* and differentiate among the traditional, interactionist, and managed-conflict views of conflict.
- Outline the conflict process.
- Contrast distributive and integrative bargaining.
- Apply the five steps of the negotiation process.
- Show how individual differences influence negotiations.

Conflict can often turn personal. It can create chaotic conditions that make it nearly impossible for employees to work as a team. However, conflict also has a less well-known positive side. We'll explain the difference between negative and positive conflicts in this chapter and provide a guide to help you understand how conflicts develop. We'll also present a topic closely akin to conflict: negotiation.

A DEFINITION OF CONFLICT

There has been no shortage of definitions of *conflict*,[1] but common to most is the idea that conflict is a perception. If no one is aware of a conflict, then it is generally agreed no conflict exists. Also needed to begin the conflict process are opposition or incompatibility and some form of interaction.

We can define **conflict**, then, as a process that begins when one party perceives another party has or is about to negatively affect something the first party cares about.[2] This definition is purposely broad. It describes that point in any ongoing activity when an interaction crosses over to become an interparty conflict. It encompasses the wide range of conflicts people experience in organizations: incompatibility of goals, differences over interpretations of facts, disagreements based on behavioral expectations, and the like. Finally, our definition is flexible enough to cover the full range of conflict levels—from overt and violent acts to subtle forms of disagreement.

TRANSITIONS IN CONFLICT THOUGHT

It is entirely appropriate to say there has been conflict over the role of conflict in groups and organizations. One school of thought has argued that conflict must be avoided—that it indicates a malfunctioning within the group.

We call this the *traditional* view. Another perspective proposes not only that conflict can be a positive force in a group but that some conflict is absolutely necessary for a group to perform effectively. We label this the *interactionist* view. Finally, recent research argues that instead of encouraging "good" or discouraging "bad" conflict, it's more important to resolve naturally occurring conflicts productively. This perspective is the *managed conflict* view. Let's take a closer look at each view.

> Conflict is an inherent part of organizational life. Indeed, some level of conflict is probably necessary for optimal organizational functioning.

The Traditional View of Conflict

The early approach to conflict assumed all conflict was bad and to be avoided. Conflict was viewed negatively and discussed with such terms as *violence, destruction,* and *irrationality* to reinforce its negative connotation. This **traditional view of conflict** was consistent with attitudes about group behavior that prevailed in the 1930s and 1940s. Conflict was a dysfunctional outcome resulting from poor communication, a lack of openness and trust between people, and the failure of managers to be responsive to the needs and aspirations of their employees.

The view that all conflict is bad certainly offers a simple approach to looking at the behavior of people who create conflict. We need merely direct our attention to the causes of conflict and correct those malfunctions to improve group and organizational performance. This view of conflict fell out of favor for a long time as researchers came to realize that some level of conflict was inevitable.

> Task conflict is more constructive than process or, especially, relationship conflict.

The Interactionist View of Conflict

The **interactionist view of conflict** encourages conflict on the grounds that a harmonious, peaceful, tranquil, and cooperative group is prone to becoming static, apathetic, and unresponsive to needs for change and innovation.[3] The major contribution of this view is recognizing that a minimal level of conflict can help keep a group viable, self-critical, and creative.

The interactionist view does not propose that all conflicts are good. Rather, **functional conflict** supports the goals of the group and improves its performance and is, thus, a constructive form of conflict. A conflict that hinders group performance is a destructive or **dysfunctional conflict**. What differentiates functional from dysfunctional conflict? The evidence indicates we need to look at the *type* of conflict—whether it's connected to task, relationship, or process.[4]

Task conflict relates to the content and goals of the work. **Relationship conflict** focuses on interpersonal relationships. **Process conflict** relates to how the work gets done. Studies demonstrate that relationship conflicts are almost always dysfunctional.[5] Why? It appears that the friction and interpersonal hostilities inherent in relationship conflicts increase personality clashes and decrease mutual understanding, which hinders the completion of organizational tasks. Unfortunately, managers spend a lot of effort resolving personality conflicts among staff members; one survey indicated this task consumes 18 percent of their time.[6]

In contrast, low levels of process conflict and low to moderate levels of task conflict can be functional, but only in very specific cases. Recent reviews have shown task conflicts have the potential to be just as disruptive as relationship conflicts.[7] For conflict to be productive, it must be kept within certain boundaries. For example, one study in China found that moderate levels of task conflict in the early development stage could increase creativity in groups, but high levels of task conflict decreased team performance, and task conflicts were unrelated to performance once the group was in the later stages of group development.[8] Intense arguments about who should do what become dysfunctional when they create uncertainty about task roles, increase the time to complete tasks, and lead members to work at cross-purposes. Low to moderate levels of task conflict stimulate discussion of ideas. This means task conflicts relate positively to creativity and innovation, but they are not related to routine task performance. Groups performing routine tasks that don't require creativity won't benefit from task conflict. Moreover, if the group is already engaged in active discussion of ideas in a nonconfrontational way, adding conflict will not help generate more ideas. Task conflict is also related to these positive outcomes only when all members share the same goals and have high levels of trust.[9] Another way of saying this is that task conflicts are related to increased performance only when all members believe the team is a safe place for taking risks and that members will not deliberately undermine or reject those who speak up.[10]

Resolution-Focused View of Conflict

Researchers, including those who had strongly advocated the interactionist view, have begun to recognize some problems with encouraging conflict.[11] As we will see, there are some very specific cases in which conflict can be beneficial. However, workplace conflicts are not productive; they take time away from job tasks or interacting with customers, and hurt feelings and anger often linger after conflicts appear to be over. People can seldom wall off their feelings into neat categories of "task" or "relationship" disagreements, so task conflicts sometimes escalate into relationship conflicts.[12] A study conducted in Taiwan and Indonesia found that when levels of relationship conflict are high, increases in task conflict are consistently related to lower levels of team performance and team member satisfaction.[13] Conflicts produce stress, which may lead people to become more close minded and adversarial.[14] Studies of conflict in laboratories also fail to take account of the reductions in trust and cooperation that occur even with relationship conflicts. Longer-term studies show that all conflicts reduce trust, respect, and cohesion in groups, which reduces their long-term viability.[15]

In sum, the traditional view was shortsighted in assuming all conflict should be eliminated. The interactionist view that conflict can stimulate active discussion without spilling over into negative, disruptive emotions is incomplete. The managed conflict perspective does recognize conflict is inevitable in most organizations, and it focuses more on productive conflict resolution. The research pendulum has swung from eliminating conflict, to encouraging limited levels of conflict, and now to finding constructive methods for resolving conflicts productively so their disruptive influence can be minimized.

THE CONFLICT PROCESS

The **conflict process** has five stages: (1) potential opposition or incompatibility, (2) cognition and personalization, (3) intentions, (4) behavior, and (5) outcomes. The process is dia-grammed in Exhibit 14-1.

Stage I: Potential Opposition or Incompatibility

The first step in the conflict process is the appearance of conditions that create opportuni-ties for conflict to arise. These conditions *need not* lead directly to conflict, but one of them is necessary if conflict is to surface. For simplicity's sake, we group the conditions (which we can also look at as causes or sources of conflict) into three general categories: communication, structure, and personal variables.

COMMUNICATION   Communication can be a source of conflict. This arises from seman-tic difficulties, misunderstandings, and "noise" in the communication channels. A review of the research suggests that differing word connotations, jargon, insufficient exchange of information, and noise in the communication channel are all barriers to communica-tion and potential antecedent conditions to conflict. Research has further demonstrated a surprising finding: the potential for conflict increases when either too little or *too much* communication takes place. Apparently, an increase in communication is functional up to a point, after which it is possible to overcommunicate, with a resultant increase in the potential for conflict.

STRUCTURE   The term *structure* in this context includes variables such as size of the group, degree of specialization in the tasks assigned to group members, jurisdictional clarity, member–goal compatibility, leadership styles, reward systems, and the degree of dependence between groups. The larger the group and the more specialized its activities, the greater the likelihood of conflict. Tenure and conflict have been found to be inversely related; the potential for conflict is greatest when group members are younger and when turnover is high. The greater the ambiguity about where responsibility for actions lies, the greater the potential for conflict to emerge. Such jurisdictional ambiguities increase intergroup fighting for control of resources and territory. Diversity of goals among groups is also a major source of conflict. Reward systems, too, create conflict when one member's gain comes at another's expense. Finally, if a group is dependent on another group (in contrast to the two being mutually independent), or if interdependence allows one group to gain at another's expense, opposing forces are stimulated.

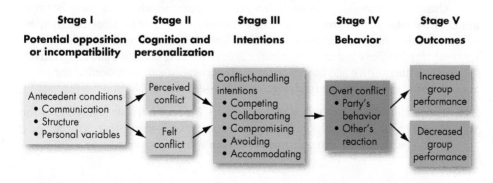

Stage I	Stage II	Stage III	Stage IV	Stage V
Potential opposition or incompatibility	**Cognition and personalization**	**Intentions**	**Behavior**	**Outcomes**

Antecedent conditions
• Communication
• Structure
• Personal variables

Perceived conflict

Felt conflict

Conflict-handling intentions
• Competing
• Collaborating
• Compromising
• Avoiding
• Accommodating

Overt conflict
• Party's behavior
• Other's reaction

Increased group performance

Decreased group performance

EXHIBIT 14-1
The Conflict Process

PERSONAL VARIABLES Our last category of potential sources of conflict is personal variables, which include personality, emotions, and values. Personality does appear to play a role in the conflict process: some people just tend to get into conflicts a lot. In particular, people high in the personality traits of disagreeableness, neuroticism, or self-monitoring are prone to tangle with other people more often, and to react poorly when conflicts occur.[16] Emotions can also cause conflict. An employee who shows up to work irate from her hectic morning commute may carry that anger with her to her 9:00 AM meeting. The problem? Her anger can annoy her colleagues, which can result in a tension-filled meeting.[17]

Stage II: Cognition and Personalization

If the conditions cited in Stage I negatively affect something one party cares about, then the potential for opposition or incompatibility becomes actualized in the second stage.

As we noted in our definition of conflict, one or more of the parties must be aware that antecedent conditions exist. However, because a conflict is a **perceived conflict** does not mean it is personalized. In other words, "A may be aware that B and A are in serious disagreement . . . but it may not make A tense or anxious, and it may have no effect whatsoever on A's affection toward B."[18] It is at the **felt conflict** level, when individuals become emotionally involved, that they experience anxiety, tension, frustration, or hostility.

Keep in mind two points. First, Stage II is important because it's where conflict issues tend to be defined, where the parties decide what the conflict is about.[19] The definition of a conflict is important because it typically delineates the set of possible settlements.

Second, emotions play a major role in shaping perceptions.[20] Negative emotions allow us to oversimplify issues, lose trust, and put negative interpretations on the other party's behavior.[21] In contrast, positive feelings increase our tendency to see potential relationships among the elements of a problem, to take a broader view of the situation, and to develop more innovative solutions.[22]

Stage III: Intentions

Intentions intervene between people's perceptions and emotions and their overt behavior. They are decisions to act in a given way.[23]

We separate out intentions as a distinct stage because we have to infer the other's intent to know how to respond to his or her behavior. Many conflicts escalate simply because one party attributes the wrong intentions to the other. There is also typically a great deal of slippage between intentions and behavior, so behavior does not always accurately reflect a person's intentions.

Using two dimensions—*cooperativeness* (the degree to which one party attempts to satisfy the other party's concerns) and *assertiveness* (the degree to which one party attempts to satisfy his own concerns)—we can identify five conflict-handling intentions: (1) *competing* (assertive and uncooperative), (2) *collaborating* (assertive and cooperative), (3) *avoiding* (unassertive and uncooperative), (4) *accommodating* (unassertive and cooperative), and (5) *compromising* (midrange on both assertiveness and cooperativeness).[24]

1. *Competing.* When one person seeks to satisfy her own interests regardless of the impact on the other parties in the conflict, that person is **competing**. You compete when you place a bet that only one person can win, for example.

2. *Collaborating.* When parties in conflict each desire to fully satisfy the concerns of all parties, there is cooperation and a search for a mutually beneficial outcome. In **collaborating**, the parties intend to solve a problem by clarifying differences rather than by accommodating various points of view. If you attempt to find a win–win solution that allows both parties' goals to be completely achieved, that's collaborating.

3. *Avoiding.* A person may recognize a conflict exists and want to withdraw from or suppress it. Examples of **avoiding** include trying to ignore a conflict and avoiding others with whom you disagree.

4. *Accommodating.* A party who seeks to appease an opponent may be willing to place the opponent's interests above his own, sacrificing to maintain the relationship. We refer to this intention as **accommodating**. Supporting someone else's opinion despite your reservations about it, for example, is accommodating.

5. *Compromising.* In **compromising**, there is no clear winner or loser. Rather, there is a willingness to ration the object of the conflict and accept a solution that provides incomplete satisfaction of both parties' concerns. The distinguishing characteristic of compromising, therefore, is that each party intends to give up something.

Intentions are not always fixed. During the course of a conflict, they might change if the parties are able to see the other's point of view or respond emotionally to the other's behavior. However, research indicates people have preferences among the five conflict-handling intentions we just described.[25] We can predict a person's intentions rather well from a combination of intellectual and personality characteristics.

Stage IV: Behavior

When most people think of conflict situations, they tend to focus on Stage IV because this is where conflicts become visible. The behavior stage includes the statements, actions, and reactions made by the conflicting parties, usually as overt attempts to implement their own intentions. As a result of miscalculations or unskilled enactments, overt behaviors sometimes deviate from these original intentions.[26]

It helps to think of Stage IV as a dynamic process of interaction. For example, you make a demand on me, I respond by arguing, you threaten me, I threaten you back, and so on. Exhibit 14-2 provides a way of visualizing conflict behavior. All conflicts exist somewhere along this continuum. At the lower part are conflicts characterized by subtle, indirect, and highly controlled forms of tension, such as a student questioning in class a point the instructor has just made. Conflict intensities escalate as they move upward along the continuum until they become highly destructive. Strikes, riots, and wars clearly fall in this upper range. Conflicts that reach the upper ranges of the continuum are almost always dysfunctional. Functional conflicts are typically confined to the lower range of the continuum.

If a conflict is dysfunctional, what can the parties do to de-escalate it? Or, conversely, what options exist if conflict is too low and needs to be increased? This brings us to techniques of **conflict management**. We have already described several as conflict-handling intentions. This shouldn't be surprising. Under ideal conditions, a person's intentions should translate into comparable behaviors.

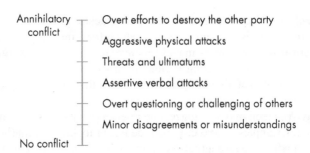

EXHIBIT 14-2

Conflict-Intensity Continuum

Source: Based on S. P. Robbins, *Managing Organizational Conflict: A Nontraditional Approach* (Upper Saddle River, NJ: Prentice Hall, 1974), pp. 93–97, and R. Glasi, "The Process of Conflict Escalation and the Roles of Third Parties," in G. B. J. Bomers and R. Peterson (eds.), *Conflict Management and Industrial Relations* (Boston: Kluwer-Nijhoff, 1982), pp. 119–140.

Stage V: Outcomes

The action–reaction interplay between the conflicting parties results in consequences. As our model demonstrates (see Exhibit 14-1), these outcomes may be functional, if the conflict improves the group's performance, or dysfunctional, if it hinders performance.

FUNCTIONAL OUTCOMES   How might conflict act as a force to increase group performance? It is hard to visualize a situation in which open or violent aggression could be functional. But it's possible to see how low or moderate levels of conflict could improve the effectiveness of a group. Let's consider some examples and then review the research evidence. Note that all our examples focus on task and process conflicts and exclude the relationship variety.

Conflict is constructive when it improves the quality of decisions, stimulates creativity and innovation, encourages interest and curiosity among group members, provides the medium through which problems can be aired and tensions released, and fosters an environment of self-evaluation and change. The evidence suggests conflict can improve the quality of decision making by allowing all points to be weighed, particularly those that are unusual or held by a minority.[27] Conflict is an antidote for groupthink. It doesn't allow the group to passively rubber-stamp decisions that may be based on weak assumptions, inadequate consideration of relevant alternatives, or other debilities. Conflict challenges the status quo and therefore furthers the creation of new ideas, promotes reassessment of group goals and activities, and increases the probability that the group will respond to change. An open discussion focused on higher-order goals can make these functional outcomes more likely. Groups that are extremely polarized do not manage their underlying disagreements effectively and tend to accept suboptimal solutions, or they avoid making decisions altogether rather than working out the conflict.[28]

Research studies in diverse settings confirm the functionality of active discussion. Groups whose members have different interests tend to produce higher-quality solutions to a variety of problems than do homogeneous groups.[29] Team members with greater differences in work styles and experience also tend to share more information with one another.[30]

DYSFUNCTIONAL OUTCOMES The destructive consequences of conflict on the performance of a group or an organization are generally well known: uncontrolled opposition breeds discontent, which acts to dissolve common ties and eventually leads to the destruction of the group. And, of course, a substantial body of literature documents how dysfunctional conflicts can reduce group effectiveness.[31] Among the undesirable consequences are poor communication, reductions in group cohesiveness, and subordination of group goals to the primacy of infighting among members. All forms of conflict—even the functional varieties—appear to reduce group member satisfaction and trust.[32] When active discussions turn into open conflicts between members, information sharing between members decreases significantly.[33] At the extreme, conflict can bring group functioning to a halt and threaten the group's survival.

MANAGING FUNCTIONAL CONFLICT If managers recognize that in some situations conflict can be beneficial, what can they do to manage conflict effectively in their organizations? Let's look at some approaches organizations are using to encourage their people to challenge the system and develop fresh ideas.

One of the keys to minimizing counterproductive conflicts is recognizing when there really is a disagreement. Many apparent conflicts are due to people using different language to discuss the same general course of action. For example, someone in marketing might focus on "distribution problems," whereas someone from operations will talk about "supply chain management" to describe essentially the same issue. Successful conflict management recognizes these different approaches and attempts to resolve them by encouraging open, frank discussion focused on interests rather than issues (we'll have more to say about this when we contrast distributive and integrative bargaining styles). Another approach is to have opposing groups pick parts of the solution that are most important to them and then focus on how each side can get its top needs satisfied. Neither side may get exactly what it wants, but both sides will get the most important parts of its agenda.[34]

Groups that resolve conflicts successfully discuss differences of opinion openly and are prepared to manage conflict when it arises.[35] The most disruptive conflicts are those that are never addressed directly. An open discussion makes it much easier to develop a shared perception of the problems at hand; it also allows groups to work toward a mutually acceptable solution. Managers need to emphasize shared interests in resolving conflicts, so groups that disagree with one another don't become too entrenched in their points of view and start to take the conflicts personally. Groups with cooperative conflict styles and a strong underlying identification to the overall group goals are more effective than groups with a competitive style.[36]

Differences across countries in conflict resolution strategies may be based on collectivistic tendencies and motives.[37] Collectivist cultures see people as deeply embedded in social situations, whereas individualist cultures see them as autonomous. As a result, collectivists are more likely to seek to preserve relationships and promote the good of the group as a whole. They will avoid direct expression of conflicts, preferring indirect methods for resolving differences of opinion. Collectivists may also be more interested in demonstrations of concern and working through third parties to resolve disputes, whereas individualists will be more likely to confront differences of opinion directly and openly.

Some research does support this theory. Compared to collectivist Japanese negotiators, their more individualist U.S. counterparts are more likely to see offers from their counterparts as unfair and to reject them. Another study revealed that whereas U.S. managers were more likely to use competing tactics in the face of conflicts, compromising and avoiding are the most preferred methods of conflict management in China.[38] Interview data, however, suggests top management teams in Chinese high-technology firms prefer collaboration even more than compromising and avoiding.[39]

Having considered conflict—its nature, causes, and consequences—we now turn to negotiation, which often resolves conflict.

NEGOTIATION

The most effective negotiators utilize different tactics for distributive and integrative bargaining; the chapter provides clear ways in order for you to improve each type of bargaining.

Negotiation permeates the interactions of almost everyone in groups and organizations. There's the obvious: labor bargains with management. There's the not-so-obvious: managers negotiate with employees, peers, and bosses; salespeople negotiate with customers; purchasing agents negotiate with suppliers. And there's the subtle: an employee agrees to cover for a colleague for a few minutes in exchange for some past or future benefit. In today's loosely structured organizations, in which members work with colleagues over whom they have no direct authority and with whom they may not even share a common boss, negotiation skills become critical.

We can define **negotiation** as a process that occurs when two or more parties decide how to allocate scarce resources.[40] Although we commonly think of the outcomes of negotiation in one-shot economic terms, like negotiating over the price of a car, every negotiation in organizations also affects the relationship between the negotiators and the way the negotiators feel about themselves.[41] Depending on how much the parties are going to interact with one another, sometimes maintaining the social relationship and behaving ethically will be just as important as achieving an immediate outcome of bargaining. Note that we use the terms *negotiation* and *bargaining* interchangeably. In this section, we contrast two bargaining strategies, provide a model of the negotiation process, ascertain the role of moods and personality traits on bargaining, review gender and cultural differences in negotiation, and take a brief look at third-party negotiations.

Bargaining Strategies

There are two general approaches to negotiation—*distributive bargaining* and *integrative bargaining*.[42] As Exhibit 14-3 shows, they differ in their goal and motivation, focus, interests, information sharing, and duration of relationship. Let's define each and illustrate the differences.

DISTRIBUTIVE BARGAINING   You see a used car advertised for sale online. It appears to be just what you've been looking to buy. You go out to see the car. It's great and you want it. The owner tells you the asking price. You don't want to pay that much. The two of you then negotiate. The negotiating strategy you're engaging in is called **distributive bargaining**. Its identifying feature is that it operates under zero-sum conditions—that is, any gain I make is at your expense and vice versa. Every dollar you can get the seller to cut from the car's price is a dollar you save, and every dollar more the seller can get from you comes at your expense. So the essence of distributive bargaining is negotiating over who gets what share of a fixed pie. By **fixed pie**, we mean a set amount of goods or

EXHIBIT 14-3
**Distributive
Versus
Integrative
Bargaining**

Bargaining Characteristic	Distributive Bargaining	Integrative Bargaining
Goal	Get as much of the pie as possible	Expand the pie so that both parties are satisfied
Motivation	Win–lose	Win–win
Focus	Positions ("I can't go beyond this point on this issue.")	Interests ("Can you explain why this issue is so important to you?")
Interests	Opposed	Congruent
Information sharing	Low (Sharing information will only allow other party to take advantage)	High (Sharing information will allow each party to find ways to satisfy interests of each party)
Duration of relationship	Short term	Long term

services to be divvied up. When the pie is fixed, or the parties believe it is, they tend to bargain distributively.

Probably the most widely cited example of distributive bargaining is labor–management negotiations over wages. Typically, labor's representatives come to the bargaining table determined to get as much money as possible from management. Because every cent labor negotiates increases management's costs, each party bargains aggressively and treats the other as an opponent who must be defeated.

The essence of distributive bargaining is depicted in Exhibit 14-4. Parties *A* and *B* represent two negotiators. Each has a *target point* that defines what she would like to achieve. Each also has a *resistance point,* which marks the lowest acceptable outcome—the point below which the party would break off negotiations rather than accept a less favorable settlement. The area between these two points makes up each party's aspiration range. As long as there is some overlap between *A*'s and *B*'s aspiration ranges, there exists a settlement range in which each one's aspirations can be met.

When you are engaged in distributive bargaining, research consistently shows one of the best things you can do is make the first offer, and make it an aggressive one. Making the first offer shows power; individuals in power are much more likely to make initial offers, speak first at meetings, and thereby gain the advantage.

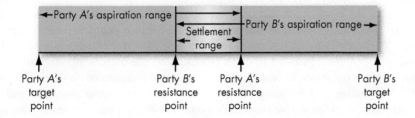

EXHIBIT 14-4
**Staking Out the
Bargaining Zone**

Another reason this is a good strategy is the anchoring bias. People tend to fixate on initial information. Once that anchoring point is set, they fail to adequately adjust it based on subsequent information. A savvy negotiator sets an anchor with the initial offer, and scores of negotiation studies show that such anchors greatly favor the person who sets them.[43]

INTEGRATIVE BARGAINING   Jake is a 5-year-old Chicago luxury boutique owned by Jim Wetzel and Lance Lawson. In the early days of the business, Wetzel and Lawson had no trouble moving millions of dollars of merchandise from many up-and-coming designers. They developed such a good rapport that many designers would send allotments to Jake without requiring advance payment. When the economy soured in 2008, Jake had trouble selling inventory, and the designers found they were not being paid for what they had shipped to the store. Despite the fact that many designers were willing to work with the store on a delayed payment plan, Wetzel and Lawson stopped returning their calls. Lamented one designer, Doo-Ri Chung, "You kind of feel this familiarity with people who supported you for so long. When they have cash-flow issues, you want to make sure you are there for them as well."[44] Ms. Chung's attitude shows the promise of **integrative bargaining**. In contrast to distributive bargaining, integrative bargaining operates under the assumption that one or more of the possible settlements can create a win–win solution. Of course, as the Jake example shows and we'll highlight later, integrative bargaining takes "two to tango"—both parties must be engaged for it to work.

In terms of intraorganizational behavior, all things being equal, integrative bargaining is preferable to distributive bargaining because the former builds long-term relationships. Integrative bargaining bonds negotiators and allows them to leave the bargaining table feeling they have achieved a victory. Distributive bargaining, however, leaves one party a loser. It tends to build animosities and deepen divisions when people have to work together on an ongoing basis. Research shows that over repeated bargaining episodes, a "losing" party who feels positive about the negotiation outcome is much more likely to bargain cooperatively in subsequent negotiations. This points to an important advantage of integrative negotiations: even when you "win," you want your opponent to feel good about the negotiation.[45]

Why, then, don't we see more integrative bargaining in organizations? The answer lies in the conditions necessary for it to succeed. These include opposing parties who are open with information and candid about their concerns, are sensitive to the other's needs and trust, and are willing to maintain flexibility.[46] Because these conditions seldom exist in organizations, it isn't surprising that negotiations often take on a win-at-any-cost dynamic.

There are ways to achieve more integrative outcomes. Individuals who bargain in teams reach more integrative agreements than those who bargain individually because more ideas are generated when more people are at the bargaining table. So, try bargaining in teams.[47] Another way to achieve higher joint-gain settlements is to put more issues on the table. The more negotiable issues introduced into a negotiation, the more opportunity for "logrolling," where issues are traded off because people have different preferences. This creates better outcomes for each side than if they negotiated each issue individually.[48] A final piece of advice is to focus on the underlying interests of both sides rather than on issues. In other words, it is better to concentrate on *why* an employee wants a raise rather than focusing just on the raise amount—some unseen potential for integrative outcomes may arise if both sides concentrate on what they really want rather than on the specific items they're bargaining over. Typically, it's easier to concentrate on underlying interests when parties to a negotiation are focused on broad, overall goals rather than on immediate outcomes of a specific decision.[49] Negotiations that occur when both parties are focused on learning and understanding the other side tend to also yield higher joint outcomes than those in which parties are more interested in their individual bottom-line outcomes.[50]

Finally, recognize that compromise may be your worst enemy in negotiating a win–win agreement. Compromising reduces the pressure to bargain integratively. After all, if you or your opponent caves in easily, it doesn't require anyone to be creative to reach a settlement. Thus, people end up settling for less than they could have obtained if they had been forced to consider the other party's interests, trade off issues, and be creative.[51] Think of the classic example in which two sisters are arguing over who gets an orange. Unknown to them, one sister wants the orange to drink the juice, whereas the other wants the orange peel to bake a cake. If one sister simply capitulates and gives the other sister the orange, they will not be forced to explore their reasons for wanting the orange, and thus they will never find the win–win solution: they could *each* have the orange because they want different parts of it!

The Negotiation Process

Exhibit 14-5 provides a simplified model of the negotiation process. It views negotiation as made up of five steps: (1) preparation and planning, (2) definition of ground rules, (3) clarification and justification, (4) bargaining and problem solving, and (5) closure and implementation.[52]

PREPARATION AND PLANNING Before you start negotiating, you need to do your homework. What's the nature of the conflict? What's the history leading up to this negotiation? Who's involved and what are their perceptions of the conflict? What do you want from the negotiation? What are *your* goals? If you're a supply manager at Dell Computer, for

EXHIBIT 14-5
The Negotiation

instance, and your goal is to get a significant cost reduction from your supplier of keyboards, make sure this goal stays paramount in your discussions and doesn't get overshadowed by other issues. It often helps to put your goals in writing and develop a range of outcomes— from "most hopeful" to "minimally acceptable"—to keep your attention focused.

You also want to assess what you think are the other party's goals. What are they likely to ask? How entrenched is their position likely to be? What intangible or hidden interests may be important to them? On what might they be willing to settle? When you can anticipate your opponent's position, you are better equipped to counter arguments with the facts and figures that support your position.

Relationships will change as a result of a negotiation, so that's another outcome to take into consideration. If you could "win" a negotiation but push the other side into resentment or animosity, it might be wiser to pursue a more compromising style. If preserving the relationship will make you seem weak and easily exploited, you may want to consider a more aggressive style. As an example of how the tone of a relationship set in negotiations matters, consider that people who feel good about the *process* of a job offer negotiation are more satisfied with their jobs and less likely to turn over a year later regardless of their actual *outcomes* from these negotiations.[53]

Once you've gathered your information, use it to develop a strategy. For example, expert chess players know ahead of time how they will respond to any given situation. As part of your strategy, you should determine your and the other side's **b**est **a**lternative **t**o a **n**egotiated **a**greement, or **BATNA**.[54] Your BATNA determines the lowest value acceptable to you for a negotiated agreement. Any offer you receive that is higher than your BATNA is better than an impasse. Conversely, you shouldn't expect success in your negotiation effort unless you're able to make the other side an offer it finds more attractive than its BATNA. If you go into your negotiation having a good idea of what the other party's BATNA is, even if you're not able to meet it, you might be able to elicit a change. Think carefully about what the other side is willing to give up. People who underestimate their opponent's willingness to give on key issues before the negotiation even starts end up with lower outcomes from a negotiation.[55]

DEFINITION OF GROUND RULES   Once you've done your planning and developed a strategy, you're ready to begin defining with the other party the ground rules and procedures of the negotiation itself. Who will do the negotiating? Where will it take place? What time constraints, if any, will apply? To what issues will negotiation be limited? Will you follow a specific procedure if an impasse is reached? During this phase, the parties will also exchange their initial proposals or demands.

CLARIFICATION AND JUSTIFICATION   When you have exchanged initial positions, both you and the other party will explain, amplify, clarify, bolster, and justify your original demands. This step needn't be confrontational. Rather, it's an opportunity for educating and informing each other on the issues, why they are important, and how you arrived at your initial demands. Provide the other party with any documentation that helps support your position.

BARGAINING AND PROBLEM SOLVING   The essence of the negotiation process is the actual give-and-take in trying to hash out an agreement. This is where both parties will undoubtedly need to make concessions.

CLOSURE AND IMPLEMENTATION   The final step in the negotiation process is formalizing the agreement you have worked out and developing any procedures necessary for implementing and monitoring it. For major negotiations—from labor–management negotiations to bargaining over lease terms to buying a piece of real estate to negotiating a job offer for a senior management position—this requires hammering out the specifics in a formal contract. For most cases, however, closure of the negotiation process is nothing more formal than a handshake.

Individual Differences in Negotiation Effectiveness

Are some people better negotiators than others? The answer is more complex than you might think. Four factors influence how effectively individuals negotiate: personality, mood/emotions, culture, and gender.

PERSONALITY TRAITS IN NEGOTIATION   Can you predict an opponent's negotiating tactics if you know something about her personality? Because personality and negotiation outcomes are related—but only weakly—the answer is, at best, "sort of." Negotiators who are agreeable or extraverted are not very successful in distributive bargaining. Why? Because extraverts are outgoing and friendly, they tend to share more information than they should. And agreeable people are more interested in finding ways to cooperate rather than to butt heads. These traits, although slightly helpful in integrative negotiations, are liabilities when interests are opposed. So the best distributive bargainer appears to be a disagreeable introvert—someone more interested in his or her own outcomes than in pleasing the other party and having a pleasant social exchange. People who are highly interested in having positive relationships with other people, and who are not very concerned about their own outcomes, are especially poor negotiators. These people tend to be very anxious about disagreements and plan to give in quickly to avoid unpleasant conflicts even before negotiations start.[56]

MOODS/EMOTIONS IN NEGOTIATION   Do moods and emotions influence negotiation? They do, but the way they do appears to depend on the type of negotiation. In distributive negotiations, it appears that negotiators in a position of power or equal status who show anger negotiate better outcomes because their anger induces concessions from their opponents. Angry negotiators also feel more focused and assertive in striking a bargain. This appears to hold true even when the negotiators are instructed to show anger despite not being truly angry. On the other hand, for those in a less powerful position, displaying anger leads to worse outcomes. Thus, if you're a boss negotiating with a peer or a subordinate, displaying anger may help you, but if you're an employee negotiating with a boss, it might hurt you.[57] So what happens when two parties have to negotiate and one has shown anger in the past? Does the other try to get revenge and act extra tough, or does this party have some residual fear that the angry negotiator might get angry again? Evidence suggests that being angry has a spillover effect, such that angry negotiators are perceived as "tough" when the parties meet a second time, which leads negotiation partners to give up more concessions again.[58]

Anxiety also appears to have an impact on negotiation. For example, one study found that individuals who experienced more anxiety about a negotiation used more deceptions in dealing with others.[59] Another study found that anxious negotiators expect lower outcomes from negotiations, respond to offers more quickly, and exit the bargaining process more quickly, which leads them to obtain worse outcomes.[60]

All these findings regarding emotions have related to distributive bargains. In integrative negotiations, in contrast, positive moods and emotions appear to lead to more integrative agreements (higher levels of joint gain). This may happen because, as we noted in a previous chapter, positive mood is related to creativity.[61]

CULTURE IN NEGOTIATIONS   One study compared U.S. and Japanese negotiators and found the generally conflict-avoidant Japanese negotiators tended to communicate indirectly and adapt their behaviors to the situation. A follow-up study showed that, whereas early offers by U.S. managers led to the anchoring effect we noted when discussing distributive negotiation, for Japanese negotiators, early offers led to more information sharing and better integrative outcomes.[62] In another study, managers with high levels of economic power from Hong Kong, which is a high power-distance country, were more cooperative in negotiations over a shared resource than German and U.S. managers, who were lower in power distance.[63] This suggests that in high power-distance countries, those in positions of power might exercise more restraint.

Another study looked at differences between U.S. and Indian negotiators.[64] Indian respondents reported having less trust in their negotiation counterparts than did U.S. respondents. These lower levels of trust were associated with lower discovery of common interests between parties, which occurred because Indian negotiators were less willing to disclose and solicit information. In both cultures, use of question-and-answer methods of negotiation were associated with superior negotiation outcomes, so although there are some cultural differences in negotiation styles, it appears that some negotiation tactics yield superior outcomes across cultures.

GENDER DIFFERENCES IN NEGOTIATIONS   Do men and women negotiate differently? And does gender affect negotiation outcomes? The answer to the first question appears to be no.[65] The answer to the second is a qualified yes.[66]

A popular stereotype is that women are more cooperative and pleasant in negotiations than are men. The evidence doesn't support this belief. However, men have been found to negotiate better outcomes than women, although the difference is relatively small. It's been postulated that men and women place unequal values on outcomes. "It is possible that a few hundred dollars more in salary or the corner office is less important to women than forming and maintaining an interpersonal relationship."[67]

Because women are expected to be "nice" and men "tough," research shows women are penalized when they initiate negotiations.[68] What's more, when women and men actually do conform to these stereotypes—women act "nice" and men "tough"—it becomes a self-fulfilling prophecy, reinforcing the stereotypical gender differences between male and female negotiators.[69] Thus, one of the reasons negotiations favor men is that women are "damned if they do, damned if they don't." Negotiate tough and they are penalized for violating a gender stereotype. Negotiate nice and it only reinforces and lets others take advantage of the stereotype.

Evidence also suggests women's own attitudes and behaviors hurt them in negotiations. Managerial women demonstrate less confidence than men in anticipation of negotiating and are less satisfied with their performance afterward, even when their performance and the outcomes they achieve are similar to those for men.[70] Women are also less likely than men to see an ambiguous situation as an opportunity for negotiation. It appears that women may unduly penalize themselves by failing to engage in negotiations that would be in their best interests. Some research suggests that women are less aggressive in negotiations because they are worried about backlash from others. There is an interesting qualifier to this result: women are more likely to engage in assertive negotiation when they are bargaining on behalf of someone else than when they are bargaining on their own behalf.[71]

SUMMARY AND IMPLICATIONS FOR MANAGERS

While many people assume conflict lowers group and organizational performance, this assumption is frequently incorrect. Conflict can be either constructive or destructive to the functioning of a group or unit. As shown in Exhibit 14-6, levels of conflict can be either too high or too low to be constructive. Either extreme hinders performance. An optimal level is one that prevents stagnation, stimulates creativity, allows tensions to be released, and initiates the seeds of change without being disruptive or preventing coordination of activities.

What advice can we give managers faced with excessive conflict and the need to reduce it? Don't assume one conflict-handling strategy will always be best. Select a strategy appropriate for the situation. Here are some guidelines:[72]

- Use *competition* when quick decisive action is needed (in emergencies), when issues are important, when unpopular actions need to be implemented (in cost cutting, enforcement of unpopular rules, discipline), when the issue is vital to the organization's welfare and you know you're right, and when others are taking advantage of noncompetitive behavior.
- Use *collaboration* to find an integrative solution when both sets of concerns are too important to be compromised, when your objective is to learn, when you want to merge insights from people with different perspectives or gain commitment by incorporating concerns into a consensus, and when you need to work through feelings that have interfered with a relationship.
- Use *avoidance* when an issue is trivial or symptomatic of other issues, when more important issues are pressing, when you perceive no chance of satisfying your concerns, when potential disruption outweighs the benefits of resolution, when people need to cool down and regain perspective, when gathering information supersedes immediate decision, and when others can resolve the conflict more effectively.
- Use *accommodation* when you find you're wrong, when you need to learn or show reasonableness, when you should allow a better position to be heard, when issues are more important to others than to yourself, when you want to satisfy others and maintain cooperation, when you can build social credits for later issues, when you are outmatched and losing (to minimize loss), when harmony and stability are especially important, and when employees can develop by learning from mistakes.
- Use *compromise* when goals are important but not worth the effort of potential disruption of more assertive approaches, when opponents with equal power are committed to mutually exclusive goals, when you seek temporary settlements to complex issues, when you need expedient solutions under time pressure, and as a backup when collaboration or competition is unsuccessful.
- Distributive bargaining can resolve disputes, but it often reduces the satisfaction of one or more negotiators because it is confrontational and focused on the short term.

EXHIBIT 14-6
Conflict and Unit Performance

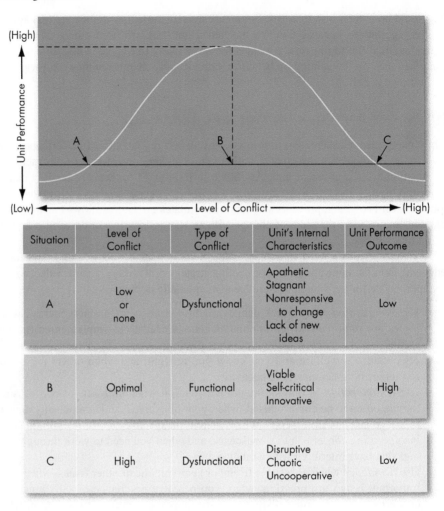

Situation	Level of Conflict	Type of Conflict	Unit's Internal Characteristics	Unit Performance Outcome
A	Low or none	Dysfunctional	Apathetic Stagnant Nonresponsive to change Lack of new ideas	Low
B	Optimal	Functional	Viable Self-critical Innovative	High
C	High	Dysfunctional	Disruptive Chaotic Uncooperative	Low

Integrative bargaining, in contrast, tends to provide outcomes that satisfy all parties and build lasting relationships.

• Make sure you set aggressive negotiating goals and try to find creative ways to achieve the objectives of both parties, especially when you value the long-term relationship with the other party. That doesn't mean sacrificing your self-interest; rather, it means trying to find creative solutions that give both parties what they really want.

PART 4: The Organization System

15

■■■

Foundations of Organization Structure

After studying this chapter, you should be able to:

- Identify the six elements of an organization's structure.
- Describe the common organizational designs.
- Compare and contrast the virtual and boundaryless organizations.
- Demonstrate how organizational structures differ.
- Analyze the behavioral implications of different organizational designs.

MyManagementLab™
⭐ **Improve Your Grade!**
Over 10 million students improved their results using the Pearson MyLabs. Visit
mymanagementlab.com for simulations, tutorials, and end-of-chapter problems.

The theme of this chapter is that organizations have different structures and that these structures have a bearing on employee attitudes and behaviors. More specifically, in the following pages, we'll define the key components that make up an organization's structure, present half a dozen or so structural designs preferable in different situations, and conclude by considering the different effects that various organizational structures have on employee behavior.

WHAT IS ORGANIZATIONAL STRUCTURE?

An **organizational structure** defines how job tasks are formally divided, grouped, and coordinated. Managers need to address six key elements when they design their organization's structure: work specialization, departmentalization, chain of command, span of control, centralization and decentralization, and formalization.[1] Exhibit 15-1 presents each of these elements as answers to an important structural question, and the following sections describe them.

EXHIBIT 15-1
**Key Design
Questions
and Answers
for Designing
the Proper
Organizational
Structure**

The Key Question	The Answer Is Provided By
1. To what degree are activities subdivided into separate jobs?	Work specialization
2. On what basis will jobs be grouped together?	Departmentalization
3. To whom do individuals and groups report?	Chain of command
4. How many individuals can a manager efficiently and effectively direct?	Span of control
5. Where does decision-making authority lie?	Centralization and decentralization
6. To what degree will there be rules and regulations to direct employees and managers?	Formalization

Work Specialization

Early in the twentieth century, Henry Ford became rich by building automobiles on an assembly line. Every Ford worker was assigned a specific, repetitive task such as putting on the right front wheel or installing the right front door. By dividing jobs into small standardized tasks that could be performed over and over, Ford was able to produce a car every 10 seconds, using employees who had relatively limited skills.

Ford demonstrated that work can be performed more efficiently if employees are allowed to specialize. Today, we use the term **work specialization**, or *division of labor,* to describe the degree to which activities in the organization are divided into separate jobs. The essence of work specialization is to divide a job into a number of steps, each completed by a separate individual. In essence, individuals specialize in doing part of an activity rather than the entirety.

By the late 1940s, most manufacturing jobs in industrialized countries featured high work specialization. Because not all employees in an organization have the same skills, management saw specialization as a means of making the most efficient use of its employees' skills and even successfully improving them through repetition. Less time is spent in changing tasks, putting away tools and equipment from a prior step, and getting ready for another. Equally important, it's easier and less costly to find and train workers to do specific and repetitive tasks, especially in highly sophisticated and complex operations. Could Cessna produce one Citation jet a year if one person had to build the entire plane alone? Not likely! Finally, work specialization increases efficiency and productivity by encouraging the creation of special inventions and machinery.

Thus, for much of the first half of the twentieth century, managers viewed work specialization as an unending source of increased productivity. And they were probably right. When specialization was not widely practiced, its introduction almost always generated higher productivity. But by the 1960s, it increasingly seemed a good thing can be carried too far. Human diseconomies from specialization began to surface in the form of boredom, fatigue, stress, low productivity, poor quality, increased absenteeism, and high turnover, which more than offset the economic advantages (see Exhibit 15-2). Managers could increase productivity now by enlarging, rather than narrowing, the scope of job activities. Giving employees a variety of activities to do, allowing them to do a whole

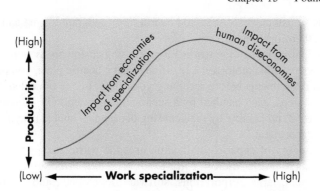

EXHIBIT 15-2

Economies and Diseconomies of Work Specialization

and complete job, and putting them into teams with interchangeable skills often achieved significantly higher output, with increased employee satisfaction.

Most managers today recognize the economies specialization provides in certain jobs and the problems when it's carried too far. High work specialization helps McDonald's make and sell hamburgers and fries efficiently and aids medical specialists in most health maintenance organizations. Amazon's Mechanical Turk program, TopCoder, and others like it have facilitated a new trend in microspecialization in which extremely small pieces of programming, data processing, or evaluation tasks are delegated to a global network of individuals by a program manager who then assembles the results.[2] For example, a manager who has a complex but routine computer program to write might send a request for specific subcomponents of the code to be written and tested by dozens of subcontracted individuals in the network (which spans the entire globe), enabling the project to be completed far more quickly than if a single programmer were writing the parts. This emerging trend suggests there still may be advantages to be had in specialization.

Departmentalization

Once jobs have been divided through work specialization, they must be grouped so common tasks can be coordinated. The basis by which jobs are grouped is called **departmentalization**.

One of the most popular ways to group activities is by *functions* performed. A manufacturing manager might organize a plant into engineering, accounting, manufacturing, personnel, and supply specialists departments. A hospital might have departments devoted to research, surgery, intensive care, accounting, and so forth. A professional football franchise might have departments entitled player personnel, ticket sales, and travel and accommodations. The major advantage of this type of functional departmentalization is efficiencies gained from putting like specialists together.

We can also departmentalize jobs by the type of *product* or *service* the organization produces. Procter & Gamble places each major product—such as Tide, Pampers, Charmin, and Pringles—under an executive who has complete global responsibility for it. The major advantage here is increased accountability for performance, because all activities related to a specific product or service are under the direction of a single manager.

When a firm is departmentalized on the basis of *geography,* or territory, the sales function, for instance, may have western, southern, midwestern, and eastern regions, each, in effect, a department organized around geography. This form is valuable when an organization's customers are scattered over a large geographic area and have similar needs based on their location.

Process departmentalization works for processing customers as well as products. If you've ever been to a state motor vehicle office to get a license plate, you probably went through several departments before receiving your plate. In one typical state, applicants go through three steps, each handled by a separate department: (1) validation by motor vehicles division, (2) processing by the licensing department, and (3) payment collection by the treasury department.

A final category of departmentalization uses the particular type of *customer* the organization seeks to reach. Microsoft, for example, is organized around four customer markets: consumers, large corporations, software developers, and small businesses. Customers in each department have a common set of problems and needs best met by having specialists for each.

As tasks have become more complex and more diverse skills have been needed to accomplish those tasks, management has turned to cross-functional teams.

Chain of Command

Although the chain of command was once a basic cornerstone in the design of organizations, it has far less importance today.[3] But contemporary managers should still consider its implications. The **chain of command** is an unbroken line of authority that extends from the top of the organization to the lowest echelon and clarifies who reports to whom.

We can't discuss the chain of command without also discussing *authority* and *unity of command*. **Authority** refers to the rights inherent in a managerial position to give orders and expect them to be obeyed. To facilitate coordination, each managerial position is given a place in the chain of command, and each manager is given a degree of authority in order to meet her responsibilities. The principle of **unity of command** helps preserve the concept of an unbroken line of authority. It says a person should have one and only one superior to whom he is directly responsible. If the unity of command is broken, an employee might have to cope with conflicting demands or priorities from several superiors, as is often the case in organization chart dotted-line reporting relationships.

Times change, and so do the basic tenets of organizational design. A low-level employee today can access information in seconds that was available only to top managers a generation ago. Operating employees are empowered to make decisions previously reserved for management. Add the popularity of self-managed and cross-functional teams as well as the creation of new structural designs that include multiple bosses, and you can see why authority and unity of command may appear to hold less relevance. Many organizations still find they can be most productive by enforcing the chain of command. Indeed, one survey of more than 1,000 managers found that 59 percent of them agreed with the statement, "There is an imaginary line in my company's organizational chart. Strategy is created by people above this line, while strategy is executed by people below the line."[4] However, this same survey found that buy-in to the organization's strategy by lower-level employees was inhibited by too much reliance on hierarchy for decision making.

Span of Control

How many employees can a manager efficiently and effectively direct? This question of **span of control** is important because it largely determines the number of levels and managers an organization has. All things being equal, the wider or larger the span, the more efficient the organization.

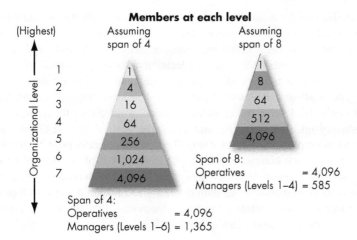

EXHIBIT 15-3

Contrasting Spans of Control

Members at each level

(Highest)

Organizational Level

Assuming span of 4

Assuming span of 8

1 — 1

2 — 4

3 — 16

4 — 64

5 — 256

6 — 1,024

7 — 4,096

1

8

64

512

4,096

Span of 8:
Operatives   = 4,096
Managers (Levels 1–4) = 585

Span of 4:
Operatives   = 4,096
Managers (Levels 1–6) = 1,365

Assume two organizations each have about 4,100 operative-level employees. One has a uniform span of four and the other a span of eight. As Exhibit 15-3 illustrates, the wider span will have two fewer levels and approximately 800 fewer managers. If the average manager makes $50,000 a year, the wider span will save $40 million a year in management salaries. Obviously, wider spans are more efficient in terms of cost. However, at some point when supervisors no longer have time to provide the necessary leadership and support, they reduce effectiveness, and employee performance suffers.

Narrow or small spans have their advocates. By keeping the span of control to five or six employees, a manager can maintain close control.[5] But narrow spans have three major drawbacks. First, they're expensive because they add levels of management. Second, they make vertical communication in the organization more complex. The added levels of hierarchy slow down decision making and tend to isolate upper management. Third, narrow spans encourage overly tight supervision and discourage employee autonomy.

The trend in recent years has been toward wider spans of control.[6] They're consistent with firms' efforts to reduce costs, cut overhead, speed decision making, increase flexibility, get closer to customers, and empower employees. However, to ensure performance doesn't suffer because of these wider spans, organizations have been investing heavily in employee training. Managers recognize they can handle a wider span best when employees know their jobs inside and out or can turn to co-workers when they have questions.

Centralization and Decentralization

Centralization refers to the degree to which decision making is concentrated at a single point in the organization. In *centralized* organizations, top managers make all the decisions, and lower-level managers merely carry out their directives. In organizations at the other extreme, *decentralized* decision making is pushed down to the managers closest to the action or even to work groups.

The concept of centralization includes only formal authority—that is, the rights inherent in a position. An organization characterized by centralization is inherently different structurally from one that's decentralized. A decentralized organization can act more quickly to solve problems, more people provide input into decisions, and employees are less likely to feel alienated from those who make decisions that affect their work lives.

Management efforts to make organizations more flexible and responsive have produced a recent trend toward decentralized decision making by lower-level managers, who are closer to the action and typically have more detailed knowledge about problems than top managers. Sears and JCPenney have given their store managers considerably more discretion in choosing what merchandise to stock. This allows those stores to compete more effectively against local merchants. Similarly, when Procter & Gamble empowered small groups of employees to make many decisions about new-product development independent of the usual hierarchy, it was able to rapidly increase the proportion of new products ready for market.[7] Research investigating a large number of Finnish organizations demonstrates that companies with decentralized research and development offices in multiple locations were better at producing innovation than companies that centralized all research and development in a single office.[8]

Formalization

Formalization refers to the degree to which jobs within the organization are standardized. If a job is highly formalized, the incumbent has a minimal amount of discretion over what to do and when and how to do it. Employees can be expected always to handle the same input in exactly the same way, resulting in a consistent and uniform output. There are explicit job descriptions, lots of organizational rules, and clearly defined procedures covering work processes in organizations in which there is high formalization. Where formalization is low, job behaviors are relatively unprogrammed, and employees have a great deal of freedom to exercise discretion in their work. Standardization not only eliminates the possibility of employees engaging in alternative behaviors, but it even removes the need for employees to consider alternatives.

The degree of formalization can vary widely between and within organizations. Publishing representatives who call on college professors to inform them of their company's new publications have a great deal of freedom in their jobs. They have only a general sales pitch, which they tailor as needed, and rules and procedures governing their behavior may be little more than the requirement to submit a weekly sales report and suggestions on what to emphasize about forthcoming titles. At the other extreme, clerical and editorial employees in the same publishing houses may need to be at their desks by 8:00 AM and follow a set of precise procedures dictated by management.

COMMON ORGANIZATIONAL DESIGNS

We now turn to three of the more common organizational designs: the *simple structure,* the *bureaucracy,* and the *matrix structure.*

The Simple Structure

What do a small retail store, an electronics firm run by a hard-driving entrepreneur, and an airline's "war room" in the midst of a pilot's strike have in common? They probably all use the **simple structure**.

We can think of the simple structure in terms of what it is *not* rather than what it is. The simple structure is not elaborate.[9] It has a low degree of departmentalization, wide spans of control, authority centralized in a single person, and little formalization.

It is a "flat" organization; it usually has only two or three vertical levels, a loose body of employees, and one individual in whom the decision-making authority is centralized.

The simple structure is most widely adopted in small businesses in which the manager and owner are one and the same. Consider a retail men's store owned and managed by Jack Gold. He employs five full-time salespeople, a cashier, and extra personnel for weekends and holidays, but Jack "runs the show." Though he is typical, large companies in times of crisis, often simplify their structures as a means of focusing their resources.

The strength of the simple structure lies in its simplicity. It's fast, flexible, and inexpensive to operate, and accountability is clear. One major weakness is that it becomes increasingly inadequate as an organization grows, because its low formalization and high centralization tend to create information overload at the top. As size increases, decision making typically becomes slower and can eventually come to a standstill as the single executive tries to continue making all the decisions. This proves the undoing of many small businesses. If the structure isn't changed and made more elaborate, the firm often loses momentum and can eventually fail. The simple structure's other weakness is that it's risky—everything depends on one person. One illness can literally destroy the organization's information and decision-making center.

The simple structure has a low degree of departmentalization, wide spans of control, authority centralized in a single person, and little formalization.

The Bureaucracy

Standardization! That's the key concept that underlies all bureaucracies. Consider the bank where you keep your checking account; the department store where you buy clothes; or the government offices that collect your taxes, enforce health regulations, or provide local fire protection. They all rely on standardized work processes for coordination and control.

The **bureaucracy** is characterized by highly routine operating tasks achieved through specialization, strictly formalized rules and regulations, tasks grouped into functional departments, centralized authority, narrow spans of control, and decision making that follows the chain of command. *Bureaucracy* is a dirty word in many people's minds. However, it does have advantages. Its primary strength is its ability to perform standardized activities in a highly efficient manner. Putting like specialties together in functional departments results in economies of scale, minimum duplication of people and equipment, and employees who can speak "the same language" among their peers. Bureaucracies can get by with less talented—and hence less costly—middle- and lower-level managers because rules and regulations substitute for managerial discretion. Standardized operations and high formalization allow decision making to be centralized. There is little need for innovative and experienced decision makers below the level of senior executives.

Listen in on a dialogue among four executives in one company: "You know, nothing happens in this place until we *produce* something," said the production executive. "Wrong," commented the research and development manager. "Nothing happens until we *design* something!" "What are you talking about?" asked the marketing executive. "Nothing happens here until we *sell* something!" The exasperated accounting manager responded, "It doesn't matter what you produce, design, or sell. No one knows what happens until we *tally up the results!*" This conversation highlights that bureaucratic specialization can create conflicts in which functional-unit goals override the overall goals of the organization.

The other major weakness of a bureaucracy is something we've all witnessed: obsessive concern with following the rules. When cases don't precisely fit the rules, there is no room for modification. The bureaucracy is efficient only as long as employees confront familiar problems with programmed decision rules.

The Matrix Structure

You'll find the **matrix structure** in advertising agencies, aerospace firms, research and development laboratories, construction companies, hospitals, government agencies, universities, management consulting firms, and entertainment companies.[10] It combines two forms of departmentalization: functional and product. Companies that use matrixlike structures include ABB, Boeing, BMW, IBM, and P&G.

The strength of functional departmentalization is putting like specialists together, which minimizes the number necessary while allowing the pooling and sharing of specialized resources across products. Its major disadvantage is the difficulty of coordinating the tasks of diverse functional specialists on time and within budget. Product departmentalization has exactly the opposite benefits and disadvantages. It facilitates coordination among specialties to achieve on-time completion and meet budget targets. It provides clear responsibility for all activities related to a product, but with duplication of activities and costs. The matrix attempts to gain the strengths of each while avoiding their weaknesses.

The most obvious structural characteristic of the matrix is that it breaks the unity-of-command concept. Employees in the matrix have two bosses: their functional department managers and their product managers.

Exhibit 15-4 shows the matrix form in a college of business administration. The academic departments of accounting, decision and information systems, marketing, and so forth are functional units. Overlaid on them are specific programs (that is, products). Thus, members in a matrix structure have a dual chain of command: to their functional department and to their product groups. A professor of accounting teaching an undergraduate course may report to the director of undergraduate programs as well as to the chairperson of the accounting department.

The strength of the matrix is its ability to facilitate coordination when the organization has a number of complex and interdependent activities. Direct and frequent contacts between different specialties in the matrix can let information permeate the organization and more quickly reach the people who need it. The matrix reduces

EXHIBIT 15-4
Matrix Structure for a College of Business Administration

Programs / Academic Departments	Undergraduate	Master's	Ph.D.	Research	Executive Development	Community Service
Accounting						
Finance						
Decision and Information Systems						
Management						
Marketing						

"bureaupathologies"—the dual lines of authority reduce people's tendency to become so busy protecting their little worlds that the organization's goals become secondary. A matrix also achieves economies of scale and facilitates the allocation of specialists by providing both the best resources and an effective way of ensuring their efficient deployment.

The major disadvantages of the matrix lie in the confusion it creates, its tendency to foster power struggles, and the stress it places on individuals.[11] Without the unity-of-command concept, ambiguity about who reports to whom is significantly increased and often leads to conflict. It's not unusual for product managers to fight over getting the best specialists assigned to their products. Bureaucracy reduces the potential for power grabs by defining the rules of the game. When those rules are "up for grabs" in a matrix, power struggles between functional and product managers result. For individuals who desire security and absence from ambiguity, this work climate can be stressful. Reporting to more than one boss introduces role conflict, and unclear expectations introduce role ambiguity. The comfort of bureaucracy's predictability is replaced by insecurity and stress.

NEW DESIGN OPTIONS

Senior managers in a number of organizations have been developing new structural options with fewer layers of hierarchy and more emphasis on opening the boundaries of the organization.[12] In this section, we describe two such designs: the *virtual organization* and the *boundaryless organization*. We'll also discuss how efforts to reduce bureaucracy and increase strategic focus have made downsizing routine.

The Virtual Organization

Why own when you can rent? That question captures the essence of the **virtual organization** (also sometimes called the *network,* or *modular,* organization), typically a small, core organization that outsources its major business functions.[13] In structural terms, the virtual organization is highly centralized, with little or no departmentalization.

The prototype of the virtual structure is today's movie-making organization. In Hollywood's golden era, movies were made by huge, vertically integrated corporations. Studios such as MGM, Warner Brothers, and 20th Century Fox owned large movie lots and employed thousands of full-time specialists—set designers, camera people, film editors, directors, and even actors. Today, most movies are made by a collection of individuals and small companies who come together and make films project by project.[14] This structural form allows each project to be staffed with the talent best suited to its demands, rather than just with the people employed by the studio. It minimizes bureaucratic overhead because there is no lasting organization to maintain. And it lessens long-term risks and their costs because there *is* no long term—a team is assembled for a finite period and then disbanded.

Philip Rosedale runs a virtual company called LoveMachine that lets employees send brief electronic messages to one another to acknowledge a job well done that can then be used to facilitate company bonuses. The company has no full-time software development staff—instead, LoveMachine outsources assignments to freelancers who submit bids for projects like debugging software or designing new features. Programmers come from or work from around the world, including Russia, India, Australia, and the United States.[15] Similarly, Newman's Own, the food products company founded by

EXHIBIT 15-5

**A Virtual
Organization**

Paul Newman, sells hundreds of millions of dollars in food every year yet employs only 28 people. This is possible because it outsources almost everything: manufacturing, procurement, shipping, and quality control.

Exhibit 15-5 shows a virtual organization in which management outsources all the primary functions of the business. The core of the organization is a small group of executives whose job is to oversee directly any activities done in-house and to coordinate relationships with the other organizations that manufacture, distribute, and perform other crucial functions for the virtual organization. The dotted lines represent the relationships typically maintained under contracts. In essence, managers in virtual structures spend most of their time coordinating and controlling external relations, typically by way of computer network links.

The major advantage of the virtual organization is its flexibility, which allows individuals with an innovative idea and little money to successfully compete against larger, more established organizations. Virtual organizations also save a great deal of money by eliminating permanent offices and hierarchical roles.[16]

Virtual organizations' drawbacks have become increasingly clear as their popularity has grown.[17] They are in a state of perpetual flux and reorganization, which means roles, goals, and responsibilities are unclear, setting the stage for political behavior. Cultural alignment and shared goals can be lost because of the low degree of interaction among members. Team members who are geographically dispersed and communicate infrequently find it difficult to share information and knowledge, which can limit innovation and slow response time. Ironically, some virtual organizations are less adaptable and innovative than those with well-established communication and collaboration networks. A leadership presence that reinforces the organization's purpose and facilitates communication is thus especially valuable.

The Boundaryless Organization

General Electric's former chairman, Jack Welch, coined the term **boundaryless organization** to describe what he wanted GE to become: a "family grocery store."[18] That is, in spite of GE's monstrous size (2010 revenues were $150 billion), Welch wanted to eliminate *vertical* and *horizontal* boundaries within it and break down *external* barriers between the company and its customers and suppliers. The boundaryless organization seeks to eliminate the chain of command, have limitless spans of control, and replace departments with empowered teams. Although GE has not yet achieved this boundary-less state—and probably never will—it has made significant progress toward that end. So have other companies, such as Hewlett-Packard, AT&T, Motorola, and 3M. Let's see what a boundaryless organization looks like and what some firms are doing to make it a reality.[19]

By removing vertical boundaries, management flattens the hierarchy and mini-mizes status and rank. Cross-hierarchical teams (which include top executives, middle managers, supervisors, and operative employees), participative decision-making prac-tices, and the use of 360-degree performance appraisals (in which peers and others above and below the employee evaluate performance) are examples of what GE is doing to break down vertical boundaries. At Oticon A/S, a $160 million-per-year Danish hearing aid manufacturer, all traces of hierarchy have disappeared. Everyone works at uniform mobile workstations, and project teams, not functions or departments, coordinate work.

Functional departments create horizontal boundaries that stifle interaction among functions, product lines, and units. The way to reduce them is to replace functional de-partments with cross-functional teams and organize activities around processes. Xerox now develops new products through multidisciplinary teams that work on a single pro-cess instead of on narrow functional tasks. Some AT&T units prepare annual budgets based not on functions or departments but on processes, such as the maintenance of a worldwide telecommunications network. Another way to lower horizontal barriers is to rotate people through different functional areas using lateral transfers. This approach turns specialists into generalists.

When fully operational, the boundaryless organization also breaks down geographic barriers. Today, most large U.S. companies see themselves as global corporations; many, like Coca-Cola and McDonald's, do as much business overseas as in the United States, and some struggle to incorporate geographic regions into their structure. The boundary-less organization provides one solution because it considers geography more of a tactical, logistical issue than a structural one. In short, the goal is to break down cultural barriers.

One way to do so is through strategic alliances.[20] Firms such as NEC Corpora-tion, Boeing, and Apple each have strategic alliances or joint partnerships with dozens of companies. These alliances blur the distinction between one organization and another as employees work on joint projects. And some companies allow customers to perform functions previously done by management. Some AT&T units receive bonuses based on customer evaluations of the teams that serve them. Finally, telecommuting is blurring or-ganizational boundaries. The security analyst with Merrill Lynch who does her job from her ranch in Montana or the software designer in Boulder, Colorado, who works for a San Francisco firm are just two of the millions of workers operating outside the physical boundaries of their employers' premises.

The Leaner Organization: Downsizing

The goal of the new organizational forms we've described is to improve agility by creat-ing a lean, focused, and flexible organization. *Downsizing* is a systematic effort to make an organization leaner by closing locations, reducing staff, or selling off business units that don't add value.

The radical shrinking of Chrysler and General Motors in recent years was a case of downsizing to survive, due to loss of market share and changes in consumer demand. Other firms, including Research in Motion (makers of the BlackBerry) and Cisco, downsize to direct all their efforts toward their core competencies.

Despite the advantages of being a lean organization, the impact of downsizing on organizational performance has been very controversial.[21] Reducing the size of the workforce has an immediately positive outcome in the form of lower-wage costs. Companies downsizing to improve strategic focus often see positive effects on stock prices after the announcement. On the other hand, among companies that only cut employees but don't restructure, profits and stock prices usually decline. Part of the problem is the effect of downsizing on employee attitudes. Those who remain often feel worried about future layoffs and may be less committed to the organization.[22] Stress reactions can lead to increased sickness absences, lower concentration on the job, and lower creativity. In companies that don't invest much in their employees, downsizing can also lead to more voluntary turnover, so vital human capital is lost. The result is a company that is more anemic than lean.

Companies can reduce negative impacts by preparing in advance, thus alleviating some employee stress and strengthening support for the new direction.[23] Here are some effective strategies for downsizing. Most are closely linked to the principles for organizational justice we've discussed previously:

- *Investment.* Companies that downsize to focus on core competencies are more effective when they invest in high-involvement work practices afterward.
- *Communication.* When employers make efforts to discuss downsizing with employees early, employees are less worried about the outcomes and feel the company is taking their perspective into account.
- *Participation.* Employees worry less if they can participate in the process in some way. Voluntary early-retirement programs or severance packages can help achieve leanness without layoffs.
- *Assistance.* Severance pay and packages, extended health care benefits, and job search assistance demonstrate a company cares about its employees and honors their contributions.

In short, companies that make themselves lean can be more agile, efficient, and productive—but only if they make cuts carefully and help employees through the process.

WHY DO STRUCTURES DIFFER?

We've described organizational designs ranging from the highly structured bureaucracy to the amorphous boundaryless organization. The other designs we discussed exist somewhere in between.

Exhibit 15-6 recaps our discussions by presenting two extreme models of organizational design. One we'll call the **mechanistic model**. It's generally synonymous with the bureaucracy in that it has highly standardized processes for work, high formalization, and more managerial hierarchy. The other extreme, the **organic model**, looks a lot like the boundaryless organization. It's flat, has fewer formal procedures for making decisions, has multiple decision makers, and favors flexible practices.[24]

The Mechanistic Model

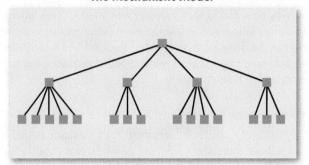

The Organic Model

- High specialization
- Rigid departmentalization
- Clear chain of command
- Narrow spans of control
- Centralization
- High formalization

- Cross-functional teams
- Cross-hierarchical teams
- Free flow of information
- Wide spans of control
- Decentralization
- Low formalization

EXHIBIT 15-6
Mechanistic Versus Organic Models

With these two models in mind, let's ask a few questions: Why are some organizations structured along more mechanistic lines, whereas others follow organic characteristics? What forces influence the choice of design? In this section, we present the major causes or determinants of an organization's structure.[25]

Organizational Strategy

Because structure is a means to achieve objectives, and objectives derive from the organization's overall strategy, it's only logical that structure should follow strategy. If management significantly changes the organization's strategy, the structure must change to accommodate.[26] Most current strategy frameworks focus on three strategy dimensions—innovation, cost minimization, and imitation—and the structural design that works best with each.[27]

To what degree does an organization introduce major new products or services? An **innovation strategy** strives to achieve meaningful and unique innovations. Obviously, not all firms pursue innovation. Apple and 3M do, but conservative retailer Marks & Spencer doesn't. Innovative firms will use competitive pay and benefits to attract top candidates and motivate employees to take risks. Some degree of mechanistic structure can actually benefit innovation. Well-developed communication channels, policies for enhancing long-term commitment, and clear channels of authority all may make it easier for rapid changes to occur smoothly.

An organization pursuing a **cost-minimization strategy** tightly controls costs, refrains from incurring unnecessary expenses, and cuts prices in selling a basic product. This describes the strategy pursued by Walmart and the makers of generic or store-label grocery products. Cost-minimizing organizations pursue fewer policies meant to develop commitment among their workforce.

Organizations following an **imitation strategy** try to both minimize risk and maximize opportunity for profit, moving new products or entering new markets only after innovators have proven their viability. Mass-market fashion manufacturers that copy designer styles follow this strategy, as do firms such as Hewlett-Packard and Caterpillar. They follow smaller and more innovative competitors with superior products, but only after competitors have demonstrated the market is there.

Organization Size

An organization's size significantly affects its structure.[28] Organizations that employ 2,000 or more people tend to have more specialization, more departmentalization, more vertical levels, and more rules and regulations than do small organizations. However, size becomes less important as an organization expands. Why? At around 2,000 employees, an organization is already fairly mechanistic; 500 more employees won't have much impact. But adding 500 employees to an organization of only 300 is likely to significantly shift it toward a more mechanistic structure.

Technology

Technology describes the way an organization transfers inputs into outputs. Every organization has at least one technology for converting financial, human, and physical resources into products or services. Ford Motor Company uses an assembly-line process to make its products. Colleges may use a number of instructional technologies—the ever-popular lecture method, case analysis, the experiential exercise, programmed learning, and online instruction and distance learning. Regardless, organizational structures adapt to their technology.

Numerous studies have examined the technology–structure relationship.[29] What differentiates technologies is their *degree of routineness*. Routine activities are characterized by automated and standardized operations. Examples are injection-mold production of plastic knobs, automated transaction processing of sales transactions, and the printing and binding of this book. Nonroutine activities are customized and require frequent revision and updating. They include furniture restoring, custom shoemaking, genetic research, and the writing and editing of this book. In general, organizations engaged in nonroutine activities tend to prefer organic structures, whereas those performing routine activities prefer mechanistic structures.

Environment

An organization's **environment** includes outside institutions or forces that can affect its performance, such as suppliers, customers, competitors, government regulatory agencies, and public pressure groups. Dynamic environments create significantly more uncertainty for managers than do static ones. To minimize uncertainty, managers may broaden their structure to sense and respond to threats. For example, most companies, including Pepsi and Southwest Airlines, have added social networking departments to counter negative information posted on blogs. Or companies may form strategic alliances with other companies.

Any organization's environment has three dimensions: capacity, volatility, and complexity.[30] *Capacity* refers to the degree to which the environment can support growth. Rich and growing environments generate excess resources, which can buffer the organization in times of relative scarcity.

Volatility describes the degree of instability in the environment. A dynamic environment with a high degree of unpredictable change makes it difficult for management to make accurate predictions. Because information technology changes at a rapid place, for instance, more organizations' environments are becoming volatile.

Finally, *complexity* is the degree of heterogeneity and concentration among environmental elements. Simple environments—like the tobacco industry, where the methods of production, competitive environment, regulatory pressures, and the like haven't changed in quite some time—are homogeneous and concentrated. Environments characterized by heterogeneity and dispersion—like the broadband industry—are complex and diverse, with numerous competitors.

The arrows indicate movement toward higher uncertainty. Organizations that operate in environments characterized as scarce, dynamic, and complex face the greatest degree of uncertainty because they have high unpredictability, little room for error, and a diverse set of elements in the environment to monitor constantly. Given this three-dimensional definition of *environment,* we can offer some general conclusions about environmental uncertainty and structural arrangements. The more scarce, dynamic, and complex the environment, the more organic a structure should be. The more abundant, stable, and simple the environment, the more the mechanistic structure will be preferred.

ORGANIZATIONAL DESIGNS AND EMPLOYEE BEHAVIOR

We opened this chapter by implying that an organization's structure can have significant effects on its members. What might those effects be?

A review of the evidence leads to a pretty clear conclusion: you can't generalize! Not everyone prefers the freedom and flexibility of organic structures. Different factors stand out in different structures as well. In highly formalized, heavily structured, mechanistic organizations, the level of fairness in formal policies and procedures is a very important predictor of satisfaction. In more personal, individually adaptive organic organizations, employees value interpersonal justice more.[31] Some people are most productive and satisfied when work tasks are standardized and ambiguity minimized—that is, in mechanistic structures. So, any discussion of the effect of organizational design on employee behavior has to address individual differences. To do so, let's consider employee preferences for work specialization, span of control, and centralization.[32]

The evidence generally indicates that *work specialization* contributes to higher employee productivity—but at the price of reduced job satisfaction. However, work specialization is not an unending source of higher productivity. Problems start to surface, and productivity begins to suffer, when the human diseconomies of doing repetitive and narrow tasks overtake the economies of specialization. As the workforce has become more highly educated and desirous of jobs that are intrinsically rewarding, we seem to reach the point at which productivity begins to decline as a function of specialization more quickly than in the past.

There is still a segment of the workforce that prefers the routine and repetitiveness of highly specialized jobs. Some individuals want work that makes minimal intellectual demands and provides the security of routine; for them, high work specialization is a source of job satisfaction. The question, of course, is whether they represent 2 percent of the workforce or 52 percent. Research suggests the "real" answer is closer to 2 percent than 52 percent. The answer often will vary by job, organization, and labor market. Given that some self-selection operates in the choice of careers, we might conclude that negative behavioral outcomes from high specialization are most likely to surface in professional jobs occupied by individuals with high needs for personal growth and diversity.

It is safe to say no evidence supports a relationship between *span of control* and employee satisfaction or performance. Although it is intuitively attractive to argue that large spans might lead to higher employee performance because they provide more distant supervision and more opportunity for personal initiative, the research fails to support this notion. Some people like to be left alone; others prefer the security of a boss who is quickly available at all times. Consistent with several of the contingency theories of leadership discussed in Chapter 12. Consistent with several contingency theories of leadership, we would expect factors such as employees' experiences, abilities, and the degree of structure in their tasks to explain when wide or narrow spans of control are likely to contribute to their performance and job satisfaction. However, some evidence indicates that a *manager's* job satisfaction increases as the number of employees supervised increases.

We find fairly strong evidence linking *centralization* and job satisfaction. In general, less centralized organizations have a greater amount of autonomy. And autonomy appears positively related to job satisfaction. But, again, while one employee may value freedom, another may find autonomous environments frustratingly ambiguous.

Our conclusion: to maximize employee performance and satisfaction, managers must take individual differences, such as experience, personality, and the work task, into account. Culture should factor in, too.

We can draw one obvious insight: other things equal, people don't select employers randomly. They are attracted to, are selected by, and stay with organizations that suit their personal characteristics.[33] Job candidates who prefer predictability are likely to seek out and take employment in mechanistic structures, and those who want autonomy are more likely to end up in an organic structure. Thus, the effect of structure on employee behavior is undoubtedly reduced when the selection process facilitates proper matching of individual characteristics with organizational characteristics.

Globalization, strategic alliances, customer-organization links, and telecommuting are all examples of practices that reduce external boundaries.

Although research is slim, it does suggest national culture influences the preference for structure.[34] Organizations that operate with people from high power-distance cultures, such as Greece, France, and most of Latin America, find their employees are much more accepting of mechanistic structures than are employees from low power-distance countries. So consider cultural differences along with individual differences when predicting how structure will affect employee performance and satisfaction.

SUMMARY AND IMPLICATIONS FOR MANAGERS

The theme of this chapter is that an organization's internal structure contributes to explaining and predicting behavior. That is, in addition to individual and group factors, the structural relationships in which people work have a bearing on employee attitudes and behavior. What's the basis for this argument? To the degree that an organization's structure reduces ambiguity for employees and clarifies concerns such as "What am I supposed to do?" "How am I supposed to do it?" "To whom do I report?" and "To whom do I go if I have a problem?" it shapes their attitudes and facilitates and motivates them to higher levels of performance.

- Although specialization can bring efficiency, excessive specialization also can breed dissatisfaction and reduced motivation.

- Formal hierarchies offer advantages like unification of mission and goals, while employees in excessively rigid hierarchies can feel they have no power or autonomy. As with specialization, the key is striking the right balance.
- Virtual and boundaryless forms are changing the face of many organizations. Contemporary managers should thoroughly understand their implications and recognize advantages and potential pitfalls.
- Organizational downsizing can lead to major cost savings and focus organizations around their core competencies, but it can leave workers dissatisfied and worried about the future of their jobs.
- When determining an appropriate organizational form, managers will need to consider scarcity, dynamism, and complexity of the environment and balance the organic and mechanistic elements appropriate to their organization's environment.

MyManagementLab

Go to **MyManagementLab.com** to access study plans, interactive lectures, and videos as well as Auto-graded writing questions and the following Assisted-graded writing question.

15-1. MyManagementLab Only—comprehensive writing assignment for this chapter.

16

■ ■ ■

Organizational Culture

After studying this chapter, you should be able to:

- Define *organizational culture*, and describe its common characteristics.
- Compare the functional and dysfunctional effects of organizational culture on people and the organization.
- Identify the factors that create and sustain an organization's culture.
- Show how culture is transmitted to employees.
- Demonstrate how an ethical culture can be created.
- Show how national culture may affect the way organizational culture is transported to a different country.

Just as individuals have personalities, so, too, do organizations. In Chapter 5, we found that individuals have relatively enduring and stable traits that help us predict their attitudes and behaviors. In this chapter 5, we propose that organizations, like people, can be characterized as, for example, rigid, friendly, warm, innovative, or conservative. These traits, in turn, can then be used to predict attitudes and behaviors of the people within these organizations.

The culture of any organization, although it may be hard to measure precisely, nevertheless exists and is generally recognized by its employees. We call this variable *organizational culture*. Just as tribal cultures have totems and taboos that dictate how each member will act toward fellow members and outsiders, organizations have cultures that govern how members behave. In this chapter, we'll discuss just what organizational culture is, how it affects employee attitudes and behavior, where it comes from, and whether or not it can be changed.

WHAT IS ORGANIZATIONAL CULTURE?

An executive once was asked what he thought *organizational culture* meant. He gave essentially the same answer a U.S. Supreme Court justice once gave in attempting to define pornography: "I can't define it, but I know it when I see it." We, however, need a basic definition of organizational culture to better understand the phenomenon. In this section we propose one and review several related ideas.

A Definition of *Organizational Culture*

Organizational culture refers to a system of shared meaning held by members that distinguishes the organization from other organizations.[1] Seven primary characteristics seem to capture the essence of an organization's culture:[2]

> An organization's culture develops over many years and is rooted in deeply held values to which employees are strongly committed.

1. *Innovation and Risk Taking.* The degree to which employees are encouraged to be innovative and take risks.
2. *Attention to Detail.* The degree to which employees are expected to exhibit precision, analysis, and attention to detail.
3. *Outcome Orientation.* The degree to which management focuses on results or outcomes rather than on the techniques and processes used to achieve them.
4. *People Orientation.* The degree to which management decisions take into consideration the effect of outcomes on people within the organization.
5. *Team Orientation.* The degree to which work activities are organized around teams rather than individuals.
6. *Aggressiveness.* The degree to which people are aggressive and competitive rather than easygoing.
7. *Stability.* The degree to which organizational activities emphasize maintaining the status quo in contrast to growth.

Each of these characteristics exists on a continuum from low to high. Appraising the organization on them, then, gives a composite picture of its culture and a basis for the shared understanding members have about the organization, how things are done in it, and the way they are supposed to behave.

Culture Is a Descriptive Term

Organizational culture shows how employees perceive the characteristics of an organization's culture, not whether they like them—that is, it's a descriptive term. This is important because it differentiates culture from job satisfaction.

Research on organizational culture has sought to measure how employees see their organization: Does it encourage teamwork? Does it reward innovation? Does it stifle initiative? In contrast, *job satisfaction* seeks to measure how employees feel about the organization's expectations, reward practices, and the like. Although the two terms have overlapping characteristics, keep in mind that *organizational culture* is descriptive, whereas *job satisfaction* is evaluative.

Do Organizations Have Uniform Cultures?

Organizational culture represents a common perception the organization's members hold. We should therefore expect individuals with different backgrounds or at different levels in the organization to describe its culture in similar terms.[3]

That doesn't mean, however, that there are no subcultures. Most large organizations have a dominant culture and numerous subcultures.[4] A **dominant culture** expresses the **core values** a majority of members share and that give the organization its distinct personality.[5] **Subcultures** tend to develop in large organizations to reflect common problems or experiences members face in the same department or location. The purchasing department can have a subculture that includes the core values of the dominant culture plus additional values unique to members of that department.

If organizations were composed only of numerous subcultures, organizational culture as an independent variable would be significantly less powerful. It is the "shared meaning" aspect of culture that makes it such a potent device for guiding and shaping behavior. That's what allows us to say, for example, that the Zappos culture values customer care and dedication over speed and efficiency, and to use that information to better understand the behavior of Zappos executives and employees.[6] But subcultures can influence members' behavior, too.

Strong Versus Weak Cultures

It's possible to differentiate between strong and weak cultures.[7] If most employees (responding to management surveys) have the same opinions about the organization's mission and values, the culture is strong; if opinions vary widely, the culture is weak.

In a **strong culture**, the organization's core values are both intensely held and widely shared.[8] The more members who accept the core values and the greater their commitment, the stronger the culture and the greater its influence on member behavior, because the high degree of sharedness and intensity creates a climate of high behavioral control. Nordstrom employees know in no uncertain terms what is expected of them, and these expectations go a long way in shaping their behavior. In contrast, Nordstrom competitor Macy's, which has struggled through an identity crisis, is working to remake its culture.

A strong culture should reduce employee turnover because it demonstrates high agreement about what the organization represents. Such unanimity of purpose builds cohesiveness, loyalty, and organizational commitment. These qualities, in turn, lessen employees' propensity to leave.[9] One study, for instance, found that the more employees agreed on customer orientation in a service organization, the higher the profitability of the business unit.[10] Another study found that when team managers and team members disagreed about perceptions of organizational support, there were more negative moods among team members, and the performance of teams was lower.[11] These negative effects are especially strong when managers believe the organization provides more support than employees think it does.

Culture Versus Formalization

We've seen that high formalization creates predictability, orderliness, and consistency. A strong culture achieves the same end without the need for written documentation.[12] Therefore, we should view formalization and culture as two different roads to a common destination. The stronger an organization's culture, the less management needs to be concerned with developing formal rules and regulations to guide employee behavior. Those guides will be internalized in employees when they accept the organization's culture.

WHAT DO CULTURES DO?

Let's review the role culture performs and whether it can ever be a liability for an organization.

Culture's Functions

First, culture has a boundary-defining role: it creates distinctions between one organization and others. Second, it conveys a sense of identity for organization members. Third, culture facilitates commitment to something larger than individual self-interest. Fourth, it enhances the stability of the social system. Culture is the social glue that helps hold the organization together by providing standards for what employees should say and do. Finally, it is a sense-making and control mechanism that guides and shapes employees' attitudes and behavior. This last function is of particular interest to us.[13] Culture defines the rules of the game.

Today's trend toward decentralized organizations makes culture more important than ever, but ironically it also makes establishing a strong culture more difficult. When formal authority and control systems are reduced, culture's *shared meaning* can point everyone in the same direction. However, employees organized in teams may show greater allegiance to their team and its values than to the organization as a whole. In virtual organizations, the lack of frequent face-to-face contact makes establishing a common set of norms very difficult. Strong leadership that communicates frequently about common goals and priorities is especially important in innovative organizations.[14]

Individual–organization "fit"—that is, whether the applicant's or employee's attitudes and behavior are compatible with the culture—strongly influences who gets a job offer, a favorable performance review, or a promotion. It's no coincidence that Disney theme park employees appear almost universally attractive, clean, and wholesome with bright smiles. The company selects employees who will maintain that image. On the job, a strong culture supported by formal rules and regulations ensures they will act in a relatively uniform and predictable way.

Culture Creates Climate

If you've worked with someone whose positive attitude inspired you to do your best, or with a lackluster team that drained your motivation, you've experienced the effects of climate. **Organizational climate** refers to the shared perceptions organizational members have about their organization and work environment.[15] This aspect of culture is like team spirit at the organizational level. When everyone has the same general feelings about what's important or how well things are working, the effect of these attitudes will be more than the sum of the individual parts. One meta-analysis found that across dozens of different samples, psychological climate was strongly related to individuals' level of job satisfaction, involvement, commitment, and motivation.[16] A positive overall workplace climate has been linked to higher customer satisfaction and financial performance as well.[17]

Dozens of dimensions of climate have been studied, including safety, justice, diversity, and customer service.[18] A person who encounters a positive climate for performance will think about doing a good job more often and will believe others support his success. Someone who encounters a positive climate for diversity will feel more comfortable collaborating with co-workers regardless of their demographic background. Climates can interact with one another to produce behavior. For example, a positive climate for worker empowerment can lead to higher levels of performance in organizations that also have a climate for personal accountability.[19] Climate also influences the habits people adopt. If the climate for safety is positive, everyone wears safety gear and follows safety procedures even if individually they wouldn't normally think very often about being safe—indeed, many studies have shown that a positive safety climate decreases the number of documented injuries on the job.[20]

Culture as a Liability

Culture can enhance organizational commitment and increase the consistency of employee behavior, clearly benefits to an organization. Culture is valuable to employees too, because it spells out how things are done and what's important. But we shouldn't ignore the potentially dysfunctional aspects of culture, especially a strong one, on an organization's effectiveness.

INSTITUTIONALIZATION   When an organization undergoes **institutionalization** and becomes *institutionalized*—that is, it is valued for itself and not for the goods or services it produces—it takes on a life of its own, apart from its founders or members.[21] It doesn't go out of business even if its original goals are no longer relevant. Acceptable modes of behavior become largely self-evident to members, and although this isn't entirely negative, it does mean behaviors and habits that should be questioned and analyzed become taken for granted, which can stifle innovation and make maintaining the organization's culture an end in itself.

BARRIERS TO CHANGE   Culture is a liability when the shared values don't agree with those that further the organization's effectiveness. This is most likely when an organization's environment is undergoing rapid change, and its entrenched culture may no longer be appropriate.[22] Consistency of behavior, an asset in a stable environment, may then burden the organization and make it difficult to respond to changes.

BARRIERS TO DIVERSITY   Hiring new employees who differ from the majority in race, age, gender, disability, or other characteristics creates a paradox:[23] management wants to demonstrate support for the differences these employees bring to the workplace, but newcomers who wish to fit in must accept the organization's core cultural values and current mix. Because diverse behaviors and unique strengths are likely to diminish as people attempt to assimilate, strong cultures can become liabilities when they effectively eliminate these advantages. A strong culture that condones prejudice, supports bias, or becomes insensitive to people who are different can even undermine formal corporate diversity policies.

BARRIERS TO ACQUISITIONS AND MERGERS   Historically, when management looked at acquisition or merger decisions, the key factors were financial advantage and product synergy. In recent years, cultural compatibility has become the primary concern.[24] All things being equal, whether the acquisition actually works seems to have more to do with how well the two organizations' cultures match up.

A survey by consulting firm A. T. Kearney revealed that 58 percent of mergers failed to reach their financial goals.[25] As one expert commented, "Mergers have an unusually high failure rate, and it's always because of people issues"—in other words, conflicting organizational cultures. The $183 billion merger between America Online (AOL) and Time Warner in 2001 was the largest in U.S. corporate history. It was also a disaster. Only 2 years later, the stock had fallen an astounding 90 percent, and the new company reported what was then the largest financial loss in U.S. history. To this day,

Time Warner stock—trading around \$32 per share in late 2011—remains at a fraction of its former price (around \$200 per share before the merger). Culture clash is commonly argued to be one of the causes of AOL Time Warner's problems. As one expert noted, "In some ways the merger of AOL and Time Warner was like the marriage of a teenager to a middle-aged banker. The cultures were vastly different. There were open collars and jeans at AOL. Time Warner was more buttoned-down."[26]

CREATING AND SUSTAINING CULTURE

An organization's culture doesn't pop out of thin air, and once established it rarely fades away. What influences the creation of a culture? What reinforces and sustains it once it's in place?

How a Culture Begins

An organization's current customs, traditions, and general way of doing things are largely due to what it has done before and how successful it was in doing it. This leads us to the ultimate source of an organization's culture: its founders.[27] Free of previous customs or ideologies, founders have a vision of what the organization should be, and the firm's small size makes it easy to impose that vision on all members.

Culture creation occurs in three ways.[28] First, founders hire and keep only employees who think and feel the same way they do. Second, they indoctrinate and socialize these employees to their way of thinking and feeling. And finally, the founders' own behavior encourages employees to identify with them and internalize their beliefs, values, and assumptions. When the organization succeeds, the founders' personality becomes embedded in the culture.

The fierce, competitive style and disciplined, authoritarian nature of Hyundai, the giant Korean conglomerate, exhibits the same characteristics often used to describe founder Chung Ju-Yung. Other founders with immeasurable impact on their organization's culture include Bill Gates at Microsoft, Ingvar Kamprad at IKEA, Herb Kelleher at Southwest Airlines, Fred Smith at FedEx, and Richard Branson at the Virgin Group.

Keeping a Culture Alive

Once a culture is in place, practices within the organization maintain it by giving employees a set of similar experiences.[29] The selection process, performance evaluation criteria, training and development activities, and promotion procedures ensure those hired fit in with the culture, reward those who support it, and penalize (or even expel) those who challenge it. Three forces play a particularly important part in sustaining a culture: selection practices, the actions of top management, and socialization methods. Let's look at each.

SELECTION   The explicit goal of the selection process is to identify and hire individuals with the knowledge, skills, and abilities to perform successfully. The final decision, because it's significantly influenced by the decision maker's judgment of how well the candidates will fit into the organization, identifies people whose values are essentially consistent with at least a good portion of the organization's.[30] Selection also provides information to applicants. Those who perceive a conflict between their values and those of the organization can remove themselves from the applicant pool. Selection thus becomes a two-way street, allowing employer or applicant to avoid a mismatch and sustaining an organization's culture by selecting out those who might attack or undermine its core values.

W. L. Gore & Associates, the maker of Gore-Tex fabric used in outerwear, prides itself on its democratic culture and teamwork. There are no job titles at Gore, nor bosses or chains of command. All work is done in teams. In Gore's selection process, teams of employees put job applicants through extensive interviews to ensure they can deal with the level of uncertainty, flexibility, and teamwork that's normal in Gore plants. Not surprisingly, W. L. Gore appears regularly on *Fortune*'s list of "100 Best Companies to Work For" (number 31 in 2011).[31]

TOP MANAGEMENT   The actions of top management also have a major impact on the organization's culture.[32] Through words and behavior, senior executives establish norms that filter through the organization about, for instance, whether risk taking is desirable, how much freedom managers give employees, what is appropriate dress, and what actions earn pay raises, promotions, and other rewards.

The culture of supermarket chain Wegmans—which believes driven, happy, and loyal employees are more eager to help one another and provide exemplary customer service—is a direct result of the beliefs of the Wegman family. The chain began in 1930 when brothers John and Walter Wegman opened their first grocery store in Rochester, New York. Its focus on fine foods quickly separated it from other grocers—a focus maintained by the company's employees, many of whom are hired based on their interest in food. In 1950, Walter's son Robert became president and added generous employee benefits such as profit sharing and fully paid medical coverage. Now Robert's son Danny is president, and he has continued the Wegmans tradition of taking care of employees. To date, Wegmans has paid more than $54 million in college scholarships for its employees, both full time and part time. Pay is well above market average, making annual turnover for full-time employees a mere 6 percent, according to the Food Marketing Institute. (The industry average is 24 percent.) Wegmans regularly appears on *Fortune*'s list as well; it was number 3 in 2011.

SOCIALIZATION   No matter how good a job the organization does in recruiting and selection, new employees need help adapting to the prevailing culture. That help is **socialization**.[33] For example, all Marines must go through boot camp, where they prove their commitment and learn the "Marine way." The consulting firm Booz Allen Hamilton begins its process of bringing new employees onboard even before they start their first day of work. New recruits go to an internal web portal to learn about the company and engage in some activities that help them understand the culture of the organization. After they start work, they continue to learn about the organization through an ongoing social networking application that links new workers with more established members of the firm and helps ensure that culture is transmitted over time.[34]

We can think of socialization as a process with three stages: prearrival, encounter, and metamorphosis.[35] This process, shown in Exhibit 16-1, has an impact on the new employee's work productivity, commitment to the organization's objectives, and eventual decision to stay with the organization.

The **prearrival stage** recognizes that each individual arrives with a set of values, attitudes, and expectations about both the work and the organization. One major purpose of a business school, for example, is to socialize business students to the attitudes and

Socialization process   **Outcomes**

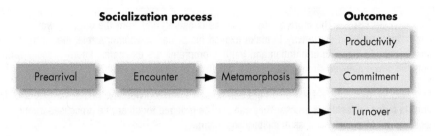

EXHIBIT 16-1
A Socialization
Model

behaviors business firms want. Newcomers to high-profile organizations with a strong market position will make their own assumptions about what it must be like to work there.[36] Most new recruits will expect Nike to be dynamic and exciting, a prestigious law firm to be high in pressure and rewards, and the Marine Corps to require both discipline and courage. No matter how well managers think they can socialize newcomers, however, the most important predictor of future behavior is past behavior. What people know before they join the organization, and how proactive their personality is, are critical predictors of how well they adjust to a new culture.[37]

One way to capitalize on prehire characteristics in socialization is to use the selection process to inform prospective employees about the organization as a whole. We've also seen how the selection process ensures the inclusion of the "right type"—those who will fit in. "Indeed, the ability of the individual to present the appropriate face during the selection process determines his ability to move into the organization in the first place. Thus, success depends on the degree to which the aspiring member has correctly anticipated the expectations and desires of those in the organization in charge of selection."[38]

On entry into the organization, the new member enters the **encounter stage** and confronts the possibility that expectations—about the job, co-workers, the boss, and the organization in general—may differ from reality. If expectations were fairly accurate, the encounter stage merely cements earlier perceptions. However, this is often not the case. At the extreme, a new member may become disillusioned enough to resign. Proper recruiting and selection should significantly reduce that outcome, along with encouraging friendship ties in the organization—newcomers are more committed when friends and co-workers help them "learn the ropes."[39]

Finally, to work out any problems discovered during the encounter stage, the new member changes or goes through the **metamorphosis stage**. The options presented in Exhibit 16-2 are alternatives designed to bring about the desired metamorphosis. Most research suggests there are two major "bundles" of socialization practices. The more management relies on formal, collective, fixed, and serial socialization programs while emphasizing divestiture, the more likely newcomers' differences will be stripped away and replaced by standardized predictable behaviors. These *institutional* practices are common in police departments, fire departments, and other organizations that value rule following and order. Programs that are informal, individual, random, and variable, while emphasizing investiture are more likely to give newcomers an innovative sense of their role and methods of working. Creative fields, such as research and development, advertising, and filmmaking, rely on these *individual* practices. Most research suggests high levels of institutional practices encourage person–organization fit and high levels of commitment, whereas individual practices produce more role innovation.[40]

EXHIBIT 16-2
Entry Socialization Options

FORMAL VS. INFORMAL   The more a new employee is segregated from the ongoing work setting and differentiated in some way to make explicit his or her newcomer's role, the more formal socialization is. Specific orientation and training programs are examples. Informal socialization puts the new employee directly into the job, with little or no special attention.

INDIVIDUAL VS. COLLECTIVE   New members can be socialized individually. This describes how it's done in many professional offices. They can also be grouped together and processed through an identical set of experiences, as in military boot camp.

FIXED VS. VARIABLE   This refers to the time schedule in which newcomers make the transition from outsider to insider. A fixed schedule establishes standardized stages of transition. This characterizes rotational training programs. It also includes probationary periods, such as the 8- to 10-year "associate" status used by accounting and law firms before deciding on whether or not a candidate is made a partner. Variable schedules give no advance notice of their transition timetable. Variable schedules describe the typical promotion system, in which one is not advanced to the next stage until one is "ready."

SERIAL VS. RANDOM   Serial socialization is characterized by the use of role models who train and encourage the newcomer. Apprenticeship and mentoring programs are examples. In random socialization, role models are deliberately withheld. New employees are left on their own to figure things out.

INVESTITURE VS. DIVESTITURE   Investiture socialization assumes that the newcomer's qualities and qualifications are the necessary ingredients for job success, so these qualities and qualifications are confirmed and supported. Divestiture socialization tries to strip away certain characteristics of the recruit. Fraternity and sorority "pledges" go through divestiture socialization to shape them into the proper role.

The three-part entry socialization process is complete when new members have internalized and accepted the norms of the organization and their work group, are confident in their competence, and feel trusted and valued by their peers. They understand the system—not only their own tasks but the rules, procedures, and informally accepted practices as well. Finally, they know what is expected of them and what criteria will be used to measure and evaluate their work. As Exhibit 16-2 showed, successful metamorphosis should have a positive impact on new employees' productivity and their commitment to the organization, while reducing their propensity to leave the organization.

Researchers have begun to examine how employee attitudes change during socialization by measuring at several points over the first few months. One study has documented patterns of "honeymoons" and "hangovers" for new workers, showing the period of initial adjustment is often marked by decreases in job satisfaction as their idealized hopes come into contact with the reality of organizational life.[41] Other research suggests role conflict and role overload for newcomers rise over time, and workers with the largest increases in these role problems experience the largest decreases in commitment and satisfaction.[42] It may be that the initial adjustment period for newcomers presents increasing demands and difficulties, at least in the short term.

EXHIBIT 16-3
How Organization Cultures Form

Summary: How Cultures Form

Exhibit 16-3 summarizes how an organization's culture is established and sustained. The original culture derives from the founder's philosophy and strongly influences hiring criteria as the firm grows. Top managers' actions set the general climate, including what is acceptable behavior and what is not. The way employees are socialized will depend both on the degree of success achieved in matching new employees' values to those of the organization in the selection process, and on top management's preference for socialization methods.

HOW EMPLOYEES LEARN CULTURE

Culture is transmitted to employees in a number of forms, the most potent being stories, rituals, material symbols, and language.

Stories

When Henry Ford II was chairman of Ford Motor Company, you would have been hard pressed to find a manager who hadn't heard how he reminded his executives, when they got too arrogant, "It's my name that's on the building." The message was clear: Henry Ford II ran the company.

A number of senior Nike executives spend much of their time serving as corporate storytellers.[43] When they tell how co-founder (and Oregon track coach) Bill Bowerman went to his workshop and poured rubber into his wife's waffle iron to create a better running shoe, they're talking about Nike's spirit of innovation. When new hires hear tales of Oregon running star Steve Prefontaine's battles to make running a professional sport and attain better performance equipment, they learn of Nike's commitment to helping athletes.

Stories such as these circulate through many organizations, anchoring the present in the past and legitimating current practices. They typically include narratives about the organization's founders, rule breaking, rags-to-riches successes, reductions in the workforce, relocation of employees, reactions to past mistakes, and organizational coping.[44] Employees also create their own narratives about how they came to either fit or not fit with the organization during the process of socialization, including first days on the job, early interactions with others, and first impressions of organizational life.[45]

Rituals

Rituals are repetitive sequences of activities that express and reinforce the key values of the organization—what goals are most important and which people are important as well as which are expendable.[46] One of the best known rituals is Walmart's company chant.

Begun by the company's founder, the late Sam Walton, as a way to motivate and unite his workforce, this chant has become a ritual that bonds workers and reinforces Walton's belief in the contribution his employees made to the company's success. Similar corporate chants are used by IBM, Ericsson, Novell, Deutsche Bank, and PricewaterhouseCoopers.[47]

Material Symbols

Alcoa headquarters doesn't look like your typical head-office operation. There are few individual offices, even for senior executives. The space is essentially made up of cubicles, common areas, and meeting rooms. This informality conveys to employees that Alcoa values openness, equality, creativity, and flexibility. Some corporations provide their top executives with chauffeur-driven limousines and a corporate jet. Other CEOs drive the company car themselves and travel in the economy section.

The layout of corporate headquarters, the types of automobiles top executives are given, and the presence or absence of corporate aircraft are a few examples of **material symbols**. Others include the size of offices, the elegance of furnishings, executive perks, and attire.[48] These convey to employees who is important, the degree of egalitarianism top management desires, and the kinds of behavior that are appropriate, such as risk taking, conservative, authoritarian, participative, individualistic, or social.

Language

Many organizations and subunits within them use language to help members identify with the culture, attest to their acceptance of it, and help preserve it. Unique terms describe equipment, officers, key individuals, suppliers, customers, or products that relate to the business. New employees may at first be overwhelmed by acronyms and jargon that, once assimilated, act as a common denominator to unite members of a given culture or subculture.

CREATING AN ETHICAL ORGANIZATIONAL CULTURE

The organizational culture most likely to shape high ethical standards among its members is high in risk tolerance, low to moderate in aggressiveness, and focused on means as well as outcomes.[49] This type of culture takes a long-term perspective and balances the rights of multiple stakeholders, including employees, stockholders, and the community. Managers are supported for taking risks and innovating, discouraged from engaging in unbridled competition, and guided to heed not just to *what* goals are achieved but also *how*.

If the culture is strong and supports high ethical standards, it should have a very powerful and positive influence on employee behavior. Examples of organizations that have failed to establish proper codes of ethical conduct can be found in the media nearly every day. Some actively deceive customers or clients. Others produce products that harm consumers or the environment, or they harass or discriminate against certain groups of employees. Others are more subtle and cover up or fail to report wrongdoing. The negative consequences of a systematic culture of unethical behavior can be severe and include customer boycotts, fines, lawsuits, and government regulation of an organization's practices.

What can managers do to create a more ethical culture? They can adhere to the following principles:[50]

- *Be a Visible Role Model.* Employees will look to the actions of top management as a benchmark for appropriate behavior. Send a positive message.
- *Communicate Ethical Expectations.* Minimize ethical ambiguities by sharing an organizational code of ethics that states the organization's primary values and ethical rules employees must follow.
- *Provide Ethical Training.* Set up seminars, workshops, and training programs to reinforce the organization's standards of conduct, clarify what practices are impermissible, and address potential ethical dilemmas.
- *Visibly Reward Ethical Acts and Punish Unethical Ones.* Appraise managers on how their decisions measure up against the organization's code of ethics. Review the means as well as the ends. Visibly reward those who act ethically and conspicuously punish those who don't.
- *Provide Protective Mechanisms.* Provide formal mechanisms so employees can discuss ethical dilemmas and report unethical behavior without fear of reprimand. These might include ethical counselors, ombudsmen, or ethical officers.

The work of setting a positive ethical climate has to start at the top of the organization.[51] A study of 195 managers demonstrated that when top management emphasizes strong ethical values, supervisors are more likely to practice ethical leadership. Positive ethical attitudes transfer down to line employees, who show lower levels of deviant behavior and higher levels of cooperation and assistance. A study involving auditors found perceived pressure from organizational leaders to behave unethically was associated with increased intentions to engage in unethical practices.[52] Clearly the wrong type of organizational culture can negatively influence employee ethical behavior. Finally, employees whose ethical values are similar to those of their department are more likely to be promoted, so we can think of ethical culture as flowing from the bottom up as well.[53]

CREATING A POSITIVE ORGANIZATIONAL CULTURE

At first blush, creating a positive culture may sound hopelessly naïve or like a Dilbert-style conspiracy. The one thing that makes us believe this trend is here to stay, however, are signs that management practice and OB research are converging.

It is possible to form ethical cultures and positive organizational cultures, but the means by which such cultures are attained are quite different.

A **positive organizational culture** emphasizes building on employee strengths, rewards more than it punishes, and emphasizes individual vitality and growth.[54] Let's consider each of these areas.

Building on Employee Strengths

Although a positive organizational culture does not ignore problems, it does emphasize showing workers how they can capitalize on their strengths. As management guru Peter Drucker said, "Most Americans do not know what their strengths are. When you ask them, they look at you with a blank stare, or they respond in terms of subject knowledge, which is the wrong answer." Wouldn't it be better to be in an organizational culture that helped you discover your strengths and learn how to make the most of them?

Larry Hammond used this approach when you'd least expect it: during his firm's darkest days. Hammond is CEO of Auglaize Provico, an agribusiness company based in

Ohio. In the midst of the firm's worst financial struggles, when it had to lay off one-quarter of its workforce, Hammond decided to try a different approach. Rather than dwell on what was wrong, he took advantage of what was right. "If you really want to [excel], you have to know yourself—you have to know what you're good at, and you have to know what you're not so good at," says Hammond. With the help of Gallup consultant Barry Conchie, Hammond focused on discovering and using employee strengths and helped the company turn itself around. "You ask Larry [Hammond] what the difference is, and he'll say that it's individuals using their natural talents," says Conchie.[55]

Rewarding More Than Punishing

Although most organizations are sufficiently focused on extrinsic rewards such as pay and promotions, they often forget about the power of smaller (and cheaper) rewards such as praise. Part of creating a positive organizational culture is "catching employees doing something right." Many managers withhold praise because they're afraid employees will coast or because they think praise is not valued. Employees generally don't ask for praise, and managers usually don't realize the costs of failing to give it.

Consider Elïzbieta Górska-Kolodziejczyk, a plant manager for International Paper's facility in Kwidzyn, Poland. Employees work in a bleak windowless basement. Staffing is roughly one-third its prior level, while production has tripled. These challenges had done in the previous three managers. So when Górska-Kolodziejczyk took over, although she had many ideas about transforming the organization, at the top were recognition and praise. She initially found it difficult to give praise to those who weren't used to it, especially men. "They were like cement at the beginning," she said. "Like cement." Over time, however, she found they valued and even reciprocated praise. One day a department supervisor pulled her over to tell her she was doing a good job. "This I do remember, yes," she said.[56]

Emphasizing Vitality and Growth

No organization will get the best from employees who see themselves as mere cogs in the machine. A positive culture recognizes the difference between a job and a career. It supports not only what the employee contributes to organizational effectiveness but also how the organization can make the employee more effective—personally and professionally.

Although it may take more creativity to encourage employee growth in some types of industries, consider the food industry. At Masterfoods in Belgium, Philippe Lescornez leads a team of employees including Didier Brynaert, who works in Luxembourg, nearly 150 miles away. Brynaert was considered a good sales promoter who was meeting expectations when Lescornez decided Brynaert's job could be made more important if he were seen less as just another sales promoter and more as an expert on the unique features of the Luxembourg market. So Lescornez asked Brynaert for information he could share with the home office. He hoped that by raising Brynaert's profile in Brussels, he could create in him a greater sense of ownership for his remote sales territory. "I started to communicate much more what he did to other people [within the company], because there's quite some distance between the Brussels office and the section he's working in. So I started to communicate, communicate, communicate. The more I communicated, the more he started to provide material," says Lescornez. As a result, "Now he's recognized as the specialist for Luxembourg—the guy who is able to build a strong relationship with the Luxembourg clients," says Lescornez. What's good for Brynaert is, of course, also good for Lescornez, who gets credit for helping Brynaert grow and develop.[57]

Limits of Positive Culture

Is a positive culture a cure-all? Though companies such as GE, Xerox, Boeing, and 3M have embraced aspects of a positive organizational culture, it is a new enough idea for us to be uncertain about how and when it works best.

   Not all cultures value being positive as much as U.S. culture does, and, even within U.S. culture, there surely are limits to how far we should go to preserve a positive culture. For example, Admiral, a British insurance company, has established a Ministry of Fun in its call centers to organize poem writings, foosball, conker (a British game involving chestnuts), and fancy-dress days. When does the pursuit of a positive culture start to seem coercive or even Orwellian? As one critic notes, "Promoting a social orthodoxy of positiveness focuses on a particular constellation of desirable states and traits but, in so doing, can stigmatize those who fail to fit the template."[58] There may be benefits to establishing a positive culture, but an organization also needs to be objective and not pursue it past the point of effectiveness.

GLOBAL IMPLICATIONS

We considered global cultural values (collectivism–individualism, power distance, and so on) in Chapter 5. Here our focus is a bit narrower: how is organizational culture affected by a global context? Organizational culture is so powerful it often transcends national boundaries. But that doesn't mean organizations should, or could, ignore local culture.

   Organizational cultures often reflect national culture. The culture at AirAsia, a Malaysian-based airline, emphasizes informal dress so as not to create status differences. The carrier has lots of parties, participative management, and no private offices, reflecting Malaysia's relatively collectivistic culture. The culture of US Airways does not reflect the same degree of informality. If US Airways were to set up operations in Malaysia or merge with AirAsia, it would need to take these cultural differences into account.

   One of the primary things U.S. managers can do is to be culturally sensitive. The United States is a dominant force in business and in culture—and with that influence comes a reputation. "We are broadly seen throughout the world as arrogant people, totally self-absorbed and loud," says one U.S. executive. Companies such as American Airlines, Lowe's, Novell, ExxonMobil, and Microsoft have implemented training programs to sensitize their managers to cultural differences. Some ways in which U.S. managers can be culturally sensitive include talking in a low tone of voice, speaking slowly, listening more, and avoiding discussions of religion and politics.

   The management of ethical behavior is one area where national culture can rub up against corporate culture.[59] U.S. managers endorse the supremacy of anonymous market forces and implicitly or explicitly view profit maximization as a moral obligation for business organizations. This worldview sees bribery, nepotism, and favoring personal contacts as highly unethical. Any action that deviates from profit maximization may indicate that inappropriate or corrupt behavior may be occurring. In contrast, managers in developing economies are more likely to see ethical decisions as embedded in a social environment. That means doing special favors for family and friends is not only

Organizational culture and national culture are not the same thing, though to some degree, an organization's culture reflects the dominant values of its host country.

appropriate but possibly even an ethical responsibility. Managers in many nations also view capitalism skeptically and believe the interests of workers should be put on a par with the interests of shareholders.

U.S. employees are not the only ones who need to be culturally sensitive. Three times a week, employees at the Canadian unit of Japanese video game maker Koei begin the day by standing next to their desks, facing their boss, and saying "Good morning" in unison. Employees then deliver short speeches on topics that range from corporate principles to 3D game engines. Koei also has employees punch a time clock and asks women to serve tea to top executive guests. Although these practices are consistent with Koei's culture, they do not fit Canadian culture very well. "It's kind of like school," says one Canadian employee.[60]

SUMMARY AND IMPLICATIONS FOR MANAGERS

Employees form an overall subjective perception of the organization based on factors such as degree of risk tolerance, team emphasis, and support of people. This overall perception becomes, in effect, the organization's culture or personality and affects employee performance and satisfaction, with stronger cultures having greater impact.

- Just as people's personalities tend to be stable over time, so too do strong cultures. This makes a strong culture difficult for managers to change if it becomes mismatched to its environment. Changing an organization's culture is a long and difficult process. Thus, at least in the short term, managers should treat their organization's culture as relatively fixed.
- One of the most important managerial implications of organizational culture relates to selection decisions. Hiring individuals whose values don't align with those of the organization is likely to yield employees who lack motivation and commitment, and who are dissatisfied with their jobs and the organization.[61] Not surprisingly, "misfits" have considerably higher turnover rates.
- An employee's performance also depends to a considerable degree on knowing what to do and not do. Understanding the right way to do a job indicates proper socialization.
- As a manager, you can shape the culture of your work environment, sometimes as much as it shapes you. All managers can especially do their part to create an ethical culture.

MyManagementLab

Go to **MyManagementLab.com** to access study plans, interactive lectures, and videos as well as Auto-graded writing questions and the following Assisted-graded writing question.

16-1. MyManagementLab Only—comprehensive writing assignment for this chapter.

17

■■■

Organizational Change and Stress Management

After studying this chapter, you should be able to:

- Identify forces that act as stimulants to change.
- Describe the sources of resistance to change.
- Compare the four main approaches to managing organizational change.
- Demonstrate two ways of creating a culture for change.
- Describe the causes and consequences of work stress.

This chapter is about change and stress. We describe environmental forces that require firms to change, why people and organizations often resist change, and how this resistance can be overcome. We review processes for managing organizational change. Then we move to the topic of stress and its sources and consequences. In closing, we discuss what individuals and organizations can do to better manage stress levels.

FORCES FOR CHANGE

No company today is in a particularly stable environment. Even those with dominant market share must change, sometimes radically. Even though Apple has been successful with its iPad, the growing number of competitors in the field of tablet computers suggests that Apple will need to continually update and innovate to keep ahead of the market.

"Change or die!" is thus the rallying cry among today's managers worldwide. In a number of places in this book, we've discussed the *changing nature of the workforce*. Almost every organization must adjust to a multicultural environment, demographic changes, immigration, and outsourcing. *Technology* is continually changing jobs and organizations. It is not hard to imagine the very idea of an office becoming an antiquated concept in the near future.

The housing and financial sectors recently have experienced extraordinary *economic shocks*, leading to the elimination, bankruptcy, or acquisition of some of the best-known U.S. companies, including Bear Stearns, Merrill Lynch, Lehman Brothers, Countrywide Financial, Washington Mutual, and Ameriquest. Tens of thousands of jobs were lost and may never return. After years of declining numbers of bankruptcies, the global recession caused the bankruptcy of auto manufacturers General Motors and Chrysler, retailers Borders and Sharper Image, and myriad other organizations.

Competition is changing. Competitors are as likely to come from across the ocean as from across town. Successful organizations will be fast on their feet, capable of developing new products rapidly and getting them to market quickly. In other words, they'll be flexible and will require an equally flexible and responsive workforce. Increasingly, in the United States and Europe, the government regulates business practices, including executive pay.

Social trends don't remain static either. Consumers who are otherwise strangers now meet and share product information in chat rooms and blogs. Companies must continually adjust product and marketing strategies to be sensitive to changing social trends, as Liz Claiborne did when it sold off fashion brands (such as Ellen Tracy), de-emphasized large vendors such as Macy's, streamlined operations, and cut staff. Consumers, employees, and organizational leaders are more sensitive to environmental concerns. "Green" practices are quickly becoming expected rather than optional.

Not even globalization's strongest proponents could have imagined how *world politics* would change in recent years. We've seen a major set of financial crises that have rocked global markets, a dramatic rise in the power and influence of China, and dramatic shakeups in government across the Arab world. Throughout the industrialized world, businesses—particularly in the banking and financial sectors—have come under new scrutiny.

RESISTANCE TO CHANGE

Our egos are fragile, and we often see change as threatening. One recent study showed that even when employees are shown data that suggest they need to change, they latch onto whatever data they can find that suggests they are okay and don't need to change.[1] Employees who have negative feelings about a change cope by not thinking about it, increasing their use of sick time, and quitting. All these reactions can sap the organization of vital energy when it is most needed.[2]

One of the most well-documented findings from studies of individual and organizational behavior is that organizations and their members resist change.

Resistance to change can be positive if it leads to open discussion and debate.[3]

These responses are usually preferable to apathy or silence and can indicate that members of the organization are engaged in the process, providing change agents an opportunity to explain the change effort. Change agents can also use resistance to modify the change to fit the preferences of other members of the organization. When they treat resistance only as a threat, rather than a point of view to be discussed, they may increase dysfunctional conflict.

Resistance doesn't necessarily surface in standardized ways. It can be overt, implicit, immediate, or deferred. It's easiest for management to deal with overt and immediate resistance, such as complaints, a work slowdown, or a strike threat. The greater challenge is managing resistance that is implicit or deferred. Because behavioral responses such as loss of motivation, increased errors, or heightened absenteeism can have many causes, they are more subtle and more difficult to recognize for what they are. Deferred actions also cloud the link between the change and the reaction to it and may surface weeks, months, or even years later. Or a single change of little inherent impact may be the straw that breaks the camel's back because resistance to earlier changes has been deferred and stockpiled.

Exhibit 17-1 summarizes major forces for resistance to change, categorized by their sources. Individual sources reside in human characteristics such as perceptions, personalities, and needs. Organizational sources reside in the structural makeup of organizations themselves.

It's worth noting that not all change is good. Speed can lead to bad decisions, and sometimes those initiating change fail to realize the full magnitude of the effects

---

INDIVIDUAL SOURCES

Habit—To cope with life's complexities, we rely on habits or programmed responses. But when confronted with change, this tendency to respond in our accustomed ways becomes a source of resistance.

Security—People with a high need for security are likely to resist change because it threatens feelings of safety.

Economic factors—Changes in job tasks or established work routines can arouse economic fears if people are concerned that they won't be able to perform the new tasks or routines to their previous standards, especially when pay is closely tied to productivity.

Fear of the unknown—Change substitutes ambiguity and uncertainty for the unknown.

Selective information processing—Individuals are guilty of selectively processing information in order to keep their perceptions intact. They hear what they want to hear and they ignore information that challenges the world they've created.

ORGANIZATIONAL SOURCES

Structural inertia—Organizations have built-in mechanisms—like their selection processes and formalized regulations—to produce stability. When an organization is confronted with change, this structural inertia acts as a counterbalance to sustain stability.

Limited focus of change—Organizations are made up of a number of interdependent subsystems. One can't be changed without affecting the others. So limited changes in subsystems tend to be nullified by the larger system.

Group inertia—Even if individuals want to change their behavior, group norms may act as a constraint.

Threat to expertise—Changes in organizational patterns may threaten the expertise of specialized groups.

Threat to established power relationships—Any redistribution of decision-making authority can threaten long-established power relationships within the organization.

Threat to established resource allocations—Groups in the organization that control sizable resources often see change as a threat. They tend to be content with the way things are.

EXHIBIT 17-1

Sources of Resistance to Change

or their true costs. Rapid, transformational change is risky, and some organizations have collapsed for this reason.[4] Change agents need to carefully think through the full implications.

Overcoming Resistance to Change

Eight tactics can help change agents deal with resistance to change.[5] Let's review them briefly.

EDUCATION AND COMMUNICATION   Communicating the logic of a change can reduce employee resistance on two levels. First, it fights the effects of misinformation and poor communication: if employees receive the full facts and clear up misunderstandings, resistance should subside. Second, communication can help "sell" the need for change by packaging it properly.[6] A study of German companies revealed changes are most effective when a company communicates a rationale that balances the interests of various stakeholders (shareholders, employees, community, customers) rather than those of shareholders only.[7] Another study of a changing organization in the Philippines found that formal change information sessions decreased employee anxiety, while providing high-quality information about the change increased commitment to it.[8]

PARTICIPATION   It's difficult to resist a change decision in which we've participated. Assuming participants have the expertise to make a meaningful contribution, their involvement can reduce resistance, obtain commitment, and increase the quality of the change decision. However, against these advantages are the negatives: potential for a poor solution and great consumption of time.

BUILDING SUPPORT AND COMMITMENT   When employees' fear and anxiety are high, counseling and therapy, new-skills training, or a short paid leave of absence may facilitate adjustment. When managers or employees have low emotional commitment to change, they favor the status quo and resist it.[9] Employees are also more accepting of changes when they are committed to the organization as a whole.[10] So, firing up employees and emphasizing their commitment to the organization overall can also help them emotionally commit to the change rather than embrace the status quo.

DEVELOP POSITIVE RELATIONSHIPS   People are more willing to accept changes if they trust the managers implementing them.[11] One study surveyed 235 employees from a large housing corporation in the Netherlands that was experiencing a merger. Those who had a more positive relationship with their supervisors, and who felt the work environment supported development, were much more positive about the change process.[12] Another set of studies found that individuals who were dispositionally resistant to change felt more positive about the change if they trusted the change agent.[13] This research suggests that if managers are able to facilitate positive relationships, they may be able to overcome resistance to change even among those who ordinarily don't like changes.

IMPLEMENTING CHANGES FAIRLY   One way organizations can minimize negative impact is to make sure change is implemented fairly. As we saw in Chapter 7, procedural fairness is especially important when employees perceive an outcome as negative, so it's crucial that employees see the reason for the change and perceive its implementation as consistent and fair.[14]

MANIPULATION AND COOPTATION   *Manipulation* refers to covert influence attempts. Twisting facts to make them more attractive, withholding information, and creating false rumors to get employees to accept change are all examples of manipulation. If management threatens to close a manufacturing plant whose employees are resisting an across-the-board pay cut, and if the threat is actually untrue, management is using manipulation. *Cooptation*, on the other hand, combines manipulation and participation. It seeks to "buy off" the leaders of a resistance group by giving them a key role, seeking their advice not to find a better solution but to get their endorsement. Both manipulation and cooptation are relatively inexpensive ways to gain the support of adversaries, but they can backfire if the targets become aware they are being tricked or used. Once that's discovered, the change agent's credibility may drop to zero.

SELECTING PEOPLE WHO ACCEPT CHANGE   Research suggests the ability to easily accept and adapt to *change* is related to personality—some people simply have more positive attitudes about change than others.[15] Such individuals are open to experience, take a positive attitude toward change, are willing to take risks, and are flexible in their behavior. One study of managers in the United States, Europe, and Asia found those with a positive self-concept and high risk tolerance coped better with organizational change. A study of 258 police officers found those higher in growth-needs strength, internal locus of control, and internal work motivation had more positive attitudes about organizational change efforts.[16] Individuals higher in general mental ability are also better able to learn and adapt to changes in the workplace.[17] In sum, an impressive body of evidence shows organizations can facilitate change by selecting people predisposed to accept it.

Besides selecting individuals who are willing to accept changes, it is also possible to select teams that are more adaptable. Studies have shown that teams that are strongly motivated by learning about and mastering tasks are better able to adapt to changing environments.[18] This research suggests that it may be necessary to consider not just individual motivation, but also group motivation when trying to implement changes.

COERCION   Last on the list of tactics is *coercion*, the application of direct threats or force on the resisters. If management really is determined to close a manufacturing plant whose employees don't acquiesce to a pay cut, the company is using coercion. Other examples are threats of transfer, loss of promotions, negative performance evaluations, and a poor letter of recommendation. The advantages and drawbacks of coercion are approximately the same as for manipulation and cooptation.

APPROACHES TO MANAGING ORGANIZATIONAL CHANGE

Now we turn to several approaches to managing change: Lewin's classic three-step model of the change process, Kotter's eight-step plan, action research, and organizational development.

Lewin's Three-Step Model

Kurt Lewin argued that successful change in organizations should follow three steps: **unfreezing** the status quo, **movement** to a desired end state, and **refreezing** the new change to make it permanent.[19] (See Exhibit 17-2.)

EXHIBIT 17-2
Lewin's Three-Step Change Model

Unfreezing → Movement → Refreezing

EXHIBIT 17-3
Unfreezing the Status Quo

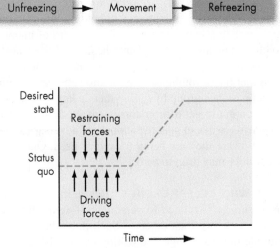

The status quo is an equilibrium state. To move from equilibrium—to overcome the pressures of both individual resistance and group conformity—unfreezing must happen in one of three ways (see Exhibit 17-3.) The **driving forces**, which direct behavior away from the status quo, can be increased. The **restraining forces**, which hinder movement away from equilibrium, can be decreased. A third alternative is to combine the first two approaches. Companies that have been successful in the past are likely to encounter restraining forces because people question the need for change.[20] Similarly, research shows that companies with strong cultures excel at incremental change but are overcome by restraining forces against radical change.[21]

Research on organizational change has shown that, to be effective, the actual change has to happen quickly.[22] Organizations that build up to change do less well than those that get to and through the movement stage quickly.

Once change has been implemented, to be successful, the new situation must be refrozen so it can be sustained over time. Without this last step, change will likely be short-lived and employees will attempt to revert to the previous equilibrium state. The objective of refreezing, then, is to stabilize the new situation by balancing the driving and restraining forces.

Kotter's Eight-Step Plan for Implementing Change

John Kotter of the Harvard Business School built on Lewin's three-step model to create a more detailed approach for implementing change.[23] Kotter began by listing common mistakes managers make when trying to initiate change. They may fail to create a sense of urgency about the need for change, create a coalition for managing the change process, have a vision for change and effectively communicate it, remove obstacles that could impede the vision's achievement, provide short-term and achievable goals, or anchor the changes into the organization's culture. They may also declare victory too soon.

Kotter then established eight sequential steps to overcome these problems. They're listed in Exhibit 17-4. Notice how Kotter's first four steps essentially extrapolate Lewin's

EXHIBIT 17-4
Kotter's Eight-Step Plan for Implementing Change

1. Establish a sense of urgency by creating a compelling reason for why change is needed.
2. Form a coalition with enough power to lead the change.
3. Create a new vision to direct the change and strategies for achieving the vision.
4. Communicate the vision throughout the organization.
5. Empower others to act on the vision by removing barriers to change and encouraging risk taking and creative problem solving.
6. Plan for, create, and reward short-term "wins" that move the organization toward the new vision.
7. Consolidate improvements, reassess changes, and make necessary adjustments in the new programs.
8. Reinforce the changes by demonstrating the relationship between new behaviors and organizational success.

"unfreezing" stage. Steps 5, 6, and 7 represent "movement," and the final step works on "refreezing." So Kotter's contribution lies in providing managers and change agents with a more detailed guide for successfully implementing change.

Organizational Development

Organizational development (OD) is a collection of change methods that try to improve organizational effectiveness and employee well-being.[24]

OD methods value human and organizational growth, collaborative and participative processes, and a spirit of inquiry.[25] Contemporary OD borrows heavily from postmodern philosophy in placing heavy emphasis on the subjective ways in which people see their environment. The focus is on how individuals make sense of their work environment. The change agent may take the lead in OD, but there is a strong emphasis on collaboration. These are the underlying values in most OD efforts:

1. *Respect for People.* Individuals are perceived as responsible, conscientious, and caring. They should be treated with dignity and respect.
2. *Trust and Support.* An effective and healthy organization is characterized by trust, authenticity, openness, and a supportive climate.
3. *Power Equalization.* Effective organizations de-emphasize hierarchical authority and control.
4. *Confrontation.* Problems should be openly confronted, not swept under the rug.
5. *Participation.* The more engaged in the decisions they are, the more people affected by a change will be committed to implementing them.

What are some OD techniques or interventions for bringing about change? Here are five.

1. *Survey Feedback.* One tool for assessing attitudes held by organizational members, identifying discrepancies among member perceptions, and solving these differences is the **survey feedback** approach.[26] Everyone in an organization can participate in survey feedback, but of key importance is the organizational "family"—the manager of any given unit and the employees who report directly to him or her. All usually complete a questionnaire about their perceptions and attitudes on a range of topics, including decision-making practices; communication effectiveness; coordination among units; and satisfaction with the organization, job, peers, and immediate supervisor.

Data from this questionnaire are tabulated with data pertaining to an individual's specific "family" and to the entire organization and then distributed to employees. These data become the springboard for identifying problems and clarifying issues that may be creating difficulties for people. Particular attention is given to encouraging discussion and ensuring it focuses on issues and ideas and not on attacking individuals. For instance, are people listening? Are new ideas being generated? Can decision making, interpersonal relations, or job assignments be improved? Answers should lead the group to commit to various remedies for the problems identified.

2. *Process Consultation.* Managers often sense their unit's performance can be improved but are unable to identify what to improve and how. The purpose of **process consultation (PC)** is for an outside consultant to assist a client, usually a manager, "to perceive, understand, and act upon process events" with which the manager must deal.[27]

   PC is similar to sensitivity training in assuming we can improve organizational effectiveness by dealing with interpersonal problems and in emphasizing involvement. But PC is more task directed, and consultants are there to "give the client 'insight' into what is going on around him, within him, and between him and other people."[28] They do not solve the organization's problems but rather guide or coach the client to solve her own problems after *jointly* diagnosing what needs improvement. The client develops the skill to analyze processes within his unit and can continue to call on it long after the consultant is gone.

3. *Team Building.* We've noted throughout this book that organizations increasingly rely on teams to accomplish work tasks. **Team building** uses high-interaction group activities to increase trust and openness among team members, improve coordinative efforts, and increase team performance.[29] Team building typically includes goal-setting, development of interpersonal relations among team members, role analysis to clarify each member's role and responsibilities, and team process analysis. It may emphasize or exclude certain activities, depending on the purpose of the development effort and the specific problems with which the team is confronted.

4. *Intergroup Development.* A major area of concern in OD is dysfunctional conflict among groups. **Intergroup development** seeks to change groups' attitudes, stereotypes, and perceptions about each other. Here, training sessions closely resemble diversity training (in fact, diversity training largely evolved from intergroup development in OD), except rather than focusing on demographic differences, they focus on differences among occupations, departments, or divisions within an organization. Among several approaches for improving intergroup relations, a popular one emphasizes problem solving.[30] Each group meets independently to list its perceptions of itself and of the other group and how it believes the other group perceives it. The groups share their lists, discuss similarities and differences, and look for the causes of disparities. Once they have identified the causes of the difficulty, the groups move to the integration phase—developing solutions to improve relations between them. Subgroups can be formed of members from each of the conflicting groups to conduct further diagnosis and formulate alternative solutions.

5. *Appreciative Inquiry.* Most OD approaches are problem centered. They identify a problem or set of problems, then look for a solution. **Appreciative inquiry (AI)** instead accentuates the positive.[31] Rather than looking for problems to fix, it seeks to identify the unique qualities and special strengths of an organization, which members can build on to improve performance. That is, AI focuses on an organization's

successes rather than its problems. The AI process consists of four steps—discovery, dreaming, design, and destiny—often played out in a large-group meeting over a 2- or 3-day time period and overseen by a trained change agent. *Discovery* sets out to identify what people think are the organization's strengths. Employees recount times they felt the organization worked best or when they specifically felt most satisfied with their jobs. In *dreaming*, employees use information from the discovery phase to speculate on possible futures, such as what the organization will be like in 5 years. In *design*, participants find a common vision of how the organization will look in the future and agree on its unique qualities. For the fourth step, participants seek to define the organization's *destiny* or how to fulfill their dreams, and they typically write action plans and develop implementation strategies.

CREATING A CULTURE FOR CHANGE

We've considered how organizations can *adapt* to change. But recently, some OB scholars have focused on a more proactive approach—how organizations can *embrace* change by transforming their cultures. In this section, we review two such approaches: stimulating an innovative culture and creating a learning organization.

Various approaches can be used to manage organizational change and for developing a culture for change; it is unlikely one approach is always best in every situation.

Stimulating a Culture of Innovation

How can an organization become more innovative? An excellent model is W. L. Gore, the $2.6 billion-per-year company best known as the maker of Gore-Tex fabric.[32] Gore has developed a reputation as one of the most innovative U.S. companies by developing a stream of diverse products—including guitar strings, dental floss, medical devices, and fuel cells.

What's the secret of Gore's success? What can other organizations do to duplicate its track record for innovation? Although there is no guaranteed formula, certain characteristics surface repeatedly when researchers study innovative organizations. We've grouped them into structural, cultural, and human resource categories. Change agents should consider introducing these characteristics into their organization to create an innovative climate. Before we look at these characteristics, however, let's clarify what we mean by innovation.

DEFINITION OF INNOVATION We said change refers to making things different. **Innovation**, a more specialized kind of change, is a new idea applied to initiating or improving a product, process, or service.[33] So all innovations imply change, but not all changes necessarily introduce new ideas or lead to significant improvements. Innovations can range from small incremental improvements, such as netbook computers, to radical breakthroughs, such as Nissan's electric Leaf car.

SOURCES OF INNOVATION *Structural variables* have been the most studied potential source of innovation.[34] A comprehensive review of the structure–innovation relationship leads to the following conclusions:[35]

1. Organic structures positively influence innovation. Because they're lower in vertical differentiation, formalization, and centralization, organic organizations facilitate the flexibility, adaptation, and cross-fertilization that make the adoption of innovations easier.

2. Long tenure in management is associated with innovation. Managerial tenure apparently provides legitimacy and knowledge of how to accomplish tasks and obtain desired outcomes.

3. Innovation is nurtured when there are slack resources. Having an abundance of resources allows an organization to afford to purchase innovations, bear the cost of instituting them, and absorb failures.

4. Interunit communication is high in innovative organizations.[36] These organizations are high users of committees, task forces, cross-functional teams, and other mechanisms that facilitate interaction across departmental lines.

Innovative organizations tend to have similar *cultures*. They encourage experimentation. They reward both successes and failures. They celebrate mistakes. Unfortunately, in too many organizations, people are rewarded for the absence of failures rather than for the presence of successes. Such cultures extinguish risk taking and innovation. People will suggest and try new ideas only when they feel such behaviors exact no penalties. Managers in innovative organizations recognize that failures are a natural by-product of venturing into the unknown.

Within the *human resources* category, innovative organizations actively promote the training and development of their members so they keep current, offer high job security so employees don't fear getting fired for making mistakes, and encourage individuals to become champions of change. Once a new idea is developed, **idea champions** actively and enthusiastically promote it, build support, overcome resistance, and ensure it's implemented.[37] Champions have common personality characteristics: extremely high self-confidence, persistence, energy, and a tendency to take risks. They also display characteristics associated with transformational leadership—they inspire and energize others with their vision of an innovation's potential and their strong personal conviction about their mission. Idea champions are good at gaining the commitment of others, and their jobs provide considerable decision-making discretion; this autonomy helps them introduce and implement innovations.[38]

Do successful idea champions do things differently in different cultures? Yes.[39] People in collectivist cultures prefer appeals for cross-functional support for innovation efforts; people in high power distance cultures prefer champions to work closely with those in authority to approve innovative activities before work is begun; and the higher the uncertainty avoidance of a society, the more champions should work within the organization's rules and procedures to develop the innovation. These findings suggest that effective managers will alter their organization's championing strategies to reflect cultural values. So, for instance, although idea champions in Russia might succeed by ignoring budgetary limitations and working around confining procedures, champions in Austria, Denmark, Germany, or other cultures high in uncertainty avoidance will be more effective by closely following budgets and procedures.

Sergio Marcchione, CEO of Fiat-Chrysler, has acted as idea champion for the single objective of updating the pipeline of vehicles for Chrysler. To facilitate this change, he has radically dismantled the bureaucracy, tearing up Chrysler's organization chart and introducing a flatter structure with himself at the lead. As a result, the company introduced a more innovative line of vehicles and planned to redesign or significantly refresh 75 percent of its lineup in 2010 alone.[40]

WORK STRESS AND ITS MANAGEMENT

Friends say they're stressed from greater workloads and longer hours because of down-sizing at their companies. Parents worry about the lack of job stability and reminisce about a time when a job with a large company implied lifetime security. We read surveys in which employees complain about the stress of trying to balance work and family responsibilities.[41] Indeed, work is, for most people, the most important source of stress in life. What are the causes and consequences of stress, and what can individuals and organizations do to reduce it?

What Is Stress?

Stress is a dynamic condition in which an individual is confronted with an opportunity, demand, or resource related to what the individual desires and for which the outcome is perceived to be both uncertain and important.[42] This is a complicated definition. Let's look at its components more closely.

Although stress is typically discussed in a negative context, it is not necessarily bad in and of itself; it also has a positive value.[43] It's an opportunity when it offers potential gain. Consider, for example, the superior performance an athlete or stage performer gives in a "clutch" situation. Such individuals often use stress positively to rise to the occasion and perform at their maximum. Similarly, many professionals see the pressures of heavy workloads and deadlines as positive challenges that enhance the quality of their work and the satisfaction they get from their job.

Recently, researchers have argued that **challenge stressors**—or stressors associated with workload, pressure to complete tasks, and time urgency—operate quite differently from **hindrance stressors**—or stressors that keep you from reaching your goals (for example, red tape, office politics, confusion over job responsibilities). Although research is just starting to accumulate, early evidence suggests challenge stressors produce less strain than hindrance stressors.[44]

> Change is often stressful to individuals, but, like change, researchers are beginning to accept that not all stress is harmful.

Researchers have sought to clarify the conditions under which each type of stress exists. It appears that employees who have a stronger affective commitment to their organization can transfer psychological stress into greater focus and higher sales performance, whereas employees with low levels of commitment perform worse under stress.[45] And when challenge stress increases, those with high levels of organizational support have higher role-based performance, but those with low levels of organizational support do not.[46]

More typically, stress is associated with **demands** and **resources**. Demands are responsibilities, pressures, obligations, and uncertainties individuals face in the work-place. Resources are things within an individual's control that he can use to resolve the demands. Let's discuss what this demands–resources model means.[47]

When you take a test at school or undergo your annual performance review at work, you feel stress because you confront opportunities and performance pressures. A good performance review may lead to a promotion, greater responsibilities, and a higher salary. A poor review may prevent you from getting a promotion. An extremely poor review might even result in your being fired. To the extent you can apply resources to the demands on you—such as being prepared, placing the exam or review in perspective, or obtaining social support—you will feel less stress.

Research suggests adequate resources help reduce the stressful nature of demands when demands and resources match. If emotional demands are stressing you, having emotional resources in the form of social support is especially important. If the demands are cognitive—say, information overload—then job resources in the form of computer support or information are more important. Thus, under the demands–resources perspective, having resources to cope with stress is just as important in offsetting it as demands are in increasing it.[48]

Consequences of Stress

Stress shows itself in a number of ways, such as high blood pressure, ulcers, irritability, difficulty making routine decisions, loss of appetite, accident proneness, and the like. These symptoms fit under three general categories: physiological, psychological, and behavioral symptoms.[49]

PHYSIOLOGICAL SYMPTOMS   Most early concern with stress was directed at physiological symptoms because most researchers were specialists in the health and medical sciences. Their work led to the conclusion that stress could create changes in metabolism, increase heart and breathing rates and blood pressure, bring on headaches, and induce heart attacks.

Evidence now clearly suggests stress may have wide-ranging harmful physiological effects. One study linked stressful job demands to increased susceptibility to upper-respiratory illnesses and poor immune system functioning, especially for individuals with low self-efficacy.[50] A long-term study conducted in the United Kingdom found that job strain was associated with higher levels of coronary heart disease.[51] Still another study conducted with Danish human services workers found that higher levels of psychological burnout at the work-unit level were related to significantly higher levels of sickness absence.[52] Many other studies have shown similar results linking work stress to a variety of indicators of poor health.

PSYCHOLOGICAL SYMPTOMS   Job dissatisfaction is "the simplest and most obvious psychological effect" of stress.[53] But stress shows itself in other psychological states—for instance, tension, anxiety, irritability, boredom, and procrastination. For example, a study that tracked physiological responses of employees over time found that stress due to high workloads was related to higher blood pressure and lower emotional well-being.[54]

Jobs that make multiple and conflicting demands or that lack clarity about the incumbent's duties, authority, and responsibilities increase both stress and dissatisfaction.[55] Similarly, the less control people have over the pace of their work, the greater their stress and dissatisfaction. Jobs that provide a low level of variety, significance, autonomy, feedback, and identity appear to create stress and reduce satisfaction and involvement in the job.[56] Not everyone reacts to autonomy in the same way, however. For those with an external locus of control, increased job control increases the tendency to experience stress and exhaustion.[57]

BEHAVIORAL SYMPTOMS   Research on behavior and stress has been conducted across several countries and over time, and the relationships appear relatively consistent. Behavior-related stress symptoms include reductions in productivity, absence, and turnover, as well as changes in eating habits, increased smoking or consumption of alcohol, rapid speech, fidgeting, and sleep disorders.[58]

Managing Stress

Because low to moderate levels of stress can be functional and lead to higher performance, management may not be concerned when employees experience them. Employees, however, are likely to perceive even low levels of stress as undesirable. It's not unlikely, therefore, for employees and management to have different notions of what constitutes an acceptable level of stress on the job. What management may consider to be "a positive stimulus that keeps the adrenaline running" is very likely to be seen as "excessive pressure" by the employee. Keep this in mind as we discuss individual and organizational approaches toward managing stress.[59]

INDIVIDUAL APPROACHES   An employee can take personal responsibility for reducing stress levels. Individual strategies that have proven effective include time-management techniques, increased physical exercise, relaxation training, and expanded social support networks.

Many people manage their time poorly. The well-organized employee, like the well-organized student, can often accomplish twice as much as the person who is poorly organized. So an understanding and utilization of basic time-management principles can help individuals better cope with tensions created by job demands.[60] A few of the best-known time-management principles are (1) making daily lists of activities to be accomplished, (2) prioritizing activities by importance and urgency, (3) scheduling activities according to the priorities set, (4) knowing your daily cycle and handling the most demanding parts of your job when you are most alert and productive, and (5) avoiding electronic distractions like frequently checking e-mail, which can limit attention and reduce efficiency.[61] These time-management skills can help minimize procrastination by focusing efforts on immediate goals and boosting motivation even in the face of tasks that are less desirable.[62]

Physicians have recommended noncompetitive *physical exercise*, such as aerobics, walking, jogging, swimming, and riding a bicycle, as a way to deal with excessive stress levels. These activities increase lung capacity, lower the at-rest heart rate, and provide a mental diversion from work pressures, effectively reducing work-related levels of stress.[63]

Individuals can also teach themselves to reduce tension through *relaxation techniques* such as meditation, hypnosis, and deep breathing. The objective is to reach a state of deep physical relaxation, in which you focus all your energy on release of muscle tension.[64] Deep relaxation for 15 or 20 minutes a day releases strain and provides a pronounced sense of peacefulness, as well as significant changes in heart rate, blood pressure, and other physiological factors. A growing body of research shows that simply taking breaks from work at routine intervals can facilitate psychological recovery and reduce stress significantly and may improve job performance, and these effects are even greater if relaxation techniques are employed.[65]

As we have noted, friends, family, or work colleagues can provide an outlet when stress levels become excessive. Expanding your *social support network* provides someone to hear your problems and offer a more objective perspective on a stressful situation than your own.

ORGANIZATIONAL APPROACHES   Several organizational factors that cause stress—particularly task and role demands—are controlled by management and thus can be modified or changed. Strategies to consider include improved employee selection and job placement, training, realistic goal-setting, redesign of jobs, increased employee involvement, improved organizational communication, employee sabbaticals, and corporate wellness programs.

Certain jobs are more stressful than others but, as we've seen, individuals differ in their response to stressful situations. We know individuals with little experience or an external locus of control tend to be more prone to stress. *Selection and placement* decisions should take these facts into consideration. Obviously, management shouldn't restrict hiring to only experienced individuals with an internal locus, but such individuals may adapt better to high-stress jobs and perform those jobs more effectively. Similarly, *training* can increase an individual's self-efficacy and thus lessen job strain.

We discussed *goal-setting* in Chapter 7. Individuals perform better when they have specific and challenging goals and receive feedback on their progress toward these goals. Goals can reduce stress as well as provide motivation.[66] Employees who are highly committed to their goals and see purpose in their jobs experience less stress because they are more likely to perceive stressors as challenges rather than hindrances. Specific goals perceived as attainable clarify performance expectations. In addition, goal feedback reduces uncertainties about actual job performance. The result is less employee frustration, role ambiguity, and stress.

Redesigning jobs to give employees more responsibility, more meaningful work, more autonomy, and increased feedback can reduce stress because these factors give employees greater control over work activities and lessen dependence on others. But as we noted in our discussion of work design, not all employees want enriched jobs. The right redesign for employees with a low need for growth might be less responsibility and increased specialization. If individuals prefer structure and routine, reducing skill variety should also reduce uncertainties and stress levels.

Role stress is detrimental to a large extent because employees feel uncertain about goals, expectations, how they'll be evaluated, and the like. By giving these employees a voice in the decisions that directly affect their job performance, management can increase employee control and reduce role stress. Thus, managers should consider *increasing employee involvement* in decision making, because evidence clearly shows that increases in employee empowerment reduce psychological strain.[67]

Increasing formal *organizational communication* with employees reduces uncertainty by lessening role ambiguity and role conflict. Given the importance that perceptions play in moderating the stress–response relationship, management can also use effective communications as a means to shape employee perceptions. Remember that what employees categorize as demands, threats, or opportunities at work is an interpretation and that interpretation can be affected by the words and actions communicated by management.

Our final suggestion is organizationally supported **wellness programs**. These typically provide workshops to help people quit smoking, control alcohol use, lose weight, eat better, and develop a regular exercise program; they focus on the employee's total physical and mental condition.[68] Some help employees improve their psychological health as well. A meta-analysis of 36 programs designed to reduce stress (including wellness programs) showed that interventions to help employees reframe stressful situations and use active coping strategies appreciably reduced stress levels.[69] Most wellness programs assume employees need to take personal responsibility for their physical and mental health and that the organization is merely a means to that end.

SUMMARY AND IMPLICATIONS FOR MANAGERS

The need for change has been implied throughout this text. "A casual reflection on change should indicate that it encompasses almost all of our concepts in the organizational behavior literature."[70] For instance, think about attitudes, motivation, work teams, communication, leadership, organizational structures, human resource practices, and organizational cultures. Change was an integral part in our discussion of each. If environments were perfectly static, if employees' skills and abilities were always up to date and incapable of deteriorating, and if tomorrow were always exactly the same as today, organizational change would have little or no relevance to managers. But the real world is turbulent, requiring organizations and their members to undergo dynamic change if they are to perform at competitive levels.

- Managers are the primary change agents in most organizations. By the decisions they make and their role-modeling behaviors, they shape the organization's change culture.
- Management decisions related to structural design, cultural factors, and human resource policies largely determine the level of innovation within the organization.
- Management policies and practices will determine the degree to which the organization learns and adapts to changing environmental factors.
- The existence of work stress, in and of itself, need not imply lower performance. The evidence indicates that stress can be either a positive or a negative influence on employee performance.
- Low to moderate amounts of stress enable many people to perform their jobs better by increasing their work intensity, alertness, and ability to react. This is especially true if stress arises due to challenges on the job rather than hindrances that prevent employees from doing their jobs effectively.
- However, a high level of stress, or even a moderate amount sustained over a long period, eventually takes its toll, and performance declines.

MyManagementLab

Go to **MyManagementLab.com** to access study plans, interactive lectures, and videos as well as Auto-graded writing questions and the following Assisted-graded writing question.

17-1. MyManagementLab Only—comprehensive writing assignment for this chapter.

EPILOGUE

The end of a book typically has the same meaning to an author that it has to the reader: It generates feelings of both accomplishment and relief. As both of us rejoice at having completed our tour of the essential concepts in organizational behavior, this is a good time to examine where we've been and what it all means.

The underlying theme of this book has been that the behavior of people at work is not a random phenomenon. Employees are complex entities, but their attitudes and behavior can nevertheless be explained and predicted with a reasonable degree of accuracy. Our approach has been to look at organizational behavior at three levels: the individual, the group, and the organization system.

We started with the individual and reviewed the major psychological contributions to understanding why individuals act as they do. We found that many of the individual differences among employees can be systematically labeled and categorized, and therefore generalizations can be made. For example, we know that individuals with a conventional type of personality are better matched to certain jobs in corporate management than are people with investigative personalities. So placing people into jobs that are compatible with their personality types should result in higher-performing and more satisfied employees.

Next, our analysis moved to the group level. We argued that the understanding of group behavior is more complex than merely multiplying what we know about individuals by the number of members in the group, because people act differently in a group than when they are alone. We demonstrated how roles, norms, leadership styles, power relationships, and other similar group factors affect the behavior of employees.

Finally, we overlaid system-wide variables on our knowledge of individual and group behavior to further improve our understanding of organizational behavior. Major emphasis was given to showing how an organization's structure, design, and culture affect both the attitudes and the behavior of employees.

It may be tempting to criticize the stress this book placed on theoretical concepts, but as noted psychologist Kurt Lewin is purported to have said, "There is nothing so practical as a good theory." Of course, it's also true that there is nothing so impractical as a good theory that leads nowhere. To avoid presenting theories that lead nowhere, this book included a wealth of examples and illustrations. And we regularly stopped to inquire about the implications of theory for the practice of management. The result has been the presentation of numerous concepts that, individually, offer some insights into behavior, but which, when taken together, provide a complex system to help you explain, predict, and control organizational behavior.

ENDNOTES

CHAPTER 1

1. See, for instance, C. Penttila, "Hiring Hardships," *Entrepreneur* (October 2002), pp. 34–35.
2. S. E. Humphrey, J. D. Nahrgang, and F. P. Morgeson, "Integrating Motivational, Social, and Contextual Work Design Features: A Meta-Analytic Summary and Theoretical Extension of the Work Design Literature," *Journal of Applied Psychology* 92, no. 5 (2007), pp. 1332–1356.
3. I. S. Fulmer, B. Gerhart, and K. S. Scott, "Are the 100 Best Better? An Empirical Investigation of the Relationship Between Being a 'Great Place to Work' and Firm Performance," *Personnel Psychology* (Winter 2003), pp. 965–993.
4. See, for instance, C. Heath and S. B. Sitkin, "Big-B Versus Big-O: What Is *Organizational* about Organizational Behavior?" *Journal of Organizational Behavior* (February 2001), pp. 43–58. For a review of what one eminent researcher believes *should* be included in organizational behavior, based on survey data, see J. B. Miner, "The Rated Importance, Scientific Validity, and Practical Usefulness of Organizational Behavior Theories: A Quantitative Review," *Academy of Management Learning & Education* (September 2003), pp. 250–268.
5. D. M. Rousseau and S. McCarthy, "Educating Managers from an Evidence-Based Perspective," *Academy of Management Learning & Education* 6, no. 1 (2007), pp. 84–101; and S. L. Rynes, T. L. Giluk, and K. G. Brown, "The Very Separate Worlds of Academic and Practitioner Periodicals in Human Resource Management: Implications for Evidence-Based Management," *Academy of Management Journal* 50, no. 5 (2007), pp. 987–1008.
6. Quote from Ken Cohen, ExxonMobil vice president of public and government affairs, at www.exxonmobileperspectives.com/2012/01/31/the-facts-behind-exxonmobils-earnings/.
7. M. Toossi, "A New Look at Long-Term Labor Force Projections to 2050," *Monthly Labor Review* (November 2006), pp. 19–20.
8. See, for instance, M. Workman and W. Bommer, "Rede Signing Computer Call Center Work: A Longitudinal Field Experiment," *Journal of Organizational Behavior* (May 2004), pp. 317–337.
9. See, for instance, V. S. Major, K. J. Klein, and M. G. Ehrhart, "Work Time, Work Interference with Family, and Psychological Distress," *Journal of Applied Psychology* (June 2002), pp. 427–436; D. Brady, "Rethinking the Rat Race," *BusinessWeek* (August 26, 2002), pp. 142–143; and J. M. Brett and L. K. Stroh, "Working 61 Plus Hours a Week: Why Do Managers Do It?" *Journal of Applied Psychology* (February 2003), pp. 67–78.
10. See, for instance, *The 2002 National Study of the Changing Workforce* (New York: Families and Work Institute, 2002); and W. J. Casper and L. C. Buffardi, "Work-Life Benefits and Job Pursuit Intentions: The Role of Anticipated Organizational Support," *Journal of Vocational Behavior* 65, no. 3 (2004), pp. 391–410.
11. Cited in S. Armour, "Workers Put Family First Despite Slow Economy, Jobless Fears," *USA Today* (June 6, 2002), p. 38.
12. S. Shellenbarger, "What Job Candidates Really Want to Know: Will I Have a Life?" *Wall Street Journal* (November 17, 1999), p. B1; and "U.S. Employers Polish Image to Woo a Demanding New Generation," *Manpower Argus* (February 2000), p. 2.
13. W. Bailey and A. Spicer, "When Does National Identity Matter? Convergence and Divergence in International Business Ethics," *Academy of Management Journal* 50, no. 6 (2007), pp. 1462–1480; and A. B. Oumlil and J. L. Balloun, "Ethical Decision-Making Differences between American and Moroccan Managers," *Journal of Business Ethics* 84, no. 4 (2009), pp. 457–478.
14. J. Merritt, "For MBAs, Soul-Searching 101," *BusinessWeek* (September 16, 2002), pp. 64–66; and S. Greenhouse, "The Mood at Work: Anger and Anxiety," *New York Times* (October 29, 2002), p. E1.
15. See, for instance, G. R. Weaver, L. K. Trevino, and P. L. Cochran, "Corporate Ethics Practices in the Mid-1990's: An Empirical Study of the Fortune 1000," *Journal of Business Ethics* (February 1999), pp. 283–294; and C. De Mesa Graziano, "Promoting Ethical Conduct: A Review of Corporate Practices," *Strategic Investor Relations* (Fall 2002), pp. 29–35.
16. D. M. Mayer, M. Kuenzi, R. Greenbaum, M. Bardes, and R. Salvador, "How Low Does Ethical Leadership Flow? Test of a Trickle-Down Model," *Organizational Behavior and Human Decision Processes* 108, no. 1 (2009), pp. 1–13; and A. Ardichvili, J. A. Mitchell, and D. Jondle, "Characteristics of Ethical Business Cultures," *Journal of Business Ethics* 85, no. 4 (2009), pp. 445–451.

CHAPTER 2

1. M. DiNatale and S. Boraas, "The Labor Force Experience of Women from Generation X," *Monthly Labor Review* (March 2002), pp. 1–15.
2. See, for example, F. Welch, "Catching Up: Wages of Black Men," *The American Economic Review* 93, no. 2 (2003), pp. 320–325; A. Sakamoto, H. Wu, and J. M. Tzeng, "The Declining Significance of Race Among American Men During the Latter Half of the Twentieth Century," *Demography* 37 (January 2000), pp. 41–51; and A Sakamoto, K. A. Goyette, and C. Kim, "Socioeconomic Attainments of Asian Americans," *Annual Review of Sociology* 35, (2009), pp. 255–276.
3. J. Schram, *SHRM Workplace Forecast* (Alexandria, VA: Society for Human Resource Management, 2006).
4. D. A. Harrison, K. H. Price, J. H. Gavin, and A. T. Florey, "Time, Teams, and Task Performance: Changing Effects of Surface- and Deep-Level Diversity on Group Functioning," *Academy of Management Journal* 45, no. 5 (2002), pp. 1029–1045; and A. H. Eagly and J. L. Chin, "Are Memberships in Race, Ethnicity, and Gender Categories Merely Surface Characteristics?" *American Psychologist* 65 (2010), pp. 934–935.

5. P. Chattopadhyay, M. Tluchowska, and E. George, "Identifying the Ingroup: A Closer Look at the Influence of Demographic Dissimilarity on Employee Social Identity," *Academy of Management Review* 29, no. 2 (2004), pp. 180–202; and P. Chattopadhyay, "Beyond Direct and Symmetrical Effects: The Influence of Demographic Dissimilarity on Organizational Citizenship Behavior," *Academy of Management Journal* 42, no. 3 (1999), pp. 273–287.

6. L. M. Cortina, "Unseen Injustice: Incivility as Modern Discrimination in Organizations," *Academy of Management Review* 33, no. 1 (2008), pp. 55–75.

7. R. J. Grossman, "Keep Pace with Older Workers," *HR Magazine* (May 2008), pp. 39–46.

8. K. A. Wrenn and T. J. Maurer, "Beliefs About Older Workers' Learning and Development Behavior in Relation to Beliefs About Malleability of Skills, Age-Related Decline, and Control," *Journal of Applied Social Psychology* 34, no. 2 (2004), pp. 223–242; and R. A. Posthuma and M. A. Campion, "Age Stereotypes in the Workplace: Common Stereotypes, Moderators, and Future Research Directions," *Journal of Management* 35 (2009), pp. 158–188.

9. T. W. H. Ng and D. C. Feldman, "Re-examining the Relationship Between Age and Voluntary Turnover," *Journal of Vocational Behavior* 74 (2009), pp. 283–294.

10. T. W. H. Ng and D. C. Feldman, "The Relationship of Age to Ten Dimensions of Job Performance," *Journal of Applied Psychology* 93 (2008), pp. 392–423.

11. Cited in K. Labich, "The New Unemployed," *Fortune* (March 8, 1993), p. 43.

12. See Ng and Feldman, "The Relationship of Age to Ten Dimensions of Job Performance."

13. T. W. H. Ng and D. C. Feldman, "The Relationship of Age with Job Attitudes: A Meta-Analysis," *Personnel Psychology* 63 (2010), pp. 677–718.

14. K. M. Kacmar and G. R. Ferris, "Theoretical and Methodological Considerations in the Age–Job Satisfaction Relationship," *Journal of Applied Psychology* (April 1989), pp. 201–207; and W. A. Hochwarter, G. R. Ferris, P. L. Perrewe, L. A. Witt, and C. Kiewitz, "A Note on the Nonlinearity of the Age–Job Satisfaction Relationship," *Journal of Applied Social Psychology* (June 2001), pp. 1223–1237.

15. F. Kunze, S. A. Boehm, and H. Bruch, "Age Diversity, Age Discrimination Climate and Performance Consequences—A Cross Organizational Study," *Journal of Organizational Behavior* 32 (2011), pp. 264–290.

16. See E. M. Weiss, G. Kemmler, E. A. Deisenhammer, W. W. Fleischhacker, and M. Delazer, "Sex Differences in Cognitive Functions," *Personality and Individual Differences* (September 2003), pp. 863–875; and A. F. Jorm, K. J. Anstey, H. Christensen, and B. Rodgers, "Gender Differences in Cognitive Abilities: The Mediating Role of Health State and Health Habits," *Intelligence* (January 2004), pp. 7–23.

17. See M. M. Black and E. W. Holden, "The Impact of Gender on Productivity and Satisfaction Among Medical School Psychologists," *Journal of Clinical Psychology in Medical Settings* (March 1998), pp. 117–131.

18. M. E. Heilman and T. G. Okimoto, "Why Are Women Penalized for Success at Male Tasks? The Implied Communality Deficit," *Journal of Applied Psychology* 92, no. 1 (2007), pp. 81–92.

19. D. R. Avery, P. F. McKay, and D. C. Wilson "What are the Odds? How Demographic Similarity Affects the Prevalence of Perceived Employment Discrimination," *Journal of Applied Psychology* 93 (2008), pp. 235–249.

20. C. Kirchmeyer, "The Different Effects of Family on Objective Career Success Across Gender: A Test of Alternative Explanations," *Journal of Vocational Behavior* 68, no. 2 (2006), pp. 323–346; and C. Guillaume and S. Pochic, "What Would You Sacrifice? Access to Top Management and the Work-Life Balance," *Gender, Work & Organization* 16, no. 1 (2009), pp. 14–36.

21. Guillaume and Pochic, "What Would You Sacrifice? Access to Top Management and the Work-Life Balance."

22. P. W. Hom, L. Roberson, and A. D. Ellis, "Challenging Conventional Wisdom About Who Quits: Revelations from Corporate America," *Journal of Applied Psychology* 93, no. 1 (2008), pp. 1–34.

23. See, for instance, K. D. Scott and E. L. McClellan, "Gender Differences in Absenteeism," *Public Personnel Management* (Summer 1990), pp. 229–253; and A. VandenHeuvel and M. Wooden, "Do Explanations of Absenteeism Differ for Men and Women?" *Human Relations* (November 1995), pp. 1309–1329.

24. See, for instance, M. Tait, M. Y. Padgett, and T. T. Baldwin, "Job and Life Satisfaction: A Reevaluation of the Strength of the Relationship and Gender Effects as a Function of the Date of the Study," *Journal of Applied Psychology* (June 1989), pp. 502–507; and M. B. Grover, "Daddy Stress," *Forbes* (September 6, 1999), pp. 202–208.

25. S. Halrynjo, "Men's Work-Life Conflict: Career, Care and Self-Realization: Patterns of Privileges and Dilemmas," *Gender, Work & Organization* 16, no. 1 (2009), pp. 98–125; and S. Jayson, "Gender Roles See a 'Conflict' Shift," *USA Today* (March 26, 2009), p. 1A.

26. M. E. Heilman and T. G. Okimoto, "Motherhood: A Potential Source of Bias in Employment Decisions," *Journal of Applied Psychology* 93, no. 1 (2008), pp. 189–198.

27. J. L. Raver and L. H. Nishii, "Once, Twice, or Three Times as Harmful? Ethnic Harassment, Gender Harassment, and Generalized Workplace Harassment," *Journal of Applied Psychology* 95 (2010), pp. 236–254.

28. D. R. Avery, J. A. Richeson, M R. Hebl, and N. Ambady, "It Does Not Have to Be Uncomfortable: The Role of Behavioral Scripts in Black-White Interracial Interactions," *Journal of Applied Psychology* 94 (2009), pp. 1382–1393.

29. J. M. McCarthy, C. H. Van Iddekinge, and M. A. Campion, "Are Highly Structured Job Interviews Resistant to Demographic Similarity Effects?" *Personnel Psychology* 63 (2010), pp. 325–359; and G. N. Powell and D. A. Butterfield, "Exploring the Influence of Decision Makers' Race and Gender on Actual Promotions to Top Management," *Personnel Psychology* 55, no. 2 (2002), pp. 397–428.

30. D. A. Kravitz, D. M. Mayer, L. M. Leslie, and D. Lev-Arey, "Understanding Attitudes Toward Affirmative Action Programs in Employment: Summary and Meta-Analysis of 35 Years of Research," *Journal of Applied Psychology* 91 (2006), pp. 1013–1036.

31. D. R. Avery, P F. McKay, and D. C. Wilson "What Are the Odds? How Demographic Similarity Affects the Prevalence of Perceived Employment Discrimination," *Journal of Applied Psychology* 93 (2008), pp. 235–249.

32. J. M. Sacco, C. R. Scheu, A. M. Ryan, and N. Schmitt, "An Investigation of Race and Sex Similarity Effects in Interviews: A Multilevel Approach to Relational Demography," *Journal of Applied Psychology* 88, no. 5 (2003), pp. 852–865; and

P. F. McKay and M. A. McDaniel, "A Reexamination of Black-White Mean Differences in Work Performance: More Data, More Moderators," *Journal of Applied Psychology* 91, no. 3 (2006), pp. 538–554.

33. P. Bobko, P. L. Roth, and D. Potosky, "Derivation and Implications of a Meta-Analytic Matrix Incorporating Cognitive Ability, Alternative Predictors, and Job Performance," *Personnel Psychology* (Autumn 1999), pp. 561–589.

34. M. J. Ree, T. R. Carretta, and J. R. Steindl, "Cognitive Ability," in N. Anderson, D. S. Ones, H. K. Sinangil, and C. Viswesvaran (eds.), *Handbook of Industrial, Work, and Organizational Psychology*, vol. 1 (London: Sage Publications, 2001), pp. 219–232.

35. W. T. Dickens and J. R. Flynn, "Black Americans Reduce the Racial IQ Gap: Evidence from Standardization Samples," *Psychological Science* 17 (2006), pp. 913–920; and C. Murray, "The Magnitude and Components of Change in the Black-White IQ Difference from 1920 to 1991: A Birth Cohort Analysis of the Woodcock-Johnson Standardizations," *Intelligence* 35, no. 44 (2007), pp. 305–318.

36. See J. P. Rushton and A. R. Jenson, "Thirty Years of Research on Race Differences in Cognitive Ability," *Psychology, Public Policy, and the Law* 11, no. 2 (2005), pp. 235–295; and R. E. Nisbett, "Heredity, Environment, and Race Differences in IQ: A Commentary on Rushton and Jensen (2005)," *Psychology, Public Policy, and the Law* 11, no. 2 (2005), pp. 302–310.

37. P. F. McKay, D. R. Avery, and M. A. Morris, "Mean Racial-Ethnic Differences in Employee Sales Performance: The Moderating Role of Diversity Climate," *Personnel Psychology* 61, no. 2 (2008), pp. 349–374.

38. *Americans with Disabilities Act,* 42 U.S.C. § 12101, et seq. (1990).

39. S. G. Goldberg, M. B. Killeen, and B. O'Day, "The Disclosure Conundrum: How People with Psychiatric Disabilities Navigate Employment," *Psychology, Public Policy, and Law* 11, no. 3 (2005), pp. 463–500; M. L. Ellison, Z. Russinova, K. L. MacDonald-Wilson, and A. Lyass, "Patterns and Correlates of Workplace Disclosure Among Professionals and Managers with Psychiatric Conditions," *Journal of Vocational Rehabilitation* 18, no. 1 (2003), pp. 3–13.

40. L. R. Ren, R. L. Paetzold, and A. Colella, "A Meta-Analysis of Experimental Studies on the Effects of Disability on Human Resource Judgments," *Human Resource Management Review* 18, no. 3 (2008), pp. 191–203.

41. S. Almond and A. Healey, "Mental Health and Absence from Work: New Evidence from the UK Quarterly Labour Force Survey," *Work, Employment, and Society* 17, no. 4 (2003), pp. 731–742.

42. E. Louvet, "Social Judgment Toward Job Applicants with Disabilities: Perception of Personal Qualities and Competences," *Rehabilitation Psychology* 52, no. 3 (2007), pp. 297–303; and W. D. Gouvier, S. Sytsma-Jordan, and S. Mayville, "Patterns of Discrimination in Hiring Job Applicants with Disabilities: The Role of Disability Type, Job Complexity, and Public Contact," *Rehabilitation Psychology* 48, no. 3 (2003), pp. 175–181.

43. A. Colella, A. S. DeNisi, and A. Varma, "The Impact of Ratee's Disability on Performance Judgments and Choice as Partner: The Role of Disability-Job Fit Stereotypes and Interdependence of Rewards," *Journal of Applied Psychology* 83, no. 1 (1998), pp. 102–111.

44. J. M. Czajka and A. S. DeNisi, "Effects of Emotional Disability and Clear Performance Standards on Performance Ratings," *Academy of Management Journal* 31, no. 2 (1988), pp. 394–404.

45. B. S. Bell and K. J. Klein, "Effect of Disability, Gender, and Job Level on Ratings of Job Applicants," *Rehabilitation Psychology* 46, no. 3 (2001), pp. 229–246; and Louvet, "Social Judgment Toward Job Applicants with Disabilities: Perception of Personal Qualities and Competences."

46. T. W. H. Ng and D. C. Feldman, "Organizational Tenure and Job Performance," *Journal of Management* 36, (2010), pp. 1220–1250.

47. I. R. Gellatly, "Individual and Group Determinants of Employee Absenteeism: Test of a Causal Model," *Journal of Organizational Behavior* (September 1995), pp. 469–485.

48. P. O. Popp and J. A. Belohlav, "Absenteeism in a Low Status Work Environment," *Academy of Management Journal* (September 1982), p. 681.

49. R. W. Griffeth, P. W. Hom, and S. Gaertner, "A Meta-analysis of Antecedents and Correlates of Employee Turnover: Update, Moderator Tests, and Research Implications for the Next Millennium," *Journal of Management* 26, no. 3 (2000), pp. 463–488.

50. M. R. Barrick and R. D. Zimmerman, "Hiring for Retention and Performance," *Human Resource Management* 48 (2009), pp. 183–206.

51. W. van Breukelen, R. van der Vlist, and H. Steensma, "Voluntary Employee Turnover: Combining Variables from the 'Traditional' Turnover Literature with the Theory of Planned Behavior," *Journal of Organizational Behavior* 25, no. 7 (2004), pp. 893–914.

52. M. Elias, "USA's Muslims Under a Cloud," *USA Today* (August 10, 2006), pp. 1D, 2D; and R. R. Hastings, "Muslims Seek Acknowledgement of Mainstream Americans," *HR Week* (May 11, 2007), p. 1.

53. E. B. King and A. S. Ahmad, "An Experimental Field Study of Interpersonal Discrimination Toward Muslim Job Applicants," *Personnel Psychology* 63 (2010), pp. 881–906.

54. See, for example, E. B. King and J. M. Cortina, "The Social and Economic Imperative of Lesbian, Gay, Bisexual, and Transgendered Supportive Organizational Policies," *Industrial and Organizational Psychology: Perspectives on Science and Practice* 3 (2010), pp. 69–78.

55. *HRC Corporate Equality Index,* 2011, www.hrc.org/documents/HRC-CEI-2011-Final.pdf; and R. R. Hastings, "Necessity Breeds Inclusion: Reconsidering 'Don't Ask, Don't Tell,'" *HR Week* (January 2007), pp. 1–2.

56. B. R. Ragins, "Disclosure Disconnects: Antecedents and Consequences of Disclosing Invisible Stigmas Across Life Domains," *Academy of Management Review* 33 (2008), pp. 194–215.

57. B. Leonard, "Transgender Issues Test Diversity Limits," *HR Magazine* (June 2007), pp. 32–34.

58. L. S. Gottfredson, "The Challenge and Promise of Cognitive Career Assessment," *Journal of Career Assessment* 11, no. 2 (2003), pp. 115–135.

59. M. D. Dunnette, "Aptitudes, Abilities, and Skills," in M. D. Dunnette (ed.), *Handbook of Industrial and Organizational Psychology* (Chicago: Rand McNally, 1976), pp. 478–483.

60. J. W. B. Lang, M. Kersting, U. R. Hülscheger, and J. Lang, "General Mental Ability, Narrower Cognitive Abilities, and Job Performance: The Perspective of the Nested-Factors Model of Cognitive Abilities" *Personnel Psychology* 63 (2010), pp. 595–640.

61. N. Barber, "Educational and Ecological Correlates of IQ: A Cross-National Investigation," *Intelligence* (May–June 2005), pp. 273–284.

62. J. F. Salgado, N. Anderson, S. Moscoso, C. Bertua, F. de Fruyt, and J. P. Rolland, "A Meta-analytic Study of General Mental Ability Validity for Different Occupations in the European Community," *Journal of Applied Psychology* (December 2003), pp. 1068–1081; and F. L. Schmidt and J. E. Hunter, "Select on Intelligence," in E. A. Locke (ed.), *Handbook of Principles of Organizational Behavior* (Malden, MA: Blackwell, 2004).

63. Y. Ganzach, "Intelligence and Job Satisfaction," *Academy of Management Journal* 41, no. 5 (1998), pp. 526–539; and Y. Ganzach, "Intelligence, Education, and Facets of Job Satisfaction," *Work and Occupations* 30, no. 1 (2003), pp. 97–122.

64. E. A. Fleishman, "Evaluating Physical Abilities Required by Jobs," *Personnel Administrator* (June 1979), pp. 82–92.

65. D. R. Avery, "Reactions to Diversity in Recruitment Advertising: Are the Differences Black and White?" *Journal of Applied Psychology* 88, no. 4 (2003), pp. 672–679; P. F. McKay and D. R. Avery, "What Has Race Got to Do with It? Unraveling the Role of Racioethnicity in Job Seekers' Reactions to Site Visits," *Personnel Psychology* 59, no. 2 (2006), pp. 395–429; and D. R. Avery and P. F. McKay, "Target Practice: An Organizational Impression Management Approach to Attracting Minority and Female Job Applicants," *Personnel Psychology* 59, no. 1 (2006), pp. 157–187.

66. M. R. Buckley, K. A. Jackson, M. C. Bolino, J. G. Veres, and H. S. Field, "The Influence of Relational Demography on Panel Interview Ratings: A Field Experiment," *Personnel Psychology* 60 (2007), pp. 627–646; J. M. Sacco, C. R. Scheu, A. M. Ryan, and N. Schmitt, "An Investigation of Race and Sex Similarity Effects in Interviews: A Multilevel Approach to Relational Demography," *Journal of Applied Psychology* 88 (2003), pp. 852–865; and J. C. Ziegert and P. J. Hanges, "Employment Discrimination: The Role of Implicit Attitudes, Motivation, and a Climate for Racial Bias," *Journal of Applied Psychology* 90 (2005), pp. 553–562.

67. J. Schaubroeck and S. S. K. Lam, "How Similarity to Peers and Supervisor Influences Organizational Advancement in Different Cultures," *Academy of Management Journal* 45 (2002), pp. 1120–1136.

68. P. F. McKay, D. R. Avery, and M. A. Morris, "Mean Racial-Ethnic Differences in Employee Sales Performance: The Moderating Role of Diversity Climate," *Personnel Psychology* 61, no. 2 (2008), pp. 349–374.

69. A. S. Tsui, T. D. Egan, and C. A. O'Reilly, "Being Different: Relational Demography and Organizational Attachment," *Administrative Science Quarterly* 37 (1992), pp. 547–579; and J. M. Sacco and N. Schmitt, "A Dynamic Multilevel Model of Demographic Diversity and Misfit Effects," *Journal of Applied Psychology* 90 (2005), pp. 203–231.

70. P. F. McKay, D. R. Avery, S. Tonidandel, M. A. Morris, M. Hernandez, and M. R. Hebl, "Racial Differences in Employee Retention: Are Diversity Climate Perceptions the Key?" *Personnel Psychology* 60, no. 1 (2007), pp. 35–62.

71. S. T. Bell, "Deep-Level Composition Variables as Predictors of Team Performance: A Meta–Analysis," *Journal of Applied Psychology* 92, no. 3 (2007), pp. 595–615; S. K. Horwitz and I. B. Horwitz, "The Effects of Team Diversity on Team Outcomes: A Meta-Analytic Review of Team Demography," *Journal of Management* 33, no. 6 (2007), pp. 987–1015;

G. L. Stewart, "A Meta-Analytic Review of Relationships Between Team Design Features and Team Performance," *Journal of Management* 32, no. 1 (2006), pp. 29–54; and A. Joshi and H. Roh, "The Role of Context in Work Team Diversity Research: A Meta-Analytic Review," *Academy of Management Journal* 52, no. 3 (2009), pp. 599–627.

72. A. C. Homan, J. R. Hollenbeck, S. E. Humphrey, D. Van Knippenberg, D. R. Ilgen, and G. A. Van Kleef, "Facing Differences with an Open Mind: Openness to Experience, Salience of Intragroup Differences, and Performance of Diverse Work Groups," *Academy of Management Journal* 51, no. 6 (2008), pp. 1204–1222.

73. E. Kearney and D. Gebert, "Managing Diversity and Enhancing Team Outcomes: The Promise of Transformational Leadership," *Journal of Applied Psychology* 94, no. 1 (2009), pp. 77–89.

74. C. L. Holladay and M. A. Quiñones, "The Influence of Training Focus and Trainer Characteristics on Diversity Training Effectiveness," *Academy of Management Learning and Education* 7, no. 3 (2008), pp. 343–354; and R. Anand and M. Winters, "A Retrospective View of Corporate Diversity Training from 1964 to the Present," *Academy of Management Learning and Education* 7, no. 3 (2008), pp. 356–372.

75. Q. M. Roberson and C. K. Stevens, "Making Sense of Diversity in the Workplace: Organizational Justice and Language Abstraction in Employees' Accounts of Diversity-Related Incidents," *Journal of Applied Psychology* 91 (2006), pp. 379–391; and D. A. Harrison, D. A. Kravitz, D. M. Mayer, L. M. Leslie, and D. Lev-Arey, "Understanding Attitudes Toward Affirmative Action Programs in Employment: Summary and Meta-Analysis of 35 Years of Research," *Journal of Applied Psychology* 91 (2006), pp. 1013–1036.

76. A. Kalev, F. Dobbin, and E. Kelly, "Best Practices or Best Guesses? Assessing the Efficacy of Corporate Affirmative Action and Diversity Policies," *American Sociological Review* 71, no. 4 (2006), pp. 589–617.

77. R. J. Crisp and R. N. Turner, "Cognitive Adaptation to the Experience of Social and Cultural Diversity," *Psychological Bulletin* 137 (2011), pp. 242–266.

78. A. Sippola and A. Smale, "The Global Integration of Diversity Management: A Longitudinal Case Study," *International Journal of Human Resource Management* 18, no. 11 (2007), pp. 1895–1916.

79. A. Pomeroy, "Cultivating Female Leaders," *HR Magazine* (February 2007), pp. 44.

CHAPTER 3

1. S. J. Breckler, "Empirical Validation of Affect, Behavior, and Cognition as Distinct Components of Attitude," *Journal of Personality and Social Psychology* (May 1984), pp. 1191–1205.

2. A. W. Wicker, "Attitude Versus Action: The Relationship of Verbal and Overt Behavioral Responses to Attitude Objects," *Journal of Social Issues* (Autumn 1969), pp. 41–78.

3. L. Festinger, *A Theory of Cognitive Dissonance* (Stanford, CA: Stanford University Press, 1957).

4. See, for instance, L. R. Fabrigar, R. E. Petty, S. M. Smith, and S. L. Crites, "Understanding Knowledge Effects on Attitude-Behavior Consistency: The Role of Relevance, Complexity, and Amount of Knowledge," *Journal of Personality and Social Psychology* 90, no. 4 (2006), pp. 556–577; and

D. J. Schleicher, J. D. Watt, and G. J. Greguras, "Reexamining the Job Satisfaction-Performance Relationship: The Complexity of Attitudes," *Journal of Applied Psychology* 89, no. 1 (2004), pp. 165–177.

5. See, for instance, J. Nocera, "If It's Good for Philip Morris, Can It Also Be Good for Public Health?" *New York Times* (June 18, 2006).

6. See L. R. Glasman and D. Albarracín, "Forming Attitudes That Predict Future Behavior: A Meta-Analysis of the Attitude–Behavior Relation," *Psychological Bulletin* (September 2006), pp. 778–822; I. Ajzen, "Nature and Operation of Attitudes," in S. T. Fiske, D. L. Schacter, and C. Zahn-Waxler (eds.), *Annual Review of Psychology,* vol. 52 (Palo Alto, CA: Annual Reviews, 2001), pp. 27–58; and M. Riketta, "The Causal Relation Between Job Attitudes and Performance: A Meta-Analysis of Panel Studies," *Journal of Applied Psychology* 93, no. 2 (2008), pp. 472–481.

7. Ibid.

8. D. A. Harrison, D. A. Newman, and P. L. Roth, "How Important Are Job Attitudes? Meta-Analytic Comparisons of Integrative Behavioral Outcomes and Time Sequences," *Academy of Management Journal* 49, no. 2 (2006), pp. 305–325.

9. D. P. Moynihan and S. K. Pandey, "Finding Workable Levers Over Work Motivation: Comparing Job Satisfaction, Job Involvement, and Organizational Commitment," *Administration & Society* 39, no. 7 (2007), pp. 803–832.

10. See, for example, J. M. Diefendorff, D. J. Brown, and A. M. Kamin, "Examining the Roles of Job Involvement and Work Centrality in Predicting Organizational Citizenship Behaviors and Job Performance," *Journal of Organizational Behavior* (February 2002), pp. 93–108.

11. Based on G. J. Blau and K. R. Boal, "Conceptualizing How Job Involvement and Organizational Commitment Affect Turnover and Absenteeism," *Academy of Management Review* (April 1987), p. 290.

12. G. Chen and R. J. Klimoski, "The Impact of Expectations on Newcomer Performance in Teams as Mediated by Work Characteristics, Social Exchanges, and Empowerment," *Academy of Management Journal* 46, no. 5 (2003), pp. 591–607; A. Ergeneli, G. Saglam, and S. Metin, "Psychological Empowerment and Its Relationship to Trust in Immediate Managers," *Journal of Business Research* (January 2007), pp. 41–49; and S. E. Seibert, S. R. Silver, and W. A. Randolph, "Taking Empowerment to the Next Level: A Multiple-Level Model of Empowerment, Performance, and Satisfaction," *Academy of Management Journal* 47, no. 3 (2004), pp. 332–349.

13. B. J. Avolio, W. Zhu, W. Koh, and P. Bhatia, "Transformational Leadership and Organizational Commitment: Mediating Role of Psychological Empowerment and Moderating Role of Structural Distance," *Journal of Organizational Behavior* 25, no. 8 (2004), pp. 951–968.

14. J. M. Diefendorff, D. J. Brown, A. M. Kamin, and R. G. Lord, "Examining the Roles of Job Involvement and Work Centrality in Predicting Organizational Citizenship Behaviors and Job Performance," *Journal of Organizational Behavior* (February 2002), pp. 93–108.

15. M. R. Barrick, M. K. Mount, and J. P. Strauss, "Antecedents of Involuntary Turnover Due to a Reduction in Force," *Personnel Psychology* 47, no. 3 (1994), pp. 515–535.

16. O. N. Solinger, W. van Olffen, and R. A. Roe, "Beyond the Three-Component Model of Organizational Commitment," *Journal of Applied Psychology* 93 (2008), pp. 70–83.

17. B. J. Hoffman, C. A. Blair, J. P. Meriac, and D. J. Woehr, "Expanding the Criterion Domain? A Quantitative Review of the OCB Literature," *Journal of Applied Psychology* 92, no. 2 (2007), pp. 555–566.

18. T. A. Wright and D. G. Bonett, "The Moderating Effects of Employee Tenure on the Relation Between Organizational Commitment and Job Performance: A Meta-Analysis," *Journal of Applied Psychology* (December 2002), pp. 1183–1190.

19. T. W. H. Ng, D. C. Feldman, and S. S. K. Lam, "Psychological Contract Breaches, Organizational Commitment, and Innovation-Related Behaviors: A Latent Growth Modeling Approach," *Journal of Applied Psychology* 95 (2010), pp. 744–751.

20. See, for instance, K. Bentein, C. Vandenberghe, R. Vandenberg, and F. Stinglhamber, "The Role of Change in the Relationship between Commitment and Turnover: A Latent Growth Modeling Approach," *Journal of Applied Psychology* 90 (2005), pp. 468–482; and J. D. Kammeyer-Mueller, C. R. Wanberg, T. M. Glomb, and D. Ahlburg, "The Role of Temporal Shifts in Turnover Processes: It's About Time." *Journal of Applied Psychology* 90 (2005), pp. 644–658.

21. J. P. Hausknecht, N. J. Hiller, and R. J. Vance, "Work-Unit Absenteeism: Effects of Satisfaction, Commitment, Labor Market Conditions, and Time," *Academy of Management Journal* 51 (2008), pp. 1223–1245.

22. L. Rhoades, R. Eisenberger, and S. Armeli, "Affective Commitment to the Organization: The Contribution of Perceived Organizational Support," *Journal of Applied Psychology* 86, no. 5 (2001), pp. 825–836.

23. C. Vandenberghe, K. Bentein, R. Michon, J. Chebat, M. Tremblay, and J. Fils, "An Examination of the Role of Perceived Support and Employee Commitment in Employee–Customer Encounters," *Journal of Applied Psychology* 92, no. 4 (2007), pp. 1177–1187; and P. Eder and R. Eisenberger, "Perceived Organizational Support: Reducing the Negative Influence of Coworker Withdrawal Behavior," *Journal of Management* 34, no. 1 (2008), pp. 55–68.

24. J. Farh, R. D. Hackett, and J. Liang, "Individual-Level Cultural Values as Moderators of Perceived Organizational Support—Employee Outcome Relationships in China: Comparing the Effects of Power Distance and Traditionality," *Academy of Management Journal* 50, no. 3 (2007), pp. 715–729.

25. B. L. Rich, J. A. Lepine, and E. R. Crawford, "Job Engagement: Antecedents and Effects on Job Performance," *Academy of Management Journal* 53 (2010), pp. 617–635.

26. J. K. Harter, F. L. Schmidt, and T. L. Hayes, "Business-Unit-Level Relationship Between Employee Satisfaction, Employee Engagement, and Business Outcomes: A Meta-Analysis," *Journal of Applied Psychology* 87, no. 2 (2002), pp. 268–279.

27. R. J. Vance, "Employee Engagement and Commitment: A Guide to Understanding, Measuring, and Increasing Engagement in Your Organization" on www.shrm.org.

28. N. R. Lockwood, *Leveraging Employee Engagement for Competitive Advantage* (Alexandria, VA: Society for Human Resource Management, 2007); and R. J. Vance, *Employee Engagement and Commitment* (Alexandria, VA: Society for Human Resource Management, 2006).

29. W. H. Macey and B. Schneider, "The Meaning of Employee Engagement," *Industrial and Organizational Psychology* 1 (2008), pp. 3–30; A. Saks, "The Meaning and Bleeding of Employee Engagement: How Muddy Is the Water?"

Industrial and Organizational Psychology 1 (2008), pp. 40–43.

30. L. Rhoades and R. Eisenberger, "Perceived Organizational Support: A Review of the Literature," *Journal of Applied Psychology* 87, no. 4 (2002), pp. 698–714; and R. L. Payne and D. Morrison, "The Differential Effects of Negative Affectivity on Measures of Well-Being Versus Job Satisfaction and Organizational Commitment," *Anxiety, Stress & Coping: An International Journal* 15, no. 3 (2002), pp. 231–244.

31. For problems with the concept of job satisfaction, see R. Hodson, "Workplace Behaviors," *Work and Occupations* (August 1991), pp. 271–290; and H. M. Weiss and R. Cropanzano, "Affective Events Theory: A Theoretical Discussion of the Structure, Causes and Consequences of Affective Experiences at Work," in B. M. Staw and L. L. Cummings (eds.), *Research in Organizational Behavior,* vol. 18 (Greenwich, CT: JAI Press, 1996), pp. 1–3.

32. The Wyatt Company's 1989 national WorkAmerica study identified 12 dimensions of satisfaction: Work organization, working conditions, communications, job performance and performance review, co-workers, supervision, company management, pay, benefits, career development and training, job content and satisfaction, and company image and change.

33. See E. Spector, *Job Satisfaction: Application, Assessment, Causes, and Consequences* (Thousand Oaks, CA: Sage, 1997), p. 3.

34. J. Wanous, A. E. Reichers, and M. J. Hudy, "Overall Job Satisfaction: How Good Are Single-Item Measures?" *Journal of Applied Psychology* (April 1997), pp. 247–252.

35. A. F. Chelte, J. Wright, and C. Tausky, "Did Job Satisfaction Really Drop During the 1970s?" *Monthly Labor Review* (November 1982), pp. 33–36; "Job Satisfaction High in America, Says Conference Board Study," *Monthly Labor Review* (February 1985), p. 52; K. Bowman, "Attitudes About Work, Chores, and Leisure in America," *AEI Opinion Studies* (August 25, 2003); and J. Pepitone, "U.S. Job Satisfaction Hits 22-Year Low," *CNNMoney.com* (January 5, 2010).

36. W. K. Balzer, J. A. Kihm, P. C. Smith, J. L. Irwin, P. D. Bachiochi, C. Robie, E. F. Sinar, and L. F. Parra, *Users' Manual for the Job Descriptive Index (JDI; 1997 Revision) and the Job in General Scales* (Bowling Green, OH: Bowling Green State University, 1997).

37. M. J. Gelfand, M. Erez, and Z. Aycan, "Cross-Cultural Organizational Behavior," Annual Review of Psychology 58 (2007), pp. 479–514; and A. S. Tsui, S. S. Nifadkar, and A. Y. Ou, "Cross-National, Cross-Cultural Organizational Behavior Research: Advances, Gaps, and Recommendations," Journal of Management (June 2007), pp. 426–478.

38. M. Benz and B. S. Frey, "The Value of Autonomy: Evidence from the Self-Employed in 23 Countries," working paper 173, Institute for Empirical Research in Economics, University of Zurich, November 2003 (ssrn.com/abstract[equals]475140); and P. Warr, Work, Happiness, and Unhappiness (Mahwah, NJ: Laurence Erlbaum, 2007).

39. J. Barling, E. K. Kelloway, and R. D. Iverson, "High-Quality Work, Job Satisfaction, and Occupational Injuries," *Journal of Applied Psychology* 88, no. 2 (2003), pp. 276–283; and F. W. Bond and D. Bunce, "The Role of Acceptance and Job Control in Mental Health, Job Satisfaction, and Work Performance," *Journal of Applied Psychology* 88, no. 6 (2003), pp. 1057–1067.

40. S. E. Humphrey, J. D. Nahrgang, and F. P. Morgeson, "Integrating Motivational, Social, and Contextual Work Design Features: A Meta-Analytic Summary and Theoretical Extension of the Work Design Literature," *Journal of Applied Psychology* 92, no. 5 (2007), pp. 1332–1356; and D. S. Chiaburu and D. A. Harrison, "Do Peers Make the Place? Conceptual Synthesis and Meta-Analysis of Coworker Effect on Perceptions, Attitudes, OCBs, and Performance," *Journal of Applied Psychology* 93, no. 5 (2008), pp. 1082–1103.

41. E. Diener, E. Sandvik, L. Seidlitz, and M. Diener, "The Relationship Between Income and Subjective Well-Being: Relative or Absolute?" *Social Indicators Research* 28 (1993), pp. 195–223.

42. E. Diener and M. E. P. Seligman, "Beyond Money: Toward an Economy of Well-Being," *Psychological Science in the Public Interest* 5, no. 1 (2004), pp. 1–31; and A. Grant, "Money = Happiness? That's Rich: Here's the Science Behind the Axiom," *The (South Mississippi) Sun Herald* (January 8, 2005).

43. T. A. Judge and C. Hurst, "The Benefits and Possible Costs of Positive Core Self-Evaluations: A Review and Agenda for Future Research," in D. Nelson and C. L. Cooper (eds.), *Positive Organizational Behavior* (London, UK: Sage Publications, 2007), pp. 159–174.

44. See D. Farrell, "Exit, Voice, Loyalty, and Neglect as Responses to Job Dissatisfaction: A Multidimensional Scaling Study," *Academy of Management Journal* (December 1983), pp. 596–606; C. E. Rusbult, D. Farrell, G. Rogers, and A. G. Mainous III, "Impact of Exchange Variables on Exit, Voice, Loyalty, and Neglect: An Integrative Model of Responses to Declining Job Satisfaction," *Academy of Management Journal* (September 1988), pp. 599–627; M. J. Withey and W. H. Cooper, "Predicting Exit, Voice, Loyalty, and Neglect," *Administrative Science Quarterly* (December 1989), pp. 521–539; J. Zhou and J. M. George, "When Job Dissatisfaction Leads to Creativity: Encouraging the Expression of Voice," *Academy of Management Journal* (August 2001), pp. 682–696; J. B. Olson-Buchanan and W. R. Boswell, "The Role of Employee Loyalty and Formality in Voicing Discontent," *Journal of Applied Psychology* (December 2002), pp. 1167–1174; and A. Davis-Blake, J. P. Broschak, and E. George, "Happy Together? How Using Nonstandard Workers Affects Exit, Voice, and Loyalty Among Standard Employees," *Academy of Management Journal* 46, no. 4 (2003), pp. 475–485.

45. R. B. Freeman, "Job Satisfaction as an Economic Variable," *American Economic Review* (January 1978), pp. 135–141.

46. T. A. Judge, C. J. Thoresen, J. E. Bono, and G. K. Patton, "The Job Satisfaction–Job Performance Relationship: A Qualitative and Quantitative Review," *Psychological Bulletin* (May 2001), pp. 376–407.

47. C. Ostroff, "The Relationship Between Satisfaction, Attitudes, and Performance: An Organizational Level Analysis," *Journal of Applied Psychology* (December 1992), pp. 963–974; A. M. Ryan, M. J. Schmit, and R. Johnson, "Attitudes and Effectiveness: Examining Relations at an Organizational Level," *Personnel Psychology* (Winter 1996), pp. 853–882; and J. K. Harter, F. L. Schmidt, and T. L. Hayes, "Business-Unit Level Relationship Between Employee Satisfaction, Employee Engagement, and Business Outcomes: A Meta-Analysis," *Journal of Applied Psychology* (April 2002), pp. 268–279.

48. See P. Podsakoff, S. B. MacKenzie, J. B. Paine, and D. G. Bachrach, "Organizational Citizenship Behaviors: A Critical Review of the Theoretical and Empirical Literature and

Suggestions for Future Research," *Journal of Management* 26, no. 3 (2000), pp. 513–563.

49. B. J. Hoffman, C. A. Blair, J. P. Maeriac, and D. J. Woehr, "Expanding the Criterion Domain? A Quantitative Review of the OCB Literature," *Journal of Applied Psychology* 92, no. 2 (2007), pp. 555–566.

50. S. L. Blader and T. R. Tyler, "Testing and Extending the Group Engagement Model: Linkages Between Social Identity, Procedural Justice, Economic Outcomes, and Extrarole Behavior," *Journal of Applied Psychology* 94, no. 2 (2009), pp. 445–464.

51. D. S. Chiaburu and D. A. Harrison, "Do Peers Make the Place? Conceptual Synthesis and Meta-Analysis of Coworker Effect on Perceptions, Attitudes, OCBs, and Performance," *Journal of Applied Psychology* 93, no. 5 (2008), pp. 1082–1103.

52. R. Ilies, I. S. Fulmer, M. Spitzmuller, and M. D. Johnson, "Personality and Citizenship Behavior: The Mediating Role of Job Satisfaction," *Journal of Applied Psychology* 94 (2009), pp. 945–959.

53. R. Ilies, B. A. Scott, and T. A. Judge, "The Interactive Effects of Personal Traits and Experienced States on Intraindividual Patterns of Citizenship Behavior," *Academy of Management Journal* 49 (2006), pp. 561–575.

54. See, for instance, D. J. Koys, "The Effects of Employee Satisfaction, Organizational Citizenship Behavior, and Turnover on Organizational Effectiveness: A Unit-Level, Longitudinal Study," *Personnel Psychology* (Spring 2001), pp. 101–114; and C. Vandenberghe, K. Bentein, R. Michon, J. Chebat, M. Tremblay, and J. Fils, "An Examination of the Role of Perceived Support and Employee Commitment in Employee-Customer Encounters," *Journal of Applied Psychology* 92, no. 4 (2007), pp. 1177–1187; and M. Schulte, C. Ostroff, S. Shmulyian, and A. Kinicki, "Organizational Climate Configurations: Relationships to Collective Attitudes, Customer Satisfaction, and Financial Performance," *Journal of Applied Psychology* 94 (2009), pp. 618–634.

55. J. M. O'Brien, "Zappos Knows How to Kick It," *Fortune* (February 2, 2009), pp. 55–60.

56. T. Frank, "Report: Low Morale May Hurt Airport Security," *USA Today* (June 25, 2008), p. 3A; and J. Bailey, "Fliers Fed Up? The Employees Feel the Same," *New York Times* (December 22, 2007), pp. A1, A18.

57. E. A. Locke, "The Nature and Causes of Job Satisfaction," in M. D. Dunnette (ed.), *Handbook of Industrial and Organizational Psychology* (Chicago: Rand McNally, 1976), p. 1331; K. D. Scott and G. S. Taylor, "An Examination of Conflicting Findings on the Relationship Between Job Satisfaction and Absenteeism: A Meta-Analysis," *Academy of Management Journal* (September 1985), pp. 599–612; and R. Steel and J. R. Rentsch, "Influence of Cumulation Strategies on the Long-Range Prediction of Absenteeism," *Academy of Management Journal* (December 1995), pp. 1616–1634.

58. J. P. Hausknecht, N. J. Hiller, and R. J. Vance, "Work-Unit Absenteeism: Effects of Satisfaction, Commitment, Labor Market Conditions, and Time," *Academy of Management Journal* 51, no. 6 (2008), pp. 1123–1245.

59. W. Hom and R. W. Griffeth, *Employee Turnover* (Cincinnati, OH: South-Western Publishing, 1995); R. W. Griffeth, P. W. Hom, and S. Gaertner, "A Meta-Analysis of Antecedents and Correlates of Employee Turnover: Update, Moderator Tests, and Research Implications for the Next Millennium," *Journal of Management* 26, no. 3 (2000), p. 479.

60. T. H. Lee, B. Gerhart, I. Weller, and C. O. Trevor, "Understanding Voluntary Turnover: Path-Specific Job Satisfaction Effects and the Importance of Unsolicited Job Offers," *Academy of Management Journal* 51, no. 4 (2008), pp. 651–671.

61. P. E. Spector, S. Fox, L. M. Penney, K. Bruursema, A. Goh, and S. Kessler, "The Dimensionality of Counterproductivity: Are All Counterproductive Behaviors Created Equal?" *Journal of Vocational Behavior* 68, no. 3 (2006), pp. 446–460; and D. S. Chiaburu and D. A. Harrison, "Do Peers Make the Place? Conceptual Synthesis and Meta-Analysis of Coworker Effect on Perceptions, Attitudes, OCBs, and Performance," *Journal of Applied Psychology* 93, no. 5 (2008), pp. 1082–1103.

62. K. Holland, "Inside the Minds of Your Employees," *New York Times* (January 28, 2007), p. B1; "Study Sees Link Between Morale and Stock Price," *Workforce Management* (February 27, 2006), p. 15; and "The Workplace as a Solar System," *New York Times* (October 28, 2006), p. B5.

63. E. White, "How Surveying Workers Can Pay Off," *Wall Street Journal* (June 18, 2007), p. B3.

64. Harrison, D. A., Newman, D. A., & Roth, P. L., "How Important Are Job Attitudes?: Meta-analytic Comparisons for Integrative Behavioral Outcomes and Time Sequences," *Academy of Management Journal*, no. 49 (2006), pp. 320–321.

CHAPTER 4

1. See, for instance, C. D. Fisher and N. M. Ashkanasy, "The Emerging Role of Emotions in Work Life: An Introduction," *Journal of Organizational Behavior,* Special Issue 2000, pp. 123–129; N. M. Ashkanasy, C. E. J. Hartel, and W. J. Zerbe (eds.), *Emotions in the Workplace: Research, Theory, and Practice* (Westport, CT: Quorum Books, 2000); N. M. Ashkanasy and C. S. Daus, "Emotion in the Workplace: The New Challenge for Managers," *Academy of Management Executive* (February 2002), pp. 76–86; and N. M. Ashkanasy, C. E. J. Hartel, and C. S. Daus, "Diversity and Emotion: The New Frontiers in Organizational Behavior Research," *Journal of Management* 28, no. 3 (2002), pp. 307–338.

2. See, for example, L. L. Putnam and D. K. Mumby, "Organizations, Emotion and the Myth of Rationality," in S. Fineman (ed.), *Emotion in Organizations* (Thousand Oaks, CA: Sage, 1993), pp. 36–57; and J. Martin, K. Knopoff, and C. Beckman, "An Alternative to Bureaucratic Impersonality and Emotional Labor: Bounded Emotionality at the Body Shop," *Administrative Science Quarterly* (June 1998), pp. 429–469.

3. B. E. Ashforth and R. H. Humphrey, "Emotion in the Workplace: A Reappraisal," *Human Relations* (February 1995), pp. 97–125.

4. S. G. Barsade and D. E. Gibson, "Why Does Affect Matter in Organizations?" *Academy of Management Perspectives* (February 2007), pp. 36–59.

5. See N. H. Frijda, "Moods, Emotion Episodes and Emotions," in M. Lewis and J. M. Haviland (eds.), *Handbook of Emotions* (New York: Guilford Press, 1993), pp. 381–403.

6. H. M. Weiss and R. Cropanzano, "Affective Events Theory: A Theoretical Discussion of the Structure, Causes and Consequences of Affective Experiences at Work," in B. M. Staw and L. L. Cummings (eds.), *Research in Organizational Behavior,* vol. 18 (Greenwich, CT: JAI Press, 1996), pp. 17–19.

7. See P. Ekman and R. J. Davidson (eds.), *The Nature of Emotions: Fundamental Questions* (Oxford, UK: Oxford University Press, 1994).

8. Frijda, "Moods, Emotion Episodes and Emotions," p. 381.

9. See Ekman and Davidson (eds.), *The Nature of Emotions.*

10. See, for example, P. Ekman, "An Argument for Basic Emotions," *Cognition and Emotion* (May/July 1992), pp. 169–200; C. E. Izard, "Basic Emotions, Relations Among Emotions, and Emotion–Cognition Relations," *Psychological Bulletin* (November 1992), pp. 561–565; and J. L. Tracy and R. W. Robins, "Emerging Insights into the Nature and Function of Pride," *Current Directions in Psychological Science* 16, no. 3 (2007), pp. 147–150.

11. R. C. Solomon, "Back to Basics: On the Very Idea of 'Basic Emotions,'" *Journal for the Theory of Social Behaviour* 32, no. 2 (June 2002), pp. 115–144.

12. Weiss and Cropanzano, "Affective Events Theory," pp. 20–22.

13. Cited in R. D. Woodworth, *Experimental Psychology* (New York: Holt, 1938).

14. D. Watson, L. A. Clark, and A. Tellegen, "Development and Validation of Brief Measures of Positive and Negative Affect: The PANAS Scales," *Journal of Personality and Social Psychology* (1988), pp. 1063–1070.

15. A. Ben-Ze'ev, *The Subtlety of Emotions* (Cambridge, MA: MIT Press, 2000), p. 94.

16. Ben-Ze'ev, *The Subtlety of Emotions,* p. 99.

17. J. T. Cacioppo and W. L. Gardner, "Emotion," in *Annual Review of Psychology,* vol. 50 (Palo Alto, CA: Annual Reviews, 1999), pp. 191–214.

18. S. Oishi, E. Diener, and C. Napa Scollon, "Cross-Situational Consistency of Affective Experiences Across Cultures," *Journal of Personality & Social Psychology* 86, no. 3 (2004), pp. 460–472.

19. Eid and Diener, "Norms for Experiencing Emotions in Different Cultures."

20. L. M. Poverny and S. Picascia, "There Is No Crying in Business," *Womensmedia.com,* October 20, 2009, www.womensmedia.com/new/Crying-at-Work.shtml.

21. A. R. Damasio, *Descartes' Error: Emotion, Reason, and the Human Brain* (New York: Quill, 1994).

22. Ibid.

23. J. Haidt, "The New Synthesis in Moral Psychology," *Science* 316 (May 18, 2007), pp. 998, 1002; I. E. de Hooge, R. M. A. Nelissen, S. M. Breugelmans, and M. Zeelenberg, "What is Moral about Guilt? Acting 'Prosocially' at the Disadvantage of Others," *Journal of Personality and Social Psychology* 100 (2011), pp. 462–473; and C. A. Hutcherson and J. J. Gross, "The Moral Emotions: A Social-Functionalist Account of Anger, Disgust, and Contempt," *Journal of Personality and Social Psychology* 100 (2011), pp. 719–737.

24. R. J. Larsen and E. Diener, "Affect Intensity as an Individual Difference Characteristic: A Review," *Journal of Research in Personality* 21 (1987), pp. 1–39.

25. D. Watson, *Mood and Temperament* (New York: Guilford Press, 2000).

26. J. J. A. Denissen, L. Butalid, L. Penke, and M. A. G. van Aken, "The Effects of Weather on Daily Mood: A Multilevel Approach," *Emotion* 8, no. 5 (2008), pp. 662–667; M. C. Keller, B. L. Fredrickson, O. Ybarra, S. Côté, K. Johnson, J. Mikels, A. Conway, and T. Wagner, "A Warm Heart and a Clear Head: The Contingent Effects of Weather on Mood and Cognition," *Psychological Science* 16 (2005) pp. 724–731; and Watson, *Mood and Temperament.*

27. Watson, *Mood and Temperament,* p. 100.

28. J. A. Fuller, J. M. Stanton, G. G. Fisher, C. Spitzmüller, S. S. Russell, and P. C. Smith, "A Lengthy Look at the Daily Grind: Time Series Analysis of Events, Mood, Stress, and Satisfaction," *Journal of Applied Psychology* 88, no. 6 (December 2003), pp. 1019–1033.

29. A. M. Isen, "Positive Affect as a Source of Human Strength," in L. G. Aspinwall and U. Staudinger (eds.), *The Psychology of Human Strengths* (Washington, DC: American Psychological Association, 2003), pp. 179–195.

30. Watson, *Mood and Temperament.*

31. *Sleep in America Poll* (Washington, DC: National Sleep Foundation, 2005), www.kintera.org/atf/cf/%7Bf6bf2668-a1b4-4fe8-8d1a-a5d39340d9cb%7D/2005_summary_of_findings.pdf.

32. M. Lavidor, A. Weller, and H. Babkoff, "How Sleep Is Related to Fatigue," *British Journal of Health Psychology* 8 (2003), pp. 95–105; and J. J. Pilcher and E. Ott, "The Relationships Between Sleep and Measures of Health and Well-Being in College Students: A Repeated Measures Approach," *Behavioral Medicine* 23 (1998), pp. 170–178.

33. E. K. Miller and J. D. Cohen, "An Integrative Theory of Prefrontal Cortex Function," *Annual Review of Neuroscience* 24 (2001), pp. 167–202.

34. B. A. Scott and T. A. Judge, "Insomnia, Emotions, and Job Satisfaction: A Multilevel Study," *Journal of Management* 32, no. 5 (2006), pp. 622–645.

35. P. R. Giacobbi, H. A. Hausenblas, and N. Frye, "A Naturalistic Assessment of the Relationship Between Personality, Daily Life Events, Leisure-Time Exercise, and Mood," *Psychology of Sport & Exercise* 6, no. 1 (January 2005), pp. 67–81.

36. L. L. Carstensen, M. Pasupathi, M. Ulrich, and J. R. Nesselroade, "Emotional Experience in Everyday Life Across the Adult Life Span," *Journal of Personality and Social Psychology* 79, no. 4 (2000), pp. 644–655.

37. M. LaFrance and M. Banaji, "Toward a Reconsideration of the Gender–Emotion Relationship," in M. Clark (ed.), *Review of Personality and Social Psychology,* vol. 14 (Newbury Park, CA: Sage, 1992), pp. 178–197; and A. M. Kring and A. H. Gordon, "Sex Differences in Emotion: Expression, Experience, and Physiology," *Journal of Personality and Social Psychology* (March 1998), pp. 686–703.

38. M. G. Gard and A. M. Kring, "Sex Differences in the Time Course of Emotion," *Emotion* 7, no. 2 (2007), pp. 429–437; M. Jakupcak, K. Salters, K. L. Gratz, and L. Roemer, "Masculinity and Emotionality: An Investigation of Men's Primary and Secondary Emotional Responding," *Sex Roles* 49 (2003), pp. 111–120; and M. Grossman and W. Wood, "Sex Differences in Intensity of Emotional Experience: A Social Role Interpretation," *Journal of Personality and Social Psychology* (November 1992), pp. 1010–1022.

39. A. H. Fischer, P. M. Rodriguez Mosquera, A. E. M. van Vianen, and A. S. R. Manstead, "Gender and Culture Differences in Emotion," *Emotion* 4 (2004), pp. 84–87.

40. L. F. Barrett and E. Bliss-Moreau, "She's Emotional. He's Having a Bad Day: Attributional Explanations for Emotion Stereotypes," *Emotion* 9 (2009), pp. 649–658.

41. D. V. Becker, D. T. Kenrick, S. L. Neuberg, K. C. Blackwell, and D. M. Smith, "The Confounded Nature of Angry Men and Happy Women," *Journal of Personality and Social Psychology* 92 (2007), pp. 179–190.

42. P. Ekman, W. V. Friesen, and M. O'Sullivan, "Smiles When Lying," in P. Ekman and E. L. Rosenberg (eds.), *What the*

Face Reveals: Basic and Applied Studies of Spontaneous Expression Using the Facial Action Coding System (FACS) (London: Oxford University Press, 1997), pp. 201–216.

43. A. Grandey, "Emotion Regulation in the Workplace: A New Way to Conceptualize Emotional Labor," *Journal of Occupational Health Psychology* 5, no. 1 (2000), pp. 95–110; and R. Cropanzano, D. E. Rupp, and Z. S. Byrne, "The Relationship of Emotional Exhaustion to Work Attitudes, Job Performance, and Organizational Citizenship Behavior," *Journal of Applied Psychology* (February 2003), pp. 160–169.

44. A. R. Hochschild, "Emotion Work, Feeling Rules, and Social Structure," *American Journal of Sociology* (November 1979), pp. 551–575; W.-C. Tsai, "Determinants and Consequences of Employee Displayed Positive Emotions," *Journal of Management* 27, no. 4 (2001), pp. 497–512; M. W. Kramer and J. A. Hess, "Communication Rules for the Display of Emotions in Organizational Settings," *Management Communication Quarterly* (August 2002), pp. 66–80; and J. M. Diefendorff and E. M. Richard, "Antecedents and Consequences of Emotional Display Rule Perceptions," *Journal of Applied Psychology* (April 2003), pp. 284–294.

45. B. M. DePaulo, "Nonverbal Behavior and Self-Presentation," *Psychological Bulletin* (March 1992), pp. 203–243.

46. J. M. Diefendorff and G. J. Greguras, "Contextualizing Emotional Display Rules: Examining the Roles of Targets and Discrete Emotions in Shaping Display Rule Perceptions," *Journal of Management* 35 (2009), pp. 880–898.

47. Solomon, "Back to Basics."

48. C. M. Brotheridge and R. T. Lee, "Development and Validation of the Emotional Labour Scale," *Journal of Occupational & Organizational Psychology* 76 (2003), pp. 365–379.

49. A. A. Grandey, "When 'The Show Must Go On': Surface Acting and Deep Acting as Determinants of Emotional Exhaustion and Peer-Rated Service Delivery," *Academy of Management Journal* (February 2003), pp. 86–96; and A. A. Grandey, D. N. Dickter, and H. Sin, "The Customer Is Not Always Right: Customer Aggression and Emotion Regulation of Service Employees," *Journal of Organizational Behavior* 25 (2004), pp. 397–418.

50. J. M. Diefendorff, R. J. Erickson, A. A. Grandey, and J. J. Dahling, "Emotional Display Rules as Work Unit Norms: A Multilevel Analysis of Emotional Labor among Nurses," *Journal of Occupational Health Psychology* 16 (2011), pp. 170–186.

51. J. P. Trougakos, D. J. Beal, S. G. Green, and H. M. Weiss, "Making the Break Count: An Episodic Examination of Recovery Activities, Emotional Experiences, and Positive Affective Displays," *Academy of Management Journal* 51 (2008), pp. 131–146.

52. This section is based on Daniel Goleman, *Emotional Intelligence* (New York: Bantam, 1995); P. Salovey and D. Grewal, "The Science of Emotional Intelligence," *Current Directions in Psychological Science* 14, no. 6 (2005), pp. 281–285; M. Davies, L. Stankov, and R. D. Roberts, "Emotional Intelligence: In Search of an Elusive Construct," *Journal of Personality and Social Psychology* (October 1998), pp. 989–1015; D. Geddes and R. R. Callister, "Crossing the Line(s): A Dual Threshold Model of Anger in Organizations," *Academy of Management Review* 32, no. 3 (2007), pp. 721–746.

53. C. Cherniss, "The Business Case for Emotional Intelligence," *Consortium for Research on Emotional Intelligence in Organizations*, 1999, www.eiconsortium.org/reports/business_case_for_ei.html.

54. K. S. Law, C. Wong, and L. J. Song, "The Construct and Criterion Validity of Emotional Intelligence and Its Potential Utility for Management Studies," *Journal of Applied Psychology* 89, no. 3 (2004), pp. 483–496.

55. H. A. Elfenbein and N. Ambady, "Predicting Workplace Outcomes from the Ability to Eavesdrop on Feelings," *Journal of Applied Psychology* 87, no. 5 (October 2002), pp. 963–971.

56. D. L. Joseph and D. A. Newman, "Emotional Intelligence: An Integrative Meta-Analysis and Cascading Model," *Journal of Applied Psychology* 95 (2010), pp. 54–78.

57. R. Bar-On, D. Tranel, N. L. Denburg, and A. Bechara, "Exploring the Neurological Substrate of Emotional and Social Intelligence," *Brain* 126, no. 8 (August 2003), pp. 1790–1800.

58. P. A. Vernon, K. V. Petrides, D. Bratko, and J. A. Schermer, "A Behavioral Genetic Study of Trait Emotional Intelligence," *Emotion* 8, no. 5 (2008), pp. 635–642.

59. E. A. Locke, "Why Emotional Intelligence Is an Invalid Concept," *Journal of Organizational Behavior* 26, no. 4 (June 2005), pp. 425–431.

60. J. D. Mayer, R. D. Roberts, and S. G. Barsade, "Human Abilities: Emotional Intelligence," *Annual Review of Psychology* 59 (2008), pp. 507–536; H. A. Elfenbein, "Emotion in Organizations: A Review and Theoretical Integration," *Academy of Management Annals* 1 (2008), pp. 315–386; and D. L. Joseph and D. A. Newman, "Emotional Intelligence: An Integrative Meta-Analysis and Cascading Model," *Journal of Applied Psychology* 95 (2010), pp. 54–78.

61. J. M. Conte, "A Review and Critique of Emotional Intelligence Measures," *Journal of Organizational Behavior* 26, no. 4 (June 2005), pp. 433–440; and M. Davies, L. Stankov, and R. D. Roberts, "Emotional Intelligence," pp. 989–1015.

62. T. Decker, "Is Emotional Intelligence a Viable Concept?" *Academy of Management Review* 28, no. 2 (April 2003), pp. 433–440; and Davies, Stankov, and Roberts, "Emotional Intelligence."

63. D. L. Joseph and D. A. Newman, "Emotional Intelligence: An Integrative Meta-Analysis and Cascading Model," *Journal of Applied Psychology* 95 (2010), pp. 54–78.

64. F. J. Landy, "Some Historical and Scientific Issues Related to Research on Emotional Intelligence," *Journal of Organizational Behavior* 26, no. 4 (June 2005), pp. 411–424.

65. S. L. Koole, "The Psychology of Emotion Regulation: An Integrative Review," *Cognition and Emotion* 23 (2009), pp. 4–41.

66. S. Srivastava, M. Tamir, K. M. McGonigal, O. P. John, and J. J. Gross, "The Social Costs of Emotional Suppression: A Prospective Study of the Transition to College," *Journal of Personality and Social Psychology* 96 (2009), pp. 883–897; Y. Liu, L. M. Prati, P. L. Perrewé, and R. A. Brymer, "Individual Differences in Emotion Regulation, Emotional Experiences at Work, and Work-Related Outcomes: A Two-Study Investigation," *Journal of Applied Social Psychology* 40 (2010), pp. 1515–1538; and H. A. Wadlinger and D. M. Isaacowitz, "Fixing our Focus: Training Attention to Regulate Emotion," *Personality and Social Psychology Review* 15 (2011), pp. 75–102.

67. L. K. Barber, P. G. Bagsby, and D. C. Munz, "Affect Regulation Strategies for Promoting (or Preventing) Flourishing Emotional Health," *Personality and Individual Differences* 49 (2010), pp. 663–666.

68. J. Park and M. R. Banaji, "Mood and Heuristics: The Influence of Happy and Sad States on Sensitivity and Bias in Stereotyping," *Journal of Personality and Social Psychology* 78, no. 6 (2000), pp. 1005–1023.

69. See A. M. Isen, "Positive Affect and Decision Making," in M. Lewis and J. M. Haviland-Jones (eds.), *Handbook of Emotions,* 2nd ed. (New York: Guilford, 2000), pp. 261–277.

70. L. B. Alloy and L. Y. Abramson, "Judgment of Contingency in Depressed and Nondepressed Students: Sadder but Wiser?" *Journal of Experimental Psychology: General* 108 (1979), pp. 441–485.

71. N. Ambady and H. M. Gray, "On Being Sad and Mistaken: Mood Effects on the Accuracy of Thin-Slice Judgments," *Journal of Personality and Social Psychology* 83, no. 4 (2002), pp. 947–961.

72. S. Lyubomirsky, L. King, and E. Diener, "The Benefits of Frequent Positive Affect: Does Happiness Lead to Success?" *Psychological Bulletin* 131, no. 6 (2005), pp. 803–855; and M. Baas, C. K. W. De Dreu, and B. A. Nijstad, "A Meta-Analysis of 25 Years of Mood-Creativity Research: Hedonic Tone, Activation, or Regulatory Focus," *Psychological Bulletin* 134 (2008), pp. 779–806.

73. M. J. Grawitch, D. C. Munz, and E. K. Elliott, "Promoting Creativity in Temporary Problem-Solving Groups: The Effects of Positive Mood and Autonomy in Problem Definition on Idea-Generating Performance," *Group Dynamics* 7, no. 3 (September 2003), pp. 200–213.

74. S. Lyubomirsky, L. King, and E. Diener, "The Benefits of Frequent Positive Affect: Does Happiness Lead to Success?" *Psychological Bulletin* 131, no. 6 (2005), pp. 803–855.

75. N. Madjar, G. R. Oldham, and M. G. Pratt, "There's No Place Like Home? The Contributions of Work and Nonwork Creativity Support to Employees' Creative Performance," *Academy of Management Journal* 45, no. 4 (2002), pp. 757–767.

76. J. M. George and J. Zhou, "Understanding When Bad Moods Foster Creativity and Good Ones Don't: The Role of Context and Clarity of Feelings," *Journal of Applied Psychology* 87, no. 4 (August 2002), pp. 687–697; and J. P. Forgas and J. M. George, "Affective Influences on Judgments and Behavior in Organizations: An Information Processing Perspective," *Organizational Behavior and Human Decision Processes* 86, no. 1 (2001), pp. 3–34.

77. C. K. W. De Dreu, M. Baas, and B. A. Nijstad, "Hedonic Tone and Activation Level in the Mood-Creativity Link: Toward a Dual Pathway to Creativity Model," *Journal of Personality and Social Psychology* 94, no. 5 (2008), pp. 739–756; J. M. George and J. Zhou, "Dual Tuning in a Supportive Context: Joint Contributions of Positive Mood, Negative Mood, and Supervisory Behaviors to Employee Creativity," *Academy of Management Journal* 50, no. 3 (2007), pp. 605–622.

78. A. Erez and A. M. Isen, "The Influence of Positive Affect on the Components of Expectancy Motivation," *Journal of Applied Psychology* 87, no. 6 (2002), pp. 1055–1067.

79. R. Ilies and T. A. Judge, "Goal Regulation Across Time: The Effect of Feedback and Affect," *Journal of Applied Psychology* 90, no. 3 (May 2005), pp. 453–467.

80. W. Tsai, C. Chen, and H. Liu, "Test of a Model Linking Employee Positive Moods and Task Performance," *Journal of Applied Psychology* 92, no. 6 (2007), pp. 1570–1583.

81. K. M. Lewis, "When Leaders Display Emotion: How Followers Respond to Negative Emotional Expression of Male and Female Leaders," *Journal of Organizational Behavior,* March 2000, pp. 221–234; and J. M. George, "Emotions and Leadership: The Role of Emotional Intelligence," *Human Relations* (August 2000), pp. 1027–1055.

82. Ashforth and Humphrey, "Emotion in the Workplace," p. 116.

83. J. E. Bono, H. J. Foldes, G. Vinson, and J. P. Muros, "Workplace Emotions: The Role of Supervision and Leadership," *Journal of Applied Psychology* 92, no. 5 (2007), pp. 1357–1367.

84. G. A. Van Kleef, C. K. W. De Dreu, and A. S. R. Manstead, "The Interpersonal Effects of Emotions in Negotiations: A Motivated Information Processing Approach," *Journal of Personality and Social Psychology* 87, no. 4 (2004), pp. 510–528; and G. A. Van Kleef, C. K. W. De Dreu, and A. S. R. Manstead, "The Interpersonal Effects of Anger and Happiness in Negotiations," *Journal of Personality and Social Psychology* 86, no. 1 (2004), pp. 57–76.

85. E. van Dijk, G. A. Van Kleef, W. Steinel, and I. van Beest, "A Social Functional Approach to Emotions in Bargaining: When Communicating Anger Pays and When It Backfires," *Journal of Personality and Social Psychology* 94, no. 4 (2008), pp. 600–614.

86. K. M. O'Connor and J. A. Arnold, "Distributive Spirals: Negotiation Impasses and the Moderating Role of Disputant Self-Efficacy," *Organizational Behavior and Human Decision Processes* 84, no. 1 (2001), pp. 148–176.

87. B. Shiv, G. Loewenstein, A. Bechara, H. Damasio, and A. R. Damasio, "Investment Behavior and the Negative Side of Emotion," *Psychological Science* 16, no. 6 (2005), pp. 435–439.

88. W.-C. Tsai and Y.-M. Huang, "Mechanisms Linking Employee Affective Delivery and Customer Behavioral Intentions," *Journal of Applied Psychology* (October 2002), pp. 1001–1008.

89. Grandey, "When 'The Show Must Go On.' "

90. See P. B. Barker and A. A. Grandey, "Service with a Smile and Encounter Satisfaction: Emotional Contagion and Appraisal Mechanisms," *Academy of Management Journal* 49, no. 6 (2006), pp. 1229–1238; and S. D. Pugh, "Service with a Smile: Emotional Contagion in the Service Encounter," *Academy of Management Journal* (October 2001), pp. 1018–1027.

91. D. E. Rupp and S. Spencer, "When Customers Lash Out: The Effects of Customer Interactional Injustice on Emotional Labor and the Mediating Role of Emotions, *Journal of Applied Psychology* 91, no. 4 (2006), pp. 971–978; and Tsai and Huang, "Mechanisms Linking Employee Affective Delivery and Customer Behavioral Intentions."

92. R. Ilies and T. A. Judge, "Understanding the Dynamic Relationships Among Personality, Mood, and Job Satisfaction: A Field Experience Sampling Study," *Organizational Behavior and Human Decision Processes* 89 (2002), pp. 1119–1139.

93. R. Rau, "Job Strain or Healthy Work: A Question of Task Design," *Journal of Occupational Health Psychology* 9, no. 4 (October 2004), pp. 322–338; and R. Rau and A. Triemer, "Overtime in Relation to Blood Pressure and Mood During Work, Leisure, and Night Time," *Social Indicators Research* 67, no. 1–2 (June 2004), pp. 51–73.

94. Z. Song, M. Foo, and M. A. Uy, "Mood Spillover and Crossover Among Dual-Earner Couples: A Cell Phone Event Sampling Study," *Journal of Applied Psychology* 93, no. 2 (2008), pp. 443–452.

95. T. A. Judge and R. Ilies, "Affect and Job Satisfaction: A Study of Their Relationship at Work and at Home," *Journal of Applied Psychology* 89 (2004), pp. 661–673.

96. See R. J. Bennett and S. L. Robinson, "Development of a Measure of Workplace Deviance," *Journal of Applied Psychology,* June 2000, pp. 349–360; see also P. R. Sackett and C. J. DeVore, "Counterproductive Behaviors at Work," in N. Anderson, D. S. Ones, H. K. Sinangil, and C. Viswesvaran (eds.), *Handbook of Industrial, Work & Organizational Psychology,* vol. 1 (Thousand Oaks, CA: Sage, 2001), pp. 145–164.

97. Bedeian, "Workplace Envy," p. 54.

98. S. C. Douglas, C. Kiewitz, M. Martinko, P. Harvey, Y. Kim, and J. U. Chun, "Cognitions, Emotions, and Evaluations: An Elaboration Likelihood Model for Workplace Aggression," *Academy of Management Review* 33, no. 2 (2008), pp. 425–451.

99. K. Lee and N. J. Allen, "Organizational Citizenship Behavior and Workplace Deviance: The Role of Affect and Cognition," *Journal of Applied Psychology* 87, no. 1 (2002), pp. 131–142; T. A. Judge, B. A. Scott, and R. Ilies, "Hostility, Job Attitudes, and Workplace Deviance: Test of a Multilevel Model," *Journal of Applied Psychology* 91, no. 1 (2006), 126–138; and S. Kaplan, J. C. Bradley, J. N. Luchman, and D. Haynes, "On the Role of Positive and Negative Affectivity in Job Performance: A Meta-Analytic Investigation," *Journal of Applied Psychology* 94, no. 1 (2009), pp. 162–176.

100. R. D. Iverson and P. J. Erwin, "Predicting Occupational Injury: The Role of Affectivity," *Journal of Occupational and Organizational Psychology* 70, no. 2 (1997), pp. 113–128; and Kaplan, Bradley, Luchman, and Haynes, "On the Role of Positive and Negative Affectivity in Job Performance: A Meta-Analytic Investigation."

101. A. M. Isen, A. A. Labroo, and P. Durlach, "An Influence of Product and Brand Name on Positive Affect: Implicit and Explicit Measures," *Motivation & Emotion* 28, no. 1 (March 2004), pp. 43–63.

102. T. Sy, S. Côté, and R. Saavedra, "The Contagious Leader: Impact of the Leader's Mood on the Mood of Group Members, Group Affective Tone, and Group Processes," *Journal of Applied Psychology* 90, no. 2 (2005), pp. 295–305.

103. P. Totterdell, "Catching Moods and Hitting Runs: Mood Linkage and Subjective Performance in Professional Sports Teams," *Journal of Applied Psychology* 85, no. 6 (2000), pp. 848–859.

104. S. Nelton, "Emotions in the Workplace," *Nation's Business* (February 1996), p. 25.

CHAPTER 5

1. G. W. Allport, *Personality: A Psychological Interpretation* (New York: Holt, Rinehart & Winston, 1937), p. 48. For a brief critique of current views on the meaning of personality, see R. T. Hogan and B. W. Roberts, "Introduction: Personality and Industrial and Organizational Psychology," in B. W. Roberts and R. Hogan (eds.), *Personality Psychology in the Workplace* (Washington, DC: American Psychological Association, 2001), pp. 11–12.

2. K. I. van der Zee, J. N. Zaal, and J. Piekstra, "Validation of the Multicultural Personality Questionnaire in the Context of Personnel Selection," *European Journal of Personality* 17, Suppl. 1 (2003), pp. S77–S100.

3. S. A. Birkeland, T. M. Manson, J. L. Kisamore, M. T. Brannick, and M. A. Smith, "A Meta-Analytic Investigation of Job Applicant Faking on Personality Measures," *International Journal of Selection and Assessment* 14, no. 14 (2006), pp. 317–335.

4. See R. Ilies, R. D. Arvey, and T. J. Bouchard, "Darwinism, Behavioral Genetics, and Organizational Behavior: A Review and Agenda for Future Research," *Journal of Organizational Behavior* 27, no. 2 (2006), pp. 121–141; and W. Johnson, E. Turkheimer, I. I. Gottesman, and T. J. Bouchard, Jr., "Beyond Heritability: Twin Studies in Behavioral Research," *Current Directions in Psychological Science* 18, no. 4 (2009), pp. 217–220.

5. S. Srivastava, O. P. John, and S. D. Gosling, "Development of Personality in Early and Middle Adulthood: Set Like Plaster or Persistent Change?" *Journal of Personality and Social Psychology* 84, no. 5 (2003), pp. 1041–1053; and B. W. Roberts, K. E. Walton, and W. Viechtbauer, "Patterns of Mean-Level Change in Personality Traits Across the Life Course: A Meta-Analysis of Longitudinal Studies," *Psychological Bulletin* 132, no. 1 (2006), pp. 1–25.

6. S. E. Hampson and L. R. Goldberg, "A First Large Cohort Study of Personality Trait Stability Over the 40 Years Between Elementary School and Midlife," *Journal of Personality and Social Psychology* 91, no. 4 (2006), pp. 763–779.

7. See A. H. Buss, "Personality as Traits," *American Psychologist* 44, no. 11 (1989), pp. 1378–1388; R. R. McCrae, "Trait Psychology and the Revival of Personality and Culture Studies," *American Behavioral Scientist* 44, no. 1 (2000), pp. 10–31; and L. R. James and M. D. Mazerolle, *Personality in Work Organizations* (Thousand Oaks, CA: Sage, 2002).

8. See, for instance, G. W. Allport and H. S. Odbert, "Trait Names, A Psycholexical Study," *Psychological Monographs,* no. 47 (1936); and R. B. Cattell, "Personality Pinned Down," *Psychology Today* (July 1973), pp. 40–46.

9. R. B. Kennedy and D. A. Kennedy, "Using the Myers-Briggs Type Indicator in Career Counseling," *Journal of Employment Counseling* 41, no. 1 (2004), pp. 38–44.

10. See, for instance, D. J. Pittenger, "Cautionary Comments Regarding the Myers-Briggs Type Indicator," *Consulting Psychology Journal: Practice and Research* 57, no. 3 (2005), pp. 10–221; L. Bess and R. J. Harvey, "Bimodal Score Distributions and the Myers-Briggs Type Indicator: Fact or Artifact?" *Journal of Personality Assessment* 78, no. 1 (2002), pp. 176–186; R. M. Capraro and M. M. Capraro, "Myers-Briggs Type Indicator Score Reliability Across Studies: A Meta-Analytic Reliability Generalization Study," *Educational & Psychological Measurement* 62, no. 4 (2002), pp. 590–602; and R. C. Arnau, B. A. Green, D. H. Rosen, D. H. Gleaves, and J. G. Melancon, "Are Jungian Preferences Really Categorical? An Empirical Investigation Using Taxometric Analysis," *Personality & Individual Differences* 34, no. 2 (2003), pp. 233–251.

11. See, for example, I. Oh, G. Wang, and M. K. Mount, "Validity of Observer Ratings of the Five-Factor Model of Personality Traits: A Meta-Analysis," *Journal of Applied Psychology* 96, no. 4 (2011), pp. 762–773; and M. R. Barrick and M. K. Mount, "Yes, Personality Matters: Moving On to More Important Matters," *Human Performance* 18, no. 4 (2005), pp. 359–372.

12. W. Fleeson and P. Gallagher, "The Implications of Big Five Standing for the Distribution of Trait Manifestation in Behavior: Fifteen Experience-Sampling Studies and a Meta-Analysis,"

Journal of Personality and Social Psychology 97, no. 6 (2009), pp. 1097–1114.

13. See, for instance, I. Oh and C. M. Berry, "The Five-Factor Model of Personality and Managerial Performance: Validity Gains Through the Use of 360 Degree Performance Ratings," *Journal of Applied Psychology* 94, no. 6 (2009), pp. 1498–1513; G. M. Hurtz and J. J. Donovan, "Personality and Job Performance: The Big Five Revisited," *Journal of Applied Psychology* 85, no. 6 (2000), pp. 869–879; J. Hogan and B. Holland, "Using Theory to Evaluate Personality and Job-Performance Relations: A Socioanalytic Perspective," *Journal of Applied Psychology* 88, no. 1 (2003), pp. 100–112; and M. R. Barrick and M. K. Mount, "Select on Conscientiousness and Emotional Stability," in E. A. Locke (ed.), *Handbook of Principles of Organizational Behavior* (Malden, MA: Blackwell, 2004), pp. 15–28.

14. M. K. Mount, M. R. Barrick, and J. P. Strauss, "Validity of Observer Ratings of the Big Five Personality Factors," *Journal of Applied Psychology* 79, no. 2 (1994), p. 272. Additionally confirmed by G. M. Hurtz and J. J. Donovan, "Personality and Job Performance: The Big Five Revisited"; and Oh and Berry, "The Five-Factor Model of Personality and Managerial Performance."

15. A. E. Poropat, "A Meta-Analysis of the Five-Factor Model of Personality and Academic Performance," *Psychological Bulletin* 135, no. 2 (2009), pp. 322–338.

16. A. M. Cianci, H. J. Klein, and G. H. Seijts, "The Effect of Negative Feedback on Tension and Subsequent Performance: The Main and Interactive Effects of Goal Content and Conscientiousness," *Journal of Applied Psychology* 95, no. 4 (2010), pp. 618–630.

17. H. Le, I. Oh, S. B. Robbins, R. Ilies, E. Holland, and P. Westrick, "Too Much of a Good Thing: Curvilinear Relationships Between Personality Traits and Job Performance," *Journal of Applied Psychology* 96, no. 1 (2011), pp. 113–133.

18. T. Bogg and B. W. Roberts, "Conscientiousness and Health-Related Behaviors: A Meta-Analysis of the Leading Behavioral Contributors to Mortality," *Psychological Bulletin* 130, no. 6 (2004), pp. 887–919.

19. G. J. Feist, "A Meta-Analysis of Personality in Scientific and Artistic Creativity," *Personality and Social Psychology Review* 2, no. 4 (1998), pp. 290–309; C. Robert and Y. H. Cheung, "An Examination of the Relationship Between Conscientiousness and Group Performance on a Creative Task," *Journal of Research in Personality* 44, no. 2 (2010), pp. 222–231; and M. Batey, T. Chamorro-Premuzic, and A. Furnham, "Individual Differences in Ideational Behavior. Can the Big Five and Psychometric Intelligence Predict Creativity Scores?" *Creativity Research Journal* 22, no. 1 (2010), pp. 90–97.

20. R. J. Foti and M. A. Hauenstein, "Pattern and Variable Approaches in Leadership Emergence and Effectiveness," *Journal of Applied Psychology* 92, no. 2 (2007), pp. 347–355.

21. L. I. Spirling and R. Persaud, "Extraversion as a Risk Factor," *Journal of the American Academy of Child & Adolescent Psychiatry* 42, no. 2 (2003), p. 130.

22. B. Weiss, and R. S. Feldman, "Looking Good and Lying to Do It: Deception as an Impression Management Strategy in Job Interviews," *Journal of Applied Social Psychology* 36, no. 4 (2006), pp. 1070–1086.

23. R. Ilies, I. S. Fulmer, M. Spitzmuller, and M. D. Johnson, "Personality and Citizenship Behavior: The Mediating Role

24. of Job Satisfaction," *Journal of Applied Psychology* 94, no. 4 (2009), pp. 945–959.

24. See, for instance, S. Yamagata, A. Suzuki, J. Ando, Y. Ono, K. Yutaka, N. Kijima, et al., "Is the Genetic Structure of Human Personality Universal? A Cross-Cultural Twin Study from North America, Europe, and Asia," *Journal of Personality and Social Psychology* 90, no. 6 (2006), pp. 987–998; H. C. Triandis and E. M. Suh, "Cultural Influences on Personality," *Annual Review of Psychology* 53, no. 1 (2002), pp. 133–160; and R. R. McCrae, P. T. Costa Jr., T. A. Martin, V. E. Oryol, A. A. Rukavishnikov, I. G. Senin, et al., "Consensual Validation of Personality Traits Across Cultures," *Journal of Research in Personality* 38, no. 2 (2004), pp. 179–201.

25. A. T. Church and M. S. Katigbak, "Trait Psychology in the Philippines," *American Behavioral Scientist* 44, no. 1, (2000), pp. 73–94.

26. J. F. Salgado, "The Five Factor Model of Personality and Job Performance in the European Community," *Journal of Applied Psychology* 82, no. 1 (1997), pp. 30–43.

27. T. A. Judge and J. E. Bono, "A Rose by Any Other Name . . . Are Self-Esteem, Generalized Self-Efficacy, Neuroticism, and Locus of Control Indicators of a Common Construct?" in B. W. Roberts and R. Hogan (eds.), *Personality Psychology in the Workplace* (Washington, DC: American Psychological Association, 2001), pp. 93–118.

28. A. Erez and T. A. Judge, "Relationship of Core Self-Evaluations to Goal Setting, Motivation, and Performance," *Journal of Applied Psychology* 86, no. 6 (2001), pp. 1270–1279.

29. A. N. Salvaggio, B. Schneider, L. H. Nishi, D. M. Mayer, A. Ramesh, and J. S. Lyon, "Manager Personality, Manager Service Quality Orientation, and Service Climate: Test of a Model," *Journal of Applied Psychology* 92, no. 6 (2007), pp. 1741–1750; B. A. Scott and T. A. Judge, "The Popularity Contest at Work: Who Wins, Why, and What Do They Receive?" *Journal of Applied Psychology* 94, no. 1 (2009), pp. 20–33; and T. A. Judge and C. Hurst, "How the Rich (and Happy) Get Richer (and Happier): Relationship of Core Self-Evaluations to Trajectories in Attaining Work Success," *Journal of Applied Psychology* 93, no. 4 (2008), pp. 849–863.

30. A. M. Grant and A. Wrzesniewksi, "I Won't Let You Down . . . or Will I? Core Self-Evaluations, Other-Orientation, Anticipated Guilt and Gratitude, and Job Performance," *Journal of Applied Psychology* 95, no. 1 (2010), pp. 108–121.

31. U. Malmendier and G. Tate, "CEO Overconfidence and Corporate Investment," *Journal of Finance* 60, no. 6 (2005), pp. 2661–2700.

32. R. Sandomir, "Star Struck," *New York Times* (January 12, 2007), pp. C10, C14.

33. R. Christie and F. L. Geis, *Studies in Machiavellianism* (New York: Academic Press, 1970), p. 312; and S. R. Kessler, A. C. Bandelli, P. E. Spector, W. C. Borman, C. E. Nelson, L. M. Penney, "Re-Examining Machiavelli: A Three-Dimensional Model of Machiavellianism in the Workplace," *Journal of Applied Social Psychology* 40, no. 8 (2010), pp. 1868–1896.

34. J. J. Dahling, B. G. Whitaker, and P. E. Levy, "The Development and Validation of a New Machiavellianism Scale," *Journal of Management* 35, no. 2 (2009), pp. 219–257.

35. Christie and Geis, *Studies in Machiavellianism.*

36. P. Cramer and C. J. Jones, "Narcissism, Identification, and Longitudinal Change in Psychological Health: Dynamic Predictions," *Journal of Research in Personality* 42, no. 5

(2008), pp. 1148–1159; B. M. Galvin, D. A. Waldman, and P. Balthazard, "Visionary Communication Qualities as Mediators of the Relationship between Narcissism and Attributions of Leader Charisma," *Personnel Psychology* 63, no. 3 (2010), pp. 509–537; and T. A. Judge, R. F. Piccolo, and T. Kosalka, "The Bright and Dark Sides of Leader Traits: A Review and Theoretical Extension of the Leader Trait Paradigm," *The Leadership Quarterly* 20, no. 6 (2009), pp. 855–875.

37. M. Maccoby, "Narcissistic Leaders: The Incredible Pros, the Inevitable Cons," *The Harvard Business Review* (January–February 2000), pp. 69–77, www.maccoby.com/Articles/NarLeaders.shtml.

38. W. K. Campbell and C. A. Foster, "Narcissism and Commitment in Romantic Relationships: An Investment Model Analysis," *Personality and Social Psychology Bulletin* 28, no. 4 (2002), pp. 484–495.

39. T. A. Judge, J. A. LePine, and B. L. Rich, "The Narcissistic Personality: Relationship with Inflated Self-Ratings of Leadership and with Task and Contextual Performance," *Journal of Applied Psychology* 91, no. 4 (2006), pp. 762–776.

40. C. J. Resick, D. S. Whitman, S. M. Weingarden, and N. J. Hiller, "The Bright-Side and Dark-Side of CEO Personality: Examining Core Self-Evaluations, Narcissism, Trans-formational Leadership, and Strategic Influence," *Journal of Applied Psychology* 94, no. 6 (2009), pp. 1365–1381.

41. See M. Snyder, *Public Appearances/Private Realities: The Psychology of Self-Monitoring* (New York: W. H. Freeman, 1987); and S. W. Gangestad and M. Snyder, "Self-Monitoring: Appraisal and Reappraisal," *Psychological Bulletin* 126, no. 4 (2000), pp. 530–555.

42. F. J. Flynn and D. R. Ames, "What's Good for the Goose May Not Be as Good for the Gander: The Benefits of Self-Monitoring for Men and Women in Task Groups and Dyadic Conflicts," *Journal of Applied Psychology* 91, no. 2 (2006), pp. 272–281; and Snyder, *Public Appearances/Private Realities*.

43. D. V. Day, D. J. Shleicher, A. L. Unckless, and N. J. Hiller, "Self-Monitoring Personality at Work: A Meta-Analytic Investigation of Construct Validity," *Journal of Applied Psychology* 87, no. 2 (2002), pp. 390–401.

44. H. Oh and M. Kilduff, "The Ripple Effect of Personality on Social Structure: Self-Monitoring Origins of Network Brokerage," *Journal of Applied Psychology* 93, no. 5 (2008), pp. 1155–1164; and A. Mehra, M. Kilduff, and D. J. Brass, "The Social Networks of High and Low Self-Monitors: Implications for Workplace Performance," *Administrative Science Quarterly* 46, no. 1 (2001), pp. 121–146.

45. E. Reeve, "A History of Donald Trump's Net Worth Publicity," *The Atlantic*, (April 21, 2011), www.theatlanticwire.com.

46. R. N. Taylor and M. D. Dunnette, "Influence of Dogmatism, Risk-Taking Propensity, and Intelligence on Decision-Making Strategies for a Sample of Industrial Managers," *Journal of Applied Psychology* 59, no. 4 (1974), pp. 420–423.

47. I. L. Janis and L. Mann, *Decision Making: A Psychological Analysis of Conflict, Choice, and Commitment* (New York: The Free Press, 1977); W. H. Stewart Jr. and L. Roth, "Risk Propensity Differences Between Entrepreneurs and Managers: A Meta-Analytic Review," *Journal of Applied Psychology* 86, no. 1 (2001), pp. 145–153; J. B. Miner and N. S. Raju, "Risk Propensity Differences Between Managers and Entrepreneurs and Between Low- and High-Growth Entrepreneurs: A Reply in a More Conservative Vein," *Journal of Applied Psychology* 89, no. 1 (2004), pp. 3–13;

and W. H. Stewart Jr. and P. L. Roth, "Data Quality Affects Meta-Analytic Conclusions: A Response to Miner and Raju (2004) Concerning Entrepreneurial Risk Propensity," *Journal of Applied Psychology* 89, no. 1 (2004), pp. 14–21.

48. J. K. Maner, J. A. Richey, K. Cromer, M. Mallott, C. W. Lejuez, T. E. Joiner, and N. B. Schmidt, "Dispositional Anxiety and Risk-Avoidant Decision Making," *Personality and Individual Differences* 42, no. 4 (2007), pp. 665–675.

49. J. M. Crant, "Proactive Behavior in Organizations," *Journal of Management* 26, no. 3 (2000), p. 436.

50. S. E. Seibert, M. L. Kraimer, and J. M. Crant, "What Do Proactive People Do? A Longitudinal Model Linking Proactive Personality and Career Success," *Personnel Psychology* 54, no. 4 (2001), pp. 845–874.

51. T. S. Bateman and J. M. Crant, "The Proactive Component of Organizational Behavior: A Measure and Correlates," *Journal of Organizational Behavior* 14, no. 2 (1993), pp. 103–118; and J. M. Crant and T. S. Bateman, "Charismatic Leadership Viewed from Above: The Impact of Proactive Personality," *Journal of Organizational Behavior* 21, no. 1 (2000), pp. 63–75.

52. N. Li, J. Liang, and J. M. Crant, "The Role of Proactive Personality in Job Satisfaction and Organizational Citizenship Behavior: A Relational Perspective," *Journal of Applied Psychology* 95, no. 2 (2010), pp. 395–404.

53. Crant, "Proactive Behavior in Organizations," p. 436.

54. See, for instance, R. C. Becherer and J. G. Maurer, "The Proactive Personality Disposition and Entrepreneurial Behavior Among Small Company Presidents," *Journal of Small Business Management* 37, no. 1 (1999), pp. 28–36.

55. S. E. Seibert, J. M. Crant, and M. L. Kraimer, "Proactive Personality and Career Success," *Journal of Applied Psychology* 84, no. 3 (1999), pp. 416–427; Seibert, Kraimer, and Crant, "What Do Proactive People Do?" p. 850; D. J. Brown, R. T. Cober, K. Kane, P. E. Levy, and J. Shalhoop, "Proactive Personality and the Successful Job Search: A Field Investigation with College Graduates," *Journal of Applied Psychology* 91, no. 3 (2006), pp. 717–726; and J. D. Kammeyer-Mueller and C. R. Wanberg, "Unwrapping the Organizational Entry Process: Disentangling Multiple Antecedents and Their Pathways to Adjustment," *Journal of Applied Psychology* 88, no. 5 (2003), pp. 779–794.

56. B. M. Meglino and M. A. Korsgaard, "Considering Situational and Dispositional Approaches to Rational Self-Interest: An Extension and Response to De Dreu (2006)," *Journal of Applied Psychology* 91, no. 6 (2006), pp. 1253–1259; and B. M. Meglino and M. A. Korsgaard, "Considering Rational Self-Interest as a Disposition: Organizational Implications of Other Orientation," *Journal of Applied Psychology* 89, no. 6 (2004), pp. 946–959.

57. M. A. Korsgaard, B. M. Meglino, S. W. Lester, and S. S. Jeong, "Paying You Back or Paying Me Forward: Understanding Rewarded and Unrewarded Organizational Citizenship Behavior," *Journal of Applied Psychology* 95, no. 2 (2010), pp. 277–290.

58. Grant and Wrzesniewski, "I Won't Let You Down . . . Or Will I?; C. K. W. De Dreu, "Self-Interest and Other-Orientation in Organizational Behavior: Implications for Job Performance, Prosocial Behavior, and Personal Initiative," *Journal of Applied Psychology* 94, no. 4 (2009), pp. 913–926.

59. M. Rokeach, *The Nature of Human Values* (New York: The Free Press, 1973), p. 5.

60. M. Rokeach and S. J. Ball-Rokeach, "Stability and Change in American Value Priorities, 1968–1981," *American*

Psychologist 44, no. 5 (1989), pp. 775–784; and A. Bardi, J. A. Lee, N. Hofmann-Towfigh, and G. Soutar, "The Structure of Intraindividual Value Change," *Journal of Personality and Social Psychology* 97, no. 5 (2009), pp. 913–929.

61. S. Roccas, L. Sagiv, S. H. Schwartz, and A. Knafo, "The Big Five Personality Factors and Personal Values," *Personality and Social Psychology Bulletin* 28, no. 6 (2002), pp. 789–801.

62. See, for instance, B. M. Meglino and E. C. Ravlin, "Individual Values in Organizations: Concepts, Controversies, and Research," *Journal of Management* 24, no. 3 (1998), p. 355.

63. Rokeach, *The Nature of Human Values,* p. 6.

64. J. M. Munson and B. Z. Posner, "The Factorial Validity of a Modified Rokeach Value Survey for Four Diverse Samples," *Educational and Psychological Measurement* 40, no. 4 (1980), pp. 1073–1079; and W. C. Frederick and J. Weber, "The Values of Corporate Managers and Their Critics: An Empirical Description and Normative Implications," in W. C. Frederick and L. E. Preston (eds.), *Business Ethics: Research Issues and Empirical Studies* (Greenwich, CT: JAI Press, 1990), pp. 123–144.

65. Frederick and Weber, "The Values of Corporate Managers and Their Critics," pp. 123–144.

66. Ibid., p. 132.

67. J. L. Holland, *Making Vocational Choices: A Theory of Vocational Personalities and Work Environments* (Odessa, FL: Psychological Assessment Resources, 1997).

68. See, for example, J. L. Holland and G. D. Gottfredson, "Studies of the Hexagonal Model: An Evaluation (or, The Perils of Stalking the Perfect Hexagon)," *Journal of Vocational Behavior* 40, no. 2 (1992), pp. 158–170; and T. J. Tracey and J. Rounds, "Evaluating Holland's and Gati's Vocational-Interest Models: A Structural Meta-Analysis," *Psychological Bulletin* 113, no. 2 (1993), pp. 229–246.

69. C. H. Van Iddekinge, D. J. Putka, and J. P. Campbell, "Reconsidering Vocational Interests for Personnel Selection: The Validity of an Interest-Based Selection Test in Relation to Job Knowledge, Job Performance, and Continuance Intentions," *Journal of Applied Psychology* 96, no. 1 (2011), pp. 13–33.

70. S. A. Woods and S. E. Hampson, "Predicting Adult Occupational Environments from Gender and Childhood Personality Traits," *Journal of Applied Psychology* 95, no. 6 (2010), pp. 1045–1057.

71. See B. Schneider, H. W. Goldstein, and D. B. Smith, "The ASA Framework: An Update," *Personnel Psychology* 48, no. 4 (1995), pp. 747–773; B. Schneider, D. B. Smith, S. Taylor, and J. Fleenor, "Personality and Organizations: A Test of the Homogeneity of Personality Hypothesis," *Journal of Applied Psychology* 83, no. 3 (1998), pp. 462–470; W. Arthur Jr., S. T. Bell, A. J. Villado, and D. Doverspike, "The Use of Person-Organization Fit in Employment Decision-Making: An Assessment of Its Criterion-Related Validity," *Journal of Applied Psychology* 91, no. 4 (2006), pp. 786–801; and J. R. Edwards, D. M. Cable, I. O. Williamson, L. S. Lambert, and A. J. Shipp, "The Phenomenology of Fit: Linking the Person and Environment to the Subjective Experience of Person–Environment Fit," *Journal of Applied Psychology* 91, no. 4 (2006), pp. 802–827.

72. Based on T. A. Judge and D. M. Cable, "Applicant Personality, Organizational Culture, and Organization Attraction," *Personnel Psychology* 50, no. 2 (1997), pp. 359–394.

73. M. L. Verquer, T. A. Beehr, and S. E. Wagner, "A Meta-Analysis of Relations Between Person–Organization Fit and Work Attitudes," *Journal of Vocational Behavior* 63, no. 3 (2003), pp. 473–489; and J. C. Carr, A. W. Pearson, M. J. Vest, and S. L. Boyar, "Prior Occupational Experience, Anticipatory Socialization, and Employee Retention," *Journal of Management* 32, no. 32 (2006), pp. 343–359.

74. A. Ramesh and M. J. Gelfand, "Will They Stay or Will They Go? The Role of Job Embeddedness in Predicting Turnover in Individualistic and Collectivistic Cultures," *Journal of Applied Psychology* 95, no. 5 (2010), pp. 807–823.

75. G. Hofstede, *Cultures and Organizations: Software of the Mind* (London: McGraw-Hill, 1991); G. Hofstede, "Cultural Constraints in Management Theories," *Academy of Management Executive* 7, no. 1 (1993), pp. 81–94; G. Hofstede and M. F. Peterson, "National Values and Organizational Practices," in N. M. Ashkanasy, C. M. Wilderom, and M. F. Peterson (eds.), *Handbook of Organizational Culture and Climate* (Thousand Oaks, CA: Sage, 2000), pp. 401–416; and G. Hofstede, *Culture's Consequences: Comparing Values, Behaviors, Institutions, and Organizations Across Nations,* 2nd ed. (Thousand Oaks, CA: Sage, 2001). For criticism of this research, see B. McSweeney, "Hofstede's Model of National Cultural Differences and Their Consequences: A Triumph of Faith—A Failure of Analysis," *Human Relations* 55, no. 1 (2002), pp. 89–118.

76. G. Ailon, "Mirror, Mirror on the Wall: *Culture's Consequences* in a Value Test of Its Own Design," *Academy of Management Review* 33, no. 4 (2008), pp. 885–904; M. H. Bond, "Reclaiming the Individual from Hofstede's Ecological Analysis—A 20-Year Odyssey: Comment on Oyserman et al. (2002), *Psychological Bulletin* 128, no. 1 (2002), pp. 73–77; and G. Hofstede, "The Pitfalls of Cross-National Survey Research: A Reply to the Article by Spector et al. on the Psychometric Properties of the Hofstede Values Survey Module 1994," *Applied Psychology: An International Review* 51, no. 1 (2002), pp. 170–178.

77. V. Taras, B. L. Kirkman, and P. Steel, "Examining the Impact of Culture's Consequences: A Three-Decade, Multilevel, Meta-Analytic Review of Hofstede's Cultural Value Dimensions," *Journal of Applied Psychology* 95, no. 5 (2010), pp. 405–439.

78. M. Javidan and R. J. House, "Cultural Acumen for the Global Manager: Lessons from Project GLOBE," *Organizational Dynamics* 29, no. 4 (2001), pp. 289–305; and R. J. House, P. J. Hanges, M. Javidan, and P. W. Dorfman (eds.), *Leadership, Culture, and Organizations: The GLOBE Study of 62 Societies* (Thousand Oaks, CA: Sage, 2004).

79. P. C. Early, "Leading Cultural Research in the Future: A Matter of Paradigms and Taste," *Journal of International Business Studies* 37, no. 6 (2006), pp. 922–931; G. Hofstede, "What Did GLOBE Really Measure? Researchers' Minds Versus Respondents' Minds," *Journal of International Business Studies* 37, no. 6 (2006), pp. 882–896; and M. Javidan, R. J. House, P. W. Dorfman, P. J. Hanges, and M. S. de Luque, "Conceptualizing and Measuring Cultures and Their Consequences: A Comparative Review of GLOBE's and Hofstede's Approaches," *Journal of International Business Studies* 37, no. 6 (2006), pp. 897–914.

80. R. P. Tett and D. D. Burnett, "A Personality Trait–Based Interactionist Model of Job Performance," *Journal of Applied Psychology* 88, no. 3 (2003), pp. 500–517.

CHAPTER 6

1. H. H. Kelley, "Attribution in Social Interaction," in E. Jones et al. (eds.), *Attribution: Perceiving the Causes of Behavior* (Morristown, NJ: General Learning Press, 1972); and M. J. Martinko, P. Harvey, and M. T. Dasborough, "Attribution Theory in the Organizational Sciences: A Case of Unrealized Potential," *Journal of Organizational Behavior* 32, no. 1 (2011), pp. 144–149.

2. See L. Ross, "The Intuitive Psychologist and His Shortcomings," in L. Berkowitz (ed.), *Advances in Experimental Social Psychology*, vol. 10 (Orlando, FL: Academic Press, 1977), pp. 174–220; and A. G. Miller and T. Lawson, "The Effect of an Informational Option on the Fundamental Attribution Error," *Personality and Social Psychology Bulletin* 15, no. 2 (1989), pp. 194–204.

3. See, for instance, N. Epley and D. Dunning, "Feeling 'Holier Than Thou': Are Self-Serving Assessments Produced by Errors in Self- or Social Prediction?" *Journal of Personality and Social Psychology* 76, no. 6 (2000), pp. 861–875; M. Goerke, J. Moller, S. Schulz-Hardt, U. Napiersky, and D. Frey, "'It's Not My Fault—But Only I Can Change It': Counterfactual and Prefactual Thoughts of Managers," *Journal of Applied Psychology* 89, no. 2 (2004), pp. 279–292; and E. G. Hepper, R. H. Gramzow, and C. Sedikides, "Individual Differences in Self-Enhancement and Self-Protection Strategies: An Integrative Analysis," *Journal of Personality* 78, no. 2 (2010), pp. 781–814.

4. See, for instance, A. H. Mezulis, L. Y. Abramson, J. S. Hyde, and B. L. Hankin, "Is There a Universal Positivity Bias in Attributions: A Meta-Analytic Review of Individual, Developmental, and Cultural Differences in the Self-Serving Attributional Bias," *Psychological Bulletin* 130, no. 5 (2004), pp. 711–747; C. F. Falk, S. J. Heine, M. Yuki, and K. Takemura, "Why Do Westerners Self-Enhance More than East Asians?" *European Journal of Personality* 23, no. 3 (2009), pp. 183–203; and F. F. T. Chiang and T. A. Birtch, "Examining the Perceived Causes of Successful Employee Performance: An East–West Comparison," *International Journal of Human Resource Management* 18, no. 2 (2007), pp. 232–248.

5. S. Nam, "Cultural and Managerial Attributions for Group Performance," unpublished doctoral dissertation, University of Oregon. Cited in R. M. Steers, S. J. Bischoff, and L. H. Higgins, "Cross-Cultural Management Research," *Journal of Management Inquiry,* December 1992, pp. 325–326.

6. T. Menon, M. W. Morris, C. Y. Chiu, and Y. Y. Hong, "Culture and the Construal of Agency: Attribution to Individual Versus Group Dispositions," *Journal of Personality and Social Psychology* 76, no. 5 (1999), pp. 701–717; and R. Friedman, W. Liu, C. C. Chen, and S. S. Chi, "Causal Attribution for Interfirm Contract Violation: A Comparative Study of Chinese and American Commercial Arbitrators," *Journal of Applied Psychology* 92, no. 3 (2007), pp. 856–864.

7. J. Spencer-Rodgers, M. J. Williams, D. L. Hamilton, K. Peng, and L. Wang, "Culture and Group Perception: Dispositional and Stereotypic Inferences about Novel and National Groups," *Journal of Personality and Social Psychology* 93, no. 4 (2007), pp. 525–543.

8. J. D. Brown, "Across the (Not So) Great Divide: Cultural Similarities in Self-Evaluative Processes," *Social and Personality Psychology Compass* 4, no. 5 (2010), pp. 318–330.

9. A. Zhang, C. Reyna, Z. Qian, and G. Yu, "Interpersonal Attributions of Responsibility in the Chinese Workplace: A Test of Western Models in a Collectivistic Context," *Journal of Applied Social Psychology* 38, no. 9 (2008), pp. 2361–2377; and A. Zhang, F. Xia, and C. Li, "The Antecedents of Help Giving in Chinese Culture: Attribution, Judgment of Responsibility, Expectation Change and the Reaction of Affect," *Social Behavior and Personality* 35, no. 1 (2007), pp. 135–142.

10. See P. Rosenzweig, *The Halo Effect* (New York: The Free Press, 2007); I. Dennis, "Halo Effects in Grading Student Projects," *Journal of Applied Psychology* 92, no. 4 (2007), pp. 1169–1176; C. E. Naquin and R. O. Tynan, "The Team Halo Effect: Why Teams Are Not Blamed for Their Failures," *Journal of Applied Psychology* 88, no. 2 (2003), pp. 332–340; and T. M. Bechger, G. Maris, and Y. P. Hsiao, "Detecting Halo Effects in Performance-Based Evaluations," *Applied Psychological Measurement* 34, no. 8 (2010), pp. 607–619.

11. S. E. Asch, "Forming Impressions of Personality," *Journal of Abnormal and Social Psychology* 41, no. 3 (1946), pp. 258–290.

12. J. L. Hilton and W. von Hippel, "Stereotypes," *Annual Review of Psychology* 47 (1996), pp. 237–271.

13. See, for example, C. Ostroff and L. E. Atwater, "Does Whom You Work with Matter? Effects of Referent Group Gender and Age Composition on Managers' Compensation," *Journal of Applied Psychology* 88, no. 4 (2003), pp. 725–740; M. E. Heilman, A. S. Wallen, D. Fuchs, and M. M. Tamkins, "Penalties for Success: Reactions to Women Who Succeed at Male Gender-Typed Tasks," *Journal of Applied Psychology* 89, no. 3 (2004), pp. 416–427; V. K. Gupta, D. B. Turban, and N. M. Bhawe, "The Effect of Gender Stereotype Activation on Entrepreneurial Intentions," *Journal of Applied Psychology* 93, no. 5 (2008), pp. 1053–1061; and R. A. Posthuma and M. A. Campion, "Age Stereotypes in the Workplace: Common Stereotypes, Moderators, and Future Research Directions," *Journal of Management* 35, no. 1 (2009), pp. 158–188.

14. See, for example, N. Dasgupta, D. DeSteno, L. A. Williams, and M. Hunsinger, "Fanning the Flames of Prejudice: The Influence of Specific Incidental Emotions on Implicit Prejudice," *Emotion* 9, no. 4 (2009), pp. 585–591; and J. C. Ziegert and P. C. Hanges, "Strong Rebuttal for Weak Criticisms: Reply to Blanton et al. (2009)," *Journal of Applied Psychology* 94, no. 3 (2009), pp. 590–597.

15. J. L. Eberhardt, P. G. Davies, V. J. Purdie-Vaughns, and S. L. Johnson, "Looking Deathworthy: Perceived Stereotypicality of Black Defendants Predicts Capital-Sentencing Outcomes," *Psychological Science* 17, no. 5 (2006), pp. 383–386.

16. A. S. Rosette, G. J. Leonardelli, and K. W. Phillips, "The White Standard: Racial Bias in Leader Categorization," *Journal of Applied Psychology* 93, no. 4 (2008), pp. 758–777.

17. R. Sanders, *The Executive Decisionmaking Process: Identifying Problems and Assessing Outcomes* (Westport, CT: Quorum, 1999).

18. See H. A. Simon, "Rationality in Psychology and Economics," *Journal of Business* (October 1986), pp. 209–224; and E. Shafir and R. A. LeBoeuf, "Rationality," *Annual Review of Psychology* 53 (2002), pp. 491–517.

19. For a review of the rational decision-making model, see M. H. Bazerman and D. A. Moore, *Judgment in Managerial Decision Making,* 7th ed. (Hoboken, NJ: Wiley, 2008).

20. J. G. March, *A Primer on Decision Making* (New York: The Free Press, 2009); and D. Hardman and C. Harries, "How Rational Are We?" *Psychologist* (February 2002), pp. 76–79.

21. Bazerman and Moore, *Judgment in Managerial Decision Making*.

22. J. E. Russo, K. A. Carlson, and M. G. Meloy, "Choosing an Inferior Alternative," *Psychological Science* 17, no. 10 (2006), pp. 899–904.

23. D. Kahneman, "Maps of Bounded Rationality: Psychology for Behavioral Economics," *The American Economic Review* 93, no. 5 (2003), pp. 1449–1475; and J. Zhang, C. K. Hsee, and Z. Xiao, "The Majority Rule in Individual Decision Making," *Organizational Behavior and Human Decision Processes* 99 (2006), pp. 102–111.

24. See H. A. Simon, *Administrative Behavior,* 4th ed. (New York: The Free Press, 1997); and M. Augier, "Simon Says: Bounded Rationality Matters," *Journal of Management Inquiry* (September 2001), pp. 268–275.

25. G. Gigerenzer, "Why Heuristics Work," *Perspectives on Psychological Science* 3, no. 1 (2008), pp. 20–29; and A. K. Shah and D. M. Oppenheimer, "Heuristics Made Easy: An Effort-Reduction Framework," *Psychological Bulletin* 134, no. 2 (2008), pp. 207–222.

26. See A. W. Kruglanski and G. Gigerenzer, "Intuitive and Deliberate Judgments Are Based on Common Principles," *Psychological Review* 118 (2011), pp. 97–109.

27. E. Dane and M. G. Pratt, "Exploring Intuition and Its Role in Managerial Decision Making," *Academy of Management Review* 32, no. 1 (2007), pp. 33–54; and J. A. Hicks, D. C. Cicero, J. Trent, C. M. Burton, and L. A. King, "Positive Affect, Intuition, and Feelings of Meaning," *Journal of Personality and Social Psychology* 98 (2010), pp. 967–979.

28. P. D. Brown, "Some Hunches About Intuition," *New York Times* (November 17, 2007), p. B5.

29. S. P. Robbins, *Decide & Conquer: Making Winning Decisions and Taking Control of Your Life* (Upper Saddle River, NJ: Financial Times/Prentice Hall, 2004), p. 13.

30. S. Plous, *The Psychology of Judgment and Decision Making* (New York: McGraw-Hill, 1993), p. 217.

31. C. R. M. McKenzie, M. J. Liersch, and I. Yaniv, "Overconfidence in Interval Estimates: What Does Expertise Buy You," *Organizational Behavior and Human Decision Processes* 107 (2008), pp. 179–191.

32. B. Fischhoff, P. Slovic, and S. Lichtenstein, "Knowing with Certainty: The Appropriateness of Extreme Confidence," *Journal of Experimental Psychology: Human Perception and Performance* (November 1977), pp. 552–564.

33. J. Kruger and D. Dunning, "Unskilled and Unaware of It: How Difficulties in Recognizing One's Own Incompetence Leads to Inflated Self-Assessments," *Journal of Personality and Social Psychology* (November 1999), pp. 1121–1134; and R. P. Larrick, K. A. Burson, and J. B. Soll, "Social Comparison and Confidence: When Thinking You're Better than Average Predicts Overconfidence (and When It Does Not)" *Organizational Behavior and Human Decision Processes* 102 (2007), pp. 76–94.

34. K. M. Hmieleski and R. A. Baron, "Entrepreneurs' Optimism and New Venture Performance: A Social Cognitive Perspective," *Academy of Management Journal* 52, no. 3 (2009), pp. 473–488.

35. See, for instance, J. P. Simmons, R. A. LeBoeuf, and L. D. Nelson, "The Effect of Accuracy Motivation on Anchoring and Adjustment: Do People Adjust from Their Provided Anchors?" *Journal of Personality and Social Psychology* 99 (2010), pp. 917–932.

36. C. Janiszewski and D. Uy, "Precision of the Anchor Influences the Amount of Adjustment," *Psychological Science* 19, no. 2 (2008), pp. 121–127.

37. See E. Jonas, S. Schultz-Hardt, D. Frey, and N. Thelen, "Confirmation Bias in Sequential Information Search after Preliminary Decisions," *Journal of Personality and Social Psychology* (April 2001), pp. 557–571; and W. Hart, D. Albarracín, A. H. Eagly, I. Brechan, M. Lindberg, and L. Merrill, "Feeling Validated Versus Being Correct: A Meta-Analysis of Selective Exposure to Information," *Psychological Bulletin* 135 (2009), pp. 555–588.

38. See A. Tversky and D. Kahneman, "Availability: A Heuristic for Judging Frequency and Probability," in D. Kahneman, P. Slovic, and A. Tversky (eds.), *Judgment Under Uncertainty: Heuristics and Biases* (Cambridge, UK: Cambridge University Press, 1982), pp. 163–178; and B. J. Bushman and G. L. Wells, "Narrative Impressions of Literature: The Availability Bias and the Corrective Properties of Meta-Analytic Approaches," *Personality and Social Psychology Bulletin* (September 2001), pp. 1123–1130.

39. G. Morgenson, "Debt Watchdogs: Tamed or Caught Napping?" *The New York Times* (December 7, 2009), pp. 1, 32.

40. See B. M. Staw, "The Escalation of Commitment to a Course of Action," *Academy of Management Review* (October 1981), pp. 577–587; K. Fai, E. Wong, M. Yik, and J. Y. Y. Kwong, "Understanding the Emotional Aspects of Escalation of Commitment: The Role of Negative Affect," *Journal of Applied Psychology* 91, no. 2 (2006), pp. 282–297; and A. Zardkoohi, "Do Real Options Lead to Escalation of Commitment? Comment," *Academy of Management Review* (January 2004), pp. 111–119.

41. B. M. Staw, "Knee-Deep in the Big Muddy: A Study of Escalating Commitment to a Chosen Course of Action," *Organizational Behavior and Human Performance* 16 (1976), pp. 27–44; and S. Schulz-Hardt, B. Thurow Kröning, and D. Frey, "Preference-Based Escalation: A New Interpretation for the Responsibility Effect in Escalating Commitment and Entrapment," *Organizational Behavior and Human Decision Processes* 108 (2009), pp. 175–186.

42. K. F. E. Wong and J. Y. Y. Kwong, "The Role of Anticipated Regret in Escalation of Commitment," *Journal of Applied Psychology* 92, no. 2 (2007), pp. 545–554.

43. K. F. E. Wong, J. Y. Y. Kwong, and C. K. Ng, "When Thinking Rationally Increases Biases: The Role of Rational Thinking Style in Escalation of Commitment," *Applied Psychology: An International Review* 57, no. 2 (2008), pp. 246–271.

44. See, for instance, A. James and A. Wells, "Death Beliefs, Superstitious Beliefs and Health Anxiety," *British Journal of Clinical Psychology* (March 2002), pp. 43–53; and U. Hahn and P. A. Warren, "Perceptions of Randomness: Why Three Heads Are Better than One," *Psychological Review* 116 (2009), pp. 454–461.

45. See, for example, D. J. Keys and B. Schwartz, "Leaky Rationality: How Research on Behavioral Decision Making Challenges Normative Standards of Rationality," *Psychological Science* 2, no. 2 (2007), pp. 162–180; and U. Simonsohn, "Direct Risk Aversion: Evidence from Risky Prospects Valued Below Their Worst Outcomes," *Psychological Science* 20, no. 6 (2009), pp. 686–692.

46. J. K. Maner, M. T. Gailliot, D. A. Butz, and B. M. Peruche, "Power, Risk, and the Status Quo: Does Power Promote

Riskier or More Conservative Decision Making," *Personality and Social Psychology Bulletin* 33, no. 4 (2007), pp. 451–462.

47. A. Chakraborty, S. Sheikh, and N. Subramanian, "Termination Risk and Managerial Risk Taking," *Journal of Corporate Finance* 13 (2007), pp. 170–188.

48. R. L. Guilbault, F. B. Bryant, J. H. Brockway, and E. J. Posavac, "A Meta-Analysis of Research on Hindsight Bias," *Basic and Applied Social Psychology* (September 2004), pp. 103–117; and L. Werth, F. Strack, and J. Foerster, "Certainty and Uncertainty: The Two Faces of the Hindsight Bias," *Organizational Behavior and Human Decision Processes* (March 2002), pp. 323–341.

49. J. Bell, "The Final Cut?" *Oregon Business* 33, no. 5 (2010), p. 27.

50. This section is based on T. Gärling, E. Kirchler, A. Lewis, and F. van Raaij, "Psychology, Financial Decision Making, and Financial Crises," *Psychological Science in the Public Interest* 10 (2009), pp.1–47; T. Zaleskiewicz, "Financial Forecasts During the Crisis: Were Experts More Accurate than Laypeople?" *Journal of Economic Psychology* 32 (2011), pp. 384–390; and G. A. Akerlof and R. J. Shiller, *Animal Spirits: How Human Psychology Drives the Economy and Why It Matters for Global Capitalism* (Princeton, NJ: Princeton University Press, 2009).

51. A. Wildavsky, *The Politics of the Budgetary Process* (Boston: Little, Brown, 1964).

52. G. F. Cavanagh, D. J. Moberg, and M. Valasquez, "The Ethics of Organizational Politics," *Academy of Management Journal* (June 1981), pp. 363–374.

53. See, for example, T. Machan, ed., *Commerce and Morality* (Totowa, NJ: Rowman and Littlefield, 1988).

54. T. M. Amabile, "A Model of Creativity and Innovation in Organizations," in B. M. Staw and L. L. Cummings (eds.), *Research in Organizational Behavior*, vol. 10 (Greenwich, CT: JAI Press, 1988), p. 126; and J. E. Perry-Smith and C. E. Shalley, "The Social Side of Creativity: A Static and Dynamic Social Network Perspective," *Academy of Management Review* (January 2003), pp. 89–106.

55. G. J. Feist and F. X. Barron, "Predicting Creativity from Early to Late Adulthood: Intellect, Potential, and Personality," *Journal of Research in Personality* (April 2003), pp. 62–88.

56. R. W. Woodman, J. E. Sawyer, and R. W. Griffin, "Toward a Theory of Organizational Creativity," *Academy of Management Review* (April 1993), p. 298; J. M. George and J. Zhou, "When Openness to Experience and Conscientiousness Are Related to Creative Behavior: An Interactional Approach," *Journal of Applied Psychology* (June 2001), pp. 513–524; and E. F. Rietzschel, C. K. W. de Dreu, and B. A. Nijstad, "Personal Need for Structure and Creative Performance: The Moderating Influence of Fear of Invalidity," *Personality and Social Psychology Bulletin* (June 2007), pp. 855–866.

57. A. K. Leung, W. W. Maddux, A. D. Galinsky, and C. Chiu, "Multicultural Experience Enhances Creativity," *American Psychologist* 63, no. 3 (2008), pp. 169–180.

58. This section is based on T. M. Amabile, "Motivating Creativity in Organizations: On Doing What You Love and Loving What You Do," *California Management Review* 40, no. 1 (Fall 1997), pp. 39–58.

59. M. Baas, C. K. W. De Dreu, and B. A. Nijstad, "A Meta-Analysis of 25 Years of Mood-Creativity Research: Hedonic Tone, Activation, or Regulatory Focus?" *Psychological Bulletin* 134, no. 6 (2008), pp. 779–806.

60. J. Zhou, "When the Presence of Creative Coworkers Is Related to Creativity: Role of Supervisor Close Monitoring, Developmental Feedback, and Creative Personality," *Journal of Applied Psychology* 88, no. 3 (June 2003), pp. 413–422.

61. J. E. Perry-Smith, "Social Yet Creative: The Role of Social Relationships in Facilitating Individual Creativity," *Academy of Management Journal* 49, no. 1 (2006), pp. 85–101.

62. G. Park, D. Lubinski, and C. P. Benbow, "Contrasting Intellectual Patterns Predict Creativity in the Arts and Sciences," *Psychological Science* 18, no. 11 (2007), pp. 948–952.

63. See C. E. Shalley, J. Zhou, and G. R. Oldham, "The Effects of Personal and Contextual Characteristics on Creativity: Where Should We Go from Here?" *Journal of Management* (November 2004), pp. 933–958; G. Hirst, D. Van Knippenberg, and J. Zhou, "A Cross-Level Perspective on Employee Creativity: Goal Orientation, Team Learning Behavior, and Individual Creativity," *Academy of Management Journal* 52, no. 2 (2009), pp. 280–293; and C. E. Shalley, L. L. Gilson, and T. C. Blum, "Interactive Effects of Growth Need Strength, Work Context, and Job Complexity on Self-Reported Creative Performance," *Academy of Management Journal* 52, no. 3 (2009), pp. 489–505.

64. T. Jackson, "Cultural Values and Management Ethics: A 10-Nation Study," *Human Relations* (October 2001), pp. 1267–1302; see also J. B. Cullen, K. P. Parboteeah, and M. Hoegl, "Cross-National Differences in Managers' Willingness to Justify Ethically Suspect Behaviors: A Test of Institutional Anomie Theory," *Academy of Management Journal* (June 2004), pp. 411–421.

65. W. Chow Hou, "To Bribe or Not to Bribe?" *Asia, Inc.* (October 1996), p. 104.

66. P. Digh, "Shades of Gray in the Global Marketplace," *HR Magazine* (April 1997), p. 91.

CHAPTER 7

1. See, for example, G. P. Latham and C. C. Pinder, "Work Motivation Theory and Research at the Dawn of the Twenty-First Century," *Annual Review of Psychology* 56 (2005), pp. 485–516; and C. Pinder, *Work Motivation in Organizational Behavior*, 2nd ed. (London, UK: Psychology Press, 2008).

2. R. Wagner and J. K. Harter, *12: The Elements of Great Managing* (Washington, DC: Gallup Press, 2006).

3. "The 2008 Wasting Time at Work Survey Reveals a Record Number of People Waste Time at Work," Salary.com (2008), www.salary.com.

4. See, for instance, Pinder, *Work Motivation in Organizational Behavior*.

5. A. Maslow, *Motivation and Personality* (New York: Harper & Row, 1954).

6. G. Hofstede, "Motivation, Leadership, and Organization: Do American Theories Apply Abroad?" *Organizational Dynamics* (Summer 1980), p. 55.

7. See, for example, E. E. Lawler III and J. L. Suttle, "A Causal Correlation Test of the Need Hierarchy Concept," *Organizational Behavior and Human Performance* 7, no. 2 (1972), pp. 265–287; D. T. Hall and K. E. Nougaim, "An Examination of Maslow's Need Hierarchy in an Organizational Setting," *Organizational Behavior and Human Performance* 3, no. 1 (1968), pp. 12–35; and J. Rauschenberger, N. Schmitt, and J. E. Hunter, "A Test of the Need Hierarchy Concept by a

Markov Model of Change in Need Strength," *Administrative Science Quarterly* 25, no. 4 (1980), pp. 654–670.

8. M. A. Wahba and L. G. Bridwell, "Maslow Reconsidered: A Review of Research on the Need Hierarchy Theory," *Organizational Behavior and Human Performance* 15, no. 2 (1976), pp. 212–240.

9. D. T. Kenrick, V. Griskevicius, S. L. Neuberg, and M. Schaller, "Renovating the Pyramid of Needs: Contemporary Extensions Built on Ancient Foundations," *Perspectives on Psychological Science* 5, no. 3 (2010), pp. 292–314.

10. D. McGregor, *The Human Side of Enterprise* (New York: McGraw-Hill, 1960). For an updated analysis of Theory X and Theory Y constructs, see R. E. Kopelman, D. J. Prottas, and D. W. Falk, "Construct Validation of a Theory X/Y Behavior Scale," *Leadership and Organization Development Journal* 31, no. 2 (2010), pp. 120–135.

11. F. Herzberg, B. Mausner, and B. Snyderman, *The Motivation to Work* (New York: Wiley, 1959).

12. R. J. House and L. A. Wigdor, "Herzberg's Dual-Factor Theory of Job Satisfaction and Motivations: A Review of the Evidence and Criticism," *Personnel Psychology* 20, no. 4 (1967), pp. 369–389; D. P. Schwab and L. L. Cummings, "Theories of Performance and Satisfaction: A Review," *Industrial Relations* 9, no. 4 (1970), pp. 403–430; and J. Phillipchuk and J. Whittaker, "An Inquiry into the Continuing Relevance of Herzberg's Motivation Theory," *Engineering Management Journal* 8 (1996), pp. 15–20.

13. D. C. McClelland, *The Achieving Society* (New York: Van Nostrand Reinhold, 1961); J. W. Atkinson and J. O. Raynor, *Motivation and Achievement* (Washington, DC: Winston, 1974); D. C. McClelland, *Power: The Inner Experience* (New York: Irvington, 1975); and M. J. Stahl, *Managerial and Technical Motivation: Assessing Needs for Achievement, Power, and Affiliation* (New York: Praeger, 1986).

14. D. C. McClelland and D. G. Winter, *Motivating Economic Achievement* (New York: The Free Press, 1969); and J. B. Miner, N. R. Smith, and J. S. Bracker, "Role of Entrepreneurial Task Motivation in the Growth of Technologically Innovative Firms: Interpretations from Follow-up Data," *Journal of Applied Psychology* 79, no. 4 (1994), pp. 627–630.

15. McClelland, *Power;* D. C. McClelland and D. H. Burnham, "Power Is the Great Motivator," *Harvard Business Review* (March/April 1976), pp. 100–110; and R. E. Boyatzis, "The Need for Close Relationships and the Manager's Job," in D. A. Kolb, I. M. Rubin, and J. M. McIntyre, *Organizational Psychology: Readings on Human Behavior in Organizations,* 4th ed. (Upper Saddle River, NJ: Prentice Hall, 1984), pp. 81–86.

16. D. G. Winter, "The Motivational Dimensions of Leadership: Power, Achievement, and Affiliation," in R. E. Riggio, S. E. Murphy, and F. J. Pirozzolo (eds.), *Multiple Intelligences and Leadership* (Mahwah, NJ: Lawrence Erlbaum, 2002), pp. 119–138.

17. J. B. Miner, *Studies in Management Education* (New York: Springer, 1965).

18. Ibid.

19. E. Deci and R. Ryan (eds.), *Handbook of Self-Determination Research* (Rochester, NY: University of Rochester Press, 2002); R. Ryan and E. Deci, "Self-Determination Theory and the Facilitation of Intrinsic Motivation, Social Development, and Well-Being," *American Psychologist* 55, no. 1 (2000), pp. 68–78; and M. Gagné and E. L. Deci, "Self-Determination Theory and Work Motivation," *Journal of Organizational Behavior* 26, no. 4 (2005), pp. 331–362.

20. See, for example, E. L. Deci, R. Koestner, and R. M. Ryan, "A Meta-Analytic Review of Experiments Examining the Effects of Extrinsic Rewards on Intrinsic Motivation," *Psychological Bulletin* 125, no. 6 (1999), pp. 627–668; G. J. Greguras and J. M. Diefendorff, "Different Fits Satisfy Different Needs: Linking Person-Environment Fit to Employee Commitment and Performance Using Self-Determination Theory," *Journal of Applied Psychology* 94, no. 2 (2009), pp. 465–477; and D. Liu, X. Chen, and X. Yao, "From Autonomy to Creativity: A Multilevel Investigation of the Mediating Role of Harmonious Passion," *Journal of Applied Psychology* 96, no. 2 (2011), pp. 294–309.

21. R. Eisenberger and L. Rhoades, "Incremental Effects of Reward on Creativity," *Journal of Personality and Social Psychology* 81, no. 4 (2001), 728–741; and R. Eisenberger, W. D. Pierce, and J. Cameron, "Effects of Reward on Intrinsic Motivation—Negative, Neutral, and Positive: Comment on Deci, Koestner, and Ryan (1999)," *Psychological Bulletin* 125, no. 6 (1999), pp. 677–691.

22. M. Burgess, M. E. Enzle, and R. Schmaltz, "Defeating the Potentially Deleterious Effects of Externally Imposed Deadlines: Practitioners' Rules-of-Thumb," *Personality and Social Psychology Bulletin* 30, no. 7 (2004), pp. 868–877.

23. K. M. Sheldon, A. J. Elliot, and R. M. Ryan, "Self-Concordance and Subjective Well-being in Four Cultures," *Journal of Cross-Cultural Psychology* 35, no. 2 (2004), pp. 209–223.

24. J. E. Bono and T. A. Judge, "Self-Concordance at Work: Toward Understanding the Motivational Effects of Transformational Leaders," *Academy of Management Journal* 46, no. 5 (2003), pp. 554–571.

25. J. P. Meyer, T. E. Becker, and C. Vandenberghe, "Employee Commitment and Motivation: A Conceptual Analysis and Integrative Model," *Journal of Applied Psychology* 89, no. 6 (2004), pp. 991–1007.

26. W. A. Kahn, "Psychological Conditions of Personal Engagement and Disengagement at Work," *Academy of Management Journal* 33, no. 4 (1990), pp. 692–724.

27. www.gallup.com/consulting/52/Employee-Engagement.aspx

28. J. K. Harter, F. L. Schmidt, and T. L. Hayes, "Business-Unit-Level Relationship Between Employee Satisfaction, Employee Engagement, and Business Outcomes: A Meta-Analysis," *Journal of Applied Psychology* 87, no. 2 (2002), pp. 268–279.

29. M. S. Christian, A. S. Garza, and J. E. Slaughter, "Work Engagement: A Quantitative Review and Test of Its Relations with Task and Contextual Performance," *Personnel Psychology* 64, no. 1 (2011), pp. 89–136.

30. W. B. Schaufeli, A. B. Bakker, and W. van Rhenen, "How Changes in Job Demands and Resources Predict Burnout, Work Engagement, and Sickness Absenteeism," *Journal of Organizational Behavior* 30, no. 7 (2009), pp. 893–917; E. R. Crawford, J. A. LePine, and B. L. Rich, "Linking Job Demands and Resources to Employee Engagement and Burnout: A Theoretical Extension and Meta-Analytic Test," *Journal of Applied Psychology* 95, no. 5 (2010), pp. 834–848; and D. Xanthopoulou, A. B. Bakker, E. Demerouti, and W. B. Schaufeli, "Reciprocal Relationships Between Job Resources, Personal Resources, and Work Engagement," *Journal of Vocational Behavior* 74, no. 3 (2009), pp. 235–244.

31. B. L. Rich, J. A. LePine, and E. R. Crawford, "Job Engagement: Antecedents and Effects on Job Performance," *Academy of Management Journal* 53, no. 3 (2010), pp. 617–635.

32. M. Tims, A. B. Bakker, and D. Xanthopoulou, "Do Transformational Leaders Enhance Their Followers' Daily Work Engagement?" *Leadership Quarterly* 22, no. 1 (2011), pp. 121–131; and F. O. Walumbwa, P. Wang, H. Wang, J. Schaubroeck, and B. J. Avolio, "Psychological Processes Linking Authentic Leadership to Follower Behaviors," *Leadership Quarterly* 21, no. 5 (2010), pp. 901–914.

33. D. A. Newman and D. A. Harrison, "Been There, Bottled That: Are State and Behavioral Work Engagement New and Useful Construct 'Wines?'" *Industrial and Organizational Psychology* 1, no. 1 (2008), pp. 31–35; A. J. Wefald and R. G. Downey, "Job Engagement in Organizations: Fad, Fashion, or Folderol," *Journal of Organizational Behavior* 30, no. 1 (2009), pp. 141–145.

34. See, for example, Rich, LePine, and Crawford, "Job Engagement: Antecedents and Effects on Job Performance"; and Christian, Garza, and Slaughter, "Work Engagement: A Quantitative Review and Test of Its Relations with Task and Contextual Performance."

35. J. M. George, "The Wider Context, Costs, and Benefits of Work Engagement," *European Journal of Work and Organizational Psychology* 20, no. 1 (2011), pp. 53–59; and J. R. B. Halbesleben, J. Harvey, and M. C. Bolino, "Too Engaged? A Conservation of Resources View of the Relationship Between Work Engagement and Work Interference with Family," *Journal of Applied Psychology* 94, no. 6 (2009), pp. 1452–1465.

36. E. A. Locke, "Toward a Theory of Task Motivation and Incentives," *Organizational Behavior and Human Performance* 3, no. 2 (1968), pp. 157–189.

37. P. C. Earley, P. Wojnaroski, and W. Prest, "Task Planning and Energy Expended: Exploration of How Goals Influence Performance," *Journal of Applied Psychology* 72, no. 1 (1987), pp. 107–114.

38. See M. E. Tubbs, "Goal Setting: A Meta-Analytic Examination of the Empirical Evidence," *Journal of Applied Psychology* 71, no. 3 (1986), pp. 474–483; and E. A. Locke and G. P. Latham, "New Directions in Goal-Setting Theory," *Current Directions in Psychological Science* 15, no. 5 (2006), pp. 265–268.

39. E. A. Locke and G. P. Latham, "Building a Practically Useful Theory of Goal Setting and Task Motivation," *American Psychologist* 57, no. 2 (2002), pp. 705–717.

40. J. M. Ivancevich and J. T. McMahon, "The Effects of Goal Setting, External Feedback, and Self-Generated Feedback on Outcome Variables: A Field Experiment," *Academy of Management Journal* 25, no. 2 (1982), pp. 359–372; and E. A. Locke, "Motivation Through Conscious Goal Setting," *Applied and Preventive Psychology* 5, no. 2 (1996), pp. 117–124.

41. See, for example, G. P. Latham, M. Erez, and E. A. Locke, "Resolving Scientific Disputes by the Joint Design of Crucial Experiments by the Antagonists: Application to the Erez-Latham Dispute Regarding Participation in Goal Setting," *Journal of Applied Psychology* 73, no. 4 (1988), pp. 753–772; T. D. Ludwig and E. S. Geller, "Assigned Versus Participative Goal Setting and Response Generalization: Managing Injury Control among Professional Pizza Deliverers," *Journal of Applied Psychology* 82, no. 2 (1997), pp. 253–261; and S. G. Harkins and M. D. Lowe, "The Effects of Self-Set Goals on Task Performance," *Journal of Applied Social Psychology* 30, no. 1 (2000), pp. 1–40.

42. M. Erez, P. C. Earley, and C. L. Hulin, "The Impact of Participation on Goal Acceptance and Performance: A Two-Step Model," *Academy of Management Journal* 28, no. 1 (1985), pp. 50–66.

43. E. A. Locke, "The Motivation to Work: What We Know," *Advances in Motivation and Achievement* 10 (1997), pp. 375–412; and Latham, Erez, and Locke, "Resolving Scientific Disputes by the Joint Design of Crucial Experiments by the Antagonists," pp. 753–772.

44. Ibid.

45. J. R. Hollenbeck, C. R. Williams, and H. J. Klein, "An Empirical Examination of the Antecedents of Commitment to Difficult Goals," *Journal of Applied Psychology* 74, no. 1 (1989), pp. 18–23. See also J. C. Wofford, V. L. Goodwin, and S. Premack, "Meta-Analysis of the Antecedents of Personal Goal Level and of the Antecedents and Consequences of Goal Commitment," *Journal of Management* 18, no. 3 (1992), pp. 595–615; M. E. Tubbs, "Commitment as a Moderator of the Goal-Performance Relation: A Case for Clearer Construct Definition," *Journal of Applied Psychology* 78, no. 1 (1993), pp. 86–97; and J. E. Bono and A. E. Colbert, "Understanding Responses to Multi-Source Feedback: The Role of Core Self-Evaluations," *Personnel Psychology* 58, no. 1 (2005), pp. 171–203.

46. See R. E. Wood, A. J. Mento, and E. A. Locke, "Task Complexity as a Moderator of Goal Effects: A Meta-Analysis," *Journal of Applied Psychology* 72, no. 3 (1987), pp. 416–425; R. Kanfer and P. L. Ackerman, "Motivation and Cognitive Abilities: An Integrative/Aptitude-Treatment Interaction Approach to Skill Acquisition," *Journal of Applied Psychology* 74, no. 4 (1989), pp. 657–690; T. R. Mitchell and W. S. Silver, "Individual and Group Goals When Workers Are Interdependent: Effects on Task Strategies and Performance," *Journal of Applied Psychology* 75, no. 2 (1990), pp. 185–193; and A. M. O'Leary-Kelly, J. J. Martocchio, and D. D. Frink, "A Review of the Influence of Group Goals on Group Performance," *Academy of Management Journal* 37, no. 5 (1994), pp. 1285–1301.

47. D. F. Crown, "The Use of Group and Groupcentric Individual Goals for Culturally Heterogeneous and Homogeneous Task Groups: An Assessment of European Work Teams," *Small Group Research* 38, no. 4 (2007), pp. 489–508; J. Kurman, "Self-Regulation Strategies in Achievement Settings: Culture and Gender Differences," *Journal of Cross-Cultural Psychology* 32, no. 4 (2001), pp. 491–503; and M. Erez and P. C. Earley, "Comparative Analysis of Goal-Setting Strategies Across Cultures," *Journal of Applied Psychology* 72, no. 4 (1987), pp. 658–665.

48. C. Sue-Chan and M. Ong, "Goal Assignment and Performance: Assessing the Mediating Roles of Goal Commitment and Self-Efficacy and the Moderating Role of Power Distance," *Organizational Behavior and Human Decision Processes* 89, no. 2 (2002), pp. 1140–1161.

49. G. P. Latham and E. A. Locke, "Enhancing the Benefits and Overcoming the Pitfalls of Goal Setting," *Organizational Dynamics* 35, no. 6, pp. 332–340; L. D. Ordóñez, M. E. Schweitzer, A. D. Galinsky, and M. Bazerman, "Goals Gone Wild: The Systematic Side Effects of Overprescribing Goal Setting," *Academy of Management Perspectives* 23, no. 1 (2009), pp. 6–16; and E. A. Locke and G. P. Latham, "Has Goal Setting Gone Wild, or Have Its Attackers Abandoned Good Scholarship?" *Academy of Management Perspectives* 23, no. 1 (2009), pp. 17–23.

50. S. J. Perry, L. A. Witt, L. M. Penney, and L. Atwater, "The Downside of Goal-Focused Leadership: The Role of Personality in Subordinate Exhaustion," *Journal of Applied Psychology* 95, no. 6 (2010), pp. 1145–1153.

51. See, for example, A. D. Sajkovic, E. A. Locke, and E. S. Blair, "A First Examination of the Relationships Between Primed Subconscious Goals, Assigned Conscious Goals, and Task Performance," *Journal of Applied Psychology* 91, no. 5 (2006), pp. 1172–1180; G. P. Latham, A. D. Stajkovic, and E. A. Locke, "The Relevance and Viability of Subconscious Goals in the Workplace," *Journal of Management* 36, no. 1 (2010), pp. 234–255; and A. Schantz and G. P. Latham, "An Exploratory Field Experiment on the Effect of Subconscious and Conscious Goals on Employee Performance," *Organizational Behavior and Human Decision Processes* 109, no. 1 (2009), pp. 9–17.

52. "KEYGroup Survey Finds Nearly Half of All Employees Have No Set Performance Goals," *IPMA-HR Bulletin* (March 10, 2006), p. 1; S. Hamm, "SAP Dangles a Big, Fat Carrot," *BusinessWeek* (May 22, 2006), pp. 67–68; and "P&G CEO Wields High Expectations but No Whip," *USA Today* (February 19, 2007), p. 3B.

53. See, for instance, S. J. Carroll and H. L. Tosi, *Management by Objectives: Applications and Research* (New York: Macmillan, 1973); and R. Rodgers and J. E. Hunter, "Impact of Management by Objectives on Organizational Productivity," *Journal of Applied Psychology* 76, no. 2 (1991), pp. 322–336.

54. A. Bandura, *Self-Efficacy: The Exercise of Control* (New York: Freeman, 1997).

55. A. D. Stajkovic and F. Luthans, "Self-Efficacy and Work-Related Performance: A Meta-Analysis," *Psychological Bulletin* 124, no. 2 (1998), pp. 240–261; and A. Bandura, "Cultivate Self-Efficacy for Personal and Organizational Effectiveness," in E. Locke (ed.), *Handbook of Principles of Organizational Behavior* (Malden, MA: Blackwell, 2004), pp. 120–136.

56. M. Salanova, S. Llorens, and W. B. Schaufeli, "Yes I Can, I Feel Good, and I Just Do It! On Gain Cycles and Spirals of Efficacy Beliefs, Affect, and Engagement," *Applied Psychology* 60, no. 2 (2011), pp. 255–285.

57. P. Tierney and S. M. Farmer, "Creative Self-Efficacy Development and Creative Performance Over Time," *Journal of Applied Psychology* 96, no. 2 (2011), pp. 277–293.

58. A. Bandura and D. Cervone, "Differential Engagement in Self-Reactive Influences in Cognitively-Based Motivation," *Organizational Behavior and Human Decision Processes* 38, no. 1 (1986), pp. 92–113.

59. Bandura, *Self-Efficacy.*

60. R. C. Rist, "Student Social Class and Teacher Expectations: The Self-Fulfilling Prophecy in Ghetto Education," *Harvard Educational Review* 70, no. 3 (2000), pp. 266–301.

61. D. Eden, "Self-Fulfilling Prophecies in Organizations," in J. Greenberg (ed.), *Organizational Behavior: The State of the Science,* 2nd ed. (Mahwah, NJ: Lawrence Erlbaum, 2003), pp. 91–122.

62. Ibid.

63. C. L. Holladay and M. A. Quiñones, "Practice Variability and Transfer of Training: The Role of Self-Efficacy Generality," *Journal of Applied Psychology* 88, no. 6 (2003), pp. 1094–1103.

64. E. C. Dierdorff, E. A. Surface, and K. G. Brown, "Frame-of-Reference Training Effectiveness: Effects of Goal Orientation and Self-Efficacy on Affective, Cognitive, Skill-Based, and Transfer Outcomes," *Journal of Applied Psychology* 95, no. 6 (2010), pp. 1181–1191; and R. Grossman, and E. Salas, "The Transfer of Training: What Really Matters," *International Journal of Training and Development* 15, no. 2 (2011), pp. 103–120.

65. T. A. Judge, C. L. Jackson, J. C. Shaw, B. Scott, and B. L. Rich, "Self-Efficacy and Work-Related Performance: The Integral Role of Individual Differences," *Journal of Applied Psychology* 92, no. 1 (2007), pp. 107–127.

66. Ibid.

67. J. S. Adams, "Inequity in Social Exchanges," in L. Berkowitz (ed.), *Advances in Experimental Social Psychology* (New York: Academic Press, 1965), pp. 267–300.

68. P. S. Goodman, "An Examination of Referents Used in the Evaluation of Pay," *Organizational Behavior and Human Performance* 12, no. 2 (1974), pp. 170–195; W. Scholl, E. A. Cooper, and J. F. McKenna, "Referent Selection in Determining Equity Perception: Differential Effects on Behavioral and Attitudinal Outcomes," *Personnel Psychology* 40, no. 1 (1987), pp. 113–127; and M. L. Williams, M. A. McDaniel, and N. T. Nguyen, "A Meta-Analysis of the Antecedents and Consequences of Pay Level Satisfaction," *Journal of Applied Psychology* 91, no. 2 (2006), pp. 392–413.

69. C. T. Kulik and M. L. Ambrose, "Personal and Situational Determinants of Referent Choice," *Academy of Management Review* 17, no. 2 (1992), pp. 212–237.

70. See, for example, E. Walster, G. W. Walster, and W. G. Scott, *Equity: Theory and Research* (Boston: Allyn & Bacon, 1978); and J. Greenberg, "Cognitive Reevaluation of Outcomes in Response to Underpayment Inequity," *Academy of Management Journal,* March 1989, pp. 174–184.

71. P. S. Goodman and A. Friedman, "An Examination of Adams' Theory of Inequity," *Administrative Science Quarterly* 16, no. 3 (1971), pp. 271–288; R. P. Vecchio, "An Individual-Differences Interpretation of the Conflicting Predictions Generated by Equity Theory and Expectancy Theory," *Journal of Applied Psychology* 66, no. 4 (1981), pp. 470–481; R. T. Mowday, "Equity Theory Predictions of Behavior in Organizations," in R. Steers, L. W. Porter, and G. Bigley (eds.), *Motivation and Work Behavior,* 6th ed. (New York: McGraw-Hill, 1996), pp. 111–131; R. W. Griffeth and S. Gaertner, "A Role for Equity Theory in the Turnover Process: An Empirical Test," *Journal of Applied Social Psychology* 31, no. 5 (2001), pp. 1017–1037; and L. K. Scheer, N. Kumar, and J.-B. E. M. Steenkamp, "Reactions to Perceived Inequity in U.S. and Dutch Interorganizational Relationships," *Academy of Management* 46, no. 3 (2003), pp. 303–316.

72. See, for example, R. C. Huseman, J. D. Hatfield, and E. W. Miles, "A New Perspective on Equity Theory: The Equity Sensitivity Construct," *Academy of Management Journal* 12, no. 2 (1987), pp. 222–234; K. S. Sauley and A. G. Bedeian, "Equity Sensitivity: Construction of a Measure and Examination of Its Psychometric Properties," *Journal of Management* 26, no. 5 (2000), pp. 885–910; and J. A. Colquitt, "Does the Justice of One Interact with the Justice of Many? Reactions to Procedural Justice in Teams," *Journal of Applied Psychology* 89, no. 4 (2004), pp. 633–646.

73. See, for instance, J. A. Colquitt, D. E. Conlon, M. J. Wesson, C. O. L. H. Porter, and K. Y. Ng, "Justice at the Millennium: A Meta-Analytic Review of the 25 Years of Organizational Justice Research," *Journal of Applied Psychology* 86, no. 3 (2001), pp. 425–445; T. Simons and Q. Roberson, "Why Managers Should Care About Fairness: The Effects of Aggregate Justice Perceptions on Organizational Outcomes," *Journal of Applied Psychology* 88, no. 3 (2003), pp. 432–443; and B. C. Holtz and C. M. Harold, "Fair Today, Fair

Tomorrow? A Longitudinal Investigation of Overall Justice Perceptions," *Journal of Applied Psychology* 94, no. 5 (2009), pp. 1185–1199.

74. K. Leung, K. Tong, and S. S. Ho, "Effects of Interactional Justice on Egocentric Bias in Resource Allocation Decisions," *Journal of Applied Psychology* 89, no. 3 (2004), pp. 405–415; and L. Francis-Gladney, N. R. Manger, and R. B. Welker, "Does Outcome Favorability Affect Procedural Fairness as a Result of Self-Serving Attributions," *Journal of Applied Social Psychology* 40, no. 1 (2010), pp. 182–194.

75. See, for example, R. Cropanzano, J. H. Stein, and T. Nadisic, *Social Justice and the Experience of Emotion* (New York: Routledge/Taylor and Francis Group, 2011).

76. D. P. Skarlicki and D. E. Rupp, "Dual Processing and Organizational Justice: The Role of Rational Versus Experiential Processing in Third-Party Reactions to Workplace Mistreatment," *Journal of Applied Psychology* 95, no. 5 (2010), pp. 944–952.

77. G. S. Leventhal, "What Should Be Done with Equity Theory? New Approaches to the Study of Fairness in Social Relationships," in K. Gergen, M. Greenberg, and R. Willis (eds.), *Social Exchange: Advances in Theory and Research* (New York: Plenum, 1980), pp. 27–55.

78. J. C. Shaw, E. Wild, and J. A. Colquitt, "To Justify or Excuse? A Meta-Analytic Review of the Effects of Explanations," *Journal of Applied Psychology* 88, no. 3 (2003), pp. 444–458.

79. D. P. Skarlicki and R. Folger, "Retaliation in the Workplace: The Roles of Distributive, Procedural, and Interactional Justice," *Journal of Applied Psychology* 82, no. 3 (1997), pp. 434–443; and D. A. Jones, "Getting Even with One's Supervisor and One's Organization: Relationships Among Types of Injustice, Desires for Revenge, and Counterproductive Work Behavior," *Journal of Organizational Behavior* 30, no. 4 (2009), pp. 525–542.

80. R. Cropanzano, C. A. Prehar, and P. Y. Chen, "Using Social Exchange Theory to Distinguish Procedural from Interactional Justice," *Group & Organization Management* 27, no. 3 (2002), pp. 324–351; and S. G. Roch and L. R. Shanock, "Organizational Justice in an Exchange Framework: Clarifying Organizational Justice Dimensions," *Journal of Management* 32, no. 2 (2006), pp. 299–322.

81. Colquitt, Conlon, Wesson, Porter, and Ng, "Justice at the Millennium," pp. 425–445.

82. J. K. Giacobbe-Miller, D. J. Miller, and V. I. Victorov, "A Comparison of Russian and U.S. Pay Allocation Decisions, Distributive Justice Judgments, and Productivity Under Different Payment Conditions," *Personnel Psychology* 51, no. 1 (1998), pp. 137–163.

83. M. C. Bolino and W. H. Turnley, "Old Faces, New Places: Equity Theory in Cross-Cultural Contexts," *Journal of Organizational Behavior* 29, no. 1 (2008), pp. 29–50.

84. B. A. Scott, J. A. Colquitt, and E. L. Paddock, "An Actor-Focused Model of Justice Rule Adherence and Violation: The Role of Managerial Motives and Discretion," *Journal of Applied Psychology* 94, no. 3 (2009), pp. 756–769.

85. L. J. Barclay and D. P. Skarlicki, "Healing the Wounds of Organizational Injustice: Examining the Benefits of Expressive Writing," *Journal of Applied Psychology* 94, no. 2 (2009), pp. 511–523.

86. R. Fischer and P. B. Smith, "Reward Allocation and Culture: A Meta-Analysis," *Journal of Cross-Cultural Psychology* 34, no. 3 (2003), pp. 251–268.

87. F. F. T. Chiang and T. Birtch, "The Transferability of Management Practices: Examining Cross-National Differences in Reward Preferences," *Human Relations* 60, no. 9 (2007), pp. 1293–1330; A. E. Lind, T. R. Tyler, and Y. J. Huo, "Procedural Context and Culture: Variation in the Antecedents of Procedural Justice Judgments," *Journal of Personality and Social Psychology* 73, no. 4 (1997), pp. 767–780; M. J. Gelfand, M. Erez, and Z. Aycan, "Cross-Cultural Organizational Behavior," *Annual Review of Psychology* 58, (2007), pp. 479–514.

88. V. H. Vroom, *Work and Motivation* (New York: Wiley, 1964).

89. For criticism, see H. G. Heneman III and D. P. Schwab, "Evaluation of Research on Expectancy Theory Prediction of Employee Performance," *Psychological Bulletin* 78, no. 1 (1972), pp. 1–9; T. R. Mitchell, "Expectancy Models of Job Satisfaction, Occupational Preference and Effort: A Theoretical, Methodological and Empirical Appraisal," *Psychological Bulletin* 81, no. 12 (1974), pp. 1053–1077; and W. Van Eerde and H. Thierry, "Vroom's Expectancy Models and Work-Related Criteria: A Meta-Analysis," *Journal of Applied Psychology* 81, no. 5 (1996), pp. 575–586. For support, see L. W. Porter and E. E. Lawler III, *Managerial Attitudes and Performance* (Homewood, IL: Irwin, 1968); and J. J. Donovan, "Work Motivation," in N. Anderson et al. (eds.), *Handbook of Industrial, Work & Organizational Psychology*, vol. 2 (Thousand Oaks, CA: Sage, 2001), pp. 56–59.

90. Vroom refers to these three variables as expectancy, instrumentality, and valence, respectively.

91. J. Nocera, "The Anguish of Being an Analyst," *New York Times* (March 4, 2006), pp. B1, B12.

92. R. J. House, H. J. Shapiro, and M. A. Wahba, "Expectancy Theory as a Predictor of Work Behavior and Attitudes: A Re-evaluation of Empirical Evidence," *Decision Sciences* 5, no. 3 (1974), pp. 481–506.

93. This section is based on F. J. Landy and W. S. Becker, "Motivation Theory Reconsidered," in L. L. Cummings and B. M. Staw (eds.), *Research in Organizational Behavior,* vol. 9 (Greenwich, CT: JAI Press, 1987), pp. 24–35.

CHAPTER 8

1. J. R. Hackman and G. R. Oldham, "Motivation Through the Design of Work: Test of a Theory," *Organizational Behavior and Human Performance* 16, no. 2 (1976), pp. 250–279; and J. R. Hackman and G. R. Oldham, *Work Redesign* (Reading, MA: Addison-Wesley, 1980).

2. J. R. Hackman, "Work Design," in J. R. Hackman and J. L. Suttle (eds.), *Improving Life at Work* (Santa Monica, CA: Goodyear, 1977), p. 129.

3. See B. T. Loher, R. A. Noe, N. L. Moeller, and M. P. Fitzgerald, "A Meta-Analysis of the Relation of Job Characteristics to Job Satisfaction," *Journal of Applied Psychology* 70, no. 2 (1985), pp. 280–289; S. J. Zaccaro and E. F. Stone, "Incremental Validity of an Empirically Based Measure of Job Characteristics," *Journal of Applied Psychology* 73, no. 2 (1988), pp. 245–252; J. R. Rentsch and R. P. Steel, "Testing the Durability of Job Characteristics as Predictors of Absenteeism over a Six-Year Period," *Personnel Psychology* 51, no. 2 (1998), pp. 165–190; S. J. Behson, E. R. Eddy, and S. J. Lorenzet, "The Importance of the Critical Psychological States in the Job Characteristics Model: A Meta-Analytic

and Structural Equations Modeling Examination," *Current Research in Social Psychology* 51, no. 12 (2000), pp. 170–189; and S. E. Humphrey, J. D. Nahrgang, and F. P. Morgeson, "Integrating Motivational, Social, and Contextual Work Design Features: A Meta-Analytic Summary and Theoretical Extension of the Work Design Literature," *Journal of Applied Psychology* 92, no. 5 (2007), pp. 1332–1356.

4. T. A. Judge, S. K. Parker, A. E. Colbert, D. Heller, and R. Ilies, "Job Satisfaction: A Cross-Cultural Review," in N. Anderson, D. S. Ones (eds.), *Handbook of Industrial, Work and Organizational Psychology*, vol. 2 (Thousand Oaks, CA: Sage Publications, 2002), pp. 25–52.

5. B. M. Meglino and A. M. Korsgaard, "The Role of Other Orientation in Reactions to Job Characteristics," *Journal of Management* 33, no. 1 (2007), pp. 57–83.

6. M. F. Peterson and S. A. Ruiz-Quintanilla, "Cultural Socialization as a Source of Intrinsic Work Motivation," *Group & Organization Management* 28, no. 2 (2003), pp. 188–216.

7. C. Ansberry, "In the New Workplace, Jobs Morph to Suit Rapid Pace of Change," *Wall Street Journal* (March 22, 2002), p. A1.

8. T. Silver, "Rotate Your Way to Higher Value," *Baseline* (March/April 2010), p. 12; and J. J. Salopek, "Coca-Cola Division Refreshes Its Talent with Diversity Push on Campus," *Workforce Management Online* (March 2011), www.workforce.com.

9. J. Ortega, "Job Rotation as a Learning Mechanism," *Management Science* 47, no. 10 (2001), pp. 1361–1370.

10. A. Christini and D. Pozzoli, "Workplace Practices and Firm Performance in Manufacturing: A Comparative Study of Italy and Britain," *International Journal of Manpower* 31, no. 7 (2010), pp. 818–842; K. Kaymaz, "The Effects of Job Rotation Practices on Motivation: A Research on Managers in the Automotive Organizations," *Business and Economics Research Journal* 1, no. 3 (2010), pp. 69–86.

11. Hackman and Oldham, *Work Redesign.*

12. A. M. Grant, E. M. Campbell, G. Chen, K. Cottone, D. Lapedis, and K. Lee, "Impact and the Art of Motivation Maintenance: The Effects of Contact with Beneficiaries on Persistence Behavior," *Organizational Behavior and Human Decision Processes* 103, no. 1 (2007), pp. 53–67.

13. A. M. Grant, J. E. Dutton, and B. D. Rosso, "Giving Commitment: Employee Support Programs and the Prosocial Sensemaking Process," *Academy of Management Journal* 51, no. 5 (2008), pp. 898–918.

14. See, for example, R. W. Griffin, "Effects of Work Redesign on Employee Perceptions, Attitudes, and Behaviors: A Long-Term Investigation," *Academy of Management Journal* 34, no. 2 (1991), pp. 425–435; and M. Subramony, "A Meta-Analytic Investigation of the Relationship between HRM Bundles and Firm Performance," *Human Resource Management* 48, no. 5 (2009), pp. 745–768.

15. R. D. Pritchard, M. M. Harrell, D. DiazGrandos, and M. J. Guzman, "The Productivity Measurement and Enhancement System: A Meta-Analysis," *Journal of Applied Psychology* 93, no. 3 (2008), pp. 540–567.

16. F. P. Morgeson, M. D. Johnson, M. A. Campion, G. J. Medsker, and T. V. Mumford, "Understanding Reactions to Job Redesign: A Quasi-Experimental Investigation of the Moderating Effects of Organizational Contact on Perceptions of Performance Behavior," *Personnel Psychology* 59, no. 2 (2006), pp. 333–363.

17. Cited in K. Palmer, "The New Mommy Track," *U.S. News and World Report* (September 3, 2007), pp. 40–45.

18. Cited in "Flextime Gains in Popularity in Germany," *Manpower Argus* (September 2000), p. 4; and Y. Yanadori and T. Kato, "Work and Family Practices in Japanese Firms: Their Scope, Nature, and Impact on Employee Turnover," *International Journal of Human Resource Management* 20, no. 2 (2009), pp. 439–456.

19. 20 S. Westcott, "Beyond Flextime: Trashing the Workweek," *Inc.* (August 2008), p. 30.

20. See, for example, D. A. Ralston and M. F. Flanagan, "The Effect of Flextime on Absenteeism and Turnover for Male and Female Employees," *Journal of Vocational Behavior* 26, no. 2 (1985), pp. 206–217; B. B. Baltes, T. E. Briggs, J. W. Huff, J. A. Wright, and G. A. Neuman, "Flexible and Compressed Workweek Schedules: A Meta-Analysis of Their Effects on Work-Related Criteria," *Journal of Applied Psychology* 84, no. 4 (1999), pp. 496–513; K. M. Shockley, and T. D. Allen, "When Flexibility Helps: Another Look at the Availability of Flexible Work Arrangements and Work–Family Conflict," *Journal of Vocational Behavior* 71, no. 3 (2007), pp. 479–493; J. G. Grzywacz, D. S. Carlson, and S. Shulkin, "Schedule Flexibility and Stress: Linking Formal Flexible Arrangements and Perceived Flexibility to Employee Health." *Community, Work, and Family* 11, no. 2 (2008), pp. 199–214; and L. A. McNall, A. D. Masuda, and J. M. Nicklin, "Flexible Work Arrangements, Job Satisfaction, and Turnover Intentions: The Mediating Role of Work-to-Family Enrichment," *Journal of Psychology* 144, no. 1 (2010), pp. 61–81.

21. K. M. Shockley and T. D. Allen, "Investigating the Missing Link in Flexible Work Arrangement Utilization: An Individual Difference Perspective," *Journal of Vocational Behavior* 76, no. 1 (2010), pp. 131–142.

22. J. LaReau, "Ford's 2 Julies Share Devotion—and Job," *Automotive News* (October 25, 2010), p. 4.

23. Society for Human Resource Management, *2008 Employee Benefits* (Alexandria, VA: Author, 2008).

24. S. Shellenbarger, "Two People, One Job: It Can Really Work," *The Wall Street Journal* (December 7, 1994), p. B1.

25. "Job-Sharing: Widely Offered, Little Used," *Training* (November 1994), p. 12.

26. C. Dawson, "Japan: Work-Sharing Will Prolong the Pain," *BusinessWeek* (December 24, 2001), p. 46.

27. Shellenbarger, "Two People, One Job," p. B1.

28. See, for example, E. J. Hill, M. Ferris, and V. Martinson, "Does It Matter Where You Work? A Comparison of How Three Work Venues (Traditional Office, Virtual Office, and Home Office) Influence Aspects of Work and Personal/Family Life," *Journal of Vocational Behavior* 63, no. 2 (2003), pp. 220–241; B. Williamson, "Managing Virtual Workers," *Bloomberg Businessweek* (July 16, 2009), www.businessweek.com, and B. A. Lautsch and E. E. Kossek, "Managing a Blended Workforce: Telecommuters and Non-Telecommuters," *Organizational Dynamics* 40, no. 1 (2010), pp. 10–17.

29. J. Tozzi, "Home-Based Businesses Increasing," *Bloomberg Businessweek* (January 25, 2010), www.businessweek.com.

30. Society for Human Resource Management, *2008 Employee Benefits*.

31. See, for instance, M. Conlin, "The Easiest Commute of All," *BusinessWeek* (December 12, 2005), p. 78; S. Shellenbarger, "Telework Is on the Rise, but It Isn't Just Done from Home Anymore," *Wall Street Journal* (January 23, 2001), p. B1;

and E. O'Keefe, "Teleworking Grows But Still a Rarity," *Washington Post* (February 22, 2011), p. B3.

32. Conlin, "The Easiest Commute of All."

33. E. E. Kossek, B. A. Lautsch, S. C. Eaton, "Telecommuting, Control, and Boundary Management: Correlates of Policy Use and Practice, Job Control, and Work-Family Effectiveness," *Journal of Vocational Behavior* 68, no. 2 (2006), pp. 347–367.

34. J. M. Stanton and J. L. Barnes-Farrell, "Effects of Electronic Performance Monitoring on Personal Control, Task Satisfaction, and Task Performance," *Journal of Applied Psychology* 81, no. 6 (1996), pp. 738–745; and L. Taskin and F. Bridoux, "Telework: A Challenge to Knowledge Transfer in Organizations," *International Journal of Human Resource Management* 21, no. 13 (2010), pp. 2503–2520.

35. See, for example, P. Brotherton, "For Teleworkers, Less Is Definitely More," *T & D* 65 (March 2011), p. 29; and M. Virick, N. DaSilva, and K. Arrington, "Moderators of the Curvilinear Relation Between Extent of Telecommuting and Job and Life Satisfaction: The Role of Performance Outcome Orientation and Worker Type," *Human Relations* 63, no. 1 (2010), pp. 137–154.

36. J. Welch and S. Welch, "The Importance of Being There," *BusinessWeek* (April 16, 2007), p. 92; Z. I. Barsness, K. A. Diekmann, and M. L. Seidel, "Motivation and Opportunity: The Role of Remote Work, Demographic Dissimilarity, and Social Network Centrality in Impression Management," *Academy of Management Journal* 48, no. 3 (2005), pp. 401–419.

37. F. P. Morgeson and S. E. Humphrey, "The Work Design Questionnaire (WDQ): Developing and Validating a Comprehensive Measure for Assessing Job Design and the Nature of Work," *Journal of Applied Psychology* 91, no. 6 (2006), pp. 1321–1339; S. E. Humphrey, J. D. Nahrgang, and F. P. Morgeson, "Integrating Motivational, Social, and Contextual Work Design Features: A Meta-Analytic Summary and Theoretical Extension of the Work Design Literature," *Journal of Applied Psychology* 92, no. 5 (2007), pp. 1332–1356; and R. Takeuchi, D. P. Lepak, H. Wang, and K. Takeuchi, "An Empirical Examination of the Mechanisms Mediating Between High-Performance Work Systems and the Performance of Japanese Organizations," *Journal of Applied Psychology* 92, no. 4 (2007), pp. 1069–1083.

38. See, for example, the increasing body of literature on empowerment, such as D. P. Ashmos, D. Duchon, R. R. McDaniel Jr., and J. W. Huonker, "What a Mess! Participation as a Simple Managerial Rule to 'Complexify' Organizations," *Journal of Management Studies* 39, no. 2 (2002), pp. 189–206; S. E. Seibert, S. R. Silver, and W. A. Randolph, "Taking Empowerment to the Next Level: A Multiple-Level Model of Empowerment, Performance, and Satisfaction," *Academy of Management Journal* 47, no. 3 (2004), pp. 332–349; M. M. Butts, R. J. Vandenberg, D. M. DeJoy, B. S. Schaffer, and M. G. Wilson, "Individual Reactions to High Involvement Work Processes: Investigating the Role of Empowerment and Perceived Organizational Support," *Journal of Occupational Health Psychology* 14, no. 2 (2009), pp. 122–136; R. Park, E. Applebaum, and D. Kruse, "Employee Involvement and Group Incentives in Manufacturing Companies: A Multi-Level Analysis," *Human Resource Management Journal* 20, no. 3 (2010), pp. 227–243; and D. C. Jones, P. Kalmi, and A. Kauhanen, "How Does Employee Involvement Stack Up? The Effects of Human Resource Management Policies in a Retail Firm," *Industrial Relations* 49, no. 1 (2010), pp. 1–21.

39. See, for instance, A. Sagie and Z. Aycan, "A Cross-Cultural Analysis of Participative Decision-Making in Organizations," *Human Relations* 56, no. 4 (2003), pp. 453–473; and J. Brockner, "Unpacking Country Effects: On the Need to Operationalize the Psychological Determinants of Cross-National Differences," in R. M. Kramer and B. M. Staw (eds.), *Research in Organizational Behavior,* vol. 25 (Oxford, UK: Elsevier, 2003), pp. 336–340.

40. C. Robert, T. M. Probst, J. J. Martocchio, R. Drasgow, and J. J. Lawler, "Empowerment and Continuous Improvement in the United States, Mexico, Poland, and India: Predicting Fit on the Basis of the Dimensions of Power Distance and Individualism," *Journal of Applied Psychology* 85, no. 5 (2000), pp. 643–658.

41. Z. X. Chen and S. Aryee, "Delegation and Employee Work Outcomes: An Examination of the Cultural Context of Mediating Processes in China," *Academy of Management Journal* 50, no. 1 (2007), pp. 226–238.

42. F. Heller, E. Pusic, G. Strauss, and B. Wilpert, *Organizational Participation: Myth and Reality* (Oxford, UK: Oxford University Press, 1998).

43. See, for instance, K. L. Miller and P. R. Monge, "Participation, Satisfaction, and Productivity: A Meta-Analytic Review," *Academy of Management Journal* (December 1986), pp. 727–753; J. A. Wagner III, "Participation's Effects on Performance and Satisfaction: A Reconsideration of Research Evidence," *Academy of Management Review* 19, no. 2 (1994), pp. 312–330; C. Doucouliagos, "Worker Participation and Productivity in Labor-Managed and Participatory Capitalist Firms: A Meta-Analysis," *Industrial and Labor Relations Review* 49, no. 1 (1995), pp. 58–77; J. A. Wagner III, C. R. Leana, E. A. Locke, and D. M. Schweiger, "Cognitive and Motivational Frameworks in U.S. Research on Participation: A Meta-Analysis of Primary Effects," *Journal of Organizational Behavior* 18, no. 1 (1997), pp. 49–65; A. Pendleton and A. Robinson, "Employee Stock Ownership, Involvement, and Productivity: An Interaction-Based Approach," *Industrial and Labor Relations Review* 64, no. 1 (2010), pp. 3–29.

44. D. K. Datta, J. P. Guthrie, and P. M. Wright, "Human Resource Management and Labor Productivity: Does Industry Matter? *Academy of Management Journal* 48, no. 1 (2005), pp. 135–145; C. M. Riordan, R. J. Vandenberg, and H. A. Richardson, "Employee Involvement Climate and Organizational Effectiveness." *Human Resource Management* 44, no. 4 (2005), pp. 471–488; and J. Kim, J. P. MacDuffie, and F. K. Pil, "Employee Voice and Organizational Performance: Team Versus Representative Influence," *Human Relations* 63, no. 3 (2010), pp. 371–394.

45. Cotton, *Employee Involvement,* p. 114.

46. See, for example, M. Gilman and P. Marginson, "Negotiating European Works Council: Contours of Constrained Choice," *Industrial Relations Journal* 33, no. 1 (2002), pp. 36–51; J. T. Addison and C. R. Belfield, "What Do We Know About the New European Works Council? Some Preliminary Evidence from Britain," *Scottish Journal of Political Economy* 49, no. 4 (2002), pp. 418–444; and B. Keller, "The European Company Statute: Employee Involvement—and Beyond," *Industrial Relations Journal* 33, no. 5 (2002), pp. 424–445.

47. Cotton, *Employee Involvement,* pp. 129–130, 139–140.

48. Ibid., p. 140.

49. E. White, "Opportunity Knocks, and It Pays a Lot Better," *Wall Street Journal* (November 13, 2006), p. B3.

50. P. S. Goodman and P. P. Pan, "Chinese Workers Pay for Wal-Mart's Low Prices," *Washington Post* (February 8, 2004), p. A1.

51. M. Sabramony, N. Krause, J. Norton, and G. N. Burns "The Relationship Between Human Resource Investments and Organizational Performance: A Firm-Level Examination of Equilibrium Theory," *Journal of Applied Psychology* 93, no. 4 (2008), pp. 778–788.

52. See, for example, B. Martinez, "Teacher Bonuses Emerge in Newark," *Wall Street Journal*, (April 21, 2011), p. A.15; and D. Weber, "Seminole Teachers to Get Bonuses Instead of Raises," *Orlando Sentinel* (January 19, 2011), www.orlandosentinel.com.

53. Based on J. R. Schuster and P. K. Zingheim, "The New Variable Pay: Key Design Issues," *Compensation & Benefits Review* (March/April 1993), p. 28; K. S. Abosch, "Variable Pay: Do We Have the Basics in Place?" *Compensation & Benefits Review* (July–August 1998), pp. 12–22; and K. M. Kuhn and M. D. Yockey, "Variable Pay as a Risky Choice: Determinants of the Relative Attractiveness of Incentive Plans," *Organizational Behavior and Human Decision Processes* 90, no. 2 (2003), pp. 323–341.

54. B. Wysocki Jr., "Chilling Reality Awaits Even the Employed," *The Wall Street Journal* (November 5, 2001), p. A1; and J. C. Kovac, "Sour Economy Presents Compensation Challenges," *Employee Benefit News* (July 1, 2008), p. 18.

55. G. D. Jenkins Jr., N. Gupta, A. Mitra, and J. D. Shaw, "Are Financial Incentives Related to Performance? A Meta-Analytic Review of Empirical Research," *Journal of Applied Psychology* 83, no. 5 (1998), pp. 777–787; and S. L. Rynes, B. Gerhart, and L. Parks, "Personnel Psychology: Performance Evaluation and Pay for Performance," *Annual Review of Psychology* 56, no. 1 (2005), pp. 571–600.

56. N. Byrnes, "Pain, But No Layoffs at Nucor," *BusinessWeek* (March 26, 2009), www.businessweek.com.

57. G. E. Ledford Jr., "Paying for the Skills, Knowledge, and Competencies of Knowledge Workers," *Compensation & Benefits Review*, (July/August 1995), pp. 55–62; B. Murray and B. Gerhart, "An Empirical Analysis of a Skill-Based Pay Program and Plant Performance Outcomes," *Academy of Management Journal* 41, no. 1 (1998), pp. 68–78; J. R. Thompson and C. W. LeHew, "Skill-Based Pay as an Organizational Innovation," *Review of Public Personnel Administration* 20, no. 1 (2000), pp. 20–40; and J. D. Shaw, N. Gupta, A. Mitra, and G. E. Ledford, Jr., "Success and Survival of Skill-Based Pay Plans," *Journal of Management* 31, no. 1 (2005), pp. 28–49.

58. A. Mitra, N. Gupta, and J. D. Shaw, "A Comparative Examination of Traditional and Skill-Based Pay Plans," *Journal of Managerial Psychology* 26, no. 4 (2011), pp. 278–296.

59. E. C. Dierdorff and E. A. Surface, "If You Pay for Skills, Will They Learn? Skill Change and Maintenance under a Skill-Based Pay System," *Journal of Management* 34, no.4 (2008), pp. 721–743.

60. F. Giancola, "Skill-Based Pay—Issues for Consideration," *Benefits and Compensation Digest* 44, no. 5 (2007), pp. 1–15.

61. N. Chi and T. Han, "Exploring the Linkages Between Formal Ownership and Psychological Ownership for the Organization: The Mediating Role of Organizational Justice," *Journal of Occupational and Organizational Psychology* 81, no. 4 (2008), pp. 691–711.

62. See, for instance, D. O. Kim, "Determinants of the Survival of Gainsharing Programs," *Industrial & Labor Relations Review* 53, no. 1 (1999), pp. 21–42; "Why Gainsharing Works Even Better Today Than in the Past," *HR Focus* (April 2000), pp. 3–5; L. R. Gomez-Mejia, T. M. Welbourne, and R. M. Wiseman, "The Role of Risk Sharing and Risk Taking Under Gainsharing," *Academy of Management Review* 25, no. 3 (2000), pp. 492–507; M. Reynolds, "A Cost-Reduction Strategy That May Be Back," *Healthcare Financial Management* (January 2002), pp. 58–64; and M. R. Dixon, L. J. Hayes, and J. Stack, "Changing Conceptions of Employee Compensation," *Journal of Organizational Behavior Management* 23, no. 2–3 (2003), pp. 95–116; I. M. Leitman, R. Levin, M. J. Lipp, L. Sivaprasad, C. J. Karalakulasingam, D. S. Bernard, P. Friedmann, and D. J. Shulkin, "Quality and Financial Outcomes from Gainsharing for Inpatient Admissions: A Three-Year Experience," *Journal of Hospital Medicine* 5, no. 9 (2010), pp. 501–517.

63. T. M. Welbourne and C. J. Ferrante, "To Monitor or Not to Monitor: A Study of Individual Outcomes from Monitoring One's Peers under Gainsharing and Merit Pay," *Group & Organization Management* 33, no. 2 (2008), pp. 139–162.

64. A. A. Buchko, "The Effects of Employee Ownership on Employee Attitudes: A Test of Three Theoretical Perspectives," *Work and Occupations* 19, no. 1 (1992), 59–78; and R. P. Garrett, "Does Employee Ownership Increase Innovation?" *New England Journal of Entrepreneurship* 13, no. 2, (2010), pp. 37–46.

65. D. McCarthy, E. Reeves, and T. Turner, "Can Employee Share-Ownership Improve Employee Attitudes and Behaviour?" *Employee Relations* 32, no. 4 (2010), pp. 382–395.

66. A. Pendleton and A. Robinson, "Employee Stock Ownership, Involvement, and Productivity: An Interaction-Based Approach," *Industrial and Labor Relations Review* 64, no. 1 (2010), pp. 3–29.

67. X. Zhang, K. M. Bartol, K. G. Smith, M. D. Pfarrer, and D. M. Khanin, "CEOs on the Edge: Earnings Manipulation and Stock-Based Incentive Misalignment," *Academy of Management Journal* 51, no. 2 (2008), pp. 241–258.

68. D. D'Art and T. Turner, "Profit Sharing, Firm Performance, and Union Influence in Selected European Countries," *Personnel Review* 33, no. 3 (2004), pp. 335–350; and D. Kruse, R. Freeman, and J. Blasi, *Shared Capitalism at Work: Employee Ownership, Profit and Gain Sharing, and Broad-Based Stock Options* (Chicago: University of Chicago Press, 2010).

69. A. Bayo-Moriones and M. Larraza-Kintana, "Profit-Sharing Plans and Affective Commitment: Does the Context Matter?" *Human Resource Management* 48, no. 2 (2009), pp. 207–226.

70. T. M. Welbourne and L. R. Gomez-Mejia, "Gainsharing: A Critical Review and a Future Research Agenda," *Journal of Management* 21, no. 3 (1995), pp. 559–609.

71. C. B. Cadsby, F. Song, and F. Tapon, "Sorting and Incentive Effects of Pay for Performance: An Experimental Investigation," *Academy of Management Journal* 50, no. 2 (2007), pp. 387–405.

72. S. C. L. Fong and M. A. Shaffer, "The Dimensionality and Determinants of Pay Satisfaction: A Cross-Cultural Investigation of a Group Incentive Plan," *International Journal of Human Resource Management* 14, no. 4 (2003), pp. 559–580.

73. See, for instance, M. W. Barringer and G. T. Milkovich, "A Theoretical Exploration of the Adoption and Design of Flexible Benefit Plans: A Case of Human Resource Innovation," *Academy of Management Review* 23, no. 2 (1998), pp. 305–324; D. Brown, "Everybody Loves Flex," *Canadian HR Reporter* (November 18, 2002), p. 1; J. Taggart, "Putting Flex Benefits Through Their Paces," *Canadian HR Reporter* (December 2, 2002), p. G3; and N. D. Cole and D. H. Flint, "Perceptions of Distributive and Procedural Justice in Employee Benefits: Flexible Versus Traditional Benefit Plans," *Journal of Managerial Psychology* 19, no. 1 (2004), pp. 19–40.

74. P. Stephens, "Flex Plans Gain in Popularity," *CA Magazine* (January/February 2010), p. 10.

75. D. Lovewell, "Flexible Benefits: Benefits on Offer," *Employee Benefits* (March 2010), p. S15.

76. S. E. Markham, K. D. Scott, and G. H. McKee, "Recognizing Good Attendance: A Longitudinal, Quasi-Experimental Field Study," *Personnel Psychology* 55, no. 3 (2002), p. 641; and S. J. Peterson and F. Luthans, "The Impact of Financial and Nonfinancial Incentives on Business Unit Outcomes over Time," *Journal of Applied Psychology* 91, no. 1 (2006), pp. 156–165.

77. A. D. Stajkovic and F. Luthans, "Differential Effects of Incentive Motivators on Work Performance," *Academy of Management Journal* 4, no. 3 (2001), p. 587. See also F. Luthans and A. D. Stajkovic, "Provide Recognition for Performance Improvement," in E. A. Locke (ed.), *Handbook of Principles of Organizational Behavior* (Malden, MA: Blackwell, 2004), pp. 166–180.

78. L. Shepherd, "Special Report on Rewards and Recognition: Getting Personal," *Workforce Management* (September 2010), pp. 24–29.

79. L. Shepherd, "On Recognition, Multinationals Think Globally," *Workforce Management* (September 2010), p. 26.

80. R. J. Long and J. L. Shields, "From Pay to Praise? Non-Case Employee Recognition in Canadian and Australian Firms," *International Journal of Human Resource Management* 21, no. 8 (2010), pp. 1145–1172.

CHAPTER 9

1. L. R. Sayles, "Work Group Behavior and the Larger Organization," in C. Arensburg et al. (eds.), *Research in Industrial Relations* (New York: Harper & Row, 1957), pp. 131–145.

2. J. F. McGrew, J. G. Bilotta, and J. M. Deeney, "Software Team Formation and Decay: Extending the Standard Model for Small Groups," *Small Group Research* 30, no. 2 (1999), pp. 209–234.

3. B. W. Tuckman, "Developmental Sequences in Small Groups," *Psychological Bulletin,* June 1965, pp. 384–399; B. W. Tuckman and M. C. Jensen, "Stages of Small-Group Development Revisited," *Group and Organizational Studies,* December 1977, pp. 419–427; M. F. Maples, "Group Development: Extending Tuckman's Theory," *Journal for Specialists in Group Work* (Fall 1988), pp. 17–23; and K. Vroman and J. Kovacich, "Computer-Mediated Interdisciplinary Teams: Theory and Reality," *Journal of Interprofessional Care* 16, no. 2 (2002), pp. 159–170.

4. J. E. Mathieu and T. L. Rapp, "Laying the Foundation for Successful Team Performance Trajectories: The Roles of Team Charters and Performance Strategies," *Journal of Applied Psychology* 94, no. 1 (2009), pp. 90–103; and E. C. Dierdorff, S. T. Bell, and J. A. Belohlav, "The Power of 'We': Effects of Psychological Collectivism on Team Performance Over Time," *Journal of Applied Psychology* 96, no. 2 (2011), pp. 247–262.

5. C. J. G. Gersick, "Time and Transition in Work Teams: Toward a New Model of Group Development," *Academy of Management Journal* (March 1988), pp. 9–41; C. J. G. Gersick, "Marking Time: Predictable Transitions in Task Groups," *Academy of Management Journal* (June 1989), pp. 274–309; M. J. Waller, J. M. Conte, C. B. Gibson, and M. A. Carpenter, "The Effect of Individual Perceptions of Deadlines on Team Performance," *Academy of Management Review* (October 2001), pp. 586–600; and A. Chang, P. Bordia, and J. Duck, "Punctuated Equilibrium and Linear Progression: Toward a New Understanding of Group Development," *Academy of Management Journal* (February 2003), pp. 106–117.

6. Gersick, "Time and Transition in Work Teams"; and Gersick, "Marking Time."

7. A. Seers and S. Woodruff, "Temporal Pacing in Task Forces: Group Development or Deadline Pressure?" *Journal of Management* 23, no. 2 (1997), pp. 169–187.

8. See M. F. Peterson et al., "Role Conflict, Ambiguity, and Overload: A 21-Nation Study," *Academy of Management Journal* (April 1995), pp. 429–452; and I. H. Settles, R. M. Sellers, and A. Damas Jr., "One Role or Two? The Function of Psychological Separation in Role Conflict," *Journal of Applied Psychology* (June 2002), pp. 574–582.

9. For a review of the research on group norms, see J. R. Hackman, "Group Influences on Individuals in Organizations," in M. D. Dunnette and L. M. Hough (eds.), *Handbook of Industrial & Organizational Psychology,* 2nd ed., vol. 3 (Palo Alto, CA: Consulting Psychologists Press, 1992), pp. 235–250. For a more recent discussion, see M. G. Ehrhart and S. E. Naumann, "Organizational Citizenship Behavior in Work Groups: A Group Norms Approach," *Journal of Applied Psychology* (December 2004), pp. 960–974.

10. Adapted from P. S. Goodman, E. Ravlin, and M. Schminke, "Understanding Groups in Organizations," in L. L. Cummings and B. M. Staw (eds.), *Research in Organizational Behavior,* vol. 9 (Greenwich, CT: JAI Press, 1987), p. 159.

11. E. Mayo, *The Human Problems of an Industrial Civilization* (New York: Macmillan, 1933); and F. J. Roethlisberger and W. J. Dickson, *Management and the Worker* (Cambridge, MA: Harvard University Press, 1939).

12. C. A. Kiesler and S. B. Kiesler, *Conformity* (Reading, MA: Addison-Wesley, 1969); and R. B. Cialdini and N. J. Goldstein, "Social Influence: Compliance and Conformity," *Annual Review of Psychology* 55 (2004), pp. 591–621.

13. S. E. Asch, "Effects of Group Pressure upon the Modification and Distortion of Judgments," in H. Guetzkow (ed.), *Groups, Leadership and Men* (Pittsburgh: Carnegie Press, 1951), pp. 177–190; and S. E. Asch, "Studies of Independence and Conformity: A Minority of One Against a Unanimous Majority," *Psychological Monographs: General and Applied* 70, no. 9 (1956), pp. 1–70.

14. R. Bond and P. B. Smith, "Culture and Conformity: A Meta-Analysis of Studies Using Asch's (1952, 1956) Line Judgment Task," *Psychological Bulletin* (January 1996), pp. 111–137.

15. See S. L. Robinson and A. M. O'Leary-Kelly, "Monkey See, Monkey Do: The Influence of Work Groups on the Antisocial Behavior of Employees," *Academy of Management Journal*

(December 1998), pp. 658–672; R. J. Bennett and S. L. Robinson, "The Past, Present, and Future of Workplace Deviance," in J. Greenberg (ed.), *Organizational Behavior: The State of the Science,* 2nd ed. (Mahwah, NJ: Erlbaum, 2003), pp. 237–271; and C. M. Berry, D. S. Ones, and P. R. Sackett, "Interpersonal Deviance, Organizational Deviance, and Their Common Correlates: A Review and Meta-Analysis," *Journal of Applied Psychology* 92, no. 2 (2007), pp. 410–424.

16. C. M. Pearson, L. M. Andersson, and C. L. Porath, "Assessing and Attacking Workplace Civility," *Organizational Dynamics* 29, no. 2 (2000), p. 130; see also C. Pearson, L. M. Andersson, and C. L. Porath, "Workplace Incivility," in S. Fox and P. E. Spector (eds.), *Counterproductive Work Behavior: Investigations of Actors and Targets* (Washington, DC: American Psychological Association, 2005), pp. 177–200.

17. S. Lim, L. M. Cortina, V. J. Magley, "Personal and Workgroup Incivility: Impact on Work and Health Outcomes," *Journal of Applied Psychology* 93, no. 1 (2008), pp. 95–107.

18. Robinson and O'Leary-Kelly, "Monkey See, Monkey Do"; and T. M. Glomb and H. Liao, "Interpersonal Aggression in Workgroups: Social Influence, Reciprocal, and Individual Effects," *Academy of Management Journal* 46 (2003), pp. 486–496.

19. P. Bamberger and M. Biron, "Group Norms and Excessive Absenteeism: The Role of Peer Referent Others," *Organizational Behavior and Human Decision Processes* 103, no. 2 (2007), pp. 179–196; and A. Väänänen, N. Tordera, M. Kivimäki, A. Kouvonen, J. Pentti, A. Linna, and J. Vahtera, "The Role of Work Group in Individual Sickness Absence Behavior," *Journal of Health & Human Behavior* 49, no. 4 (2008), pp. 452–467.

20. M. S. Cole, F. Walter, and H. Bruch, "Affective Mechanisms Linking Dysfunctional Behavior to Performance in Work Teams: A Moderated Mediation Study," *Journal of Applied Psychology* 93, no. 5 (2008), pp. 945–958.

21. A. Erez, H. Elms, and E. Fong, "Lying, Cheating, Stealing: It Happens More in Groups," paper presented at the European Business Ethics Network Annual Conference, Budapest, Hungary, August 30, 2003.

22. S. L. Robinson and M. S. Kraatz, "Constructing the Reality of Normative Behavior: The Use of Neutralization Strategies by Organizational Deviants," in R. W. Griffin and A. O'Leary-Kelly (eds.), *Dysfunctional Behavior in Organizations: Violent and Deviant Behavior* (Greenwich, CT: JAI Press, 1998), pp. 203–220.

23. See J. Berger, M. H. Fisek, R. Z. Norman, and M. Zelditch, *Status Characteristics and Social Interaction: An Expected States Approach* (New York: Elsevier, 1977).

24. Cited in Hackman, "Group Influences on Individuals in Organizations," p. 236.

25. R. R. Callister and J. A. Wall Jr., "Conflict Across Organizational Boundaries: Managed Care Organizations Versus Health Care Providers," *Journal of Applied Psychology* 86, no. 4 (2001), pp. 754–763; and P. Chattopadhyay, W. H. Glick, and G. P. Huber, "Organizational Actions in Response to Threats and Opportunities," *Academy of Management Journal* 44, no. 5 (2001), pp. 937–955.

26. P. F. Hewlin, "Wearing the Cloak: Antecedents and Consequences of Creating Facades of Conformity," *Journal of Applied Psychology* 94, no. 3 (2009), pp. 727–741.

27. J. A. Wiggins, F. Dill, and R. D. Schwartz, "On 'Status-Liability,'" *Sociometry* (April/May 1965), pp. 197–209.

28. See J. M. Levine and R. L. Moreland, "Progress in Small Group Research," in J. T. Spence, J. M. Darley, and D. J. Foss (eds.), *Annual Review of Psychology,* vol. 41 (Palo Alto, CA: Annual Reviews, 1990), pp. 585–634; S. D. Silver, B. P. Cohen, and J. H. Crutchfield, "Status Differentiation and Information Exchange in Face-to-Face and Computer-Mediated Idea Generation," *Social Psychology Quarterly* (1994), pp. 108–123; and J. M. Twenge, "Changes in Women's Assertiveness in Response to Status and Roles: A Cross-Temporal Meta-Analysis, 1931–1993," *Journal of Personality and Social Psychology* (July 2001), pp. 133–145.

29. G. H. Seijts and G. P. Latham, "The Effects of Goal Setting and Group Size on Performance in a Social Dilemma," *Canadian Journal of Behavioural Science* 32, no. 2 (2000), pp. 104–116.

30. M. E. Shaw, *Group Dynamics: The Psychology of Small Group Behavior,* 3rd ed. (New York: McGraw-Hill, 1981).

31. See, for instance, D. R. Comer, "A Model of Social Loafing in Real Work Groups," *Human Relations* (June 1995), pp. 647–667; S. M. Murphy, S. J. Wayne, R. C. Liden, and B. Erdogan, "Understanding Social Loafing: The Role of Justice Perceptions and Exchange Relationships," *Human Relations* (January 2003), pp. 61–84; and R. C. Liden, S. J. Wayne, R. A. Jaworski, and N. Bennett, "Social Loafing: A Field Investigation," *Journal of Management* (April 2004), pp. 285–304.

32. W. Moede, "Die Richtlinien der Leistungs-Psychologie," *Industrielle Psychotechnik* 4 (1927), pp. 193–207. See also D. A. Kravitz and B. Martin, "Ringelmann Rediscovered: The Original Article," *Journal of Personality and Social Psychology* (May 1986), pp. 936–941.

33. See, for example, J. A. Shepperd, "Productivity Loss in Performance Groups: A Motivation Analysis," *Psychological Bulletin* (January 1993), pp. 67–81; and S. J. Karau and K. D. Williams, "Social Loafing: A Meta-Analytic Review and Theoretical Integration," *Journal of Personality and Social Psychology* (October 1993), pp. 681–706.

34. S. G. Harkins and K. Szymanski, "Social Loafing and Group Evaluation," *Journal of Personality and Social Psychology* (December 1989), pp. 934–941.

35. A. Gunnthorsdottir and A. Rapoport, "Embedding Social Dilemmas in Intergroup Competition Reduces Free-Riding," *Organizational Behavior and Human Decision Processes* 101 (2006), pp. 184–199; and E. M. Stark, J. D. Shaw, and M. K. Duffy, "Preference for Group Work, Winning Orientation, and Social Loafing Behavior in Groups," *Group and Organization Management* 32, no. 6 (2007), pp. 699–723.

36. B. Mullen and C. Cooper, "The Relation Between Group Cohesiveness and Performance: An Integration," *Psychological Bulletin* (March 1994), pp. 210–227; P. M. Podsakoff, S. B. MacKenzie, and M. Ahearne, "Moderating Effects of Goal Acceptance on the Relationship Between Group Cohesiveness and Productivity," *Journal of Applied Psychology* (December 1997), pp. 974–983; and D. J. Beal, R. R. Cohen, M. J. Burke, and C. L. McLendon, "Cohesion and Performance in Groups: A Meta-Analytic Clarification of Construct Relations," *Journal of Applied Psychology* (December 2003), pp. 989–1004.

37. Ibid.

38. Based on J. L. Gibson, J. M. Ivancevich, and J. H. Donnelly Jr., *Organizations,* 8th ed. (Burr Ridge, IL: Irwin, 1994), p. 323.

39. D. S. Staples and L. Zhao, "The Effects of Cultural Diversity in Virtual Teams Versus Face-to-Face Teams," *Group Decision and Negotiation* (July 2006), pp. 389–406.

40. N. Chi, Y. Huang, and S. Lin, "A Double-Edged Sword? Exploring the Curvilinear Relationship Between Organizational Tenure Diversity and Team Innovation: The Moderating Role of Team-Oriented HR Practices," *Group and Organization Management* 34, no. 6 (2009), pp. 698–726.

41. K. J. Klein, A. P. Knight, J. C. Ziegert, B. C. Lim, and J. L. Saltz, "When Team Members' Values Differ: The Moderating Role of Team Leadership," *Organizational Behavior and Human Decision Processes* 114, no. 1 (2011), pp. 25–36; and G. Park and R. P. DeShon, "A Multilevel Model of Minority Opinion Expression and Team Decision-Making Effectiveness," *Journal of Applied Psychology* 95, no. 5 (2010), pp. 824–833.

42. M. Rigoglioso, "Diverse Backgrounds and Personalities Can Strengthen Groups," *Standford Knowledgebase* (August 15, 2006), www.stanford.edu/group/knowledgebase/.

43. K. W. Phillips and D. L. Loyd, "When Surface and Deep-Level Diversity Collide: The Effects on Dissenting Group Members," *Organizational Behavior and Human Decision Processes* 99 (2006), pp. 143–160; and S. R. Sommers, "On Racial Diversity and Group Decision Making: Identifying Multiple Effects of Racial Composition on Jury Deliberations," *Journal of Personality and Social Psychology* (April 2006), pp. 597–612.

44. E. Mannix and M. A. Neale, "What Differences Make a Difference? The Promise and Reality of Diverse Teams in Organizations," *Psychological Science in the Public Interest* (October 2005), pp. 31–55.

45. N. Foote, E. Matson, L. Weiss, and E. Wenger, "Leveraging Group Knowledge for High-Performance Decision-Making," *Organizational Dynamics* 31, no. 2 (2002), pp. 280–295.

46. See N. R. F. Maier, "Assets and Liabilities in Group Problem Solving: The Need for an Integrative Function," *Psychological Review* (April 1967), pp. 239–249; G. W. Hill, "Group Versus Individual Performance: Are *N[plus]*1 Heads Better Than One?" *Psychological Bulletin* (May 1982), pp. 517–539; M. D. Johnson and J. R. Hollenbeck, "Collective Wisdom as an Oxymoron: Team-Based Structures as Impediments to Learning," in J. Langan-Fox, C. L. Cooper, and R. J. Klimoski (eds), *Research Companion to the Dysfunctional Workplace: Management Challenges and Symptoms* (Northampton, MA: Edward Elgar Publishing, 2007), pp. 319–331; and R. F. Martell and M. R. Borg, "A Comparison of the Behavioral Rating Accuracy of Groups and Individuals," *Journal of Applied Psychology* (February 1993), pp. 43–50.

47. D. Gigone and R. Hastie, "Proper Analysis of the Accuracy of Group Judgments," *Psychological Bulletin* (January 1997), pp. 149–167; and B. L. Bonner, S. D. Sillito, and M. R. Baumann, "Collective Estimation: Accuracy, Expertise, and Extroversion as Sources of Intra-Group Influence," *Organizational Behavior and Human Decision Processes* 103 (2007), pp. 121–133.

48. See, for example, W. C. Swap and Associates, *Group Decision Making* (Newbury Park, CA: Sage, 1984).

49. I. L. Janis, *Groupthink* (Boston: Houghton Mifflin, 1982); W. Park, "A Review of Research on Groupthink," *Journal of Behavioral Decision Making* (July 1990), pp. 229–245; J. N. Choi and M. U. Kim, "The Organizational Application of Groupthink and Its Limits in Organizations," *Journal of Applied Psychology* (April 1999), pp. 297–306; and W. W. Park, "A Comprehensive Empirical Investigation of the Relationships Among Variables of the Groupthink Model," *Journal of Organizational Behavior* (December 2000), pp. 873–887.

50. Janis, *Groupthink.*

51. G. Park and R. P. DeShon, "A Multilevel Model of Minority Opinion Expression and Team Decision-Making Effectiveness," *Journal of Applied Psychology* 95, no. 5 (2010), pp. 824–833.

52. M. E. Turner and A. R. Pratkanis, "Mitigating Groupthink by Stimulating Constructive Conflict," in C. De Dreu and E. Van de Vliert (eds.), *Using Conflict in Organizations* (London: Sage, 1997), pp. 53–71.

53. J. A. Goncalo, E. Polman, and C. Maslach, "Can Confidence Come Too Soon? Collective Efficacy, Conflict, and Group Performance over Time," *Organizational Behavior and Human Decision Processes* 113, no. 1 (2010), pp. 13–24.

54. See N. R. F. Maier, *Principles of Human Relations* (New York: Wiley, 1952); I. L. Janis, *Groupthink: Psychological Studies of Policy Decisions and Fiascoes,* 2nd ed. (Boston: Houghton Mifflin, 1982); N. Richardson Ahlfinger and J. K. Esser, "Testing the Groupthink Model: Effects of Promotional Leadership and Conformity Predisposition," *Social Behavior & .Personality* 29, no. 1 (2001), pp. 31–41; and S. Schultz-Hardt, F. C. Brodbeck, A. Mojzisch, R. Kerschreiter, and D. Frey, "Group Decision Making in Hidden Profile Situations: Dissent as a Facilitator for Decision Quality," *Journal of Personality and Social Psychology* 91, no. 6 (2006), pp. 1080–1093.

55. See D. J. Isenberg, "Group Polarization: A Critical Review and Meta-Analysis," *Journal of Personality and Social Psychology* (December 1986), pp. 1141–1151; J. L. Hale and F. J. Boster, "Comparing Effect Coded Models of Choice Shifts," *Communication Research Reports* (April 1988), pp. 180–186; and P. W. Paese, M. Bieser, and M. E. Tubbs, "Framing Effects and Choice Shifts in Group Decision Making," *Organizational Behavior and Human Decision Processes* (October 1993), pp. 149–165.

56. R. D. Clark III, "Group-Induced Shift Toward Risk: A Critical Appraisal," *Psychological Bulletin* (October 1971), pp. 251–270; M. Brauer and C. M. Judd, "Group Polarization and Repeated Attitude Expression: A New Take on an Old Topic," *European Review of Social Psychology* 7, (1996), pp. 173–207; and M. P. Brady and S. Y. Wu, "The Aggregation of Preferences in Groups: Identity, Responsibility, and Polarization," *Journal of Economic Psychology* 31, no. 6 (2010), pp. 950–963.

57. Z. Krizan and R. S. Baron, "Group Polarization and Choice-Dilemmas: How Important Is Self-Categorization?" *European Journal of Social Psychology* 37, no. 1 (2007), pp. 191–201.

58. A. F. Osborn, *Applied Imagination: Principles and Procedures of Creative Thinking,* 3rd ed. (New York: Scribner, 1963). See also R. P. McGlynn, D. McGurk, V. S. Effland, N. L. Johll, and D. J. Harding, "Brainstorming and Task Performance in Groups Constrained by Evidence," *Organizational Behavior and Human Decision Processes* (January 2004), pp. 75–87; and R. C. Litchfield, "Brainstorming Reconsidered: A Goal-Based View," *Academy of Management Review* 33, no. 3 (2008), pp. 649–668.

59. N. L. Kerr and R. S. Tindale, "Group Performance and Decision-Making," *Annual Review of Psychology* 55 (2004), pp. 623–655.

60. See A. L. Delbecq, A. H. Van deVen, and D. H. Gustafson, *Group Techniques for Program Planning: A Guide to Nominal and Delphi Processes* (Glenview, IL: Scott Foresman, 1975); and P. B. Paulus and H.-C. Yang, "Idea Generation in Groups: A Basis for Creativity in Organizations," *Organizational Behavior and Human Decision Processing* (May 2000), pp. 76–87.

61. C. Faure, "Beyond Brainstorming: Effects of Different Group Procedures on Selection of Ideas and Satisfaction with the Process," *Journal of Creative Behavior* 38 (2004), pp. 13–34.

62. T. P. Verney, "Role Perception Congruence, Performance, and Satisfaction," in D. J. Vredenburgh and R. S. Schuler (eds.), *Effective Management: Research and Application,* Proceedings of the 20th Annual Eastern Academy of Management, Pittsburgh, PA (May 1983), pp. 24–27. Ibid. A. G. Bedeian and A. A. Armenakis, "A Path-Analytic Study of the Consequences of Role Conflict and Ambiguity," *Academy of Management Journal* (June 1981), pp. 417–424; and P. L. Perrewe, K. L. Zellars, G. R. Ferris, A. M. Rossi, C. J. Kacmar, and D. A. Ralston, "Neutralizing Job Stressors: Political Skill as an Antidote to the Dysfunctional Consequences of Role Conflict," *Academy of Management Journal* (February 2004), pp. 141–152.

63. Ibid.

64. A. G. Bedeian and A. A. Armenakis, "A Path-Analytic Study of the Consequences of Role Conflict and Ambiguity," *Academy of Management Journal* (June 1981), pp. 417–424; and P. L. Perrewe, K. L. Zellars, G. R. Ferris, A. M. Rossi, C. J. Kacmar, and D. A. Ralston, "Neutralizing Job Stressors: Political Skill as an Antidote to the Dysfunctional Consequences of Role Conflict," *Academy of Management Journal* (February 2004), pp. 141–152.

65. Shaw, *Group Dynamics.*

66. B. Mullen, C. Symons, L. Hu, and E. Salas, "Group Size, Leadership Behavior, and Subordinate Satisfaction," *Journal of General Psychology* (April 1989), pp. 155–170.

CHAPTER 10

1. This section is based on J. R. Katzenbach and D. K. Smith, *The Wisdom of Teams* (Cambridge, MA: Harvard University Press, 1993), pp. 21, 45, 85; and D. C. Kinlaw, *Developing Superior Work Teams* (Lexington, MA: Lexington Books, 1991), pp. 3–21.

2. J. Mathieu, M. T. Maynard, T. Rapp, and L. Gilson, "Team Effectiveness 1997–2007: A Review of Recent Advancements and a Glimpse into the Future," *Journal of Management* 34, no. 3 (2008), pp. 410–476.

3. J. H. Shonk, *Team-Based Organizations* (Homewood, IL: Business One Irwin, 1992); and M. A. Verespej, "When Workers Get New Roles," *IndustryWeek* (February 3, 1992), p. 11.

4. G. Bodinson and R. Bunch, "AQP's National Team Excellence Award: Its Purpose, Value and Process," *The Journal for Quality and Participation* (Spring 2003), pp. 37–42.

5. See, for example, A. Erez, J. A. LePine, and H. Elms, "Effects of Rotated Leadership and Peer Evaluation on the Functioning and Effectiveness of Self-Managed Teams: A Quasi-experiment," *Personnel Psychology* (Winter 2002), pp. 929–948.

6. See, for instance, C. W. Langfred, "Too Much of a Good Thing? Negative Effects of High Trust and Individual Autonomy in Self-Managing Teams," *Academy of Management Journal* (June 2004), pp. 385–399.

7. C. W. Langfred, "The Downside of Self-Management: A Longitudinal Study of the Effects of Conflict on Trust, Autonomy, and Task Interdependence in Self-Managing Teams," *Academy of Management Journal* 50, no. 4 (2007), pp. 885–900.

8. J. Devaro, "The Effects of Self-Managed and Closely Managed Teams on Labor Productivity and Product Quality: An Empirical Analysis of a Cross-Section of Establishments," *Industrial Relations* 47, no. 4 (2008), pp. 659–698.

9. A. Shah, "Starbucks Strives for Instant Gratification with Via Launch," *PR Week* (December 2009), p. 15.

10. B. Freyer and T. A. Stewart, "Cisco Sees the Future," *Harvard Business Review* (November 2008), pp. 73–79.

11. See, for example, L. L. Martins, L. L. Gilson, and M. T. Maynard, "Virtual Teams: What Do We Know and Where Do We Go from Here?" *Journal of Management* (November 2004), pp. 805–835; and B. Leonard, "Managing Virtual Teams," *HR Magazine* (June 2011), pp. 39–42.

12. J. R. Mesmer-Magnus, L. A. DeChurch, M. Jimenez-Rodriguez, J. Wildman, and M. Shuffler, "A Meta-Analytic Investigation of Virtuality and Information Sharing in Teams," *Organizational Behavior and Human Decision Processes* 115, no. 2 (2011), pp. 214–225.

13. A. Malhotra, A. Majchrzak, and B. Rosen, "Leading Virtual Teams," *Academy of Management Perspectives* (February 2007), pp. 60–70; and J. M. Wilson, S. S. Straus, and B. McEvily, "All in Due Time: The Development of Trust in Computer-Mediated and Face-to-Face Teams," *Organizational Behavior and Human Decision Processes* 19 (2006), pp. 16–33.

14. See, for instance, J. R. Hackman, "The Design of Work Teams," in J. W. Lorsch (ed.), *Handbook of Organizational Behavior* (Upper Saddle River, NJ: Prentice Hall, 1987), pp. 315–342; and M. A. Campion, G. J. Medsker, and C. A. Higgs, "Relations Between Work Group Characteristics and Effectiveness: Implications for Designing Effective Work Groups," *Personnel Psychology* (Winter 1993), pp. 823–850.

15. D. E. Hyatt and T. M. Ruddy, "An Examination of the Relationship Between Work Group Characteristics and Performance: Once More into the Breech," *Personnel Psychology* (Autumn 1997), p. 555.

16. This model is based on M. A. Campion, E. M. Papper, and G. J. Medsker, "Relations Between Work Team Characteristics and Effectiveness: A Replication and Extension," *Personnel Psychology* (Summer 1996), pp. 429–452; Hyatt and Ruddy, "An Examination of the Relationship Between Work Group Characteristics and Performance," pp. 553–585; S. G. Cohen and D. E. Bailey, "What Makes Teams Work: Group Effectiveness Research from the Shop Floor to the Executive Suite," *Journal of Management* 23, no. 3 (1997), pp. 239–290; L. Thompson, *Making the Team* (Upper Saddle River, NJ: Prentice Hall, 2000), pp. 18–33; and J. R. Hackman, *Leading Teams: Setting the Stage for Great Performance* (Boston: Harvard Business School Press, 2002).

17. See G. L. Stewart and M. R. Barrick, "Team Structure and Performance: Assessing the Mediating Role of Intrateam Process and the Moderating Role of Task Type," *Academy of Management Journal* (April 2000), pp. 135–148.

18. Hyatt and Ruddy, "An Examination of the Relationship Between Work Group Characteristics and Performance," p. 577.

19. P. Balkundi and D. A. Harrison, "Ties, Leaders, and Time in Teams: Strong Inference About Network Structure's Effects on Team Viability and Performance," *Academy of Management Journal* 49, no. 1 (2006), pp. 49–68; G. Chen, B. L. Kirkman, R. Kanfer, D. Allen, and B. Rosen, "A Multilevel Study of Leadership, Empowerment, and Performance in Teams," *Journal of Applied Psychology* 92, no. 2 (2007), pp. 331–346; L. A. DeChurch and M. A. Marks, "Leadership in Multiteam Systems," *Journal of Applied Psychology* 91, no. 2 (2006), pp. 311–329; A. Srivastava, K. M. Bartol, and E. A. Locke, "Empowering Leadership in Management Teams: Effects on Knowledge Sharing, Efficacy, and Performance," *Academy of Management Journal* 49, no. 6 (2006), pp. 1239–1251; and J. E. Mathieu, K. K. Gilson, and T. M. Ruddy, "Empowerment and Team Effectiveness: An Empirical Test of an Integrated Model," *Journal of Applied Psychology* 91, no. 1 (2006), pp. 97–108.

20. J. B. Carson, P. E. Tesluk, and J. A. Marrone, "Shared Leadership in Teams: An Investigation of Antecedent Conditions and Performance," *Academy of Management Journal* 50, no. 5 (2007), pp. 1217–1234.

21. K. T. Dirks, "Trust in Leadership and Team Performance: Evidence from NCAA Basketball," *Journal of Applied Psychology* (December 2000), pp. 1004–1012; M. Williams, "In Whom We Trust: Group Membership as an Affective Context for Trust Development," *Academy of Management Review* (July 2001), pp. 377–396; and J. Schaubroeck, S. S. K. Lam, and A. C. Peng, "Cognition-Based and Affect-Based Trust as Mediators of Leader Behavior Influences on Team Performance," *Journal of Applied Psychology,* Online First Publication (February 7, 2011), doi: 10.1037/a0022625.

22. See F. Aime, C. J. Meyer, and S. E. Humphrey, "Legitimacy of Team Rewards: Analyzing Legitimacy as a Condition for the Effectiveness of Team Incentive Designs," *Journal of Business Research* 63, no. 1 (2010), pp. 60–66; and P. A. Bamberger and R. Levi, "Team-Based Reward Allocation Structures and the Helping Behaviors of Outcome-Interdependent Team Members," *Journal of Managerial Psychology* 24, no. 4 (2009), pp. 300–327; and M. J. Pearsall, M. S. Christian, and A. P. J. Ellis, "Motivating Interdependent Teams: Individual Rewards, Shared Rewards, or Something in Between?" *Journal of Applied Psychology* 95, no. 1 (2010), pp. 183–191.

23. R. R. Hirschfeld, M. H. Jordan, H. S. Feild, W. F. Giles, and A. A. Armenakis, "Becoming Team Players: Team Members' Mastery of Teamwork Knowledge as a Predictor of Team Task Proficiency and Observed Teamwork Effectiveness," *Journal of Applied Psychology* 91, no. 2 (2006), pp. 467–474; and K. R. Randall, C. J. Resick, and L. A. DeChurch, "Building Team Adaptive Capacity: The Roles of Sense-giving and Team Composition," *Journal of Applied Psychology* 96, no. 3 (2011), pp. 525–540.

24. H. Moon, J. R. Hollenbeck, and S. E. Humphrey, "Asymmetric Adaptability: Dynamic Team Structures as One-Way Streets," *Academy of Management Journal* 47, no. 5 (October 2004), pp. 681–695; A. P. J. Ellis, J. R. Hollenbeck, and D. R. Ilgen, "Team Learning: Collectively Connecting the Dots," *Journal of Applied Psychology* 88, no. 5 (October 2003), pp. 821–835; C. L. Jackson and J. A. LePine, "Peer Responses to a Team's Weakest Link: A Test and Extension of LePine and Van Dyne's Model," *Journal of Applied Psychology* 88, no. 3 (June 2003), pp. 459–475; and J. A. LePine, "Team Adaptation and Postchange Performance: Effects of Team Composition

in Terms of Members' Cognitive Ability and Personality," *Journal of Applied Psychology* 88, no. 1 (February 2003), pp. 27–39.

25. S. T. Bell, "Deep-Level Composition Variables as Predictors of Team Performance: A Meta-Analysis," *Journal of Applied Psychology* 92, no. 3 (2007), pp. 595–615; and M. R. Barrick, G. L. Stewart, M. J. Neubert, and M. K. Mount, "Relating Member Ability and Personality to Work-Team Processes and Team Effectiveness," *Journal of Applied Psychology* (June 1998), pp. 377–391.

26. T. A. O'Neill and N. J. Allen, "Personality and the Prediction of Team Performance," *European Journal of Personality* 25, no. 1 (2011), pp. 31–42.

27. Ellis, Hollenbeck, and Ilgen, "Team Learning"; C. O. L. H. Porter, J. R. Hollenbeck, and D. R. Ilgen, "Backing Up Behaviors in Teams: The Role of Personality and Legitimacy of Need," *Journal of Applied Psychology* 88, no. 3 (June 2003), pp. 391–403; A. Colquitt, J. R. Hollenbeck, and D. R. Ilgen, "Computer-Assisted Communication and Team Decision-Making Performance: The Moderating Effect of Openness to Experience," *Journal of Applied Psychology* 87, no. 2 (April 2002), pp. 402–410; J. A. LePine, J. R. Hollenbeck, D. R. Ilgen, and J. Hedlund, "The Effects of Individual Differences on the Performance of Hierarchical Decision Making Teams: Much More Than G," *Journal of Applied Psychology* 82 (1997), pp. 803–811; Jackson and LePine, "Peer Responses to a Team's Weakest Link"; and LePine, "Team Adaptation and Postchange Performance."

28. Barrick, Stewart, Neubert, and Mount, "Relating Member Ability and Personality to Work-Team Processes and Team Effectiveness," p. 388; and S. E. Humphrey, J. R. Hollenbeck, C. J. Meyer, and D. R. Ilgen, "Trait Configurations in Self-Managed Teams: A Conceptual Examination of the Use of Seeding for Maximizing and Minimizing Trait Variance in Teams," *Journal of Applied Psychology* 92, no. 3 (2007), pp. 885–892.

29. S. E. Humphrey, F. P. Morgeson, and M. J. Mannor, "Developing a Theory of the Strategic Core of Teams: A Role Composition Model of Team Performance," *Journal of Applied Psychology* 94, no. 1 (2009), pp. 48–61.

30. C. Margerison and D. McCann, *Team Management: Practical New Approaches* (London: Mercury Books, 1990).

31. K. Y. Williams and C. A. O'Reilly III, "Demography and Diversity in Organizations: A Review of 40 Years of Research," in B. M. Staw and L. L. Cummings (eds.), *Research in Organizational Behavior,* vol. 20 (Stamford, CT: JAI Press, 1998) pp. 77–140; and A. Joshi, "The Influence of Organizational Demography on the External Networking Behavior of Teams," *Academy of Management Review* (July 2006), pp. 583–595.

32. A. Joshi and H. Roh, "The Role of Context in Work Team Diversity Research: A Meta-Analytic Review," *Academy of Management Journal* 52, no. 3 (2009), pp. 599–-627; S. K. Horwitz and I. B. Horwitz, "The Effects of Team Diversity on Team Outcomes: A Meta-Analytic Review of Team Demography," *Journal of Management* 33, no. 6 (2007), pp. 987–1015; and S. T. Bell, A. J. Villado, M. A. Lukasik, L. Belau, and A. L. Briggs, "Getting Specific about Demographic Diversity Variable and Team Performance Relationships: A Meta-Analysis," *Journal of Management* 37, no. 3 (2011), pp. 709–743.

33. S. J. Shin and J. Zhou, "When Is Educational Specialization Heterogeneity Related to Creativity in Research and

Development Teams? Transformational Leadership as a Moderator," *Journal of Applied Psychology* 92, no. 6 (2007), pp. 1709–1721; and K. J. Klein, A. P. Knight, J. C. Ziegert, B. C. Lim, and J. L. Saltz, "When Team Members' Values Differ: The Moderating Role of Team Leadership," *Organizational Behavior and Human Decision Processes* 114, no. 1 (2011), pp. 25–36.

34. W. E. Watson, K. Kumar, and L. K. Michaelsen, "Cultural Diversity's Impact on Interaction Process and Performance: Comparing Homogeneous and Diverse Task Groups," *Academy of Management Journal* (June 1993), pp. 590–602; P. C. Earley and E. Mosakowski, "Creating Hybrid Team Cultures: An Empirical Test of Transnational Team Functioning," *Academy of Management Journal* (February 2000), pp. 26–49; and S. Mohammed and L. C. Angell, "Surface- and Deep-Level Diversity in Workgroups: Examining the Moderating Effects of Team Orientation and Team Process on Relationship Conflict," *Journal of Organizational Behavior* (December 2004), pp. 1015–1039.

35. Watson, Kumar, and Michaelsen, "Cultural Diversity's Impact on Interaction Process and Performance."

36. D. F. Crown, "The Use of Group and Groupcentric Individual Goals for Culturally Heterogeneous and Homogeneous Task Groups: An Assessment of European Work Teams," *Small Group Research* 38, no. 4 (2007), pp. 489–508.

37. D. Coutu, "Why Teams Don't Work" *Harvard Business Review* (May 2009), pp. 99–105. The evidence in this section is described in Thompson, *Making the Team*, pp. 65–67. See also L. A. Curral, R. H. Forrester, and J. F. Dawson, "It's What You Do and the Way That You Do It: Team Task, Team Size, and Innovation-Related Group Processes," *European Journal of Work & Organizational Psychology* 10, no. 2 (June 2001), pp. 187–204; R. C. Liden, S. J. Wayne, and R. A. Jaworski, "Social Loafing: A Field Investigation," *Journal of Management* 30, no. 2 (2004), pp. 285–304; and J. A. Wagner, "Studies of Individualism–Collectivism: Effects on Cooperation in Groups," *Academy of Management Journal* 38, no. 1 (February 1995), pp. 152–172.

38. "Is Your Team Too Big? Too Small? What's the Right Number? *Knowledge@Wharton* (June 14, 2006), pp. 1–5.

39. Hyatt and Ruddy, "An Examination of the Relationship Between Work Group Characteristics and Performance"; J. D. Shaw, M. K. Duffy, and E. M. Stark, "Interdependence and Preference for Group Work: Main and Congruence Effects on the Satisfaction and Performance of Group Members," *Journal of Management* 26, no. 2 (2000), pp. 259–279; and S. A. Kiffin-Peterson and J. L. Cordery, "Trust, Individualism, and Job Characteristics of Employee Preference for Teamwork," *International Journal of Human Resource Management* (February 2003), pp. 93–116.

40. J. A. LePine, R. F. Piccolo, C. L. Jackson, J. E. Mathieu, and J. R. Saul, "A Meta-Analysis of Teamwork Processes: Tests of a Multidimensional Model and Relationships with Team Effectiveness Criteria," *Personnel Psychology* 61 (2008), pp. 273–307.

41. I. D. Steiner, *Group Processes and Productivity* (New York: Academic Press, 1972).

42. J. A. LePine, R. F. Piccolo, C. L. Jackson, J. E. Mathieu, and J. R. Saul, "A Meta-Analysis of Teamwork Processes: Tests of a Multidimensional Model and Relationships with Team Effectiveness Criteria"; and J. E. Mathieu and T. L. Rapp, "Laying the Foundation for Successful Team Performance Trajectories: The Roles of Team Charters and Performance

Strategies," *Journal of Applied Psychology* 94, no. 1 (2009), pp. 90–103.

43. J. E. Mathieu and W. Schulze, "The Influence of Team Knowledge and Formal Plans on Episodic Team Process—Performance Relationships," *Academy of Management Journal* 49, no. 3 (2006), pp. 605–619.

44. A. N. Pieterse, D. van Knippenberg, and W. P. van Ginkel, "Diversity in Goal Orientation, Team Reflexivity, and Team Performance," *Organizational Behavior and Human Decision Processes* 114, no. 2 (2011), pp. 153–164.

45. A. Gurtner, F. Tschan, N. K. Semmer, and C. Nagele, "Getting Groups to Develop Good Strategies: Effects of Reflexivity Interventions on Team Process, Team Performance, and Shared Mental Models," *Organizational Behavior and Human Decision Processes* 102 (2007), pp. 127–142; M. C. Schippers, D. N. Den Hartog, and P. L. Koopman, "Reflexivity in Teams: A Measure and Correlates," *Applied Psychology: An International Review* 56, no. 2 (2007), pp. 189–211; and C. S. Burke, K. C. Stagl, E. Salas, L. Pierce, and D. Kendall, "Understanding Team Adaptation: A Conceptual Analysis and Model," *Journal of Applied Psychology* 91, no. 6 (2006), pp. 1189–1207.

46. A. N. Pieterse, D. van Knippenberg, and W. P. van Ginkel, "Diversity in Goal Orientation, Team Reflexivity, and Team Performance," *Organizational Behavior and Human Decision Processes* 114, no. 2 (2011), pp. 153–164.

47. E. Weldon and L. R. Weingart, "Group Goals and Group Performance," *British Journal of Social Psychology* (Spring 1993), pp. 307–334. See also R. P. DeShon, S. W. J. Kozlowski, A. M. Schmidt, K. R. Milner, and D. Wiechmann, "A Multiple-Goal, Multilevel Model of Feedback Effects on the Regulation of Individual and Team Performance," *Journal of Applied Psychology* (December 2004), pp. 1035–1056.

48. K. Tasa, S. Taggar, and G. H. Seijts, "The Development of Collective Efficacy in Teams: A Multilevel and Longitudinal Perspective," *Journal of Applied Psychology* 92, no. 1 (2007), pp. 17–27; D. I. Jung and J. J. Sosik, "Group Potency and Collective Efficacy: Examining Their Predictive Validity, Level of Analysis, and Effects of Performance Feedback on Future Group Performance," *Group & Organization Management* (September 2003), pp. 366–391; and R. R. Hirschfeld and J. B. Bernerth, "Mental Efficacy and Physical Efficacy at the Team Level: Inputs and Outcomes Among Newly Formed Action Teams," *Journal of Applied Psychology* 93, no. 6 (2008), pp. 1429–1437.

49. S. Mohammed, L. Ferzandi, and K. Hamilton, "Metaphor No More: A 15-Year Review of the Team Mental Model Construct," *Journal of Management* 36, no. 4 (2010), pp. 876–910.

50. A. P. J. Ellis, "System Breakdown: The Role of Mental Models and Transactive Memory on the Relationships Between Acute Stress and Team Performance," *Academy of Management Journal* 49, no. 3 (2006), pp. 576–589.

51. S. W. J. Kozlowski and D. R. Ilgen, "Enhancing the Effectiveness of Work Groups and Teams," *Psychological Science in the Public Interest* (December 2006), pp. 77–124; and B. D. Edwards, E. A. Day, W. Arthur Jr., and S. T. Bell, "Relationships Among Team Ability Composition, Team Mental Models, and Team Performance," *Journal of Applied Psychology* 91, no. 3 (2006), pp. 727–736.

52. L. A. DeChurch and J. R. Mesmer-Magnus, "The Cognitive Underpinnings of Effective Teamwork: A Meta-Analysis," *Journal of Applied Psychology* 95, no. 1 (2010), pp. 32–53.

53. J. Farh, C. Lee, and C.I.C. Farh, "Task Conflict and Team Creativity: A Question of How Much and When," *Journal of Applied Psychology* 95, no. 6 (2010), pp. 1173–1180.

54. K. J. Behfar, R. S. Peterson, E. A. Mannix, and W. M. K. Trochim, "The Critical Role of Conflict Resolution in Teams: A Close Look at the Links Between Conflict Type, Conflict Management Strategies, and Team Outcomes," *Journal of Applied Psychology* 93, no. 1 (2008), pp. 170–188.

55. K. H. Price, D. A. Harrison, and J. H. Gavin, "Withholding Inputs in Team Contexts: Member Composition, Interaction Processes, Evaluation Structure, and Social Loafing," *Journal of Applied Psychology* 91, no. 6 (2006), pp. 1375–1384.

56. See, for instance, B. L. Kirkman and D. L. Shapiro, "The Impact of Cultural Values on Employee Resistance to Teams: Toward a Model of Globalized Self-Managing Work Team Effectiveness," *Academy of Management Review,* July 1997, pp. 730–757; and B. L. Kirkman, C. B. Gibson, and D. L. Shapiro, "'Exporting' Teams: Enhancing the Implementation and Effectiveness of Work Teams in Global Affiliates," *Organizational Dynamics* 30, no. 1 (2001), pp. 12–29.

57. G. Hertel, U. Konradt, and K. Voss, "Competencies for Virtual Teamwork: Development and Validation of a Web-Based Selection Tool for Members of Distributed Teams," *European Journal of Work and Organizational Psychology* 15, no. 4 (2006), pp. 477–504.

58. E. Kearney, D. Gebert, and S. C. Voelpel, "When and How Diversity Benefits Teams: The Importance of Team Members' Need for Cognition," *Academy of Management Journal* 52, no. 3 (2009), pp. 581–598.

59. H. M. Guttman, "The New High-Performance Player," *The Hollywood Reporter* (October 27, 2008), www .hollywoodreporter.com.

60. J. S. DeMatteo, L. T. Eby, and E. Sundstrom, "Team-Based Rewards: Current Empirical Evidence and Directions for Future Research," in B. M. Staw and L. L. Cummings (eds.), *Research in Organizational Behavior,* vol. 20 (Stamford, CT: JAI Press, 1998), pp. 141–183.

61. T. Erickson and L. Gratton, "What It Means to Work Here," *BusinessWeek* (January 10, 2008), www.businessweek.com.

62. M. D. Johnson, J. R. Hollenbeck, S. E. Humphrey, D. R. Ilgen, D. Jundt, and C. J. Meyer, "Cutthroat Cooperation: Asymmetrical Adaptation to Changes in Team Reward Structures," *Academy of Management Journal* 49, no. 1 (2006), pp. 103–119.

63. C. E. Naquin and R. O. Tynan, "The Team Halo Effect: Why Teams Are Not Blamed for Their Failures," *Journal of Applied Psychology,* April 2003, pp. 332–340.

64. A. B. Drexler and R. Forrester, "Teamwork—Not Necessarily the Answer," *HR Magazine* (January 1998), pp. 55–58.

CHAPTER 11

1. D. K. Berlo, *The Process of Communication* (New York: Holt, Rinehart & Winston, 1960), pp. 30–32; see also K. Byron, "Carrying Too Heavy a Load? The Communication and Miscommunication of Emotion by Email," *The Academy of Management Review* 33, no. 2 (2008), pp. 309–327.

2. J. Langan-Fox, "Communication in Organizations: Speed, Diversity, Networks, and Influence on Organizational Effectiveness, Human Health, and Relationships," in N. Anderson, D. S. Ones, H. K. Sinangil, and C. Viswesvaran

(Eds.), *Handbook of Industrial, Work and Organizational Psychology*, vol. 2 (Thousand Oaks, CA: Sage, 2001), p. 190.

3. R. L. Simpson, "Vertical and Horizontal Communication in Formal Organizations," *Administrative Science Quarterly* (September 1959), pp. 188–196; A. G. Walker and J. W. Smither, "A Five-Year Study of Upward Feedback: What Managers Do with Their Results Matter," *Personnel Psychology* (Summer 1999), pp. 393–424; and J. W. Smither and A. G. Walker, "Are the Characteristics of Narrative Comments Related to Improvement in Multirater Feedback Ratings Over Time?" *Journal of Applied Psychology* 89, no. 3 (June 2004), pp. 575–581.

4. P. Dvorak, "How Understanding the 'Why' of Decisions Matters," *Wall Street Journal* (March 19, 2007), p. B3.

5. T. Neeley and P. Leonardi, "Effective Managers Say the Same Thing Twice (or More)," *Harvard Business Review* (May 2011), pp. 38–39.

6. T. Waghorn, "How One Company Gets Its Employees Innovating," *Wall Street Journal* (March 15, 2010), p. 1.

7. E. Nichols, "Hyper-Speed Managers," *HR Magazine* (April 2007), pp. 107–110.

8. L. Dulye, "Get Out of Your Office," *HR Magazine* (July 2006), pp. 99–101.

9. L. S. Rashotte, "What Does That Smile Mean? The Meaning of Nonverbal Behaviors in Social Interaction," *Social Psychology Quarterly* (March 2002), pp. 92–102.

10. J. Fast, *Body Language* (Philadelphia: M. Evan, 1970), p. 7.

11. A. Mehrabian, *Nonverbal Communication* (Chicago: Aldine-Atherton, 1972).

12. N. M. Henley, "Body Politics Revisited: What Do We Know Today?" in P. J. Kalbfleisch and M. J. Cody (eds.), *Gender, Power, and Communication in Human Relationships* (Hillsdale, NJ: Lawrence Erlbaum, 1995), pp. 27–61.

13. See, for example, N. B. Kurland and L. H. Pelled, "Passing the Word: Toward a Model of Gossip and Power in the Workplace," *Academy of Management Review* (April 2000), pp. 428–438; and G. Michelson, A. van Iterson, and K. Waddington, "Gossip in Organizations: Contexts, Consequences, and Controversies," *Group and Organization Management* 35, no. 4 (2010), pp. 371–390.

14. G. Van Hoye and F. Lievens, "Tapping the Grapevine: A Closer Look at Word-of-Mouth as a Recruitment Source," *Journal of Applied Psychology* 94, no. 2 (2009), pp. 341–352.

15. K. Davis, "Management Communication and the Grapevine," *Harvard Business Review* (September/October 1953), pp. 43–49.

16. R. L. Rosnow and G. A. Fine, *Rumor and Gossip: The Social Psychology of Hearsay* (New York: Elsevier, 1976).

17. J. K. Bosson, A. B. Johnson, K. Niederhoffer, and W. B. Swann, Jr., "Interpersonal Chemistry Through Negativity: Bonding by Sharing Negative Attitudes About Others," *Personal Relationships* 13 (2006), pp. 135–150.

18. T. J. Grosser, V. Lopez-Kidwell, and G. Labianca, "A Social Network Analysis of Positive and Negative Gossip in Organizational Life," *Group and Organization Management* 35, no. 2 (2010), pp. 177–212.

19. B. Gates, "How I Work," *Fortune* (April 17, 2006), www .money.cnn.com.

20. D. Brady, "*!#?@ the E-mail. Can We Talk?" *BusinessWeek* (December 4, 2006), p. 109.

21. E. Binney, "Is E-mail the New Pink Slip?" *HR Magazine* (November 2006), pp. 32–33; and R. L. Rundle, "Critical Case: How an Email Rant Jolted a Big HMO," *Wall Street Journal* (April 24, 2007), pp. A1, A16.

22. S. Hourigan, "62 Trillion Spam Emails Cause Huge Carbon Footprint," *Courier Mail* (April 17, 2009), www.news.com.au/couriermail.

23. R. Stross, "The Daily Struggle to Avoid Burial by E-Mail," *New York Times* (April 21, 2008), p. BU5; and H. Rhodes, "You've Got Mail . . . Again," *Gainesville Sun* (September 29, 2008), pp. 1D, 6D.

24. C. Byron, "Carrying Too Heavy a Load? The Communication and Miscommunication of Emotion by Email," *Academy of Management Review* 33, no. 2 (2008), pp. 309–327.

25. D. Goleman, "Flame First, Think Later: New Clues to E-mail Misbehavior," *New York Times* (February 20, 2007), p. D5; and E. Krell, "The Unintended Word," *HR Magazine* (August 2006), pp. 50–54.

26. J. E. Hall, M. T. Kobata, and M. Denis, "Employees and E-mail Privacy Rights," *Workforce Management* (June 2010), p. 10.

27. R. Zeidner, "Keeping E-mail in Check," *HR Magazine* (June 2007), pp. 70–74; "E-mail May Be Hazardous to Your Career," *Fortune* (May 14, 2007), p. 24; and J. D. Glater, "Open Secrets," *The New York Times* (June 27, 2008), pp. B1, B5.

28. A. Williams, "Mind Your BlackBerry or Mind Your Manners," *The New York Times* (June 21, 2009), www.nytimes.com.

29. "Survey Finds Mixed Reviews on Checking E-mail During Meetings," *IPMA-HR Bulletin* (April 27, 2007), p. 1.

30. K. Gurchiek, "Shoddy Writing Can Trip Up Employees, Organizations," *SHRM Online* (April 27, 2006), pp. 1–2.

31. T. Henneman, "Companies Making Friends with Social Media," *Workforce Management*, (April 2010), p. 4.

32. D. Lidsky, "It's Not Just Who You Know," *Fast Company* (May 2007), p. 56.

33. "Bosses Battle Risk by Firing E-mail, IM & Blog Violators," *IPMA-HR Bulletin* (January 12, 2007), pp. 1–2; G. Krants, "Blogging with a Vendetta," *Workforce Week* 8, no. 25 (June 10, 2007), www.workforce.com/section/quick_takes/49486_3.html; B. Leonard, "Blogs Can Present New Challenges to Employers," *SHRM Online* (March 13, 2006), pp. 1–2; and J. Greenwald, "Monitoring Communications? Know Legal Pitfalls," *Workforce Management Online* (February 2011), www.workforce.com.

34. E. Agnvall, "Meetings Go Virtual," *HR Magazine* (January 2009), pp. 74–77.

35. C. Huff, "Staying Afloat in a Digital Flood," *Workforce Management Online* (July 2008), www.workforce.com.

36. M. Richtel, "Lost in E-mail, Tech Firms Face Self-Made Beast," *The New York Times* (June 14, 2008), pp. A1, A14; and M. Johnson, "Quelling Distraction," *HR Magazine* (August 2008), pp. 43–46.

37. P. Briñol, R. E. Petty, and J. Barden, "Happiness Versus Sadness as a Determinant of Thought Confidence in Persuasion: A Self-Validation Analysis," *Journal of Personality and Social Psychology* 93, no. 5 (2007), pp. 711–727.

38. R. C. Sinclair, S. E. Moore, M. M. Mark, A. S. Soldat, and C. A. Lavis, "Incidental Moods, Source Likeability, and Persuasion: Liking Motivates Message Elaboration in Happy People," *Cognition and Emotion* 24, no. 6 (2010), pp. 940–961; and V. Griskevicius, M. N. Shiota, and S. L. Neufeld, "Influence of Different Positive Emotions on Persuasion Processing: A Functional Evolutionary Approach," *Emotion* 10, no. 2 (2010), pp. 190–206.

39. J. Sandberg, "The Jargon Jumble," *Wall Street Journal* (October 24, 2006), p. B1.

40. E. W. Morrison and F. J. Milliken, "Organizational Silence: A Barrier to Change and Development in a Pluralistic World," *Academy of Management Review* 25, no. 4 (2000), pp. 706–725; and B. E. Ashforth and V. Anand, "The Normalization of Corruption in Organizations," *Research in Organizational Behavior* 25 (2003), pp. 1–52.

41. F. J. Milliken, E. W. Morrison, and P. F. Hewlin, "An Exploratory Study of Employee Silence: Issues That Employees Don't Communicate Upward and Why," *Journal of Management Studies* 40, no. 6 (2003), pp. 1453–1476.

42. S. Tangirala and R. Ramunujam, "Employee Silence on Critical Work Issues: The Cross-Level Effects of Procedural Justice Climate," *Personnel Psychology* 61, no. 1 (2008), pp. 37–68; and F. Bowen and K. Blackmon, "Spirals of Silence: The Dynamic Effects of Diversity on Organizational Voice," *Journal of Management Studies* 40, no. 6 (2003), pp. 1393–1417.

43. B. R. Schlenker and M. R. Leary, "Social Anxiety and Self-Presentation: A Conceptualization and Model," *Psychological Bulletin* 92 (1982), pp. 641–669; and L. A. Withers, and L. L. Vernon, "To Err Is Human: Embarrassment, Attachment, and Communication Apprehension," *Personality and Individual Differences* 40, no. 1 (2006), pp. 99–110.

44. See, for instance, S. K. Opt and D. A. Loffredo, "Rethinking Communication Apprehension: A Myers-Briggs Perspective," *Journal of Psychology* (September 2000), pp. 556–570; and B. D. Blume, G. F. Dreher, and T. T. Baldwin, "Examining the Effects of Communication Apprehension within Assessment Centres," *Journal of Occupational and Organizational Psychology* 83, no. 3 (2010), pp. 663–671.

45. See, for example, J. A. Daly and J. C. McCroskey, "Occupational Desirability and Choice as a Function of Communication Apprehension," *Journal of Counseling Psychology* 22, no. 4 (1975), pp. 309–313; and T. L. Rodebaugh, "I Might Look OK, But I'm Still Doubtful, Anxious, and Avoidant: The Mixed Effects of Enhanced Video Feedback on Social Anxiety Symptoms," *Behaviour Research & Therapy* 42, no. 12 (December 2004), pp. 1435–1451.

46. B. M. Depaulo, D. A. Kashy, S. E. Kirkendol, M. M. Wyer, and J. A. Epstein, "Lying in Everyday Life," *Journal of Personality and Social Psychology* 70, no. 5 (1996), pp. 979–995; and K. B. Serota, T. R. Levine, and F. J. Boster, "The Prevalence of Lying in America: Three Studies of Self-Reported Lies," *Human Communication Research* 36, no. 1. (2010), pp. 2–25.

47. DePaulo, Kashy, Kirkendol, Wyer, and Epstein, "Lying in Everyday Life"; and C. E. Naquin, T. R. Kurtzberg, and L. Y. Belkin, "The Finer Points of Lying Online: E-Mail Versus Pen and Paper," *Journal of Applied Psychology* 95, no. 2 (2010), pp. 387–394.

48. A. Vrij, P. A. Granhag, and S. Porter, "Pitfalls and Opportunities in Nonverbal and Verbal Lie Detection," *Psychological Science in the Public Interest* 11, no. 3 (2010), pp. 89–121.

49. R. E. Axtell, *Gestures: The Do's and Taboos of Body Language Around the World* (New York: Wiley, 1991); Watson Wyatt Worldwide, "Effective Communication: A Leading Indicator of Financial Performance—2005/2006 Communication ROI Study," www.watsonwyatt.com/research/resrender.asp?id=w-868; and A. Markels, "Turning the Tide at P&G," *U.S. News & World Report* (October 30, 2006), p. 69.

50. See M. Munter, "Cross-Cultural Communication for Managers," *Business Horizons* (May/June 1993), pp. 75–76;

and H. Ren and B. Gray, "Repairing Relationship Conflict: How Violation Types and Culture Influence the Effectiveness of Restoration Rituals," *Academy of Management Review* 34, no. 1 (2009), pp. 105–126.

51. See E. T. Hall, *Beyond Culture* (Garden City, NY: Anchor Press/Doubleday, 1976); W. L. Adair, "Integrative Sequences and Negotiation Outcome in Same- and Mixed-Culture Negotiations," *International Journal of Conflict Management* 14, no. 3–4 (2003), pp. 1359–1392; W. L. Adair and J. M. Brett, "The Negotiation Dance: Time, Culture, and Behavioral Sequences in Negotiation," *Organization Science* 16, no. 1 (2005), pp. 33–51; E. Giebels and P. J. Taylor, "Interaction Patterns in Crisis Negotiations: Persuasive Arguments and Cultural Differences," *Journal of Applied Psychology* 94, no. 1 (2009), pp. 5–19; and M. G. Kittler, D. Rygl, and A. Mackinnon, "Beyond Culture or Beyond Control? Reviewing the Use of Hall's High-/Low-Context Concept," *International Journal of Cross-Cultural Management* 11, no. 1 (2011), pp. 63–82.

52. N. Adler, *International Dimensions of Organizational Behavior,* 4th ed. (Cincinnati, OH: South-Western Publishing, 2002), p. 94.

53. See, for example. R. S. Schuler, "A Role Perception Transactional Process Model for Organizational Communication-Outcome Relationships," *Organizational Behavior and Human Performance* (April 1979), pp. 268–291.

54. J. P. Walsh, S. J. Ashford, and T. E. Hill, "Feedback Obstruction: The Influence of the Information Environment on Employee Turnover Intentions," *Human Relations* (January 1985), pp. 23–46.

55. S. A. Hellweg and S. L. Phillips, "Communication and Productivity in Organizations: A State-of-the-Art Review," in *Proceedings of the 40th Annual Academy of Management Conference,* Detroit, 1980, pp. 188–192. See also B. A. Bechky, "Sharing Meaning Across Occupational Communities: The Transformation of Understanding on a Production Floor," *Organization Science* 14, no. 3 (May/June 2003), pp. 312–330.

CHAPTER 12

1. J. G. Geier, "A Trait Approach to the Study of Leadership in Small Groups," *Journal of Communication* (December 1967), pp. 316–323.

2. S. A. Kirkpatrick and E. A. Locke, "Leadership: Do Traits Matter?" *Academy of Management Executive* (May 1991), pp. 48–60; and S. J. Zaccaro, R. J. Foti, and D. A. Kenny, "Self-Monitoring and Trait-Based Variance in Leadership: An Investigation of Leader Flexibility Across Multiple Group Situations," *Journal of Applied Psychology* (April 1991), pp. 308–315.

3. T. A. Judge, J. E. Bono, R. Ilies, and M. W. Gerhardt, "Personality and Leadership: A Qualitative and Quantitative Review," *Journal of Applied Psychology* (August 2002), pp. 765–780.

4. D. R. Ames and F. J. Flynn, "What Breaks a Leader: The Curvilinear Relation Between Assertiveness and Leadership," *Journal of Personality and Social Psychology* 92, no. 2 (2007), pp. 307–324.

5. K. Ng, S. Ang, and K. Chan, "Personality and Leader Effectiveness: A Moderated Mediation Model of Leadership Self-Efficacy, Job Demands, and Job Autonomy," *Journal of Applied Psychology* 93, no. 4 (2008), pp. 733–743.

6. This section is based on J. M. George, "Emotions and Leadership: The Role of Emotional Intelligence," *Human Relations* (August 2000), pp. 1027–1055; C.-S. Wong and K. S. Law, "The Effects of Leader and Follower Emotional Intelligence on Performance and Attitude: An Exploratory Study," *Leadership Quarterly* (June 2002), pp. 243–274; and J. Antonakis, N. M. Ashkanasy, and M. T. Dasborough, "Does Leadership Need Emotional Intelligence?" *Leadership Quarterly* 20 (2009), pp. 247–261.

7. R. H. Humphrey, J. M. Pollack, and T. H. Hawver, "Leading with Emotional Labor," *Journal of Managerial Psychology* 23 (2008), pp. 151–168.

8. F. Walter, M. S. Cole, and R. H. Humphrey, "Emotional Intelligence: Sine Qua Non of Leadership or Folderol?" *Academy of Management Perspectives* (February 2011), pp. 45–59.

9. S. Côté, P. N. Lopez, P. Salovey, and C. T. H. Miners, "Emotional Intelligence and Leadership Emergence in Small Groups," *Leadership Quarterly* 21 (2010), pp. 496–508.

10. R. G. Lord, C. L. DeVader, and G. M. Alliger, "A Meta-Analysis of the Relation Between Personality Traits and Leadership Perceptions: An Application of Validity Generalization Procedures," *Journal of Applied Psychology* (August 1986), pp. 402–410; and J. A. Smith and R. J. Foti, "A Pattern Approach to the Study of Leader Emergence," *Leadership Quarterly* (Summer 1998), pp. 147–160.

11. R. M. Stogdill and A. E. Coons (eds.), *Leader Behavior: Its Description and Measurement,* Research Monograph no. 88 (Columbus: Ohio State University, Bureau of Business Research, 1951). This research is updated in C. A. Schriesheim, C. C. Cogliser, and L. L. Neider, "Is It 'Trustworthy'? A Multiple-Levels-of-Analysis Reexamination of an Ohio State Leadership Study, with Implications for Future Research," *Leadership Quarterly* (Summer 1995), pp. 111–145; and T. A. Judge, R. F. Piccolo, and R. Ilies, "The Forgotten Ones? The Validity of Consideration and Initiating Structure in Leadership Research," *Journal of Applied Psychology* (February 2004), pp. 36–51.

12. D. Akst, "The Rewards of Recognizing a Job Well Done," *Wall Street Journal* (January 31, 2007), p. D9.

13. Judge, Piccolo, and Ilies, "The Forgotten Ones?"

14. M. Javidan, P. W. Dorfman, M. S. de Luque, and R. J. House, "In the Eye of the Beholder: Cross Cultural Lessons in Leadership from Project GLOBE," *Academy of Management Perspectives* (February 2006), pp. 67–90.

15. F. E. Fiedler, *A Theory of Leadership Effectiveness* (New York: McGraw-Hill, 1967).

16. S. Shiflett, "Is There a Problem with the LPC Score in LEADER MATCH?" *Personnel Psychology* (Winter 1981), pp. 765–769.

17. F. E. Fiedler, M. M. Chemers, and L. Mahar, *Improving Leadership Effectiveness: The Leader Match Concept* (New York: Wiley, 1977).

18. Cited in R. J. House and R. N. Aditya, "The Social Scientific Study of Leadership," *Journal of Management* 23, no. 3 (1997), p. 422.

19. L. H. Peters, D. D. Hartke, and J. T. Pohlmann, "Fiedler's Contingency Theory of Leadership: An Application of the Meta-Analysis Procedures of Schmidt and Hunter," *Psychological Bulletin* (March 1985), pp. 274–285; C. A. Schriesheim, B. J. Tepper, and L. A. Tetrault, "Least Preferred Coworker Score, Situational Control, and Leadership Effectiveness: A Meta-Analysis of Contingency Model

Performance Predictions," *Journal of Applied Psychology* (August 1994), pp. 561–573; and R. Ayman, M. M. Chemers, and F. Fiedler, "The Contingency Model of Leadership Effectiveness: Its Levels of Analysis," *Leadership Quarterly* (Summer 1995), pp. 147–167.

20. House and Aditya, "The Social Scientific Study of Leadership."

21. See, for instance, R. W. Rice, "Psychometric Properties of the Esteem for the Least Preferred Coworker (LPC) Scale," *Academy of Management Review* (January 1978), pp. 106–118; C. A. Schriesheim, B. D. Bannister, and W. H. Money, "Psychometric Properties of the LPC Scale: An Extension of Rice's Review," *Academy of Management Review* (April 1979), pp. 287–290; and J. K. Kennedy, J. M. Houston, M. A. Korgaard, and D. D. Gallo, "Construct Space of the Least Preferred Coworker (LPC) Scale," *Educational and Psychological Measurement* (Fall 1987), pp. 807–814.

22. See E. H. Schein, *Organizational Psychology,* 3rd ed. (Upper Saddle River, NJ: Prentice Hall, 1980), pp. 116–117; and B. Kabanoff, "A Critique of Leader Match and Its Implications for Leadership Research," *Personnel Psychology* (Winter 1981), pp. 749–764.

23. X. Zhou and C. A. Schriesheim, "Supervisor–Subordinate Convergence in Descriptions of Leader–Member Exchange (LMX) Quality: Review and Testable Propositions," *Leadership Quarterly* 20, no. 6 (2009), pp. 920–932; G. B. Graen and M. Uhl-Bien, "Relationship-Based Approach to Leadership: Development of Leader–Member Exchange (LMX) Theory of Leadership Over 25 Years: Applying a Multi-Domain Perspective," *Leadership Quarterly* (Summer 1995), pp. 219–247; R. C. Liden, R. T. Sparrowe, and S. J. Wayne, "Leader–Member Exchange Theory: The Past and Potential for the Future," in G. R. Ferris (ed.), *Research in Personnel and Human Resource Management,* vol. 15 (Greenwich, CT: JAI Press, 1997), pp. 47–119; and C. A. Schriesheim, S. L. Castro, X. Zhou, and F. J. Yammarino, "The Folly of Theorizing 'A' but Testing 'B': A Selective Level-of-Analysis Review of the Field and a Detailed Leader–Member Exchange Illustration," *Leadership Quarterly* (Winter 2001), pp. 515–551.

24. B. Erdogan and T. N. Bauer, "Differentiated Leader–Member Exchanges: The Buffering Role of Justice Climate," *Journal of Applied Psychology* 95, no. 6 (2010), pp. 1104–1120; R. C. Liden, S. J. Wayne, and D. Stilwell, "A Longitudinal Study of the Early Development of Leader–Member Exchanges," *Journal of Applied Psychology* (August 1993), pp. 662–674; S. J. Wayne, L. M. Shore, W. H. Bommer, and L. E. Tetrick, "The Role of Fair Treatment and Rewards in Perceptions of Organizational Support and Leader–Member Exchange," *Journal of Applied Psychology* 87, no. 3 (June 2002), pp. 590–598; and S. S. Masterson, K. Lewis, and B. M. Goldman, "Integrating Justice and Social Exchange: The Differing Effects of Fair Procedures and Treatment on Work Relationships," *Academy of Management Journal* 43, no. 4 (August 2000), pp. 738–748.

25. D. Duchon, S. G. Green, and T. D. Taber, "Vertical Dyad Linkage: A Longitudinal Assessment of Antecedents, Measures, and Consequences," *Journal of Applied Psychology* (February 1986), pp. 56–60; Liden, Wayne, and Stilwell, "A Longitudinal Study on the Early Development of Leader–Member Exchanges"; and M. Uhl-Bien, "Relationship Development as a Key Ingredient for Leadership Development," in S. E. Murphy and R. E. Riggio (eds.),

Future of Leadership Development (Mahwah, NJ: Lawrence Erlbaum, 2003) pp. 129–147.

26. R. Vecchio and D. M. Brazil, "Leadership and Sex-Similarity: A Comparison in a Military Setting," *Personnel Psychology* 60 (2007), pp. 303–335.

27. See, for instance, C. R. Gerstner and D. V. Day, "Meta-Analytic Review of Leader–Member Exchange Theory: Correlates and Construct Issues," *Journal of Applied Psychology* (December 1997), pp. 827–844; R. Ilies, J. D. Nahrgang, and F. P. Morgeson, "Leader–Member Exchange and Citizenship Behaviors: A Meta-Analysis," *Journal of Applied Psychology* 92, no. 1 (2007), pp. 269–277; and Z. Chen, W. Lam, and J. A. Zhong, "Leader–Member Exchange and Member Performance: A New Look at Individual-Level Negative Feedback-Seeking Behavior and Team-Level Empowerment Culture," *Journal of Applied Psychology* 92, no. 1 (2007), pp. 202–212.

28. B. Erdogan and T. N. Bauer, "Differentiated Leader-Member Exchanges: The Buffering Role of Justice Climate," *Journal of Applied Psychology* 95, no. 6 (2010), pp. 1104–1120.

29. M. Ozer, "Personal and Task-Related Moderators of Leader-Member Exchange Among Software Developers," *Journal of Applied Psychology* 93, no. 5 (2008), pp. 1174–1182.

30. M. Weber, *The Theory of Social and Economic Organization,* A. M. Henderson and T. Parsons (trans.) (New York: The Free Press, 1947).

31. J. A. Conger and R. N. Kanungo, "Behavioral Dimensions of Charismatic Leadership," in J. A. Conger, R. N. Kanungo, and Associates (eds.), *Charismatic Leadership* (San Francisco: Jossey-Bass, 1988), p. 79.

32. J. A. Conger and R. N. Kanungo, *Charismatic Leadership in Organizations* (Thousand Oaks, CA: Sage, 1998); and R. Awamleh and W. L. Gardner, "Perceptions of Leader Charisma and Effectiveness: The Effects of Vision Content, Delivery, and Organizational Performance," *Leadership Quarterly* (Fall 1999), pp. 345–373.

33. R. J. House and J. M. Howell, "Personality and Charismatic Leadership," *Leadership Quarterly* 3 (1992), pp. 81–108; D. N. Den Hartog and P. L. Koopman, "Leadership in Organizations," in N. Anderson and D. S. Ones (eds.), *Handbook of Industrial, Work and Organizational Psychology,* vol. 2 (Thousand Oaks, CA: Sage, 2002), pp. 166–187.

34. See J. A. Conger and R. N. Kanungo, "Training Charismatic Leadership: A Risky and Critical Task," *Charismatic Leadership* (San Francisco: Jossey-Bass, 1988), pp. 309–323; A. J. Towler, "Effects of Charismatic Influence Training on Attitudes, Behavior, and Performance," *Personnel Psychology* (Summer 2003), pp. 363–381; and M. Frese, S. Beimel, and S. Schoenborn, "Action Training for Charismatic Leadership: Two Evaluations of Studies of a Commercial Training Module on Inspirational Communication of a Vision," *Personnel Psychology* (Autumn 2003), pp. 671–697.

35. R. J. Richardson and S. K. Thayer, *The Charisma Factor: How to Develop Your Natural Leadership Ability* (Upper Saddle River, NJ: Prentice Hall, 1993).

36. J. M. Howell and P. J. Frost, "A Laboratory Study of Charismatic Leadership," *Organizational Behavior and Human Decision Processes* (April 1989), pp. 243–269. See also Frese, Beimel, and Schoenborn, "Action Training for Charismatic Leadership."

37. B. Shamir, R. J. House, and M. B. Arthur, "The Motivational Effects of Charismatic Leadership: A Self-Concept Theory," *Organization Science* (November 1993), pp. 577–594.

38. D. N. Den Hartog, A. H. B. De Hoogh, and A. E. Keegan, "The Interactive Effects of Belongingness and Charisma on Helping and Compliance," *Journal of Applied Psychology* 92, no. 4 (2007), pp. 1131–1139.

39. A. Erez, V. F. Misangyi, D. E. Johnson, M. A. LePine, and K. C. Halverson, "Stirring the Hearts of Followers: Charismatic Leadership as the Transferal of Affect," *Journal of Applied Psychology* 93, no. 3 (2008), pp. 602–615. For reviews on the role of vision in leadership, see S. J. Zaccaro, "Visionary and Inspirational Models of Executive Leadership: Empirical Review and Evaluation," in S. J. Zaccaro (ed.), *The Nature of Executive Leadership: A Conceptual and Empirical Analysis of Success* (Washington, DC: American Psychological Association, 2001), pp. 259–278; and M. Hauser and R. J. House, "Lead Through Vision and Values," in E. A. Locke (ed.), *Handbook of Principles of Organizational Behavior* (Malden, MA: Blackwell, 2004), pp. 257–273.

40. D. A. Waldman, B. M. Bass, and F. J. Yammarino, "Adding to Contingent-Reward Behavior: The Augmenting Effect of Charismatic Leadership," *Group and Organization Studies,* December 1990, pp. 381–394; and S. A. Kirkpatrick and E. A. Locke, "Direct and Indirect Effects of Three Core Charismatic Leadership Components on Performance and Attitudes," *Journal of Applied Psychology* (February 1996), pp. 36–51.

41. A. H. B. de Hoogh, D. N. Den Hartog, P. L. Koopman, H. Thierry, P. T. van den Berg, and J. G. van der Weide, "Charismatic Leadership, Environmental Dynamism, and Performance," *European Journal of Work and Organizational Psychology* (December 2004), pp. 447–471; S. Harvey, M. Martin, and D. Stout, "Instructor's Transformational Leadership: University Student Attitudes and Ratings," *Psychological Reports* (April 2003), pp. 395–402; and D. A. Waldman, M. Javidan, and P. Varella, "Charismatic Leadership at the Strategic Level: A New Application of Upper Echelons Theory," *Leadership Quarterly* (June 2004), pp. 355–380.

42. R. J. House, "A 1976 Theory of Charismatic Leadership," in J. G. Hunt and L. L. Larson (eds.), *Leadership: The Cutting Edge* (Carbondale: Southern Illinois University Press, 1977), pp. 189–207; and House and Aditya, "The Social Scientific Study of Leadership," p. 441.

43. J. C. Pastor, M. Mayo, and B. Shamir, "Adding Fuel to Fire: The Impact of Followers' Arousal on Ratings of Charisma," *Journal of Applied Psychology* 92, no. 6 (2007), pp. 1584–1596.

44. A. H. B. De Hoogh and D. N. Den Hartog, "Neuroticism and Locus of Control as Moderators of the Relationships of Charismatic and Autocratic Leadership with Burnout," *Journal of Applied Psychology* 94, no. 4 (2009), pp. 1058–1067.

45. F. Cohen, S. Solomon, M. Maxfield, T. Pyszczynski, and J. Greenberg, "Fatal Attraction: The Effects of Mortality Salience on Evaluations of Charismatic, Task-Oriented, and Relationship-Oriented Leaders," *Psychological Sciences* (December 2004), pp. 846–851; and M. G. Ehrhart and K. J. Klein, "Predicting Followers' Preferences for Charismatic Leadership: The Influence of Follower Values and Personality," *Leadership Quarterly* (Summer 2001), pp. 153–179.

46. H. L. Tosi, V. Misangyi, A. Fanelli, D. A. Waldman, and F. J. Yammarino, "CEO Charisma, Compensation, and Firm Performance," *Leadership Quarterly* (June 2004), pp. 405–420.

47. See, for instance, R. Khurana, *Searching for a Corporate Savior: The Irrational Quest for Charismatic CEOs* (Princeton, NJ: Princeton University Press, 2002); and J. A. Raelin, "The Myth of Charismatic Leaders," *Training and Development* (March 2003), pp. 47–54.

48. B. M. Galvin, D. A. Waldman, and P. Balthazard, "Visionary Communication Qualities as Mediators of the Relationship between Narcissism and Attributions of Leader Charisma," *Personnel Psychology* 63, no. 3 (2010), pp. 509–537.

49. See, for instance, B. M. Bass, B. J. Avolio, D. I. Jung, and Y. Berson, "Predicting Unit Performance by Assessing Transformational and Transactional Leadership," *Journal of Applied Psychology* (April 2003), pp. 207–218; and T. A. Judge and R. F. Piccolo, "Transformational and Transactional Leadership: A Meta-Analytic Test of Their Relative Validity," *Journal of Applied Psychology* (October 2004), pp. 755–768.

50. B. M. Bass, "Leadership: Good, Better, Best," *Organizational Dynamics* (Winter 1985), pp. 26–40; and J. Seltzer and B. M. Bass, "Transformational Leadership: Beyond Initiation and Consideration," *Journal of Management* (December 1990), pp. 693–703.

51. T. R. Hinkin and C. A. Schriesheim, "An Examination of 'Nonleadership': From Laissez-Faire Leadership to Leader Reward Omission and Punishment Omission," *Journal of Applied Psychology* 93, no. 6 (2008), pp. 1234–1248.

52. S. J. Shin and J. Zhou, "Transformational Leadership, Conservation, and Creativity: Evidence from Korea," *Academy of Management Journal* (December 2003), pp. 703–714; V. J. García-Morales, F. J. Lloréns-Montes, and A. J. Verdú-Jover, "The Effects of Transformational Leadership on Organizational Performance Through Knowledge and Innovation," *British Journal of Management* 19, no. 4 (2008), pp. 299–313; and S. A. Eisenbeiss, D. van Knippenberg, and S. Boerner, "Transformational Leadership and Team Innovation: Integrating Team Climate Principles," *Journal of Applied Psychology* 93, no. 6 (2008), pp. 1438–1446.

53. Y. Ling, Z. Simsek, M. H. Lubatkin, and J. F. Veiga, "Transformational Leadership's Role in Promoting Corporate Entrepreneurship: Examining the CEO-TMT Interface," *Academy of Management Journal* 51, no. 3 (2008), pp. 557–576.

54. X. Zhang and K. M. Bartol, "Linking Empowering Leadership and Employee Creativity: The Influence of Psychological Empowerment, Intrinsic Motivation, and Creative Process Engagement," *Academy of Management Journal* 53, no. 1 (2010), pp. 107–128.

55. A. E. Colbert, A. E. Kristof-Brown, B. H. Bradley, and M. R. Barrick, "CEO Transformational Leadership: The Role of Goal Importance Congruence in Top Management Teams," *Academy of Management Journal* 51, no. 1 (2008), pp. 81–96.

56. D. Zohar and O. Tenne-Gazit, "Transformational Leadership and Group Interaction as Climate Antecedents: A Social Network Analysis," *Journal of Applied Psychology* 93, no. 4 (2008), pp. 744–757.

57. F. O. Walumbwa, B. J. Avolio, and W. Zhu, "How Transformational Leadership Weaves Its Influence on Individual Job Performance: The Role of Identification and Efficacy Beliefs," *Personnel Psychology* 61, no. 4 (2008), pp. 793–825.

58. J. E. Bono and T. A. Judge, "Self-Concordance at Work: Toward Understanding the Motivational Effects of

Transformational Leaders," *Academy of Management Journal* (October 2003), pp. 554–571; Y. Berson and B. J. Avolio, "Transformational Leadership and the Dissemination of Organizational Goals: A Case Study of a Telecommunication Firm," *Leadership Quarterly* (October 2004), pp. 625–646; and J. Schaubroeck, S. S. K. Lam, and S. E. Cha, "Embracing Transformational Leadership: Team Values and the Impact of Leader Behavior on Team Performance," *Journal of Applied Psychology* 92, no. 4 (2007), pp. 1020–1030.

59. J. R. Baum, E. A. Locke, and S. A. Kirkpatrick, "A Longitudinal Study of the Relation of Vision and Vision Communication to Venture Growth in Entrepreneurial Firms," *Journal of Applied Psychology* (February 2000), pp. 43–54.

60. B. J. Avolio, W. Zhu, W. Koh, and P. Bhatia, "Transformational Leadership and Organizational Commitment: Mediating Role of Psychological Empowerment and Moderating Role of Structural Distance," *Journal of Organizational Behavior* (December 2004), pp. 951–968; and T. Dvir, N. Kass, and B. Shamir, "The Emotional Bond: Vision and Organizational Commitment Among High-Tech Employees," *Journal of Organizational Change Management* 17, no. 2 (2004), pp. 126–143.

61. R. T. Keller, "Transformational Leadership, Initiating Structure, and Substitutes for Leadership: A Longitudinal Study of Research and Development Project Team Performance," *Journal of Applied Psychology* 91, no. 1 (2006), pp. 202–210.

62. Y. Gong, J. Huang, and J. Farh, "Employee Learning Orientation, Transformational Leadership, and Employee Creativity: The Mediating Role of Employee Creative Self-Efficacy," *Academy of Management Journal* 52, no. 4 (2009), pp. 765–778.

63. G. Wang, I. Oh, S. H. Courtright, and A. E. Colbert, "Transformational Leadership and Performance Across Criteria and Levels: A Meta-Analytic Review of 25 Years of Research," *Group and Organization Management* 36, no. 2 (2011), pp. 223–270.

64. Y. Ling, Z. Simsek, M. H. Lubatkin, and J. F. Veiga, "The Impact of Transformational CEOs on the Performance of Small- to Medium-Sized Firms: Does Organizational Context Matter?" *Journal of Applied Psychology* 93, no. 4 (2008), pp. 923–934.

65. Schaubroeck, Lam, and Cha, "Embracing Transformational Leadership."

66. B. L. Kirkman, G. Chen, J. Farh, Z. X. Chen, and K. B. Lowe, "Individual Power Distance Orientation and Follower Reactions to Transformational Leaders: A Cross-Level, Cross-Cultural Examination," *Academy of Management Journal* 52, no. 4 (2009), pp. 744–764.

67. J. Liu, O. Siu, and K. Shi, "Transformational Leadership and Employee Well-Being: The Mediating Role of Trust in the Leader and Self-Efficacy," *Applied Psychology: An International Review* 59, no. 3 (2010), pp. 454–479.

68. X. Wang and J. M. Howell, "Exploring the Dual-Level Effects of Transformational Leadership on Followers," *Journal of Applied Psychology* 95, no. 6 (2010), pp. 1134–1144.

69. H. Hetland, G. M. Sandal, and T. B. Johnsen, "Burnout in the Information Technology Sector: Does Leadership Matter?" *European Journal of Work and Organizational Psychology* 16, no. 1 (2007), pp. 58–75; and K. B. Lowe, K. G. Kroeck, and N. Sivasubramaniam, "Effectiveness Correlates of Transformational and Transactional Leadership: A Meta-Analytic Review of the MLQ Literature," *Leadership Quarterly* (Fall 1996), pp. 385–425.

70. See, for instance, J. Barling, T. Weber, and E. K. Kelloway, "Effects of Transformational Leadership Training on Attitudinal and Financial Outcomes: A Field Experiment," *Journal of Applied Psychology* (December 1996), pp. 827–832; and T. Dvir, D. Eden, and B. J. Avolio, "Impact of Transformational Leadership on Follower Development and Performance: A Field Experiment," *Academy of Management Journal* (August 2002), pp. 735–744.

71. R. J. House, M. Javidan, P. Hanges, and P. Dorfman, "Understanding Cultures and Implicit Leadership Theories Across the Globe: An Introduction to Project GLOBE," *Journal of World Business* (Spring 2002), pp. 3–10.

72. D. E. Carl and M. Javidan, "Universality of Charismatic Leadership: A Multi-Nation Study," paper presented at the National Academy of Management Conference, Washington, DC (August 2001), p. 29.

73. N. Beccalli, "European Business Forum Asks: Do Companies Get the Leaders They Deserve?" *European Business Forum* (2003), www.pwcglobal.com/extweb/pwcpublications.nsf/DocID/D1EC3380F589844585256D7300346A1B.

74. See B. J. Avolio, W. L. Gardner, F. O. Walumbwa, F. Luthans, and D. R. May, "Unlocking the Mask: A Look at the Process by Which Authentic Leaders Impact Follower Attitudes and Behaviors," *Leadership Quarterly* (December 2004), pp. 801–823; W. L. Gardner and J. R. Schermerhorn Jr., "Performance Gains Through Positive Organizational Behavior and Authentic Leadership," *Organizational Dynamics* (August 2004), pp. 270–281; and M. M. Novicevic, M. G. Harvey, M. R. Buckley, J. A. Brown-Radford, and R. Evans, "Authentic Leadership: A Historical Perspective," *Journal of Leadership and Organizational Behavior* 13, no. 1 (2006), pp. 64–76.

75. C. Tan, "CEO Pinching Penney in a Slowing Economy," *Wall Street Journal* (January 31, 2008), pp. 1–2; and A. Carter, "Lighting a Fire Under Campbell," *BusinessWeek* (December 4, 2006), pp. 96–101.

76. R. Ilies, F. P. Morgeson, and J. D. Nahrgang, "Authentic Leadership and Eudaemonic Well-being: Understanding Leader-follower Outcomes," *Leadership Quarterly* 16 (2005), pp. 373–394; B. Levin, "Raj Rajaratnam Did Not Appreciate Rajat Gupta's Attempt to Leave The Goldman Board, Join 'The Billionaire Circle,'" *NetNet with John Carney* (March 14, 2011). Retrieved July 26, 2011, from http://www.cnbc.com/.

77. This section is based on E. P. Hollander, "Ethical Challenges in the Leader–Follower Relationship," *Business Ethics Quarterly* (January 1995), pp. 55–65; J. C. Rost, "Leadership: A Discussion About Ethics," *Business Ethics Quarterly* (January 1995), pp. 129–142; L. K. Treviño, M. Brown, and L. P. Hartman, "A Qualitative Investigation of Perceived Executive Ethical Leadership: Perceptions from Inside and Outside the Executive Suite," *Human Relations* (January 2003), pp. 5–37; and R. M. Fulmer, "The Challenge of Ethical Leadership," *Organizational Dynamics* 33, no. 3 (2004), pp. 307–317.

78. J. L. Lunsford, "Piloting Boeing's New Course," *Wall Street Journal* (June 13, 2006), pp. B1, B3.

79. J. M. Burns, *Leadership* (New York: Harper & Row, 1978).

80. J. M. Howell and B. J. Avolio, "The Ethics of Charismatic Leadership: Submission or Liberation?" *Academy of Management Executive* (May 1992), pp. 43–55.

81. D. van Knippenberg, D. De Cremer, and B. van Knippenberg, "Leadership and Fairness: The State of the Art," *European Journal of Work and Organizational Psychology* 16, no. 2 (2007), pp. 113–140.

82. K. M. Kacmar, D. G. Bachrach, K. J. Harris, and S. Zivnuska, "Fostering Good Citizenship Through Ethical Leadership: Exploring the Moderating Role of Gender and Organizational Politics," *Journal of Applied Psychology,* Advance Online Publication (December 13, 2010), doi: 10.1037/a0021872; F. O. Walumbwa and J. Schaubroeck, "Leader Personality Traits and Employee Voice Behavior: Mediating Roles of Ethical Leadership and Work Group Psychological Safety," *Journal of Applied Psychology* 94, no. 5 (2009), pp. 1275–1286.

83. M. E. Brown and L. K. Treviño, "Socialized Charismatic Leadership, Values Congruence, and Deviance in Work Groups," *Journal of Applied Psychology* 91, no. 4 (2006), pp. 954–962.

84. M. E. Brown and L. K. Treviño, "Leader-Follower Values Congruence: Are Socialized Charismatic Leaders Better Able to Achieve It?" *Journal of Applied Psychology* 94, no. 2 (2009), pp. 478–490.

85. D. van Dierendonck, "Servant Leadership: A Review and Synthesis," *Journal of Management* 37, no. 4 (2011), pp. 1228–1261.

86. F. Walumbwa, C. A. Hartnell, and A. Oke, "Servant Leadership, Procedural Justice Climate, Service Climate, Employee Attitudes, and Organizational Citizenship Behavior: A Cross-Level Investigation," *Journal of Applied Psychology* 95, no. 3 (2010), pp. 517–529.

87. D. De Cremer, D. M. Mayer, M. van Dijke, B. C. Schouten, and M. Bardes, "When Does Self-Sacrificial Leadership Motivate Prosocial Behavior? It Depends on Followers' Prevention Focus," *Journal of Applied Psychology* 2009, no. 4 (2009), pp. 887–899.

88. J. Hu and R. C. Liden, "Antecedents of Team Potency and Team Effectiveness: An Examination of Goal and Process Clarity and Servant Leadership," *Journal of Applied Psychology,* Online first publication (February 14, 2011), doi: 10.1037/a0022465.

89. M. J. Neubert, K. M. Kacmar, D. S. Carlson, L. B. Chonko, and J. A. Roberts, "Regulatory Focus as a Mediator of the Influence of Initiating Structure and Servant Leadership on Employee Behavior," *Journal of Applied Psychology* 93, no. 6 (2008), pp. 1220–1233.

90. T. Menon, J. Sim, J. Ho-Ying Fu, C. Chiu, and Y. Hong, "Blazing the Trail Versus Trailing the Group: Culture and Perceptions of the Leader's Position," *Organizational Behavior and Human Decision Processes* 113, no. 1 (2010), pp. 51–61.

91. D. M. Rousseau, S. B. Sitkin, R. S. Burt, and C. Camerer, "Not So Different After All: A Cross-Discipline View of Trust," *Academy of Management Review* (July 1998), pp. 393–404; and J. A. Simpson, "Psychological Foundations of Trust," *Current Directions in Psychological Science* 16, no. 5 (2007), pp. 264–268.

92. See, for instance, K. Dirks and D. Ferrin, "Trust in Leadership: Meta-Analytic Findings and Implications for Research and Practice," *Journal of Applied Psychology* 87, no.4 (2002), pp. 611–628; D. I. Jung and B. J. Avolio, "Opening the Black Box: An Experimental Investigation of the Mediating Effects of Trust and Value Congruence on Transformational and Transactional Leadership," *Journal of Organizational Behavior* (December 2000), pp. 949–964; and A. Zacharatos, J. Barling, and R. D. Iverson, "High-Performance Work Systems and Occupational Safety," *Journal of Applied Psychology* (January 2005), pp. 77–93.

93. D. E. Zand, *The Leadership Triad: Knowledge, Trust, and Power* (New York: Oxford University Press, 1997), p. 89.

94. Based on L. T. Hosmer, "Trust: The Connecting Link Between Organizational Theory and Philosophical Ethics," *Academy of Management Review* (April 1995), p. 393; R. C. Mayer, J. H. Davis, and F. D. Schoorman, "An Integrative Model of Organizational Trust," *Academy of Management Review* (July 1995), pp. 709–734; and F. D. Schoorman, R. C. Mayer, and J. H. Davis, "An Integrative Model of Organizational Trust: Past, Present, and Future," *Academy of Management Review* 32, no. 2 (2007), pp. 344–354.

95. J. Schaubroeck, S. S. K. Lam, and A. C. Peng, "Cognition-Based and Affect-Based Trust as Mediators of Leader Behavior Influences on Team Performance." *Journal of Applied Psychology,* Advance online publication (February 7, 2011), doi: 10.1037/a0022625.

96. J. R. Detert and E. R. Burris, "Leadership Behavior and Employee Voice: Is the Door Really Open?" *Academy of Management Journal* 50, no. 4 (2007), pp. 869–884.

97. Colquitt, Scott, and LePine, "Trust, Trustworthiness, and Trust Propensity."

98. Comment by Jim Collins, cited in J. Useem, "Conquering Vertical Limits," *Fortune* (February 19, 2001), p. 94.

99. See, for instance, J. R. Meindl, "The Romance of Leadership as a Follower-centric Theory: A Social Constructionist Approach," *Leadership Quarterly* (Fall 1995), pp. 329–341; and B. Schyns, J. Felfe, and H. Blank, "Is Charisma Hyper-Romanticism? Empirical Evidence from New Data and a Meta-Analysis," *Applied Psychology: An International Review* 56, no. 4 (2007), pp. 505–527.

100. R. G. Lord, C. L. DeVader, and G. M. Alliger, "A Meta-Analysis of the Relation Between Personality Traits and Leadership Perceptions: An Application of Validity Generalization Procedures," *Journal of Applied Psychology* (August 1986), pp. 402–410.

101. J. R. Meindl, S. B. Ehrlich, and J. M. Dukerich, "The Romance of Leadership," *Administrative Science Quarterly* (March 1985), pp. 78–102; and M. C. Bligh, J. C. Kohles, C. L. Pearce, J. E. Justin, and J. F. Stovall, "When the Romance Is Over: Follower Perspectives of Aversive Leadership," *Applied Psychology: An International Review* 56, no. 4 (2007), pp. 528–557.

102. B. R. Agle, N. J. Nagarajan, J. A. Sonnenfeld, and D. Srinivasan, "Does CEO Charisma Matter?" *Academy of Management Journal* 49, no. 1 (2006), pp. 161–174.

103. Bligh, Kohles, Pearce, Justin, and Stovall, "When the Romance Is Over."

104. Schyns, Felfe, and Blank, "Is Charisma Hyper-Romanticism?"

105. J. Cassidy, "Subprime Suspect: The Rise and Fall of Wall Street's First Black C.E.O.," *New Yorker* (March 31, 2008), pp. 78–91.

106. A. S. Rosette, G. J. Leonardelli, and K. W. Phillips, "The White Standard: Racial Bias in Leader Categorization," *Journal of Applied Psychology* 93, no. 4 (2008), pp. 758–777.

107. A. M. Koenig, A. H. Eagly, A. A. Mitchell, and T. Ristikari, "Are Leader Stereotypes Masculine? A Meta-Analysis of Three Research Paradigms," *Psychological Bulletin* 137, no. 4 (2011), pp. 616–642.

108. M. Van Vugt and B. R. Spisak, "Sex Differences in the Emergence of Leadership During Competitions Within and Between Groups," *Psychological Science* 19, no. 9 (2008), pp. 854–858.

109. Ibid.

110. S. D. Dionne, F. J. Yammarino, L. E. Atwater, and L. R. James, "Neutralizing Substitutes for Leadership Theory: Leadership Effects and Common-Source Bias," *Journal of Applied Psychology,* 87 (2002), pp. 454–464; and J. R. Villa, J. P. Howell, P. W. Dorfman, and D. L. Daniel, "Problems with Detecting Moderators in Leadership Research Using Moderated Multiple Regression," *Leadership Quarterly* 14 (2002), pp. 3–23.

111. L. A. Hambley, T. A. O'Neill, and T. J. B. Kline, "Virtual Team Leadership: The Effects of Leadership Style and Communication Medium on Team Interaction Styles and Outcomes," *Organizational Behavior and Human Decision Processes* 103 (2007), pp. 1–20; and B. J. Avolio and S. S. Kahai, "Adding the 'E' to E-Leadership: How It May Impact Your Leadership," *Organizational Dynamics* 31, no. 4 (2003), pp. 325–338.

112. S. J. Zaccaro and P. Bader, "E-Leadership and the Challenges of Leading E-Teams: Minimizing the Bad and Maximizing the Good," *Organizational Dynamics* 31, no. 4 (2003), pp. 381–385.

113. C. E. Naquin and G. D. Paulson, "Online Bargaining and Interpersonal Trust," *Journal of Applied Psychology* (February 2003), pp. 113–120.

CHAPTER 13

1. R. M. Kanter, "Power Failure in Management Circuits," *Harvard Business Review* (July–August 1979), p. 65.

2. Based on B. M. Bass, *Bass and Stogdill's Handbook of Leadership,* 3rd ed. (New York: The Free Press, 1990).

3. D. Carney, "Powerful People Are Better Liars," *Harvard Business Review* (May 2010), pp. 32–33.

4. A. J. Ferguson, M. E. Ormiston, and H. Moon, "From Approach to Inhibition: The Influence of Power on Responses to Poor Performers," *Journal of Applied Psychology* 95, no. 2 (2010), pp. 305–320.

5. J. R. P. French Jr. and B. Raven, "The Bases of Social Power," in D. Cartwright (ed.), *Studies in Social Power* (Ann Arbor, MI: University of Michigan, Institute for Social Research, 1959), pp. 150–167; B. J. Raven, "The Bases of Power: Origins and Recent Developments," *Journal of Social Issues* (Winter 1993), pp. 227–251; and G. Yukl, "Use Power Effectively," in E. A. Locke (ed.), *Handbook of Principles of Organizational Behavior* (Malden, MA: Blackwell, 2004), pp. 242–247.

6. E. A. Ward, "Social Power Bases of Managers: Emergence of a New Factor," *Journal of Social Psychology* (February 2001), pp. 144–147.

7. S. R. Giessner and T. W. Schubert, "High in the Hierarchy: How Vertical Location and Judgments of Leaders' Power Are Interrelated," *Organizational Behavior and Human Decision Processes* 104, no. 1 (2007), pp. 30–44.

8. P. M. Podsakoff and C. A. Schriesheim, "Field Studies of French and Raven's Bases of Power: Critique, Reanalysis, and Suggestions for Future Research," *Psychological Bulletin* (May 1985), pp. 387–411; T. R. Hinkin and C. A. Schriesheim, "Development and Application of New Scales to Measure the French and Raven (1959) Bases of Social Power," *Journal of Applied Psychology* (August 1989), pp. 561–567; and P. P. Carson, K. D. Carson, and C. W. Roe, "Social Power Bases: A Meta-Analytic Examination of Interrelationships and Outcomes," *Journal of Applied Social Psychology* 23, no. 14 (1993), pp. 1150–1169.

9. S. Perman, "Translation Advertising: Where Shop Meets Hip Hop," *Time* (August 30, 2010), www.time.com.

10. M. van Dijke, D. De Cremer, and D. M. Mayer, "The Role of Authority Power in Explaining Procedural Fairness Effects," *Journal of Applied Psychology* 95, no. 3 (2010), pp. 488–502.

11. See, for example, D. Kipnis and S. M. Schmidt, "Upward-Influence Styles: Relationship with Performance Evaluations, Salary, and Stress," *Administrative Science Quarterly* (December 1988), pp. 528–542; G. Yukl and J. B. Tracey, "Consequences of Influence Tactics Used with Subordinates, Peers, and the Boss," *Journal of Applied Psychology* (August 1992), pp. 525–535; G. Blickle, "Influence Tactics Used by Subordinates: An Empirical Analysis of the Kipnis and Schmidt Subscales," *Psychological Reports* (February 2000), pp. 143–154; and G. Yukl, "Use Power Effectively," pp. 249–252.

12. G. Yukl, *Leadership in Organizations,* 5th ed. (Upper Saddle River, NJ: Prentice Hall, 2002), pp. 141–174; G. R. Ferris, W. A. Hochwarter, C. Douglas, F. R. Blass, R. W. Kolodinksy, and D. C. Treadway, "Social Influence Processes in Organizations and Human Resource Systems," in G. R. Ferris and J. J. Martocchio (eds.), *Research in Personnel and Human Resources Management,* vol. 21 (Oxford, UK: JAI Press/Elsevier, 2003), pp. 65–127; and C. A. Higgins, T. A. Judge, and G. R. Ferris, "Influence Tactics and Work Outcomes: A Meta-Analysis," *Journal of Organizational Behavior* (March 2003), pp. 89–106.

13. C. M. Falbe and G. Yukl, "Consequences for Managers of Using Single Influence Tactics and Combinations of Tactics," *Academy of Management Journal* (July 1992), pp. 638–653.

14. R. E. Petty and P. Briñol, "Persuasion: From Single to Multiple to Metacognitive Processes," *Perspectives on Psychological Science* 3, no. 2 (2008), pp. 137–147.

15. J. Badal, "Getting a Raise from the Boss," *Wall Street Journal* (July 8, 2006), pp. B1, B5.

16. Yukl, *Leadership in Organizations.*

17. Ibid.

18. Falbe and Yukl, "Consequences for Managers of Using Single Influence Tactics and Combinations of Tactics."

19. A. W. Kruglanski, A. Pierro, and E. T. Higgins, "Regulatory Mode and Preferred Leadership Styles: How Fit Increases Job Satisfaction," *Basic and Applied Social Psychology* 29, no. 2 (2007), pp. 137–149; and A. Pierro, L. Cicero, and B. H. Raven, "Motivated Compliance with Bases of Social Power," *Journal of Applied Social Psychology* 38, no. 7 (2008), pp. 1921–1944.

20. P. P. Fu and G. Yukl, "Perceived Effectiveness of Influence Tactics in the United States and China," *Leadership Quarterly* (Summer 2000), pp. 251–266; O. Branzei, "Cultural Explanations of Individual Preferences for Influence Tactics in Cross-Cultural Encounters," *International Journal of Cross Cultural Management* (August 2002), pp. 203–218; G. Yukl, P. P. Fu, and R. McDonald, "Cross-Cultural Differences in Perceived Effectiveness of Influence Tactics for Initiating or Resisting Change," *Applied Psychology: An International Review* (January 2003), pp. 66–82; and P. P. Fu, T. K. Peng, J. C. Kennedy, and G. Yukl, "Examining the Preferences of Influence Tactics in Chinese Societies: A Comparison of Chinese Managers in Hong Kong, Taiwan, and Mainland China," *Organizational Dynamics* 33, no. 1 (2004), pp. 32–46.

21. C. J. Torelli and S. Shavitt, "Culture and Concepts of Power," *Journal of Personality and Social Psychology* 99, no. 4 (2010), pp. 703–723.

22. Fu and Yukl, "Perceived Effectiveness of Influence Tactics in the United States and China."

23. S. J. Heine, "Making Sense of East Asian Self-Enhancement," *Journal of Cross-Cultural Psychology* (September 2003), pp. 596–602.

24. G. R. Ferris, D. C. Treadway, P. L. Perrewé, R. L. Brouer, C. Douglas, and S. Lux, "Political Skill in Organizations," *Journal of Management* (June 2007), pp. 290–320; K. J. Harris, K. M. Kacmar, S. Zivnuska, and J. D. Shaw, "The Impact of Political Skill on Impression Management Effectiveness," *Journal of Applied Psychology* 92, no. 1 (2007), pp. 278–285; W. A. Hochwarter, G. R. Ferris, M. B. Gavin, P. L. Perrewé, A. T. Hall, and D. D. Frink," Political Skill as Neutralizer of Felt Accountability–Job Tension Effects on Job Performance Ratings: A Longitudinal Investigation," *Organizational Behavior and Human Decision Processes* 102 (2007), pp. 226–239; and D. C. Treadway, G. R. Ferris, A. B. Duke, G. L. Adams, and J. B. Tatcher, "The Moderating Role of Subordinate Political Skill on Supervisors' Impressions of Subordinate Ingratiation and Ratings of Subordinate Interpersonal Facilitation," *Journal of Applied Psychology* 92, no. 3 (2007), pp. 848–855.

25. M. C. Andrews, K. M. Kacmar, and K. J. Harris, "Got Political Skill? The Impact of Justice on the Importance of Political Skills for Job Performance." *Journal of Applied Psychology* 94, no. 6 (2009), pp. 1427–1437.

26. C. Anderson, S. E. Spataro, and F. J. Flynn, "Personality and Organizational Culture as Determinants of Influence," *Journal of Applied Psychology* 93, no. 3 (2008), pp. 702–710.

27. Mintzberg, *Power In and Around Organizations*, p. 26. See also K. M. Kacmar and R. A. Baron, "Organizational Politics: The State of the Field, Links to Related Processes, and an Agenda for Future Research," in G. R. Ferris (ed.), *Research in Personnel and Human Resources Management,* vol. 17 (Greenwich, CT: JAI Press, 1999), pp. 1–39; and G. R. Ferris, D. C. Treadway, R. W. Kolokinsky, W. A. Hochwarter, C. J. Kacmar, and D. D. Frink, "Development and Validation of the Political Skill Inventory," *Journal of Management* (February 2005), pp. 126–152.

28. S. B. Bacharach and E. J. Lawler, "Political Alignments in Organizations," in R. M. Kramer and M. A. Neale (eds.), *Power and Influence in Organizations* (Thousand Oaks, CA: Sage, 1998), pp. 68–69.

29. A. Drory and T. Romm, "The Definition of Organizational Politics: A Review," *Human Relations* (November 1990), pp. 1133–1154; and R. S. Cropanzano, K. M. Kacmar, and D. P. Bozeman, "Organizational Politics, Justice, and Support: Their Differences and Similarities," in R. S. Cropanzano and K. M. Kacmar (eds.), *Organizational Politics, Justice and Support: Managing Social Climate at Work* (Westport, CT: Quorum Books, 1995), pp. 1–18; and G. R. Ferris and W. A. Hochwarter, "Organizational Politics," in S. Zedeck (ed.), *APA Handbook of Industrial and Organizational Psychology,* vol. 3 (Washington, DC: American Psychological Association, 2011), pp. 435–459.

30. D. A. Buchanan, "You Stab My Back, I'll Stab Yours: Management Experience and Perceptions of Organization Political Behavior," *British Journal of Management* 19, no. 1 (2008), pp. 49–64.

31. J. Pfeffer, *Power: Why Some People Have It—And Others Don't* (New York: HarperCollins, 2010).

32. Drory and Romm, "The Definition of Organizational Politics."

33. S. M. Rioux and L. A. Penner, "The Causes of Organizational Citizenship Behavior: A Motivational Analysis," *Journal of Applied Psychology* (December 2001), pp. 1306–1314; M. A. Finkelstein and L. A. Penner, "Predicting Organizational Citizenship Behavior: Integrating the Functional and Role Identity Approaches," *Social Behavior and Personality* 32, no. 4 (2004), pp. 383–398; and J. Schwarzwald, M. Koslowsky, and M. Allouf, "Group Membership, Status, and Social Power Preference," *Journal of Applied Social Psychology* 35, no. 3 (2005), pp. 644–665.

34. See, for example, G. R. Ferris, G. S. Russ, and P. M. Fandt, "Politics in Organizations," in R. A. Giacalone and P. Rosenfeld (eds.), *Impression Management in the Organization* (Hillsdale, NJ: Lawrence Erlbaum, 1989), pp. 155–156; and W. E. O'Connor and T. G. Morrison, "A Comparison of Situational and Dispositional Predictors of Perceptions of Organizational Politics," *Journal of Psychology* (May 2001), pp. 301–312.

35. Farrell and Petersen, "Patterns of Political Behavior in Organizations," *Academy of Management Review* 7, no. 3 (1982), pp. 403–412.

36. G. R. Ferris and K. M. Kacmar, "Perceptions of Organizational Politics," *Journal of Management* (March 1992), pp. 93–116.

37. See, for example, P. M. Fandt and G. R. Ferris, "The Management of Information and Impressions: When Employees Behave Opportunistically," *Organizational Behavior and Human Decision Processes* (February 1990), pp. 140–158; Ferris, Russ, and Fandt, "Politics in Organizations," p. 147; and J. M. L. Poon, "Situational Antecedents and Outcomes of Organizational Politics Perceptions," *Journal of Managerial Psychology* 18, no. 2 (2003), pp. 138–155.

38. Ferris and Hochwarter, "Organizational Politics."

39. W. A. Hochwarter, C. Kiewitz, S. L. Castro, P. L. Perrewe, and G. R. Ferris, "Positive Affectivity and Collective Efficacy as Moderators of the Relationship Between Perceived Politics and Job Satisfaction," *Journal of Applied Social Psychology* (May 2003), pp. 1009–1035; and C. C. Rosen, P. E. Levy, and R. J. Hall, "Placing Perceptions of Politics in the Context of Feedback Environment, Employee Attitudes, and Job Performance," *Journal of Applied Psychology* 91, no. 1 (2006), pp. 211–230.

40. G. R. Ferris, D. D. Frink, M. C. Galang, J. Zhou, K. M. Kacmar, and J. L. Howard, "Perceptions of Organizational Politics: Prediction, Stress-Related Implications, and Outcomes," *Human Relations* (February 1996), pp. 233–266; and E. Vigoda, "Stress-Related Aftermaths to Workplace Politics: The Relationships Among Politics, Job Distress, and Aggressive Behavior in Organizations," *Journal of Organizational Behavior* (August 2002), pp. 571–591.

41. S. Aryee, Z. Chen, and P. S. Budhwar, "Exchange Fairness and Employee Performance: An Examination of the Relationship Between Organizational Politics and Procedural Justice," *Organizational Behavior and Human Decision Processes* (May 2004), pp. 1–14; and K. M. Kacmar, D. P. Bozeman, D. S. Carlson, and W. P. Anthony, "An Examination of the Perceptions of Organizational Politics Model." *Human Relations* 52, no. 3 (1999), pp. 383–416.

42. C. Kiewitz, W. A. Hochwarter, G. R. Ferris, and S. L. Castro, "The Role of Psychological Climate in Neutralizing the Effects of Organizational Politics on Work Outcomes," *Journal of Applied Social Psychology* (June 2002), pp. 1189–1207; and M. C. Andrews, L. A. Witt, and K. M. Kacmar,

"The Interactive Effects of Organizational Politics and Exchange Ideology on Manager Ratings of Retention," *Journal of Vocational Behavior* (April 2003), pp. 357–369.

43. O. J. Labedo, "Perceptions of Organisational Politics: Examination of the Situational Antecedent and Consequences Among Nigeria's Extension Personnel," *Applied Psychology: An International Review* 55, no. 2 (2006), pp. 255–281.

44. Kacmar, Bozeman, Carlson, and Anthony, "An Examination of the Perceptions of Organizational Politics Model," p. 389.

45. Ibid., p. 409.

46. K. M. Kacmar, D. G. Bachrach, K. J. Harris, and S. Zivnuska, "Fostering Good Citizenship Through Ethical Leadership: Exploring the Moderating Role of Gender and Organizational Politics," *Journal of Applied Psychology* 96 (2011), pp. 633–642.

47. B. E. Ashforth and R. T. Lee, "Defensive Behavior in Organizations: A Preliminary Model," *Human Relations* (July 1990), pp. 621–648.

48. M. Valle and P. L. Perrewe, "Do Politics Perceptions Relate to Political Behaviors? Tests of an Implicit Assumption and Expanded Model," *Human Relations* (March 2000), pp. 359–386.

49. M. R. Leary and R. M. Kowalski, "Impression Management: A Literature Review and Two-Component Model," *Psychological Bulletin* (January 1990), pp. 34–47.

50. See, for instance, W. L. Gardner and M. J. Martinko, "Impression Management in Organizations," *Journal of Management* (June 1988), pp. 321–338; M. C. Bolino and W. H. Turnley, "More Than One Way to Make an Impression: Exploring Profiles of Impression Management," *Journal of Management* 29, no. 2 (2003), pp. 141–160; S. Zivnuska, K. M. Kacmar, L. A. Witt, D. S. Carlson, and V. K. Bratton, "Interactive Effects of Impression Management and Organizational Politics on Job Performance," *Journal of Organizational Behavior* (August 2004), pp. 627–640; and M. C. Bolino, K. M. Kacmar, W. H. Turnley, and J. B. Gilstrap, "A Multi-Level Review of Impression Management Motives and Behaviors," *Journal of Management* 34, no. 6 (2008), pp. 1080–1109.

51. M. Snyder and J. Copeland, "Self-monitoring Processes in Organizational Settings," in R. A. Giacalone and P. Rosenfeld (eds.), *Impression Management in the Organization* (Hillsdale, NJ: Lawrence Erlbaum, 1989), p. 11; Bolino and Turnley, "More Than One Way to Make an Impression"; and W. H. Turnley and M. C. Bolino, "Achieved Desired Images While Avoiding Undesired Images: Exploring the Role of Self-Monitoring in Impression Management," *Journal of Applied Psychology* (April 2001), pp. 351–360.

52. Leary and Kowalski, "Impression Management," p. 40.

53. J. Ham and R. Vonk, "Impressions of Impression Management: Evidence of Spontaneous Suspicion of Ulterior Motivation." *Journal of Experimental Social Psychology* 47, no. 2 (2011), pp. 466–471; and W. M. Bowler, J. R. B. Halbesleben, and J. R. B. Paul, "If You're Close with the Leader, You Must Be a Brownnose: The Role of Leader–Member Relationships in Follower, Leader, and Coworker Attributions of Organizational Citizenship Behavior Motives." *Human Resource Management Review* 20, no. 4 (2010), pp. 309–316.

54. C. Lebherz, K. Jonas, and B. Tomljenovic, "Are We Known by the Company We Keep? Effects of Name Dropping on First Impressions," *Social Influence* 4, no. 1 (2009), pp. 62–79.

55. J. R. B. Halbesleben, W. M. Bowler, M. C. Bolino, and W. H Turnley, "Organizational Concern, Prosocial Values, or Impression Management? How Supervisors Attribute Motives to Organizational Citizenship Behavior," *Journal of Applied Social Psychology* 40, no. 6 (2010), pp. 1450–1489.

56. Ferris, Russ, and Fandt, "Politics in Organizations."

57. Z. I. Barsness, K. A. Diekmann, and M. L. Seidel, "Motivation and Opportunity: The Role of Remote Work, Demographic Dissimilarity, and Social Network Centrality in Impression Management," *Academy of Management Journal* 48, no. 3 (2005), pp. 401–419.

58. A. P. J. Ellis, B. J. West, A. M. Ryan, and R. P. DeShon, "The Use of Impression Management Tactics in Structural Interviews: A Function of Question Type?" *Journal of Applied Psychology* (December 2002), pp. 1200–1208.

59. C. K. Stevens and A. L. Kristof, "Making the Right Impression: A Field Study of Applicant Impression Management During Job Interviews," *Journal of Applied Psychology* 80 (1995), pp. 587–606; L. A. McFarland, A. M. Ryan, and S. D. Kriska, "Impression Management Use and Effectiveness Across Assessment Methods," *Journal of Management* 29, no. 5 (2003), pp. 641–661; C. A. Higgins and T. A. Judge, "The Effect of Applicant Influence Tactics on Recruiter Perceptions of Fit and Hiring Recommendations: A Field Study," *Journal of Applied Psychology* 89, no. 4 (2004), pp. 622–632; and W. C. Tsai, C. C. Chen, and S. F. Chiu, "Exploring Boundaries of the Effects of Applicant Impression Management Tactics in Job Interviews," *Journal of Management* (February 2005), pp. 108–125.

60. D. C. Gilmore and G. R. Ferris, "The Effects of Applicant Impression Management Tactics on Interviewer Judgments," *Journal of Management* 15, no. 4 (1989), pp. 557–564.

61. Stevens and Kristof, "Making the Right Impression."

62. C. A. Higgins, T. A. Judge, and G. R. Ferris, "Influence Tactics and Work Outcomes: A Meta-Analysis," *Journal of Organizational Behavior* (March 2003), pp. 89–106.

63. Ibid.

64. K. J. Harris, K. M. Kacmar, S. Zivnuska, and J. D. Shaw, "The Impact of Political Skill on Impression Management Effectiveness," *Journal of Applied Psychology* 92, no. 1 (2007), pp. 278–285; and D. C. Treadway, G. R. Ferris, A. B. Duke, G. L. Adams, and J. B. Thatcher, "The Moderating Role of Subordinate Political Skill on Supervisors' Impressions of Subordinate Ingratiation and Ratings of Subordinate Interpersonal Facilitation," *Journal of Applied Psychology* 92, no. 3 (2007), pp. 848–855.

65. J. D. Westphal and I. Stern, "Flattery Will Get You Everywhere (Especially if You Are a Male Caucasian): How Ingratiation, Boardroom Behavior, and Demographic Minority Status Affect Additional Board Appointments of U.S. Companies," *Academy of Management Journal* 50, no. 2 (2007), pp. 267–288.

66. See T. Romm and A. Drory, "Political Behavior in Organizations: A Cross-Cultural Comparison," *International Journal of Value Based Management* 1 (1988), pp. 97–113; and E. Vigoda, "Reactions to Organizational Politics: A Cross-Cultural Examination in Israel and Britain," *Human Relations* (November 2001), pp. 1483–1518.

67. J. L. T. Leong, M. H. Bond, and P. P. Fu, "Perceived Effectiveness of Influence Strategies in the United States and Three Chinese Societies," *International Journal of Cross Cultural Management* (May 2006), pp. 101–120.

68. Y. Miyamoto and B. Wilken, "Culturally Contingent Situated Cognition: Influencing Other People Fosters Analytic Perception in the United States but Not in Japan," *Psychological Science* 21, no. 11 (2010), pp. 1616–1622.

69. E. Vigoda, "Reactions to Organizational Politics," p. 1512.

70. Ibid., p. 1510.

CHAPTER 14

1. See, for instance, D. Tjosvold, "Defining Conflict and Making Choices About Its Management: Lighting the Dark Side of Organizational Life," *International Journal of Conflict Management* 17, no. 2 (2006), pp. 87–95; and M. A. Korsgaard, S. S. Jeong, D. M. Mahony, and A. H. Pitariu, "A Multilevel View of Intragroup Conflict," *Journal of Management* 34, no. 6 (2008), pp. 1222–1252.

2. K. W. Thomas, "Conflict and Negotiation Processes in Organizations," in M. D. Dunnette and L. M. Hough (eds.), *Handbook of Industrial and Organizational Psychology*, 2nd ed., vol. 3 (Palo Alto, CA: Consulting Psychologists Press, 1992), pp. 651–717.

3. For a comprehensive review of the interactionist approach, see C. De Dreu and E. Van de Vliert (eds.), *Using Conflict in Organizations* (London: Sage, 1997).

4. See K. A. Jehn, "A Multimethod Examination of the Benefits and Detriments of Intragroup Conflict," *Administrative Science Quarterly* (June 1995), pp. 256–282; K. A. Jehn, "A Qualitative Analysis of Conflict Types and Dimensions in Organizational Groups," *Administrative Science Quarterly* (September 1997), pp. 530–557; K. A. Jehn and E. A. Mannix, "The Dynamic Nature of Conflict: A Longitudinal Study of Intragroup Conflict and Group Performance," *Academy of Management Journal* (April 2001), pp. 238–251; and C. K. W. De Dreu and L. R. Weingart, "Task Versus Relationship Conflict, Team Performance, and Team Member Satisfaction: A Meta-Analysis," *Journal of Applied Psychology* (August 2003), pp. 741–749.

5. J. Yang and K. W. Mossholder, "Decoupling Task and Relationship Conflict: The Role of Intragroup Emotional Processing," *Journal of Organizational Behavior* 25, no. 5 (August 2004), pp. 589–605; and N. Gamero, V. González-Romá, and J. M. Peiró, "The Influence of Intra-Team Conflict on Work Teams' Affective Climate: A Longitudinal Study," *Journal of Occupational and Organizational Psychology* 81, no. 1 (2008), pp. 47–69.

6. "Survey Shows Managers Have Their Hands Full Resolving Staff Personality Conflicts," *IPMA-HR Bulletin* (November 3, 2006).

7. De Dreu and Weingart, "Task Versus Relationship Conflict, Team Performance, and Team Member Satisfaction."

8. J. Farh, C. Lee, and C. I. C. Farh, "Task Conflict and Team Creativity: A Question of How Much and When," *Journal of Applied Psychology* 95, no. 6 (2010), pp. 1173–1180.

9. C. K.W. De Dreu and M. A. West, "Minority Dissent and Team Innovation: The Importance of Participation in Decision Making," *Journal of Applied Psychology* 86, no. 6 (2001), pp. 1191–1201.

10. B. H. Bradley, B. E. Postlewaite, A. C. Klotz, M. R. Hamdani, and K. G. Brown, "Reaping the Benefits of Task Conflict in Teams: The Critical Role of Team Psychological Safety Climate," *Journal of Applied Psychology*, Advance publication, (July 4, 2011), doi: 10.1037/a0024200.

11. C. K. W. De Dreu, "The Virtue and Vice of Workplace Conflict: Food for (Pessimistic) Thought," *Journal of Organizational Behavior* 29, no. 1 (2008), pp. 5–18.

12. R. S. Peterson and K. J. Behfar, "The Dynamic Relationship Between Performance Feedback, Trust, and Conflict in Groups: A Longitudinal Study," *Organizational Behavior and Human Decision Process* 92, no. 1–2 (2003), pp. 102–112.

13. J. D. Shaw, J. Zhu, M. K. Duffy, K. L. Scott, H. Shih, and E. Susanto, "A Contingency Model of Conflict and Team Effectiveness," *Journal of Applied Psychology* 96, no. 2 (2011), pp. 391–400.

14. L. M. Penny and P. E. Spector, "Job Stress, Incivility, and Counterproductive Work Behavior: The Moderating Role of Negative Affectivity," *Journal of Organizational Behavior* 26, no. 7 (2005), pp. 777–796.

15. K. A. Jehn, L. Greer, S. Levine, and G. Szulanski, "The Effects of Conflict Types, Dimensions, and Emergent States on Group Outcomes," *Group Decision and Negotiation* 17, no. 6 (2008), pp. 465–495.

16. T. M. Glomb and H. Liao, "Interpersonal Aggression in Work Groups: Social Influence, Reciprocal, and Individual Effects," *Academy of Management Journal* 46, no. 4 (2003), pp. 486–496; and V. Venkataramani and R. S. Dalal, "Who Helps and Harms Whom? Relational Aspects of Interpersonal Helping and Harming in Organizations," *Journal of Applied Psychology* 92, no. 4 (2007), pp. 952–966.

17. R. Friedman, C. Anderson, J. Brett, M. Olekalns, N. Goates, and C. C. Lisco, "The Positive and Negative Effects of Anger on Dispute Resolution: Evidence from Electronically Mediated Disputes," *Journal of Applied Psychology* (April 2004), pp. 369–376.

18. L. R. Pondy, "Organizational Conflict: Concepts and Models," *Administrative Science Quarterly* (September 1967), p. 302.

19. See, for instance, R. L. Pinkley, "Dimensions of Conflict Frame: Disputant Interpretations of Conflict," *Journal of Applied Psychology* (April 1990), pp. 117–126; and R. L. Pinkley and G. B. Northcraft, "Conflict Frames of Reference: Implications for Dispute Processes and Outcomes," *Academy of Management Journal* (February 1994), pp. 193–205.

20. A. M. Isen, A. A. Labroo, and P. Durlach, "An Influence of Product and Brand Name on Positive Affect: Implicit and Explicit Measures," *Motivation and Emotion* (March 2004), pp. 43–63.

21. Ibid.

22. P. J. D. Carnevale and A. M. Isen, "The Influence of Positive Affect and Visual Access on the Discovery of Integrative Solutions in Bilateral Negotiations," *Organizational Behavior and Human Decision Processes* (February 1986), pp. 1–13.

23. Thomas, "Conflict and Negotiation Processes in Organizations."

24. Ibid.

25. See R. A. Baron, "Personality and Organizational Conflict: Effects of the Type A Behavior Pattern and Self-monitoring," *Organizational Behavior and Human Decision Processes* (October 1989), pp. 281–296; R. J. Volkema and T. J. Bergmann, "Conflict Styles as Indicators of Behavioral Patterns in Interpersonal Conflicts," *Journal of Social Psychology* (February 1995), pp. 5–15; and J. A. Rhoades, J. Arnold, and C. Jay, "The Role of Affective Traits and Affective States in Disputants' Motivation and Behavior During Episodes of Organizational Conflict," *Journal of Organizational Behavior* (May 2001), pp. 329–345.

26. Thomas, "Conflict and Negotiation Processes in Organizations."

27. See, for instance, K. A. Jehn, "Enhancing Effectiveness: An Investigation of Advantages and Disadvantages of Value-Based Intragroup Conflict," *International Journal of Conflict Management* (July 1994), pp. 223–238; R. L. Priem, D. A. Harrison, and N. K. Muir, "Structured Conflict and Consensus Outcomes in Group Decision Making," *Journal of Management* 21, no. 4 (1995), pp. 691–710; and K. A. Jehn and E. A. Mannix, "The Dynamic Nature of Conflict: A Longitudinal Study of Intragroup Conflict and Group Performance," *Academy of Management Journal* (April 2001), pp. 238–251.

28. B. A. Nijstad and S. C. Kaps, "Taking the Easy Way Out: Preference Diversity, Decision Strategies, and Decision Refusal in Groups," *Journal of Personality and Social Psychology* 94, no. 5 (2008), pp. 860–870.

29. R. L. Hoffman, "Homogeneity of Member Personality and Its Effect on Group Problem-Solving," *Journal of Abnormal and Social Psychology* (January 1959), pp. 27–32; R. L. Hoffman and N. R. F. Maier, "Quality and Acceptance of Problem Solutions by Members of Homogeneous and Heterogeneous Groups," *Journal of Abnormal and Social Psychology* (March 1961), pp. 401–407; and P. Pitcher and A. D. Smith, "Top Management Team Heterogeneity: Personality, Power, and Proxies," *Organization Science* (January–February 2001), pp. 1–18.

30. M. E. Zellmer-Bruhn, M. M. Maloney, A. D. Bhappu, and R. Salvador, "When and How Do Differences Matter? An Exploration of Perceived Similarity in Teams," *Organizational Behavior and Human Decision Processes* 107, no. 1 (2008), pp. 41–59.

31. For example, see J. A. Wall Jr. and R. R. Callister, "Conflict and Its Management," *Journal of Management* 21, no. 3 (1995) pp. 523–526, for evidence supporting the argument that conflict is almost uniformly dysfunctional. See also P. J. Hinds and D. E. Bailey, "Out of Sight, Out of Sync: Understanding Conflict in Distributed Teams," *Organization Science* (November–December 2003), pp. 615–632.

32. Jehn, Greer, Levine, and Szulanski, "The Effects of Conflict Types, Dimensions, and Emergent States on Group Outcomes."

33. Zellmer-Bruhn, Maloney, Bhappu, and Salvador, "When and How Do Differences Matter?"

34. J. Fried, "I Know You Are, But What Am I?" *Inc.* (July–August 2010), pp. 39–40.

35. K. J. Behfar, R. S. Peterson, E. A. Mannix, and W. M. K. Trochim, "The Critical Role of Conflict Resolution in Teams: A Close Look at the Links Between Conflict Type, Conflict Management Strategies, and Team Outcomes," *Journal of Applied Psychology* 93, no. 1 (2008), pp. 170–188; A. G. Tekleab, N. R. Quigley, and P. E. Tesluk, "A Longitudinal Study of Team Conflict, Conflict Management, Cohesion, and Team Effectiveness," *Group and Organization Management* 34, no. 2 (2009), pp. 170–205; and E. Van de Vliert, M. C. Euwema, and S. E. Huismans, "Managing Conflict with a Subordinate or a Superior: Effectiveness of Conglomerated Behavior," *Journal of Applied Psychology* 80 (1995), pp. 271–281.

36. A. Somech, H. S. Desivilya, and H. Lidogoster, "Team Conflict Management and Team Effectiveness: The Effects of Task Interdependence and Team Identification," *Journal of Organizational Behavior* 30, no. 3 (2009), pp. 359–378.

37. H. R. Markus and S. Kitayama, "Culture and the Self: Implications for Cognition, Emotion, and Motivation," *Psychological Review* 98, no. 2 (1991), pp. 224–253; and H. Ren and B. Gray, "Repairing Relationship Conflict: How Violation Types and Culture Influence the Effectiveness of Restoration Rituals," *Academy of Management Review* 34, no. 1 (2009), pp. 105–126.

38. M. J. Gelfand, M. Higgins, L. H. Nishii, J. L. Raver, A. Dominguez, F. Murakami, S. Yamaguchi, and M. Toyama, "Culture and Egocentric Perceptions of Fairness in Conflict and Negotiation," *Journal of Applied Psychology* (October 2002), pp. 833–845; and Z. Ma, "Chinese Conflict Management Styles and Negotiation Behaviours: An Empirical Test," *International Journal of Cross Cultural Management* (April 2007), pp. 101–119.

39. P. P. Fu, X. H. Yan, Y. Li, E. Wang, and S. Peng, "Examining Conflict-Handling Approaches by Chinese Top Management Teams in IT Firms," *International Journal of Conflict Management* 19, no. 3 (2008), pp. 188–209.

40. M. H. Bazerman, J. R. Curhan, D. A. Moore, and K. L. Valley, "Negotiation," *Annual Review of Psychology* 51 (2000), pp. 279–314.

41. See, for example, D. R. Ames, "Assertiveness Expectancies: How Hard People Push Depends on the Consequences They Predict," *Journal of Personality and Social Psychology* 95, no. 6 (2008), pp. 1541–1557; and J. R. Curhan, H. A. Elfenbein, and H. Xu, "What Do People Value When They Negotiate? Mapping the Domain of Subjective Value in Negotiation," *Journal of Personality and Social Psychology* 91, no. 3 (2006), pp. 493–512.

42. R. Lewicki, D. Saunders, and B. Barry, *Negotiation,* 6th ed. (New York: McGraw-Hill/Irwin, 2009).

43. J. C. Magee, A. D. Galinsky, and D. H. Gruenfeld, "Power, Propensity to Negotiate, and Moving First in Competitive Interactions," *Personality and Social Psychology Bulletin* (February 2007), pp. 200–212.

44. E. Wilson, "The Trouble with Jake," *New York Times* (July 15, 2009), www.nytimes.com.

45. J. R. Curhan, H. A. Elfenbein, and H. Xu, "What Do People Value When They Negotiate? Mapping the Domain of Subjective Value in Negotiation," *Journal of Personality and Social Psychology* 91, no. 3 (2006), pp. 493–512.

46. Thomas, "Conflict and Negotiation Processes in Organizations."

47. P. M. Morgan and R. S. Tindale, "Group vs. Individual Performance in Mixed-Motive Situations: Exploring an Inconsistency," *Organizational Behavior and Human Decision Processes* (January 2002), pp. 44–65.

48. C. E. Naquin, "The Agony of Opportunity in Negotiation: Number of Negotiable Issues, Counterfactual Thinking, and Feelings of Satisfaction," *Organizational Behavior and Human Decision Processes* (May 2003), pp. 97–107.

49. M. Giacomantonio, C. K. W. De Dreu, and L. Mannetti, "Now You See It, Now You Don't: Interests, Issues, and Psychological Distance in Integrative Negotiation," *Journal of Personality and Social Psychology* 98, no. 5 (2010), pp. 761–774.

50. F. S. Ten Velden, B. Beersma, and C. K. W. De Dreu, "It Takes One to Tango: The Effect of Dyads' Epistemic Motivation Composition in Negotiation," *Personality and Social Psychology Bulletin* 36, no. 11 (2010), pp. 1454–1466.

51. C. K. W. De Dreu, L. R. Weingart, and S. Kwon, "Influence of Social Motives on Integrative Negotiation: A Meta-Analytic

Review and Test of Two Theories," *Journal of Personality and Social Psychology* (May 2000), pp. 889–905.

52. This model is based on R. J. Lewicki, "Bargaining and Negotiation," *Exchange: The Organizational Behavior Teaching Journal* 6, no. 2 (1981), pp. 39–40.

53. J. R. Curhan, H. A. Elfenbein, and G. J. Kilduff, "Getting Off on the Right Foot: Subjective Value Versus Economic Value in Predicting Longitudinal Job Outcomes from Job Offer Negotiations," *Journal of Applied Psychology* 94, no. 2 (2009), pp. 524–534.

54. M. H. Bazerman and M. A. Neale, *Negotiating Rationally* (New York: The Free Press, 1992), pp. 67–68.

55. R. P. Larrick and G. Wu, "Claiming a Large Slice of a Small Pie: Asymmetric Disconfirmation in Negotiation," *Journal of Personality and Social Psychology* 93, no. 2 (2007), pp. 212–233.

56. E. T. Amanatullah, M. W. Morris, and J. R. Curhan, "Negotiators Who Give Too Much: Unmitigated Communion, Relational Anxieties, and Economic Costs in Distributive and Integrative Bargaining," *Journal of Personality and Social Psychology* 95, no. 3 (2008), pp. 723–738; and D. S. DeRue, D. E. Conlon, H. Moon, and H. W. Willaby, "When Is Straightforwardness a Liability in Negotiations? The Role of Integrative Potential and Structural Power," *Journal of Applied Psychology* 94, no. 4 (2009), pp. 1032–1047.

57. G. A. Gan Kleef and S. Côté, "Expressing Anger in Conflict: When It Helps and When It Hurts," *Journal of Applied Psychology* 92, no. 6 (2007), pp. 1157–1569; J. M. Brett, M. Olekalns, R. Friedman, N. Goates, C. Anderson, C. C. Lisco, "Sticks and Stones: Language, Face, and Online Dispute Resolution," *Academy of Management Journal* 50, no. 1 (2007), pp. 85–99; and J. R. Overbeck, M. A. Neale, and C. L. Govan, "I Feel, Therefore You Act: Intrapersonal and Interpersonal Effects of Emotion on Negotiations as a Function of Social Power," *Organizational Behavior and Human Decision Processes* 112, no. 2 (2010), pp. 126–139.

58. G. A. Van Kleef and C. K. W. De Dreu, "Longer-Term Consequences of Anger Expression in Negotiation: Retaliation or Spillover?" *Journal of Experimental Social Psychology* 46, no. 5 (2010), pp. 753–760.

59. M. Olekalns and P. L Smith, "Mutually Dependent: Power, Trust, Affect, and the Use of Deception in Negotiation," *Journal of Business Ethics* 85, no. 3 (2009), pp. 347–365.

60. A. W. Brooks and M. E. Schweitzer, "Can Nervous Nellie Negotiate? How Anxiety Causes Negotiators to Make Low First Offers, Exit Early, and Earn Less Profit," *Organizational Behavior and Human Decision Processes* 115, no. 1 (2011), pp. 43–54.

61. S. Kopelman, A. S. Rosette, and L. Thompson, "The Three Faces of Eve: Strategic Displays of Positive, Negative, and Neutral Emotions in Negotiations," *Organizational Behavior and Human Decision Processes* 99 (2006), pp. 81–101.

62. W. L. Adair, T. Okumura, and J. M. Brett, "Negotiation Behavior When Cultures Collide: The United States and Japan," *Journal of Applied Psychology* (June 2001), pp. 371–385; and W. L. Adair, L. Weingart, and J. Brett, "The Timing and Function of Offers in U.S. and Japanese Negotiations," *Journal of Applied Psychology* 92, no. 4 (2007), pp. 1056–1068.

63. S. Kopelman, "The Effect of Culture and Power on Cooperation in Commons Dilemmas: Implications for Global Resource Management," *Organizational Behavior and Human Decision Processes* 108, no. 1 (2009), pp. 153–163.

64. B. C. Gunia, J. M. Brett, A. K. Nandkeolyar, and D. Kamdar, "Paying a Price: Culture, Trust, and Negotiation Consequences," *Journal of Applied Psychology* 96, no. 4 (2010), pp. 774–789.

65. C. Watson and L. R. Hoffman, "Managers as Negotiators: A Test of Power Versus Gender as Predictors of Feelings, Behavior, and Outcomes," *Leadership Quarterly* (Spring 1996), pp. 63–85.

66. A. E. Walters, A. F. Stuhlmacher, and L. L. Meyer, "Gender and Negotiator Competitiveness: A Meta-Analysis," *Organizational Behavior and Human Decision Processes* (October 1998), pp. 1–29; and A. F. Stuhlmacher and A. E. Walters, "Gender Differences in Negotiation Outcome: A Meta-Analysis," *Personnel Psychology* (Autumn 1999), pp. 653–677.

67. Stuhlmacher and Walters, "Gender Differences in Negotiation Outcome," p. 655.

68. H. R. Bowles, L. Babcock, and L. Lei, "Social Incentives for Gender Differences in the Propensity to Initiate Negotiations," *Faculty Research Working Papers Series* (Cambridge, MA: Harvard University—John F. Kennedy School of Government, 2005).

69. L. J. Kray, A. D. Galinsky, and L. Thompson, "Reversing the Gender Gap in Negotiations: An Exploration of Stereotype Regeneration," *Organizational Behavior and Human Decision Processes* (March 2002), pp. 386–409.

70. D. A. Small, M. Gelfand, L. Babcock, and H. Gettman, "Who Goes to the Bargaining Table? The Influence of Gender and Framing on the Initiation of Negotiation," *Journal of Personality and Social Psychology* 93, no. 4 (2007), pp. 600–613.

71. E. T. Amanatullah and M. W. Morris, "Negotiating Gender Roles: Gender Differences in Assertive Negotiating Are Mediated by Women's Fear of Backlash and Attenuated When Negotiating on Behalf of Others," *Journal of Personality and Social Psychology* 98, no. 2 (2010), pp. 256–267.

72. K. W. Thomas, "Toward Multidimensional Values in Teaching: The Example of Conflict Behaviors," *Academy of Management Review* (July 1977), p. 487.

CHAPTER 15

1. See, for instance, R. L. Daft, *Organization Theory and Design,* 10th ed. (Cincinnati, OH: South-Western Publishing, 2010).

2. T. W. Malone, R. J. Laubacher, and T. Johns, "The Age of Hyperspecialization," *Harvard Business Review* (July–August 2011), pp. 56–65.

3. C. Hymowitz, "Managers Suddenly Have to Answer to a Crowd of Bosses," *Wall Street Journal* (August 12, 2003), p. B1.

4. See, for instance, "How Hierarchy Can Hurt Strategy Execution," *Harvard Business Review* (July–August 2010), pp. 74–75.

5. See, for instance, J. H. Gittell, "Supervisory Span, Relational Coordination, and Flight Departure Performance: A Reassessment of Postbureaucracy Theory," *Organization Science* (July–August 2001), pp. 468–483.

6. J. Child and R. G. McGrath, "Organizations Unfettered: Organizational Form in an Information-Intensive Economy," *Academy of Management Journal* (December 2001), pp. 1135–1148.

7. B. Brown and S. D. Anthony, "How P&G Tripled Its Innovation Success Rate," *Harvard Business Review* (June 2011), pp. 64–72.

8. A. Leiponen and C. E. Helfat, "Location, Decentralization, and Knowledge Sources for Innovation," *Organization Science* 22, no. 3 (2011), pp. 641–658.

9. H. Mintzberg, *Structure in Fives: Designing Effective Organizations* (Upper Saddle River, NJ: Prentice Hall, 1983), p. 157.

10. L. R. Burns and D. R. Wholey, "Adoption and Abandonment of Matrix Management Programs: Effects of Organizational Characteristics and Interorganizational Networks," *Academy of Management Journal* (February 1993), pp. 106–138; J. R. Galbraith, *Designing Matrix Organizations that Actually Work: How IBM, Procter & Gamble, and Others Design for Success* (San Francisco: Jossey Bass, 2009); and E. Krell, "Managing the Matrix," *HR Magazine* (April 2011), pp. 69–71.

11. See, for instance, T. Sy and L. S. D'Annunzio, "Challenges and Strategies of Matrix Organizations: Top-Level and Mid-Level Managers' Perspectives," *Human Resource Planning* 28, no. 1 (2005), pp. 39–48; and T. Sy and S. Cote, "Emotional Intelligence: A Key Ability to Succeed in the Matrix Organization," *Journal of Management Development* 23, no. 5 (2004), pp. 437–455.

12. N. Anand and R. L. Daft, "What Is the Right Organization Design?" *Organizational Dynamics* 36, no. 4 (2007), pp. 329–344.

13. See, for instance, R. E. Miles and C. C. Snow, "The New Network Firm: A Spherical Structure Built on Human Investment Philosophy," *Organizational Dynamics* (Spring 1995), pp. 5–18; D. Pescovitz, "The Company Where Everybody's a Temp," *New York Times Magazine* (June 11, 2000), pp. 94–96; B. Hedberg, G. Dahlgren, J. Hansson, and N. Love, *Virtual Organizations and Beyond* (New York: Wiley, 2001); N. S. Contractor, S. Wasserman, and K. Faust, "Testing Multitheoretical, Multilevel Hypotheses About Organizational Networks: An Analytic Framework and Empirical Example," *Academy of Management Review* 31, no. 3 (2006) pp. 681–703; and Y. Shin, "A Person-Environment Fit Model for Virtual Organizations," *Journal of Management* (October 2004), pp. 725–743.

14. J. Bates, "Making Movies and Moving On," *Los Angeles Times* (January 19, 1998), p. A1.

15. D. Dahl, "Want a Job? Let the Bidding Begin," *Inc.* (March 2011), pp. 94–96.

16. J. Schramm, "At Work in a Virtual World," *HR Magazine* (June 2010), p. 152.

17. C. B. Gibson and J. L. Gibbs, "Unpacking the Concept of Virtuality: The Effects of Geographic Dispersion, Electronic Dependence, Dynamic Structure, and National Diversity on Team Innovation," *Administrative Science Quarterly* 51, no. 3 (2006), pp. 451–495; H. M. Latapie and V. N. Tran, "Subculture Formation, Evolution, and Conflict Between Regional Teams in Virtual Organizations," *The Business Review* (Summer 2007), pp. 189–193; and S. Davenport and U. Daellenbach, "'Belonging' to a Virtual Research Center: Exploring the Influence of Social Capital Formation Processes on Member Identification in a Virtual Organization" *British Journal of Management* 22, no. 1 (2011), pp. 54–76.

18. "GE: Just Your Average Everyday $60 Billion Family Grocery Store," *IndustryWeek* (May 2, 1994), pp. 13–18.

19. The following is based on D. D. Davis, "Form, Function and Strategy in Boundaryless Organizations," in A. Howard (ed.), *The Changing Nature of Work* (San Francisco: Jossey-Bass, 1995), pp. 112–138; R. L. Cross, A. Yan, and M. R. Louis, "Boundary Activities in 'Boundaryless' Organizations: A Case Study of a Transformation to a Team-Based Structure," *Human Relations* (June 2000), pp. 841–868; and R. Ashkenas, D. Ulrich, T. Jick, and S. Kerr, *The Boundaryless Organization: Breaking the Chains of Organizational Structure*, revised and updated (San Francisco: Jossey-Bass, 2002).

20. See, for example, U. Wassmer, "Alliance Portfolios: A Review and Research Agenda," *Journal of Management* 36, no. 1 (2010), pp 141–171; A. M. Hess and F. T. Rothaemel, "When Are Assets Complementary? Star Scientists, Strategic Alliances, and Innovation in the Pharmaceutical Industry," *Strategic Management Journal* 32, no. 8 (2011), pp. 895–909; and J. A. Adegbesan and M. J. Higgins, "The Intra-Alliance Division of Value Created through Collaboration," *Strategic Management Journal* 32, no. 2 (2011), pp. 187–211.

21. See J. P. Guthrie and D. K. Datta, "Dumb and Dumber: The Impact of Downsizing on Firm Performance as Moderated by Industry Conditions," *Organization Science* 19, no. 1 (2008), pp. 108–123; and K. P. De Meuse, T. J. Bergmann, P. A. Vanderheiden, and C. E. Roraff, "New Evidence Regarding Organizational Downsizing and a Firm's Financial Performance: A Long-Term Analysis," *Journal of Managerial Issues* 16, no. 2 (2004), pp. 155–177.

22. See, for example, C. O. Trevor and A. J. Nyberg, "Keeping Your Headcount When All About You Are Losing Theirs: Downsizing, Voluntary Turnover Rates, and the Moderating Role of HR Practices," *Academy of Management Journal* 51, no. 2 (2008), pp. 259–276; T. M. Probst, S. M. Stewart, M. L. Gruys, and B. W. Tierney, "Productivity, Counterproductivity and Creativity: The Ups and Downs of Job Insecurity," *Journal of Occupational and Organizational Psychology* 80, no. 3 (2007), pp. 479–497; and C. P. Maertz, J. W. Wiley, C. LeRouge, and M. A. Campion, "Downsizing Effects on Survivors: Layoffs, Offshoring, and Outsourcing," *Industrial Relations* 49, no. 2 (2010), pp. 275–285.

23. C. D. Zatzick, and R. D. Iverson, "High-Involvement Management and Workforce Reduction: Competitive Advantage or Disadvantage?" *Academy of Management Journal* 49, no. 5 (2006), pp. 999–1015; A. Travaglione, and B. Cross, "Diminishing the Social Network in Organizations: Does There Need to Be Such a Phenomenon as 'Survivor Syndrome' After Downsizing?" *Strategic Change* 15, no. 1 (2006), pp. 1–13; and J. D. Kammeyer-Mueller, H. Liao, and R. D. Arvey, "Downsizing and Organizational Performance: A Review of the Literature from a Stakeholder Perspective," *Research in Personnel and Human Resources Management* 20 (2001), pp. 269–329.

24. T. Burns and G. M. Stalker, *The Management of Innovation* (London: Tavistock, 1961); and J. A. Courtright, G. T. Fairhurst, and L. E. Rogers, "Interaction Patterns in Organic and Mechanistic Systems," *Academy of Management Journal* (December 1989), pp. 773–802.

25. This analysis is referred to as a contingency approach to organization design. See, for instance, J. M. Pennings, "Structural Contingency Theory: A Reappraisal," in B. M. Staw and L. L. Cummings (eds.), *Research in Organizational Behavior,* vol. 14 (Greenwich, CT: JAI Press, 1992), pp. 267–309; J. R. Hollenbeck, H. Moon, A. P. J. Ellis, B. J. West, D. R. Ilgen, L. Sheppard, C. O. L. H. Porter, and J. A. Wagner III,

"Structural Contingency Theory and Individual Differences: Examination of External and Internal Person-Team Fit," *Journal of Applied Psychology* (June 2002), pp. 599–606; and A. Drach-Zahavy and A. Freund, "Team Effectiveness Under Stress: A Structural Contingency Approach," *Journal of Organizational Behavior* 28, no. 4 (2007), pp. 423–450.

26. The strategy–structure thesis was originally proposed in A. D. Chandler Jr., *Strategy and Structure: Chapters in the History of the Industrial Enterprise* (Cambridge, MA: MIT Press, 1962). For an updated analysis, see T. L. Amburgey and T. Dacin, "As the Left Foot Follows the Right? The Dynamics of Strategic and Structural Change," *Academy of Management Journal* (December 1994), pp. 1427–1452.

27. See R. E. Miles and C. C. Snow, *Organizational Strategy, Structure, and Process* (New York: McGraw-Hill, 1978); D. C. Galunic and K. M. Eisenhardt, "Renewing the Strategy–Structure–Performance Paradigm," in B. M. Staw and L. L. Cummings (eds.), *Research in Organizational Behavior*, vol. 16 (Greenwich, CT: JAI Press, 1994), pp. 215–255; and S. M. Toh, F. P. Morgeson, and M. A. Campion, "Human Resource Configurations: Investigating Fit with the Organizational Context," *Journal of Applied Psychology* 93, no. 4 (2008), pp. 864–882.

28. See, for instance, P. M. Blau and R. A. Schoenherr, *The Structure of Organizations* (New York: Basic Books, 1971); D. S. Pugh, "The Aston Program of Research: Retrospect and Prospect," in A. H. Van de Ven and W. F. Joyce (eds.), *Perspectives on Organization Design and Behavior* (New York: Wiley, 1981), pp. 135–166; R. Z. Gooding and J. A. Wagner III, "A Meta-Analytic Review of the Relationship Between Size and Performance: The Productivity and Efficiency of Organizations and Their Subunits," *Administrative Science Quarterly* (December 1985), pp. 462–481; and A. C. Bluedorn, "Pilgrim's Progress: Trends and Convergence in Research on Organizational Size and Environments," *Journal of Management* (Summer 1993), pp. 163–192.

29. See C. Perrow, "A Framework for the Comparative Analysis of Organizations," *American Sociological Review* (April 1967), pp. 194–208; J. Hage and M. Aiken, "Routine Technology, Social Structure, and Organizational Goals," *Administrative Science Quarterly* (September 1969), pp. 366–377; C. C. Miller, W. H. Glick, Y. Wang, and G. P. Huber, "Understanding Technology-Structure Relationships: Theory Development and Meta-Analytic Theory Testing," *Academy of Management Journal* (June 1991), pp. 370–399; and W. D. Sine, H. Mitsuhashi, and D. A. Kirsch, "Revisiting Burns and Stalker: Formal Structure and New Venture Performance in Emerging Economic Sectors," *Academy of Management Journal* 49, no. 1 (2006), pp. 121–132.

30. G. G. Dess and D. W. Beard, "Dimensions of Organizational Task Environments," *Administrative Science Quarterly* (March 1984), pp. 52–73; E. A. Gerloff, N. K. Muir, and W. D. Bodensteiner, "Three Components of Perceived Environmental Uncertainty: An Exploratory Analysis of the Effects of Aggregation," *Journal of Management* (December 1991), pp. 749–768; and O. Shenkar, N. Aranya, and T. Almor, "Construct Dimensions in the Contingency Model: An Analysis Comparing Metric and Non-metric Multivariate Instruments," *Human Relations* (May 1995), pp. 559–580.

31. C. S. Spell and T. J. Arnold, "A Multi-Level Analysis of Organizational Justice and Climate, Structure, and Employee Mental Health," *Journal of Management* 33, no. 5 (2007),

pp. 724–751; and M. L. Ambrose and M. Schminke, "Organization Structure as a Moderator of the Relationship Between Procedural Justice, Interactional Justice, Perceived Organizational Support, and Supervisory Trust," *Journal of Applied Psychology* 88, no. 2 (2003), pp. 295–305.

32. See, for instance, Spell and Arnold, "A Multi-Level Analysis of Organizational Justice Climate, Structure, and Employee Mental Health"; J. D. Shaw and N. Gupta, "Job Complexity, Performance, and Well-Being: When Does Supplies-Values Fit Matter? *Personnel Psychology* 57, no. 4 (2004), 847–879; and C. Anderson and C. E. Brown, "The Functions and Dysfunctions of Hierarchy," *Research in Organizational Behavior* 30 (2010), pp. 55–89.

33. See, for instance, R. E. Ployhart, J. A. Weekley, and K. Baughman, "The Structure and Function of Human Capital Emergence: A Multilevel Examination of the Attraction-Selection-Attrition Model," *Academy of Management Journal* 49, no. 4 (2006), pp. 661–677.

34. See, for example, P. R. Harris and R. T. Moran, *Managing Cultural Differences,* 5th ed. (Houston, TX: Gulf Publishing, 1999).

CHAPTER 16

1. See, for example, E. H. Schein, "Culture: The Missing Concept in Organization Studies," *Administrative Science Quarterly* 41, no. 2 (1996), pp. 229–240.

2. This seven-item description is based on C. A. O'Reilly III, J. Chatman, and D. F. Caldwell, "People and Organizational Culture: A Profile Comparison Approach to Assessing Person-Organization Fit," *Academy of Management Journal* (September 1991), pp. 487–516; and J. A. Chatman and K. A. Jehn, "Assessing the Relationship Between Industry Characteristics and Organizational Culture: How Different Can You Be?" *Academy of Management Journal* (June 1994), pp. 522–553.

3. The view that there will be consistency among perceptions of organizational culture has been called the "integration" perspective. For a review of this perspective and conflicting approaches, see D. Meyerson and J. Martin, "Cultural Change: An Integration of Three Different Views," *Journal of Management Studies* (November 1987), pp. 623–647; and P. J. Frost, L. F. Moore, M. R. Louis, C. C. Lundberg, and J. Martin (eds.), *Reframing Organizational Culture* (Newbury Park, CA: Sage, 1991).

4. See J. M. Jermier, J. W. Slocum Jr., L. W. Fry, and J. Gaines, "Organizational Subcultures in a Soft Bureaucracy: Resistance Behind the Myth and Facade of an Official Culture," *Organization Science* (May 1991), pp. 170–194; and P. Lok, R. Westwood, and J. Crawford, "Perceptions of Organisational Subculture and their Significance for Organisational Commitment," *Applied Psychology: An International Review* 54, no. 4 (2005), pp. 490–514.

5. D. A. Hoffman and L. M. Jones, "Leadership, Collective Personality, and Performance," *Journal of Applied Psychology* 90, no. 3 (2005), pp. 509–522.

6. T. Hsieh, "Zappos's CEO on Going to Extremes for Customers," *Harvard Business Review* (July–August 2010), pp. 41–45.

7. See, for example, G. G. Gordon and N. DiTomaso, "Predicting Corporate Performance from Organizational Culture," *Journal of Management Studies* (November 1992), pp. 793–798;

J. B. Sorensen, "The Strength of Corporate Culture and the Reliability of Firm Performance," *Administrative Science Quarterly* (March 2002), pp. 70–91; and J. Rosenthal and M. A. Masarech, "High-Performance Cultures: How Values Can Drive Business Results," *Journal of Organizational Excellence* (Spring 2003), pp. 3–18.

8. Y. Wiener, "Forms of Value Systems: A Focus on Organizational Effectiveness and Cultural Change and Maintenance," *Academy of Management Review* (October 1988), p. 536; and B. Schneider, A. N. Salvaggio, and M. Subirats, "Climate Strength: A New Direction for Climate Research," *Journal of Applied Psychology* 87 (2002), pp. 220–229.

9. R. T. Mowday, L. W. Porter, and R. M. Steers, *Employee Linkages: The Psychology of Commitment, Absenteeism, and Turnover* (New York: Academic Press, 1982); C. Vandenberghe, "Organizational Culture, Person-Culture Fit, and Turnover: A Replication in the Health Care Industry," *Journal of Organizational Behavior* (March 1999), pp. 175–184; and M. Schulte, C. Ostroff, S. Shmulyian, and A. Kinicki, "Organizational Climate Configurations: Relationships to Collective Attitudes, Customer Satisfaction, and Financial Performance," *Journal of Applied Psychology* 94, no. 3 (2009), pp. 618–634.

10. J. W. Grizzle, A. R. Zablah, T. J. Brown, J. C. Mowen, and J. M. Lee, "Employee Customer Orientation in Context: How the Environment Moderates the Influence of Customer Orientation on Performance Outcomes," *Journal of Applied Psychology* 94, no. 5 (2009), pp. 1227–1242.

11. M. R. Bashshur, A. Hernández, and V. González-Romá, "When Managers and Their Teams Disagree: A Longitudinal Look at the Consequences of Differences in Perceptions of Organizational Support," *Journal of Applied Psychology* 96, no. 3 (2011), pp. 558–573.

12. S. L. Dolan and S. Garcia, "Managing by Values: Cultural Redesign for Strategic Organizational Change at the Dawn of the Twenty-First Century," *Journal of Management Development* 21, no. 2 (2002), pp. 101–117.

13. See C. A. O'Reilly and J. A. Chatman, "Culture as Social Control: Corporations, Cults, and Commitment," in B. M. Staw and L. L. Cummings (eds.), *Research in Organizational Behavior*, vol. 18 (Greenwich, CT: JAI Press, 1996), pp. 157–200. See also M. Pinae Cunha, "The 'Best Place to Be': Managing Control and Employee Loyalty in a Knowledge-Intensive Company," *Journal of Applied Behavioral Science* (December 2002), pp. 481–495.

14. Y. Ling, Z. Simsek, M. H. Lubatkin, and J. F. Veiga, "Transformational Leadership's Role in Promoting Corporate Entrepreneurship: Examining the CEO-TMT Interface," *Academy of Management Journal* 51, no. 3 (2008), pp. 557–576; and A. Malhotra, A. Majchrzak, and B. Rosen, Benson, "Leading Virtual Teams," *Academy of Management Perspectives* 21, no. 1 (2007), pp. 60–70.

15. D. Denison, "What Is the Difference Between Organizational Culture and Organizational Climate? A Native's Point of View on a Decade of Paradigm Wars," *Academy of Management Review* 21 (1996) pp. 519–654; and L. R. James, C. C. Choi, C. E. Ko, P. K. McNeil, M. K. Minton, M. A. Wright, and K. Kim, "Organizational and Psychological Climate: A Review of Theory and Research," *European Journal of Work and Organizational Psychology* 17, no. 1 (2008), pp. 5–32.

16. J. Z. Carr, A. M. Schmidt, J. K. Ford, and R. P. DeShon, "Climate Perceptions Matter: A Meta-Analytic Path Analysis Relating Molar Climate, Cognitive and Affective States, and Individual Level Work Outcomes," *Journal of Applied Psychology* 88, no. (2003), pp. 605–619.

17. Schulte, Ostroff, Shmulyian, and Kinicki, "Organizational Climate Configurations: Relationships to Collective Attitudes, Customer Satisfaction, and Financial Performance."

18. See, for example, Z. S. Byrne, J. Stoner, K. R. Thompson, and W. Hochwarter, "The Interactive Effects of Conscientiousness, Work Effort, and Psychological Climate on Job Performance," *Journal of Vocational Behavior* 66, no. 2 (2005), pp. 326–338; D. S. Pugh, J. Dietz, A. P. Brief, and J. W. Wiley, "Looking Inside and Out: The Impact of Employee and Community Demographic Composition on Organizational Diversity Climate," *Journal of Applied Psychology* 93, no. 6 (2008), pp. 1422–1428; J. C. Wallace, E. Popp, and S. Mondore, "Safety Climate as a Mediator Between Foundation Climates and Occupational Accidents: A Group-Level Investigation," *Journal of Applied Psychology* 91, no. 3 (2006), pp. 681–688; and K. H. Ehrhart, L. A. Witt, B. Schneider, and S. J. Perry, "Service Employees Give as They Get: Internal Service as a Moderator of the Service Climate-Service Outcomes Link," *Journal of Applied Psychology* 96, no. 2 (2011), pp. 423–431.

19. J C. Wallace, P. D. Johnson, K. Mathe, and J. Paul, "Structural and Psychological Empowerment Climates, Performance, and the Moderating Role of Shared Felt Accountability: A Managerial Perspective," *Journal of Applied Psychology* 96, no. 3 (2011), pp. 840–850.

20. J. M. Beus, S. C. Payne, M. E. Bergman, and W. Arthur, "Safety Climate and Injuries: An Examination of Theoretical and Empirical Relationships," *Journal of Applied Psychology* 95, no. 4 (2010), pp. 713–727.

21. R. L. Jepperson, "Institutions, Institutional Effects, and Institutionalism," in W. W. Powell and P. J. DiMaggio (eds.), *The New Institutionalism in Organizational Analysis* (Chicago: University of Chicago Press, 1991), pp. 143–163; G. F. Lanzara and G. Patriotta, "The Institutionalization of Knowledge in an Automotive Factory: Templates, Inscriptions, and the Problems of Durability," *Organization Studies* 28, no. 5 (2007), pp. 635–660; and T. B. Lawrence, M. K. Mauws, B. Dyck, and R. F. Kleysen, "The Politics of Organizational Learning: Integrating Power into the 4I Framework," *Academy of Management Review* (January 2005), pp. 180–191.

22. Sorensen, "The Strength of Corporate Culture and the Reliability of Firm Performance."

23. See T. Cox Jr., *Cultural Diversity in Organizations: Theory, Research & Practice* (San Francisco: Berrett-Koehler, 1993), pp. 162–170; L. Grensing-Pophal, "Hiring to Fit Your Corporate Culture," *HR Magazine* (August 1999), pp. 50–54; and D. L. Stone, E. F. Stone-Romero, and K. M. Lukaszewski, "The Impact of Cultural Values on the Acceptance and Effectiveness of Human Resource Management Policies and Practices," *Human Resource Management Review* 17, no. 2 (2007), pp. 152–165.

24. S. Cartwright and C. L. Cooper, "The Role of Culture Compatibility in Successful Organizational Marriages," *Academy of Management Executive* (May 1993), pp. 57–70; R. A. Weber and C. F. Camerer, "Cultural Conflict and Merger Failure: An Experimental Approach," *Management Science* (April 2003), pp. 400–412; and I. H. Gleibs, A. Mummendey, and P. Noack, "Predictors of Change in Postmerger Identification During a Merger Process: A Longitudinal Study," *Journal of Personality and Social Psychology* 95, no. 5 (2008), pp. 1095–1112.

25. P. Gumbel, "Return of the Urge to Merge," *Time Europe Magazine* (July 13, 2003), www.time.com/time/europe/magazine/article/0,13005,901030721-464418,00.html.

26. S. F. Gale, "Memo to AOL Time Warner: Why Mergers Fail—Case Studies," *Workforce Management* (February 2003), www.workforce.com; and W. Bock, "Mergers, Bubbles, and Steve Case," *Wally Bock's Monday Memo* (January 20, 2003), www.mondaymemo.net/030120feature.htm.

27. E. H. Schein, "The Role of the Founder in Creating Organizational Culture," *Organizational Dynamics* (Summer 1983), pp. 13–28.

28. E. H. Schein, "Leadership and Organizational Culture," in F. Hesselbein, M. Goldsmith, and R. Beckhard (eds.), *The Leader of the Future* (San Francisco: Jossey-Bass, 1996), pp. 61–62.

29. See, for example, J. R. Harrison and G. R. Carroll, "Keeping the Faith: A Model of Cultural Transmission in Formal Organizations," *Administrative Science Quarterly* (December 1991), pp. 552–582; and D. E. Bowen and C. Ostroff, "The 'Strength' of the HRM System, Organizational Climate Formation, and Firm Performance," *Academy of Management Review* 29 (2004), pp. 203–221.

30. B. Schneider, H. W. Goldstein, and D. B. Smith, "The ASA Framework: An Update," *Personnel Psychology* (Winter 1995), pp. 747–773; D. M. Cable and T. A. Judge, "Interviewers' Perceptions of Person-Organization Fit and Organizational Selection Decisions," *Journal of Applied Psychology* (August 1997), pp. 546–561; M. L. Verquer, T. A. Beehr, and S. H. Wagner, "A Meta-Analysis of Relations Between Person-Organization Fit and Work Attitudes," *Journal of Vocational Behavior* (December 2003), pp. 473–489; and W. Li, Y. Wang, P. Taylor, K. Shi, and D. He, "The Influence of Organizational Culture on Work-Related Personality Requirement Ratings: A Multilevel Analysis," *International Journal of Selection and Assessment* 16, no. 4 (2008), pp. 366–384.

31. R. Levering and M. Moskowitz, "And the Winners Are . . .," *Fortune* (January 20, 2011), http://money.cnn.com/magazines/fortune/bestcompanies/2011/full_list/.

32. D. C. Hambrick and P. A. Mason, "Upper Echelons: The Organization as a Reflection of Its Top Managers," *Academy of Management Review* (April 1984), pp. 193–206; M. A. Carpenter, M. A. Geletkanycz, and W. G. Sanders, "Upper Echelons Research Revisited: Antecedents, Elements, and Consequences of Top Management Team Composition," *Journal of Management* 30, no. 6 (2004), pp. 749–778, and H. Wang, A. S. Tsui, and K. R. Xin, "CEO Leadership Behaviors, Organizational Performance, and Employees' Attitudes," *The Leadership Quarterly* 22, no. 1 (2011), pp. 92–105.

33. See, for instance, J. P. Wanous, *Organizational Entry*, 2nd ed. (New York: Addison-Wesley, 1992); D. M. Cable and C. K. Parsons, "Socialization Tactics and Person-Organization Fit," *Personnel Psychology* (Spring 2001), pp. 1–23; and T. N. Bauer, T. Bodner, B. Erdogan, D. M. Truxillo, and J. S. Tucker, "Newcomer Adjustment During Organizational Socialization: A Meta-Analytic Review of Antecedents, Outcomes, and Methods," *Journal of Applied Psychology* 92, no. 3 (2007), pp. 707–721.

34. G. Kranz, "Training That Starts Before the Job Begins," *Workforce Management Online* (July 2009), www.workforce.com.

35. D. C. Feldman, "The Multiple Socialization of Organization Members," *Academy of Management Review* (April 1981), p. 310.

36. C. J. Collins, "The Interactive Effects of Recruitment Practices and Product Awareness on Job Seekers' Employer Knowledge and Application Behaviors," *Journal of Applied Psychology* 92, no. 1 (2007), pp. 180–190.

37. J. D. Kammeyer-Mueller and C. R. Wanberg, "Unwrapping the Organizational Entry Process: Disentangling Multiple Antecedents and Their Pathways to Adjustment," *Journal of Applied Psychology* 88 (2003), pp. 779–794; E. W. Morrison, "Longitudinal Study of the Effects of Information Seeking on Newcomer Socialization," *Journal of Applied Psychology* 78 (2003), pp. 173–183; and M. Wangm Y. Zhan, E. McCune, and D. Truxillo, "Understanding Newcomers' Adaptability and Work-Related Outcomes: Testing the Mediating Roles of Perceived P-E Fit Variables," *Personnel Psychology* 64, no. 1 (2011), pp. 163–189.

38. Van Maanen and Schein, "Career Development," p. 59. J. Van Maanen and E. H. Schein, "Career Development," in J. R. Hackman and J. L. Suttle (eds.), *Improving Life at Work* (Santa Monica, CA: Goodyear Publishing, 1977), pp. 30–95.

39. E. W. Morrison, "Newcomers' Relationships: The Role of Social Network Ties During Socialization," *Academy of Management Journal* 45 (2002), pp. 1149–1160.

40. T. N. Bauer, T. Bodner, B. Erdogan, D. M. Truxillo, and J. S. Tucker, "Newcomer Adjustment During Organizational Socialization: A Meta-Analytic Review of Antecedents, Outcomes, and Methods," *Journal of Applied Psychology* 92, no. 3 (2007), pp. 707–721.

41. W. R. Boswell, A. J. Shipp, S. C., Payne, and S. S. Culbertson, "Changes in Newcomer Job Satisfaction Over Time: Examining the Pattern of Honeymoons and Hangovers," *Journal of Applied Psychology* 94, no. 4 (2009), pp. 844–858.

42. C. Vandenberghe, A. Panaccio, K. Bentein, K. Mignonac, and P. Roussel, "Assessing Longitudinal Change of and Dynamic Relationships Among Role Stressors, Job Attitudes, Turnover Intention, and Well-Being in Neophyte Newcomers," *Journal of Organizational Behavior* 32, no. 4 (2011), pp. 652–671.

43. E. Ransdell, "The Nike Story? Just Tell It!" *Fast Company* (January–February 2000), pp. 44–46; and A. Muccino, "Exclusive Interview with Chuck Eichten," *Liquid Brand Summit Blog* (February 4, 2011), http://blog.liquidbrandsummit.com/.

44. D. M. Boje, "The Storytelling Organization: A Study of Story Performance in an Office-Supply Firm," *Administrative Science Quarterly* (March 1991), pp. 106–126; and M. Ricketts and J. G. Seiling, "Language, Metaphors, and Stories: Catalysts for Meaning Making in Organizations," *Organization Development Journal* (Winter 2003), pp. 33–431.

45. A. J. Shipp and K. J. Jansen, "Reinterpreting Time in Fit Theory: Crafting and Recrafting Narratives of Fit in Medias Res," *Academy of Management Review* 36, no. 1 (2011), pp. 76–101.

46. See G. Islam and M. J. Zyphur, "Rituals in Organizations: A Review and Expansion of Current Theory," *Group and Organization Management* 34, no. 1 (2009), pp. 114–139.

47. V. Matthews, "Starting Every Day with a Shout and a Song," *Financial Times* (May 2, 2001), p. 11; and M. Gimein, "Sam Walton Made Us a Promise," *Fortune* (March 18, 2002), pp. 121–130.

48. M. G. Pratt and A. Rafaeli, "Artifacts and Organizations: Understanding Our Objective Reality," in A. Rafaeli and M. G. Pratt, *Artifacts and Organizations: Beyond Mere Symbolism* (Mahwah, NJ: Lawrence Erlbaum, 2006), pp. 279–288.

49. See B. Victor and J. B. Cullen, "The Organizational Bases of Ethical Work Climates," *Administrative Science Quarterly* (March 1988), pp. 101–125; R. L. Dufresne, "An Action Learning Perspective on Effective Implementation of Academic Honor Codes," *Group & Organization Management* (April 2004), pp. 201–218; and A. Ardichvilli, J. A. Mitchell, and D. Jondle, "Characteristics of Ethical Business Cultures," *Journal of Business Ethics* 85, no. 4 (2009), pp. 445–451.

50. J. P. Mulki, J. F. Jaramillo, and W. B. Locander, "Critical Role of Leadership on Ethical Climate and Salesperson Behaviors," *Journal of Business Ethics* 86, no. 2 (2009), pp. 125–141; M. Schminke, M. L. Ambrose, and D. O. Neubaum, "The Effect of Leader Moral Development on Ethical Climate and Employee Attitudes," *Organizational Behavior and Human Decision Processes* 97, no. 2 (2005), pp. 135–151; and M. E. Brown, L. K. Treviño, and D. A. Harrison, "Ethical Leadership: A Social Learning Perspective for Construct Development and Testing," *Organizational Behavior and Human Decision Processes* 97, no. 2 (2005), pp. 117–134.

51. D. M. Mayer, M. Kuenzi, R. Greenbaum, M. Bardes, and S. Salvador, "How Low Does Ethical Leadership Flow? Test of a Trickle-Down Model," *Organizational Behavior and Human Decision Processes* 108, no. 1 (2009), pp. 1–13.

52. B. Sweeney, D. Arnold, and B. Pierce, "The Impact of Perceived Ethical Culture of the Firm and Demographic Variables on Auditors' Ethical Evaluation and Intention to Act Decisions," *Journal of Business Ethics* 93, no. 4 (2010), pp. 531–551.

53. M. L. Gruys, S. M. Stewart, J. Goodstein, M. N. Bing, and A. C. Wicks, "Values Enactment in Organizations: A Multi-Level Examination," *Journal of Management* 34, no. 4 (2008), pp. 806–843.

54. D. L. Nelson and C. L. Cooper (eds.), *Positive Organizational Behavior* (London: Sage, 2007); K. S. Cameron, J. E. Dutton, and R. E. Quinn (eds.), *Positive Organizational Scholarship: Foundations of a New Discipline* (San Francisco: Berrett-Koehler, 2003); and F. Luthans and C. M. Youssef, "Emerging Positive Organizational Behavior," *Journal of Management* (June 2007), pp. 321–349.

55. J. Robison, "Great Leadership Under Fire," *Gallup Leadership Journal* (March 8, 2007), pp. 1–3.

56. R. Wagner and J. K. Harter, *12: The Elements of Great Managing* (New York: Gallup Press, 2006).

57. R. Wagner and J. K. Harter, "Performance Reviews Without the Anxiety," *Gallup Leadership Journal* (July 12, 2007), pp. 1–4; and Wagner and Harter, *12: The Elements of Great Managing*.

58. S. Fineman, "On Being Positive: Concerns and Counterpoints," *Academy of Management Review* 31, no. 2 (2006), pp. 270–291.

59. D. J. McCarthy and S. M. Puffer, "Interpreting the Ethicality of Corporate Governance Decision in Russia: Utilizing Integrative Social Contracts Theory to Evaluate the Relevance of Agency Theory Norms," *Academy of Management Review* 33, no. 1 (2008), pp. 11–31.

60. P. Dvorak, "A Firm's Culture Can Get Lost in Translation," *Wall Street Journal* (April 3, 2006), pp. B1, B3; K. Kranhold, "The Immelt Era, Five Years Old, Transforms GE," *Wall Street Journal* (September 11, 2006), pp. B1, B3; and S. McCartney, "Teaching Americans How to Behave Abroad," *Wall Street Journal* (April 11, 2006), pp. D1, D4.

61. J. A. Chatman, "Matching People and Organizations: Selection and Socialization in Public Accounting Firms," *Administrative Science Quarterly* (September 1991), pp. 459–484;

and A. E. M. Van Vianen, "Person-Organization Fit: The Match Between Newcomers' and Recruiters' Preferences for Organizational Cultures," *Personnel Psychology* (Spring 2000), pp. 113–149.

CHAPTER 17

1. P. G. Audia and S. Brion, "Reluctant to Change: Self-Enhancing Responses to Diverging Performance Measures," *Organizational Behavior and Human Decision Processes* 102 (2007), pp. 255–269.

2. M. Fugate, A. J. Kinicki, and G. E. Prussia, "Employee Coping with Organizational Change: An Examination of Alternative Theoretical Perspectives and Models," *Personnel Psychology* 61, no. 1 (2008), pp. 1–36.

3. J. D. Ford, L. W. Ford, and A. D'Amelio, "Resistance to Change: The Rest of the Story," *Academy of Management Review* 33, no. 2 (2008), pp. 362–377.

4. M. T. Hannan, L. Pólos, and G. R. Carroll, "The Fog of Change: Opacity and Asperity in Organizations," *Administrative Science Quarterly* (September 2003), pp. 399–432.

5. J. P. Kotter and L. A. Schlesinger, "Choosing Strategies for Change," *Harvard Business Review* (March–April 1979), pp. 106–114.

6. J. E. Dutton, S. J. Ashford, R. M. O'Neill, and K. A. Lawrence, "Moves That Matter: Issue Selling and Organizational Change," *Academy of Management Journal* (August 2001), pp. 716–736.

7. P. C. Fiss and E. J. Zajac, "The Symbolic Management of Strategic Change: Sensegiving via Framing and Decoupling," *Academy of Management Journal* 49, no. 6 (2006), pp. 1173–1193.

8. A. E. Rafferty and S. L. D. Restubog, "The Impact of Change Process and Context on Change Reactions and Turnover During a Merger," *Journal of Management* 36, no. 5 (2010), pp. 1309–1338.

9. Q. N. Huy, "Emotional Balancing of Organizational Continuity and Radical Change: The Contribution of Middle Managers," *Administrative Science Quarterly* (March 2002), pp. 31–69; D. M. Herold, D. B. Fedor, and S. D. Caldwell, "Beyond Change Management: A Multilevel Investigation of Contextual and Personal Influences on Employees' Commitment to Change," *Journal of Applied Psychology* 92, no. 4 (2007), pp. 942–951; and G. B. Cunningham, "The Relationships Among Commitment to Change, Coping with Change, and Turnover Intentions," *European Journal of Work and Organizational Psychology* 15, no. 1 (2006), pp. 29–45.

10. R. Peccei, A. Giangreco, and A. Sebastiano, "The Role of Organizational Commitment in the Analysis of Resistance to Change: Co-predictor and Moderator Effects," *Personnel Review* 40, no. 2 (2011), pp. 185–204.

11. J. P. Kotter, "Leading Change: Why Transformational Efforts Fail," *Harvard Business Review* 85 (January 2007), p. 96–103.

12. K. van Dam, S. Oreg, and B. Schyns, "Daily Work Contexts and Resistance to Organisational Change: The Role of Leader-Member Exchange, Development Climate, and Change Process Characteristics," *Applied Psychology: An International Review* 57, no. 2 (2008), pp. 313–334.

13. S. Oreg and N. Sverdlik, "Ambivalence toward Imposed Change: The Conflict between Dispositional Resistance to Change and the Orientation toward the Change Agent," *Journal of Applied Psychology* 96, no. 2 (2011), pp. 337–349.

14. D. B. Fedor, S. Caldwell, and D. M. Herold, "The Effects of Organizational Changes on Employee Commitment: A Multilevel Investigation," *Personnel Psychology* 59 (2006), pp. 1–29; and R. D. Foster, "Resistance, Justice, and Commitment to Change," *Human Resource Development Quarterly* 21, no. 1 (2010), pp. 3–39.

15. S. Oreg, "Personality, Context, and Resistance to Organizational Change," *European Journal of Work and Organizational Psychology* 15, no. 1 (2006), pp. 73–101.

16. S. M. Elias, "Employee Commitment in Times of Change: Assessing the Importance of Attitudes Toward Organizational Change," *Journal of Management* 35, no. 1 (2009), pp. 37–55.

17. J. W. B. Lang and P. D. Bliese, "General Mental Ability and Two Types of Adaptation to Unforeseen Change: Applying Discontinuous Growth Models to the Task-Change Paradigm," *Journal of Applied Psychology* 94, no. 2 (2009), pp. 411–428.

18. C. O. L. H. Porter, J. W. Webb, and C. I. Gogus, "When Goal Orientations Collide: Effects of Learning and Performance Orientation on Team Adaptability in Response to Workload Imbalance," *Journal of Applied Psychology* 95, no. 5 (2010), pp. 935–943.

19. K. Lewin, *Field Theory in Social Science* (New York: Harper & Row, 1951).

20. P. G. Audia, E. A. Locke, and K. G. Smith, "The Paradox of Success: An Archival and a Laboratory Study of Strategic Persistence Following Radical Environmental Change," *Academy of Management Journal* (October 2000), pp. 837–853; and P. G. Audia and S. Brion, "Reluctant to Change: Self-Enhancing Responses to Diverging Performance Measures," *Organizational Behavior and Human Decision Processes* 102, no. 2 (2007), pp. 255–269.

21. J. B. Sorensen, "The Strength of Corporate Culture and the Reliability of Firm Performance," *Administrative Science Quarterly* (March 2002), pp. 70–91.

22. J. Amis, T. Slack, and C. R. Hinings, "The Pace, Sequence, and Linearity of Radical Change," *Academy of Management Journal* (February 2004), pp. 15–39; and E. Autio, H. J. Sapienza, and J. G. Almeida, "Effects of Age at Entry, Knowledge Intensity, and Imitability on International Growth," *Academy of Management Journal* (October 2000), pp. 909–924.

23. J. P. Kotter, "Leading Changes: Why Transformation Efforts Fail," *Harvard Business Review* (March–April 1995), pp. 59–67; and J. P. Kotter, *Leading Change* (Harvard Business School Press, 1996).

24. For a sampling of various OD definitions, see H. K. Sinangil and F. Avallone, "Organizational Development and Change," in N. Anderson, D. S. Ones, H. K. Sinangil, and C. Viswesvaran (eds.), *Handbook of Industrial, Work and Organizational Psychology*, vol. 2 (Thousand Oaks, CA: Sage, 2001), pp. 332–335; and R. J. Marshak and D. Grant, "Organizational Discourse and New Organization Development Practices," *British Journal of Management* 19, no. 1 (2008), pp. S7–S19.

25. See, for instance, R. Lines, "Influence of Participation in Strategic Change: Resistance, Organizational Commitment and Change Goal Achievement," *Journal of Change Management* (September 2004), pp. 193–215.

26. J. E. Edwards and M. D. Thomas, "The Organizational Survey Process: General Steps and Practical Considerations," in P. Rosenfeld, J. E. Edwards, and M. D. Thomas (eds.), *Improving Organizational Surveys: New Directions, Methods, and Applications* (Newbury Park, CA: Sage, 1993), pp. 3–28.

27. E. H. Schein, *Process Consultation: Its Role in Organizational Development*, 2nd ed. (Reading, MA: Addison-Wesley, 1988), p. 9. See also E. H. Schein, *Process Consultation Revisited: Building Helpful Relationships* (Reading, MA: Addison-Wesley, 1999).

28. Schein, *Process Consultation.*

29. W. W. G. Dyer, W. G. Dyer, and J. H. Dyer, *Team Building: Proven Strategies for Improving Team Performance* (Hoboken, NJ: Jossey-Bass, 2007).

30. U. Wagner, L. Tropp, G. Finchilescu, and C. Tredoux (eds.), *Improving Intergroup Relations* (New York: Wiley-Blackwell, 2008).

31. See, for example, R. Fry, F. Barrett, J. Seiling, and D. Whitney (eds.), *Appreciative Inquiry & Organizational Transformation: Reports from the Field* (Westport, CT: Quorum, 2002); J. K. Barge and C. Oliver, "Working with Appreciation in Managerial Practice," *Academy of Management Review* (January 2003), pp. 124–142; and D. van der Haar and D. M. Hosking, "Evaluating Appreciative Inquiry: A Relational Constructionist Perspective," *Human Relations* (August 2004), pp. 1017–1036.

32. A. Harrington, "Who's Afraid of a New Product?" *Fortune* (November 10, 2003), pp. 189–192; C. C. Manz, F. Shipper, and G. L. Stewart, "Everyone a Team Leader: Shared Influence at W. L. Gore and Associates," *Organizational Dynamics* 38, no. 3 (2009), pp. 239–244.

33. See, for instance, R. M. Kanter, "When a Thousand Flowers Bloom: Structural, Collective and Social Conditions for Innovation in Organizations," in B. M. Staw and L. L. Cummings (eds.), *Research in Organizational Behavior*, vol. 10 (Greenwich, CT: JAI Press, 1988), pp. 169–211.

34. F. Damanpour, "Organizational Innovation: A Meta-Analysis of Effects of Determinants and Moderators," *Academy of Management Journal* (September 1991), p. 557.

35. Ibid., pp. 555–590; and G. Westerman, F. W. McFarlan, and M. Iansiti, "Organization Design and Effectiveness over the Innovation Life Cycle," *Organization Science* 17, no. 2 (2006), pp. 230–238.

36. See P. R. Monge, M. D. Cozzens, and N. S. Contractor, "Communication and Motivational Predictors of the Dynamics of Organizational Innovation," *Organization Science* (May 1992), pp. 250–274; P. Schepers and P. T. van den Berg, "Social Factors of Work-Environment Creativity," *Journal of Business and Psychology* 21, no. 3 (2007), pp. 407–428.

37. D. L. Day, "Raising Radicals: Different Processes for Championing Innovative Corporate Ventures," *Organization Science* (May 1994), pp. 148–172; and M. E. Mullins, S. W. J. Kozlowski, N. Schmitt, and A. W. Howell, "The Role of the Idea Champion in Innovation: The Case of the Internet in the Mid-1990s," *Computers in Human Behavior* 24, no. 2 (2008), pp. 451–467.

38. J. M. Howell and C. A. Higgins, "Champions of Change: Identifying, Understanding, and Supporting Champions of Technological Innovations," *Organizational Dynamics* 19 (1990), pp. 40–55.

39. See S. Shane, S. Venkataraman, and I. MacMillan, "Cultural Differences in Innovation Championing Strategies," *Journal of Management* 21, no. 5 (1995), pp. 931–952.

40. A. Taylor, "Chrysler's Speed Merchant," *Fortune* (September 6, 2010), pp. 77–82.

41. See, for instance, S. Armour, "Rising Job Stress Could Affect Bottom Line," *USA Today* (July 29, 2003), p. 1B; and J. Schramm, "Work/Life on Hold," *HR Magazine* 53 (October 2008), p. 120.

42. Adapted from R. S. Schuler, "Definition and Conceptualization of Stress in Organizations," *Organizational Behavior and Human Performance* (April 1980), p. 189. For an updated review of definitions, see C. L. Cooper, P. J. Dewe, and M. P. O'Driscoll, *Organizational Stress: A Review and Critique of Theory, Research, and Applications* (Thousand Oaks, CA: Sage, 2002).

43. See, for instance, M. A. Cavanaugh, W. R. Boswell, M. V. Roehling, and J. W. Boudreau, "An Empirical Examination of Self-Reported Work Stress Among U.S. Managers," *Journal of Applied Psychology* (February 2000), pp. 65–74.

44. N. P. Podsakoff, J. A. LePine, and M. A. LePine, "Differential Challenge-Hindrance Stressor Relationships with Job Attitudes, Turnover Intentions, Turnover, and Withdrawal Behavior: A Meta-Analysis," *Journal of Applied Psychology* 92, no. 2 (2007), pp. 438–454; and J. A. LePine, M. A. LePine, and C. L. Jackson, "Challenge and Hindrance Stress: Relationships with Exhaustion, Motivation to Learn, and Learning Performance," *Journal of Applied Psychology* (October 2004), pp. 883–891.

45. L. W. Hunter and S. M. B. Thatcher, "Feeling the Heat: Effects of Stress, Commitment, and Job Experience on Job Performance," *Academy of Management Journal* 50, no. 4 (2007), pp. 953–968.

46. J. C. Wallace, B. D. Edwards, T. Arnold, M. L. Frazier, and D. M. Finch, "Work Stressors, Role-Based Performance, and the Moderating Influence of Organizational Support," *Journal of Applied Psychology* 94, no. 1 (2009), pp. 254–262.

47. N. W. Van Yperen and O. Janssen, "Fatigued and Dissatisfied or Fatigued but Satisfied? Goal Orientations and Responses to High Job Demands," *Academy of Management Journal* (December 2002), pp. 1161–1171; and N. W. Van Yperen and M. Hagedoorn, "Do High Job Demands Increase Intrinsic Motivation or Fatigue or Both? The Role of Job Control and Job Social Support," *Academy of Management Journal* (June 2003), pp. 339–348.

48. J. de Jonge and C. Dormann, "Stressors, Resources, and Strain at Work: A Longitudinal Test of the Triple-Match Principle," *Journal of Applied Psychology* 91, no. 5 (2006), pp. 1359–1374.

49. Schuler, "Definition and Conceptualization of Stress," pp. 200-205; and R. L. Kahn and M. Byosiere, "Stress in Organizations," in M. D. Dunnette and L. M. Hough (eds.), *Handbook of Industrial and Organizational Psychology,* 2nd ed., vol. 3 (Palo Alto, CA: Consulting Psychologists Press, 1992), pp. 604–610.

50. J. Schaubroeck, J. R. Jones, and J. L. Xie, "Individual Differences in Utilizing Control to Cope with Job Demands: Effects on Susceptibility to Infectious Disease," *Journal of Applied Psychology* (April 2001), pp. 265–278.

51. M. Kivimäki, J. Head, J. E. Ferrie, E. Brunner, M. G. Marmot, J. Vahtera, and M. J. Shipley, "Why Is Evidence on Job Strain and Coronary Heart Disease Mixed? An Illustration of Measurement Challenges in the Whitehall II Study," *Psychosomatic Medicine* 68, no. 3 (2006), pp. 398–401.

52. M. Borritz, K. B. Christensen, U. Bültmann, R. Rugulies, T. Lund, I Andersen, E. Villadsen, F. Didreichsen, and T. S. Krisensen, "Impact on Burnout and Psychosocial Work Characteristics on Future Long-Term Sickness Absence, Prospective Results of the Danish PUMA Study Among Human Service Workers," *Journal of Occupational and Environmental Medicine* 52, no. 10 (2010), pp. 964–970.

53. B. D. Steffy and J. W. Jones, "Workplace Stress and Indicators of Coronary-Disease Risk," *Academy of Management Journal* 31, no. 3 (1988), pp. 686–698.

54. R. Illies, N. Dimotakis, and I. E. DePater, "Psychological and Physiological Reactions to High Workloads: Implications for Well-Being," *Personnel Psychology* 63, no. 2 (2010), pp. 407–463.

55. D. Örtqvist and J. Wincent, "Prominent Consequences of Role Stress: A Meta-Analytic Review," *International Journal of Stress Management*, 13, no. 4 (2006), pp. 399–422.

56. J. R. Hackman and G. R. Oldham, "Development of the Job Diagnostic Survey," *Journal of Applied Psychology* (April 1975), pp. 159–170; J. J. Hakanen, A. B. Bakker, and M. Jokisaari, "A 35-Year Follow-Up Study on Burnout Among Finnish Employees," *Journal of Occupational Health Psychology* 16, no. 3 (2011), pp. 345–360; E. R. Crawford, J. A. Lepine, and B. L. Rich, "Linking Job Demands and Resources to Employee Engagement and Burnout," *Journal of Applied Psychology* 95, no. 5 (September 1995), pp. 834–848; and G. A. Chung-Yan, "The Nonlinear Effects of Job Complexity and Autonomy on Job Satisfaction, Turnover, and Psychological Well-Being," *Journal of Occupational Health Psychology* 15, no. 3 (2010), pp. 237–251.

57. L. L. Meier, N. K. Semmer, A. Elfering, and N. Jacobshagen, "The Double Meaning of Control: Three-Way Interactions Between Internal Resources, Job Control, and Stressors at Work," *Journal of Occupational Health Psychology* 13, no. 3 (2008), pp. 244–258.

58. E. M. de Croon, J. K. Sluiter, R. W. B. Blonk, J. P. J. Broersen, and M. H. W. Frings-Dresen, "Stressful Work, Psychological Job Strain, and Turnover: A 2-Year Prospective Cohort Study of Truck Drivers," *Journal of Applied Psychology* (June 2004), pp. 442–454; R. Cropanzano, D. E. Rupp, and Z. S. Byrne, "The Relationship of Emotional Exhaustion to Work Attitudes, Job Performance, and Organizational Citizenship Behaviors," *Journal of Applied Psychology* (February 2003), pp. 160–169; and S. Diestel and K. Schmidt, "Costs of Simultaneous Coping with Emotional Dissonance and Self-Control Demands at Work: Results from Two German Samples," *Journal of Applied Psychology* 96, no. 3 (2011), pp. 643–653.

59. The following discussion has been influenced J. M. Ivancevich, M. T. Matteson, S. M. Freedman, and J. S. Phillips, "Worksite Stress Management Interventions," *American Psychologist* (February 1990), pp. 252–261; R. Schwarzer, "Manage Stress at Work Through Preventive and Proactive Coping," in E. A. Locke (ed.), *Handbook of Principles of Organizational Behavior* (Malden, MA: Blackwell, 2004), pp. 342–355; and K. M. Richardson and H. R. Rothstein, "Effects of Occupational Stress Management Intervention Programs: A Meta-Analysis," *Journal of Occupational Health Psychology* 13, no. 1 (2008), pp. 69–93.

60. T. H. Macan, "Time Management: Test of a Process Model," *Journal of Applied Psychology* (June 1994), pp. 381–391; and B. J. C. Claessens, W. Van Eerde, C. G. Rutte, and R. A. Roe, "Planning Behavior and Perceived Control of Time at Work," *Journal of Organizational Behavior* (December 2004), pp. 937–950.

61. See, for example, G. Lawrence-Ell, *The Invisible Clock: A Practical Revolution in Finding Time for Everyone and Everything* (Seaside Park, NJ: Kingsland Hall, 2002); and B. Tracy, *Time Power* (New York: AMACOM, 2004).

62. R. W. Renn, D. G. Allen, and T. M. Huning, "Empirical Examination of Individual-Level Personality-Based Theory of Self-Management Failure," *Journal of Organizational Behavior* 32, no. 1 (2011), pp. 25–43; and P. Gröpel and P. Steel, "A Mega-Trial Investigation of Goal Setting, Interest Enhancement, and Energy on Procrastination," *Personality and Individual Differences* 45, no. 5 (2008), pp. 406–411.

63. P. Salmon, "Effects of Physical Exercise on Anxiety, Depression, and Sensitivity to Stress: A Unifying Theory," *Clinical Psychology Review* 21, no. 1 (2001), pp. 33–61.

64. K. M. Richardson and H. R. Rothstein, "Effects of Occupational Stress Management Intervention Programs: A Meta-Analysis," *Journal of Occupational Health Psychology* 13, no. 1 (2008), pp. 69–93.

65. V. C. Hahn, C. Binnewies, S. Sonnentag, and E. J. Mojza, "Learning How to Recover From Job Stress: Effects of a Recovery Training Program on Recovery, Recovery-Related Self-Efficacy, and Well-Being," *Journal of Occupational Health Psychology* 16, no. 2 (2011), pp. 202–216; and C. Binnewies, S. Sonnentag, and E. J. Mojza, "Recovery During the Weekend and Fluctuations in Weekly Job Performance: A Week-Level Study Examining Intra-Individual Relationships," *Journal of Occupational and Organizational Psychology* 83, no. 2 (2010), pp. 419–441.

66. E. R. Greenglass and L. Fiksenbaum, "Proactive Coping, Positive Affect, and Well-Being: Testing for Mediation Using Path Analysis," *European Psychologist* 14, no. 1 (2009), pp. 29–39; and P. Miquelon and R. J. Vallerand, "Goal Motives, Well-Being, and Physical Health: Happiness and Self-Realization as Psychological Resources under Challenge," *Motivation and Emotion* 30, no. 4 (2006), pp. 259–272.

67. M. M. Butts, R. J. Vandenberg, D. M. DeJoy, B. S. Schaffer, and M. G. Wilson, "Individual Reactions to High Involvement Work Processes: Investigating the Role of Empowerment and Perceived Organizational Support," *Journal of Occupational Health Psychology* 14, no. 2 (2009), pp. 122–136.

68. L. Blue, "Making Good Health Easy," *Time* (November 12, 2009), www.time.com; and M. Andrews, "Americas Best Health Plans," *US News and World Report* (November 5, 2007), pp. 54–60.

69. K. M. Richardson and H. R. Rothstein, "Effects of Occupational Stress Management Intervention Programs: A Meta-Analysis," *Journal of Occupational Health Psychology* 13, no. 1 (2008), pp. 69–93.

70. P. S. Goodman and L. B. Kurke, "Studies of Change in Organizations: A Status Report," in P. S. Goodman (ed.), *Change in Organizations* (San Francisco: Jossey-Bass, 1982), p. 1.

Glindex (Combined glossary and index)